Michigan's Upper Peninsula Almanac

Ron Jolly and Karl Bohnak

The University of Michigan Press
Ann Arbor

&

The Petoskey Publishing Company
Traverse City

Cover Design
Elizabeth Yelland and Stacey Willey

Interior Layout and Design
Stacey Willey, Elizabeth Yelland
Globe Printing, Inc., Ishpeming, MI
www.globeprinting.net

Illustrations and Photographs unless otherwise noted by
Elizabeth Yelland

Cover Photography by
Elizabeth Yelland

Photo descriptions: *Top left,* Sand Hill Point Lighthouse; *bottom left,* Tahquamenon Falls in spring; *right-hand side,* Cabin Eleven, Huron Mountain club, Huron Mountains

Acknowledgments

First, we single out the historians and historical societies throughout the Upper Peninsula who work so hard to preserve and share our heritage. Without your dedication and passion for history, this book and many other regional books would not be possible. Thank you.

Thanks to Rosemary Michelin of the J.M. Longyear Library for her help in tracing the origins of Upper Michigan's newspapers. Thanks and appreciation is also extended to the second-floor librarians at the Peter White Public Library in Marquette. Your local history section is outstanding and is a fabulous community resource. We want to also express our gratitude to the State of Michigan for its award-winning website, www.michigan.gov.

Special thanks go to: Leisa Mansfield, Director of the Sault Ste. Marie Chamber of Commerce for help in identifying the largest employers in the U.P., to the county clerks, and all the helpful employees of Upper Michigan's 15 counties for local government, population and employment figures, to Marilyn and Tom Taylor, George and Betty Tomasi, Clinton Weaner, Tom Mountz and Betsy Demaray for their interest and help in this project.

For photographs we thank: Elizabeth Yelland, Marian Strahl Boyer, Max and Henry Nedanovich, Kimber Bilby, William Wilson, Joyce Bahle, Paul Binsfeld, Stacey Willey, Rachael Poutanen, Elizabeth Daly, Fred Rydholm, The Ishpeming Ski Club and Greg Martin (Culture Chapter, author Tom Bissell).

Ron sends special thanks to his wife, Laura. Without her love and support, Ron would not have even tackled this project. Karl extends special thanks to his wife, Liz. Her gentle encouragement and suggestions helped the project move forward. Her enthusiasm and artistic eye is responsible for the beautiful book you hold in your hands.

Stacey Willey, at Globe Printing in Ishpeming Michigan, also deserves special recognition for her talent, creativity and can-do attitude. She applied long hours of technical lay out time and design consultation for the book. Her professional reputation is highly regarded in this region as a person to turn to for lay out and design of books.

CHAPTER 4 WATER

CHAPTER 5 PEOPLE

CHAPTER 6 COUNTIES AND TOWNS

CHAPTER 7 ECONOMY

CHAPTER 9 TRANSPORTATION

CHAPTER 10 EDUCATION

CHAPTER 13 SPORTS

CHAPTER 14 WILDLIFE

CHAPTER 15 ARCHITECTURE

CHAPTER 16 BIGGEST AND BEST

Chapter 1

HISTORY

Upper Peninsula Timeline

2.7 Billion years ago: Volcanic and sedimentary rocks begin their formation over what is now Upper Michigan and surrounding areas, when lava escapes the depths of the earth through rifts in the sea floor. Today, volcanic formations lie throughout the region, deep beneath glacial drift. Volcanic debris, sand, mud, and gravel released into the nearby seas later settle, forming massive layers of sedimentary rock.

1.9 Billion years ago: Most of the world's iron ore is formed during this period. This is a time of massive erosion that levels the earlier mountain range, releasing iron and silica particles into a new sea. The iron combines with atmospheric oxygen and precipitates into layers forming the Marquette and Menominee Ranges along with other iron ranges in the Lake Superior region.

1.1 Billion years ago: Intense volcanic activity takes place for about 20 million years along a great continental rift from eastern Lake Superior to Kansas. Much of the molten rock never reaches the surface, but solidifies underground to form dark-colored, coarse-grained rocks. Lava that reaches the earth's surface forms into huge overlapping flows, found now along the north shore of Lake Superior mostly as dark-colored basalt. Lake Superior agates are formed during this period in the cavities left by gas escaping the cooling lava.

600 Million To 2 Million years ago: This

The current landscape across the Upper Peninsula results mainly from glacial activity during the last ice age.

Statue of Father Marquette, his mission at St. Ignace was the second oldest established settlement in Michigan

period features advancing and retreating seas, development of plant and animal life forms, and lots of sediment. Major tectonic shifts give Upper Michigan an equatorial climate during part of this period. Evidence of this is seen in the many fossils preserved in these rocks.

2 Million years ago to 10,000 years ago: The current landscape across the Upper Peninsula results mainly from glacial activity during this period. The Upper Peninsula's present climate, with its cyclic warm and cold seasons, becomes established during this time. Glaciers "warehouse" huge quantities of the earth's water supplies, lowering ocean levels and expanding continental boundaries. Plant and animal communities migrate, adapt selectively, or become extinct with the changing climate. Upper Michigan sees the advance and retreat of several major, successive periods of continental ice sheets.

5,000 years ago: The U.P.'s climate warms enough to again support wildlife. An unknown, mysterious people mine copper. These people are sometimes called "Old Copper Indians". But almost nothing is known about them, except their mining methods, gleaned from the ancient pits and tools they left behind. Some theories have been promoted, which suggests that this copper was traded over many parts of the world (see bibliography).

Before 1000 B.C.: Woodland Amerindians appeared. These people of the Laurel culture likely moved into the area from the south and east, following the spread of wild rice into the Upper Great Lakes. These people engaged in long distance commerce, exchanging Lake Superior copper for things like Atlantic coast seashells. They navigated the waterways that would promote the fur trade nearly three thousand years later.

Before 1600: At the time of contact between Native Americans and Europeans, the Cree may have controlled most of the western Lake Superior shore with Dakota present in the south and Ojibwa in the north. By 1700, the Ojibwa control much of the region.

About 1620: Etienne Brule is the first documented European visitor to Lake Superior. He at least made it to the area of present-day Sault Ste. Marie and may have traveled the entire lake. He leaves no record of his journey.

1641: Fathers Raymbault and Jogues arrive at the falls between Lakes Huron and Superior, giving it the name Sault Ste. Marie. They establish a mission among the Chippewas (Ojibwa).

1658: Radisson and Groseilliers begin a two-year expedition around Lake Superior. They arrive back in New France with a vast quantity of furs.

1660: French Jesuit Menard attempts to establish a mission near the site of present-day L'Anse.

1669: Pere Dablon, Jesuit superior of the Sault mission, erects a church. This was the first permanent settlement on Michigan soil.

1670: The Hudson Bay Company is formed and intensive fur trading begins in the Lake Superior region.

1671: Father Marquette arrives at present-day St. Ignace with a flotilla of 200 canoes filled with Ojibwa from the Apostle Islands area on the west end of Lake Superior. Marquette establishes a mission there, making St. Ignace the second oldest settlement in Michigan.

1696: The price of furs collapses. King Louis XIV revokes all fur-trading licenses and prohibits colonials from bringing goods into the Lake Superior region.

1756: War begins between England and France, sending French influence across the region into decline.

John Johnston, father-in-law of Henry Rowe Schoolcraft, and a prominent Lake Superior fur trader.

1760: Alexander Henry, who wrote extensively about his adventures in the Lake Superior region, arrives in the Mackinac region.

1763: British are massacred at Fort Michilimackinac. Alexander Henry is saved by a Chippewa friend, Wawatam.

1766: Fishing fails resulting in famine at Sault Ste. Marie during the winter of 1766-67.

1771: First documented mining operation set up by Alexander Henry near the old Victoria mining site in present-day Ontonagon County.

1780: The English occupy Mackinac Island and erect a fort. They give up possession of it in 1795.

1783: Peace is made with the English and independence is acknowledged. Ben Franklin, having learned of the ancient copper mines on Isle Royale, supposedly helps negotiate a deal giving the island near the Canadian shore to the United States.

1793: Brit John Johnston, future father-in-law of Henry Rowe Schoolcraft, "pushes his way to the foot of Lake Superior."

1797: The Northwest Fur Company constructs a 38-foot navigation lock on the Canadian side at Sault Ste. Marie to allow larger boats to pass through the St. Marys Rapids. The lock is destroyed during the War of 1812.

1812: War again breaks out with England. The British hide war ships on Isle Royale and recapture the fort on Mackinac Island.

1815: A final peace treaty is made between the United States and Great Britain. The Brits again relinquish Fort Mackinac and Sault Ste. Marie.

1820: General Lewis Cass tours the new United States territory. He and his party, which includes Henry Rowe Schoolcraft, narrowly miss being attacked at Sault Ste. Marie by Ojibwa

TOWER OF HISTORY

The Tower of History offers one of the best views of the Sault Ste. Marie area and serves as a vertical museum.

The twisting tower of concrete reaches 210 feet into the sky and has an open-air viewing area offering a sweeping 360-degree vista of the region including the Soo Locks, the St. Mar's River, Sault Ste. Marie, Canada, and Lake Superior.

The tower was meant to be part of a new Catholic church but after it was completed in 1967 the parish pulled the plug. The original idea was to charge admission to the tower which would feature a museum-like exhibit telling the story of Christianity. Admissions would help pay for construction of the church.

The Bishop halted the project and the tower was sold for one dollar to Sault Historic Sites. Today the tower features a video on the Edison Sault Power Plant and exhibits on Native Americans of the region, logging history and Bishop Baraga. Proceeds from admissions have gone toward restoration of the neighboring St. Mary's Pro Cathederal, which was built in the 1880s.

This twisting tower of concrete reaches 210 feet into the sky.

loyal to the British. John Johnston's wife, an Ojibwa princess, persuade the Indians to lay down their arms.

1822: Henry Rowe Schoolcraft is appointed Indian agent at Sault Ste. Marie by an act of Congress. He moves to the Sault with a company of soldiers, establishing the first United States settlement in Upper Michigan.

1835: The schooner *John Jacob Astor* is launched, becoming the largest vessel to sail on Lake Superior. The ship's captain, Charles Stannard, discovers the rock that bears his name (Stannard Rock, 50 miles north of Marquette) in August. In September 1844, his brother, Ben, loses the vessel in a storm on Keweenaw Point.

1835: The "Toledo War" between Michigan and Ohio begins. Bloodshed is avoided and peace is made. Ohio gets the strip of land bordering Lake Erie that contains present-day Toledo and Michigan has to settle for the "sterile region on the shores of Lake Superior, destined by soil and climate to remain forever a wilderness." The *Detroit Free Press* called it "a region of perpetual snows—the *Ultima Thule* of our national domain in the north."

1836: The Chippewa cede a vast section of their land, which includes the area from Drummond Island to the Chocolate (now Chocolay) River. The selling price—about 12 cents an acre.

1841: State Geologist Douglass Houghton sends out a favorable report on the copper regions of the Upper Peninsula.

1842: The western portion of Upper Michigan is obtained from the Lake Superior Chippewa, effectively opening up the region to mineral exploration.

1843: Eagle River is founded. It serves as a shipping port for early mining companies of the Keweenaw.

1844: U.S. government establishes Fort Wilkins near Copper Harbor on the tip of the Keweenaw Peninsula. The fort is installed to protect settlers from Indian uprisings, which never occur. In 1846, when war breaks out with Mexico, the main garrison at the fort is deployed south. Only a skeleton, caretaking force remains. The fort is finally abandoned in 1870.

1844: Michigan's chief surveyor, William Austin Burt, and his party discover iron ore near present-day Teal Lake on September 19.

1845: Mining operations begin at the Cliff Mine. It is the first successful copper mine on the Keweenaw Peninsula. The mine is dismantled and sold for scrap iron in 1903.

William Austin Burt discovers iron ore in 1844.

1846: First mining operations begin in what is now Marquette County.

1849: A federal geologist, J.W. Foster, finds significant deposits of iron ore in the Lake Antoine area near present-day Iron Mountain.

1849: The village of Worcester, later named Marquette, is settled along the southern shore of Lake Superior.

1851: Eagle Harbor, in Keweenaw County, is laid out and recorded the next year.

1853: Construction of two locks connecting Lake Superior with the other Great Lakes begins. Despite adverse conditions, including a bout of cholera which strikes the workers, the project is completed in 1855.

1857: The first railroad, "The Marquette and Iron Mountain Railroad," is completed from Lake Superior to the Superior Mine near present-day Ishpeming.

1861: The twin villages of Houghton and Hancock are incorporated.

1864: The Peninsula Railroad completes the first line across the Peninsula from Negaunee to Escanaba. Over 31-thousand tons of iron ore are shipped between the two points that year.

1866: Escanaba is incorporated as a village and the next year, a lighthouse is established at Sand Point. Also in 1867, a charcoal iron furnace is built in Fayette by the Jackson Iron Company.

1868: A June fire destroys much of the business district of Marquette.

1871: The Calumet Company and the Hecla Company merge to form the Calumet and Hecla Mining Company. In the 1870s, C&H mines 50 percent of the nation's copper.

1871: The Great Peshtigo Fire wipes out the northeastern Wisconsin village on the evening of October 8. The fire jumps across the Menominee River into Upper Michigan, largely sparing the City of Menominee, but destroying the town Birch Creek just north of town.

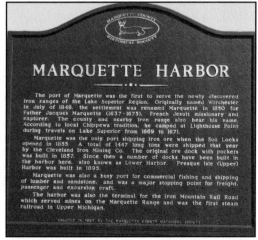

Suomi College (now Finlandia University) is established in Hancock 1896. The cornerstone of Old Main, the trust building, was erected May 30, 1898.

A quarter of its population and a number of migrant railroad workers are killed.

1872: The Chicago and Northwestern Railway reaches Escanaba and meets the Peninsula Railroad, establishing the first railway connection with the rest of the United States.

1873: The Portage Lake and Lake Superior Shipping Canal is completed. Boats can now pass through the Keweenaw Peninsula.

1877: A railroad is completed from Escanaba to Quinnesec. This allows for rapid expansion of iron mining on the Menominee Range.

1879: The first settlers come to what is now the City of Iron Mountain after iron is found there.

1883: The Milwaukee Lakeshore and Western Railroad builds tracks into Bessemer, a small settlement on the Gogebic Range. This causes a surge in settlement for the town the next year. In 1885, the village of Ironwood is platted. It also grows rapidly due to expansion of mining operations in the area.

1885: The Michigan School of Mines opens in Houghton (now Michigan Technological University). In its 110-year history, over 800 mining engineers have graduated from Michigan Tech.

1887: The village of Ironwood is largely destroyed in a September fire.

1888: The railroad comes to Sault Ste. Marie, finally connecting the first city in Upper Michigan with the "outer world" in winter. The train, carrying flour from Minneapolis, is the first train to travel from the Mississippi to the Atlantic on a route north of Lake Michigan.

1896: The year of devastating fires in Upper Michigan. In May, a large part of L'Anse is consumed by fire. In late August, a large part of the business district of Sault Ste. Marie goes up in flames. The largest fire destroys Ontonagon on August 25.

1896: Suomi College (now Finlandia University) is established in Hancock. It is the only institution of higher learning established by the Finns in North America.

1899: Northern State Normal School is founded in Marquette as a teacher's school. When the doors open, 32 students are greeted by a faculty of six.

1902: The first professional ice hockey team is formed in the Copper Country. Two years later, the Portage Lake Ice Hockey Team forms the world's first inter-city hockey league called the International Hockey League.

1910: Houghton County's population peaks at 88,098. The U.S. census 2005 estimate: 35,705.

1913: Copper Country Strike. Men strike the copper mines for an 8-hour day, higher pay, the abolishment of the one-man drill and the right to form a union. The strike finally ends in April 1914. The move to form a union fails.

1913: The Italian Hall disaster in Calumet occurs as someone yells "fire" during a Christmas party for striking workers and their families. 75 people, including 59 children and 16 adults, are crushed when they panic and rush to the stairwell.

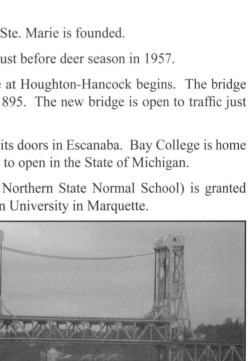

THE AMPHIDROME

The Amphidrome stood on this site from 1902 until 1927, when it burned. The first hockey game was played in the arena on December 29, 1902, when Portage Lake beat the University of Toronto, 13-2. The Amphidrome was home to the Portage Lakes, a team in the International Hockey League, ice hockey's first professional league. The building also hosted the agricultural society's annual Copper Country Fair and numerous other community events. The Houghton Warehouse Company, headed by James R. Dee, built and owned the arena. Dee, who had helped organize the International Hockey League in 1904, led the effort to rebuild the Amphidrome. This building opened in 1927 on the site of the original one and hosted professional ice hockey games until 1907. It was renamed Dee Stadium in 1943.

1923: The village of Kingsford is incorporated, named for Edward Kingsford, a key figure in Henry Ford's Upper Peninsula operations.

1926: The Barnes-Hecker Mine cave-in occurs on November 3 near Ishpeming. The accident kills 51, making it the worst mining disaster in Upper Michigan and the third worst metal-mining disaster in U.S. history. Only seven bodies are retrieved. Reclamation efforts fail and the mine is abandoned the next year.

1946: Lake Superior State University in Sault Ste. Marie is founded.

1957: The Mackinac Bridge is open to traffic just before deer season in 1957.

1957: Construction of the Portage Lift Bridge at Houghton-Hancock begins. The bridge replaces the narrow-truss swing bridge built in 1895. The new bridge is open to traffic just before Christmas in 1959.

1963: Bay De Noc Community College opens its doors in Escanaba. Bay College is home of the first Michigan Technical Education Center to open in the State of Michigan.

1963: Northern Michigan College (formerly Northern State Normal School) is granted university status and becomes Northern Michigan University in Marquette.

1970: The Delta Plaza Mall opens in Escanaba. This is the first shopping mall in the Upper Peninsula.

Portage Lift Bridge at Houghton-Hancock

NATIONAL HISTORIC LANDMARKS IN THE U.P.

County	Landmark	Date listed
Chippewa	St. Mary's Falls Ship Canal (Soo Locks Historic District, Soo Canals)	11/13/1966
Houghton	Calumet Historic District	2/10/1989
Houghton	Quincy Mining Company Historic District	3/28/1989
Mackinac	St. Ignace Mission (Father Marquette Burial Site, Marquette Mission Park, Museum of Ojibwa Culture)	10/15/1960
Mackinac/Emmet	Fort Michilimackinac	10/09/1960
Mackinac	Mackinac Island	10/15/1966
Mackinac	Grand Hotel	6/29/1989

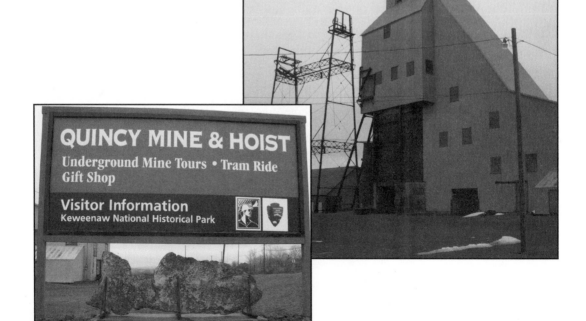

MICHIGAN HISTORICAL MARKERS – BY COUNTY
ALGER COUNTY

GRAND MARAIS

Grand Marais, which is among Michigan's oldest place names, received its name from French explorers, missionaries and traders who passed here in the 1600s. "Marais" in this case was a term used by the *voyaguers* to designate a harbor of refuge. In the 1800s Lewis Cass, Henry Schoolcraft and Douglass Houghton also found the sheltering harbor a welcome stopping place. Grand Marais's permanent settlement dates from the 1860s with the establishment of fishing and lumbering. At the turn of the century Grand Marais was a boom town served by a railroad from the south. Its mills turned out millions of board feet annually. Lumbering declined around 1910, and Grand Marais became almost a ghost town, but the fishing industry continued. Many shipping disasters have occurred at or near the harbor of refuge, which has been served by the Coast Guard since 1899. In 1942 the first radar station in Michigan was built in Grand Marais. Fishing, lumbering and tourism now give Grand Marais its livelihood.

LAKE SUPERIOR – ROADSIDE PARK 11 MILES WEST OF MUNISING

The French called it *Le lac superieur* to designate its geographical position above Lake Huron. However in area, Lake Superior stands above all other fresh water lakes in the world. The intrepid Frenchman Brule discovered it around 1622. During the 1650s and 60s French fur traders and missionaries explored this great inland sea. Within 250 years, fur-laden canoes had given way to huge boats carrying ore and grain to the world.

LOBB HOUSE – MUNISING

Built in 1905-06, it is one of the most graceful houses in Munising. This was the home of Elizabeth Lobb. Madame Lobb, as she was affectionately known, gained her wealth from a mine that was discovered on property that she and her husband Edward owned in Marquette County. Thirteen years after the death of her husband, Madame Lobb erected this handsome residence. She and her son Nathaniel operated a large brickyard in nearby Hallston until 1910. The Alger County Historical Society purchased this structure for a museum in 1974.

MIKULICH GENERAL STORE – COUNTY ROAD H-44, TRAUNIK

Traunik was the heart of a large ethnic community that developed in the early 1900s, when Slovenians settled on cut-over land. Built in 1922-23, this store was purchased by Louis Mikulich in 1925. Mikulich's store was the social and economic center for the community. In 1927, Mikulich became the postmaster and opened an office in the store. His family's residence was on the second floor. The Mikulich General Store was listed in the National Register of Historic Places in 1993.

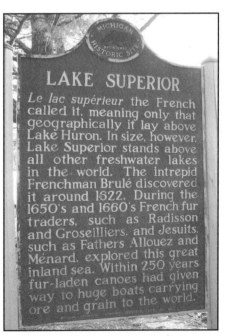

PAULSON HOUSE –AU TRAIN TOWNSHIP

Swedish pioneer Charles Paulson purchased one hundred acres of land here in 1884 and constructed this cabin for his family home. Built of hand-hewn cedar logs securely dovetailed at the corners, the house was occupied by Paulson and his wife until their deaths in 1925. At the turn of the century the three Paulson daughters were able to attend the district school which met in the upper story. Today, the restored Paulson House serves as a museum of pioneer life.

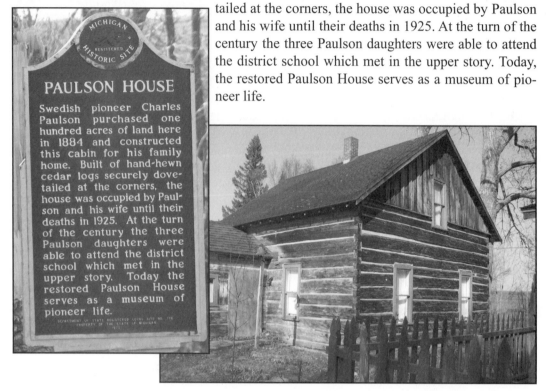

PICKLE BARREL
HOUSE/THE TEENIE WEENIES – GRAND MARAIS

The Pioneer Cooperage Company of Chicago designed this small vacation cottage, which stood on the shores of nearby Sable Lake from 1926 until about 1937. It was built for William Donahey, creator of the *Chicago Tribune* cartoon story *The Teenie Weenies*. The house was constructed as a typical barrel would have been, only on a much larger scale. The main barrel contained a living area on the first floor and a bedroom on the second. A pantry connected this barrel to a smaller single-story barrel, which housed a kitchen. Donahey spent ten summers at the cottage with his wife, Mary, also a noted author of children's books. The structure was then moved to its current site and used as a tourist information center. The Pickle Barrel House is listed in the National Register of Historic Places.

William Donahey's widely syndicated comic, *The Teenie Weenies,* debuted in the *Chicago Tribune* in 1914 and continued until the creator's death in 1970. The cartoon story featured miniature people who lived in a world of life-sized objects that to them where enormous. The popularity of these playful characters led to a contract for Donahey with the Chicago firm of Reid, Murdoch and Company, which hired the artist to create packaging and advertising for its line of food products. The Pickle Barrel House was a large-scale version of the miniature oak casks in which the company's Monarch-brand pickles were sold, and was likely intended as an advertisement for their pickle products. *Teenie Weenie* book series was translated into several languages and over one million copies were sold worldwide.

BARAGA COUNTY

JACOB AND ANNA LEINONEN HOMESTEAD – COVINGTON

This couple bought this old homestead in 1904 for $296. They ran a self sufficient farm on the site until Jacob's death in 1937. The farm has stayed in the family for three generations.

KEWEENAW BAY – BARAGA

This region's history is long and rich. Jesuit Missionary Menard wintered near what is now L'Anse in 1660-1661. Near here Father Baraga set up his mission in 1843. He and Reverend John Pitezel, the head of the neighboring Methodist mission were good friends. Furs and fish figured prominently in the bay's early history as a source of economic wealth. In the 1880s and 1890s the area's timber was cut with Baraga and Pequaming being the centers of lumbering.

Bishop Baraga Shrine located in L'Anse on the shores of Keewenaw Bay (Photo by Wilson)

L'ANSE LAC VIEUX DESERT TRAIL – L'ANSE (BISHOP BARAGA SHRINE PARKING LOT)

Near this spot ran the L'Anse-Lac Vieux Desert Trail, which crossed the interior of the Upper Peninsula of Michigan from L'Anse on Keewenaw Bay to Lac Vieux Desert on the Wisconsin border. The trail was used in prehistoric times by Native Americans as a trade and transportation route. Father Rene Menard may have followed this route in 1661 as he traveled south from Keewenaw Bay, a trip from which he never returned. The trail was later used by fur traders, early surveyors and homesteaders. The L'Anse and Lac Vieux Desert bands of Chippewa Indians used this trail into the 20th Century. Today many segments of the L'Anse-Lac Vieux Desert Trail are unpaved roads that can be traveled by car.

ZEBA INDIAN UNITED METHODIST CHURCH

Early Methodist missionaries came to Keewenaw Bay from Sault Sainte Marie by canoe. This trip often took up to two weeks to complete. Among then was John Sunday, a Chippewa who arrived in 1832 to educate and Christianize his fellow Indians. John Clark came two years later and erected a school and mission house. By 1845 this mission consisted of a farm and a church with 58 Indian and four white members. A second church, erected in 1850, was dedicated by John H. Pitezel, who served here from 1844 to 1847.

Indians from far and near came here to attend the annual camp meetings which began in 1880. The present frame church, known now as the Zeba Indian Mission Church, was erected in 1888. Completely covered with hand-made wooden shingles, this structure has changed little since its construction. The Methodist minister of L'Anse serves the congregation. The Zeba Indian United Methodist Church, the successor of the 1932 Kewawenon mission, is an area landmark.

CHIPPEWA COUNTY

CENTRAL METHODIST CHURCH – SAULT STE. MARIE

This Richardsonian Romanesque church was erected in 1892-93 according to plans by Bay City architect Dillon P. Clark. It is one of several buildings in the city constructed of red "channel rubble" sandstone discarded during a power channel excavation. The church sustained three fires, the most recent occurred on December 22, 1941, during a wartime blackout. Although the interior suffered extensive damage, the original exterior structure remains substantially unchanged.

ELMWOOD – SAULT STE. MARIE

Appointed Indian agent in 1822, Henry Rowe Schoolcraft (1793-1864) requested that the government provide a suitable structure to house the agency. Obed Walt, designer of Michigan's territorial capitol in Detroit, directed the construction of this building. Nearly 100 feet in length when completed in 1827, the Federal Style building originally had a two story central unit flanked by two single story wings. While at Elmwood, Schoolcraft, explorer and ethnologist, collected materials for his pioneering works on Indian culture which scholars still use today. These writings inspired Henry Wadsworth Longfellow's *Song of Hiawatha*. Charles T. Harvey lived here during the mid-1850s when he supervised the building of the canal and locks at Sault Ste. Marie. Elmwood's substantial alterations during the past 150 years reflect its varied uses and inhabitants.

EMERSON

Once a thriving lumbering town, Emerson is now a fishing hamlet. Just one mile south of the mouth of the Tahquamenon River (immortalized in Longfellow's poem *Hiawatha*), this settlement overlooks picturesque Whitefish Bay. The village was founded in the 1880s by Kurt Emerson, a lumberman from the Saginaw Bay area. Emerson erected a sawmill and in 1884 sold his establishment to the Chesbrough Lumber Company. Milling and lumbering operations ceased in 1912. From then on, commercial fishing became the economic bulwark of the community.

FORT BRADY

On July 6, 1822, a battalion of American troops under Col. Hugh Brady reached the Sault, thereby reconfirming the assertion of American authority over this region made by Lewis Cass in 1820. Fort Brady was built here by year's end. The French and Indians living at the little village now recognized that this remote outpost was truly part of America. The fort was removed in 1893 to a new site chosen by General Phil Sheridan.

FORT BRADY – SAULT STE. MARIE

On July 6, 1822, a battalion of American troops under Col. Hugh Brady reached the Sault, thereby reasserting American authority over this region. A fort was constructed and eventually named after the battalion's first commander. The fort was removed in 1893 to a new site chosen by General Phil Sheridan.

FORT DRUMMOND – DRUMMOND ISLAND

Forced by the Treaty of Ghent to evacuate the fort they had captured on Mackinac Island during the War of 1812, the British selected this island as an alternate military post. This stronghold was close to the traditional Indian gathering point at the Straits of Mackinac. The fort was set up in an attempt to maintain English control of the fur trade in the Upper Great Lakes. Built by Colonel Robert McDonall and his men, Fort Drummond and the nearby village at Collier's Harbor were maintained for more than a decade. The British abandoned their stronghold in 1828, six years after Drummond Island was ruled United States territory. Now summer cottages occupy this rocky countryside and only a few ruined chimneys survive as reminders of the conflict between British and American sovereignty in the Old Northwest.

JOHN JOHNSTON HOUSE – SAULT STE. MARIE

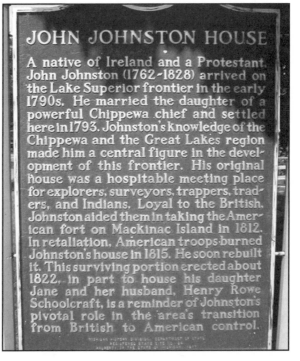

A native of Ireland and a Protestant, John Johnston (1762-1828) arrived on the Lake Superior frontier in the early 1790s. He married the daughter of a powerful Chippewa chief and settled here in 1793. Johnston's knowledge of the Chippewa and the Great Lakes region made him a central figure in the development of this frontier. His original house was a hospitable meeting place for explorers, surveyors, trappers, traders and Indians. Loyal to the British, Johnston aided them in taking the American fort on Mackinac Island in 1812. In retaliation, American troops burned Johnston's house in 1815. He soon rebuilt it. This surviving portion was erected about 1822 and stands as a reminder of Johnston's pivotal role in the area's transition from British to American control.

JOHNSTON HOMESITE – RAINS ISLAND

In 1864, John McDougal Johnston, his wife Justine, and their six children homesteaded this island. His father was the famous Sault Ste. Marie fur trader. He served as an interpreter for his brother-in-law, Indian Agent Henry R. Schoolcraft. After twelve years on Rains Island, John and Justine moved to a farm near the Sault. Two children, Anna Marie, known as Miss Molly, and Howard remained to farm the homestead. In 1892 birch bark cabins were built on this site to house visitors. Miss Molly called the spot O-non-e-gwud, an Indian name for Happy Place. The land was given to the Neebish Pioneer Association in memory of the Bagnall family in 1974 to preserve as the Johnston Conservation Area.

LAKE SUPERIOR STATE COLLEGE- SAULT STE. MARIE

In 1946 the State of Michigan assumed control of New Fort Brady, and presented it to the Michigan College of Mining and Technology, now Michigan Technological University. The Houghton based school, forced to expand by the enrollment of returning veterans, adapted the old Army buildings to college classrooms, residence halls and offices. Not until 1964, with the completion of Crawford Hall, did the campus have a building constructed for educational purposes. The school's curriculum, which at first duplicated the main campus's engineering program, was eventually broadened. On January 1, 1970 the school became a separate and autonomous four year institution called Lake Superior State College.

LARKE ROAD - SAULT STE. MARIE

Until 1962, Three Mile (Larke) Road was known simply as Larke Road. In 1876, Henry Larke (1824-1900) became the first settler along this road, making his home about one and one-half miles west of this site. He emigrated from Canada, where he farmed and made wooden pumps. From 1876 until 1897 Larke operated a dairy farm near this site. His son Richard and his daughter-in-law Lena maintained the farm until the 1940s. Around the turn of the century, a local glacial deposit and the local rural school were named in honor of the Larke family.

METHODIST INDIAN MISSION – SAULT STE. MARIE

Several Methodist ministers were active in missionary work in the "Soo" area in the 1830s. John Sunday, an Indian preacher from Canada, began missionary work in the Indian settlement at the Sault Ste. Marie Rapids around 1831. The Reverend John Clark followed in his footsteps two years later. By 1834, the mission school had thirty-five students, and three "Methodist classes" were organized with forty Indians and nineteen whites. The Michigan Conference sent William H. Brockway to the mission as superintendent in 1839. He remained for ten years, serving most of that time as chaplain for Old Fort Brady.

John H. Pitezel and John Kah-beege continued the ministerial work at this settlement. Arriving at the Sault in 1843, Pitezel found a flourishing school and farm with nearly fifty cultivated acres. He served as superintendent of the Methodist Indian District from 1848 to 1852, serving missions as far away as Minnesota. A mission house was built in 1849 at Naomikong on Whitefish Bay. As more white settlers came to the Soo in the 1850s, many of the Indians moved away. By 1861, Methodist mission work in the area was concentrated at Iroquois Point near Sault St. Marie. The Methodists sold the mission land here in 1862

NEW FORT BRADY – SAULT STE. MARIE

When Sault Ste. Marie expanded and its canal was widened, the river-front site of Fort Brady was abandoned for a higher, more strategic site selected by General Philip Sheridan. Work began in 1886, and the new fort opened in 1893. From this hilltop, New Fort Brady guarded the copper and iron ore enroute from the mineral regions of western Lake Superior through the St. Mary's ship Canal. Although never under attack, its troops were called up in 1894 during civil unrest. Their primary mission was to protect the canal until the start of World War II. At that time, 15,000 soldiers were stationed here. In 1944 the

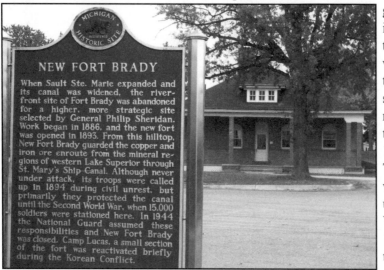

National Guard assumed these responsibilities and New Fort Brady was closed. Camp Lucas, a small section of the fort was reactivated briefly during the Korean conflict.

POST OFFICE – WHITEFISH POINT

This post office opened just six years after Whitefish Point was settled in 1871. This village served as a supply harbor and commercial fishery. Permanent residents received their mail from Sault Ste. Marie. During the summer months, mail was delivered by boat three times a week. In the winter, dog teams hauled the mail twice a month. This post office provided a link to the days before lumbermen came and cut down the area's tall stands of pine. The office here ceased operations in 1973.

ST. MARY'S PRO-CATHEDRAL – SAULT STE. MARIE

In 1853, Pope Pius IX separated the Upper Peninsula from the Diocese of Detroit and established a vicariate apostolic. Reverend Frederic Baraga, the "Apostle of the Chippewa", became vicar apostolic and made St. Mary's Church his headquarters. In 1857, the vicariate became a diocese, Baraga was named Bishop of the Sault and the log cabin known as St. Mary's became a cathedral. With the onset of mining, settlements developed in the western Upper Peninsula. Faced with the task of serving these remote parishes, Bishop Baraga obtained the pope's permission to move the seat of the diocese to Marquette. In May 1866, Baraga left St. Mary's and the parish became the pro-cathedral parish. In 1881 the present Gothic Revival-style church designed by Joseph Connolly of Toronto was erected.

SAULT STE. MARIE

In 1641, Fathers Jogues and Raymbault of Sainte Marie Mission near Georgian Bay came here and applied the name Sault de Sainte Marie or "rapids of Saint Mary" to the fast flowing segment of water that flowed past the site. Popular usage shortened it to "the Soo." This oldest city in the Midwest grew up about the mission of Fathers Dablon and Marquette, which they founded in 1668.

SHELLDRAKE

Legend has it that Territory of Michigan governor Lewis Cass and his party camped here during their 1820 expedition. This area, once a bustling lumbering community, was first settled in the mid-nineteenth century. Shelldrake is now a sleepy resort and fishing settlement. Few of the weather-beaten buildings that once faced the long boardwalk remain. This settlement is a reminder of the area's lumbering past.

WHITEFISH POINT LIGHTHOUSE

This light, the oldest on Lake Superior, began operating in 1849, though the present tower was constructed later. Long a stopping place for Indians, voyageurs, and Jesuit missionaries, the point marks the course change for ore boats and other ships navigating this treacherous coastline to and from St. Mary's Canal. Since 1971, the light, fog signal, and radio beacon have been automated and controlled from Sault Ste. Marie.

Whitefish Point Lighthouse

WHITEFISH TOWNSHIP

In 1849, the Whitefish Point lighthouse was put into service. Soon after the township was organized in 1888, lumber towns such as Emerson and Shelldrake emerged at the mouth of the Tahquamenon and Shelldrake rivers. Paradise was established in 1925. In the 1920s, lumbering declined and fires burned the cutover land, creating rich soil for blueberries. Cranberry and blueberry cultivation, as well as commercial fishing on Whitefish Bay, sustained the area's economy.

DELTA COUNTY

ESCANABA RIVER

This is the land of the Chippewa Indians and the legendary Hiawatha. Indian villages existed along the banks of the river when the first white men came to this region in the 1600s. The Indians named the river for the flat rocks over which it runs. In *The Song of Hiawatha*, Longfellow described how Hiawatha "crossed the rushing Esconaba" in pursuit of Mudjekeewis, whom he slew to avenge the death of his mother. The last Indian lands in the Upper Peninsula were ceded to the United States in 1842. This closed an era that began about 10,000 years ago.

A sawmill was built at the mouth of the Escanaba River in 1838. Another mill was built in the early 1840s where a power dam now stands. Government surveyors were surprised to discover these mills and a small settlement here in 1844. These mills were all water- powered. The region was first famous for its vast white pine forests. Lumber milled here helped build Chicago and later rebuild it after the great fire of 1871. Hardwood flooring in large quantities was produced in the region. At the turn of the century, the I. Stephenson Co., with mills at the river mouth, was the largest producer of lumber in the world.

INDIAN TRAIL – MASON TOWNSHIP

The trail that begins here was one of the most important in the Upper Peninsula. The Noquets, an Algonquian tribe, lived in this area and used the trail in their frequent travels between Lake Michigan and Lake Superior. In places, the trail is deeply worn from centuries of use. Beginning in the early 1800s, the Northwest Fur Company and the American Fur Company established posts at Grand Island, near the Lake Superior end of the trail. Traders, lumbermen and others continued to use this route until a county road was built. The U.S. Forest Service has reconstructed the trail and maintains it for hiking and riding.

LITTLE BAY DE NOC – LUDINGTON STREET DOCK, ESCANABA

The Noquet (or Noc) Indians, who once lived along these shores, gave this bay its name. Here at Sand Point in 1844, Douglass Houghton came with his party of government surveyors to chart the land to the north. In 1864, the first ore dock was built on the shore of this deep harbor, from which the ores of all three of Michigan's rich iron ranges have been shipped. Escanaba, which was incorporated in 1866, was one of the earliest lumbering centers in the Upper Peninsula. Sawmills were built here as early as 1836. Up the west shore of the bay, Gladstone was founded in 1887 by Senator W. D. Washburn to serve as a rail-lake terminal. Here, as at other points such as Ford River, Masonville, Rapid River, and Garth, the major source of income was timber products.

LUDINGTON HOTEL - ESCANABA

In 1864, E. Gaynor built the Gaynor House hotel, which he renamed the Ludington House in 1871 after lumberman Nelson Ludington. In the late 1800s, proprietor John Christie enlarged the hotel and renamed the establishment the New Ludington Hotel. An advertisement in the 1893 *Michigan Gazetteer and Business Directory* read, "New Ludington Hotel - The Largest and Only hotel in the city having Baths, Steam Heat and Electric Call Bells - $2.00 per day." The hotel exemplifies Queen Anne resort architecture, popular in the 1880s and 1890s.

DICKINSON COUNTY

ARDIS FURNACE – IRON MOUNTAIN

Inventor John T. Jones of Iron Mountain recognized the economic potential of the low-grade iron ore of the Upper Peninsula. He developed a method for processing the ore and built an experimental furnace in 1908, named for his daughter Ardis, to test his theory. The furnace, a huge metal tube lined with

House of Ludington, Escanaba

firebrick, was placed on an incline and charged with ore. The whole device was rotated with an electric motor. Iron suitable for mill use was discharged from the lower end of the tube. The experiment was plagued with financial and mechanical problems and by the end of World War I, the Ardis was dismantled. Jones moved on to other mining endeavors. Elements of the Jones method were later incorporated into successful processing operations for low-grade iron ores.

CARNEGIE LIBRARY – IRON MOUNTAIN

While in Iron Mountain on business during 1901, Andrew Carnegie saw the need for a library on the Menominee Iron Range, which was then a prospering area. He donated $15,000 for this building. Serving the community for over seventy years, the Neo-Classical Revival structure designed by James E. Clancy was one of the earliest Carnegie libraries in the Great Lake State. In 1971, this edifice became the Menominee Range Museum, featuring the history of its namesake.

Menominee Range Museum

CORNISH PUMP – IRON MOUNTAIN

When the E.P. Allis Company of Milwaukee built this pump in 1890/91, it was heralded as the nation's largest steam-driven pumping engine. On January 3, 1893, the massive engine, designed by Edwin C. Reynolds, began lifting 200 hundred tons of water per minute at "D" shaft of the Chapin Iron Mine. In 1896, underground conditions shifted the engine out of alignment and it was dismantled. The Oliver Iron Mining Company purchased and rebuilt it at shaft "C" of the Ludington Mine in 1907. It de-watered the combined Chapin, Ludington and Hamilton mines until 1914 when it was replaced by electric pumps. The device is patterned after similar pumps used in tin mines in Cornwall, England. The Cornish Pump boasts a fly-wheel forty feet in diameter, which weighs 160 tons and averaged ten revolutions per minute. The pump was listed in the National Register of Historic Places in 1981.

DICKINSON COUNTY COURTHOUSE AND JAIL – IRON MOUNTAIN

In 1873, John Lane Buell exposed one of the richest deposits of iron ore in the world. His discovery, known as the Menominee Iron Range, led to the development of the area and the subsequent creation of Dickinson County in 1891. The last of Michigan's eighty-three counties to be organized, it was named for Donald Dickinson, a prominent Detroit attorney and postmaster general in the first administration of President Grover Cleveland (1885 - 1889). Three of Michigan's largest iron mines were located in Iron Mountain, which had an abundant supply of water power and was served by two major railroads. Iron Mountain became a center of commerce and distribution for the range and was the natural location for the county seat once the county organized.

This Richardsonian Romanesque courthouse erected in 1896 - 97, is constructed of rock-faced brick trimmed with Portage Entry sandstone. James E. Clancy, a locally recognized architect who specialized in public buildings on the Menominee Iron Range, designed the courthouse. County offices opened here only five years after Dickinson County was created by act of the Michigan State Legislature. The jail, designed to complement the larger structure, originally had thirty-four cells for male prisoners and two wards for juvenile and female prisoners on the first floor, with the sheriff's quarters on the first and second floors.

MARY OF IMMACULATE LOURDES CHURCH – IRON MOUNTAIN

In the late nineteenth and early twentieth centuries Italian immigrants came to Iron Mountain to work in the iron mines. In 1890, Italian Catholics from the community organized what was popularly known as "the Italian Church." That year they built a frame church near this site. The church burned in 1893 and was rebuilt. In April 1902, Father G. Pietro Sinopoli arrived here. Within two months he formed a church building committee. Four thousand dollars was raised and in June Father Sinopoli began excavating the foundation. The church was completed in December and dedicated to Mary Immaculate of Lourdes on January 1, 1903.

This church reflects the heritage and building techniques of the Italian immigrants who erected it. The church with its bell tower fashioned after a campanile, is strikingly reminiscent of Renaissance parish churches in Italy. Masons and volunteers hauled sandstone from a quarry one mile south of here to build the exterior walls. The Menominee Stained Glass Works created at least three of the windows, including the choir loft window designed by Father Sinopoli. The church was listed in the National Register of Historic Places in 1990.

MENOMINEE IRON RANGE — QUINNESEC

This range is named for the Menominee River which runs through part of it. It is one of three great iron districts in the Upper Peninsula. In 1846, surveyor William Austin Burt, the discoverer of the Marquette Iron Range, noted signs of iron ore in the Crystal Falls area. In 1849, federal geologist J. W. Foster found ore near Lake Antoine and two years later he and J. D. Whitney confirmed Burt's report on the Crystal Falls district. The first mining activity began in 1872 at the Breen Mine where ore had been discovered in the 60s by the Breen brothers, timber cruisers from Menominee. Development of the range was delayed until a railroad could be built from Escanaba. The Breen and Vulcan mine shipped 10,405 tons of ore in 1877 when the railroad was built as far as Quinnesec. By 1880, it reached Iron Mountain and Florence and tracks were laid to Crystal Falls and Iron River by 1882. Twenty-two mines made shipments of ore that year. A few crumbling ruins are all that remain of most of them, but in subsequent decades more mines were developed which produced vast amounts of ore for America's iron and steel mills.

NORWAY SPRING — QUINNESEC

In 1878, a sawmill was erected here. It was the first industry in the Norway - Vulcan area. John O'Callaghan owned this mill, which supplied lumber to area mines until 1902. In 1903, the Norway Spring was caused by a 1,094 foot hole which was drilled by the Oliver Mining Company in search of iron ore. The hole cuts several steeply dipping porous strata that trap water at the higher elevations to the north. The difference in elevation causes pressure. This pressure is released by the drilled hole demonstrating the principle of the artesian well. On the slope to the north are the obscure workings of the Few and Munro mines, which operated from 1903-1922. They are now owned by the Ford Motor Company.

GOGEBIC COUNTY

COPPER PEAK: CHIPPEWA HILL — N. BLACK RIVER VALLEY PARKWAY, IRONWOOD

At an altitude of 1,500 feet, or 300 feet above the surrounding terrain, this location was the southernmost area in Michigan to offer a prospect of producing copper in commercial amounts. The Chippewa Copper Mining Company began work here in 1845, sinking a still visible tunnel into the granite rock. No copper was ever produced, although around 1900 the Old Peak Company made further explorations. In 1970, a 280-foot ski slide, the highest in the world, was completed on the peak in time for the western hemisphere's first international ski flying tournament here. Skiers recorded flights of nearly 500 feet from this slide.

CURRY HOUSE — IRONWOOD

Here lived Solomon S. Curry, pioneer in the mining industry of the Ironwood area. Curry, a progressive, broad-minded man, was also instrumental in the building of the city of Ironwood, which through his efforts grew from a wilderness to one of the major cities in northern Michigan. A Democrat, Curry was elected State Representative in 1874 and was a candidate for lieutenant governor in 1896. Restored to its original appearance, the Curry House has Tiffany windows, nineteenth century light fixtures, and ornate woodwork.

GOGEBIC IRON RANGE – BESSEMER

The Gogebic was the last of the three great iron ore fields opened in the Upper Peninsula and northern Wisconsin. Beginning in 1848 with Dr. A. Randall, federal and state geologists mapped the ore formations almost perfectly long before any ore was mined. Based on his 1871 studies, Geologist Raphael Pumpelly picked out lands for purchase, which years later became the sites of the wealthy Newport and Geneva Mines. The first mine to go into production was the Colby. In 1884 it shipped 1,022 tons of ore in railroad flat cars to Milwaukee. By 1890, more than thirty mines had shipped ore from this range. Many quickly ran out of good ore and were shut down. Others took their place as richer ore bodies were found. Virtually all mining here was underground, as attested to by many shafts and cave-ins. The soft hematite ores common on this range were usually sent in ore cars to Ashland and Escanaba. From these locations they were loaded on ore boats and taken to America's steel mills.

IRONWOOD CITY HALL

This building served as city hall for Ironwood, which was settled in 1885 as the commercial center of the Gogebic iron mining district. Ironwood incorporated as a city in 1889 and erected the building one year later. Designed by George Mennie, this structure is made of Lake Superior sandstone and brick. It initially contained a jail, fire station, library and city offices. Later, the fire and police departments exclusively occupied the building. Firemen hung their hoses to dry from the 85 foot tower.

NEWPORT HILL – IRONWOOD

On October 8, 1871, geologist Raphael Pumpelly of Harvard University discovered one of the iron ore formations that created Gogebic County's "boom era." The Newport Mine, named for Pumpelly's home in Rhode Island, began operations in 1884. By the time the mine shut down in 1966, 255 million tons of iron ore had been shipped from Gogebic County and 67 million tons from adjoining Iron County, Wisconsin

The Calumet Theater was once named the Red Jacket Town Hall and Opera House.

NORRIE PARK – IRONWOOD

This recreational area was named in honor of A. Lanfear Norrie, who in 1882 began to explore for iron ore on the Gogebic Range. His discovery resulted in the opening of the Norrie Mine in Ironwood. Soon other mines, such as the Ashland, Aurora, Pabst and Newport were booming. Ironwood is said to have been named after a mining captain, James Wood, who was nicknamed "Iron" Wood. After a destructive fire in 1887, the community was rebuilt.

HOUGHTON COUNTY
CALUMET THEATER

One of the first municipal theaters in America, the Calumet opened on March 20, 1900, It was called "the greatest social event ever known in copperdom's metropolis." The theater contained a magnificent stage and elegant interior decorations, including an electrified copper chandelier. For over a decade, Copper Country audiences witnessed a broad panorama of American legitimate theater. Many prominent stage personalities, both American and European, trod the boards of the Calumet. By the 1920s, motion pictures replaced live theater, and subsequently, live drama returned to the Calumet. The reopened community theater has resumed its position as a focal point of civic pride for the people of Calumet and the Copper Country.

THE COPPER COUNTRY

Long before Europeans reached America, a mysterious people extracted native copper in this region and worked it into articles which were used throughout the continent. French explorers learned of the vast copper deposits, but were not able to mine the metal. In 1771, an English group led by adventurer Alexander Henry tried without success to mine copper near the site of present-day Victoria. In 1841, Douglass Houghton's survey of copper resources was printed. Prospectors by the hundreds soon flocked here. Boom towns sprang up. The Phoenix was the first real mine to begin operation, but the Cliff was the first to show a profit. Soon miners were tapping the rich deposits all along the Keweenaw Peninsula's backbone. Until 1887, this was the country's leading center of copper production. This was virtually the only area of the world with any substantial native copper production. Copper is found in combination with other elements at the White Pine Mine where a great new mining operation began in the 1950s.

FINLANDIA UNIVERSITY (FORMERLY SUOMI COLLEGE) – HANCOCK

In the 1880s, large numbers of Finns immigrated to Hancock to labor in the copper and lumber industries. One immigrant was mission pastor J. K. Nikander of the Finnish Evangelical Lutheran Church of America headquartered in Hancock. He wanted to ensure seminary training in America. He feared the loss of Finnish identity for he observed that Swedish and Finnish in other areas of the U.S. did not provide seminary training. In 1896, Nikander founded Suomi College. The college's role was to preserve Finnish culture, train Lutheran ministers and teach English. During the 1920s, Suomi became a liberal arts college. In 1958, the seminary separated from the college. Four years later the Finnish Evangelical Lutheran Church of America merged with other mainstream Lutheran churches.

The cornerstone of Old Main, the first building erected at Suomi College, was laid on May 30, 1898. Jacobsville sandstone, quarried at the Portage Entry of the Keweenaw waterway, was brought here by barge, cut and used in construction of the building. Dedicated on January 21, 1900, it contained a dormitory, kitchen, laundry, classrooms, offices, library, chapel and lounge. The burgeoning college quickly outgrew this building, and in 1901 a frame structure, housing a gym, meeting hall and music center was erected on an adjacent lot. The frame building was demolished when Nikander Hall, named for Suomi's founder, J. K. Nikander, was constructed in 1939. The hall was designed by the architectural firm of Saarinen and Swanson.

FINNISH LUTHERAN CHURCH – JACOBSVILLE

In 1886, a group of Finnish immigrants banded together to organize the Jacobsville Finnish Lutheran congregation. Early worship services were held in various locations until 1888, when this simple frame structure was built. In 1890, the congregation helped organize the Finnish Evangelical Lutheran Church - Suomi Synod. In 1891, the church was placed atop its stone foundation and its tower and bell were added a year later. The well-preserved church, one of the oldest remaining structures in the community, retains its original furnishings, kerosene lamps and wood stove. It has neither electricity nor plumbing. In 1952, the congregation and church property became part of the Gloria Dei Lutheran congregation of Hancock. The church continued to be used for summer vesper services in the 1980s.

HANCOCK TOWN HALL AND FIRE HALL

The Quincy Mining Company platted Hancock in 1859; a decade after the company began mining Keewanaw copper. While many copper towns boomed and busted within a short period of time, Hancock remained stable, incorporating as a city in 1875. By 1897, Hancock's four thousand citizens wanted a government building that would reflect the city's prosperity and stature. The Quincy Company sold this lot to the city in 1898 and in January 1899 the Town Hall and Fire Hall opened.

The Marquette firm of Charlton, Gilbert and Demar designed Hancock's Town Hall and Fire Hall. The building housed city offices, the fire department, and the marshall's office and the jail. Built of Jacobsville sandstone with stepped and curved gables, it exhibits Richardsonian Romanesque, Dutch and Flemish influences. The building is listed in the National register of Historic Places.

HOUGHTON COUNTY COURTHOUSE

Organized in 1845, Houghton County once comprised the entire Keweenaw Peninsula. Eagle River was the first county seat. In 1861, after the state legislature split the county into Keweenaw and Houghton, the village of Houghton became the new seat of Houghton County government. Finnish settlers were predominant in the county. There were also Scandinavians, as well as Cornish, Germans and French Canadians. Jobs were plentiful, since Houghton County was the center of the copper boom. In 1874, Michigan produced 88 percent of the nations' copper, of which Houghton county mines supplied 79 percent. Two years later, Michigan copper production peaked at 90 percent of the nation's output. The Michigan Mining School opened in Houghton in 1886. In 1964 it was renamed Michigan Technological University.

The opulent High Victorian design of the Houghton County Courthouse testifies to the prosperity that the copper boom brought to the area in the late 19th Century. The building's irregular form and polychromatic exterior make it one of Michigan's most distinctive 19th Century courthouses. The red sandstone trim and copper roof were products of the Upper Peninsula. The architect, J. B. Sweatt, was from Marquette. Originally from Chicago, Sweatt typified the many architects who worked in Houghton and participated in the building rush that occurred during the copper boom. Dedicated on July 28, 1887, the courthouse replaced a frame structure constructed in 1862.

ITALIAN HALL – CALUMET

On December 24, 1913, area copper miners had been on strike for five months. The miners were fighting for better pay, shortened work days, safer working conditions and union recognition. That day, during a yuletide party for the striking miners and their families, someone yelled, "Fire!" Although there was no fire, 73 persons died while attempting to escape down a stairwell. Over half of those who died were children between the ages of six and ten. The perpetrator of the tragedy was never identified. The strike ended in April 1914.

The Italian Hall was built in 1908 as headquarters for Calumet's benevolent society. The Society, organized along ethnic lines, encouraged and financially aided immigrants and provided relief to victims of hardship. Following the 1913 Christmas Eve tragedy, the hall continued to be used for nearly five decades. The two-story red brick building was razed in 1984. Through the efforts of the Friends of the Italian Hall and Local 324 of the AFL-CIO, the site of the building became a memorial park dedicated ot the people who lost their lives in 1913.

MICHIGAN TECHNOLOGICAL UNIVERSITY – HOUGHTON

In 1885 the state established a mining school here in America's first great metal mining region. As the Michigan College of Mines, it achieved world-wide renown as a center of education and research in mining, metallurgy, and geology. In 1927 and again in 1964, its name was changed and the school's scope was broadened to meet industry's expanding needs. Under its present name, Michigan Technological University, it enrolls men and women in undergraduate and graduate programs in its original subjects and other branches of engineering, science, business, forestry, and liberal arts.

ST. IGNATIUS LOYOLA CHURCH – HOUGHTON

The roots of the Catholic Church in the Portage Lake area are associated with Bishop Frederic Baraga, the "Snowshoe Priest," who dedicated the original St. Ignatius Loyola Church on July 31, 1859. Before the erection of this building, Catholics in Houghton worshiped in a boarding house and later a school. The present structure was completed in 1902, after four years of construction, under the direction of Father Ivan Rezek. Father (later Monsignor) Rezek came as pastor in 1895 and remained in that position for fifty-one years. One of the most imposing edifices in Houghton, St. Ignatius Loyola Church features rockfaced sandstone facades. Beautiful stained glass windows and an elaborate Gothic altar adorn the breathtaking interior.

ST. PAUL THE APOSTLE CHURCH – CALUMET

St. Joseph Roman Catholic Church was established in 1889 by Slovenian immigrants who came to work in Copper Country mines. The wood frame church built in 1890 was destroyed by fire in 1902. The following year construction began on this elegant Romanesque church. It was designed by Erhard Brielmater of Milwaukee and was completed at a cost of $100,000 in 1908. Built of locally-quarried Jacobsville sandstone, the structure displays Cathedral-type stained glass windows from the Ford Brothers Glass Studio of Minneapolis. Its interior features a beautifully painted sixty-five foot nave. In 1966 four parishes consolidated and the name was changed to St. Paul the Apostle.

SUOMI SYNOD – LAURIUM

On March 25, 1890, nine Lutheran congregations representing 1200 Finnish immigrants assembled at Trinity Lutheran Church in Calumet. This group organized the Finnish Evangelical Lutheran Church in America - Suomi Synod. Four pastors and 17 laymen from congregations in Calumet, Hancock, Jacobsville, Republic, Ishpeming, Negaunee and Ironwood, Michigan, as well as Savo, South Dakota chose the Reverend Juho K. Nikander as the first president of the synod. By the 1920s, the synod had become a national church body with 153 congregations and thirty-six thousand members. In 1963, it merged with Lutheran churches of Swedish, German and Danish descent to form the Lutheran Church in America. Calumet's Faith Lutheran Church is a continuation of the Finnish, Swedish and Norwegian group that met at Trinity Lutheran in 1890.

TRINITY EPISCOPAL CHURCH – HOUGHTON

Many of the Cornish miners, storekeepers and mining captains who immigrated to this area during the Copper Country mining boom (1842-1860) were Anglicans. On July 17, 1860, the Reverend Samuel A. McCoskry, Episcopal Bishop of Michigan, met with nine Houghton and Hancock businessmen to establish a parish. The group held its first public worship services on September 15, 1860. At its first vestry meeting on July 13, 1861, the name Trinity Church was adopted. The present Jacobsville sandstone church was completed in 1910. Located on the site of an earlier wooden church, the present building has an interior design influenced by the Oxford Movement. The sanctuary's attractive wood carvings are the handiwork of Aloysius Lang of Oberammergau.

IRON COUNTY

FIRST ROADSIDE PARK – US-2, FOUR MILES EAST OF IRON RIVER

In 1918, the Iron County Board of Supervisors purchased this 320-acre tract of roadside virgin timber and dedicated it as a forest preserve. The following year, Iron County established Michigan's first roadside park and picnic tables. This was also quite likely America's first roadside park. Since then, similar parks have been provided by most states for the comfort and enjoyment of the traveling motorist.

INDIAN VILLAGE – COUNTY ROAD 630, STAMBAUGH TOWNSHIP

Here in October 1851, U.S. surveyor Guy H. Carleton discovered an Ojibwa (Chippewa) Indian village, cemetery and campground. Chief Edwards, last ruler of the Chicaugon Lake tribe, received a patent for this land in 1884. He and his wife Pentoga, for whom this area is named, sold the land in 1891 and moved to the Lac Vieux Desert area. By 1903, only a few burial houses and a brush fence remained of the ancient village. Iron County engineer Herbert Larson, Sr. convinced the county to buy the property and restore it as a park honoring the area's first inhabitants. It was dedicated in 1922.

IRON COUNTY

This county was set off in 1885 from Marquette and Menominee counties. The iron ore deposits found here gave the new county its name. In 1882, the railroad arrived and ore shipments began. Iron River was the first county seat, but after a celebrated struggle, the government was shifted to Crystal Falls in 1899.

The courthouse in Crystal Falls was designed by J.C. Clancy designed in the Richardsonian Romanesque tradition. Constructed of regional materials and completed in 1891, this courthouse commands a view of the city's main street and the valley below. The structure, featuring a domed courtroom with original furnishings, continues to serve a county built from "the iron and the pine."

IRON INN – IRON RIVER

Erected in 1906, this hotel is said to be the first brick commercial building in the city. The Iron Inn is known for a prohibition-era incident, which occurred in February 1920. Here, local attorney Martin McDonough challenged the right of federal Prohibition officer A. V. Dalrymple to arrest, without a warrant, people involved in a wine-making operation. This confrontation was part of the eight-day "Rum Rebellion" against federal policies of seizure relating to Prohibition. It resulted in the reaffirmation of due process in Iron County.

MACKINNON HOUSE - IRON RIVER

Built in the mid-1880s by Donald C. MacKinnon, this house is said to be one of the oldest frame houses in the area. In 1878, MacKinnon and W.H. Seddon began exploring the area for iron ore. MacKinnon and his brother Alexander platted the village of Iron River in 1881. They then filed claims for the first mines—the Nanaimo and the Beta—and helped bring in the railroad in 1882. MacKinnon also served as the first village president. His daughter Sara, born in 1894, married Martin McDonough, an attorney involved in the 1920 "Rum Rebellion" incident.

KEWEENAW COUNTY
EAGLE HARBOR HOUSE – EAGLE HARBOR

Built by the Eagle Harbor Mining Company in 1845, Eagle Harbor House opened to boarders and travelers in 1846 at the beginning of the Keweenaw copper rush. It is the last remaining log building in Eagle Harbor. In 1852, German immigrant Charles Kunz purchased the inn, adding a blacksmith shop and warehouses. Kunz became Keweenaw County's first sheriff in 1861. He owned the boardinghouse until his death in 1902. It was inherited by his nephew, Thomas E. Parks.

Although the economy was based primarily on copper mining, the Keweenaw Peninsula lured visitors with its natural beauty. Beginning in 1846, Eagle Harbor House provided safe lodging to businessmen, prospectors and travelers. County sheriff Thomas E. Parks owned the property from 1902 to 1944. He sold the business to J.C. Westlake in 1946 and his son Fred operated it until 1973. Rehabilitation begun in 1995 restored many interior features.

Photo Courtesy Travel Michigan

FORT WILKINS – COPPER HARBOR

This fort was established in 1844 to control possible Indian uprisings. Two companies of infantry stood guard at this early copper mining and shipping center. In 1846 during the Mexican War, the force was withdrawn. The fort saw a brief redeployment between 1867 and 1869.

LAKE SHORE DRIVE BRIDGE AND EAGLE RIVER

Completed in 1915, this bridge was one of two bridges erected simultaneously by the Michigan State Highway Department across Eagle River. The second was located in nearby Phoenix. Prior to 1915, a Pratt truss bridge crossed the fifty-three foot gorge here. It deteriorated and was replaced by this structure. The highway department designed the bridge, which was constructed by the Wisconsin Bridge and Iron Company of Milwaukee. The Smith-Byers-Sparks Company of Houghton provided the concrete abutments for this steel riveted Warren deck truss bridge. The main span measures 105 feet long and 17 feet wide. In 1990, this bridge was converted to pedestrian use when the adjacent timber bridge opened.

The community of Eagle River grew near the Cliff Mine. Discovered in 1844 and developed by the Pittsburgh and Boston Company, this mine was considered "the first great copper mine in the Western Hemisphere." On August 29, 1846, the *Lake Superior News and Miners' Journal* boasted that Eagle River had "the appearance of a thriving village." In 1850, Prussian immigrant Frank Knivel opened the Knivel Brewery, and in 1862 the Eagle River Fuse Company was established southeast of here on the river. The company manufactured twenty-five thousand feet of fuse per day for use in the mines. In 1861, Keweenaw County was set off from Houghton County and Eagle River became the county seat.

LUCE COUNTY

HELMER HOUSE INN – COUNTY ROAD 417, HELMER

Erected in 1881-82 this two-and-a-half-story structure was built as a mission house and Newberry's Presbyterian Church. It served as a mission station until 1888, when first postmaster Gaylord Helmer purchased it for use as a general store and hotel. In 1894, the village of Helmer became a stagecoach mail stop and Gaylord Helmer added a second structure to accommodate more travelers.

Charles and Jeanie Fyvie purchased the Helmer House Inn and store in 1904. The store housed the post office until 1920, when rural free delivery (RFD) was initiated. The Fyvie family continued to live here and operate the store and hotel until 1950. In 1981, following nearly three decades of disrepair and neglect, the building received new windows, doors, porch, roof and stone facing and was reopened as a hotel to commemorate its centennial.

JAIL AND SHERIFF'S RESIDENCE – NEWBERRY

Constructed in 1894, this graceful Queen Anne style structure served as the Luce County jail and sheriff's residence for over seventy years. The Peninsular Land Company donated the site. The architectural firm of Lovejoy and DeMar from Marquette designed this sturdy edifice from rough-hewn Jacobsville sandstone. The Luce County Historical Society rescued this building from demolition in 1975 and restored it as the Luce County Historical Museum in 1976.

LIFE SAVING STATION – TWO HEARTED RIVER AT LAKE SUPERIOR

Two-Hearted River Life Saving Station was built in 1876. It was erected at a cost of $4,790 and manned by volunteer crews. The facility, a simple two-story building with a small lookout tower, housed a lifeboat and other necessary equipment for recovering endangered sailors. An average crew consisted of six to eight experienced surfmen. In 1915 the Life Saving Service was integrated into the U.S. Coast Guard.

Several shipwrecks occurred near the mouth of the Two-Hearted River, also referred to as the Twin River and the Big Two Hearted River. Among these were the *Cleveland* (1864), the *W. W. Arnold* (1869), and the *Sumatra* (1875). Construction of the life saving station was completed here in 1876. Life savers performed brave rescues of sailors off the *Satellite* (1879) and the *Phineas S. Marsh* (1896). The station was decommissioned in the 1930s and the structure was razed in 1944.

MACKINAC COUNTY

ACROSS THE PENINSULA – US 2 AT OLD PORTAGE ROAD, MORAN TOWNSHIP

Old Portage Road, which ends near here, has been used to cross the peninsula since this shore was first settled. It closely parallels the Indian trail, which was the way of the trapper and traveler in the 17th and 18th Centuries.

BEAUMONT MEMORIAL

On June 6, 1822, Alexis St. Martin (1804-1880), a French Canadian, was accidentally shot in the stomach at this American Fur Company retail store. Dr. William Beaumont, M.D. (1786-1853), army surgeon at Fort Mackinac, nursed him back to health. Although St. Martin's physique was not impaired, his stomach wound refused to heal, leaving an opening through which the doctor could observe the digestive process. Beaumont convinced St. Martin to become the subject of a medical study of digestion and wrote several articles on the findings from these experiments. St. Martin married and fathered seventeen children. He out-lived Beaumont by twenty-seven years. The Michigan State Medical Society acquired the retail store in 1947 and, after building this memorial to Dr. Beaumont in 1953, gave the structure to the Mackinac Island State Park Commission.

AMERICAN FUR COMPANY STORE AND BEAUMONT MEMORIAL – MACKINAC ISLAND

On June 6, 1822, French-Canadian Voyageur Alexis St. Martin (1804 ~1889) was accidentally shot in the American Fur Company store located on this site. Dr. William Beaumont (1786 ~1853), The Fort Mackinac post surgeon nursed St. Martin back to health. St. Martin's wound healed but he was left with a permanent opening into his stomach. Through this opening Beaumont compared the digestibility of foods, recorded the temperature of the stomach under different conditions, and extracted and analyzed gastric juices. Beaumont conducted the first of 250 experiments with St. Martin in 1825 in the Officers' Stone Quarters at Fort Mackinac. Eight years later he published a ground breaking book on his discovery of the digestive process.

BATTLEFIELD OF 1814 – MACKINAC ISLAND

Here in this area on Aug. 4, 1814, an American force battled the British in a vain attempt to recapture the island, which the British had seized at the outbreak of the War of 1812. The Americans, under Col. George Croghan, came ashore at what is known as British Landing where they came under strong resistance as they advanced inland. An attempt to outflank the British line was repulsed by Indians hidden in the thick woods and resulted in the death of Maj. Andrew Holmes. Croghan withdrew when he found he could not defeat the British.

BIDDLE HOUSE – MACKINAC ISLAND

This house is probably the oldest on the island. Parts of it may date back to 1780. In 1822, Edward Biddle obtained a deed to the property with a $100 down payment. Biddle was a cousin of the Biddles of Philadelphia and a leading trader and citizen. For years he lived in this house with his Indian wife. The house is an example of the Quebec rural style. It is listed in the Historic American Buildings Survey and was restored by the Michigan Society of Architects and the building industry in 1959.

BOIS BLANC ISLAND (POPULAR PRONUNCIATION "BOB LO")

On August 3, 1795, Chippewa Chief Matchekewis ceded Bois Blanc to the United States as part of the treaty of Greenville. The cession also included most of Ohio, part of Indiana, sixteen strategic sites on Michigan waterways and Mackinac Island. During the War of 1812, U.S. Navy Captain Arthur Sinclair's fleet took shelter at the island while waiting to attack the British at Fort Mackinac. In 1880, the island provided a haven to alleged murderer Henry English who escaped from Pennsylvania authorities before his trial. He was apprehended on Bois Blanc by Pinkerton agents, returned to Pennsylvania and acquitted. During the twentieth century, Bois Blanc's wilderness supported a lucrative lumber industry before giving way to tourism. Although primarily a resort in 1990, the island had forty-five permanent residents.

BRITISH CANNON – MACKINAC ISLAND

Early on the morning of July 17, 1812, British troops placed a cannon on this promintory overlooking Ft. Mackinac. This move, coupled with the size of the British forces, resulted in the American garrison's surrender.

BRITISH LANDING – MACKINAC ISLAND

During the night of July 16-17, 1812, a small force of British regulars and several hundred voyageurs and Indian allies from St. Joseph Island landed here. They occupied a hill that overlooked Fort Mackinac and demanded its surrender. Lt. Porter Hanks, commander of the American garrison of 57 soldiers, did not know that war had been declared. The reconstruction of this bark chapel is dedicated to the memory of this heroic pioneer priest.

EARLY MISSIONARY BARK CHAPEL – MACKINAC ISLAND

Bark chapels were built in the Indian villages of the Great Lakes. Courageous French "black robes" lived in these primitive huts and sought to bring Christianity to the native population. One of these blackrobes, Father Claude Dablon from the mission of Sault Ste. Marie, wintered on Mackinac Island in 1670-71 and carried on missionary work here. It is in memory of this heroic pioneer priest that this reconstruction of a bark chapel is dedicated.

EPOUFETTE

Epoufette has been a fishing village since 1859. That year Amable Goudreau, born in Quebec around 1824, established a commercial fishery here. While Goudreau died in 1882, some of his descendants continued fishing operations a century later. Father Edward Jacker, then serving the St. Ignace and Mackinac missions, visited Epoufette in August 1875. He reported a thriving fishery, with nets as far as 40 miles distant, which kept two coopers busy from dawn to dusk making barrels for shipment of salted fish to distant markets.

FORT DU BUADE – ST. IGNACE

This fort was built by the French near here within a decade after Marquette had established his mission in 1671. Its name is from the family of Frontenac, the French Governor of North America. Until Detroit was founded in 1701, this was the most important French post west of Montreal. The fort's commandant had charge of all other French forts in the West. Also known as Fort Michilimackinac, it was the first of three forts which were to bear this name in the Straits area.

FORT HOLMES – MACKINAC ISLAND

Here in 1812 on the island's highest point, a blockhouse and stockade were built by the British and named Fort George. In 1814, it was the bulwark of British defenses when the American attack was repulsed. After the war the Americans renamed the post in honor of Maj. Holmes who was killed during the American assault. The fort was not maintained by the Americans however. The present blockhouse is not the original building.

GRAND HOTEL – MACKINAC ISLAND

This "grand" hotel opened in July 1887. It was built by a consortium of three companies with legislative help from Senator Francis Stockbridge. Constructed of Michigan white pine, the structure boasts a magnificent colonial porch—the longest in the world. It is a classic example of gracious living seldom seen today. One of the outstanding landmarks on the Great Lakes, it is the world's largest summer hotel.

GROS CAP AND ST. HELENA ISLAND

French fishermen came to Gros Cap early last century. They also participated in the off-shore settlement of St. Helena Island—the place ships obtained wood fuel and other supplies. In 1850, Archie and Wilson Newton set up a fishing and shipping business. The community thrived for more than thirty years.

HISTORIC FORT MACKINAC – MACKINAC ISLAND

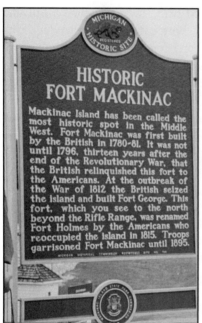

Mackinac Island has been called the most historic spot in the Middle West. Fort Mackinac was first built by the British in 1780-81. It took until 1796—thirteen years after the end of the Revolutionary War—for the British to relinquished this fort to the United States. At the onset of the War of 1812, the British seized the island and built Fort George. This fort, which you see to the north beyond the Rifle Range, was renamed Fort Holmes by the Americans who reoccupied the island in 1815. Troops garrisoned Fort Mackinac until 1895.

INDIAN DORMITORY – MACKINAC ISLAND

The Treaty of 1836 was one of the earliest attempts to consider the Indian problem in a humanitarian way. The treaty provided for "a dormitory for the Indians visiting the post." Completed in 1838, the building was designed by Indian Agent Henry R. Schoolcraft, the author of the treaty. For ten years it served as a guest house for Indians who came to the island to receive their annual payments. From 1848 to 1867 the building was used for a variety of purposes, including that of a U. S. Customs House. In 1867, it became the Mackinac Island School and served this purpose until it was closed in 1860. Four years later, the building was purchased by the Mackinac Island Park Commission. The building was restored in 1966 to conform to the original Schoolcraft plans.

ISLAND HOUSE – MACKINAC ISLAND

By the 1880s, the Island House was known as "The best family hotel on the island."

Constructed for Charles O'Malley about 1852, this building was one of the first summer hotels on Mackinac Island. Great Lakes mariner Captain Henry Van Allen purchased the hotel in 1865. He later moved it from the beach to its present location. By the 1880s, the Island House was known as "The best family hotel on the island." Mrs. Rose Van Allen Webster became proprietor about 1892. She was the wife of Colonel John Webster, whom she had met during the 1870s when he was stationed at Fort Mackinac. Mrs.

Webster added the large wings in 1895 and 1912, retaining ownership until her death in 1938. The Island House still serves as a resort hotel.

LAKE MICHIGAN – PARK ON US 2 SIX MILES WEST OF ST. IGNACE

This lake, the sixth largest in the world, was discovered in 1634 by Jean Nicolet. He explored the north shore to Green Bay looking for a passage to the Orient. The general shape of the lake was established in 1670s by Marquette and Jolliet. They named it Lake Michigan. Its elongated shape was an obstacle to transcontinental expansion, but its water soon proved a real boon to commerce.

LAKE VIEW HOTEL – MACKINAC ISLAND

Originally known as the Lake View House, this is one of the oldest continuously operated hotels on Mackinac Island. Reuben Chapman built the structure in 1858. After his death in 1860, the hotel was operated by his wife, Maria. In 1880, structure was purchased by the Chapmans' daughter, Jeannie and her husband Claude C. Cable. Later, they changed the name to the Lake View Hotel. In the 1890s as Mackinac Island became a midwestern tourist mecca, the hotel was enlarged and two large towers were added. The restaurant and bar were built in 1969 and expanded in 1975. The original portion of the hotel is a well preserved example of vernacular resort architecture. The handsome building is accented by an open, wood columned porch with a modified hipped roof and a raised basement.

LITTLE STONE CHURCH – MACKINAC ISLAND

The Union Congregational Church is affectionately known as the Little Stone Church. It was established in 1900 by eleven charter members. Local residents and summer visitors donated funds for its construction. The cornerstone was laid on August 2, 1904. This structure was built of Mackinac Island stones in an eclectic Gothic style. Installed in '94, its handsome stained glass windows tell the story of the Protestant movement on the Island. Open only during the summer, this church has been a landmark to visitors and a popular wedding site.

MACKINAC CONFERENCE – MACKINAC ISLAND

On September 6, 1943, Michigan's Republican United States Senator Arthur H. Vandenberg chaired the meeting of the Post War Advisory Council. Republican National Committee Chairman Harrison Spangler created the council to draw up a foreign policy plank for the 1944 party platform. Fearing a split between isolationists and internationalists, Spangler wanted a unified policy statement on treaty ratification and the proposed world peace organization. The resulting plank cleared the way for Republican congressional support of the United Nations and ultimately the North Atlantic Treaty Organization. Among those attending the public sessions were Governors Warren of California, Dewey of New York, Kelly of Michigan, Green of Illinois, and Senator Robert A. Taft of Ohio.

MACKINAC ISLAND

In 1670, Jesuit missionary Claude Dablon wintered here. Just over a century later, the British made it their center of military and fur trading activity. The island was occupied by the Americans in 1796. It was taken back by the British during the War of 1812 and then became the hub of John Jacob Astor's fur empire after 1817. Mackinac was already becoming a popular resort when fur trading declined in the 1830s.

MACKINAC STRAITS

Nicolet passed through the Straits in 1634 seeking a route to the Orient. Soon it became a crossroads where Indian, missionary, trapper and soldier met. From the 1600s through the War of 1812, the French, British and Americans struggled for control of this strategic waterway. In 1679, the French *Griffin* was the first sailing vessel to ply these waters. The vessel disappeared, likely sinking in the area of the Straits. The railroad reached the Straits in 1882. Until the Mackinac Bridge was opened in 1957, ferries linked the north and south.

MARKET STREET – MACKINAC ISLAND

During the peak of the fur trade, this street bustled with activity. Each July and August Indians, traders and trappers by the thousands came here with furs from throughout the Northwest. In 1817, John Jacob Astor's American Fur Co. located its headquarters on Mackinac Island. Furs with a total value of $3,000,000 went through the Market Street offices in 1822. After 1834, the fur trade moved westward.

MISSION CHURCH – MACKINAC ISLAND

This is one of Michigan's oldest Protestant churches. It was built in 1829-30 by the congregation of Presbyterian minister William Ferry. Ferry founded a nearby Indian mission in 1823. Among its more notable members were Robert Stuart and Henry Schoolcraft who served as lay leaders. About 1838, private owners bought the building. It is judged Michigan's best example of Colonial church style.

MISSION HOUSE – MACKINAC ISLAND

In 1823, the Reverend William Ferry founded a Mission on Mackinac Island on the land now known as Mission Point. Two years later he and his wife Amanda erected a building which served as a boarding school for Indian children. In 1827, 112 students attended the school. The majority of the resident pupils were *metis,* children of Indian and Euro-American parents. The mission closed in 1837. In 1849, Edward Franks opened the Mission House Hotel after adding a third story to the structure. The Franks family operated the hotel until 1939 when it was sold and converted into a rooming house. In 1946, Miles and Margaret Phillimore bought the property, which provided a base for the Moral Re-Armament movement. Around 1971, the Cathedral of Tomorrow purchased the site. Six years later the Mission House became part of the Mackinac Island State Park.

NORTHERNMOST POINT OF LAKE MICHIGAN – ROADSIDE PARK, 3 MILES EAST OF NAUBINWAY

This geographical point is of historical importance because the act of Congress which created the territory of Michigan in 1805. This point was used to mark the western boundary of this frontier governmental unit. The boundary ran up the middle of Lake Michigan "to its northern extremity, and thence due north to the northern boundary of the United States." West of this line the Upper Peninsula was originally part of Indiana Territory. In 1818, Michigan's boundary was pushed west to the Mississippi River. The territory then included all of the U.P., along with what is now Wisconsin and parts of Minnesota.

ROUND ISLAND LIGHTHOUSE

The Round Island Lighthouse was completed in 1895. It was manned by a crew of three until its beacon was replaced by an automated light in 1924. A sole caretaker occupied and operated the station from 1924 to 1947. Following the construction of a new automatic beacon near the breakwater off the south shore of Mackinac Island, the lighthouse was abandoned. The United States Forest Service now supervises the structure which is located in the Hiawatha National Forest. The lighthouse serves as a sentinel for the past, reminding visitors of the often precarious sailing and rich history of the Straits of Mackinac.

SAINTE ANNE CHURCH – MACKINAC ISLAND

In 1670, Jesuit Father Charles Dablon founded a birchbark mission chapel on Mackinac Island. The following year, Father Jacques Marquette relocated the mission at St. Ignace. Abandoned in 1706 and reestablished at Fort Michilimackinac around 1715, the new church was named Sainte Anne de Michilimackinac. During the winter of 1780 - 1781, the church building was moved across the ice to the Island. It is the nation's oldest church dedicated to Saint Anne, and maintains baptismal records dating from April 1695.

ST. IGNACE

In 1671, Pere Marquette established the Mission of St. Ignace. French troops soon after built Fort Buade. The state's second oldest white village guarded the Straits while serving as the most important French fur post in the northwest. By 1706, both the fort and mission where abandoned. It took until the 19th century before lumbering and fishing revived the town.

ST. IGNACE MISSION

Marquette operated this mission for two years. Then in 1673, he left on his great journey to the Mississippi Valley. He never returned to his mission before he died in 1675. Two years later his remains were reburied here beneath the chapel altar. In 1706, after French troops abandoned the fort, the chapel was destroyed.

SKULL CAVE – MACKINAC ISLAND

According to tradition, this is the cave in which the English fur-trader Alexander Henry hid out during the Indian uprising of 1763. He claimed the floor of the cave was covered with human bones, presumably those of area Indians.

TRINITY CHURCH – MACKINAC ISLAND

Episcopal services on Mackinac Island date from 1837, when a Bishop preached in the Mission Church. For many years the congregation met in the post Chapel at Fort Mackinac and in the Court House. In 1873, a parish was organized and in 1882 this church building was constructed. Its furnishings include an altar of hand-carved walnut, and two chancel chairs made by soldiers at the fort.

WAWASHKAMO GOLF CLUB – MACKINAC ISLAND

In 1898 Chicago cottagers founded the Wawashkamo Golf Club. By 1900, the club was incorporated and the clubhouse was built on the site of the 1814 Battle of Mackinac Island. Wawashkamo is Indian for "Crooked Trail." Golf course architect Alex B. Smith left the natural features of the site unaltered in his design for this true nine-hole Scottish links. Wawashkamo Golf Club is Michigan's oldest unchanged private nine-hole golf course.

MARQUETTE COUNTY

CLIFFS SHAFT MINE – ISHPEMING

Opened by the Iron Cliffs Co. in 1879, the mine was acquired by present owner Cleveland-Cliffs Iron Co. (now Cliffs Natural Resources) in 1891. The Cliffs Shaft was the nation's largest producer of hard specular hematite, a type of iron ore. Over 26 million tons were mined and since 1887 ore was shipped every year but one. The mine was also one of the largest Michigan iron mines—its sixty-five miles of tunnels running under most of Ishpeming, plunging to a depth of 1358 feet. In the late 1930s, there were still eight iron mines in Ishpeming. The Cliffs Shaft was the last of these and its closing in 1967 marked the end of an era.

One of the two remaining headframes of the Cliff Shaft Mine.

FATHER MARQUETTE PARK – MARQUETTE

Serving as Priests, explorers, cartographers, linguists, farmers, scientists and chroniclers, Jesuit missionaries introduced Christianity to the Great Lakes region. Among them was Father Jacques Marquette. In 1671, he brought a large contingent of Indians who had been forced east by the Sioux and established St. Ignace mission at the Straits of Mackinac. From there, Marquette and Louis Jolliet set out on their voyage to the Mississippi River in the spring of 1673. Ill before the journey began, Marquette died on May 18, 1675 during the return trip. He was 37 years old. Indians from St. Ignace later brought Marquette's remains to a chapel on the site where they were rediscovered in 1877 by Father Edward Jacker.

FIRST STEAM RAILROAD IN THE U.P. – MARQUETTE

On this site in 1852, the Green Bay and Lake Superior Rail-Road began the survey which led to the construction of the first steam railroad in the Upper Peninsula. The railroad ran from Marquette to the Jackson and Cleveland iron mines fourteen miles away. In 1855, the building of the railroad along the previously surveyed route was begun by the Iron Mountain Railroad Company. By 1857, it was hauling ore from the mines to Marquette. It later years, it became part of the Duluth, South Shore and Atlantic Railroad, which has operated since 1961 as the Soo Line. This railroad and others like it carried millions of tons of ore, the basic raw material for the rapidly developing steel industry in the United States.

ISHPEMING: HISTORIC SKI CENTER

The sport of skiing was introduced to America in the 19th Century by Scandinavian immigrants. The first ski club in Michigan and one of the first in the country was formed at Ishpeming in 1887. It held its first public ski meet on February 25, 1888. The longest ski jump during this inaugural meet was only 35 feet. Since then, this city has produced many famous ski jumpers who have gained their experience on renowned Suicide Hill. The National Ski Association was formed in Ishpeming on February 21, 1904.

JACKSON MINE – NEGAUNEE

On Sept. 19, 1844 at present-day Negaunee, government surveyor William A. Burt discovered the great Lake Superior iron ore deposits. Peculiar fluctuations in his magnetic compass led Burt to ask his men to seek the cause, and they soon returned with pieces of iron ore from out-croppings in the area. Next year, prospectors from Jackson, Michigan led by Philo M. Everett arrived at the Carp River. That summer, Ojibwa chief Marji-Gesick guided members of the party to rich iron ore deposits As a result of the discovery, the Jackson Mining Company began the first mining operation of the Lake Superior Region in 1847.

Ojibwa chief Marji-Gesick

MARQUETTE COUNTY COURTHOUSE – MARQUETTE

This Neo-Classical Revival structure designed by Charleton & Gilbert of Marquette was constructed between 1902 and 1904 at a cost of $210,000. Built of local sandstone, it is the second courthouse to occupy this site. In a case tried here in 1913, President Theodore Roosevelt won a libel suit against Ishpeming newspaper publisher George Newett and was awarded six cents, "the price of a good newspaper." Another case tried here inspired *Anatomy of a Murder*, a novel by Ishpeming resident John D. Voelker. In 1959, the courthouse was the setting of the motion picture based on the novel. The picture was directed by Otto Preminger, with musical score written and performed by Duke Ellington. The courthouse was renovated in 1982-1984 at a cost of $2.4 million.

MARQUETTE IRON RANGE – NEGAUNEE

The first of the immensely rich Lake Superior iron ore deposits were discovered on the Marquette Iron Range at Negaunee. In 1844, William A. Burt and his surveying party discovered outcroppings of

Original Jackson Mine monument in its original location early 1900s.

iron ore south of Teal Lake. This area soon became the first and remained the chief center of the range's mining. In 1847, real production first began at the Jackson Mine. Operations at the early mines were confined to extracting ore close to the surface. Underground mining began after the Civil War. A forge built on the Carp River produced iron blooms in 1848. The Pioneer Furnace in Negaunee, built in 1857-58, was the first actual blast furnace. Most ore was shipped out to be smelted. When the Iron Mountain Railroad was built in 1857, ore could be easily shipped to Marquette. At the Marquette docks, the ore was loaded aboard ships and carried through the Soo Canal to the growing industrial centers in the East. Copper, gold, silver and lead have been mined here but in only small amounts, leaving iron supreme.

NORTHERN MICHIGAN UNIVERSITY – MARQUETTE

Northern State Normal School was established by an act of the State Legislature in 1899. Its original mission was to provide teachers for Upper Peninsula schools. A four-year collegiate program was introduced in 1918 and the first Bachelor of Arts degree was conferred two years later. In the 1950s, Northern became a multipurpose institution placing emphasis on instruction, service, and research. The next year it established its own graduate program leading to the Master of Arts degree. Serving an ever increasing student body, Northern achieved university status through an act of the Legislature in 1963.

SAM COHODAS LODGE – MICHIGAMME TOWNSHIP

This lodge, built for Russian immigrant Sam Cohodas, symbolizes the Upper Peninsula's ethnic diversity. Finnish craftsmen erected this massive lodge in 1934, following plans drawn by local architect and Swedish immigrant David Anderson. The rustic log lodge is built of materials gathered within a fifteen-mile radius of the site. Cohodas was one of the nation's leading fruit wholesalers. The Sam Cohodas Lodge was listed on the National Register of Historic Places in 1991.

In 1903, Sam Cohodas (1895 - 1988) and his family left present-day Byelorussia, U.S.S.R. They joined his father who immigrated to Marinette, Wisconsin in 1900. Like many Jews, the Cohodases fled the eastern European pogroms. Cohodas, his father and brothers worked in an uncle's produce business. In 1915, Sam and his brother Harry began their own retail and wholesale company in Michigan's Copper Country. Under Sam's direction, the business boomed nationally. This lodge, erected in 1934, served as his wilderness camp from 1935 to 1972.

MENOMINEE COUNTY

CHAPPEE RAPIDS – RIVER ROAD WEST OF MENOMINEE

Stanislaus Chaput, a French-Canadian fur trader sometimes called Louis Chappee, became the first settler at the mouth of the Menominee River in the early 1800s. He fought, along with most of the Green Bay traders, in the British attack on Fort Mackinac during the War of 1812. After the war, he traded extensively in the northern Wisconsin region, working for Green Bay fur magnate John Lawe. In 1824, Chaput was forcibly deposed from his original Menominee River location by rival traders. He moved his operation a few miles upstream where he built a fortified trading post at the foot of the rapids. Until Chaput's death in the 1850s, the post at the rapids was a center of trade for the surrounding villages of Menominee Indians.

HERMANSVILLE – U.S.-2 NEAR COUNTY RD. 388

German immigrant Charles J. L. Meyer of Minden continued his family's tradition of woodworking when he founded a sash, door and blinds plant at Fond du Lac, Wisconsin. In 1878, he bought pine timberlands and founded the town of Hermansville to supply lumber to his Fond du Lac factories. The village was named for his son Herman, who served as first postmaster for the village, while the township took the Meyer family name. Meyer's son-in-law George Washington Earle helped bring the lumber company Meyer founded through difficult times. Earle led the company to pre-eminence by producing precision finished hardwood flooring on machines which Meyer designed and manufactured. The flooring factory closed in 1943.

MENOMINEE/MAIN STREET HISTORIC DISTRICT

French-Canadian voyager Louis Chaput (Chappee) came here during the late 1790s. Chaput, an agent for the American Fur Company, was the first white settler in the Menominee area. Within the next one hundred years, Menominee developed into a prosperous city, built along the waterfront with money from the booming lumber industry. By 1890, twelve steam powered mills operated here. The fishing and paper industries and the production of pig iron contributed to a broadening economic base. By 1902, the population had reached thirty thousand. As the pine forests of the Upper Peninsula were depleted, the population declined. During the 1990s, it stabilized at nine thousand.

The Main Street Historic District is comprised of buildings dating from the prosperous era of lumbering and shipping that began around 1890. Local architects and others from Chicago, Minneapolis and Green Bay designed buildings constructed of native red sandstone and locally made brick. The general store of Ludington, Wells and Van Schalk Company located at 501 First Street, served employees of the second largest lumber company in the county. The Paalzow Building at 409 First Street was built in 1895 and displays the only example in the district of a cast iron facade. The Main Street Historic District is listed in the National Register of Historic Places.

MENOMINEE AREA

This was the home of the Menominee Indians. French explorer Jean Nicolet visited them in 1634 on his futile search for a passage to the Orient. Conflict over fishing rights brought on the Sturgeon War here between the Menominee and Chippewa tribes. During the 1700s, this became a center of the fur trade. Menominee remained the Upper Peninsula's main lumber port until about 1910 when most of the trees in the area were gone. Its timber helped rebuild Chicago after the 1871 fire.

ONTONAGON COUNTY
PORCUPINE MOUNTAINS – CARP LAKE TOWNSHIP

From Lake Superior, the main range of mountains looking toward the Upper Peninsula mainland looks like a crouching porcupine, thus their name. Machinery, rock dumps, and old adits are ghostly reminders of forty mining ventures from 1846 to 1928, none of which succeeded. Some logging took place around 1916. As late as 1930, a few trappers eked out a living here. Finally in 1945, the area was made a state park to preserve its virgin splendor.

SCHOOLCRAFT COUNTY

BISHOP BARAGA'S FIRST CHURCH – MANISTIQUE

Near this site, on May 15, 1832, the Catholic missionary Father Frederic Baraga established and blessed his first church. A small building of logs and bark, it was built with the willing help of the Indians and dedicated "to the honor of God under the name and patronage of his Virginal Mother Mary." Until his death in 1868, Father Baraga labored selflessly in an area from Minnesota to Sault Ste. Marie, from Grand Rapids to Eagle Harbor. World famous as a missionary, he became upper Michigan's first Roman Catholic Bishop in 1853.

LIME KILN – MANISTIQUE TOWNSHIP

These towers are the remains of kilns used by the White Marble Lime Company founded by George Nicholson, Jr. in 1889. The kilns, which were fired by wood waste from the lumber industry, burned dolomite to produce quicklime for use as a building material and an ingredient in the manufacture of paper. As larger corporations were formed and the methods of producing lime were made more efficient, the company diversified. It established a sawmill and a shingle mill and became a dealer in forest products as well as crushed stone, cement and builders' supplies. Its operations here and in Manistique and Blaney once employed some 250 men. In 1925, the company was reorganized as the Manistique Lime and Stone Company, and continued under that name until the Depression of 1929.

THOMPSON/CHRISTMAS TREE SHIP

The *Rouse Simmons* was one of the last schooners on the Great Lakes. Built in 1868 to carry lumber, the three-masted vessel became Chicago's "Christmas Tree Ship" when Captain Herman Schuenemann purchased an interest in it in 1910. Around 1876, the Schuenemanns

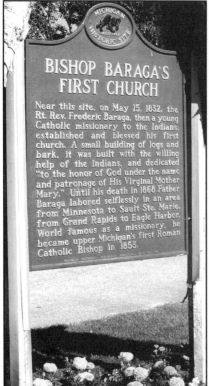

began transporting trees from northern Michigan and Wisconsin to Chicago. In November 1898, Herman's brother August perished in the wreck of the Schooner *S. Thal,* but Herman continued in the business. On November 22, 1912, the *Simmons* set sail from Thompson with a load of Christmas trees bound for Chicago. Schuenemann and his crew sailed into a severe snowstorm and gale, which took took them down near Manitowoc, Wisconsin. Herman's wife and daughters kept the Christmas tree business going until around 1934.

The Delta Lumber Company of Detroit, headed by E.L. Thompson, platted the village of Thompson in 1888. Seven different lumber companies ran the mill in the village. By 1907, the population had reached 900. Three churches and four saloons served the residents along with a general store, hotel, and a hospital. Stagecoaches carried passengers twice daily to nearby Manistique. The Thompson Railroad, used primarily for hauling logs to the docks, also took tours to the Big Spring, *Kitchitikipi.* Lumbering activities in Thompson died out quickly, and by 1919 the town's population had dropped to only 150.

GEOLOGY OF UPPER MICHIGAN

Underlying the Upper Peninsula of Michigan are two broad regions of bedrock—Precambrian and Phanerozoic. Precambrian rocks cover the western portion of the peninsula and are the far southern terminus of the Canadian Shield—the first area of the North American continent to be exposed. This shield is home to the oldest rocks and mountains in the world. The rocks date back to the Archean and Proterozoic eras, some 2.5 billion years ago. The Huron Mountains of the north-central Upper Peninsula and the Porcupine Mountains of the west are remnants of this ancient mountain range. The rich mineral resources of the region, including iron, copper, silver and gold are found in these rocks.

The eastern Upper Peninsula is underlain with rocks of the Phanerozoic eon. These are much younger rocks, dating back around 540 million years ago. These rocks were deposited by successive layers of marine sediment. Seas advanced and retreated over this region and areas to the south and east over millions of years. The sand of the seas eventually hardened to sandstone. A sandstone peculiar to the Upper Peninsula is called Jacobsville Sandstone. The Jacobsville formation can be found along the shoreline of Lake Superior from Sault Ste. Marie to Munising and Marquette, and then along the shore of Lake Superior to Keweenaw Bay as well as a good portion of the Keweenaw Peninsula. The reddish stone is found in the architecture of many of the churches and heritage buildings of the region.

About a billion years ago, a great fracture in the earth running from what is now Oklahoma to Lake Superior became volcanically active. Lava flows created mountains covering western Upper Michigan, northern Minnesota and Wisconsin. Molten magma eventually spewed out to the sides beneath the highlands of what is now Lake Superior. The area sank forming the great rock basin now occupied by the lake.

This mammoth lava flow was subjected to great pressure over time. This pressure crinkled the lava flow downward in the middle and upward on its edges into the shape of a "U." The "U" was pushed incessantly from the side and caused the edges to fracture into overlapping ridges. Isle Royale was formed in this way along with the main ridge that runs along the Keweenaw Peninsula from near Copper Harbor southwest through the high country of Ontonagon County to the Porcupine Mountains. These pressure ridges give the western highlands of the Upper Peninsula its unique, rugged character.

Eastern Upper Michigan bedrock is overlain with glacial drift. The great ice sheets advanced and retreated over about five million years. The Wisconsinan ice sheet was the last glacier to retreat and leave the area between 7,000 and 9,000 years ago. It is glacial material from this era that is found in the Upper Peninsula. As the glaciers left, their leading

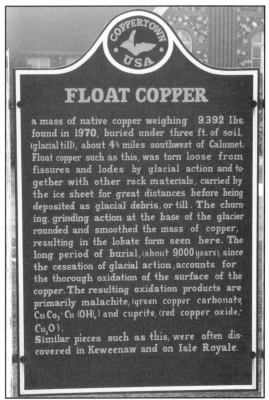

FLOAT COPPER

a mass of native copper weighing 9,392 lbs. found in 1970, buried under three ft. of soil, (glacial till), about 4½ miles southwest of Calumet. Float copper such as this, was torn loose from fissures and lodes by glacial action and together with other rock materials, carried by the ice sheet for great distances before being deposited as glacial debris, or till. The churning, grinding action at the base of the glacier rounded and smoothed the mass of copper, resulting in the lobate form seen here. The long period of burial, (about 9000 years), since the cessation of glacial action, accounts for the thorough oxidation of the surface of the copper. The resulting oxidation products are primarily malachite, (green copper carbonate $Cu\,Co_3 \cdot Cu\,(OH)_2$) and cuprite, (red copper oxide; Cu_2O).
Similar pieces such as this, were often discovered in Keweenaw and on Isle Royale.

This specimen of float copper found in 1970, weighs 9,392 lbs.

edges created high ridges. Huge lakes formed between these ridges, which eventually evolved into the Great Lakes of today.

The glaciers were ice flows thousands of feet thick. When they retreated the land began rebounding. It is still rising today—around a foot per century over the far northern portion of the Upper Peninsula. This raising of the land contributed to the difference in elevation between Lake Superior and Lakes Michigan and Huron. Lake Superior is over 20 feet higher than Michigan and Huron. For this reason, water flows from the Lake Superior basin down to the Lower Great Lakes.

In summary, the geology of Upper Michigan and Lake Superior played a large role in the development of the area. The height of Lake Superior and its resulting isolation from the Lower Lakes slowed early growth, while on the other hand, the mineral riches found in the hills of the western U.P. spurred development and contributed greatly to the growth and expansion of the United States into the 20th Century.

Chapter 2

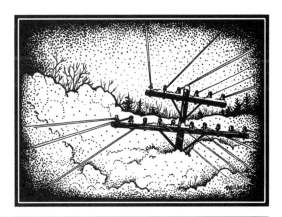

WEATHER

The Upper Peninsula of Michigan covers 16,500 square miles and is bordered by three of the Great Lakes and the State of Wisconsin on the south. Most of the land mass lies above the 45th parallel of latitude, well within the "middle latitudes" of the Northern Hemisphere. This geographical position insures Upper Michigan a vigorous, changeable climate with four distinct seasons (Though the joke is that there are only two seasons—winter and rough sledding!).

The Great Lakes modify the climate in all seasons and give rise to the infamous "lake-effect." The Lakes affect temperature and precipitation in all seasons. During the cold season, the near-shore areas are warmed by their proximity to the Great Lakes. Winter is a time of evaporation when cold, dry air draws moisture off the Lakes and drops that moisture as snow on downwind shores. In the U.P., areas downwind of Lake Superior experience this phenomenon on a regular basis owing to the predominant wind off the Lake.

The phrase "cooler near the lake" is frequently used in weather forecasts during the spring and summer. Water warms more slowly than land and this means areas along the Great Lakes shores will be as much as 30 degrees or more cooler than inland locations, especially during the spring when the lakes are coldest. Summer is a time of condensation when warmer air masses over the Great Lakes are cooled, forcing the water vapor in the air to condense forming fog. Occasionally these fog banks roll into communities along the shores. The coolest weather over the U.P. in the warm season occurs along the north shore of Lake Michigan where the predominant southerly wind blows the full length of the chilly lake.

The following charts feature a representative town from each county and illustrate average and extreme temperatures, precipitation and snowfall as well as information on the growing season and severe weather, specifically tornadoes. The chapter concludes with a section on U.P. weather extremes.

TEMPERATURE

The Upper Peninsula of Michigan's temperature pattern exhibits both continental and maritime characteristics. This means areas in the interior, away from the influence of the Great Lakes, have wide swings in temperature similar to land areas over the rest of the North American continent. At the same time, communities near the Great Lakes normally have more moderate temperatures. This is because water gains and retains heat more slowly than land.

For example, Munising, near chilly Lake Superior, has an average high temperature in May of 60 degrees. May's average high in Iron Mountain-Kingsford, far from Great Lakes influence, is 67.8 degrees. In October, Munising stays warmer near the Lake. The average low there is 37.6 degrees, while in Iron Mountain it is 34.

The terrain of Upper Michigan can sometimes trump lake-effect in certain situations. The hottest day on record occurred in Marquette, situated on the shore of Lake Superior. On July 15, 1901 a sweltering high of 108 degrees was recorded. That day a gusty southwesterly wind blew off the land. There

The last 3 winters of the 70's were cold and snowy over Upper Michigan. This is a view from Escanaba January 1979. (Photo courtesy of Delta Co. Historical Society from "So Cold A Sky".)

was no cooling influence off the Lake. In addition, the hills to the southwest of the city contributed to the warming because of a unique property of air—it warms up when it sinks. The rate of warming is approximately 5 degrees per 1000 feet. So the 800-foot hills to the city's southwest likely tacked 3 to 4 degrees on the high temperature that July day.

The following charts show the average high and low temperatures for a city in each Upper Peninsula county as well as the average mean temperature for each month. The next chart shows the warmest month and coldest month in the period of record as well as the warmest and coldest day.

Beach-goers cooling their beverages with Lake Superior ice on June 1, 1996. (Photo courtesy of the Ed Kearney collection, taken from "So Cold a Sky")

St. Ignace/Mackinac County
1971-2000 Normals

Element	JAN	FEB	MAR	APR	MAY	JUN	JUL	AUG	SEP	OCT	NOV	DEC	ANN
Max °F	24.8	26.4	35.0	46.8	59.7	69.3	75.2	74.3	65.6	53.7	40.9	30.4	50.2
Min °F	12.2	11.9	20.3	31.9	42.8	52.9	59.6	59.7	51.6	41.6	31.5	20.7	36.4
Mean °F	18.5	19.2	27.7	39.4	51.3	61.1	67.4	67.0	58.6	47.7	36.2	25.6	43.3

Temperature Extremes
Period of Record: 1973-2001

Month	High Mean°F	Year	Low Mean°F	Year	1-Day Max°F	Date	1-Day Min°F	Date
JAN	25.9	1990	6.3	1994	48	01-11-1975	-27	01-04-1981
FEB	30.2	1998	14.6	1980	54	02-27-2000	-29	02-16-1987
MAR	35.3	2000	21.0	1989	65	03-14-1995	-15	03-01-1980
APR	44.4	1987	33.7	1982	80	04-25-1990	1	04-07-1979
MAY	56.8	1998	45.2	1983	84	05-28-1987	15	05-11-1981
JUN	64.9	1991	55.8	1980	88	06-15-1976	29	06-05-1983
JUL	70.9	1983	60.2	1992	90	07-26-1999	39	07-06-1983
AUG	70.0	1983	61.7	1982	93	08-04-1985	38	08-30-1976
SEP	62.1	1999	54.1	1974	89	09-05-1999	26	09-28-1981
OCT	50.5	2000	42.6	1981	77	10-01-1995	20	10-19-1974
NOV	42.8	2001	30.3	1995	65	11-01-1999	6	11-30-1986
DEC	33.2	2001	13.7	1989	60	12-06-2001	-16	12-11-1977
Annual	47.7	1984	40.4	1978	93	08-04-1985	-29	02-16-1987
Winter	27.1	1998	15.5	1977	60	12-06-1901	-29	02-16-1987
Spring	43.2	1998	35.9	1997	84	05-28-1987	-15	03-01-1980
Summer	67.0	1983	60.1	1992	93	08-04-1985	29	06-05-1983
Fall	50.5	1998	43.6	1976	89	09-05-1999	6	11-30-1986

Sault Ste. Marie/Chippewa County
1971-2000 Normals

Element	JAN	FEB	MAR	APR	MAY	JUN	JUL	AUG	SEP	OCT	NOV	DEC	ANN
Max °F	21.5	24.5	33.6	48.0	63.2	70.7	75.7	74.1	64.8	52.8	38.9	27.2	49.6
Min °F	4.9	6.6	16.1	28.8	39.3	46.5	52.0	52.4	44.8	36.0	25.9	13.1	30.5
Mean °F	13.2	15.6	24.9	38.4	51.3	58.6	63.9	63.3	54.8	44.4	32.4	20.2	40.1

Temperature Extremes
Period of Record: 1931-2001

Month	High Mean°F	Year	Low Mean°F	Year	1-Day Max°F	Date	1-Day Min°F	Date
JAN	27.4	1932	0.8	1994	54	01-07-1932	-36	01-10-1982
FEB	29.1	1998	2.2	1934	49	02-11-1999	-37	02-08-1934
MAR	35.3	1946	16.8	1943	75	03-28-1946	-28	03-11-1948
APR	45.9	1987	29.7	1950	85	04-25-1990	-2	04-05-1982
MAY	57.6	1998	43.3	1947	89	05-30-1937	18	05-07-1966
JUN	63.4	1933	51.5	1982	93	06-26-1983	26	06-03-1982
JUL	70.2	1955	57.4	1992	97	07-01-1931	36	07-14-1950
AUG	69.8	1947	57.3	1977	98	08-05-1947	29	08-29-1982
SEP	60.9	1931	50.3	1981	95	09-08-1976	25	09-25-1947
OCT	53.9	1963	37.7	1980	81	10-12-1938	3	10-18-1935
NOV	40.7	1931	24.1	1933	74	11-03-1938	-10	11-30-1936
DEC	31.0	2001	7.3	1989	62	12-05-2001	-31	12-26-1993
Annual	47.4	1998	37.8	1950	98	08-05-1947	-37	02-08-1934
Winter	25.1	1932	10.0	1977	62	12-05-1901	-37	02-08-1934
Spring	42.9	1987	32.3	1950	89	05-30-1937	-28	03-11-1948
Summer	67.2	1955	57.4	1982	98	08-05-1947	26	06-03-1982
Fall	50.9	1931	39.7	1980	95	09-08-1976	-10	11-30-1936

Newberry/Luce County
1971-2000 Normals

Element	JAN	FEB	MAR	APR	MAY	JUN	JUL	AUG	SEP	OCT	NOV	DEC	ANN
Max °F	23.9	27.8	36.5	50.6	66.0	73.6	78.3	76.5	67.5	55.4	40.9	28.8	52.2
Min °F	8.0	9.8	17.6	29.2	40.3	48.2	53.5	53.2	45.7	36.4	26.3	14.6	31.9
Mean °F	16.0	18.8	27.1	39.9	53.2	60.9	65.9	64.9	56.6	45.9	33.6	21.7	42.0

Temperature Extremes
Period of Record: 1896-2001

Month	High Mean°F	Year	Low Mean°F	Year	1-Day Max°F	Date	1-Day Min°F	Date
JAN	26.8	1932	2.6	1912	51	01-03-1897	-30	01-26-1927
FEB	29.7	1998	2.3	1904	52	02-24-2000	-32	02-07-1899
MAR	36.7	1946	15.9	1900	74	03-28-1946	-23	03-13-1905
APR	45.8	1942	30.3	1950	82	04-25-1915	-2	04-01-1923
MAY	59.1	1998	43.6	1947	93	05-29-1986	15	05-08-1902
JUN	68.8	1919	53.7	1899	99	06-30-1931	22	06-28-1899
JUL	74.6	1921	56.4	1900	103	07-13-1936	22	07-16-1903
AUG	69.6	1947	58.2	1950	98	08-20-1916	28	08-19-1898
SEP	62.0	1921	48.7	1899	96	09-11-1931	18	09-25-1936
OCT	53.7	1947	33.9	1907	82	10-02-1922	4	10-28-1933
NOV	41.5	1902	25.5	1959	71	11-02-1990	-10	11-29-1976
DEC	30.5	1994	9.1	1989	60	12-02-1982	-22	12-17-1919
Annual	46.6	2001	36.5	1904	103	07-13-1936	-32	02-07-1999
Winter	25.9	1932	8.9	1904	60	12-02-1982	-32	02-07-1999
Spring	44.5	1998	33.1	1897	93	05-29-1986	-23	03-13-1905
Summer	68.0	1921	57.9	1992	103	07-13-1936	22	06-28-1999
Fall	51.3	1931	39.5	1896	96	09-11-1931	-10	11-29-1976

Manistique/Schoolcraft County
1971-2000 Normals

Element	JAN	FEB	MAR	APR	MAY	JUN	JUL	AUG	SEP	OCT	NOV	DEC	ANN
Max °F	24.5	26.9	34.9	46.3	58.4	67.6	73.3	73.0	64.5	53.1	40.5	29.6	49.4
Min °F	6.7	8.7	17.8	29.4	40.3	49.0	55.2	54.8	47.0	37.1	26.3	14.5	32.2
Mean °F	15.6	17.8	26.4	37.9	49.4	58.3	64.3	63.9	55.8	45.1	33.4	22.1	40.8

Temperature Extremes
Period of Record: 1948-2001

Month	High Mean°F	Year	Low Mean°F	Year	1-Day Max°F	Date	1-Day Min°F	Date
JAN	25.4	1990	5.8	1994	48	01-25-1973	-25	01-20-1994
FEB	29.6	1998	8.5	1994	49	02-15-1954	-33	02-04-1970
MAR	35.2	1973	19.6	1989	67	03-28-1998	-31	03-03-1972
APR	45.1	1955	32.4	1996	84	04-26-1990	-7	04-05-1972
MAY	56.1	1998	44.5	1997	87	05-28-1986	19	05-08-1956
JUN	63.0	1987	52.4	1969	96	06-12-1956	27	06-02-1956
JUL	71.3	1955	57.9	1992	97	07-12-1966	35	07-01-1960
AUG	70.2	1955	58.2	1950	101	08-19-1955	31	08-24-1971
SEP	61.2	1961	52.1	1974	92	09-01-1953	19	09-15-1986
OCT	54.3	1963	40.8	1988	79	10-01-1971	12	10-18-1972
NOV	41.1	1963	26.8	1995	69	11-05-1963	-6	11-29-1976
DEC	31.3	2001	11.1	1989	59	12-01-1998	-25	12-30-1976
Annual	45.3	1998	38.6	1972	101	08-19-1955	-33	02-04-1970
Winter	26.1	1998	12.8	1979	59	12-01-1998	-33	02-04-1970
Spring	42.5	1998	33.0	1996	87	05-28-1986	-31	03-03-1972
Summer	67.6	1955	57.9	1992	101	08-19-1955	27	06-02-1956
Fall	50.4	1963	41.1	1976	92	09-01-1953	-6	11-29-1976

Munising/Alger County
1971-2000 Normals

Element	JAN	FEB	MAR	APR	MAY	JUN	JUL	AUG	SEP	OCT	NOV	DEC	ANN
Max °F	22.5	25.5	33.8	45.9	60.0	68.0	73.1	71.7	62.8	51.8	38.2	27.3	48.4
Min °F	9.1	10.7	19.2	29.8	39.7	48.2	54.4	54.4	47.9	37.6	27.1	15.7	32.8
Mean °F	15.8	18.1	26.5	37.9	49.9	58.1	63.8	63.1	55.4	44.7	32.7	21.5	40.6

Temperature Extremes
Period of Record: 1943-2001

Month	High Mean°F	Year	Low Mean°F	Year	1-Day Max°F	Date	1-Day Min°F	Date
JAN	25.9	1944	7.8	1977	50	01-26-1944	-27	01-24-1948
FEB	30.2	1998	9.4	1963	57	02-17-1981	-30	02-02-1985
MAR	37.1	1946	17.4	1972	80	03-28-1946	-26	03-03-1943
APR	45.2	1955	31.3	1950	89	04-26-1990	-4	04-06-1950
MAY	57.5	1977	42.5	1945	95	05-28-1969	17	05-05-1954
JUN	65.1	1995	52.9	1982	96	06-13-1956	24	06-13-1947
JUL	71.0	1983	59.2	1992	101	07-07-1988	31	07-01-1960
AUG	72.1	1947	57.6	1950	103	08-06-1947	31	08-25-1950
SEP	61.0	1948	51.2	1974	99	09-09-1947	25	09-27-1947
OCT	56.6	1947	41.3	1976	84	10-17-1947	13	10-24-1981
NOV	40.5	2001	27.1	1959	70	11-03-1961	-9	11-25-1950
DEC	30.2	2001	13.0	1976	60	12-03-1962	-21	12-30-1976
Annual	47.8	1985	37.1	1996	103	08-06-1947	-30	02-02-1985
Winter	26.1	1998	12.7	1977	60	12-03-1962	-30	02-02-1985
Spring	43.2	1991	33.1	1996	95	05-28-1969	-26	03-03-1943
Summer	67.2	1955	59.4	1972	103	08-06-1947	24	06-13-1947
Fall	50.5	1963	40.6	1976	99	09-09-1947	-9	11-25-1950

Escanaba/Delta County
1971-2000 Normals

Element	JAN	FEB	MAR	APR	MAY	JUN	JUL	AUG	SEP	OCT	NOV	DEC	ANN
Max °F	25.2	27.7	35.8	46.1	59.6	70.0	76.0	74.6	66.5	54.5	41.5	30.3	50.7
Min °F	7.0	7.9	17.8	30.2	42.3	51.3	57.1	56.5	48.5	38.9	27.0	14.9	33.3
Mean °F	16.1	17.8	26.8	38.2	51.0	60.7	66.6	65.6	57.5	46.7	34.3	22.6	42.0

Temperature Extremes
Period of Record: 1948-2001

Month	High Mean°F	Year	Low Mean°F	Year	1-Day Max°F	Date	1-Day Min°F	Date
JAN	23.7	1990	7.3	1994	50	01-23-1967	-28	01-16-1982
FEB	27.7	1954	8.4	1979	52	02-23-1958	-30	02-17-1979
MAR	34.5	2000	19.9	1989	71	03-09-2000	-26	03-03-1972
APR	45.5	1955	32.1	1950	82	04-29-1957	-1	04-05-1972
MAY	55.8	1977	45.7	1983	91	05-30-1986	23	05-05-1954
JUN	65.1	1991	56.0	1958	98	06-29-1970	30	06-04-1990
JUL	71.8	1955	61.5	1992	96	07-05-1948	40	07-05-1967
AUG	70.7	1955	59.6	1950	100	08-21-1955	38	08-28-1986
SEP	62.2	1948	52.9	1974	96	09-01-1953	28	09-26-1965
OCT	55.2	1963	42.3	1952	82	10-10-1960	19	10-18-1972
NOV	40.7	2001	27.2	1959	71	11-10-1999	-7	11-24-1950
DEC	30.4	2001	11.9	1989	58	12-06-2001	-23	12-30-1976
Annual	46.5	1999	39.2	1972	100	08-21-1955	-30	02-17-1979
Winter	24.8	1983	12.7	1979	58	12-06-1901	-30	02-17-1979
Spring	42.0	1987	34.5	1950	91	05-30-1986	-26	03-03-1972
Summer	68.3	1955	60.8	1950	100	08-21-1955	30	06-04-1990
Fall	50.4	1963	42.5	1976	96	09-01-1953	-7	11-24-1950

Menominee-Marinette/Menominee County
1971-2000 Normals

Element	JAN	FEB	MAR	APR	MAY	JUN	JUL	AUG	SEP	OCT	NOV	DEC	ANN
Max °F	24.7	28.9	39.2	52.6	66.2	76.1	81.3	78.5	69.4	56.9	42.3	29.6	53.8
Min °F	8.2	12.4	22.0	33.2	44.8	54.2	59.7	58.1	50.4	39.4	27.5	15.0	35.4
Mean °F	16.5	20.7	30.6	42.9	55.5	65.2	70.5	68.3	59.9	48.2	34.9	22.3	44.6

Temperature Extremes
Period of Record: 1948-2001

Month	High Mean°F	Year	Low Mean°F	Year	1-Day Max°F	Date	1-Day Min°F	Date
JAN	25.3	1964	8.5	1977	50	01-26-1973	-30	01-17-1982
FEB	31.7	1998	12.5	1963	62	02-12-1999	-30	02-03-1996
MAR	39.3	1973	24.3	1996	77	03-08-2000	-20	03-01-1962
APR	49.9	1987	35.2	1950	90	04-27-1952	5	04-09-1989
MAY	64.2	1977	47.8	1983	97	05-30-1988	22	05-10-1966
JUN	71.4	1988	58.2	1982	100	06-14-1987	34	06-08-1949
JUL	76.3	1955	64.0	1992	102	07-06-1988	40	07-06-1965
AUG	75.3	1955	64.2	1950	101	08-21-1955	34	08-28-1986
SEP	64.9	1961	53.7	1974	96	09-01-1953	23	09-23-1974
OCT	59.2	1963	41.7	1988	89	10-06-1963	16	10-18-1948
NOV	43.4	2001	28.5	1995	75	11-18-1953	-8	11-24-1950
DEC	31.3	1965	10.9	1989	62	12-04-1998	-22	12-23-1983
Annual	49.5	2001	41.7	1990	102	07-06-1988	-30	01-17-1982
Winter	27.6	1998	14.6	1979	62	12-04-1998	-30	01-17-1982
Spring	48.9	1977	37.6	1950	97	05-30-1988	-20	03-01-1962
Summer	72.9	1955	63.9	1992	102	07-06-1988	34	06-08-1949
Fall	54.1	1963	44.6	1993	96	09-01-1953	-8	11-24-195

Iron Mountain-Kingsford/Dickinson County
1971-2000 Normals

Element	JAN	FEB	MAR	APR	MAY	JUN	JUL	AUG	SEP	OCT	NOV	DEC	ANN
Max °F	23.6	28.8	38.9	53.3	67.8	76.3	80.4	78.0	68.7	56.3	40.0	27.7	53.3
Min °F	0.6	4.5	16.1	28.9	40.9	50.4	55.4	53.8	44.9	34.0	22.4	9.0	30.1
Mean °F	12.1	16.7	27.5	41.1	54.4	63.4	67.9	65.9	56.8	45.2	31.2	18.4	41.7

Temperature Extremes
Period of Record: 1931-2001

Month	High Mean°F	Year	Low Mean°F	Year	1-Day Max°F	Date	1-Day Min°F	Date
JAN	24.5	1944	3.0	1994	55	01-23-1942	-33	01-27-1935
FEB	29.4	1998	3.4	1936	61	02-24-1976	-39	02-01-1938
MAR	37.8	1946	18.6	1960	77	03-09-2000	-27	03-18-1939
APR	47.7	1955	32.3	1950	94	04-22-1980	-6	04-05-1972
MAY	62.4	1977	46.8	1997	100	05-31-1934	16	05-11-1990
JUN	69.8	1933	56.0	1969	100	06-29-1931	24	06-08-1949
JUL	72.7	1983	62.2	1992	103	07-13-1936	35	07-16-1939
AUG	72.4	1947	60.4	1950	101	08-05-1947	30	08-26-1945
SEP	64.5	1931	51.7	1974	98	09-12-1998	19	09-28-1942
OCT	55.9	1947	39.8	1988	88	10-15-1947	11	10-23-1969
NOV	41.1	2001	23.6	1959	75	11-05-1975	-10	11-29-1976
DEC	29.0	1931	7.1	1989	64	12-04-1998	-26	12-30-1976
Annual	47.2	1987	39.3	1950	103	07-13-1936	-39	02-01-1938
Winter	24.9	1998	10.3	1959	64	12-04-1998	-39	02-01-1938
Spring	47.8	1977	35.5	1950	100	05-31-1934	-27	03-18-1939
Summer	69.2	1995	61.9	1992	103	07-13-1936	24	06-08-1949
Fall	51.7	1931	41.0	1993	98	09-12-1998	-10	11-29-1976

Crystal Falls/Iron County
1971-2000 Normals

Element	JAN	FEB	MAR	APR	MAY	JUN	JUL	AUG	SEP	OCT	NOV	DEC	ANN
Max °F	20.8	26.3	36.5	50.5	65.8	74.0	78.6	75.9	66.2	53.7	37.4	25.1	50.9
Min °F	-2.1	1.0	12.2	26.0	37.6	47.0	51.7	50.3	41.9	32.3	20.9	6.4	27.1
Mean °F	9.4	13.7	24.4	38.3	51.7	60.5	65.2	63.1	54.1	43.0	29.2	15.8	39.0

Temperature Extremes
Period of Record: 1962-1989

Month	High Mean°F	Year	Low Mean°F	Year	1-Day Max°F	Date	1-Day Min°F	Date
JAN	19.1	1964	-0.1	1977	51	01-26-1973	-41	01-09-1977
FEB	23.5	1984	3.3	1979	61	02-25-1976	-42	02-17-1979
MAR	33.9	1973	17.2	1984	69	03-08-1987	-35	03-01-1962
APR	44.6	1986	31.9	1975	92	04-23-1980	-10	04-05-1972
MAY	59.7	1977	44.1	1967	93	05-22-1964	12	05-04-1966
JUN	64.6	1988	53.5	1969	99	06-30-1963	25	06-02-1964
JUL	70.4	1983	60.7	1971	99	07-20-1977	33	07-06-1965
AUG	67.5	1983	56.6	1977	96	08-03-1988	29	08-29-1965
SEP	56.5	1983	48.4	1974	97	09-08-1976	19	09-23-1974
OCT	53.7	1963	37.2	1976	87	10-02-1976	2	10-23-1969
NOV	36.0	1963	21.9	1976	73	11-06-1975	-20	11-29-1976
DEC	23.5	1965	5.5	1976	58	12-03-1982	-35	12-12-1977
Annual	42.4	1987	35.7	1972	99	06-30-1963	-42	02-17-1979
Winter	19.8	1983	5.1	1979	61	02-25-1976	-42	02-17-1979
Spring	43.6	1977	34.3	1971	93	05-22-1964	-35	03-01-1962
Summer	66.6	1988	59.9	1982	99	06-30-1963	25	06-02-1964
Fall	48.4	1963	36.8	1976	97	09-08-1976	-20	11-29-1976

Ironwood/Gogebic County
1971-2000 Normals

Element	JAN	FEB	MAR	APR	MAY	JUN	JUL	AUG	SEP	OCT	NOV	DEC	ANN
Max °F	19.3	25.6	35.6	49.7	64.2	72.5	76.5	74.5	65.0	53.0	36.4	24.0	49.7
Min °F	-0.3	3.7	14.3	28.2	40.6	49.8	54.6	52.5	44.3	34.2	21.4	7.3	29.2
Mean °F	9.5	14.7	25.0	39.0	52.4	61.2	65.6	63.5	54.7	43.6	28.9	15.7	39.5

Temperature Extremes
Period of Record: 1901-2001

Month	High Mean°F	Year	Low Mean°F	Year	1-Day Max°F	Date	1-Day Min°F	Date
JAN	23.8	1944	-5.4	1912	55	01-26-1981	-41	01-17-1982
FEB	29.6	1998	-0.2	1936	62	02-25-1976	-41	02-12-1967
MAR	39.6	1910	16.1	1996	79	03-28-1946	-34	03-07-1984
APR	50.4	1915	30.3	1907	88	04-29-1970	-12	04-07-1982
MAY	62.1	1977	42.7	1907	100	05-31-1934	16	05-04-1907
JUN	69.0	1933	54.5	1982	99	06-29-1931	25	06-04-1945
JUL	73.8	1916	58.6	1992	104	07-13-1936	31	07-02-1907
AUG	73.4	1947	56.6	1977	101	08-04-1947	30	08-15-1976
SEP	63.4	1931	48.5	1918	99	09-08-1906	21	09-28-1907
OCT	56.9	1963	33.8	1917	86	10-04-1922	2	10-30-1925
NOV	41.0	2001	19.0	1995	80	11-01-1950	-18	11-30-1976
DEC	28.9	1939	5.0	1989	59	12-04-1998	-36	12-20-1983
Annual	46.4	1931	35.3	1917	104	07-13-1936	-41	01-17-1982
Winter	23.1	1998	5.9	1979	62	02-25-1976	-41	01-17-1982
Spring	46.2	1977	31.9	1996	100	05-31-1934	-34	03-07-1984
Summer	68.9	1949	58.3	1992	104	07-13-1936	25	06-04-1945
Fall	50.7	1931	38.0	1993	99	09-08-1906	-18	11-30-1976

Ontonagon/Ontonagon County
1971-2000 Normals

Element	JAN	FEB	MAR	APR	MAY	JUN	JUL	AUG	SEP	OCT	NOV	DEC	ANN
Max °F	23.8	29.6	39.2	52.7	67.1	74.9	79.1	77.6	68.2	56.7	39.8	28.0	53.1
Min °F	6.9	8.2	17.5	30.1	40.3	48.9	54.2	53.2	45.9	36.6	25.8	13.7	31.8
Mean °F	15.4	18.9	28.4	41.4	53.7	61.9	66.7	65.4	57.1	46.7	32.8	20.9	42.4

Temperature Extremes
Period of Record: 1977-2001

Month	High Mean°F	Year	Low Mean°F	Year	1-Day Max°F	Date	1-Day Min°F	Date
JAN	24.3	1990	5.8	1994	56	01-25-1981	-31	01-21-1984
FEB	32.4	1998	7.7	1979	63	02-17-1981	-42	02-17-1979
MAR	37.9	2000	20.5	1996	74	03-31-1986	-27	03-07-1984
APR	48.0	1987	34.4	1996	89	04-25-1990	0	04-07-1996
MAY	58.9	1988	46.7	1997	93	05-26-1978	18	05-01-1978
JUN	66.0	1995	56.2	1982	94	06-26-1986	25	06-21-1992
JUL	71.5	1983	60.1	1992	101	07-07-1988	32	07-01-1988
AUG	70.5	1995	61.4	1982	99	08-07-1983	34	08-16-1979
SEP	61.9	1998	52.4	1993	96	09-05-1998	25	09-22-1981
OCT	51.0	1994	42.5	1988	87	10-12-1995	15	10-24-1981
NOV	43.2	2001	26.1	1995	77	11-03-1978	-5	11-23-1989
DEC	29.2	2001	11.4	1983	62	12-03-1982	-23	12-27-1996
Annual	47.8	1999	39.7	1996	101	07-07-1988	-42	02-17-1979
Winter	26.8	1998	10.5	1979	63	02-17-1981	-42	02-17-1979
Spring	46.6	1987	34.8	1996	93	05-26-1978	-27	03-07-1984
Summer	68.3	1983	59.7	1992	101	07-07-1988	25	06-21-1992
Fall	49.7	1998	41.9	1993	96	09-05-1998	-5	11-23-1989

Houghton County Airport/Houghton County
1971-2000 Normals

Element	JAN	FEB	MAR	APR	MAY	JUN	JUL	AUG	SEP	OCT	NOV	DEC	ANN
Max °F	21.6	24.8	33.7	47.1	62.3	70.8	75.9	73.6	63.3	51.6	36.8	26.0	49.0
Min °F	7.6	9.1	17.6	29.5	40.8	49.3	55.2	54.7	46.2	36.4	25.1	13.8	32.1
Mean °F	14.6	17.0	25.7	38.3	51.6	60.1	65.6	64.2	54.8	44.0	31.0	19.9	40.6

Temperature Extremes
Period of Record: 1952-2001

Month	High Mean°F	Year	Low Mean°F	Year	1-Day Max°F	Date	1-Day Min°F	Date
JAN	23.2	1990	4.9	1994	43	01-13-1987	-26	01-21-1984
FEB	30.3	1998	6.1	1979	56	02-26-2000	-25	02-19-1966
MAR	33.6	2000	17.6	1960	65	03-31-1986	-21	03-07-1953
APR	46.3	1987	32.3	1972	88	04-25-1990	0	04-04-1954
MAY	58.2	1977	41.8	1954	95	05-28-1969	20	05-03-1954
JUN	66.1	1995	52.9	1969	96	06-14-1988	31	06-01-1964
JUL	70.9	1988	59.4	1992	102	07-07-1988	36	07-01-1960
AUG	69.5	1983	59.3	1982	97	08-19-1976	38	08-22-1952
SEP	59.0	1994	49.7	1974	92	09-03-1960	24	09-28-2000
OCT	55.2	1963	39.0	1952	86	10-02-1953	13	10-31-1954
NOV	40.0	2001	22.9	1959	71	11-03-1978	-2	11-29-1958
DEC	27.3	1994	11.4	1976	54	12-03-1962	-15	12-29-1976
Annual	44.9	1998	37.1	1972	102	07-07-1988	-26	01-21-1984
Winter	26.0	1998	10.6	1959	56	02-26-1900	-26	01-21-1984
Spring	43.8	1977	32.5	1954	95	05-28-1969	-21	03-07-1953
Summer	67.2	1995	59.2	1992	102	07-07-1988	31	06-01-1964
Fall	48.9	1963	40.2	1959	92	09-03-1960	-2	11-29-1958

Copper Harbor/Keweenaw County
1971-2000 Normals

Element	JAN	FEB	MAR	APR	MAY	JUN	JUL	AUG	SEP	OCT	NOV	DEC	ANN
Max °F	23.7	26.5	34.6	46.5	60.5	68.1	74.8	74.1	65.7	53.9	39.3	28.8	49.7
Min °F	9.7	9.8	18.6	29.6	38.8	46.8	54.5	55.9	49.0	38.9	27.8	16.6	33.0
Mean °F	16.7	18.2	26.6	38.1	49.7	57.5	64.7	65.0	57.4	46.4	33.6	22.7	41.4

Temperature Extremes
Period of Record: 1972-2001

Month	High Mean°F	Year	Low Mean°F	Year	1-Day Max°F	Date	1-Day Min°F	Date
JAN	25.1	1990	7.4	1977	46	01-08-1990	-18	01-18-1994
FEB	30.4	1998	11.1	1994	55	02-19-1994	-22	02-10-1994
MAR	35.4	2000	20.0	1989	66	03-27-1989	-19	03-07-1996
APR	43.4	1987	31.8	1996	83	04-26-1990	-2	04-08-1974
MAY	53.5	1998	44.0	1997	89	05-29-1999	16	05-07-1974
JUN	61.7	1987	51.7	1977	92	06-27-2001	32	06-21-1992
JUL	68.7	1988	58.2	1992	99	07-07-1988	42	07-13-1987
AUG	70.0	1995	62.2	1992	94	08-20-1976	38	08-25-1973
SEP	62.2	1998	53.0	1993	95	09-05-1998	30	09-29-1991
OCT	52.9	1973	42.7	1976	80	10-12-1995	21	10-31-1984
NOV	41.8	2001	27.2	1995	67	11-04-1975	-5	11-23-1976
DEC	36.3	2000	14.0	1976	65	12-02-2000	-11	12-03-1976
Annual	47.4	1987	39.0	1996	99	07-07-1988	-22	02-10-1994
Winter	27.6	1998	13.0	1977	65	12-02-1900	-22	02-10-1994
Spring	43.3	1987	32.2	1996	89	05-29-1999	-19	03-07-1996
Summer	65.3	1987	58.5	1992	99	07-07-1988	32	06-21-1992
Fall	49.9	1998	42.3	1993	95	09-05-1998	-5	11-23-1976

Herman/Baraga County
1971-2000 Normals

Element	JAN	FEB	MAR	APR	MAY	JUN	JUL	AUG	SEP	OCT	NOV	DEC	ANN
Max °F	20.1	26.1	36.2	50.3	65.5	72.9	76.6	74.1	65.2	53.1	36.2	24.3	50.1
Min °F	3.5	5.7	14.2	26.2	38.7	47.4	52.4	51.2	43.5	34.0	22.0	9.8	29.1
Mean °F	11.8	15.9	25.2	38.3	52.1	60.2	64.5	62.7	54.4	43.6	29.1	17.1	39.6

Temperature Extremes
Period of Record: 1968-2001

Month	High Mean°F	Year	Low Mean°F	Year	1-Day Max°F	Date	1-Day Min°F	Date
JAN	22.2	1990	1.5	1977	54	01-26-1973	-36	01-09-1977
FEB	27.5	1998	6.5	1979	61	02-24-1976	-40	02-17-1979
MAR	33.7	2000	17.7	1984	71	03-08-2000	-32	03-07-1984
APR	46.9	1987	31.0	1975	91	04-22-1980	-17	04-07-1982
MAY	60.8	1977	42.1	1997	93	05-28-1969	12	05-07-1974
JUN	67.3	1995	51.6	1969	96	06-27-1971	22	06-10-1972
JUL	69.5	1983	58.5	1992	96	07-28-1988	26	07-10-1968
AUG	68.2	1995	56.8	1977	95	08-19-1976	27	08-27-1968
SEP	58.2	1994	48.3	1974	95	09-07-1976	11	09-28-2000
OCT	50.3	1971	37.7	1976	86	10-02-1992	1	10-23-1969
NOV	38.5	2001	20.9	1995	73	11-03-1978	-12	11-30-1976
DEC	26.8	1994	6.9	1983	58	12-03-1982	-37	12-19-1983
Annual	46.7	1968	36.2	1972	96	06-27-1971	-40	02-17-1979
Winter	22.1	1998	7.8	1977	61	02-24-1976	-40	02-17-1979
Spring	45.2	1977	32.1	1997	93	05-28-1969	-32	03-07-1984
Summer	67.2	1995	58.4	1992	96	06-27-1971	22	06-10-1972
Fall	46.5	1994	37.9	1976	95	09-07-1976	-12	11-30-1976

City of Marquette/Marquette County
1971-2000 Normals

Element	JAN	FEB	MAR	APR	MAY	JUN	JUL	AUG	SEP	OCT	NOV	DEC	ANN
Max °F	25.1	28.8	36.8	48.0	61.0	69.7	75.6	74.4	65.9	54.7	40.4	29.5	50.8
Min °F	11.0	13.6	22.3	32.7	42.0	50.7	57.1	57.1	49.4	39.5	28.4	17.0	35.1
Mean °F	18.1	21.2	29.6	40.4	51.5	60.2	66.4	65.8	57.7	47.1	34.4	23.3	43.0

Temperature Extremes
Period of Record: 1948-2001

Month	High Mean°F	Year	Low Mean°F	Year	1-Day Max°F	Date	1-Day Min°F	Date
JAN	26.3	1990	8.3	1994	49	01-28-1989	-22	01-18-1994
FEB	32.7	1998	10.5	1979	62	02-24-1976	-24	02-03-1996
MAR	38.0	2000	21.1	1960	77	03-08-2000	-13	03-01-1962
APR	46.8	1955	32.3	1950	91	04-25-1990	4	04-03-1954
MAY	58.4	1977	44.4	1954	100	05-28-1969	22	05-05-1954
JUN	64.7	1995	54.4	1982	101	06-30-1963	31	06-08-1980
JUL	71.6	1999	59.7	1992	104	07-19-1977	41	07-05-1967
AUG	70.8	1969	58.9	1950	101	08-24-1948	40	08-16-1979
SEP	64.0	1998	52.9	1956	97	09-03-1983	30	09-27-1965
OCT	58.8	1963	42.4	1988	86	10-18-1950	19	10-23-1981
NOV	43.1	2001	26.1	1959	74	11-03-1978	-2	11-29-1976
DEC	30.9	2001	14.4	1983	60	12-03-1982	-13	12-26-1990
Annual	47.6	1998	39.5	1972	104	07-19-1977	-24	02-03-1996
Winter	28.4	1998	14.1	1979	62	02-24-1976	-24	02-03-1996
Spring	45.6	1977	34.5	1950	100	05-28-1969	-13	03-01-1962
Summer	68.1	1955	59.9	1992	104	07-19-1977	31	06-08-1980
Fall	51.8	1963	42.8	1951	97	09-03-1983	-2	11-29-1976

Marquette National Weather Service Office/Negaunee Township/Marquette County

1971-2000 Normals

Element	JAN	FEB	MAR	APR	MAY	JUN	JUL	AUG	SEP	OCT	NOV	DEC	ANN
Max °F	19.7	24.2	33.1	45.8	61.5	70.3	75.2	72.6	63.2	50.9	35.4	24.1	48.0
Min °F	3.3	5.4	14.3	26.9	39.1	48.3	53.5	52.0	43.8	34.0	22.4	10.2	29.4
Mean °F	11.5	14.8	23.7	36.4	50.3	59.3	64.4	62.3	53.5	42.5	28.9	17.2	38.7

Temperature Extremes
Period of Record: 1959-2001

Month	High Mean°F	Year	Low Mean°F	Year	1-Day Max°F	Date	1-Day Min°F	Date
JAN	22.0	1990	2.8	1994	53	01-26-1973	-32	01-09-1977
FEB	28.4	1998	5.8	1963	61	02-17-1981	-34	02-17-1979
MAR	33.1	1973	16.9	1965	71	03-08-2000	-27	03-01-1962
APR	44.6	1987	31.0	1972	92	04-22-1980	-5	04-01-1964
MAY	59.4	1977	43.6	1967	95	05-28-1969	17	05-09-1983
JUN	66.3	1995	53.2	1969	99	06-30-1963	25	06-04-1964
JUL	70.1	1983	58.4	1992	99	07-19-1977	34	07-05-1967
AUG	68.1	1995	58.5	1964	96	08-06-2001	31	08-30-1976
SEP	58.3	1998	48.5	1974	92	09-03-1983	21	09-27-1965
OCT	53.5	1963	38.0	1988	87	10-02-1992	9	10-23-1969
NOV	39.9	2001	22.4	1995	73	11-09-1999	-13	11-29-1976
DEC	27.5	1994	8.5	1976	59	12-03-1982	-28	12-20-1983
Annual	43.4	1998	36.4	1972	99	06-30-1963	-34	02-17-1979
Winter	23.5	1998	8.5	1977	61	02-17-1981	-34	02-17-1979
Spring	43.8	1977	32.6	1996	95	05-28-1969	-27	03-01-1962
Summer	66.7	1995	58.0	1992	99	06-30-1963	25	06-04-1964
Fall	47.3	1963	38.3	1976	92	09-03-1983	-13	11-29-1976

SNOW

The Upper Peninsula is famous for snow. Some of the highest annual totals east of the Rocky Mountains fall over sections of the U.P. due to the phenomenon called "lake-effect." During winter, cold air flows across the waters of the Great Lakes. The cold, dry air picks up moisture and drops it as snow (and even rain during the early part of the season in the fall).

Not all of Upper Michigan shares in the snowfall bonanza. Seasonal snowfall over the south is less than half the amount received over most northern portions. This happens because the predominant wind flow during the cold months is from the northwest—downwind from Lake Superior. Areas in the southern U.P. catch the tail-end of the lake-effect snow bands, as most of the snow falls over the higher elevations to the northwest.

Seasonal snowfall is greatest over the higher elevations adjacent to Lake Superior. The moist airflow off the lake is given added lift up the highlands. This lifting process increases the snowfall. This can be clearly seen in examining the annual snowfall difference between the City of Marquette and the National Weather Service (NWS) office near

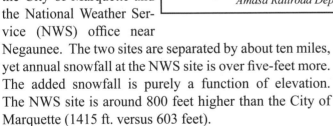
Amasa Railroad Depot

Negaunee. The two sites are separated by about ten miles, yet annual snowfall at the NWS site is over five-feet more. The added snowfall is purely a function of elevation. The NWS site is around 800 feet higher than the City of Marquette (1415 ft. versus 603 feet).

Amounts over the south vary, too. For instance, Escanaba receives an average of just less than 47 inches per winter. Manistique, around 50 miles to the east, collects close to 70 inches annually. This difference can be attributed to location. Manistique's position over the narrower portion of the Peninsula means that some of the northwesterly-wind snow bands off Lake Superior can survive and drop snow on the city. Also, its position on the north-central shore of Lake Michigan means that, on some occasions, a southerly flow off this lake can produce heavy

"FAVORITE" COLD SPOTS

While the Great Lakes greatly modify the cold, there are spots in the Upper Peninsula that get as chilly as any inland location in the Upper Midwest. These traditional cold spots are found well away from the warming influence of the Great Lakes on high plateaus sheltered from the wind or in marshy areas.

One of the notorious cold spots of the western U.P. is at Amasa in Iron County. On a typical clear, still night, Amasa may be more than 10 degrees colder than surrounding communities. During a severe cold spell in January 1994, a thermometer there registered 53 degrees below zero. National Weather Service (NWS) personnel later failed to certify this reading because of calibration and exposure issues with the thermometer. The lowest "official" reading in Upper Michigan is 48 below set at Bergland in Ontonagon County in January 1912. Other cold observations in the west come out of Champion, in Marquette County, and from an NWS cooperative observer west of Baraga.

In the eastern U.P., Rudyard and Raco in Chippewa County will often register the coldest readings in the region when the skies are clear. Clear skies are hard to come by in the winter because the prevailing wind off Lake Superior usually keeps clouds firmly entrenched. This holds true for places like Seney in Schoolcraft County and Spinich Lake in Luce County. When the skies clear though, these locations are cold-air collectors. Highway workers near Rudyard, while working on Interstate 75 in early March 1962, reported a thermometer at their work sight went below 60 degrees below zero!

Temperatures can vary widely over short distances. On a bitter cold morning in late January 1996, the Marquette County airport's FAA observers measured 37 below zero, while an NWS thermometer read 25 below. NWS personnel took a hand held thermometer to each location and verified both readings. There was a 12 degree difference over only several hundred yards!

snow. On December 12, 1989 a southerly flow blowing the full length of Lake Michigan dropped 24 inches of snow on the town. Escanaba, on the other hand, has a large mass of high ground to the northwest and is tucked on the northwest shore of Lake Michigan, sheltered, for the most part, from snow-producing southerly winds. That is why Escanaba is the center of Upper Michigan's "Banana Belt."

Occasionally, a major winter storm will bring widespread "system" snow to most of the Peninsula. These storms are the ones residents talk about for years. The storm of late January 1938 buried most of the U.P. and is considered the "granddaddy" of them all by residents who experienced it. On the other hand, while smaller in scope, the storm of early December 1995 in Sault Ste. Marie dumped more snow. Over five feet fell during a weekend storm and brought the city to a standstill. A state of emergency was declared and National Guard troops spent a week clearing the streets of snow.

Over five feet of snow fell during a weekend storm and brought Sault Ste. Marie to a standstill in December 1995. (Photos courtesy of Marcia Morse-Mullins, from "So Cold a Sky")

St. Ignace/Mackinac County
1973-2000 Averages

Element	JAN	FEB	MAR	APR	MAY	JUN	JUL	AUG	SEP	OCT	NOV	DEC	ANN
Snow(in)	20.4	9.4	6.1	2.6	0.0	0.0	0.0	0.0	0.0	0.0	3.6	15.5	57.6

Snowfall Extremes
Period of Record: 1973-2001

Month	High (in)	Year	1-Day Max (in)	Date
JAN	35.0	1990	15.0	01-10-1999
FEB	22.1	1992	7.5	02-09-1986
MAR	18.6	1986	10.0	03-14-1997
APR	20.0	1985	10.5	04-06-1985
MAY	1.0	1997	1.0	05-18-1997
JUN	0.0	-	-	-
JUL	0.0	-	-	-
AUG	0.0	-	-	-
SEP	0.0	-	-	-
OCT	0.0	-	-	-
NOV	19.3	1989	5.0	11-28-1995
DEC	46.0	1996	10.5	12-24-2000
Season (Jul-Jun)	122.5	2000-2001	15.0	01-10-1999

Sault Ste. Marie/Chippewa County
1971-2000 Averages

Element	JAN	FEB	MAR	APR	MAY	JUN	JUL	AUG	SEP	OCT	NOV	DEC	ANN
Snow(in)	34.6	19.5	15.1	7.6	0.2	0.0	0.0	0.0	0.0	2.5	16.5	36.4	132.4

Snowfall Extremes
Period of Record: 1931-2001

Month	High (in)	Year	1-Day Max (in)	Date
JAN	71.0	1982	12.2	01-25-1972
FEB	41.3	1972	12.4	02-02-1968
MAR	34.7	1964	11.8	03-05-1964
APR	25.8	1982	9.0	04-06-1979
MAY	4.6	1947	4.6	05-29-1947
JUN	0.0	-	-	-
JUL	0.0	-	-	-
AUG	0.0	-	-	-
SEP	2.7	1956	2.7	09-20-1956
OCT	11.6	1969	7.0	10-27-1969
NOV	46.8	1989	14.3	11-16-1943
DEC	98.7	1995	26.6	12-10-1995
Season (Jul-Jun)	222.0	1995-1996	26.6	12-10-1995

Newberry/Luce County
1971-2000 Averages

Element	JAN	FEB	MAR	APR	MAY	JUN	JUL	AUG	SEP	OCT	NOV	DEC	ANN
Snow(in)	33.8	19.6	15.1	6.1	0.2	0.0	0.0	0.0	0.0	0.8	11.7	26.6	113.9

Snowfall Extremes
Period of Record: 1896-2001

Month	High (in)	Year	1-Day Max (in)	Date
JAN	65.5	1978	23.0	01-04-1982
FEB	49.7	1972	13.2	02-12-1940
MAR	39.4	1923	13.0	03-14-1997
APR	28.0	1979	13.0	04-06-1985
MAY	11.9	1917	6.0	05-23-1917
JUN	0.0	-	-	-
JUL	0.0	-	-	-
AUG	0.0	-	-	-
SEP	2.0	1965	2.0	09-26-1965
OCT	11.9	1925	8.0	10-20-1905
NOV	37.2	1989	15.0	11-28-1966
DEC	58.1	1985	15.0	12-07-1917
Season (Jul-Jun)	187.5	1976-1977	23.0	01-04-1982

Manistique/Schoolcraft County
1971-2000 Averages

Element	JAN	FEB	MAR	APR	MAY	JUN	JUL	AUG	SEP	OCT	NOV	DEC	ANN
Snow(in)	21.2	13.6	9.3	1.9	0.0	0.0	0.0	0.0	0.0	0.3	4.7	18.0	69.0

Snowfall Extremes
Period of Record: 1948-2001

Month	High (in)	Year	1-Day Max (in)	Date
JAN	42.8	1979	13.0	01-27-1996
FEB	39.0	1972	12.0	02-15-2000
MAR	23.0	1951	10.0	03-24-1975
APR	16.0	1996	10.0	04-05-1977
MAY	6.0	1954	6.0	05-07-1954
JUN	0.0	-	-	-
JUL	0.0	-	-	-
AUG	0.0	-	-	-
SEP	1.2	1965	1.2	09-26-1965
OCT	6.0	1962	3.0	10-19-1989
NOV	17.6	1951	9.5	11-26-1949
DEC	42.0	1989	24.0	12-12-1989
Season (Jul-Jun)	120.0	1996-1997	24.0	12-12-1989

Munising/Alger County
1971-2000 Averages

Element	JAN	FEB	MAR	APR	MAY	JUN	JUL	AUG	SEP	OCT	NOV	DEC	ANN
Snow(in)	45.0	24.1	18.4	5.3	0.7	0.0	0.0	0.0	0.0	2.2	13.0	37.7	146.4

Snowfall Extremes
Period of Record: 1911-2001

Month	High (in)	Year	1-Day Max (in)	Date
JAN	89.7	1997	15.0	01-26-1978
FEB	55.8	1967	13.5	02-04-1966
MAR	44.4	1955	17.0	03-19-1983
APR	30.6	1953	11.0	04-08-1928
MAY	13.0	1917	10.0	05-23-1917
JUN	0.0	-	-	-
JUL	0.0	-	-	-
AUG	0.0	-	-	-
SEP	2.0	1928	2.0	09-25-1928
OCT	31.3	1925	9.0	10-21-1925
NOV	40.7	1996	12.0	11-15-1927
DEC	84.4	1958	14.0	12-15-1983
Season (Jul-Jun)	238.7	1996-1997	17.0	03-19-1983

Escanaba/Delta County
1971-2000 Averages

Element	JAN	FEB	MAR	APR	MAY	JUN	JUL	AUG	SEP	OCT	NOV	DEC	ANN
Snow(in)	12.9	8.4	8.8	2.4	0.1	0.0	0.0	0.0	0.0	0.0	3.2	10.9	46.7

Snowfall Extremes
Period of Record: 1892-2001

Month	High (in)	Year	1-Day Max (in)	Date
JAN	30.0	1969	10.8	01-20-1988
FEB	31.7	1962	12.0	02-20-1898
MAR	23.1	1972	10.8	03-24-1975
APR	12.2	1894	12.0	04-10-1894
MAY	4.0	1954	3.8	05-07-1954
JUN	0.0	-	-	-
JUL	0.3	1951	0.3	07-26-1951
AUG	0.0	-	-	-
SEP	0.3	1965	0.3	09-26-1965
OCT	0.8	1989	0.8	10-20-1989
NOV	18.9	1985	9.2	11-22-1985
DEC	28.3	1968	8.0	12-15-1987
Season (Jul-Jun)	90.0	1970-1971	12.0	04-10-1894

Menominee-Marinette/Menominee County
1971-2000 Averages

Element	JAN	FEB	MAR	APR	MAY	JUN	JUL	AUG	SEP	OCT	NOV	DEC	ANN
Snow(in)	15.8	9.9	9.1	2.7	0.1	0.0	0.0	0.0	0.0	0.1	3.2	12.8	53.7

Snowfall Extremes
Period of Record: 1919-2001

Month	High (in)	Year	1-Day Max (in)	Date
JAN	36.0	1971	17.0	01-04-1971
FEB	29.0	1985	8.5	02-11-1985
MAR	26.5	1956	12.0	03-26-1964
APR	13.0	1977	8.0	04-05-1977
MAY	3.5	1990	3.5	05-10-1990
JUN	0.0	-	-	-
JUL	0.0	-	-	-
AUG	0.0	-	-	-
SEP	0.0	-	-	-
OCT	2.3	1976	2.0	10-19-1976
NOV	17.0	1951	8.5	11-27-1995
DEC	37.2	1968	12.0	12-04-1990
Season (Jul-Jun)	83.5	1978-1979	17.0	01-04-1971

Iron Mountain-Kingsford/Dickinson County
1971-2000 Averages

Element	JAN	FEB	MAR	APR	MAY	JUN	JUL	AUG	SEP	OCT	NOV	DEC	ANN
Snow(in)	17.1	9.2	11.2	4.5	0.9	0.0	0.0	0.0	0.0	0.3	6.2	15.6	65.0

Snowfall Extremes
Period of Record: 1899-2001

Month	High (in)	Year	1-Day Max (in)	Date
JAN	43.5	1971	17.0	01-04-1971
FEB	36.8	1962	16.0	02-23-1922
MAR	36.0	1972	12.5	03-06-1959
APR	22.0	1907	12.0	04-04-1977
MAY	11.0	1990	8.0	05-11-1990
JUN	0.5	1954	0.5	06-11-1954
JUL	0.0	-	-	-
AUG	0.0	-	-	-
SEP	1.5	1965	1.5	09-26-1965
OCT	8.1	1933	7.0	10-24-1933
NOV	24.2	1948	13.0	11-26-1942
DEC	36.5	1968	13.0	12-27-1904
Season (Jul-Jun)	128.5	1938-1939	17.0	01-04-1971

Crystal Falls/Iron County
1971-2000 Averages

Element	JAN	FEB	MAR	APR	MAY	JUN	JUL	AUG	SEP	OCT	NOV	DEC	ANN
Snow(in)	18.6	11.4	13.9	4.8	0.3	0.0	0.0	0.0	0.0	1.0	8.2	18.2	76.4

Snowfall Extremes
Period of Record: 1948-2001

Month	High (in)	Year	1-Day Max (in)	Date
JAN	42.5	1971	14.0	01-07-1967
FEB	30.2	1962	12.0	02-25-1975
MAR	36.2	1972	11.8	03-19-1986
APR	15.7	1950	8.5	04-06-1957
MAY	5.5	1960	3.5	05-06-1979
JUN	0.0	-	-	-
JUL	0.0	-	-	-
AUG	0.0	-	-	-
SEP	0.0	-	-	-
OCT	9.8	1976	8.0	10-22-1976
NOV	23.6	1948	12.0	11-19-1957
DEC	43.1	1968	11.0	12-04-1970
Season (Jul-Jun)	118.1	1970-1971	14.0	01-07-1967

Ironwood/Gogebic County
1971-2000 Averages

Element	JAN	FEB	MAR	APR	MAY	JUN	JUL	AUG	SEP	OCT	NOV	DEC	ANN
Snow(in)	45.8	24.6	23.2	9.8	2.1	0.0	0.0	0.0	0.3	5.4	27.6	41.6	180.4

Snowfall Extremes
Period of Record: 1901-2001

Month	High (in)	Year	1-Day Max (in)	Date
JAN	100.7	1997	20.0	01-04-1999
FEB	58.5	1937	21.0	02-23-1922
MAR	52.0	1917	24.0	03-06-1908
APR	43.0	1928	12.0	04-19-1928
MAY	19.1	1997	8.5	05-01-1996
JUN	0.0	-	-	-
JUL	0.0	-	-	-
AUG	0.0	-	-	-
SEP	6.9	1995	6.5	09-22-1995
OCT	26.7	1967	16.0	10-21-1987
NOV	78.2	1989	20.0	11-02-1989
DEC	89.0	1968	24.0	12-16-1920
Season (Jul-Jun)	301.8	1996-1997	24.0	12-16-1920

Ontonagon/Ontonagon County
1977-2000 Averages

Element	JAN	FEB	MAR	APR	MAY	JUN	JUL	AUG	SEP	OCT	NOV	DEC	ANN
Snow(in)	55.5	23.3	18.7	6.7	1.2	0.0	0.0	0.0	0.1	2.2	25.0	55.1	187.8

Snowfall Extremes
Period of Record: 1977-2001

Month	High (in)	Year	1-Day Max (in)	Date
JAN	80.0	1982	12.0	01-18-1996
FEB	49.0	2001	14.0	02-03-1983
MAR	38.0	1979	20.0	03-25-1996
APR	28.0	1996	9.0	04-30-1996
MAY	15.0	1997	13.0	05-12-1997
JUN	0.0	-	-	-
JUL	0.0	-	-	-
AUG	0.0	-	-	-
SEP	2.0	1995	2.0	09-22-1995
OCT	9.0	1981	6.0	10-20-1982
NOV	69.0	1991	12.0	11-30-1991
DEC	98.5	1989	15.0	12-15-1981
Season (Jul-Jun)	263.0	1995-1996	20.0	03-25-1996

Houghton County Airport/Houghton County
1971-2000 Averages

Element	JAN	FEB	MAR	APR	MAY	JUN	JUL	AUG	SEP	OCT	NOV	DEC	ANN
Snow(in)	71.0	33.7	24.0	7.7	1.1	0.0	0.0	0.0	0.1	4.0	24.0	57.7	223.3

Snowfall Extremes
Period of Record: 1952-2001

Month	High (in)	Year	1-Day Max (in)	Date
JAN	110.3	1979	26.5	01-18-1996
FEB	89.8	1989	19.6	02-08-1989
MAR	63.5	1976	24.9	03-04-1985
APR	22.9	1996	13.5	04-02-1971
MAY	11.9	1954	7.5	05-07-1954
JUN	0.0	-	-	-
JUL	0.0	-	-	-
AUG	0.0	-	-	-
SEP	3.0	1995	3.0	09-22-1995
OCT	15.4	1967	11.1	10-23-1979
NOV	57.7	1959	17.0	11-12-1982
DEC	119.0	1978	17.8	12-23-1998
Season (Jul-Jun)	376.1	1978-1979	26.5	01-18-1996

Copper Harbor/Keweenaw County
1971-2000 Averages

Element	JAN	FEB	MAR	APR	MAY	JUN	JUL	AUG	SEP	OCT	NOV	DEC	ANN
Snow(in)	47.6	26.6	15.7	7.2	0.7	0.0	0.0	0.0	0.0	0.7	9.7	31.5	139.7

Snowfall Extremes
Period of Record: 1948-2001

Month	High (in)	Year	1-Day Max (in)	Date
JAN	68.9	1997	16.5	01-19-1996
FEB	50.0	1995	13.5	02-08-1989
MAR	34.5	1985	18.0	03-25-1996
APR	21.1	1996	12.0	04-01-1987
MAY	6.7	1990	6.7	05-10-1990
JUN	0.0	-	-	-
JUL	0.0	-	-	-
AUG	0.0	-	-	-
SEP	0.0	-	-	-
OCT	6.0	1976	3.0	10-19-1976
NOV	38.9	1995	12.0	11-23-1985
DEC	77.1	1989	12.5	12-31-1992
Season (Jul-Jun)	238.4	1995-1996	18.0	03-25-1996

Herman/Baraga County
1971-2000 Averages

Element	JAN	FEB	MAR	APR	MAY	JUN	JUL	AUG	SEP	OCT	NOV	DEC	ANN
Snow(in)	54.3	33.8	36.3	14.8	3.4	0.0	0.0	0.0	0.2	8.7	34.7	49.6	235.8

Snowfall Extremes
Period of Record: 1968-2001

Month	High (in)	Year	1-Day Max (in)	Date
JAN	114.0	1997	27.5	01-26-1975
FEB	76.6	1985	25.0	02-03-1983
MAR	78.1	1976	26.0	03-25-1996
APR	45.5	1996	27.5	04-05-1977
MAY	26.0	1997	17.0	05-10-1990
JUN	0.0	-	-	-
JUL	0.0	-	-	-
AUG	0.0	-	-	-
SEP	3.0	1995	3.0	09-22-1995
OCT	30.5	1979	14.4	10-20-1982
NOV	64.0	1995	13.0	11-06-1988
DEC	111.0	1996	30.0	12-19-1996
Season (Jul-Jun)	384.0	1996-1997	30.0	12-19-1996

City of Marquette/Marquette County
1971-2000 Averages

Element	JAN	FEB	MAR	APR	MAY	JUN	JUL	AUG	SEP	OCT	NOV	DEC	ANN
Snow(in)	30.9	19.5	20.9	8.2	1.1	0.0	0.0	0.0	0.2	1.7	12.2	26.2	120.9

Snowfall Extremes
Period of Record: 1948-2001

Month	High (in)	Year	1-Day Max (in)	Date
JAN	64.5	1997	13.6	01-27-1996
FEB	45.6	1960	13.5	02-12-1965
MAR	44.3	1976	17.3	03-14-1997
APR	37.7	1996	11.7	04-13-1951
MAY	12.0	1990	10.6	05-10-1990
JUN	0.0	-	-	-
JUL	0.0	-	-	-
AUG	0.0	-	-	-
SEP	5.1	1974	4.4	09-22-1974
OCT	17.5	1976	6.3	10-25-1976
NOV	36.6	1959	10.1	11-26-1950
DEC	56.9	2000	14.3	12-24-1996
Season (Jul-Jun)	188.1	1959-1960	17.3	03-14-1997

Marquette National Weather Service Office/Negaunee Township
1971-2000 Averages

Element	JAN	FEB	MAR	APR	MAY	JUN	JUL	AUG	SEP	OCT	NOV	DEC	ANN
Snow(in)	42.2	29.7	31.8	12.5	1.5	0.0	0.0	0.0	0.1	5.9	22.6	38.6	184.9

Snowfall Extremes
Period of Record: 1959-2001

Month	High (in)	Year	1-Day Max (in)	Date
JAN	91.7	1997	22.9	01-20-1988
FEB	63.6	1995	18.4	02-03-1983
MAR	60.6	1976	26.2	03-14-1997
APR	43.4	1996	15.5	04-05-1977
MAY	22.6	1990	14.2	05-10-1990
JUN	0.0	-	-	-
JUL	0.0	-	-	-
AUG	0.0	-	-	-
SEP	1.7	1993	1.7	09-29-1993
OCT	18.6	1979	13.0	10-24-1959
NOV	48.9	1991	19.2	11-27-2001
DEC	89.5	2000	23.7	12-01-1985
Season (Jul-Jun)	319.8	2001-2002	26.2	03-14-1997

Photo courtesy of Jean Carey

After three day storm of 1938, ice covers cabin, Middle Island Point, Marquette Co.

PRECIPITATION

This includes rain and melted snow. Most areas receive their lightest precipitation in the winter, when cold, dry air dominates. An exception can be found in the record of the Houghton County airport near Calumet. This high-elevation location receives its heaviest precipitation during December and January due to persistent lake-effect snow.

During the spring and summer, rainfall is fairly evenly distributed with a tendency for heavier monthly totals over inland areas like Iron Mountain and Crystal Falls. This is due to more frequent shower activity that develops over the warmer land areas. Extreme rainfall events are relatively rare, but occur on occasion. Torrential rains caused extensive flooding around Ironwood in July 1909, the Marquette area in July 1949 and Sault Ste. Marie in August 1974.

Aerial photo at mouth of Dead River showing damaged road and bridge during May 2003 flood. City of Marquette photo

Heavy rainfall in spring can bring flooding when combined with rapid snowmelt. Heavy U.P.-wide rain in tandem with snowmelt produced extensive flooding in the springs of 1960, 1985 and 2002.

The following charts show average monthly and yearly rain along with the highest monthly precipitation total and the lowest along with maximum 1-day rainfall.

View of Wakefield near the intersection of Brotherton and Pierce Streets in April 2002. (Photo courtesy of Marko Movritch from "So Cold a Sky")

St. Ignace/Mackinac County

Element	JAN	FEB	MAR	APR	MAY	JUN	JUL	AUG	SEP	OCT	NOV	DEC	ANN
Precip (in)	1.68	1.01	1.60	2.00	2.44	2.51	2.72	2.58	3.09	2.89	2.39	1.62	26.53

Precipitation Extremes
Period of Record: 1973-2001

Month	High (in)	Year	Low (in)	Year	1-Day Max (in)	Date
JAN	2.37	1989	0.00	2001	1.07	01-20-1974
FEB	2.62	1985	0.02	1998	1.00	02-24-1977
MAR	4.91	1977	0.00	2001	3.05	03-26-1996
APR	4.37	1981	0.38	1998	1.75	04-09-1980
MAY	4.85	1983	0.45	1992	1.60	05-25-1989
JUN	5.00	1990	0.40	1988	2.35	06-07-1987
JUL	6.70	1977	0.00	2001	3.00	07-03-1977
AUG	7.76	1975	0.28	1991	2.82	08-09-2001
SEP	7.90	1986	0.73	1989	1.56	09-14-1993
OCT	5.15	2001	0.54	2000	1.68	10-14-2001
NOV	6.26	1988	0.55	1999	2.26	11-05-1988
DEC	3.67	1996	0.00	1994	1.30	12-28-1984
Annual	38.33	1985	17.38	1900	3.05	03-26-1996

Sault Ste. Marie/Chippewa County

Element	JAN	FEB	MAR	APR	MAY	JUN	JUL	AUG	SEP	OCT	NOV	DEC	ANN
Precip (in)	2.64	1.60	2.41	2.57	2.50	3.00	3.14	3.47	3.71	3.32	3.40	2.91	34.67

Precipitation Extremes
Period of Record: 1931-2001

Month	High (in)	Year	Low (in)	Year	1-Day Max (in)	Date
JAN	4.52	1982	0.51	1961	1.21	01-05-1988
FEB	3.73	1971	0.21	1993	1.00	02-24-1977
MAR	4.96	1976	0.24	1937	1.38	03-15-1971
APR	5.15	1954	0.60	1949	2.34	04-26-1954
MAY	7.40	1970	0.62	1996	5.08	05-31-1970
JUN	7.35	1969	0.52	1988	2.39	06-26-1969
JUL	7.23	1996	0.57	1939	2.23	07-15-1955
AUG	9.47	1974	0.50	1947	5.92	08-03-1974
SEP	7.77	1970	0.86	1943	2.20	09-12-1984
OCT	6.84	2001	0.16	1963	1.86	10-24-1959
NOV	7.72	1988	0.87	1962	2.33	11-05-1988
DEC	6.24	1995	0.58	1994	1.46	12-09-1995
Annual	45.84	1995	22.40	1900	5.92	08-03-1974

Newberry/Luce County

Element	JAN	FEB	MAR	APR	MAY	JUN	JUL	AUG	SEP	OCT	NOV	DEC	ANN
Precip (in)	2.25	1.17	1.93	1.90	2.51	3.14	3.14	3.48	3.52	3.18	2.49	2.16	30.87

Precipitation Extremes
Period of Record: 1896-2001

Month	High (in)	Year	Low (in)	Year	1-Day Max (in)	Date
JAN	5.91	1967	0.50	1910	2.00	01-18-1999
FEB	3.74	1981	0.00	1996	1.55	02-13-1938
MAR	6.17	1977	0.00	1996	2.00	03-04-1972
APR	5.74	1960	0.00	1899	2.04	04-26-1954
MAY	7.19	1960	0.00	1905	3.59	05-31-1970
JUN	8.32	1943	0.09	1903	2.82	06-22-1961
JUL	7.44	1994	0.15	1908	4.18	07-22-1994
AUG	8.23	1988	0.15	2000	3.90	08-29-1941
SEP	8.06	1970	0.55	1904	4.10	09-01-1937
OCT	6.20	1995	0.05	1907	2.40	10-18-1923
NOV	5.97	1934	0.10	1899	1.89	11-27-1966
DEC	4.35	1977	0.00	1997	1.20	12-14-1975
Annual	45.15	1977	7.35	1910	4.18	07-22-1994

Manistique/Schoolcraft County

Element	JAN	FEB	MAR	APR	MAY	JUN	JUL	AUG	SEP	OCT	NOV	DEC	ANN
Precip (in)	1.51	0.94	1.82	2.23	2.43	3.05	3.13	3.19	3.34	2.87	2.56	1.66	28.73

Precipitation Extremes
Period of Record: 1948-2001

Month	High (in)	Year	Low (in)	Year	1-Day Max (in)	Date
JAN	5.40	1979	0.13	1995	2.48	01-24-1979
FEB	3.68	1968	0.00	1969	1.26	02-24-1977
MAR	5.52	1977	0.00	1999	1.50	03-29-1977
APR	5.32	1954	0.45	1963	2.06	04-13-1952
MAY	8.31	1960	0.34	1977	2.26	05-06-1960
JUN	6.64	1969	0.47	1970	2.51	06-28-1977
JUL	7.58	1991	0.01	2001	3.70	07-28-1991
AUG	6.39	1959	1.17	1996	2.55	08-23-1978
SEP	8.07	1954	0.74	1967	3.85	09-07-1985
OCT	6.12	1967	0.35	1952	2.58	10-08-1967
NOV	6.46	1977	0.53	1986	2.26	11-21-1992
DEC	4.01	1971	0.00	1997	1.50	12-21-1983
Annual	40.21	1979	17.22	1989	3.85	09-07-1985

Munising/Alger County

Element	JAN	FEB	MAR	APR	MAY	JUN	JUL	AUG	SEP	OCT	NOV	DEC	ANN
Precip (in)	3.19	1.94	2.36	2.03	2.63	3.01	3.27	3.20	3.92	3.66	3.27	3.35	35.83

Precipitation Extremes
Period of Record: 1911-2001

Month	High (in)	Year	Low (in)	Year	1-Day Max (in)	Date
JAN	8.11	1982	0.76	1956	1.40	01-03-2000
FEB	5.48	1985	0.41	1912	1.40	02-18-1985
MAR	5.08	1979	0.30	1912	2.23	03-06-1959
APR	5.47	1914	0.27	1984	2.45	04-28-1914
MAY	6.18	1960	0.40	1923	3.51	05-31-1970
JUN	9.12	1943	0.49	1970	2.68	06-02-1916
JUL	8.44	1911	0.57	1981	3.12	07-11-1982
AUG	7.30	1988	0.18	1991	2.50	08-15-1988
SEP	7.10	1926	0.59	1967	2.33	09-11-1978
OCT	9.23	1968	0.42	1924	2.80	10-25-1967
NOV	6.91	1948	0.65	1954	2.14	11-05-1988
DEC	8.06	1983	0.68	1994	1.41	12-15-1983
Annual	47.84	1968	19.00	1985	3.51	05-31-1970

Escanaba/Delta County

Element	JAN	FEB	MAR	APR	MAY	JUN	JUL	AUG	SEP	OCT	NOV	DEC	ANN
Precip (in)	1.44	0.95	1.87	1.95	2.74	3.02	3.36	3.52	3.20	2.49	2.53	1.46	28.53

Precipitation Extremes
Period of Record: 1892-2001

Month	High (in)	Year	Low (in)	Year	1-Day Max (in)	Date
JAN	3.12	1969	0.23	1961	1.30	01-03-1897
FEB	2.81	1893	0.06	1982	1.20	02-20-1898
MAR	4.84	1977	0.00	1895	1.49	03-27-1898
APR	5.23	1954	0.50	1971	2.01	04-19-1898
MAY	7.72	1895	0.52	1986	2.13	05-18-1949
JUN	7.91	1953	0.58	1970	3.92	06-30-1953
JUL	9.93	1951	0.44	1895	3.44	07-26-1951
AUG	6.82	1959	0.56	1969	2.87	08-12-1976
SEP	8.73	1895	0.43	1989	2.75	09-12-1984
OCT	4.78	1991	0.07	1952	2.70	10-29-1896
NOV	7.18	1985	0.61	1976	2.77	11-01-1985
DEC	2.90	1968	0.30	1960	1.16	12-14-1975
Annual	39.02	1977	20.30	1900	3.92	06-30-1953

Menominee-Marinette/Menominee County

Element	JAN	FEB	MAR	APR	MAY	JUN	JUL	AUG	SEP	OCT	NOV	DEC	ANN
Precip (in)	2.00	1.33	2.39	2.75	3.06	3.60	3.44	3.35	3.53	2.47	2.69	1.79	32.40

Precipitation Extremes
Period of Record: 1919-2001

Month	High (in)	Year	Low (in)	Year	1-Day Max (in)	Date
JAN	8.49	1996	0.00	1990	2.35	01-27-1996
FEB	4.20	1922	0.00	1990	2.16	02-21-1937
MAR	7.03	1977	0.16	1937	1.90	03-09-2000
APR	6.67	1968	0.36	1946	1.97	04-17-1968
MAY	8.81	1965	0.77	1988	5.17	05-16-1965
JUN	11.07	1996	0.56	1921	3.31	06-22-1990
JUL	7.52	1991	0.87	1981	3.96	07-28-1991
AUG	9.97	1960	0.53	1970	5.05	08-03-1960
SEP	8.38	1965	0.31	1967	2.78	09-01-1979
OCT	6.04	1967	0.06	1952	2.13	10-07-1995
NOV	8.20	1985	0.10	1976	3.36	11-01-1985
DEC	5.74	1959	0.00	1989	3.10	12-28-1959
Annual	45.27	1996	16.65	1989	5.17	05-16-1965

Iron Mountain-Kingsford/Dickinson County

Element	JAN	FEB	MAR	APR	MAY	JUN	JUL	AUG	SEP	OCT	NOV	DEC	ANN
Precip (in)	1.39	0.89	1.73	2.19	3.10	3.48	3.62	3.78	3.65	2.65	2.03	1.49	30.00

Precipitation Extremes
Period of Record: 1899-2001

Month	High (in)	Year	Low (in)	Year	1-Day Max (in)	Date
JAN	4.01	1996	0.12	1961	1.55	01-19-1996
FEB	3.55	1922	0.05	1993	1.82	02-23-1922
MAR	3.88	1942	0.05	1937	2.38	03-30-1998
APR	7.07	1951	0.23	1989	2.25	04-01-1951
MAY	6.97	1960	0.39	1986	2.90	05-16-1951
JUN	9.57	1916	0.26	1937	3.78	06-17-1951
JUL	11.35	1999	0.81	1933	4.05	07-15-1999
AUG	11.15	1941	0.18	1908	4.06	08-29-1941
SEP	6.87	1954	0.54	1909	3.15	09-01-1923
OCT	5.22	1983	0.14	1952	2.70	10-12-1983
NOV	5.91	1948	0.02	1904	1.90	11-07-1945
DEC	4.05	1927	0.04	1943	1.47	12-28-1959
Annual	48.20	1951	16.98	1910	4.06	08-29-1941

Crystal Falls/Iron County

Element	JAN	FEB	MAR	APR	MAY	JUN	JUL	AUG	SEP	OCT	NOV	DEC	ANN
Precip (in)	1.24	0.82	1.79	2.17	2.92	3.86	3.57	3.59	3.66	2.67	2.01	1.35	29.65

Precipitation Extremes
Period of Record: 1948-2001

Month	High (in)	Year	Low (in)	Year	1-Day Max (in)	Date
JAN	3.08	1950	0.09	1961	1.03	01-25-1967
FEB	2.96	1971	0.11	1958	1.09	02-12-1984
MAR	3.61	1977	0.39	1980	1.84	03-07-1973
APR	5.06	1960	0.00	2000	1.70	04-10-1950
MAY	5.95	1964	0.00	2000	3.30	05-24-1964
JUN	12.48	1981	0.00	2000	3.86	06-14-1981
JUL	8.67	1952	1.35	1963	3.50	07-01-1958
AUG	7.07	1988	0.47	1969	3.05	08-28-1960
SEP	7.99	1980	0.50	1952	2.89	09-21-1980
OCT	5.01	1970	0.32	1952	2.14	10-12-1986
NOV	5.41	1948	0.39	1981	1.62	11-02-1985
DEC	2.96	1968	0.44	1974	1.00	12-04-1970
Annual	38.69	1951	19.78	1963	3.86	06-14-1981

Ironwood/Gogebic County

Element	JAN	FEB	MAR	APR	MAY	JUN	JUL	AUG	SEP	OCT	NOV	DEC	ANN
Precip (in)	2.07	1.22	2.08	2.11	2.97	4.16	4.00	3.72	3.80	3.38	3.09	2.05	34.65

Precipitation Extremes
Period of Record: 1901-2001

Month	High (in)	Year	Low (in)	Year	1-Day Max (in)	Date
JAN	4.31	1997	0.55	1951	1.46	01-19-1996
FEB	5.42	1922	0.18	1998	3.40	02-23-1922
MAR	7.29	1926	0.04	1910	2.78	03-30-1924
APR	7.91	1960	0.48	1988	3.05	04-23-1960
MAY	7.18	1942	0.46	1948	2.02	05-21-1953
JUN	11.32	1939	0.10	1910	3.81	06-24-1946
JUL	15.44	1909	0.10	1907	6.72	07-21-1909
AUG	8.86	1941	0.48	1930	4.34	08-16-1972
SEP	10.74	1926	0.79	1939	2.54	09-03-1985
OCT	6.73	1995	0.31	1947	2.05	10-20-1937
NOV	8.16	1991	0.48	1939	5.61	11-01-1909
DEC	5.38	1927	0.27	1967	2.08	12-16-1920
Annual	52.65	1909	17.74	1907	6.72	07-21-1909

Ontonagon/Ontonagon County

Element	JAN	FEB	MAR	APR	MAY	JUN	JUL	AUG	SEP	OCT	NOV	DEC	ANN
Precip (in)	3.02	1.47	2.04	2.08	3.00	3.08	3.46	3.34	3.09	3.13	2.79	3.06	33.56

Precipitation Extremes
Period of Record: 1977-2001

Month	High (in)	Year	Low (in)	Year	1-Day Max (in)	Date
JAN	4.60	1997	1.52	1990	1.45	01-18-1996
FEB	3.99	1981	0.27	1998	1.00	02-05-1984
MAR	4.39	1979	0.23	1999	2.50	03-25-1996
APR	5.03	2001	0.48	1997	1.58	04-26-1994
MAY	5.01	1999	0.77	1986	2.25	05-26-1991
JUN	6.83	1990	0.76	1982	2.02	06-11-1986
JUL	8.09	1987	1.11	1989	2.51	07-18-1987
AUG	6.86	1988	0.70	1990	3.90	08-23-1978
SEP	6.71	1980	0.79	1989	2.31	09-05-1983
OCT	6.59	1995	0.98	2000	1.55	10-01-1981
NOV	6.53	1991	0.97	1984	1.90	11-01-1991
DEC	4.75	1985	0.46	1994	0.97	12-05-1998
Annual	42.79	1985	22.38	1994	3.90	08-23-1978

Houghton County Airport/Houghton County

Element	JAN	FEB	MAR	APR	MAY	JUN	JUL	AUG	SEP	OCT	NOV	DEC	ANN
Precip (in)	4.26	2.28	2.45	1.71	2.49	2.84	2.97	2.75	3.24	2.56	2.84	3.42	33.81

Precipitation Extremes
Period of Record: 1952-2001

Month	High (in)	Year	Low (in)	Year	1-Day Max (in)	Date
JAN	8.51	1980	0.94	2001	1.82	01-11-1980
FEB	5.11	1989	0.06	2001	1.79	02-08-1989
MAR	7.46	1976	0.21	2001	2.49	03-04-1985
APR	5.75	2001	0.32	1998	2.08	04-26-1954
MAY	5.71	1999	0.35	1986	2.84	05-26-1956
JUN	6.61	1989	0.42	1995	2.31	06-11-1954
JUL	6.19	1968	0.59	1964	2.34	07-21-1960
AUG	7.15	1955	0.23	1990	3.23	08-03-1955
SEP	6.62	1985	0.88	1952	3.06	09-03-1985
OCT	5.69	1967	0.63	1953	2.10	10-14-1954
NOV	6.91	1985	0.72	1981	1.90	11-02-1961
DEC	9.48	1983	0.09	2000	1.53	12-22-1983
Annual	53.43	1985	17.23	1900	3.23	08-03-1955

Copper Harbor/Keweenaw County

Element	JAN	FEB	MAR	APR	MAY	JUN	JUL	AUG	SEP	OCT	NOV	DEC	ANN
Precip (in)	2.87	1.56	2.00	2.05	2.81	2.86	2.70	2.72	3.14	2.71	3.10	2.53	31.05

Precipitation Extremes
Period of Record: 1948-2001

Month	High (in)	Year	Low (in)	Year	1-Day Max (in)	Date
JAN	5.00	1997	0.92	1987	1.56	01-07-1997
FEB	2.90	1985	0.40	1998	0.96	02-26-1951
MAR	3.66	1951	0.00	1999	1.38	03-30-1998
APR	3.60	1994	0.31	1949	1.88	04-06-2000
MAY	7.19	1999	0.21	1976	1.67	05-08-2000
JUN	5.84	1996	0.49	1995	3.52	06-29-1996
JUL	4.85	1987	0.78	1989	2.10	07-09-1999
AUG	9.52	1988	0.32	1990	3.65	08-22-1972
SEP	4.80	1985	0.48	1948	2.58	09-26-1973
OCT	5.02	1995	0.77	1975	1.78	10-12-1986
NOV	7.22	1988	0.42	1976	4.06	11-02-1985
DEC	4.64	1995	0.39	1994	1.12	12-15-1996
Annual	38.75	1996	13.60	1976	4.06	11-02-1985

Herman/Baraga County

Element	JAN	FEB	MAR	APR	MAY	JUN	JUL	AUG	SEP	OCT	NOV	DEC	ANN
Precip (in)	2.47	1.64	2.83	2.31	3.37	3.69	4.07	4.10	4.07	3.58	3.35	2.77	38.25

Precipitation Extremes
Period of Record: 1968-2001

Month	High (in)	Year	Low (in)	Year	1-Day Max (in)	Date
JAN	4.87	1997	1.23	1991	0.99	01-18-1996
FEB	3.94	2001	0.35	1993	1.16	02-05-1971
MAR	6.18	1976	0.76	1974	2.60	03-25-1996
APR	5.64	1985	0.44	1998	3.07	04-19-1985
MAY	9.83	1999	0.55	1986	2.13	05-20-1975
JUN	6.48	1979	0.82	1992	3.09	06-20-1972
JUL	9.64	1982	1.40	1989	3.36	07-11-1982
AUG	9.42	1987	0.54	1976	3.20	08-01-1987
SEP	8.67	1980	0.67	1989	3.12	09-11-1978
OCT	7.64	1979	1.06	1994	2.97	10-20-1982
NOV	6.77	1983	0.37	1994	1.59	11-12-1982
DEC	6.77	2000	0.56	1994	1.35	12-14-1975
Annual	54.81	1982	17.38	1998	3.36	07-11-1982

City of Marquette/Marquette County

Element	JAN	FEB	MAR	APR	MAY	JUN	JUL	AUG	SEP	OCT	NOV	DEC	ANN
Precip (in)	2.04	1.35	2.24	2.35	2.66	2.74	2.64	3.01	3.42	3.03	2.60	1.95	30.03

Precipitation Extremes
Period of Record: 1948-2001

Month	High (in)	Year	Low (in)	Year	1-Day Max (in)	Date
JAN	5.40	1997	0.51	1956	1.28	01-18-1996
FEB	3.07	1968	0.18	1993	1.28	02-12-1984
MAR	4.76	1979	0.39	1980	1.60	03-23-1979
APR	5.73	1960	0.59	2000	1.88	04-08-1980
MAY	7.70	1960	0.05	1986	2.25	05-01-1973
JUN	7.34	1951	0.77	1988	2.14	06-16-1979
JUL	10.20	1949	0.51	1998	3.93	07-28-1949
AUG	11.76	1988	0.50	1976	2.76	08-02-1988
SEP	8.25	1980	1.13	2000	2.72	09-09-1968
OCT	7.13	1959	0.21	1956	4.06	10-24-1959
NOV	7.30	1988	0.77	1986	1.95	11-27-2001
DEC	3.96	1968	0.41	1994	1.11	12-14-1975
Annual	41.54	1951	20.90	1900	4.06	10-24-1959

National Weather Service/Negaunee Township/Marquette County

Element	JAN	FEB	MAR	APR	MAY	JUN	JUL	AUG	SEP	OCT	NOV	DEC	ANN
Precip (in)	2.60	1.85	3.13	2.79	3.07	3.21	3.01	3.55	3.74	3.66	3.27	2.43	36.31

Precipitation Extremes
Period of Record: 1959-2001

Month	High (in)	Year	Low (in)	Year	1-Day Max (in)	Date
JAN	6.61	1997	0.61	1965	2.21	01-20-1988
FEB	3.68	1984	0.48	1994	1.53	02-03-1983
MAR	6.08	1979	0.32	1974	1.98	03-24-1975
APR	6.56	1985	0.90	1998	3.09	04-19-1985
MAY	7.90	1973	0.06	1986	2.90	05-29-1983
JUN	12.26	1968	0.61	1992	4.09	06-27-1968
JUL	5.60	1970	0.57	1981	2.47	07-14-1977
AUG	8.59	1988	0.56	1970	2.39	08-03-1974
SEP	7.60	1968	1.21	1989	2.61	09-11-1978
OCT	7.73	1959	0.94	1975	4.65	10-24-1959
NOV	8.25	1988	0.81	1962	2.18	11-06-1988
DEC	6.91	1968	0.37	1994	2.30	12-01-1985
Annual	51.59	1985	23.45	1962	4.65	10-24-1959

TORNADOES/SEVERE WEATHER

Tornadoes in the Upper Peninsula of Michigan are a relatively rare phenomenon. Between 1950 and 1995, there were 45 documented tornadoes in Upper Michigan. A number of these tornadoes traveled through two or more counties. Most of these tornadoes were ranked as weak (F0 or F1 on the Fujita Tornado Intensity Scale giving maximum winds up to 112 mile-per-hour). Only a few were ranked as strong F2 (113-157mph) or F3 (158-206 mph)).

Gladstone tornado of July 1992. Photo courtesy of Helen Micheau

TORNADOES BY COUNTY

ALGER COUNTY:

May 06, 1964	No injuries	$250K Damage	F2
Jul. 09, 1987	No injuries	No Damage	F1
Jul. 19, 1992	No injuries	No Damage	F0

BARAGA COUNTY:

Sep. 08, 1980	No injuries	No Damage	F0

CHIPPEWA COUNTY:

Jul. 19. 1992	2 injuries	$2.5M Damage	F2

DICKINSON COUNTY:

Apr. 21, 1974	No injuries	No Damage	F1
Jun. 14, 1981	No injuries	$2.5K Damage	F2
Jul. 11, 1987	No injuries	$25K Damage	F3
Sep. 30, 2002	No injuries	$7M Damage	F1

GOGEBIC COUNTY:

Apr. 27, 1984	No injuries	$25K Damage	F1
Aug. 03, 1988	No injuries	No Damage	F0

HOUGHTON COUNTY:

Jul. 11, 1987	No injuries	$3K Damage	F0

IRON COUNTY:

Aug. 09, 1958	No injuries	No Damage	F1
Aug. 15, 1978	2 injuries	$25K Damage	F1
Jun. 20, 1979	No injuries	$3K Damage	F0
Jun. 14, 1981	No injuries	$3K Damage	F2

KEWEENAW COUNTY:

Jul. 11, 1987   No injuries $2.5K Damage   F0

LUCE COUNTY:

Aug. 22, 1977 No injuries $25K Damage   F1

May 1, 1983   No injuries   No Damage   F0

MACKINAC COUNTY:

Jul. 14, 1984   1 injury $25K Damage   F2

Aug. 16, 1988 No injuries   No Damage   F1

MARQUETTE COUNTY:

Aug. 19, 1973 No injuries $2.5K Damage   F1

Jun. 20, 1979 No injuries   No Damage   F0

Sep. 8, 1980   No injuries   No Damage   F0

Aug. 18, 1987 No injuries $0.3K Damage   F0

MENOMINEE COUNTY:

Sep. 16, 1972 No injuries $250K Damage   F2

Jun. 08,1985   No injuries $2.5K Damage   F1

Jul. 04, 1986   12 injuries $2.5M Damage   F3

Jul. 11, 1987   No injuries $25K Damage   F3

May 28, 1991   No injuries $250K Damage   F3

May 28,1991   No injuries $250K Damage   F2

ONTONAGON COUNTY:

May 12, 1988   No injuries   No Damage   F0

SCHOOLCRAFT COUNTY:

Jul. 11, 1975   No injuries   No Damage   F0

Jul. 14, 1984   1 injury $25K Damage   F2

Jul. 11, 1987   No injuries $25K Damage   F3

The data shows that the south-central Upper Peninsula is at the greatest risk for tornadoes. One reason is that this area is often the closest to warm, humid air masses to the south. Menominee County has had the most violent tornadoes between 1950 and 1995 with three F3 twisters and two F2s. The tornado of July 4, 1986 caused the most injuries of any tornado in the recent history of Upper Michigan. Twelve people were hurt as an F3 twister cut across the county from west to east destroying a number of homes and just missing the town of Nadeau. Menominee County has also had the most damaging tornado events during this period—six with a total dollar amount at $25, 777,500.

Dickinson County's September 30, 2002 tornado was included in this table because it is the most recent significant tornado to hit the U.P., plus it did the highest dollar amount of damage—7 million. This high figure is due in part to the fact that this twister hit the densely populated area from Kingsford through Iron Mountain to Quinnesec. The figure is also biased by inflation.

Upper Michigan is much more likely to get hit by straight-line thunderstorm wind events. Particularly damaging squall lines hit Escanaba in July 1980, Marquette in August 1988, and much of the western U.P. in July 1999. Several squall-line events ravaged the west and central U.P. in the summer of 2002, while the heart of the U.P. from Gogebic County to Luce County sustained downed trees and massive power outages in August 2005.

GROWING SEASON

The traditional beginning and end of the growing season is based on the first and last date the temperature reaches 32 degrees or the freezing point of water. Most plants will not survive below a temperature of 32. The first chart in this section shows the median date, the earliest date and the latest date of certain threshold temperatures beginning with 32 degrees Fahrenheit. The second chart illustrates the length of the growing season based on these threshold temperatures.

For example, St. Ignace sees a median or average date of the last 32 degree temperature in the spring on May 11. The earliest date of the last 32 degree low temperature is April 23, while the latest date is June 5. The median date of the first "freezing" low temperature in fall is October 11. The earliest 32-degree low was observed on September 22, while the latest occurred on November 11.

The second chart shows the median or average length of the growing season based on the first and last occurrence of 32 degrees. In St. Ignace, this figure is 157 days. The shortest growing season in the period of record was 126 days, the longest 186 days.

Notice that the growing season is longest in reporting stations that are closest to a Great Lake. Interior areas of the U.P. are subject to earlier and later frosty nights because of their position away from the warming influence of the large bodies of water. To illustrate the contrast, check out Champion, one of the habitually cold spots in the U.P., which concludes this section. It is very difficult to grow tomatoes in Champion!

St. Ignace/Mackinac County
Threshold temperature, median date/last occurrence /first occurrence

Base Temp °F	Date of Last Spring Occurrence			Date of First Fall Occurrence		
	Median	Early	Late	Median	Early	Late
32	5/11	4/23	6/05	10/11	9/22	11/05
30	5/02	4/09	6/05	10/19	9/22	11/18
28	4/26	4/01	5/19	11/01	9/28	11/18
24	4/13	3/24	5/16	11/10	10/18	12/01
20	4/08	3/14	5/10	11/15	10/19	12/17
16	3/31	3/14	5/10	11/24	11/07	12/20

Length of Growing Season (Days)
Derived from 1973-2000 Averages

Base Temp °F	Median	Shortest	Longest
32	157	126	186
30	171	126	210
28	188	134	217
24	213	160	242
20	222	194	278
16	233	213	279

Sault Ste. Marie/Chippewa County
Threshold temperature, median date/last occurrence /first occurrence

Base Temp °F	Date of Last Spring Occurrence			Date of First Fall Occurrence		
	Median	Early	Late	Median	Early	Late
32	5/31	4/24	6/23	9/25	8/29	10/21
30	5/18	4/25	6/17	10/02	8/29	11/01
28	5/04	4/16	6/11	10/09	9/17	11/02
24	4/21	3/27	5/20	10/29	10/03	11/29
20	4/11	3/26	4/23	11/09	10/15	12/17
16	4/08	2/27	4/21	11/11	10/24	12/18

Length of Growing Season (Days)
Derived from 1971-2000 Averages

Base Temp °F	Median	Shortest	Longest
32	121	72	152
30	129	·86	173
28	156	106	195
24	188	148	229
20	212	181	260
16	218	186	282

Newberry/Luce County
Threshold temperature/median date/last occurrence
/first occurrence

Base Temp °F	Date of Last Spring Occurrence			Date of First Fall Occurrence		
	Median	Early	Late	Median	Early	Late
32	5/31	5/03	6/18	9/23	7/22	11/01
30	5/23	4/21	6/18	9/29	9/03	11/01
28	5/11	4/17	6/03	10/09	9/17	11/02
24	4/26	4/03	5/16	10/29	9/27	11/19
20	4/14	3/24	4/29	11/08	10/16	11/29
16	4/08	3/16	4/21	11/13	10/24	12/18

Length of Growing Season (Days)
Derived from 1971-2000 Averages

Base Temp °F	Median	Shortest	Longest
32	115	54	164
30	128	91	181
28	155	108	181
24	187	156	219
20	207	173	249
16	222	186	270

Manistique/Schoolcraft County
Threshold temperature/median date/last occurrence
/first occurrence

Base Temp °F	Date of Last Spring Occurrence			Date of First Fall Occurrence		
	Median	Early	Late	Median	Early	Late
32	5/17	4/23	6/19	9/29	8/11	11/03
30	5/07	4/21	6/19	10/10	9/14	11/07
28	4/30	4/11	6/18	10/13	9/14	11/15
24	4/18	3/24	5/15	11/06	9/15	11/29
20	4/08	3/19	4/28	11/10	9/15	12/18
16	4/06	3/15	4/14	11/21	10/19	12/18

Length of Growing Season (Days)
Derived from 1971-2000 Averages

Base Temp °F	Median	Shortest	Longest
32	133	53	180
30	150	90	200
28	162	112	215
24	205	147	241
20	216	174	269
16	228	192	277

Munising/Alger County
Threshold temperature/median date/last occurrence
/first occurrence

Base Temp °F	Date of Last Spring Occurrence			Date of First Fall Occurrence		
	Median	Early	Late	Median	Early	Late
32	5/27	4/27	7/05	10/01	8/24	10/27
30	5/17	4/25	6/19	10/08	9/21	11/12
28	5/08	4/19	6/18	10/18	9/22	11/16
24	4/28	3/27	5/22	11/02	10/03	12/07
20	4/12	3/15	5/09	11/08	10/15	12/18
16	4/07	3/13	4/20	11/17	10/16	12/28

Length of Growing Season (Days)
Derived from 1971-2000 Averages

Base Temp °F	Median	Shortest	Longest
32	130	74	178
30	151	95	188
28	164	115	200
24	192	138	255
20	212	162	277
16	235	191	279

Escanaba/Delta County
Threshold temperature/median date/last occurrence /first occurrence

Base Temp °F	Date of Last Spring Occurrence			Date of First Fall Occurrence		
	Median	Early	Late	Median	Early	Late
32	5/07	4/08	6/04	10/05	9/20	11/02
30	5/02	4/07	6/04	10/14	9/25	11/07
28	4/27	4/04	5/11	10/24	10/02	11/13
24	4/13	3/27	5/07	11/06	10/05	11/19
20	4/05	3/19	4/21	11/13	10/19	12/11
16	3/29	2/27	4/10	11/22	11/04	12/22

Length of Growing Season (Days) Derived from 1971-2000 Averages

Base Temp °F	Median	Shortest	Longest
32	158	113	183
30	166	140	205
28	184	151	205
24	206	174	227
20	224	191	259
16	232	218	283

Menominee-Marinette/Menominee County
Threshold temperature/median date/last occurrence /first occurrence

Base Temp °F	Date of Last Spring Occurrence			Date of First Fall Occurrence		
	Median	Early	Late	Median	Early	Late
32	5/08	4/20	5/27	10/03	9/14	11/01
30	4/30	4/06	5/27	10/10	9/22	11/11
28	4/23	3/26	5/11	10/18	9/22	11/15
24	4/13	3/14	5/07	11/04	9/23	11/28
20	4/05	3/14	4/19	11/12	10/14	12/20
16	3/25	2/27	4/18	11/20	10/31	12/22

Length of Growing Season (Days) Derived from 1971-2000 Averages

Base Temp °F	Median	Shortest	Longest
32	151	124	177
30	162	135	201
28	182	138	213
24	206	139	258
20	219	193	271
16	233	208	278

Iron Mountain-Kingsford/Dickinson County
Threshold temperature/median date/last occurrence /first occurrence

Base Temp °F	Date of Last Spring Occurrence			Date of First Fall Occurrence		
	Median	Early	Late	Median	Early	Late
32	5/26	5/05	6/22	9/23	9/03	10/04
30	5/17	4/23	6/11	9/25	9/03	10/17
28	5/09	4/23	5/27	10/04	9/03	11/01
24	4/28	4/05	5/13	10/14	9/23	11/07
20	4/15	3/24	5/11	11/03	10/09	11/19
16	4/09	3/14	5/11	11/09	10/18	11/29

Length of Growing Season (Days)
Derived from 1971-2000 Averages

Base Temp °F	Median	Shortest	Longest
32	117	94	145
30	134	97	170
28	148	113	182
24	171	139	204
20	199	159	234
16	216	181	261

Crystal Falls/Iron County
Threshold temperature/median date/last occurrence /first occurrence

Base Temp °F	Date of Last Spring Occurrence			Date of First Fall Occurrence		
	Median	Early	Late	Median	Early	Late
32	6/09	5/15	6/25	9/09	8/05	9/22
30	5/30	5/12	6/18	9/17	8/18	10/04
28	5/26	5/07	6/11	9/25	9/03	10/17
24	5/05	4/17	5/20	10/11	9/23	11/05
20	4/27	4/08	5/13	10/30	9/23	11/12
16	4/17	3/25	5/07	11/06	10/14	11/16

Length of Growing Season (Days)
Derived from 1971-1989 Averages

Base Temp °F	Median	Shortest	Longest
32	93	48	116
30	105	70	135
28	123	97	144
24	160	128	185
20	185	139	214
16	206	165	224

Ironwood/Gogebic County
Threshold temperature/last occurrence/first occurrence

Base Temp °F	Date of Last Spring Occurrence			Date of First Fall Occurrence		
	Median	Early	Late	Median	Early	Late
32	5/31	5/05	6/23	9/22	8/14	10/08
30	5/21	4/27	6/23	9/24	8/16	10/22
28	5/13	4/12	6/22	10/03	9/18	10/22
24	4/29	4/05	5/30	10/18	9/20	11/16
20	4/17	3/25	5/18	11/02	10/01	11/19
16	4/08	3/23	5/10	11/07	10/20	11/29

Length of Growing Season (Days)
Derived from 1971-2000 Averages

Base Temp °F	Median	Shortest	Longest
32	113	52	143
30	123	76	178
28	145	93	182
24	167	139	215
20	193	154	235
16	214	167	249

Ontonagon/Ontonagon County
Threshold temperature/last occurrence/first occurrence

Base Temp °F	Date of Last Spring Occurrence			Date of First Fall Occurrence		
	Median	Early	Late	Median	Early	Late
32	6/05	5/17	7/01	9/25	9/07	10/08
30	6/02	5/06	6/29	9/30	9/07	10/08
28	5/20	4/25	6/21	10/07	9/22	11/03
24	4/28	4/07	5/19	10/23	10/03	11/21
20	4/14	3/24	5/10	11/04	10/10	11/30
16	4/06	3/17	4/18	11/13	10/19	12/11

Length of Growing Season (Days)
Derived from 1977-2000 Averages

Base Temp °F	Median	Shortest	Longest
32	115	67	131
30	124	87	142
28	142	94	187
24	177	149	207
20	200	167	250
16	218	192	264

Houghton County Airport/Houghton County
Threshold temperature/median date/last occurrence
/first occurrence

Base Temp °F	Date of Last Spring Occurrence			Date of First Fall Occurrence		
	Median	Early	Late	Median	Early	Late
32	5/09	4/20	6/11	10/03	9/18	11/01
30	5/04	4/15	5/25	10/09	9/18	11/09
28	4/29	3/24	5/16	10/18	9/23	11/12
24	4/17	3/24	5/10	11/04	9/29	11/19
20	4/10	3/13	4/21	11/10	10/24	12/10
16	4/04	2/27	4/21	11/21	11/03	12/17

Length of Growing Season (Days)
Derived from 1971-2000 Averages

Base Temp °F	Median	Shortest	Longest
32	149	120	177
30	159	138	193
28	175	139	233
24	198	165	239
20	212	187	272
16	231	205	282

Copper Harbor/Keweenaw County
Threshold temperature/median date/last occurrence
/first occurrence

Base Temp °F	Date of Last Spring Occurrence			Date of First Fall Occurrence		
	Median	Early	Late	Median	Early	Late
32	5/19	4/28	6/21	10/09	9/24	11/01
30	5/08	4/24	5/22	10/17	9/28	12/15
28	5/04	4/23	5/22	10/30	10/08	12/15
24	4/18	3/26	5/06	11/05	10/28	12/18
20	4/10	3/17	5/07	11/18	11/01	12/21
16	4/05	3/14	5/07	12/04	11/01	1/06

Length of Growing Season (Days)
Derived from 1972-2000 Averages

Base Temp °F	Median	Shortest	Longest
32	146	94	170
30	160	148	210
28	177	152	234
24	206	178	251
20	218	202	279
16	250	217	295

Alberta/Baraga County
Threshold temperature/median date/last occurrence /first occurrence

Base Temp °F	Date of Last Spring Occurrence			Date of First Fall Occurrence		
	Median	Early	Late	Median	Early	Late
32	6/07	5/18	7/05	9/20	8/16	10/07
30	5/30	4/28	6/22	9/23	9/01	10/19
28	5/22	4/27	6/22	9/30	9/06	10/30
24	5/06	4/11	5/27	10/19	10/01	11/04
20	4/25	4/08	5/11	11/01	10/08	11/16
16	4/14	4/03	5/11	11/06	10/19	11/29

Length of Growing Season (Days)
Derived from 1971-1996 Averages

Base Temp °F	Median	Shortest	Longest
32	103	68	132
30	115	93	166
28	135	93	176
24	167	142	192
20	187	152	214
16	204	184	229

Marquette/Marquette County
Threshold temperature/median date/last occurrence /first occurrence

Base Temp °F	Date of Last Spring Occurrence			Date of First Fall Occurrence		
	Median	Early	Late	Median	Early	Late
32	5/09	4/23	6/09	10/13	9/22	11/04
30	5/04	4/06	5/31	10/21	9/30	11/15
28	4/28	4/06	5/27	10/31	10/03	11/29
24	4/13	3/20	5/08	11/08	10/19	11/29
20	4/05	3/12	4/21	11/15	10/23	12/20
16	3/28	2/27	4/14	11/23	11/03	12/27

Length of Growing Season (Days)
Derived from 1971-2000 Averages

Base Temp °F	Median	Shortest	Longest
32	155	127	189
30	173	134	220
28	180	138	220
24	207	176	254
20	228	185	278
16	242	213	283

Champion/Marquette County
Threshold temperature/median date/last occurrence
/first occurrence

Base Temp °F	Date of Last Spring Occurrence			Date of First Fall Occurrence		
	Median	Early	Late	Median	Early	Late
32	6/13	5/19	7/19	8/24	7/22	9/22
30	6/10	5/15	7/19	9/09	8/05	10/01
28	6/06	5/14	7/19	9/17	8/14	10/04
24	5/27	5/03	6/22	10/01	9/03	11/01
20	5/07	4/22	6/05	10/13	9/22	11/07
16	4/22	4/08	5/16	11/04	9/29	12/02

Length of Growing Season (Days)
Derived from 1971-2000 Averages

Base Temp °F	Median	Shortest	Longest
32	67	4	106
30	93	31	127
28	102	31	130
24	131	94	166
20	161	127	193
16	193	162	226

U.P. WEATHER EXTREMES

Hottest: 108°, July 15, 1901 **Marquette Weather Bureau (City)**

Coldest: -49 at **Humboldt, Marquette County** Feb 10, 1899

Coldest month: -7.2, **Watersmeet** January 1912

Warmest month: 76.0, July 1921 **Iron Mountain**

Hottest summer: 68.1°, 1955 **Marquette Weather Bureau (City)**

Coolest summer: 58.0°, 1992 **National Weather Service (NWS)**

Coldest winter: 5.1°, **Crystal Falls** and **Bergland**, 1978-79

Warmest winter: 30.9°, 1877-78 **Marquette Weather Bureau (City)**

Wettest month: 15.45 inches, July 1909 **Ironwood**

Driest month: 0.00 inches, January 1969 **Manistique**

Snowiest day: 29 inches, **Ishpeming** October 23, 1929

Biggest storm: 61.7 inches, **Sault Ste. Marie** December 8-11, 1995

Deepest snowcover: 63 inches, March 14, 1997 **NWS**

Snowiest month: 133.7 inches, **Delaware** December 2000

Snowiest winter: 390.4 inches, **Delaware** 1978-79

Least snowy winter: 15.8 inches, **Escanaba** 1899-1900

Highest wind: 90 mph, **Mackinac Island** November 10, 1998

SNOW PANKER

Steel-plated, 2-drum snow roller once used to "pank" (unique Upper Peninsula verb meaning to compress snow) snow on the roads of Keweenaw County. This roller was donated by Calumet Township to the Eagle River Lighthouse Museum.

Chapter 3

LAND

LAND AREA USAGE AND POPULATION DATA

The Upper Peninsula, at 16,417 square miles, represents less than a third of the total area of the state of Michigan. One reason why there seems to be more land in the U.P. than the Lower Peninsula is the population; at about 328,000 it represents only 3% of the people in the state. There's a lot more room to move around in the U.P.

Length (east to west): 320 miles (max.)

Width (north to south): 125 miles

AREA AND POPULATION DENSITY

County	Area (sq. miles)	Persons per sq. mile (2000)
Dickinson	766	35.8
Houghton	1,012	35.6
Marquette	1,821	35.5
Delta	1,170	32.9
Chippewa	1,561	24.7
Menominee	1,043	24.3
Gogebic	1,102	15.8
Mackinac	1,021	11.7
Iron	1,166	11.3
Baraga	904	9.7
Schoolcraft	1,178	7.6
Alger	918	7.6
Luce	903	7.3
Ontonagon	1,311	6.0
Keweenaw	541	4.3
Total acreage:	**16,417**	

By comparison, Wayne County has 3,356 persons per square mile, Macomb County has 1,640 persons per square mile, and Oakland County has 1,368 persons per square mile.

Marquette and Chippewa are the two largest counties in Michigan. (land area)

LARGEST COUNTIES: TOTAL AREA INCLUDING GREAT LAKES WATER (SQ. MILES)

State Rank/County	total area	land	water
1) Keweenaw	5,959.98	541.20	5,418.78
2) Alger	5,044.28	917.95	4,126.33
3) Ontonagon	3,741.37	1,311.63	2,429.74
4) Marquette	3,426.90	1,821.31	1,605.59
5) Chippewa	2,698.00	1,561.08	1.136.92
9) Mackinac	2,099.18	1,021.60	1,077.58
10) Delta	1,991.75	1,170.19	821.56
11) Luce	1,911.90	903.07	1,008.83
13) Schoolcraft	1,883.79	1,178.18	705.61
19) Houghton	1,501.54	1,011.74	489.88
20) Gogebic	1,476.54	1,101.94	374.60
23) Menominee	1,337.61	1,043.66	293.95
27) Iron	1,211.16	1,166.49	44.67
29) Baraga	1,068.56	904.16	164.40
39) Dickinson	777.20	766.42	10.78

TOP 20 HIGHEST POINTS IN MICHIGAN

The Upper Peninsula has sixteen of the twenty highest points in Michigan. Mt. Curwood was listed as the highest point in Michigan until a 1982 a U.S. Department of the Interior survey added eleven inches to Mt. Arvon.

State Rank	Name	Elevation	County	Lat/Long	Map
1	Mt. Arvon	1,979	Baraga	464520N/0880921W	Skanee South
2	Mt. Curwood	1,978	Baraga	464212N/0881425W	Mt. Curwood
3	Summit Mtn.	1,873	Marquette	462700N/0873748W	Ishpeming
4	Government Pk.	1,850	Ontonagon	464700N/0894351W	Gov't Peak
5	Wolf Mtn.	1,826	Gogebic	462630N/0894615W	Wakefield NE
6	Mt. Zion	1,722	Gogebic	462838N/0901004W	Ironwood
7	*Briar Hill**	*1,706*	*Wexford*	*442158N/0854046W*	*Harrietta*
8	Big Powderhorn	1,640	Gogebic	463015N/0900545W	Copper Peak
9	Cuyahoga Pk	1,604	Ontonagon	464849N/0894257W	Gov't. Peak
10	Copper Peak	1,558	Gogebic	463602N/0900524W	Copper Peak
11	*Cote Dame Marie*	*1,524*	*Crawford*	*443558N/0844744W*	*Cote Dame Marie*
12	Pine Mtn.	1,523	Dickinson	454959N/0880455W	Iron Mountain

13	Huron Mtn.	1,518	Marquette	465244N/0875516W	Howe Lake
14	Cloud Peak	1,514	Ontonagon	464843N/0894348W	Gov't. Peak
15	Tolonen Hill	1,506	Houghton	470210N/0884144W	South Range
16	Gratiot Mtn.	1,490	Keweenaw	472304N/0880618W	Delaware
17	*Cleary Hill*	*1,476*	*Kalkaska*	*443556N/0845300W*	*Fletcher*
18	Houghton Mtn	1,466	Keweenaw	472426N/0875630W	Lake Medora
19	Mt. Bohemia	1,465	Keweenaw	472330N/0880047W	Delaware
20	*Mt. Tom*	*1,462*	*Oscoda*	*444445N/0840803W*	*Mio*

Downstate peaks in italics

PAYMENTS IN LIEU OF TAXES (PILT)

Much of the Upper Peninsula is owned by the State of Michigan, therefore not subject to local property taxes. To make up for the shortfall to local units of government the Department of Natural Resources (DNR) makes payments based on amount of state-owned land and local property values to counties.

The payments are made by the DNR only on those public lands administered by the Department.

County	Gross acres	(2006) DNR-owned	% owned by DNR	Payment
Luce	582,654	297,747	51.1	$552,125
Dickinson	491,925	224,016	45.5	$464,114
Schoolcraft	758,095	288,492	38	$529,598
Mackinac	650,255	214,698	33.0	$445,668
Marquette	1,182,581	261,738	22.1	$526,478
Chippewa	999,960	219,689	22.0	$435,273
Alger	589,949	97,435	16.5	$194,967
Menominee	670,297	97,847	14.6	$197,503
Baraga	583,806	78,376	13.4	$170,338
Iron	760,143	84,616	11.1	$179,685
Delta	748,915	67,883	9.0	$143,027
Ontonagon	844,753	67,881	8.0	$226,695
Houghton	647,466	45,937	7.1	$97,200
Gogebic	712,033	11,766	1.6	$52,102
Keweenaw	348,468	11,196	3.2	$117,554

REAL PROPERTY TAXABLE VALUE – BY COUNTY

County	2006	% of Statewide Value
Marquette	$1,469,967,368	0.5%
Chippewa	$842,174,730	0.3%
Delta	$831,284,819	0.3%
Mackinac	$717,327,296	0.2%
Dickinson	$660,068,381	0.2%
Houghton	$559,905,035	0.2%
Menominee	$491,090,829	0.2%
Gogebic	$349,832,669	0.1%
Iron	$335,540,772	0.1%
Alger	$262,253,946	0.1%
Schoolcraft	$245,976,632	0.1%
Ontonagon	$180,529,790	0.1%
Baraga	$170,104,797	0.1%
Luce	$151,643,922	0.05%
Keweenaw	$93,456,258	0.05%

The Upper Peninsula represents about 2.6% of the taxable value of real property in Michigan.

AGRICULTURE

UPPER PENINSULA AGRICULTURE

The earliest farmers of the Upper Peninsula were Native Americans – Chippewa, Ottawa and Potawatomi – who grew wild rice and corn. In the late 1700s Jesuits, with help from local Indians, cleared land and planted crops near Sault Ste. Marie. They first planted wheat, and later grew potatoes, peas, corn and wild rice.

Family farms began to spring up as European immigrants moved to Copper Country during the mining boom of the mid-1800s. Before a family could farm they had to remove trees and stumps from the thickly-forested, rocky terrain. 19th Century farming was physically challenging work that yielded enough food for the family dinner table, and perhaps enough to sell to the growing population.

The rugged landscape of the U.P. provided the materials that fueled the industrial revolution and westward growth of the late 1800s. While mining companies extracted copper and iron ore, lumbermen were turning the thick pine forests into stumps as they cut, milled

and shipped the lumber used to build homes and businesses around the Midwest. The ancient rocky terrain of the western U.P. and the sandy, mucky soil of the eastern half were not ideal for agriculture.

Many a would-be farmer attempted to turn the stump-covered landscape into farmland. By 1919 there were 465,000 acres of farmland, but few commercial farming operations. However, there were, however, some short-lived success stories.

In the 1880s, James G. Van Tuyl planted Golden Plume celery on 25 acres near Newberry. The soil was just right, and the farm was near the Detroit, Mackinac & Marquette rail station. Before the turn of the century, Van Tuyl was shipping celery downstate and throughout the Midwest. The celery was so plentiful and popular that Newberry was known as Celery City, and many restaurant menus proudly proclaimed, "Newberry Celery Served Here!" By the 1920s, competition from downstate growers increased. They took advantage of

Dickinson County farmer circa early 1900s. Photo courtesy of Dickinson County Library.

a longer growing season, lower transportation costs, and better marketing of their different variety of celery. By the end of the decade, Newberry was no longer the Celery City.

Wild blueberries have long been a plentiful crop in the U.P. They were first picked and sold commercially in the 1870s by Native Americans and white settlers near Negaunee and Ishpeming. Blueberries thrived on the cutover land left behind by the logging industry. During the Depression, wild blueberries were picked, processed and shipped south by producers near Newberry and Sault Ste. Marie. By the time the commercial blueberry industry in the eastern U.P. peaked in the 1930s, it was shipping out 500-700 crates every day. Each July thousands of migrant workers were brought into the eastern U.P. blueberry belt where they picked by day and lived in temporary camps at night. One small plant near Newberry was canning 100 cases of berries a day before hauling them downstate. They would bring back back peaches and cherries for canning. By the 1950s, there were not enough local berries to sustain the plant, which closed in 1955. Today locals and tourists look forward to picking wild blueberries, visiting U-Pick farms, and blueberry festivals in Paradise and Marquette.

Native Americans discovered cranberries growing naturally in the swamps and bogs of the eastern U.P. before the arrival of the French missionaries. The fruit was grown commercially near Whitefish Point for a period starting in the 1870s. The bog was developed by Canadian John Clarke and Alex Barclay, a Scottish sea captain. They produced 400-500 bushels a year starting in 1890 and shipped them to neighboring states. However, the venture lasted only twenty years.

Ginseng was grown in Menominee County between 1910 and 1930. It was a tedious crop to produce, but had a high profit margin. The geopolitics of the time shut off trade routes and led to the end of the Upper Peninsula ginseng industry.

Another short-lived crop was peppermint, grown in Schoolcraft Coun-

SPECIALTY FRUITS AND VEGETABLES

Newberry was once known as "Celery City." In the early 1900s the railroad cleared land for celery farms, and Newberry became a regional center for agriculture until the 1920s.

The town of Chassell, on the Keweenaw Peninsula, was once a thriving center for strawberry production. The Chassell Heritage Center has a permanent exhibit, "Lumber Kings to Strawberry Queens," that features the strawberry industry. Each summer the town hosts a Strawberry Festival to celebrate its strawberry heritage.

ty in the late 1920s. Producers of peppermint and other crops were at a disadvantage with growers to the south as they had a shorter growing season and were farther away from major markets. Peppermint ceased to be a crop in Schoolcraft County after prices fell and the land changed hands.

FARMS AND FARMLAND – BY COUNTY

| County | Number of farms | | | Average farm size (acres) | | |
	2002	2007	Change	2002	2007	Change
Alger	67	86	+28%	223	213	-4%
Baraga	63	76	+21%	241	245	+2%
Chippewa	372	401	+8%	252	247	-2%
Delta	273	290	+6%	272	268	-1%
Dickinson	146	161	+10%	196	155	-21%
Gogebic	49	42	-19%	82	93	+13%
Houghton	158	155	-2%	164	153	-7%
Iron	106	111	+5%	296	250	-16%
Keweenaw	11	na	na	65	na	na
Luce	30	41	+37%	342	215	-37%
Mackinac	76	89	+17%	269	244	-9%
Marquette	160	144	-10%	188	209	+11%
Menominee	372	419	+13%	265	247	-7%
Ontonagon	108	104	-4%	312	296	-5%
Schoolcraft	51	66	+21%	266	405	+52%

TOTAL LAND IN FARM ACRES

County	2002	2007	Change
Menominee	98,755	103,636	+5%
Chippewa	93,924	98,967	+5%
Delta	74,242	77,762	+5%
Ontonagon	33,666	30,830	-8%
Marquette	30,073	30,092	--
Iron	31,382	27,731	-12%
Schoolcraft	13,541	26,697	+97%
Dickinson	28,658	24,889	-13%
Houghton	25,856	23,643	-9%
Mackinac	20,410	21,698	+6%
Baraga	15,174	18,644	+23%
Alger	14,969	18,357	+23%
Luce	10,262	8,819	-14%
Gogebic	4,024	3,907	-3%
Keweenaw	710	na	na

CLOVERLAND

Upper Michigan went through an awkward period about the turn of the 20th Century. The last of the white pine was rolling down the rivers in the spring. There was mile-upon-mile of stumps and slash left behind. The land stood neglected—a wasteland, ravaged by wildfires brought on by poor forest management. Promoters and developers searched for a new way to tout this once pristine wilderness. They found it in the name "Cloverland."

Originally coined by a Colonel Charles Mott, the concept of Upper Michigan as an agricultural cornucopia really took off with newspaperman Roger Andrews. He came to Menominee in 1901 to take the job of editor at the *Menominee Herald Leader*. Farmers in his region discovered rich soils where the hardwoods once grew and they began planting sugar beets. Andrews was the chief promoter of the venture, publishing a monthly paper called the *Sugar Beet News*. "Beet sugar factories are springing up on every side," he wrote. There was really only one factory on the Menominee River, but Andrews's upbeat brand of journalism did not let facts get in the way.

Andrews called U.P. business leaders together and formed the Upper Peninsula Development Bureau. Their task was to promote Cloverland to the rest of the coun-

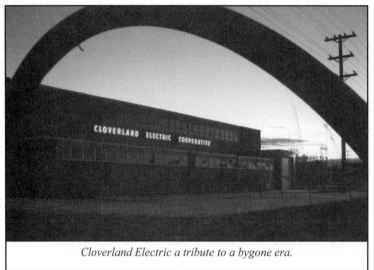

Cloverland Electric a tribute to a bygone era.

try. To that end, Andrews published the magazine *Cloverland*. In it, he sold Upper Michigan as an agricultural paradise. "The snowy season is a little longer and the snows are a little deeper than in other places farther south," he wrote, "but the air is pure, dry, and vitalizing." Of course, not all soils of the Upper Peninsula were suitable for crops like sugar beets. Much of the land was low in fertility with soils of high acid content. However, once the stumps were gone, it would be an ideal place to graze livestock—free from the drought that plagued western ranchers. Andrews pushed the idea of clover—it grew everywhere the sun shone. "If you believe in favorable climate, pure water, and lots of clover as essentials for livestock production—see Cloverland first."

The Bureau sent a representative west to sell ranchers on Cloverland. Some of them took advantage of the offer. Sheep ranchers from Utah, Idaho, Colorado, Wyoming and other western states moved in. In June 1918, a train hauling 40 Union Pacific double-decked sheep cars carrying 12,000 sheep rolled through Escanaba and drew a crowd. U.P. ranches were developed near Newberry, as far north as Ives Lake near Big Bay and even in the muck of the Seney Swamp. Ranchers were offered quite a deal: No charge on the land for the first two years, herdsmen would pay taxes on the land the third and fourth years, and in the fifth year they would pay taxes plus six percent interest on an option to purchase the property. At the end of the fifth year, 10 percent of the purchase price was due and thereafter terms would be set for future payment at six percent interest. At the time, land was selling for only $7.50 to $15 an acre.

"Cloverland" was also used to lure dairy farmers to the U.P. Immigrants with a desire to own their own land took the bait. By 1911, there were 8,000 farms in Upper Michigan. The U.S. Department of Agriculture predicted that Cloverland "is destined to become one of the best dairy sections of the United States." Andrews gushed in his magazine that "The land floweth with milk and honey for the industrious farmer, the livestock grower, the dairyman, the gardener. Nature has done her work. Man must do his share." The farmers and ranchers worked, but a combination of short growing seasons, poor soil and rising real estate taxes worked against them. Between 1920 and 1930, the amount of sheep and cattle grazing Cloverland dropped by 80 percent.

Editor-promoter Andrews saw what was coming and changed the slant of *Cloverland* magazine to tourism in 1921. By 1927, as farmers poured out of the Upper Peninsula in droves, the name *Cloverland* was dropped in favor of *Hiawathaland*. Today, while farming is still an important part of the economy, only Cloverland Drive in Ironwood and Cloverland Electric Cooperative on the east end of the Peninsula are left as reminders of an ambitious effort to turn Upper Michigan into an agricultural paradise.

ACRES OF ORCHARDS, BY COUNTY

County	Acres of orchards
Delta	72
Menominee	71
Marquette	62
Baraga	58
Houghton	32
Iron	14
Chippewa	1
Ontonagon	11
Dickinson	3
Alger	0
Gogebic	0
Keweenaw	0
Luce	0
Mackinac	0
Schoolcraft	0

MARKET VALUE OF AGRICULTURE

County	2007	2002	Change
Alger	$2,772,000	$1,511,000	+83%
Average per farm	*$32,231*	*$22,547*	*+43%*
Crop Sales $337,000 (12%) Livestock Sales $2,435,000 (88%)			
Baraga	$1,341,000	$1,120,000	+20%
Average per farm	$17,646	$17,786	-1%
Crop Sales $760,000 (57%) Livestock Sales $581,000 (43%)			
Chippewa	$9,376,000	$5,790,000	+62%
Average per farm	$23,382	$15,566	+50%
Crop Sales $409,000 (37%) Livestock Sales $5,941,000 (63%)			
Delta	$11,619,000	$10,219,000	+14%
Average per farm	$40,065	$37,433	+7%
Crop Sales $3,435,000 (37%) Livestock Sales $7,211,000 (62%)			
Dickinson	$4,565,000	$3,767,000	+21%
Average per farm	$28,353	$25,798	+10%
Crop Sales $1,978,000 (43%) Livestock Sales $2,587,000 (57%)			
Gogebic	$394,000	$201,000	+97%
Average per farm	$9,390	$4,093	+129%
Crop Sales $125,000 (32%) Livestock Sales $270,000 (68%)			
Houghton	$2,709,000	$2,821,000	-4%
Average per farm	$17,476	$17,853	-2%
Crop Sales $1,014,000 (37%) Livestock Sales $1,695,000 (63%)			
Iron	$1,949,000	$3,214,000	-39%
Average per farm	$17,560	$30,318	-42%
Crop Sales $1,437,000 (74%) Livestock Sales $512,000 (26%)			
Keweenaw	NA	NA	NA
Luce	$2,551,000	$2,635,000	-3%
Average per farm	$62,208	$87,848	-29%
Crop Sales $2,217,000 (87%) Livestock Sales $334,000 (13%)			
Mackinac	$4,298,000	$2,817,000	+53%
Average per farm	$48,288	$37,062	-61%
Crop Sales $409,000 (10%) Livestock Sales $3,888,000 (90%)			

Marquette	$3,825,000	$3,697,000	+3%
Average per farm	$26,565	$23,107	+15%

Crop Sales $1,384,000 (36%) Livestock Sales $2,442,000 (64%)

Menominee	$33,619,000	$21,190,000	+59%
Average per farm	$80,236	$56,963	+41%

Crop Sales $3,347,000 (10%) Livestock Sales $30,272,000 (90%)

Ontonagon	$1,935,000	$2,413,000	-20%
Average per farm	$18,610	$22,343	-17%

Crop Sales $752,000 (39%) Livestock Sales $1,184,000 (61%)

Schoolcraft	$2,399,000	$1,520,000	+58%
Average per farm	$36,343	$29,809	+22%

Crop Sales $1,520,000 (63%) Livestock Sales $879,000 (37%)

GOVERNMENT PAYOUTS TO FARMS

County	2007	2002	Change
Alger	$64,000	$168,000	-62%
Avg. per farm	$2,286	$14,009	-84%
Baraga	$13,000	$2,000	+661%
Avg. per farm	$828	$193	+328%
Chippewa	$43,000	$110,000	-61%
Avg. per farm	$3,563	$11,049	-68%
Delta	$299,000	$405,000	-26%
Avg. per farm	$3,649	$7,362	-50%
Dickinson	$159,000	$194,000	-18%
Avg. per farm	$3,451	$6,252	-45%
Gogebic	0	0	0
Avg. per farm	0	$9	
Houghton	$46,000	$70,000	-35%
Avg. per farm	$1,517	$2,708	-44%
Iron	$44,000	$15,000	+196%
Avg. per farm	$2,073	$736	+182%
Keweenaw	NA	NA	
Luce	NA	$13,000	
Avg. per farm	NA	$2,176	
Mackinac	$43,000	$110,000	-61%
Avg. per farm	$3,563	$11,049	-68%
Marquette	$40,000	$147,000	-73%
Avg. per farm	$3,343	$24,568	-86%
Menominee	$699,000	$1,138,000	-39%
Avg. per farm	$4,569	$11,616	-61%
Ontonagon	$27,000	$109,000	-76%
Avg. per farm	$1,153	$5,762	-80%
Schoolcraft	$7,000	$13,000	-47%
Avg. per farm	$560	$1,396	-60%

TOP COMMODITIES – BY COUNTY

(2007) County	State Top commodity	Value	Rank
Alger	Milk and other dairy products from cows	$1,675,000	60
Baraga	Cattle and calves	$383,000	71
Chippewa	Milk and other dairy products from cows	$2,808,000	52
	Sheep, goats, and their products	$288,000	5
Delta	Milk and other dairy products from cows	$4,727,000	44
	Vegetables, melons, potatoes, and sweet potatoes	$1,821,000	33
Dickinson	Milk and other dairy products from cows	$2,009,000	55
Gogebic	Cattle and calves	$130,000	79
Houghton	Milk and other dairy products from cows	$1,431,000	64
Iron	Vegetables, melons, potatoes, and sweet potatoes	$1,090,000	41
Keweenaw	NA	NA	NA
Luce	Cattle and calves	$244,000	75
Mackinac	Milk and other dairy products from cows	$2,817,000	51
Marquette	Milk and other dairy products from cows	$1,778,000	59
Menominee	Milk and other dairy products	$24,443,000	15
	Cut Christmas trees and short rotation woody crops	$491,000	11
	Cattle and calves	$4,938,000	26
	Other animals and	$696,000	11
Ontonagon	Cattle and calves	$814,000	66
Schoolcraft	Grains, oilseeds, dry beans, and dry peas	$580,000	57

USDA National Agricultural Statistics Service 2007 Census of Agriculture

BARLEY – BY COUNTY (2005)

County	Acres planted	Acres harvested	Yield Bushels	Production
Menominee	1,800	1,100	37	41,000
Delta	1,300	1,000	33	33,000
U.P. Total	5,200	3,800	37	140,000

CATTLE AND CALVES – BY COUNTY (2006)

County	All Cattle (head)	Milk Cows (head)
Menominee	17,000	7,000
Chippewa	9,000	1,000
Delta	8,000	1,500
Ontonagon	3,200	500
Dickinson	3,000	600
Mackinac	2,400	700
Alger	1,800	
Iron	1,700	
Houghton	1,400	
Schoolcraft	1,300	
Baraga	1,100	
U.P. Total	53,000	13,000

Remains of forest near Iron Mountain.
Photo courtesy Dickinson County Library.

FIRST COMMERCIAL WINERY IN THE U.P.

The Mackinaw Trail Winery opened a tasting room in 2005 near the harbor in Manistique. Owners Ralph and Laurie Stabile have set up a production facility in Iron Mountain where they use grapes from southwestern Michigan and the Traverse City area to produce their line of red, white and dessert wines. In 2006, they sold 4,000 cases and aim to double that number in the future.

Much of the U.P. is unsuitable for growing wine grapes, although the couple is scouting locations on the Garden Peninsula.

The 2005 Cabernet Franc won a gold medal at the 2005 Michigan Wine Competition.

In 2007 the Threefold Vine Winery in Garden began producing fruit wines for sale. The first grapes were planted by Andrew and Janice Green in 2002, and since then they have experimented with 30 different grape varieties on four acres of their 470 acre farm. They converted an old bean-processing barn to a wine tasting room and offer in-season tastings and tours of the farm. They raise cattle and also grow sugar beets, hay, corn, rye, pumpkins and apples.

WOODS
UPPER PENINSULA NATIONAL FORESTS
OTTAWA NATIONAL FOREST

The Ottawa National Forest contains 1.5 million acres in the western Upper Peninsula from the shore of Lake Superior to the Nicolet National Forest border in Wisconsin. The forest contains over 500 named lakes and nearly 2,000 miles of named rivers and streams. Elevations vary from around 600 feet along the Lake Superior shore to around 1800 feet in the Sylvania Wilderness.

Topography in the northern portion is most dramatic and rugged with breathtaking views, old growth white pine and hemlock along with spectacular waterfalls. There are three wilderness areas comprising about 50,000 acres in the forest. The Sylvania covers over 18,000 acres and contains 34 named lakes, some with sandy beaches other rimmed with record red and white pines. This area is in the southern portion of the forest near Watersmeet. The McCormick and Sturgeon River Gorge Wildernesses are both in the northeastern portion of the forest in the Kenton Ranger District. The McCormick contains the Yellow Dog National Wild and Scenic River, which can be accessed by foot. The Sturgeon contains the steep, rugged gorges of the Sturgeon National Wild and Scenic River. Both contain no developed campgrounds but dispersed camping is allowed.

The Ottawa is tucked in a relatively unpopulated portion of Upper Michigan. The largest towns are on the border of the forest. Ironwood on the west end is the largest with a population of 9,000. Iron River on the southeast end has about 5,000 and Ontonagon to the north approximately 2,000.

Camping areas are relatively lightly used compared with other forests in the region. The main visitor center is located near Watersmeet at the junction U.S.-Highway 2 and U.S.-Highway 45. The center is open daily from mid-May until mid-October, with more limited hours during the fall and winter seasons.

HIAWATHA NATIONAL FOREST

This forest derives its name from Henry Wadsworth's Long-fellow's celebrated poem "The Song of Hiawatha." In it he referred to the "Shining Big-sea Waters" of Lake Superior, which forms the forests north-ern boundary. The Hiawatha also opens to the shores of Lakes Michigan and Huron on its south and east boundaries. In all, the Hiawatha National For-est is bounded by 100 miles of Great Lakes shoreline.

The region was originally es-tablished in 1928 as the "Lake State Region" Forest. Later in

Cut and stacked timber near Sagola, Dickinson County

1931, President Hoover signed legislation proclaiming it the Hiawatha National Forest. Dur-ing this time, the region was devoid of timber, the result of clear-cutting practices at the turn of the century. Major fires swept over the land, especially the extremely flammable pine slash. In some areas logging and subsequent burning left the soil damaged and natural refor-estation was not occurring. The cut-over areas were referred to as "waste lands" and many logging concerns abandoned the land, which was reclaimed by the government for back tax-es. An initiative to rehabilitate the forest was proclaimed by a number of Congressional Acts.

Early foresters had little labor to take on the massive task before them. Then in the De-pression years the Civilian Conservation Corps (CCC) was established. President Roosevelt wanted "plenty of land" for CCC projects and area timber product companies were more than willing to sell their land during the Depression. The Hiawatha grew and the CCC provided the manpower for tree planting, fire suppression along with road and trail construction as well as campground construction.

The forest has been rehabilitated and provides a source of timber as well as recreation. The Hiawatha contains over 20 campgrounds within its borders; most of these campgrounds are of moderate development level. Winter recreation may be the most important aspect of tourism to local economies of the eastern Upper Peninsula. The Hiawatha National Forest has 300 miles of snowmobile trails to help support winter tourism in the area.

New lands have been acquired along with Grand Island on Lake Superior just off Munising. It is now part of the forest and a National Recreation area. The Hiawatha National Forest is the only National Forest to host six lighthouses, five of which still maintain full federal ownership.

The Hiawatha covers 879,000 acres in two regions of the central and eastern Upper Penin-sula. It contains rolling hills covered with northern hardwoods, hemlock and white pine. The flat land contains red pine, aspen and jack pine along with open and tree covered wetlands. There are approximately 775 miles of streams and rivers that empty into the Great Lakes along with 413 named lakes.

MOST FORESTED LAND – BY COUNTY

County	National forest	State forests	Total forest land Public and private
Marquette	18,040	255,663	1,027,400
Ontonagon	257,926	16,351	752,500
Chippewa	243,976	185,940	749,000
Iron	172,884	79,428	662,300
Gogebic	309,777	499	635,300
Delta	241,590	66,331	602,200
Mackinac	151,598	203,473	555,400
Schoolcraft	122,433	286,783	540,500
Houghton	156.605	44,218	540,400
Alger	127,539	93,625	531,600
Menominee	0	91,725	524,600
Baraga	44,633	69,764	508,300
Luce	0	285,962	472,700
Dickinson	0	221,673	398,200
Keweenaw	0	4,416	312,100

Source: MSU Extension Tourism Area of Expertise Team

FOREST AS A PERCENTAGE OF LAND AREA – BY COUNTY

Keweenaw	97%
Baraga	94%
Alger	92%
Gogebic	92%
Iron	89%
Marquette	88%
Mackinac	87%
Luce	86%
Ontonagon	86%
Houghton	82%
Delta	79%
Dickinson	79%
Schoolcraft	78%
Menominee	75%
Chippewa	74%
Michigan	51%

Source: U.S. Forest Service

BIG TREES IN THE U.P

Tree	County	Girth in.	Height ft.	Crown	Location
Balsam Fir	Ontonagon	84	116	33	Porcupine Mountain State Park
Striped Maple	Marquette	44	59	43	Huron Mountain Club
*Mountain Maple	Houghton	33	58	31	near Beacon Hill
Roundleaf Serviceberry	Keweenaw	16	38	30	Copper Harbor
Douglas Hawthorn	Chippewa	40	25	80	Sugar Island
Fleshy Hawthorn	Keweenaw	26	42	42	

White Spruce	Marquette	104	102	32	Huron Mountain Club
Jack Pine	Marquette	93	68	30	W. Branch Escanaba River
Jack Pine	Iron	97	70	48	Iron River
*Red Pine	Gogebic	124	124	60	Watersmeet
*Eastern White Pine	Ontonagon	200	150	53	Porcupine Mountain State Park
*Balsam Poplar	Marquette	165	128	57	Champion
*Bigtooth Aspen	Marquette	105	132	67	Huron Mountain Club
Lombardy Poplar	Schoolcraft	196	81	20	Near Fayette Historic State Park
Quaking Aspen	Dickinson	158	72	48	
*Quaking Aspen	Ontonagon	122	109	59	Porcupine Moutain State Park
Red Elderberry	Keweenaw	20	27	15	Lac La Belle
American Mt. Ash	Houghton	62	57	35	
Showy Mountain Ash	Houghton	63	37	35	
Showy Mountain Ash	Mackinac	57	58	32	7 mi. S.of Gould
Lilac	Mackinac	65	30	29	St. Ignace

•- Also a National Champion Tree

Source: Michigan Botanical Club

American Forests –dot-org lists several of the trees from the table above along with a Silver Maple in Newberry. Girth is listed at 347 inches (nearly 29 feet); its height is 115 feet, and the crown is 61 feet.

The Champion Tree Project of Copemish, Michigan lists a National Champion Yellow Birch near Gould in Mackinac County. The tree is estimated to be at least 500 years old! Its stats: a girth of 198 inches (16.5 feet), 101 feet high and a crown of 125 feet.

This National Champion Tree was cloned in 2000 by David Milarch of the Champion Tree Project in Copemish, Michigan. For more information on the Web: www.championtreeproject.org

THE TIMBER INDUSTRY IN UPPER MICHIGAN

"A horror overcomes me as I look from some heights—upon the black ground...there is no hill – no mountain – no snow peaks... [only]...terrifying forest without end, without limits...."
Missionary Father John Chebul on his first year in the U.P. wilderness 1860

The exploitation of Upper Michigan's vast forest resources proceeded slowly. The first tentative step in the development of the timber industry was the army's construction of a water-powered sawmill at Sault Ste. Marie in 1822. The army then leased it to private concerns which operated it through the 1830s. There was little interest in this timber-products venture and the mill fell into disrepair and was eventually abandoned.

It was not until 1849 that another sawmill was erected in this portion of the Upper Peninsula. James Pendill constructed a water-powered mill on a creek flowing into Whitefish Bay about 25 miles from the Sault. He employed eight men who cut timber near the mill in winter and worked the sawmill in spring. On a good day, the mill could produce between twenty-five hundred and three-thousand feet of lumber. However, the high cost of supplies, the limited local market and lack of capital conspired to bring an end to the operation by the mid-1850s. Other small sawmills popped up along the shore of Lake Superior to serve the growing mining operations of the central and western portions of the Peninsula.

To the south, the first sawmill was constructed on the Menominee River by fur trader William Farnsworth in 1831. High operation and transportation costs put the mill in debt a short time later. Eventually, the sheriff seized the property and sold it at auction. The mill changed hands several times but no one could turn a profit. Another mill was built at the mouth of the Escanaba River in 1838. A few years later, yet another mill was constructed at the mouth of Rapid River. Typically, the Escanaba River sawmill struggled until a seasoned Maine lumberman named Jefferson Sinclair relocated to the Great Lakes and saw the mill's potential. He got the backing of Milwaukee businessman Daniel Wells and, in 1846, took complete control of the Escanaba River sawmill.

Sinclair got into the ship mast business—only the tallest, straightest pine logs were cut. His business and land holdings expanded, eventually including the future sites of Escanaba, Nahma and Ford River. In 1851, Sinclair and Wells joined forces with Milwaukee businessmen Nelson and Harrison Ludington to form the N. Ludington Company. One of their lumbermen, Isaac Stephenson, worked up the ranks and eventually became a partner in the company. Stephenson became a lumber baron by the 1860s and brought competing companies in the Menominee River region together in 1867 to form the Menominee River Boom Company. This entity handled the problem of dam building and log driving, thereby reducing costs of individual companies while providing an organized approach to transporting their product downriver in the spring.

Lumbermen gradually expanded east along the north shore of Lake Michigan. Logging operations and sawmills sprang up at the mouth of the Manistique River, and at the present sites of Thompson and Nahma as well as St. Ignace.

Farther north, the pine forests adjacent to Lake Superior developed even slower. It took the completion of the Sault canal in 1855 to solve the problem of access to and from Lake Superior. Eventually, pine logging operations developed from Sault Ste. Marie west as far as Grand Marais. One of the most prominent lumbermen of the region in the 1860s was George Dawson. He entered into an agreement with a Canadian shipbuilding company for squared timbers for ship masts. His operation was located on the Two Hearted River in present-day Luce County. His 25-man crews cut and squared timbers from fall until spring and then floated the logs downriver during the spring flood. This method of logging was extremely wasteful. One squared-timber operation in the U.P. produced 202,000 feet of pine but left 600,000 feet of potential lumber on the forest floor. This practice accelerated the loss of Upper Michigan's forests and also created the worst type of fire hazard. Eventually, square timber logging was squeezed out of the Upper Peninsula by a combination of protests against the practice and the development of giant steam-powered sawmills along the south shore of Lake Superior that chewed up the best pine at an even faster rate.

The majestic white pine quickly disappeared along Great Lakes shores and near major rivers. The development of railroad transportation in the 1870s and 1880s made inland areas of Upper Michigan accessible and the final assault on the virgin white pine forest began. Logging companies like the Interior Lumber Company on the west end in Ontonagon County and the American Lumber Company out east in Luce County used the nascent Upper Peninsula railroad network to haul their product to deep-water port cities. Lumber barons like Robert Dollar, Isaac Stephenson and Russell Alger became wealthy men during the pine-logging era. However, the pine forest, considered inexhaustible a few decades earlier, was essentially depleted in the U.P. by the turn of the century. Lumbermen moved their operations to remaining pine forests out west.

Not all the lumber barons gave up on Upper Michigan's forests. Isaac Stephenson, for one, made the expensive transition to hardwood logging. Another concern that made the transition was the Wisconsin Land and Lumber Company. During the pine era, the company cut all the pine it could from its Upper Michigan holdings to supply a wooden sash, door and blind factory in Wisconsin. As pine disappeared, the company transitioned to hardwood flooring. "IXL" maple flooring was produced in the Menominee County town of Hermansville. After a rough transition during a depression in the 1890s, its flooring product became the standard of the industry.

The Bay De Noquet Lumber Company was another firm that made the transition from soft to hardwood logging. The company operated four to six logging camps each winter which cut white pine along the Sturgeon River Valley. When a camp failed to reach three-million feet of logs per year it was closed. By the late 1890s, camps consistently fell below this benchmark as the white pine was depleted. Then in 1899, the company's sawmill at Nahma burned down. The parent company, based in Oconto, Wisconsin, produced boxes and barrels and needed the hemlock and elm of the Upper Peninsula. To that end, it built a $51,000 hardwood sawmill at the Nahma site.

Hardwood could not be transported downriver like softwood pine, which forced the Bay De Noquet Company into railroading. The firm laid its first track from the Soo Line southward in 1901, but it took until 1903 for the track extension to reach the sawmill at Nahma, a mere four and a half miles south. Eventually, 65 miles of track was laid into the hardwood forest of Delta County. The company acquired several locomotives, 100 log cars, gravel cars and even a passenger car to transport lumberjacks.

As the lumber companies chewed up the forests of Upper Michigan, the remaining residents looked to farming as a source of hope. Prospective farmers and homesteaders were lured by cheap land prices. Community leaders and promoters touted the Upper Peninsula as an agricultural paradise—Cloverland (*See page* 103). In reality, the land was rocky, the soils marginal and the climate harsh. There was the problem of clearing the huge stumps left by the lumber companies. One group that thrived in this harsh environment was the Finns. Most of them were expert handlers of dynamite—needed to blast out the stumps. They also brought the concept of community organization—cooperatives—to Upper Michigan. In one instance, Finnish farmers in Ontonagon County got together and bought a thresher. A ten-dollar share gave a farmer use of the machine. Later, this co-op bought a sawmill and hay baler.

Forestry continued to evolve as the 20th Century wore on. Automaker Henry Ford brought the concept of industrial forestry to the Upper Peninsula (*See page* 303). Ford wanted a ready source of lumber for his vehicles (each Model T contained 100 board feet of hardwood) and he also wanted to use his holdings as leverage against his other timber suppliers. By 1923, the Ford holdings sprawled over four western Upper Peninsula counties and contained 400,000

THE SENEY STRETCH

The straightest, flattest, most boring section of highway in the state of Michigan runs for nearly 26 miles between Seney and Shingleton. This infamous section of highway got its name from Michigan State Police in the 1960s. A Shingleton auto mechanic who rebuilt cars would call the State Police post in Munising and advise them he would be testing a rebuilt car's engine and speedometer. The 10-mile section of Highway M-28 eastbound out of Shingleton was marked every mile—a perfect testing ground. The mechanic would choose a time when traffic was light and the post would give him a pass to "stretch 'er out." In time, the term was applied to the entire 25-mile section of highway east to Seney—the Seney Stretch.

The road runs through the Seney Swamp, more properly termed the Great Manistique Marsh. Six major rivers and streams cross the road, eventually draining into Lake Michigan. The road had its inception before World War I when the Michigan Legislature began building the State Highway system. Usually, it would absorb and improve an existing township road. So it was with the Seney Stretch. A township road running west from Seney to the little settlement of Driggs was converted into Route 25. Initially, the

acres. Henry Ford experimented with forest management techniques including removal of slash and selective cutting.

Cleveland Cliffs Iron Company also diversified into industrial forestry during the early 20th Century. The head of operations, William Gwinn Mather, nurtured an interest in conservation. Just after the turn of century, he established a game preserve on the 13,500-acre Grand Island in Munising Bay. Later, he hired a forester to oversee the CCI holdings. The company took the first small, tentative steps in forest management including reforestation. However, by the 1920s, just as Henry Ford began his Upper Peninsula experiment, CCI retreated from its forest program and clear cutting became the standard practice for the next few decades.

In general, hardwood loggers showed as little concern for the environment as their pine logging predecessors. A typical example was found on the east end of the U.P. in the Cadillac-Soo Company. The firm slashed through its 50,000-acre holdings, taking fine quality sawlogs from the best trees, while using the limbs of the trees for cord wood. Smaller trees were cut up and sent to its chemical plant. Cadillac-Soo left small branches and other slash where they fell, leaving the land worthless. By 1956, the company closed and its assets were sold. It left behind 48,000 acres of ravaged and exhausted barrens.

By the third decade of the 20th Century, hardwood logging had depleted a good share of the remaining forests of the Upper Peninsula. Slowly, the region became an important source of pulpwood. Paper mills opened in towns from Ontonagon to Menominee and Manistique. The stately pines and hardwoods were replaced by fast-growing "weed trees", heroic lumberjacks by "employees" and "cut-and-get-out" by sustainable-yield forestry.

During this time, the national forest concept took hold. It proved a boom for many lumber companies. These companies were eager to offer their cutover lands for sale to the new national forests. The average price paid for cutover land was only $1.50 per acre, but lumber companies were happy to be rid of land that had become a liability.

The Depression of the 1930s finally brought disciplined fire control efforts to Upper Michigan. With the establishment of the Civilian Conservation Corps (CCC), a ready labor supply was available to fight fires. The CCC also prepared the U.P. forests to better resist fires. Access had always been a problem in battling forest fires. Within the first seven months of the program, the Michigan CCC constructed 500 miles of truck trails, 67 miles of fire breaks, and 543 acres of emergency landing fields for observation planes. The plentiful labor force was also used to renew thousands of acres of cutover lands with new trees.

Post World War II brought the rise of the "Rubber Tire Lumberjack." This man rode to work in a car and operated a gas-powered truck or skidder. The old-style lumber camps ended with the 1950s. The flamboyant lumberjacks faded into history along with their raucous lifestyle.

Today the forests of Upper Michigan are thriving. Gone are the "wastelands" left by the "cut and get out" practices of old. While some areas of forest are still clear cut, "sustainable yield" has become the mantra of the forest industry in the U.P. In the early 21st Century, at least one logging company claims to plant more trees than it cuts down. This stewardship insures that the timber industry will continue to be a vital part of Upper Michigan's economy for generations to come.

SENEY: ONE ROUGH LUMBER TOWN

A village with a colorful and notorious past, Seney grew out of the lumbering heyday of the late 19th Century. In a 1940 publication called "Hiawatha Land," the origin of the town is credited to a railroad contractor named Seney who established his camp at the site in 1882. When the east-west Duluth, South Shore and Atlantic line was completed, Seney's camp became a meeting place and distribution point; in a short time a permanent settlement emerged.

Historian Lewis C. Reimann says the origin of the town's name is a matter of dispute. He confirms the above railroad connection, but states there are some who insist the name came from lumber-

push west to Shingleton was a slow, difficult process because of the swampy terrain. Finally in 1926, the last major stream, Commencement Creek, was bridged and the route to Shingleton was complete. The swamp contributed to the character of the road. Engineers took the shortest route west through the muck and marsh—a straight line.

At one time, the lonely section of highway had no posted speed limit and there was little in the way of police patrol. Motorists would really "stretch 'er out" gaining speeds of 90 to 100 miles-per-hour. The high speed combined with the boredom of a straight road proved a deadly mix. Many accidents resulted from drivers who became dazed or sleepy and veered off to the right onto the gravel shoulder. The startled motorist would turn the wheel sharply left, resulting in a spin-out or collision. Those who drove small cars would sometimes burn out their engines driving at high speed. By the mid-70s officials posted a 55 MPH speed limit and beefed up patrols. Immediately, the number of accidents dropped in half.

Even today after a number of road improvements including a modern rest area just west of Seney, many motorists ap-

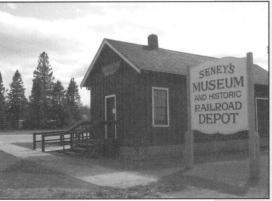

proach the Seney Stretch with a bit of trepidation. Outside of the rest area, there are no settlements or even buildings over the 25+ miles. Wildlife, mostly deer, lines the stretch at night posing a potential hazard. In the winter, the elevated roadbed, which cuts through the wide-open landscape, is subject to whiteouts. However, on a clear day when visibility is unlimited and the road is dry, some still get the urge to "stretch 'er out." If you ever find yourself in this position on the straightest, loneliest road in Michigan, remember—there is a speed limit!

The Seney Stretch: straight and flat.

jacks' mispronunciation of the name of a fur buyer named Sheeny who set up a trading post in the town. Gradually, "Sheeny" became "Seney."

Whatever the root of the name, Seney became famous throughout the Upper Great Lakes for toughness and lawlessness. At the time of its inception, several large lumber camps were already operating in the area. As the town grew, it became the natural gathering spot for lumberjacks itching to spend their wages on drinking, gambling and carousing. Businessmen in the frontier town were more than willing to satisfy these "needs." A town of 3,000 people at its peak boasted 21 saloons. "Hiawatha Land" states the town's quick growth "caused the building of stores, hotels, saloons and other places usual or common to that era in the lumbering age." What the 1940 publication may have been describing without explicitly saying in the phrase "other places" were the brothels—three in town and two up the river.

At spring break up, when the men emerged from the woods after a winter of monotonous, heavy labor, the town doubled its population. It was said a man could ask a railway agent for a ticket to hell and the agent would know immediately the man wanted to go to Seney. Whiskey and beer flowed all day and night. As the level of inebriation rose, fighting broke out. Fists, teeth and calked boots were the chief weapons, though occasionally knives were employed. The brawls kept the town's doctors busy patching wounds and splinting broken bones. Occasionally, the injuries led to death.

Danger constantly hung over the lumberjack. A limb or "widow-maker" might fall on some unsuspecting jack or a log jam on a spring drive might crush a man beneath a mountain of giant pine. Danger also lurked away from the lumbering camps. An intoxicated man might get robbed and more than a few men disappeared, victims of fights that got out of hand. However, most of the disappearances and deaths resulted from drunks who stumbled out into the bitter winter cold, fell into a snow bank and passed out.

Seney's lurid reputation spread far and wide. At one point, a sensational story appeared in a big-city newspaper titled "Ram Pasture." It detailed the horrors of human slavery in Seney. The story claimed victims were shanghaied on the frontier and then transported in box cars to lumber camps. There they were forced to work in dark forests from sun-up to sun-down; then they were herded into a great log stockade called the "Ram Pasture." There they were housed in subhuman conditions, which were so crowded the chained men had to sleep in shifts. Escape was near impossible because of the fierce dogs that guarded the stockade.

It is true that men would "sleep it off" in shifts in the town's hotels—so crowded was Seney at spring break up. And by today's standards, the $20 to $25 per month typically paid to a lumberjack is slave wages. Otherwise, the reporter, either by being misled or by purposely stretching the truth and then stretching it some more, had it all wrong. Victorian journalistic standards did not require corroborating facts with a second source, so the story ran—printed in bold headlines. Soon, most metropolitan dailies carried the story, elevating the frontier lumber town to the pinnacle of notorious legend.

Just as fast as Seney rose to prominence, it crumbled into decay. The vast white pine forests that were suppose to "supply the entire country with lumber forever" disappeared in a mere two decades. Giant trees, some eight feet in diameter with first branches several stories above the ground, were cut and hauled away indiscriminately. The tops of the trees were left where they fell, providing fuel for fires which raced across the once thick, primeval forest time and time again. The area became a "wasteland" and Seney practically a ghost town by the beginning of the 20th Century. The pine was gone and the lumberjacks, businessmen, saloon keepers, bartenders and prostitutes left.

Today, Seney is a small village of roughly 200 residents at the junction of M-28 and M-77 in Schoolcraft County. Seney did not completely die with the death of the virgin pine forests but remains as a symbol of Upper Michigan's vibrant, boisterous frontier past.

ISLANDS – BY COUNTY

CHIPPEWA COUNTY (105)

Drummond	James	Rutland	Peck
Bay	Ashman	Jim	Iroquois
Rose	Tahquamanon	Grape	Bald
LaPoint	Little Rogg	Rogg	Quarry
Fire	Howard	Wreck	Boylanger
Harbor	Standerson	Mare	Saltonstall
Little Trout	Bow	Long	Twin Sisters
Cedar	Cherry	Wilson	Harris
Burnt	Claw	Spence	Norris
Round	Gull	Sam	Willoughby
Picnic	Young	Cove	Fairbank
Adelaide	Arrow	Surveyors	Big Trout
Maple	Andrews	Cass	Little Cass
Macomb	Butterfield	Squaw	Pipe Island Twins
Pipe	Sweets	Lime	Little Lime
Hart	Love	Bass	Reef
Round	Twin	Shelter	Meade
Gravel	Espanore	Long	Garden
Bird	Bellevue	Arnold	Crab
Fisher	Surgeon	Frying Pan	Saddlebag
Albany	Edward	Canoe	Propellor
Neebish	Sugar	Pilot	Pine
Steamboat	Sand (1)	Sand (2)	the Moons
Rains	Hen	Chicken	Duck
Advance	Rock	Gem	Cook
Hog (1)	*Hog (2)*	*Hog (3)*	*Mouse*

Whitehead 105

ALGER COUNTY (5)

Grand	AuTrain	Wood	Williams	Lost

HOUGHTON COUNTY (1)

Traverse

MACKINAC COUNTY (50)

Mackinac	Round	Bois Blanc	St. Helena
Green	Big St. Martin	St. Martin	Goose
Marquette	Birch	Long	LaSalle
Little LaSalle	Government	Coryell	Island No. 8
Hill	Strongs	Rover	Naubinway
Gravel	Little Hog	Epoufette	Goat
Haven	Boot Jack	St. Ledger	Lone Susan
Echo	Gravelly	Bear	Crow
Dudley	Dollar	Rogers	Booth
Dot	Little (1)	Little (2)	Little Ellen's
Avery Point	Grover's	Cove	White Loon
Whitefish	Raspberry	Polleck's	Eagle
Penny	Boat		

DELTA COUNTY (12)

St. Martin	Gull	Little Gull	Gravelly
Poverty	Summer	Little Summer	Rocky
Round (1)	Round (2)	St. Vital	Snake

MARQUETTE COUNTY (9)

Middle	Partridge	Little Partridge	Garlic
Larus	Granite	Lighthouse*	McIntyre*
Gull*			

*Part of the Huron Islands which includes three additional unnamed islands

KEWEENAW COUNTY (83)

Manitou	Isle Royale	Little Siskivwit	Siskiwit
Redfin	Paul	Castle	Long (1)
Stone House	Menagerie	Shiverette	Outer
Inner	Channel	Wright	Malone
Ross	Hat	Schooner	Middle
Cemetery	W. Caribou	E. Caribou	Rabbit
Mott	Outer Hill	Inner Hill	Mad
Star	Davidson	Heron	Tookers
Tallman	Shaw	Lone Tree	Smithwick
Raspberry	Bat	Minong	Flag
Smith	N. Government	S. Government	Gale
Newman	Edwards	Long (2)	Third
Boys	Merritt	*Passge.*	
Pete	Battleship	Steamboat	Diamond
Net	Green (1)	Dean	Captain Kidd
Cork	Johnson	Belle	Burnt
Clay	Homer	Amygdaloid	Round
Hawk	Kamloops	Green (2)	Arch
Wilson	Taylor	Thompson	Johns
Beaver	Salt	Grace	Booth
Barnum	Washington	Bottle	

LARGEST ISLANDS OF THE GREAT LAKES

Island	Location	State/Province	Square miles
Manitoulin Island	Lake Huron/Georgian Bay	Ontario	1,068
Isle Royale	Lake Superior	Michigan	209
St. Joseph Island	Lake Huron/St. Marys River	Ontario	141
Drummond Island	Lake Huron	Michigan	134
Saint Ignace Island	Lake Superior (northern)	Ontario	106
Michipicoten Island	Lake Superior	Ontario	71
Beaver Island	Lake Michigan	Michigan	56
Cockburn Island	Lake Huron	Ontario	54
Sugar Island	Lake Nicolet/Lake George (St. Marys River)	Ontario	50
Wolfe Island	Lake Ontario	Ontario	48
Great La Cloche	Lake Huron	Ontario	36
Bois Blanc Island	Lake Huron	Michigan	35
Barrie Island	Lake Huron	Ontario	31
Parry Island	Lake Huron	Ontario	30
Simpson Island	Lake Superior	Ontario	28
Amherst Island	Lake Ontario	Ontario	27
Madeline Island	Lake Superior	Wisconsin	24
North Manitou Island	Lake Michigan	Michigan	23
Washington Island	Lake Michigan	Wisconsin	23
Grand Island	Lake Superior	Michigan	21
Neebish Island	Lake Nicolet/Munuscong Lake (St. Marys River)	Michigan	21

MACKINAC ISLAND (MACKINAC COUNTY)

Mackinac Island is one of America's favorite summer vacation spots: famous for fudge, motorless main streets, the Grand Hotel, and storybook Victorian cottages. Michigan's top summer vacation destination has thrived on tourism since the mid-1880s. By the late 1880s, the island became even more popular when the Grand Hotel opened. Visitors can rent a bicycle, a horse-pulled carriage, or walk to the island's favorite attractions, most of which bring alive the history of Mackinac Island long before it became a destination of leisure.

Area: 3.47 square miles, about three miles wide and 2 miles north to south

Shoreline: 8 miles

Highest point: Fort Holmes is 320 feet above the Straits.

Year round population: Approximately 500

Owner: 1,800 of the island's 2,200 acres (about 80%) are part of the Mackinac Island State Park. The rest is under private ownership.

Mackinac Island State Park became our 2nd National Park in 1875. (Yellowstone was first in 1872.) Mackinac became Michigan's first State Park in 1895.

Town: Harrisonville is tucked away between the airport and Grand Hotel's Jewel Golf Course. Most of the year-round residents make their home in Harrisonville.

Roads: About 144 miles of roads and trails. (61 miles within Mackinac Island State Park)

State Highway: M-185, "The Safest Highway in the Country," has never had an auto accident. The 8-mile loop around the island has no beginning and no end!

School: The Mackinac Island Public School is K-12 with less than 100 students enrolled. Average class size is six. A staff of six teachers handles all grades. All students must walk or ride a bike to school, except in the winter when snowmobiles and horse-drawn carriages are used.

Access: Ferry service operates between the island and St. Ignace in the U.P. and Mackinaw City in the Lower Peninsula between May and the end of October.

Great Lakes Air operates daily flights between the island and St. Ignace. Round trip fare is $54 during winter months.

After the Straits freeze over, usually in January, some residents cross over the "ice bridge" on foot or by snowmobile, to St. Ignace. After island residents take down their Christmas trees they are used to mark a path across the ice.

MACKINAC: NAMED BY INDIANS

Many writers claim the name Michilimackinac comes from the Chippewa word, Mi-she-mi-ki-nock, roughly translated as "tremendous mud turtle." The common story is that the Indians believed the island looked like a large turtle rising out of the water. Native American writer and historian, Andrew J. Blackbird considers this tale to be false.

Indian Dormitory built circa 1838.

In his *History of the Ottawa and Chippewa Indians of Michigan* Blackbird writes of an ancient tribe of Indians who fished the waters of the Straits and lived on Mackinac Island during the warm months. The tribe was nearly annihilated by the Seneca tribe of New York. Two members of the Straits tribe managed to survive the attack by hiding in island caves. This ancient tribe was named *Mi-shi-ne-macki naw-go*. From this word came Michilimackinac, and eventually Mackinac.

As far as we know, the first European to encounter Mackinac Island was French explorer

Jean Nicolet who in 1634 paddled his canoe from the west into the Straits. He may have possibly stopped for a breather on the island before continuing east to discover Lake Michigan. By the mid 1600s, French priests established a mission in the area and the first military fort was built. There would be a military presence on Mackinac Island for most of the following 200 years.

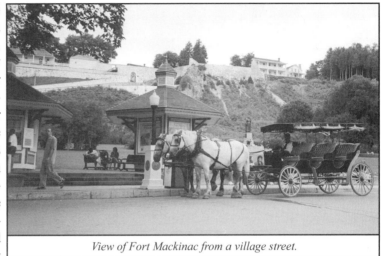
View of Fort Mackinac from a village street.

TIMELINE OF MACKINAC REGION

1634 Nicolet becomes first European on record to enter the Straits

1650's French Jesuit missionaries plant first lilacs on Mackinac Island.
These are first lilacs planted on American soil.

1670 Father Claude Dablon spent the winter on Mackinac Island. He built a chapel out of bark and ministered to the Indians. (A replica of this chapel is open to visitors.)

1671 Father Jacques Marquette establishes mission at modern-day St. Ignace.

1673 Father Marquette leaves the mission with explorer, Louis Joliet, to explore the Mississippi River. Marquette becomes ill on the return trip and dies at Ludington or Frankfort.

1677 Marquette buried at St. Ignace

A statue of Father Marquette stands in Marquette Park, dedicated in 1909, just beneath Fort Mackinac.

1679 *The Griffin*, the first commercial sailing ship on the Great Lakes reaches the Straits.

1690 French build Fort DeBaude at St. Ignace. It is later abandoned.

1701 First fur trading post built on Mackinac Island.

1715 French build Fort Michilimackinac at present day Mackinaw City.

1761 British take over the fort following the French and Indian War.

1763 Massacre at Fort Michilimackinac. Angry Chippewas, led by Chief Pontiac, kill nearly all of the British soldiers at the Fort. At least one survivor taken to Mackinac Island and hidden away in Skull Cave. British regain control the following year.

1781 During Revolutionary War, British move fort to a more secure location on Mackinac Island, and rename it Fort Mackinac. Island purchased from Chippewa Indians for 5,000 pounds.

Mackinac Island Harbor

1780s Island is becoming important link in the growing fur industry. French trappers and Indians sell their pelts to traders who ship them to Montreal, bound for Europe. The beaver, fox, and rabbit furs are coveted for hats and coats.

1783 Revolutionary War ends. British refuse to give up Fort Mackinac.

1795 British finally vacate Fort Mackinac and turn it over to Americans.

1809 John Jacob Astor opens fur trading post on Mackinac Island.

1812 War of 1812 breaks out. British troops from St. Joseph Island, armed with cannons, sneak on to Mackinac Island at night, gain high ground, and force Americans to surrender the island.

1814 American naval forces fail in attempt to take back island. 64 casualties recorded.

1815 War of 1812 ends. British hand over Fort Mackinac to Americans.

1817 John Jacob Astor builds the Stuart House, headquarters for his American Fur Company. (Now a museum). Astor dominated the fur trade after buying British-owned trading posts. After the War of 1812 Congress limited trade with Indians to U.S. owned companies.

1819 First steamboat on the Great Lakes, the *Walk-in-the-Water*, stops at Mackinac Island.

1822 American Fur Co. does $3,000,000 in business-its best year.

As furs were depleted, the industry declined. After 1850 the economy on Mackinac Island was centered on fishing.

1829 Mission Church, first Protestant church on Mackinac Island, built.

1838 Indian Dormitory built on Mackinac Island by Federal Government.

1881 Ferry service to Mackinac Island is started by the Arnold family.

Doud's Mercantile store opens. Today it's believed to be the oldest family-owned grocery store in Michigan.

1887 Grand Hotel built by railroad and steamship interests.

1894 Remaining troops leave Fort Mackinac.

1895 Mackinac Island become Michigan's first State Park.

1898 Motorized vehicles banned from island.

1946 "This Time For Keeps," starring Jimmy Durante and Esther Williams, is filmed at the Grand Hotel.

1957 Mackinac Bridge opens

1980 "Somewhere in Time," starring Christopher Reeves and Jane Seymour, is filmed at the Grand Hotel.

DRUMMOND ISLAND (CHIPPEWA COUNTY)

Drummond Island is located in Drummond Township in Chippewa County. It is the 2nd largest U.S. Island in the Great Lakes, and the 2nd largest island in Michigan. However Drummond is the largest Michigan island with a year round population.

Area: Land - 129.1 sq. miles, 36 miles in length

Water – 5.2 sq miles, includes 34 inland lakes

Shoreline: 136 miles

Ownership: 70% state owned (61% of island is state forest)

Population: 992 (2000 U.S. Census), now around 1,100; over 5,000 in summer

Housing units: 1,476 (2000 U.S. Census)

Access: The Drummond Island Ferry runs 365 days a year between DeTour Village and the ferry dock on the west side of the island.

History: Artifacts discovered on the island indicate Indians from the late Woodland period (roughly between 1200-1600) had lived on the island using it for fishing and hunting. They named the island Pont-a-gan-ipy, meaning "view of beautiful islands," referring to the dozens of smaller islands surrounding Drummond.

The British claimed Drummond Island in 1815 after they were chased from their fort on Mackinac Island. Lt. Colonel Robert McDouall attacked the American fort at the beginning of the War of 1812. Not realizing the war had begun, the Americans lost the battle and relinquished control to the Brits. McDouall was put in charge of the strategically located fort by Lt. General Sir Gordon Drummond. Although McDouall held off American troops attempting to win back control of Mackinac Island, his side lost and the fort was turned back over to Americans with the signing of the Treaty of Ghent.

In July of 1815, McDouall and about 350 British troops and families settled in on the west side of the big island, naming if for their Lt. General. They built a new fort and dozens of homes and other structures.

In 1822, McDouall lost out to the mighty pen again. The boundaries of the U.S. and Canada were redrawn and Drummond Island became U.S. territory. As the story goes, a contingent of U.S. and Canadian officials sailed through the region to confirm boundary lines and island ownership. The captain of the ship, supposedly drunk thanks to the U.S. group, sailed east around Drummond Island instead of through the DeTour Passage on the west side. Since the party had agreed that islands on the left side of the ship would be designated U.S.-owned, and those on the right as belonging to Canada, Drummond became United States property.

Without financial support from the home country McDouall left Drummond Island in 1828. By that time most of the surviving troops had also left, leaving an island inhabited by about 100 Native Americans.

White settlers began to arrive in the 1850s. Some of the first were the Daniel and Betsy Seaman family which arrived from the Mormon village on Beaver Island in 1854. The family farmed the land, raised cattle and cut lumber to sell to passing wood-fueled steam boats.

The lumber industry came to Drummond in the early 1870s with the first mill opening near present day Maxton. Scammon Cove was also a busy lumbering area. More people moved to the island, families grew and the first school was built on Townline Road in 1879. In 1891, the Free Methodist Church, the first church on the island, was also built on Townline Road.

The island population and economy grew in the late 1880s with construction of the Poe Lock in Sault Ste. Marie. Contractors set up quarry operations near present day Yacht Haven supplying limestone for lock construction into the mid 1890s.

In 1905, Maggie Walz, a Finnish immigrant, moved to the island with the intention of starting up a self-designed Finnish community. Walz' husband was killed in a mining accident near Calumet. She became involved in the women's suffrage movement, was educated at Valparaiso University in Indiana, started a Finnish language women's magazine and eventually formulated her ideas for the perfect community. After screening applicants she invited 25 Finns to settle near present day Johnswood on the south side of the island. The community grew quickly, numbering over 1,000 residents by 1908. They worked for local lumber companies, farmed the land, developed a farmer's co-op market and built a community hall. A post office opened under the name of Kreetan and Walz became the first postmaster.

The residents actively followed and discussed the growing labor movement of the day and the beginning of communism in Russia. Some advocated for a communist society in their little town. A rift developed causing Walz to leave. In the 1920s, the lumber companies shut down and most of the residents moved away.

The first tourists arrived in 1905. Five granddaughters of the Seaman's hired local Indians to build small cabins at Seastone Point, which they rented out to vacationers attracted by the fresh air and solitude. The property was sold by the Seaman family in the 1930s to Louis James Johnson of the Johnson outboard motor company, which eventually was sold to OMC and is now owned by Bombardier Recreational Products. Johnson also manufactured airplane motors including one for the first monoplane in the U.S., now on display at the Smithsonian Museum.

The island economy of the 20th century relied on tourism, fishing and some lumbering until 1942. Then, the Drummond Island Dolomite quarry opened.

The island saw major development in the 1980s when Tom Monaghan, the millionaire owner of the Detroit Tigers and founder of Dominos Pizza, built a 3,000 acre corporate retreat. The rustic, yet luxurious retreat included a hotel, conference center and The Rock, an 18-hole golf course. Monaghan sold the property in the 1990s. Since then it's been expanded and renamed the Drummond Island Resort and Conference Center.

Today the island economy is built around tourism—boating and kayaking, fishing, bicycling, golf and general rest and relaxation. It is growing as a snowmobile destination with its miles of trails and ice bridges over Pontagannissing Bay to St. Joseph Island and Canada.

Children who live on Drummond Island attend classes at DeTour Public Schools on the mainland. They travel to school by bus and ferry.

LES CHENEAUX ISLANDS (MACKINAC COUNTY)

Number of islands: 36

Ownership: 35 islands are privately owned. Government Island is the only island with public access.

The Nature Conservancy owns over 6,000 acres within the archipelago.

Largest: Marquette Island near Hessel is 6.6 square miles (4,234 sq. acres)

> 6.5 miles long and 3.5 miles wide
> LaSalle Island – 981 acres
> Hill Island – 233 acres
> Little LaSalle – 213 acres
> Strongs Island – 107 acres
> Boot Island – 87 acres
> Coryell Island – 74 acres
> St. Ledger Island – 3.91 acres
> Goat Island – 3.57 acres
> Lone Susan Island – 3.15 acres
> Haven Island – 1.78 acres
> Burnham Island – 1.61 acres
> Echo Island – 1.12 acres
> White Loon Island - .981 acres
> Little Island - .172 acres
> Pollock Island - .12 acres

Area statistics based on original Land Survey charts in Mackinac County Equalization Department.

Smallest inhabited island: Dollar Island

Shoreline: 12 miles of Lake Huron shore between Cedarville and Hessel

Population: 2,200 for Clark Township which includes Cedarville, Hessel and the islands. Summer population grows to about 8,000.

The Nature Conservancy has included the Les Cheneaux Islands in its list of "Last Great Places."

Access to islands: The only auto access is via a bridge to Hill Island east of Cedarville. Another small bridge connects Hill Island to Island # 8. All other islands are only accessible by boat. Residents use golf carts to travel around the islands.

History: The rocky islands were scraped out of the earth

LES CHENEAUX FACTS

Men's Journal magazine has listed the The Snows as one of its "25 Great Hide-outs."

Les Cheneaux has the largest number of restored wood-hulled boats in the country.

The largest one day wooden boat show in the world is held every August in Hessel.

Mertaugh's Boat Works in Hessel is the oldest Chris Craft dealer in the country.

MERTAUGH'S BOAT WORKS

E.J. Mertaugh's Boat Works opened in 1925 when longtime resident Patrick Mertaugh helped his son Eugene (E.J.) build a boathouse out of scrap lumber on the shore near Hessel. The following year Eugene signed an agreement with Chris Smith and Sons Boat Company in Algonac, Michigan. He became the company's first franchisee with exclusive rights to sell the "Chris" crafts from Bay City north into Canada.

Mertaugh sailed the wooden boats from Algonac along the Lake Huron shoreline to his shop. Some of the original boats are still around the islands today. The little boathouse built from scratch lasted 75 years, until it had to be torn down in 2000.

In 1970, E.J. turned the business over to his sons, Jack and Jim. They operated it until 1989 when it was sold to Bruce and Nancy Glupker. The Glupker's owned it until 2000 when it was sold to current owners Brad and Shelley Koster.

when the last glacier retreated northward about 10,000 years ago. Les Cheneaux Islands means "The Snows".

Native Americans paddled their birch bark canoes through the region, camping and fishing around the protected waterways of the Les Cheneaux Islands, long before the French arrived in the 1600s.

In the 17th and 18th Centuries, French voyageurs and fur traders used the island waterways as a rest stop on their commerce route between Mackinac Island and Montreal. During the Revolutionary War there were outposts on Marquette and Long Islands where lookouts would create smoke signals to warn of ships approaching the fort on Mackinac Island.

During the lumber boom in the mid-19th century, some homesteaders discovered the islands, at that time inhabited mostly by lumbermen and soldiers from nearby Mackinac Island. The island evolved from a lumber economy to a fishing and resort economy by the late 1800s.

The 1890s brought railroads and steamships farther north. This provided the means for wealthy Midwestern families from big cities like Cincinnati, Chicago and Detroit to escape the heat and pollution of summer. Hotels were built in Hessel, Cedarville and on some of the islands, as well as on Mackinac Island, Petoskey, Charlevoix, and other burgeoning resort towns. Steamers from Detroit and Cleveland delivered resorters to Hessel, and the Arnold Transit company operated a ferry between Mackinac Island and the Les Cheneaux islands.

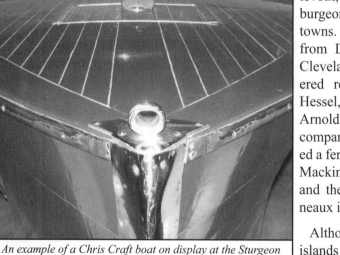

An example of a Chris Craft boat on display at the Sturgeon Bay, WI Maritime Museum.

Although the islands attracted families of wealth, including the founders of Proctor & Gamble, Eli Lilly, Armour, and such, "The Snows" were more laid back and less formal than the scene developing on Mackinac Island. Like

Mackinac Island, there were no automobiles on the Les Cheneaux Islands. Residents arrived in Cedarville or Hessel on the mainland, and had to take a boat to their island homes.

To accommodate these islanders, Mertaugh's Boat Works opened in Hessel in 1925 and is still in operation today.. Opened in 1925, it still in operation today. Mertaugh's promotes itself as the oldest Chris Craft boat dealer in the country.

The island community is considered to have the largest number of restored wood-hulled boats in the country. On the second Saturday of each August, the town of Hessel attracts over 10,000 visitors for the Antique Wooden Boat Show, the largest one day wooden boat show in the world.

In the 1990s, fishing tourism declined along with the perch population. The Chamber of Commerce outlined a strategy of eco-tourism to attract more vacationers while preserving the region's natural beauty. Since then, entrepreneurs have marketed kayak tours, bird-watching vacations and other scenic offerings. With plentiful salmon and reports of a rebound in the perch population, the islands are a favored spot for fishermen.

The Arthur Heurtley Summer Cottage built in 1902 on Marquette Island was redesigned by Frank Lloyd Wright.

BOIS BLANC ISLAND (MACKINAC COUNTY)

Bois Blanc, pronounced by locals as Bah-Blo, is 8 miles north of Cheboygan, and 4 miles to the east of Mackinac Island. Bois Blanc is French for "white wood" probably in reference to the forest of white pines that covered the middle of the island when French voyageurs first paddled by.

Area: 32 square miles, Between 12-13 miles long, 7 miles wide

Shoreline: 30 miles (approximate)

Population: 63 year round (2006 U.S. Census estimate) 1,200 – 1,600 during summer at any one time.

Access: Ferry service from Cheboygan has been offered May through November since 1932 by Plaunt Transportation. Flights are available from Cheboygan from Hoffman Flying Service.

History: There are signs that Native Americans lived or camped on Bois Blanc Island as far back as two thousand years ago. The island offered secure shelter along with good fishing and hunting. In 1795, the Treaty of Greenville signed by Chiooewa Matchekewis, ceded Bois Blanc Island and much of the Ohio territory to the U.S. Government.

GANGSTER HIDEOUT

Island lore suggests that the infamous gangster John Dillinger hid out on Bois Blanc Island in the 1930s, while recovering from plastic surgery to alter his appearance. Some say he was headed to his sister's house in Sault Ste. Marie. Dillinger and a few of his men supposedly stayed in a group of cabins, now referred to as Dillinger's cabins, on old Fire Tower Road. At the time he was a fugitive and the subject of an FBI manhunt. Dillinger may have found the remote island a safe hideout during his recovery.

John Dillinger

EMMY AWARD-WINNING INNKEEPER

Shelby Newhouse and his wife Christa operate the Insel Haus Bed and Breakfast on Bois Blanc Island. Newhouse directed the documentary "Fatima". It was narrated by Ricardo Montalban and won an Emmy award in 1984. The film examines the Catholic Miracle at Fatima in 1917. It features interviews with five witnesses to the miracle and was shot on location at the Vatican, the Basilica in Portugal, England and the U.S. After viewing the documentary, Pope John Paul II requested a Spanish version, which was produced again with narration by Ricardo Montalban.

During the War of 1812, U.S. Navy Captain Arthur Sinclair took his fleet to shelter at Bois Blanc Island before attacking the British on Mackinac Island. In 1815, the British officially relinquished Mackinac Island and the Straits region fell under U.S. control for good.

In the 1820s, merchants on Mackinac Island petitioned the U.S. government for a lighthouse on Bois Blanc Island. In 1829, two years after the island was platted, the lighthouse was built. It became only the second light on Lake Huron. A second lighthouse was constructed in 1839 after the first one was destroyed in a storm. A third lighthouse was built in 1867. It still stands as a private residence today.

By the 1880s, the mining industry was booming in the western U.P. and the shipping lanes around Bois Blanc Island were bustling with ore carriers and a new type of commerce: tourism. Wealthy families from the big Midwestern cities were sailing to northern Michigan in search of fresh air, cooler temperatures, recreation and relaxation.

In 1884, the government opened the island to settlers, attracting 71 families. The Pines Hotel opened in the summer of 1888. A life-saving station was built at Walker's Point in 1891. The next year the first resort community, Point aux Pins Association, was formed and was officially platted in 1908. Original cottages sold for between $200 and $500 dollars.

The island's towering pine trees attracted the lumber industry and by the early 1900s there were several sawmills on the island. Much of the milled lumber from Bois Blanc Island made its way into the buildings and homes of Mackinac Island where lumbering was banned.

Today the island economy is based on tourism. Unlike Mackinac Island, there are no fudge shops, carriage tours, large hotels, or any other business designed to appeal to

Shelby and Christa Newhouse

The Insel Haus Bed and Breakfast on Bois Blanc Island.

tourists. Bois Blanc Island does permit automobiles, but has no paved roads. There is one grocery store, one bar, and the Insel Haus, a beautiful B & B on the site of an old sawmill. Point aux Pins with a post office, fire station, community building, airport, and two chapels is considered the island "metropolis."

Bois Blanc's appeal is its rustic peacefulness and outdoor recreation like hunting, fishing, and hiking, mountain biking, canoeing and kayaking.

There are five inland lakes – Twin Lakes, Lake Thompson, Deer Lake, Mud Lake and Lake Mary – all hidden within the 24,000 acres of island forest. The state DNR owns 50% of the forest and manages nearly 80% of the land.

SUGAR ISLAND (CHIPPEWA COUNTY)

Sugar Island is a stones throw across the St. Marys River from Sault Ste. Marie's Aune Osborne Park. The island lies between Lake George to the west and Lake Nicolet to the east.

Area: 47.9 square miles, about 30,600 acres (about 15 miles north to south)

Shoreline: 51 miles

Once known as: *Sisibakwato Miniss*, "Sugartree Island" in Chippewa; *Ile St. George* by the French; *St. George's Island* by the British

Population: 686- Sugar Island Twp. – (2006 U.S. Census estimate)   441 (1990)

Access: The Sugar Island Ferry runs year round from the east end of Portage Ave.

The first car ferry, the *Service*, went into service in July of 1928. The fee was 45 cents. It ran until 1932 when it was replaced by the *Beaver*, which ran until 1937. A new ferry, *Scow No. 1* ran until 1944 when it was rebuilt and renamed the *Chippewa*. It ran until 1947 when the County Road Commission, which bought the ferry service two years earlier, replaced the boat with the Sugar Islander.

Early passenger service between the island and Sault Ste. Marie began in the late 19th Century. Some of the early named boats providing service include: *Willamette, Neon*, *Ferro*, *Aloha* and *Leora*.

In 1890, residents of Sugar Island petitioned the county to get permission from the Secretary of War to build a bridge between the island and the mainland. There is no record of any response from the Secretary's office.

History: Native American presence in the St. Marys River region dates back as far as 2500 BC. For centuries they used Sugar Island as a fishing base, taking advantage of the large number of whitefish in the rapids. In the spring the Indians would produce maple syrup from the thick forests of sugar maple trees that give the island its name.

The original bands of Chippewa Indians from the region date as far back as the 16th century. Their descendants make up today's Sault Ste. Marie Band of Chippewa Indians. The Chippewa, Ottawa and Potawatomi tribes ceded most of the U.P., including Sugar Island, to the government in the 1836 Treaty of Washington. In exchange the islands in the St. Marys River were reserved for the tribes for a period of five years. An 1855 Treaty gave the Chippewa tribe permanent ownership of a few parcels of land on Sugar Island.

The first white settler was Michael Payment. In 1848, he bought land at the northern tip

Sugar Island Ferry

of the island in an area now known as Payment. The native Canadian supported his expanding family by farming and logging.

In 1849, Philetus Church set up a store on the northeast portion of the island where he traded with the Garden River Indians across the river in Canada. Church became the first person to commercially manufacture raspberry jam using fruit picked by his trading partners across the river. He also chopped wood and sold it to passing steamboats along with ice and vegetables. In 1862, Church built a sawmill. The house he built for his family at the same time still stands today and is listed on the National Register of Historic Places.

The 1870 population of Sugar Island was 238, which included 48 families, most of them engaged in farming of hay, vegetables and maple syrup. Other occupations included lumbering, sawmill workers, and boat builders. Along with the existing Native American population, many island residents were from Canada, while a number of Finns relocated from the Western U.P.

Tom Wilson was the son of Scottish immigrants who farmed hay on Sugar Island. As a young man Wilson was invited aboard a passing ship that was shorthanded. He accepted the offer and never returned the island. Before long he captained his own ship and in 1872 became a shipbuilder, founding Wilson Transit Co. Wilson Transit built the *Spokane*, the first steel steamer on the Great Lakes. His boats were the first to use electric lights, gyrocompasses and radio telephones. Wilson died in 1900 and his company was eventually sold and became a division of Litton Industries, Inc.

Sugar Island Township was officially organized in 1850. The first post office opened near Payment in 1857 and closed four years later. Another post office opened in Payment in 1892 and remained open until 1942. Other post offices include: Homestead, 1906-1945; Laramie, 1906-1945; Baie de Wasai, 1908-1911; Brassar, 1911-1939; and Willwalk, 1917-1929.

In 1856, the first island church, Holy Angels, was built in the same area. In 1861, Father Frederic Baraga built St. Joseph's Church for Chippewa Indians living on the western side of the island across from Gem Island, an area Baraga called Minisheing.

The first island school opened near Payment in 1863. Eventually there were five schools on the island: Payment, Brassar, Roosevelt, Harding School near Baie de Wasai and the Hiawatha School in Willwalk. The schools accommodated children through the 8th grade. Senior high students had to attend class on the mainland. With a declining population the schools were consolidated over time until 1969 when the last classes were held on the island. Today students attend class in Sault Ste. Marie.

Population on the island peaked at about 700 in 1940. Until then the main occupations were logging and farming.

The island drew vacationers from the big cities to the south who were attracted by its beauty and remote location. It was not a resort community like the ones developing on Mackinac Island or the Les Cheneaux islands. However in 1915, a Kalamzoo company bought 600 acres near Shingle Bay with the announced intention of building a hotel and resort community. The land was platted but never developed.

There was a military presence during World War II. The U.S. Army established an anti-aircraft station near the present day Hilltop Bar. About 50 men were stationed on Sugar Island.

After World War II there was a movement to bring the newly-formed United Nations headquarters to Sugar Island. Former Michigan governor Chase Osborn led the drive, noting that the island was strategically situated between the U.S. and Canada along a peaceful border. There was talk of building a tunnel from the Soo to Sugar Island, and a bridge on the west side that would connect with Ontario. The U.N. eventually settled on New York City, but the effort did draw international attention to Sugar Island.

Osborn, former owner of the Sault Evening News, also lobbied for a bridge over the Straits of Mackinac long before it became a reality. He donated much of his personal money and energies to the Sault Ste. Marie community, including 3,000 acres on the southwest shore of Sugar Island that he gave to the University of Michigan. The Osborn Preserve is across from his beloved Duck Island, where he and his wife are buried.

Sugar Island was one of the last locations in the continental U.S. to receive electricity. The big day came on December 21, 1953 when Cloverland Electric Company finished extending electric power across the river. Until then residents relied on kerosene-powered generators or other forms of power.

The first telephone on the island was installed at the ferry dock in 1960. The first private phone service came in 1964 when a phone was installed at the Bayview Store.

NEEBISH ISLAND (CHIPPEWA COUNTY)

Neebish Island lies just south of Sugar Island and west of the Canadian St. Joseph Island. To the west lies the town of Barbeau in Chippewa County.

The Island is divided by a shallow, muddy creek. Big Neebish is north, Little Neebish is on the south side.

Neebish is said to be a Chippewa word meaning "where the water boils," referring to the rapids that raced by the western shore. The once strong rapids were weakened in 1908 after a shipping channel was dug to the north for ships using the Soo Locks.

Area: 21.5 square miles

Access: Via the ferry, April 1st through January 15th

Ownership: Four acres are owned by the state, the rest is held privately.

Population: 66

History: The first white settlers began arriving in the 1880s and began lumbering activities. In 1885 the island's first postmaster was appointed for a small settlement known as Neebish on the southeast side of the island.

Another settlement Oak Ridge, or Oak Ridge Park, was established in 1890 on the west side of the island near the present day location of the ferry dock. A post office was established there in 1911 and remained open until 1942. The population of Oak Ridge grew to about 200 by 1927.

A Sailor's Encampment was set up at the southern tip of the island in the middle 19th Century to serve as a resting spot for the crews of passing steamers unwilling to navigate the narrow, unmarked passages at night.

In 1894, the Army Corps of Engineers finished work on the Middle Neebish Channel along the northeast side of the island. The new channel shaved 11 miles from the journey up the St. Marys River to Lake Superior.

In 1907, a light tower was built on the north end of the island and the Coast Guard had a lookout camp on the island during World War II.

Today the island is a destination for vacationers who can camp or rent a cabin at Neebish Island Resort, which also operates a small store. It replaced the island store that burned down in the mid 1990s. The island offers bird-watching, hunting, fishing, rest and relaxation, and a great vantage point for watching passing freighters.

GRAND ISLAND (ALGER COUNTY)

Area: 22.4 sq. miles (14,300 acres), about 8 miles in length and 3 miles wide

Shoreline: 35 miles

Population: 45 (U.S. Census, 2000)

Access: By ferryboat which makes four daily trips (in season) from the mainland to William's Landing. Boat dock is located on M-28 between Munising and Christmas.

Grand Island Ferry & Tour operates a passenger ferry to and from Grand Island. The boat leaves from the Grand Island Landing near Munising and arrives at Williams Landing on Grand Island.

When the ice bridge is solid, usually during January and February, the island can be reached by snowmobile or cross country skis.

Distance from mainland: About one-half mile from Munising

History: Prehistoric man used Grand Island as a source for food and tools over four thousand years ago. The Grand Island Archeological Program started in 2001 by Illinois State University and Hiawatha National Forest has discovered artifacts dating to 2200 BC.

In the 1500s, Ojibwe Indians arrived on the southern shore of Lake Superior and set up seasonal villages on the southern shore of Grand Island where they fished with spears and nets. The natives also

East Channel Lighthouse (no longer in use).

hunted deer, moose, and beaver, planted corn and squash, tapped trees for maple syrup, and used the hard quartzite rock found on the island for making cutting and scraping tools. Theses seasonal Ojibwe communities were well established by the time French priests and explorers arrived in the mid 1600s.

Fur traders of the late 18th century found Grand Island to be a strategic point in their travels. The British Northwest Company built a fur trading post on the island in the late 1790s, which later belonged to the Hudson Bay Company. In 1814, it was taken over by John Jacob Astor's American Fur Trading Co. In 1820, General Lewis Cass and explorer Henry Rowe School-craft first visited the island while leading an expedition along the Lake Superior shoreline. During this visit, a young Native American named Powers-of-the-Air related a story that later became the basis for Henry W. Longfellow's epic poem *Song of Hiawatha*.

The first permanent white settlers on Grand Island were Abraham and Anna Williams and their children. They arrived on the island in 1841 at the invitation of the chief of the Grand Island Band of Anishnabeg who admired Williams's blacksmith skills. At the time the Williams family moved from their home in Sault Ste. Marie, there were an estimated 100 Indians living on Grand Island. Abraham Williams lived on the island with his family until his death in 1871. Williams Landing on the south shore of Grand Island is named after him.

The first lighthouse on the island was built in 1855 on a cliff on the northern point of the island. In 1867, the wooden lighthouse was replaced by a brick lighthouse and light keeper's residence. Today it is the home of Loren Graham, author of *A Face in the Rock: The Tale of a Grand Island Chippewa*. The book is the story of the Grand Island Ojibwe Indian named Powers-of-the-Air (see box). Another lighthouse was built in 1868 on the east side of the island. The one-and-a-half story wooden structure includes a keeper's house. In 1908, range lights were built in Munising, which led to the closing of the East Channel Light. Today it is privately owned, but open for tours.

In 1900, the Island was purchased by the Cleveland Cliffs Iron Company of Ishpeming. Company president William Mather created a wild game preserve, bringing to the island exotic species such as albino deer, mountain goats, moose, caribou and other non-native animals. Many of the animals were killed off by wolves, something Mather did not anticipate and eventually the surviving exotics were captured and moved to parks in other states.

FACE IN THE ROCK

Carved in 1820 on Lake Superior shore near Au Train. Erosion is accelerating. Above is a recent photo, while below is a photo taken in 1962.

During the first half of the 1900s, Grand Island was accessible to resorters who could stay at the Hotel Williams. Visitors came to hunt, fish, boat or hike. The resort closed in 1959, eight years after Mather died. During his lifetime Mather did not allow logging on the island, opting to preserve the old-growth forests. Shortly after his death Cleveland Cliffs began logging operations on the island that lasted into the 1980s.

In 1989, Cleveland Cliffs sold the island for $3.5 million to the non-profit group Trust for Public Land. The land was then purchased by the federal government and a National Recreation Area was created for bikers, hikers and campers.

ISLE ROYALE (KEWEENAW COUNTY)

Total area: 893 sq. miles (571,790 acres) including Isle Royale and 20 smaller islands

Total land area: 209 sq. miles (133,781 acres)

The archipelago is 45 miles long and nine miles wide at its widest point

Distance from shore: about 15 miles from Ontario, the nearest mainland shoreline, and 56 miles from Keweenaw County, the nearest Michigan shoreline

"The Ranger" leaving from Houghton.

The "Isle Royale Queen" departing from Copper Harbor.

Ownership: 843 sq. miles is federal, 51 sq. miles is non-federal

Population: 0

Access: By ferry boat from Copper Harbor, Houghton and Grand Portage Minnesota.

From Copper Harbor: The Queen III ferry takes about 4.5 hours to make the 56-mile trip to Rock Harbor. Ferry service is available mid-May through the end of September.

From Houghton: The Ranger III ferry takes about 6.5 hours to make the 73-mile trip to Rock Harbor. Ferry service is available from early June through mid-September.

From Grand Portage, MN: The Voyageur II takes about 3 hours to make the 22-mile trip to Windigo. The Voyageur II also makes trip around Isle Royale to drop off and pick up mail and backpackers. Its stops include Rock Harbor. Service is available from early May through the end of September.

There is also a seaplane service out of Houghton that makes 30-minute flights to either Rock Harbor, or Windigo.

History: The history of Isle Royale begins with the "Copper People" of the Archaic Age (6000 B.C. through

500 B.C.). This group of unknown origin came to Isle Royale and mined copper, most likely using fire, water and mauls made from island rocks.. Some of the remains discovered on the island by archaeologists date back to 3500-4000 B.C. There are ancient copper pits along the Stoll Trail on Scoville Point that date back to 2500 B.C. Copper mined by these ancient Indians was traded and transported around the Great Lakes, with artifacts discovered in New York, Illinois and Indiana. Indian activity on Isle Royale in the form of copper mining, fishing and tapping maple trees was probably at its zenith between 800–1600.

The first known Europeans to visit the island were the Jesuits in about 1670. They were soon followed by French fur trappers. The French claimed the island in 1671, adding a touch of royalty to its name in honor of King Louis XIV.

The island was used by Ojibwa for net fishing, hunting, and maple syrup production during the 1600s and 1700s. The archipelago also saw use during this period as a base for fur traders and commercial fishermen. By the 1840s when white miners arrived, the only signs of Indian activity were a camp on Sugar Mountain where maple syrup was produced and a fishing camp on Grace Island.

COUNTY RENAMED

In 1875, the island archipelago was severed from Keweenaw County, and renamed Isle Royale County. It lasted as its own county until 1897 when it was dissolved and reincorporated into Keweenaw County.

Ancient copper mine site on Isle Royale

The island came under U.S. control in 1783 as part of the Treaty of Paris. It has been written that Jesuits familiar with Isle Royale told Ben Franklin about the ancient cooper mines there. Franklin, who was defining borders for the Jefferson administration, drew the U.S. boundary line north of Isle Royale, even though the island lay much closer to Canada.

Commercial fishing began to flourish during the first half of the 19th Century led by the fur companies of the day. The North West Company opened a trading post in 1800 and during the 1830s, the American Fur Company established the largest fishing operation of the century. They employed 33 people spread over seven different fishing camps. The large commercial operations closed down by mid-century due to poor economic conditions. They were replaced by smaller, independent commercial fishing posts.

Modern copper mining on Isle Royale began in 1843. By the 1870s, there were several mining operations and small settlements on the island. Minong Mine was the largest operation, employing about 150 workers who lived with their families in the town of Island Mine. When Isle Royale split from Keweenaw County in 1875, Island Mine became the county seat. The mining industry faded by the end of the century due to light production and the challenge and expense of transporting copper back to the mainland. During this period, an active timber industry logged most of the mature forests on the island.

The commercial fishing industry dominated the early 1900s, with over 100 men earning a living from the abundant population of trout, whitefish and herring. Many were recent immigrants from Sweden, Norway and Finland. These fishermen built small cabins and docks on the shore and most sold their catch to the A. Booth and Sons Company, which dominated the market. By 1930, the fishermen were facing more regulations, getting lower prices for their catch and competing with a new invasive species—the sea lamprey. Some fishermen stayed on the islands to open small hotels as the island became a draw for summer resorters.

The first resort to open was the John's Hotel built in 1894. Steamship companies followed suit by opening seven resort hotels on Isle Royale and Washington Island. The Windigo Copper Company built the Singer Resort on Washington Island, and the Washington Club on Isle Royale. Other resorts were established at Snug Harbor, Tooker's Island, Davidson Island, and Minong Island. Guests escaped the heat and smells of summer in the big city to enjoy the cooler and fresher air of Lake Superior. Resorts offered tennis, fishing, dancing, shuffleboard, and a comfortable place for rest and relaxation. The Belle Isle Resort built a nine-hole golf course by hauling soil from McCargoe Cove to improve their turf.

Families from Michigan, Minnesota, and other nearby states bought some of the smaller islands in Tobin Harbor and south of Belle Isle where they built summer homes. By the mid-1930s a small newspaper, *The Tobin Talkie*, was published for summer residents around Tobin Harbor.

In the 1920s, Detroit outdoor writer Albert Stoll led a drive to prevent further development on the island. On March 3, 1931, the Isle Royale Park Commission was established, which allowed it to receive federal money to acquire land from private owners. In 1936, a forest fire that started in the slash piles of a pulpwood operation destroyed twenty per cent of the island. The Civilian Conservation Corp was called in to fight the fire and rebuild the infrastructure that was destroyed. Four years later Isle Royale became a National Park.

National Park Status: Isle Royale National Park was authorized by Congress on March 3, 1931 by President Herbert Hoover. Isle Royale National Park was established on April 3, 1940 by President Franklin D. Roosevelt. The park was designated part of the National Wilderness Preservation System in 1976, under the Wilderness Act. In 1981 Isle Royale was designated an International Biosphere Reserve by the United Nations. It is part of a program designed to protect examples of the different ecosystems of the world and to encourage research. It represents the northern lake-forest biome.

Housekeeping cabin available for rent on the island.

Camping and lodging: On Isle Royale National Park, lodging is available at Rock Harbor Lodge. Rock Harbor Lodge was built as a guest house around 1900. It is now managed by National Park Concessions, Inc. and is open May through September. The lodge, which is located along the shore of Rock Harbor, includes rooms with a private bath, a dinning room, store, snack bar, gift shop, marina, motorboats, guided fishing and sightseeing tours.

There are 88 three-sided sleeping shelters on Isle Royale. They provide a convenient source of shelter, especially during bad weather. The front of each shelter is screened to provide relief from the insects. Availability is on a first-come, first-served basis.

Isle Royale has 165 miles of scenic hiking trails and 36 campgrounds for backpackers and recreational boaters.

The 40-mile Greenstone Ridge Trail runs the length of the island between Windigo and Rock Harbor. There are six designated camping sites along the trail. Most hikers will devote five or six days to hike the full 40 miles, which includes Mount Desor the highest point on the island at 1,394 feet above sea level.

Wildlife: Isle Royale provides a rich natural environment for wildlife. The island is best known for its population of wolves and moose, but it is also home to red fox, beaver, lynx, snowshoe hare, mink, river otters, osprey, and bald eagles.

WOLF POPULATION

1996-97	1997-98	1998-99	1999-2000	2000-01	2001-02
24	14	25	29	19	17
2002-03	2003-04	2004-05	2005-06	2006-07	2007-08
19	29	30	30	21	23

According to researchers the wolves of Isle Royale are descendants of a lone female wolf who probably walked over the frozen lake waters from Minnesota in the late 1940s.

The annual winter study of the wolf and moose population started in 1958, and is the longest running predator-prey research project in the world.

MOOSE POPULATION (EST.)

After reaching a historic peak of almost 2,500 animals in 1995, Isle Royale moose were reduced by starvation to an estimated 500 after the severe winter of 1996.

1997	1998	1999	2000	2001	2002
500	700	750	850	900	1,100
2003	2004	2005	2006	2007	2008
900	750	540	450	385	650

Researchers believe that increasing temperatures are one reason for a decline in the moose population. In hotter weather moose are more vulnerable to ticks, which can cause weakening. They are then also less likely to forage for food.

Retired Michigan Technological University wildlife biologist Rolf Peterson says the discovery of moose on Isle Royale goes back to 1904. They thrived on a plentiful food supply free from the threat of predators until the arrival of wolves in the late 1940s.

For more information on the Isle Royale Wolf and Moose research project visit: www.isleroyalewolf.org

The study is conducted by School of Forest Services and Environmental Science at Michigan Technological University, with funding provided by the National Park Service, National Science Foundation, Earthwatch, and the Robert Bateman endowment at the Michigan Tech Fund.

Photo by E Daly

SHIPWRECKS

There are 10 shipwrecks around the island which are a mecca for divers. The shipwrecks are naturally preserved in Lake Superior's frigid waters.

Ship	Type	Size	Year
Cumberland	Wooden Side Wheeler	214 ft.	1877
Algoma	Steel passenger ship	264 ft.	1885
Chisholm	Wooden bulk freighter	270 ft.	1898
Monarch	Wooden packet	259 ft.	1906
Chester A. Congdon	Steel bulk freighter	532 ft.	1918
Glenlyon	Steel bulk freighter	328 ft.	1924
Kamloops	Steel canaler	250 ft.	1927
America	Steel packet passenger ship	183 ft.	1928
George M. Cox	Steel passenger ship	233 ft.	1933
Emperor	Steel bulk freighter	525 ft.	1947
Tug in Five Finger Bay	Wooden fish tug	40 ft.	unknown

There are four lighthouses on Isle Royale; The Rock Lighthouse, The Red Sandstone Isle Royale Lighthouse, The Passage Island Lighthouse, and the Rock of Ages Lighthouse.

Great Lakes gale washes waves over a freighter
(Courtesy of Superior View, Marquette)

MISCELLANEOUS

-Isle Royale contains 42 inland lakes.

-About 80% of the park is underwater

- The highest point on the island is Mount Desor at 1,394 feet (425 m), or about 800 feet (240 m) above lake level.

-Siskiwit Lake's Ryan Island is the largest island in the largest lake on the largest island in the broadest freshwater lake in the world.

-Isle Royale is part of the United States because it appeared in the wrong place in Lake Superior on John Mitchell's Map that was used in the treaty of Paris, 1782-83.

-Automobiles and other wheeled vehicles are not permitted on the island. Approved modes of transportation include hiking, boating, canoeing and kayaking

-Rock of Ages Lighthouse contained a second-order Fresnel lens which was the largest sized lens on the Great Lakes. View this magnificent lens at the Windigo Visitor Center.

AUTRAIN ISLAND (ALGER COUNTY)

Area in Acres: 106 acres

How far from shore: about a mile from shore at its closest point, situated roughly midway between Marquette to the west and Munising to the east

Ownership: privately owned

Access: no public access

History: This Island has been up for sale since the mid-90s. As of 2007, shoreline lots have been subdivided and offered at prices starting at $174,500.

PARTRIDGE ISLAND (MARQUETTE COUNTY)

Area in Acres: Approximately 60

How far from shore: About a mile northwest of Presque Isle, 2 miles from Marquette

Ownership: Privately owned

Access: No public access

History: The Island briefly took center stage as a destination in the 1890s. Marquette pioneer entrepreneur John M. Longyear built a pavilion on Partridge Island in 1894. His steamers, *City of Baltimore* and later, The *City of Marquette*, carried Marquette residents to the island for Saturday night dances. The enterprise was successful for a couple of years until the boat dock at the island was taken out by storms and ice. In the winter of 1898, the pavilion was skidded along the ice to Presque Isle where it served as a gathering place for years.

Partridge Island

Today, Partridge Island's most prominent residents are a pair of nesting eagles occupying the top limbs of a giant white pine on the island's south side. The island is owned by the Middle Island Point camper's association.

GRANITE ISLAND (MARQUETTE COUNTY)

Granite Island Lighthouse

Area in Acres: 2.49

How far from shore: Approximately 12 miles northwest of Marquette

Ownership: Scott and Martine Holman, Bay City, Michigan

Access: Privately owned

History: The Ojibwa called this granite outcropping 12 miles northwest of Marquette "Na-Be-Quon" (canoe with a hump). The earliest explorers found the island nearly impossible to get onto because of the rocky, jagged cliffs which promoted a dangerous lake surge even on calm days. The need for a lighthouse on this rock outcropping was recognized soon after navigation picked up on Lake Superior following the opening of the Sault Canal. In 1866, calls for a lighthouse were made because "The Marquette light cannot be seen by vessels coming from Portage until they are almost abreast of the light and have passed Granite Island, which is directly in their track."

Construction of the light was begun at the opening of navigation in 1868. Just getting the supplies onto the "rock" was difficult:

"The island (granite rock) rises almost perpendicularly out of Lake Superior, with deep water all around it. Whatever was landed had to be moved from the steamer to the top of the island, which is sixty feet above the water. At ten feet above the water a platform was erected, from which a track was laid to the summit of the island, where a portable steam engine was placed, for the purpose of hauling up a track upon which all the materials were carried."

Much of the top of the island had to be blasted to get a suitable place for construction of the buildings. The job was completed by the close of the season and went into operation the next year. In 1879, a fog bell was set up as an additional aid to mariners approaching Marquette from up the lake. The island was manned with keepers (three of whom died by drowning) until 1939 when it was automated.

The island and buildings were purchased in 2000 by a Bay City business owner who renovated the lighthouse and uses it as a seasonal residence.

HURON ISLANDS (MARQUETTE COUNTY)

Area in acres: 147

How far off shore: The chain of eight islands is about three miles off northern Marquette County or about 5 miles east of Point Abbaye

Population: Uninhabited

Ownership: Owned by the U.S. Fish and Wildlife Service and designated as the Huron Island Wilderness Area

Huron Island Lighthouse

Access: Would-be visitors are advised that only those with appropriate vessels, equipment and navigation experience should approach these islands as the waters around them are treacherous. Sightseeing trips are available to the island chain out of Marquette Harbor. Go to: http://www.uncleducky.com

History: Pierre Radisson referred to the Huron Islands as "three beautiful islands" when he wrote about his 1659 voyage across Lake Superior. There are actually 8 islands in the chain, mostly small rock outcroppings surrounded by dangerous shoals. The Huron Islands are often shrouded in thick fog making navigation around the islands even more hazardous.

On May 29, 1860, the side-wheeler *Arctic* ran aground on the easternmost island. Captain Miller was able to save his crew, passengers (which included some cattle) and cargo, but the *Arctic* was eventually smashed to kindling by the pounding waves. Newspaper coverage of the incident intensified the calls for a lighthouse there and in 1866, Congress answered with an appropriation of $17,000. A site was chosen on West Huron Island at the highest point on the rock outcropping, some 163 feet above lake level.

Construction began just after opening of navigation in 1868. Workers had to blast through granite to construct a road from shore to the construction site. Quarried granite from the island was used to build the 1 ½ story structure. After the privy, oil house, boat dock and tramway were completed the light shone for the first time on October 20, 1868.

It took until 1880 before funding for a fog signal was forthcoming. The fog-signal building had to be constructed near the water over 500 yards from the lighthouse. A 19th Century fog signal required large amounts of water to operate. The problem of getting enough water to the site was a formidable one. Initially a dam of cement and boulders was constructed as a storage basin for rain and snow melt. Violent seas and ice broke up the dam the following winter, so a separate pump house was constructed for a steam-powered pump to draw water up the cliff from the lake.

Much labor was required to keep the signal going during fog events. 1887 was the keepers' busiest year as they shoveled tons of coal to keep the signal's whistle screaming for 361 hours.

During the 20th Century many changes took place. Early in the century, the light's wick lamp was upgraded to incandescent oil vapor. Then in the 1930s, a diesel-powered generator brought electricity to the island. By 1961, a solar-powered 45,000 candlepower electric oscillating light was installed in the station's lantern. Finally in 1972, the Coast Guard boarded up the buildings and left the island for the last time.

UPPER PENINSULA REGION LIGHTHOUSE MAP

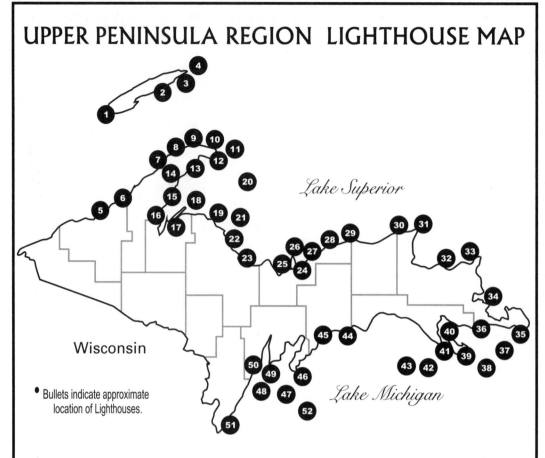

Lake Superior

Wisconsin

Lake Michigan

• Bullets indicate approximate location of Lighthouses.

1) Rock of Ages
2) Isle Royale(Menagerie Isle)
3) Rock Harbor
4) Passage
5) Ontonagon
6) Fourteen Mile Point
7) Keweenaw Waterway Upper Entrance
8) Sand Hills
9) Copper Harbor
10) Eagle Harbor
11) Manitou Island
12) Gull Rock
13) Mendota (Bete Grise)
14) Eagle River
15) Portage River
16) Portage Lake Lower Entrance
17) Sand Point
18) Huron Island

19) Big Bay Point
20) Stannard Rock
21) Granite Island
22) Presque Isle Harbor
23) Marquette Harbor
24) Munising Range
25) Grand Island West Channel
26) Grand Island North
27) Grand Island East Channel
28) Au Sable Point
29) Grand Marias Harbor
30) Crisp Point
31) Whitefish Point
32) Point Iroquois
33) Cedar Point (Round Island Point) Rear Range
34) Round Island
35) DeTour
36) Martin Reef

37) Spectacle Reef
38) Poe Reef
39) Bois Blanc
40) Round
41) St Helena
42) White Shoal
43) Grays Reef
44) Seul Choix Point
45) Manistique
46) Peninsula Point
47) St Martin Island
48) Minneapolis Shoal
49) Stonington Peninsula
50) Sand Point
51) Menominee North Pier
52) Poverty Island

Chapter 4

WATER

THE GREAT LAKES

About 88% of the boundary around the Upper Peninsula is Great Lakes shoreline, including Lakes Superior, Michigan and Huron.

LAKE SUPERIOR

This immense freshwater lake is considered young geologically, at an estimated age of 10,000 years old. However, it is nestled in the Precambrian rocks of the Canadian Shield—among the oldest exposed bedrock in the world.

The Ojibwa, primary native settlers along its shores, called it Gichigami, or Great Water. Ojibwa lore named Nanibijou, the Spirit of the Deep Sea Water, as protector of the lake. The frightful great horned lynx or sea lion Mishepehsu was the spirit that could not be trusted. This Manitou or evil spirit would stir the waters and drown people in sudden storms.

The first white man to see Lake Superior is purported to be Frenchman Etienne Brule who reached the Great Water in about 1620. In 1659, Sieur de Groseiller and Pierre Radisson made a trip to Gichigami. Ten years later, Radisson wrote about the beauty he encountered during the journey: "We went along the shore, which is most delightful and wondrous, for its nature that made it so pleasant to the eye, the spirit and the belly." He also alluded to the peril travelers could encounter: "We saw banks of sand so

This pictograph is of the sea serpent Mishepeshu found on the eastern Canadian shore of Lake Superior.

high…[the]…place is very dangerous when there is a storm, for there is no landing place…After that we came to a most remarkable place. It is a bank of rocks that the Indians make sacrifices to. (Pictured Rocks) The coast of rocks is five or six leagues in length and there is scarcely a place to put a boat in in safety from the waves." Not long afterward, the French Jesuits traveled extensively along its shores establishing missions at the present-day site of Sault Ste. Marie and La Pointe on Madeline Island on the western end of the lake during the latter part of the 17th Century.

"SONG OF HIAWATHA"

By the shores of Gitche Gumee,

By the shining Big-Sea-Water,

Stood the wigwam of Nokomis,

Daughter of the Moon, Nokomis.

Dark behind it rose the forest,

Rose the black and gloomy pine-trees,

Rose the firs with cones upon them;

Bright before it beat the water,

Beat the clear and sunny water,

Beat the shining Big-Sea-Water…

—from Henry Wadsworth Longfellow

The British took control of the Lake Superior region in the late 18th Century. Adventurer Alexander Henry explored the lake and its shores extensively. In his search for gold, he built the first documented ship of any size on the Lake. His exploration party took a 40-ton sloop to a small eastern Lake Superior island in the spring of 1771. No gold was found, but the party discovered a large herd of stunted caribou there—hence, the island's name today, Caribou.

Henry Rowe Schoolcraft was part of the first permanent American settlement at Sault Ste. Marie from 1822-1833. He took five trips along the full length of the Lake during his stay. On one trip in the summer of 1831, he was inspired to write one of the more cogent descriptions of the beauty and immensity of Lake Superior:

"He who, for the first time lifts his eyes upon the expanse, is amazed and delighted at its magnitude. Vastness is the term by which it is, more than any other, described. Clouds robed in sunshine, hanging in fleecy or nebular masses above-a bright, pure illimitable plain of water-blue mountains, or dim islands in the distance—a shore of green foliage on the one hand—a waste of waters on the other. These are the primary objects on which the eye rests."

The vastness which Schoolcraft alluded to can be put into perspective by the fact that the states of Connecticut, Massachusetts, Rhode Island and Vermont would fit into Lake Superior's surface area. The lake is about the size of South Carolina. This immense surface area means the wind can blow across over 200 miles of open water raising huge waves. The pioneers of the region discovered this quickly. In 1845, Philo M. Everett, who began the first iron mine near the shores of the Superior, wrote: "The Lake is one of the most boisterous in the world. I have seen it when our sails would not flop and in fifteen minutes blowing a gale and the seas in a few minutes more running as high as a house."

This fact, along with its desolate shores and cold water—much of the year the surface water temperature is around 40 degrees or lower—made the prospect of shipwreck on Lake Superior all the more terrifying. Lake captains of the late 20th Century were shown that even their large, modern freighters could become a victim of Superior when the Edmund Fitzgerald went down in a November gale in 1975.

Lake Superior, with its vastness, the clarity of its water, the wild beauty of its rocky shores and sandy beaches is one of the most unique locations in the world.

LAKE SUPERIOR

LAKE SUPERIOR – DEPTH

Lake Superior is the deepest of the five Great Lakes.

Average depth:

483 ft. (147 m)

Deepest point:

1,333 ft. (406.2 m)

The deepest spot is about 40 miles (64 kilometers) off the shore of Munising.

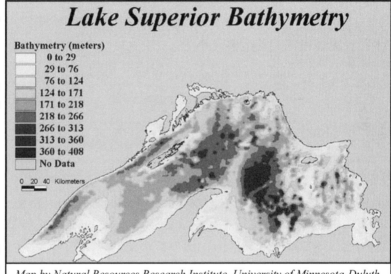

Lake Superior Bathymetry

Bathymetry (meters)
- 0 to 29
- 29 to 76
- 76 to 124
- 124 to 171
- 171 to 218
- 218 to 266
- 266 to 313
- 313 to 360
- 360 to 408
- No Data

0 20 40 Kilometers

Map by Natural Resources Research Institute, University of Minnesota-Duluth.

OTHER GREAT LAKES – DEEPEST POINTS

Lake Michigan	923 ft.	(281 m)
Lake Ontario	802 ft.	(244 m)
Lake Huron	750 ft.	(229 m)
Lake Erie	212 ft.	(64 m)

LAKE SUPERIOR – AREA

Lake Superior has the largest surface area of any freshwater lake in the world, larger than the state of South Carolina.

Surface area:	31,700 sq. mi.	(82,102 sq. km)
Max. length:	350 miles	(563 km)
Max. breadth:	160 miles	(257 km)

OTHER GREAT LAKES – SURFACE AREA

Lake Huron	22,973 sq. miles	(59,499 sq.km)
Lake Michigan	22,278 sq. miles	(57,699 sq.km)
Lake Erie	9,906 sq. miles	(25,656 sq. km)
Lake Ontario	7,340 sq. miles	(19,010 sq. km)

LAKE SUPERIOR – VOLUME

Only two other lakes in the world, Lake Baikal in Siberia and Lake Tanganyika in East Africa, hold more fresh water than Lake Superior. Lake Superior could hold all of the water from the other four Great Lakes, along with three more Lake Eries!

Cubic miles of water: 2,935 (12,232 cubic km)

OTHER GREAT LAKES – CUBIC MILES

Lake Michigan	1,180 (4,918 cubic km)
Lake Huron	850 (3,543 cubic km)
Lake Ontario	393 (1,638 cubic km)
Lake Erie	116 (483 cubic km)

LAKE SUPERIOR - SHORELINE

Total shoreline: 1,826 miles (2,938 km)

Total shoreline including islands: 27,256 miles (43,864 km)

Miles of Lake Superior shoreline (state rank) – by county

Keweenaw	424	(2)
Chippewa	421	(3)
Alger	120	(7)
Marquette	79	(10)
Baraga	70	(13)
Ontonagon	56	(17)
Houghton	51	(19)
Luce	31	(26)
Gogebic	30	(27)

The lake's elevation is approximately 600 feet (183 m) above sea level.

Other names for Lake Superior:

- *Gichigami,* "big water" by the Ojibwa. In Longfellow's *Song of Hiawatha* he spelled it *Gitche Gumee.*

- *Lake Conde* by Father Hennepin in *A Description of Louisiana.*

- *Le lac superieur* meaning "upper lake" by French Explorers. In English the name translated to Lake Superior.

Major water sources of Lake Superior include about 200 rivers including: the Nipigon, Michipicoten, and Kaministiquia rivers in Canada, and the St. Louis, Pigeon, White, and Brule rivers in Wisconosin.

Lake Superior drains into Lake Huron through the St. Marys River. Drainage through the locks and canals is regulated by the International Lake Superior Board of Control.

LAKE MICHIGAN

LAKE MICHIGAN - DEPTH

Average depth:	279 ft. (85 m)
Deepest point:	923 ft. (281 m)
(2nd deepest Great Lake)	
Lake Superior	1,333 ft.(406 m)
Lake Michigan	923 ft (281 m)
Lake Ontario	802 ft (144 m)
Lake Huron	750 ft (229 m)
Lake Erie	212 ft. (65 m)

The deepest points of Lake Michigan lie about 20 to 30 miles off the shore of Manistee and Benzie counties.

LAKE MICHIGAN - AREA

Surface area: 22,278 (including Green Bay)

Other Great Lakes

Lake Superior	31,700 sq. miles (82,102 sq. km)
Lake Huron	22,973 sq. miles (59,499 sq.km)
Lake Erie	9,906 sq. miles (25,656 sq. km)
Lake Ontario	7,340 sq. miles (19,010 sq. km)

Lake Michigan is 317 miles (510 meters) long and 118 miles (190 meters) wide.

Lake Michigan is the third largest Great Lake and the sixth largest freshwater lake in the world.

Technically Lake Michigan and Lake Huron are one lake connected by the Straits of Mackinac. As one lake with a surface area of over 45,000 square miles, it is the largest freshwater lake in the world.

LAKE MICHIGAN - VOLUME

Total volume:	1,180 cubic miles	(4,918 cubic km)
Lake Superior	2,934 cubic miles	(12,229 cubic km)
Lake Huron	850 cubic miles	(3,543 cubic km)
Lake Ontario	393 cubic miles	(1,638 cubic km)
Lake Erie	116 cubic miles	(483 cubic km)

MAJOR WATER SOURCES OF LAKE MICHIGAN

Fox River- Green Bay, Wisconsin

Grand River - Grand Haven, Wisconsin

Kalamazoo River – Saugatuck, Michigan

Lake Michigan flows into Lake Huron, which drains into Lake St. Clair

LAKE MICHIGAN - SHORELINE

Total miles of shoreline (including islands): 1,638

Miles of Lake Michigan shoreline (state rank) – by county

Mackinac	298	(3)
Delta	199	(4)
Schoolcraft	46	(21)
Menominee	41	(22)

States that border Lake Michigan: Michigan, Illinois, Indiana, Wisconsin

Lake Michigan is the only Great Lake entirely inside the United States.

LAKE MICHIGAN – WATER LEVEL

Average: 579 ft. above sea level (176 m)

The water level of Lake Michigan fluctuates slightly on a daily basis. The changes are easier to measure on a season-to-season or year-to-year basis. The water level is generally lowest in the winter for two reasons: precipitation, in the form of snow, remains piled on land, instead of draining into the lake, and drier air increases evaporation. In the summer months water levels rise after snow and ice run off into the lake.

The main cause of changing water levels is weather. High precipitation amounts mean high lake levels. Drier air results in less water evaporating from the lake, and lower average temperatures slow evaporation.

Lake levels affect property values, shipping, recreation, and the environment. During high water levels in the mid 1980s some shoreline homeowners watched their beaches disappear, and in some cases, saw their homes crumble into the advancing lake. High water levels led to increased shoreline erosion and damage from flooding. The effects of low water levels that began in 2004 have had a negative economic impact on the Great Lakes. Freighters must carry lighter loads to avoid running aground in shallower waters; many Great Lakes marinas cannot operate without the aid of costly dredging; and many lakefront properties once lined with inviting sandy beaches have been transformed to mucky, weed-filled wetlands.

Modern day high water record: 582.35 ft. above sea level   October, 1986

Modern day low water record: 576.05 ft. above sea level   March, 1964

FORMERLY KNOWN AS

- *Grand Lac*, by Champlain.
- *Lake of the Stinking Water*
- *Lake of the Puants* (French called Winnebago Indians "Puans")
- *Lac St. Joseph* by Allouez.
- *Lac des Illinois* on 1679 map.
- Indian name for the Lake was *Lake Michigami*.
- *Lake Dauphin* by Father Louis Hennepin

LAKE HURON

LAKE HURON – DEPTH

Average depth:	195ft. (59 m)
Deepest point:	750 ft. (229 m)

The deepest part of Lake Huron is in the middle of the lake east of Alpena.

Other Great Lakes – deepest points

Lake Superior	1,333 ft.	(406 m)
Lake Michigan	923 ft.	(281 m)
Lake Ontario	802 ft.	(244 m)
Lake Erie	212 ft.	(64 m)

LAKE HURON – AREA

Lake Huron is the second largest Great Lake by surface area and the fifth largest freshwater lake in the world. It contains Georgian Bay and Saginaw Bay, the two largest bays on the Great Lakes. Georgian Bay alone is large enough to be considered among the 20 largest lakes in the world.

Surface area:	23,000 sq. mi. (59,600 sq. km)
Max. length:	206 miles (332 km)
Max. breadth:	183 miles (245 km)
Other Great Lakes	
Lake Superior	31,700 sq. miles (82,102 sq. km)
Lake Michigan	22,278 sq. miles (57,699 sq. km)
Lake Erie	9,906 sq. miles (25,656 sq. km)
Lake Ontario	7,340 sq. miles (19,010 sq. km)

LAKE HURON – VOLUME

Cubic miles of water: 850 (3,540 cubic km)

Other Great Lakes – cubic miles

Lake Superior	2,934	(12,229 cubic km)
Lake Michigan	1,180	(4,918 cubic km)
Lake Ontario	393	(1,638 cubic km)
Lake Erie	116	(483 cubic km)

LAKE HURON - SHORELINE

Total shoreline (including islands): 3,827 miles (6,157 km)

Shoreline (not including islands: 1,850 miles (2,977 km)

Lake Huron has the longest shoreline of the Great Lakes, counting the shorelines of its 30,000 islands.

Manitoulin Island is the largest freshwater island in the world.

MILES OF LAKE HURON SHORELINE – BY COUNTY

Chippewa	45
Mackinac	unknown

WATER LEVELS

Normal high level: 582 feet   Normal low level: 579 feet

Early explorers listed Georgian Bay as a sixth Great Lake because it is nearly separated from the rest of Lake Huron by Manitoulin Island and the Bruce Peninsula.

Huron receives the flow from both Lake Superior and Lake Michigan, but water flows faster through Lake Huron.

Huron was the first of the Great Lakes to be discovered by European explorers.

Shipwrecks are scattered throughout the lake Five bottomland preserves in Michigan, and a national park in Ontario designated to protect the most historically significant wrecks.

References: Lake Huron brochure, 1990, Michigan Sea Grant

Outlet: St. Clair River to Lake Erie

Name: Since its French discoverers knew nothing as yet of the other lakes, they called it La Mer Douce, the sweet or fresh-water sea. A Sanson map in 1656 refers to the lake as Karegnondi, simply meaning "lake" in the Petan Indian language.

GREAT LAKES WATER LEVELS

The levels of Lakes Superior, Michigan and Huron have varied significantly through recorded history. Geologists estimate that Lake Superior has been as much as 220 feet higher than the current mean level and as much as 300 feet lower. The main driving force behind modern variance in water levels is precipitation falling on the lakes and their tributaries' watersheds.

The lowest level on Lake Superior was reached in 1926. Not coincidentally, Marquette had its driest year on record the year before in 1925. The lowest levels on Michigan and Huron occurred during the Dust Bowl era of the 1930s and during an extended drought in the 1960s. Highest levels on all three basins were in the 1980s during a time of heavy rain and snow in the Western Great Lakes.

Water levels affect everyone living along the shores of the lakes and their tributaries. High water levels will cause serious erosion and loss of shorelines during storms. The intense winter storm of December 1-2, 1985 caused serious damage to a number of structures on the Lake Superior shore.

Low water levels affect commercial navigation, recreational boating, marinas and beaches. During the recent low-water levels that began in 1998, some marinas had to dredge boat slips, channels and harbors along the Great Lakes shores. In 2000, lake freighters were forced into "light loading" carrying 5-8 percent less cargo, forcing prices higher. In the summer of 2007, Transportation Line, Inc. could not use its Wenonah ferry for service between Grand Portage, Minnesota and Isle Royale due to low water levels in Grand Portage Bay. It was able to use the smaller Voyageur II ferry.

The following charts and graphs showing the water levels of the Western Great Lakes. Note that the difference between high and low levels is only 2 to 3 feet. That seemingly small variance can have a large impact.

LAKE SUPERIOR

	Jan	Feb	Mar	Apr	May	Jun	Jul	Aug	Sep	Oct	Nov	Dec
Mean	601.5	601.3	601.2	601.3	601.6	601.9	602.1	602.2	602.2	602.1	602.00	601.8
Max	602.7 1986	602.5 1986	602.4 1986	602.6 1986	602.8 1986	602.9 1986	603.1 1950	603.2 1952	603.2 1985	603.4 1985	603.3 1985	603.1 1985
Min	599.8 1926	599.6 1926	599.5 1926	599.5 1926	599.6 1926	599.9 1926	600.3 1926	600.5 1926	600.8 1926	600.7 1925	600.4 1925	600.1 1925

LAKES MICHIGAN-HURON

Mean	578.5	578.4	578.5	578.8	579.1	579.3	579.4	579.4	579.2	579.00	578.8	578.6
Max	581.3 1987	581.1 1986	581.1 1986	581.5 1986	581.6 1986	581.8 1986	582.0 1986	582.0 1986	582.0 1986	582.3 1986	582.0 1986	581.6 1986
Min	576.1 1965	576.1 1964	576.0 1964	576.1 1964	576.6 1964	576.6 1964	576.7 1964	576.7 1964	576.6 1964	576.4 1964	576.3 1964	576.2 1964

GREAT LAKES SHORELINE

County	Miles of shore	Lake
Chippewa	456	Superior/Huron
Keweenaw	424	Superior
Mackinac	298	Michigan/Huron
Delta	199	Michigan
Alger	120	Superior
Marquette	79	Superior
Baraga	70	Superior
Ontonagon	56	Superior
Houghton	51	Superior
Schoolcraft	46	Michigan
Menominee	41	Michigan
Luce	31	Superior
Gogebic	30	Superior
Dickinson	0	
Iron	0	

INLAND LAKES

Five of the largest lakes in Michigan lie in the Upper Peninsula.

Top Twenty Largest Inland Lakes in Michgan

Lake	Sq. miles	County
1) Houghton Lake	31.3	Roscommon
2) Torch Lake	29.4	Antrim
3) Lake Charlevoix	27.0	Charlevoix
4) Burt Lake	26.8	Cheboygan
5) Mullet Lake	26.0	Cheboygan
6) Lake Gogebic	**20.9**	**Gogebic**
7) Black Lake	15.8	Cheboygan
8) Manistique	**15.8**	**Mackinac/Luce**
9) Crystal Lake	15.8	Benzie
10) Portage Lake	**15.1**	**Houghton**
11) Higgins Lake	15.0	Roscommon
12) Fletcher Pond	14.0	Alpena
13) Hubbard Lake	13.8	Alcona

14) Lake Leelanau	13.0		Leelanau
15) Indian Lake	**12.5**		**Schoolcraft**
16) Elk Lake	12.1		Antrim
17) Michigamme Res.	**11.3**		**Iron**
18) Glen Lake	9.8		Leelanau
19) Grand Lake	8.8		Presque Isle
20) Long Lake	8.8		Presque Isle

LARGEST INLAND LAKES IN THE UPPER PENINSULA

Lake	Area (acres)	Sq. miles	County
Lake Gogebic	12,800	20.9	Gogebic
Manistique Lake	10,130	15.8	Mackinac
Portage Lake	9,640	15.1	Houghton
Indian Lake	8,000	12.5	Schoolcraft
Lake Michigamme	4,360	6.8	Marquette
Lac Vieux	4,300	6.7	Gogebic
Brevoort Lake	4,230	6.6	Mackinac
S. Manistique Lake (Whitefish Lake)	4,001	6.25	Mackinac
Peavy Pond	3,500	5.5	Iron County
Dead River Basin	3,274	5.1	Marquette
Torch Lake	2,659	4.2	Houghton
Bond Falls Flowage	2,100	3.3	Ontonagon
Milakokia Lake	1,956	3.0	Mackinac
Lake Independence	1,860	2.9	Marquette
N. Manistique Lake	1,722	2.7	Luce
McDonald Lake	1,600	2.5	Schoolcraft
Gratiot Lake	1,438	2.25	Keweenaw
Dollarville Flooding	1,400	2.2	Luce
Betsy Lake	1,300	2.0	Luce
Lac LaBelle	1,146	1.8	Keweenaw
Chicagon Lake	1,100	1.7	Iron
Moss Lake	1,080	1.7	Delta

LARGEST INLAND LAKES – BY COUNTY

ALGER COUNTY

Lake	Surface	Deepest point
Au Train River Basin	1,022 acres	
Au Train Lake	830 acres	30 ft.
Beaver Lake	765 acres	37 ft.
Grand Sable Lake	627 acres	85 ft.
Round Lake	475 acres	
Sixteen Mile Lake	442 acres	10 ft.
Nawakwa Lake	399 acres	35 ft.
Lake Stella	314 acres	15 ft.
Nevins Lake	287acres	18 ft.
Deer Lake	266 acres	70 ft.
Kingston Lake	250 acres	
Echo Lake	224 acres	
Fish Lake	150 acres	30 ft.
Branch Lake (West)	137 acres	
Nugent Lake	126 acres	
Cook Lake	125 acres	15 ft.
Perch Lake	121 acres	30 ft.
Mitchell Lake	121 acres	30 ft.
Long Lake	117 acres	
Lost Lake	106 acres	15 ft.

BARAGA COUNTY

Lake	Surface	Deepest point
Lake Michigamme	4,260 acres	
Ned Lake	816 acres	20 ft.
Pricket Dam Backwater	810 acres	30 ft.
Vermilac (Worm) Lake	622 acres	7 ft.
King Lake	508 acres	22 ft.
Beaufort Lake	462 acres	35 ft.
Craig Lake	307 acres	25 ft.

Ruth Lake	192 acres	36 ft.
Parent Lake	182 acres	10 ft.
Crooked Lake	180 acres	30 ft.
George Lake	160 acres	40 ft.
Big Lake	127 acres	34 ft.
Coon Lake	126 acres	45 ft.

CHIPPEWA COUNTY

Lake	Surface	Deepest point
Caribou Lake	825 acres	20 ft.
Carp (Big Trout) Lake	560 acres	35 ft.
Hulbert Lake	557 acres	
Sheephead Lake	490 acres	
First Lake	337 acres	
Bass Lake	265 acres	12 ft.
Pat's Lake	256 acres	
Second Lake	250 acres	
Fourth Lake	243 acres	
Piatt Lake	230 acres	60 ft.
Pendills Lake	230 acres	11 ft.
Carlton Lake	187 acres	
Frenchman's Lake	174 acres	25 ft.
And Wegwaas Lake		
Monocle Lake	146 acres	55 ft.

DELTA COUNTY

Lake	Surface	Deepest point
Moss Lake	1,080 acres	5 ft.
Round Lake	475 acres	56 ft.
Chandler Falls	187 acres	
Boney Falls Dam	171 acres	
Chicago Lake	158 acres	15 ft.
*East Corner Lake	151 acres	40 ft.
(Corner Lakes Chain)		

Gooseneck Lake	139 acres	30 ft.
Lake Sixteen	131 acres	5 ft.
Sandstrom Lake	107 acres	3 ft.
Dana Lake	98 acres	25 ft.

*Lies partially in Alger County

DICKINSON COUNTY

Lake	Surface	Deepest point
Lake Antoine	748 acres	25 ft.
Twin Falls Flowage	641 acres	10 ft.
Fume Lake/Little Fumee	507 acres	
South Lake	345 acres	
Hardwood Impoundment	309 acres	
Sawyer Lake	241 acres	25 ft.
Badwater Lake	220 acres	
No Name Lake	203 acres	
Silver Lake	188 acres	23 ft.
Pond #2	150 acres	
Kates Lake	119 acres	
Silver Lake	118 acres	
Quinnesec Falls (Big)	117 acres	
Carney Lake	105 acres	35 ft.
No Name Lake	103 acres	
Six Mile Lake	100 acres	22 ft.

GOGEBIC COUNTY

Lake	Surface	Deepest point
Lake Gogebic	12,800 acres	30 ft.
*Lac Vieux	4,260 acres	38 ft. (Wisc.) 17 ft. (Mich.)
Thousand Island Lake	1,078 acres	
Presque Isle Flowage	875 acres	
Clark Lake	820 acres	74 ft.
Big Lake	802 acres	
Duck Lake	616 acres	25 ft.

Crooked Lake	565 acres	
Chaney Lake	520 acres	
Cisco Lake	506 acres	20 ft.
Whitefish Lake	500 acres	52 ft.
Langford Lake	470 acres	10 ft.
Tenderfoot Lake	442 acres	
Sucker Lake	439 acres	20 ft.
McDonald Lake	387 acres	10 ft.
West Bay Lake	361 acres	
Loon Lake	358 acres	53 ft.
Deer Island Lake	346 acres	53 ft.
Mamie Lake	341 acres	
Beaton's Lake	323 acres	80 ft.
Marion Lake	317 acres	
Pomeroy Lake	303 acres	

*Lies partially in Wisconsin

HOUGHTON COUNTY

Lake	Surface	Deepest point
Portage Lake	10,970 acres	
Torch Lake	2,659 acres	
Otter Lake	935 acres	29 ft.
Pricket Dam Backwater	810 acres	56 ft.
Rice Lake	680 acres	9 ft.
Lake Roland	292 acres	40 ft.
Lake Gerald	349 acres	40 ft.
Bear Lake	180 acres	
Mud Lake	179 acres	
Bob Lake	133 acres	
Sandy Lake	101 acres	9 ft.
Pike Lake	83 acres	51 ft.
Six Mile Lake	81 acres	
Lake Thirteen	80 acres	20 ft.
Lower Dam Lake	80 acres	
No Name Lake	80 acres	
Pike Lake	80 acres	
Red Ridge Dam Pond	80 acres	

IRON COUNTY

Lake	Surface	Deepest point
Michigamme Reservoir	5,220 acres	
Peavy Pond (Reservoir)	2,673 acres	
Chicagon Lake	1,100 acres	115 ft.
Perch Lake	1,030 acres	14 ft.
Michigamme Lake	675 acres	
Hagerman Lake	584 acres	55 ft.
Smoky Lake	580 acres	45 ft.
Lake Ottawa (Pickerel)	550 acres	85 ft.
Sunset Lake	545 acres	54 ft.
Paint Lake	405 acres	15 ft.
Iron Lake	396 acres	45 ft.
Tamarack Lake	330 acres	18 ft.
Cable Lake	320 acres	30 ft.
Emily Lake	320 acres	32 ft.
Mallard Lake	318 acres	
Stanley Lake	310 acres	39 ft.
Bone Lake	293 acres	
Golden Lake	285 acres	100 ft.

KEWEENAW COUNTY

Lake	Surface	Deepest point
*Siskiwit Lake	4,500 acres	
Gratiot Lake	1,438 acres	70 ft.
Lac LaBelle	1,146 acres	38 ft.
*Lake Desor	1,050 acres	
Lake Medora	695 acres	30 ft.
*Lake Richie	520 acres	
*Feldtmann Lake	461 acres	
*Sargent Lake	368 acres	
Deer Lake	332 acres	10 ft.
Schlatter Lake	280 acres	
*Chickenbone Lake	237 acres	
Lake Fanny Hooe	231 acres	40 ft.
Lake Bailey	204 acres	9 ft.

Lake	Surface	Deepest point
*Lake Halloran	187 acres	
*Intermediate Lake	162 acres	
Lake Upson	160 acres	
*Lake Whittlesey	156 acres	
*Lake Harvey	137 acres	
*Hatchet Lake	131 acres	
*Angleworm Lake	120 acres	
Lake Addie	120 acres	
Thayers Lake	116 acres	10 ft.

* - located in Isle Royale National Park

LUCE COUNTY

Lake	Surface	Deepest point
*Manistique Lake	10,130 acres	20 ft.
N. Manistique (Round)	1,722 acres	50 ft.
Betsy Lake	1,376 acres	7 ft.
Blind Sucker River Flowage	1,050 acres	
Muskallonge Lake	786 acres	20 ft.
Bodi Lake	306 acres	48 ft.
Pike Lake	292 acres	43 ft.
Pullup Lake	178 acres	
Bone Lake	147 acres	
(Little Two Hearted Lake #1)		
Mud Lake	153 acres	5 ft.
Clark Lake	144 acres	
Bass Lake	145 acres	74 ft.
Perch Lake	125 acres	50 ft.
East Lake	122 acres	22 ft.

*Lies partially in Mackinac County

MACKINAC COUNTY

Lake	Surface	Deepest point
*Manistique Lake	10,130 acres	20 ft.
Brevoort Lake	4,230 acres	20 ft.
S. Manistique Lake	4,001 acres	29 ft.
(Whitefish Lake)		

Lake	Surface	Deepest point
Milakokia Lake	1,958 acres	26 ft.
Millecoquin Lake	1,062 acres	12 ft.
East Lake	995 acres	2 ft.
Black Creek Flowage	820 acres	
Round Lake	600 acres	
Hay Lake	445 acres	4 ft.
Strouble Lake	351 acres	9 ft.
Chain Lake	324 acres	
Thompson Lake	260 acres	
Mitten Lake	217 acres	
Duel Lake	205 acres	
Mud Lake	200 acres	
Shoepac Lake	154 acres	
No Name Lake	150 acres	
Little Brevoort Lake	144 acres	11 ft.

* - *Lies partially in Luce County*

Teal Lake, Negaunee

MARQUETTE COUNTY

Lake	Surface	Deepest point
Dead River Storage Basin	2,704 acres	
Lake Independence	2,071 acres	30 ft.
Empire Mine Tailings Basin	764 acres	
Greenwood Reservoir	1,400 acres	30 ft.

Lake	Surface	Deepest point
*Silver Lake Basin	1,214 acres	50 ft.
Deer Lake Basin	897 acres	35 ft.
Mountain Lake	810 acres	
Tailings Pond	706 acres	
Tailings Pond	622 acres	
Ives Lake	467 acres	
Teal Lake	466 acres	32 ft.
Little Lake	454 acres	50 ft.
Goose Lake	395 acres	15 ft.
Conway Lake	366 acres	
Rush Lake	298 acres	
Pine Lake	272 acres	
Bass Lake	266 acres	25 ft.
Squaw (Long) Lake	247 acres	80 ft.
Schweitzer Creek Flowage	245 acres	
Big Chief Lake	221 acres	
Witch Lake	209 acres	95 ft.

*Silver Lake Basin drained during the flood of May 2003 and was reduced to its original pre-dammed size of about 440 acres. The basin is now being restored.

MENOMINEE COUNTY

Lake	Surface	Deepest point
Chalk Hills Impoundment (Menominee River)	1,002 acres	30 ft.
White Rapids Lake (Menominee River)	465 acres	30 ft.
Hayward Lake	422 acres	5 ft.
North Lake	301 acres	4 ft.
Marinette Upper Dam	297 acres	
Grand Rapids Impoundment	295 acres	
Merryman Lake	190 acres	
Hermansville Lake	180 acres	5 ft.
Walton River Dam	175 acres	
Menominee Lower Dam	150 acres	
Bass and Baker Lakes	105 acres	10 ft.
Resort Lake	100 acres	
Snakey Lake	100 acres	

ONTONAGON COUNTY

Lake	Surface	Deepest point
*Lake Gogebic	14,781 acres	35 ft.
Bond Falls Flowage	2,118 acres	
Tailing Pond	464 acres	
Victoria Reservoir	260 acres	
Lake of the Clouds	133 acres	
Mirror Lake	83 acres	40 ft.
Kostelnick Creek Flowage	74 acres	
Sleepy Pond	70 acres	
County Line Lake	67 acres	
Six Mile Lake	66 acres	
County Line Lake	65 acres	45 ft.

SCHOOLCRAFT COUNTY

Lake	Surface	Deepest point
Indian Lake	8,659 acres	15 ft.
McDonald Lake	1,440 acres	10 ft.
Gulliver Lake	836 acres	28 ft.
M Pool	660 acres	
E Pool	540 acres	
C 2 Pool	530 acres	
Marsh Creek Pool	461 acres	
C 3 Pool	410 acres	
Thunder Lake	361 acres	23 ft.
A 2 Pool	340 acres	
C Pool	320 acres	
Bass Lake	293 acres	
F Pool	270 acres	
A Pool	250 acres	
B Pool	225 acres	
D 1 Pool	210 acres	
T Pool	210 acres	

Lake	Surface	Deepest point
J Pool	205 acres	
G Pool	200 acres	
Straits Lake	189 acres	25 ft.
Ross Lake	184 acres	20 ft.
Petes Lake	180acres	37 ft.
Grassy Lake	176 acres	30 ft.
Triangle Lake	175 acres	

MOST WATER (INLAND LAKES, PONDS, STREAMS AND RIVERS) - BY COUNTY

County	Square miles of inland water
Chippewa	112
Mackinac	71
Marquette	51
Keweenaw	48
Iron	45
Schoolcraft	44
Gogebic	42
Houghton	30
Alger	29
Delta	26
Baraga	25
Luce	24
Ontonagon	17
Dickinson	11
Menominee	8

Mehl Lake located in Marquette County near Gwinn.

COMBINED ACRES OF INLAND LAKES, MANMADE LAKES AND PONDS – BY COUNTY

County	Acres	State rank
Marquette	30,062	4
Iron	29,456	5
Gogebic	29,199	6

Lake	Surface	State Rank
Schoolcraft	28,801	7
Mackinac	28,547	8
Houghton	20,324	11
Luce	15,271	16
Alger	14,235	17
Chippewa	11,624	24
Ontonagon	10,994	27
Baraga	10,152	33
Dickinson	6,181	47
Delta	5,977	49
Menominee	4,633	57
Keweenaw	2,775	66

NUMBER OF INLAND LAKES – BY COUNTY

County	# of inland lakes	# of lakes over 50 acres
Marquette	298	87
Gogebic	222	78
Iron	213	87
Schoolcraft	203	79
Chippewa	192	34
Alger	182	51
Luce	141	29
Mackinac	121	34
Baraga	114	38
Houghton	89	25
Dickinson	84	30
Delta	83	20
Keweenaw	74	14
Menominee	46	17
Ontonagon	44	9

WATERFALLS - BY COUNTY

ALGER COUNTY

Alger Falls: 1 mile S of Munising at intersection of M-94 & M28

Au Train Falls: 8 miles S of Au Train or .1 mile N of M-94 on Power Dam Rd

Chapel Falls: Off H-58 in Pictured Rocks Natl Lakeshore between Miners & Sable Falls

Laughing Whitefish Falls: 2 miles N of Sundell

Miners Falls: Within Pictured Rocks Natl Lakeshore, 3.5 miles N of H-58 on Miners Castle Rock

Mosquito Falls: Mosquito River, 10.5 miles NE of Munising

Rudolph Olson Memorial Falls: 1.2 miles NE of Munising at intersection of H-58 & Washington St

Sable Falls: 1.5 miles W of Grand Marais on H-58

Scott Falls: South side of M-28, east side of Lake Superior's Au Train Bay

Wagner Falls: 1.5 miles S of Munising on M-94, turn S on M-94, approximately .5 miles

Whitefish Falls: Whitefish River, 4 miles NE of Trenary on west side of U.S.-41

Munising Falls: Follow M-28 through town till the Sand Point Road Junction directly in town. Head north, it will be on your right.

BARAGA COUNTY

Big Eric's Falls: From L'Anse, 19 miles NE on Skanee Rd, right on Eric's Rd, 1 mile to falls

Canyon Falls: From L'Anse, S on U.S.-41 8 miles to Canyon Falls Roadside Park

Silver Falls: Silver River, 6 miles NE of L'Anse on Skanee Rd

Slate River Falls 11 miles from L'Anse on Skanee Rd, cross bridge, falls in on the right

Tibbets Falls: 2 miles West of Covington, turn N on Plains Rd

Power House Falls: U.S.-41 S of L'Anse, turn West on Power Dam Rd, cross tracks, straight on dirt road, turn right, follow to falls

Falls River Falls: Downtown L'Anse, 2 blocks West of blinker light

CHIPPEWA COUNTY

Lower Tahquamenon Falls: 10 miles W of Paradise on M-123

DELTA COUNTY

Rapid River Falls: 7 miles N of Rapid River on west side of U.S.-41

DICKINSON COUNTY

Fumee Falls: On Fumee Creek off US-2 in Quinnesec

Sturgeon Falls Dam: Menominee River, 3.5 miles SW of Loretto

Unnamed Falls: Menominee River, Between Hydraulic Falls Dam & Piers Gorge on Menominee River. 1 mile S of Quinnesec

GOGEBIC COUNTY

Ajibikoka Falls: Brush Lake, 4.5 miles NE of Watersmeet

Bathtub Falls: Carp River, 21 miles N of Thomaston

Gorge Falls: Black River, 10.5 miles N of Bessemer

Great Conglomerate Falls: Black River, 10 miles N of Bessemer

Kakabika Falls: From US-2 go approximately 14 miles W of Watersmeet, take Co. Rd. 527 N approx. .5 miles

Mex-I-Min-E Falls: Middle Branch of the Ontonagon River, 6 miles NE of Watersmeet

Manabezho Falls: Presque Isle River, 10 miles N of Thomaston

Manido Falls: Presque Isle River, 12 miles N of Thomaston

Nawadaha Falls: Presque Isle River, 12 miles N of Thomaston

Potawatomi Falls: Black River, 10.5 miles N of Bessemer

Rainbow Falls: Black River, 12 miles N of Bessemer

Sandstone Falls: Black River, 12 miles N of Bessemer

Shining Cloud Falls: 9 miles W of White Pine on the Carp River, 21 miles N of Thomaston

Traders Falls: Little Carp River, 20 miles N of Thomaston

Trappers Falls: Little Carp River, 17 miles N of Thomaston

Unnamed Falls: Pinkerton Creek, Located in the Porcupine Mtns Wilderness State Park

Yondota Falls: Presque Isle River, 3 miles N of Marenisco

HOUGHTON COUNTY

Duppy Falls: 5 miles S of Kenton off Forest Highway 16

Hungarian Falls: Hungarian Creek, 1 mile SW of Lake Linden

Jumbo Falls: 1.5 miles W of Kenton on M-28, 1.5 miles S of FR-4580 approximately .5 miles E on gravel road, turn S to gravel pit

Sparrow Rapids: East Branch of Ontonagon River, 2.5 miles NW of Kenton

Wyandotte Falls: Misery River, 1.5 miles SW of Twin Lakes

IRON COUNTY

Chicagon Falls: Chicagon Creek, 7 miles NW of Crystal Falls

Chipmunk Falls: Net River, 6.5 miles NW of Amasa

Horse Race Rapids: Paint River, 7.5 miles SE of Crystal Falls

Snake Rapids: Net River, 7 miles W of Amasa

KEWEENAW COUNTY

Eagle River Falls: In Eagle River on M-26

Haven Falls: Haven Creek, 8 miles SE of Eagle Harbor

Jacobs Falls: Approximately 3 miles NE of Eagle Harbor

Manganese Falls: In Copper Harbor follow U.S.-41 E to Lake Manganese Rd, turn right, approximately .7 miles

Silver River Falls: Silver River, 3 miles E of Eagle Harbor

Siskiwit Falls: On Isle Royale, at the outlet to Siskiwit Lake

LUCE COUNTY

Upper Tahquamenon Falls: 14 miles W of Paradise on M-12

Upper Tahquamenon Falls: Second largest waterfall east of the Mississippi River

MARQUETTE COUNTY

Alder Falls: Alder Creek, 2.5 miles SE of Big Bay

Big Pup Creek Falls: 4 miles S of Big Bay

Black River Falls: Black River, 8 miles SW of Ishpeming

Carp River Falls: 2.5 miles SW of Marquette

Cliff Falls: 12 miles W of Big Bay

Dead River Falls: 3 miles NW of Marquette

Frohling Falls: 6 miles N of Little Lake

Little Garlic Falls: 11 miles NW of Marquette

Morgan Falls: Morgan Creek, 3.5 miles SW of Marquette

Reany Falls: 5 miles NW of Marquette

Unnamed Falls: 2.5 miles SW of Marquette

Warner Falls: .5 mile S of Palmer on M-35

Yellow Dog (Hills) Creek: 5 miles S of Big Bay

MENOMINEE COUNTY

Pemene Falls: Menominee River, 6.5 miles S of Faithorn

ONTONAGON COUNTY

Bond Falls near Paulding, Ontonagon County.

Agate Falls: 7 miles SE of Bruce Crossing at roadside park

Bond Falls: Middle branch of Ontonagon River, 3.5 miles E of Paulding

Cascade Falls: West branch of the Ontonagon River, 6.5 miles NE of Bergland

Greenstone Falls: Located within the Porcupine Mountains Wilderness State Park

Greenwood Falls: Big Iron River, 4 miles N of White Pine

Nonesuch Falls: Iron River, 1.5 miles W of White Pine

O-Kun-De-Kun Falls: Baltimore River, 8 miles N of Bruce Crossing

Overlooked Falls: Located within Porcupine Mountains Wilderness State Park

Pewabeck Falls: Little Iron River, 6 miles SE of Silver City

Trap Falls: Carp River inlet, 5 miles SW of Silver City

Overlooked Falls: Located within Porcupine Mountains Wilderness State Park

Pewabeck Falls: Little Iron River, 6 miles SE of Silver City

Trap Falls: Carp River inlet, 5 miles SW of Silver City

RIVERS

ST. MARYS RIVER

The St. Marys River flows east and southward about 72 miles from Lake Superior to Lake Huron. It has long been a key transportation route through the interior of North America. Archaeological evidence shows that the river has been the site of human habitation for more than 4,500 years. For more than 2,000 years it was the "cultural heartland" for the Ojibwe people. Later it was the main northern link for explorers, fur traders, settlers and the military.

Etienne Brule is credited with being the first European to explore the St. Marys to its source at Lake Superior. French missionaries named the rapids which flow near the origin of the river in honor of the Virgin Mary. The name was then extended to the entire river. The first permanent American settlement on its shores was established at Sault Ste. Marie in 1822. The river became the international boundary between the United States and Canada about this time.

The first lock at the St. Marys rapids was built for canoes by the North West Company, a British interest, in 1798. A direct shipping route from Lake Huron to Lake Superior was finally facilitated in 1855 with the opening of the American locks and canal. The Canadian Sault Ship Canal was completed 40 years later, spurred on by the *Chicora* incident of 1870. The steamer *Chicora* carried an expeditionary force of British regulars and Canadian militia who were traveling to quell an uprising at Fort Garry on the Red River in Manitoba. The soldiers were denied passage through the American locks on the grounds that a military vessel from a foreign country could not use the locks. The soldiers had to disembark and transport themselves and their supplies on the Ontario side. This incident became a rallying point for the construction of an all-Canadian lock system.

Today, the St. Marys offers a variety of recreational opportunities including sightseeing, boating and fishing. The major sightseeing attractions are the Sault Locks, both on the American and Canadian sides. The lower river which leads to the North Channel of Lake Huron is recognized as one of the world's finest sailing areas. Powerboats also take center stage each summer for the annual River Rampage races at Sault Ste. Marie. Fishing for walleye, pike, bass, lake trout, and especially whitefish have always been popular. However, introduced salmon and rainbow trout have now become the dominant sport fishing species.

LONGEST RIVERS (IN MILES)

River	Miles	County
Menominee	100	Iron, Dickinson, Menominee
St. Marys	72	Chippewa
Manistique River	67	Luce, Schoolcraft
Escanaba River	46	Marquette, Delta
Brule River	43	Iron
Michigamme River	40.5	Luce, Schoolcraft
Paint River	38	Iron
Indian River	36	Alger, Schoolcraft
Fox River	32	Schoolcraft
Black River	28.5	Gogebic
Ontonagon – South Branch	26.5	Ontonagon
Ontonagon – Mainstream	24	Ontonagon
Two Hearted River	20.5	Luce
Ontonagon – Middle Branch	20.25	Ontonagon
Presque Isle River	17.5	Gogebic, Ontonagon
Montreal River	16.5	Gogebic
Ford River	14.75	Delta
Sturgeon River	13	Delta
Whitefish River	13	Delta
Ontonagon – East Branch	7.5	Ontonagon

Source: Canoeing Michigan Rivers by Jerry Dennis and Craig Date, copyright 1986, Friede Publications

Piers Gorge on the Menominee features a stretch of Class IV rapids

MENOMINEE RIVER

This is the longest river in the Upper Peninsula of Michigan flowing 100 miles from its origin at the confluence of the Brule and Michigamme Rivers about 12 miles northwest of Iron Mountain in Iron County. The river forms the border between Michigan and Wisconsin and has some 100 tributaries flowing into it. The shoreline is mostly wild and scenic and provides many opportunities for viewing wildlife between the cities of Iron Mountain and Menominee where it empties into Green Bay.

One of the prime wildlife species inhabiting the Menominee River shoreline are bald eagles. Several eagles' nests are constructed in large pine trees at the shore. The majestic bird is often seen soaring high above the tree tops or fishing in shallow water. Loons, osprey and other waterfowl are also common.

The Menominee contains a short stretch of whitewater rapids at Piers Gorge. This section of river downstream from Norway and Niagara is not navigable for general canoeing. However, it has become a destination for expert class kayakers in the eastern U.S. There are also commercial concerns that offer whitewater rafting trips through the gorge. An undeveloped ½ to ¾-mile trail winds along the gorge on the Michigan side.

The river is also a fishing destination. Walleye are most sought after in spring when the season opens and the water still holds the chill of the past winter. Smallmouth bass and northern pike are also caught and salmon, brown trout and splake provide fishing action along the shore of Green Bay near the mouth of the river.

BLUE RIBBON TROUT STREAMS

Stream	County	Upstream	Downstream	Miles
Brule River	Iron	M-73	M-189	12.5
Cooks Run	Iron	US-2	Paint River	6
Fence River	Iron	E. Branch	T45N, R13W, Sec. 35	12
Ford River	Dickinson	T43N, R30W, Sec 15	Henderson	16
Fox River	Schoolcraft	Spring Pond	Seney	18
Fox River	Schoolcraft	M-77	Luce County Line	15
Iron River	Iron	Raft Lake	Iron River	12.5
Ontonagon River (East Branch)	Houghton	Lower Dam Falls	Sparrow Rapids	13
Ontonagon River (Middle Branch)	Gogebic and Ontonagon	R45N, R39W, Sec 19	Ontonagon County Line	12
		Bond Falls	M-28	10.5
Paint River	Iron	USFS Rd 149	Gibbs City	18
Sturgeon River (West Branch)	Houghton	W. Br. Sturgeon Falls	M-38	5
Tahquamenon River (East Branch)	Chippewa	Strongs Corner	T46N, R7W, Sec 9	19
Two Hearted	Luce	T48N, R12W, Sec 12 Of Two Hearted River	Junction w/East Branch	36

Source: Michigan DNR

WILD AND SCENIC RIVERS

River	County
Black River	Gogebic
Scenic:	14
Total miles:	14

From the Ottawa National Forest boundary to Lake Superior.

Carp River	Mackinac
Wild:	12.4
Scenic:	9.3
Recreational:	6.1
Total miles:	27.8

From T43N, R5W, Section 30 to Lake Huron.

Indian River	Schoolcraft
Scenic:	12
Recreational:	39
Total miles	51

From Hovey Lake to Indian Lake.

Ontonagon	Ontonagon
Wild:	42.9
Scenic	41
Recreational	73.5
Total miles:	157.4

East Branch from its origin to the boundary of the Ottawa National Forest; the Middle Branch from its origin to the northern boundary of the national forest; the Cisco Branch from Cisco Lake Dam to Ten-Mile Creek; the West Branch from Cascade Falls to Victoria Reservoir

Paint River	Iron
Recreational:	51
Total miles:	51

The North Branch from its origin to where it meets the South Branch; the South Branch from its origin to where it meets the North Branch; the main stem from the confluence of the North and South Branch to the boundary of the Ottawa National Forest.

Presque Isle River	Gogebic and Ontonagon
Scenic:	19
Recreational:	38
Total miles:	57

The main stem from where the East and West Branch meet to Minnewawa Falls; the East, South and West Branches within the Ottawa National Forest.

Listed by Canoe Magazine as one of the ten rivers in North America that define the outer edge of whitewater paddling.

Sturgeon River   **Delta**
Scenic: 21.7
Recreational   22.2
Total miles: 43.9
From the north line of Section 26, T43N, R19W, to Lake Michigan.

Sturgeon River   **Delta**
Wild: 16.5
Scenic   8.5
Total miles: 25
From its entry into the Ottawa National Forest to the northern boundary of the forest.

Tahquamenon River
(East Branch)   **Luce and Chippewa**
Wild: 3.2
Recreational: 10
Total miles: 13.2
From its origin to the boundary of the Hiawatha National Forest.

Whitefish River   **Delta**
Scenic: 31.5
Recreational: 2.1
Total miles: 33.6

The main stem from where the East and West Branches meet to Lake Michigan; The East Branch from County Rd. 003 to the West Branch; the West Branch from County Rd. 444 to the East Branch.

Yellow Dog River   **Marquette**
Wild: 4
Total miles: 4
From its origin at Bulldog Lake Dam to the Ottawa National Forest boundary.

ACRES OF WATER – BY COUNTY

County	Total water	Inland water	Great Lakes water
Keweenaw	5,418	48	5,371
Alger	4,126	29	4,097
Ontonagon	2,430	17	2,413
Marquette	1,605	51	1,554
Chippewa	1,137	112	1,025
Mackinac	1,078	71	1,006
Luce	1,009	24	985
Delta	822	26	796
Schoolcraft	706	44	662
Houghton	490	30	460
Gogebic	375	42	332
Menominee	294	8	286
Baraga	164	25	140
Iron	45	45	0
Dickinson	11	11	0

Source: Geographic Identification Code Scheme (GICS) CD-ROM, U.S. Bureau of the Census. Compiled by the Michigan Information Center, Department of Management and Budget.

Chapter 5

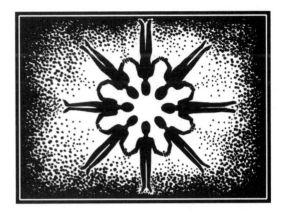

PEOPLE

UPPER PENINSULA PIONEERS

The Upper Peninsula's natural resources have drawn people of different cultures, races and nationalities since the glaciers receded some 10,000 years ago. Ancient miners came to extract copper. Woodland Indians hunted, fished and gathered berries and wild rice. Finally, pioneers of European descent established permanent settlements to exploit mineral and lumber resources. The following biographical sketches include a representative founding settler for each region of Upper Michigan.

JAMES KIRK PAUL (ONTONAGON COUNTY)

James Kirk Paul was the first white settler of Ontonagon. Born near Richmond, Virginia in 1813, Paul was a wanderer and adventurer through much of his life. He traveled with his uncle to the Ohio Valley region at the age of 15. The teenager left his uncle, and drifted west to St. Louis where he worked on the Mississippi for a few years. He later went up the Missouri River where he established a trading post then went back east where he became one of the early settlers of Chicago. Afterwards, Paul enlisted and fought in the Black Hawk War. At its conclusion, he went to the lead region of southwestern Wisconsin where he met a man who told him about the famous, huge copper boulder on the Ontonagon River in the Lake Superior region.

Determined to make his fortune, Paul set up an expedition with the goal of getting the boulder out and selling it. In the spring of 1842, he and his party made the difficult journey up the Wisconsin River to its headwaters, then across a portage to the headwaters of the Montreal River to its mouth where they then floated on Lake Superior to the mouth of the Ontonagon River. At its mouth, Paul built a cabin in which he stored his supplies. The Chippewa of the

James Kirk Paul

region were suspicious of the ambitious explorer and would not give him any help in locating the boulder. After a long, tedious march into the wilderness upriver, Paul's team finally located the treasure on the west branch of the Ontonagon. Paul immediately built a cabin near the boulder and made plans to take it out.

A two-and-a-half mile route down the west branch to the main river was determined to be impassable due to a series of rapids and a waterfall, so an overland passage was planned. This route was three miles through the dense woods and was riddled with hills and valleys as well as a bluff several hundred feet high. The iron-willed Paul began construction of a road through the wilderness, but winter came on before it could be finished. Paul spent the winter in his "rock cabin" as he called it and resumed work on the road in the spring of 1843. As plans were being readied to transport the rock over the road by means of a crude truck over movable track, the party was surprised by the arrival of another party of explorers. This government-sponsored group came with orders from the Secretary of War to bring the rock to Washington.

Paul claimed the rock by pre-emption and held off the government party with a loaded gun. Negotiations were held and it was agreed that Paul could take out the boulder and receive a reasonable compensation for it. Once he got it down to Lake Superior, another dispute arose over compensation. An agent for the government ordered the boulder loaded on a revenue cutter waiting at the mouth of the River. Paul again pulled his gun and threatened to kill the first person who touched the rock without his permission. Finally, a check for $1800 was issued to Paul and he surrendered the rock.

After the boulder incident, Paul began to plan a town site. He had both sides of the Ontonagon surveyed near the mouth and turned his cabin on the north side of the river into a general store. When other settlers arrived, Paul's claim on the south side of the river was threatened. Similar to the boulder incident, Paul resorted to firearms to protect what he felt was his. A shooting war broke out and at one point, he was shot and wounded seriously enough to require surgery up the lakeshore in Eagle River. Another time, he shot one of his enemies in the knee.

James Kirk Paul eventually prevailed and operated a hotel called the Paul House until his death in 1881. A biographer described him "as a man devoid of fear and possessed of a will of iron. Impatient of contradiction, he never allowed the offender to escape unpunished. By his courage and determined will he won the respect of his enemies and the confidence of his friends…who, in speaking of the departed pioneer, are disposed to touch lightly on his faults, and remember only his many manly and noble qualities." (There are conflicting versions of the Ontonagon Boulder's removal. For another version, see Chapter 16 "Biggest and Best")

DANIEL D. BROCKWAY (KEWEENAW COUNTY)

Daniel Brockway was one of the earliest settlers of the western Lake Superior region. He was born in Vermont in 1815. As a child he lived in New York and in 1836 he moved to the Michigan territory. There he married Lucena Harris, the daughter of a well-known pioneer of the Kalamazoo region.

The Brockways returned to his boyhood home after their marriage and lived there several years. In 1843, Brockway was appointed blacksmith and mechanic to the Indian Department of the Lake Superior region located on Keweenaw Bay near present-day L'Anse. Brockway set out with his wife and brother in spring 1843 and arrived at the Sault Portage in June of that year. There they waited six weeks and three days for the schooner *John Jacob Astor* to take them to L'Anse. The Brockways stayed in L'Anse for next three years.

As the fame of the copper region to the north increased, Brockway decided to move to Copper Harbor. On May 1, 1846, he, his wife and three small children, along with two Chippewa guides, set out in a small boat. They coasted the bay and lakeshore and arrived at the frontier settlement on May 3. There they found the few inhabitants of the community living in tents. Brockway built a wood-frame house, the first in Copper Harbor, and opened it as a hotel.

Daniel Brockway was a potent force in the development of northern portion of the Copper Country. In 1849, Brockway was employed as an agent for the Northwest Mine. He later discovered the Cape Mine and was instrumental in forming that company and acted as agent for a year. In 1861, he moved to Eagle River where he kept a hotel for two years. He then moved back to Copper Harbor and opened a mercantile store with a son-in-law which he operated until 1869. The Brockways relocated downstate for a few years to work the family farm which Lucena's father owned. They then moved back to the Keweenaw in 1872.

Daniel and his son Albert opened a general store, D.D. Brockway and Son, near the Cliff Mine which they operated for many years. 1879 marked a trip by Daniel to the Black Hills in search of gold. On his return trip in December, he and seven passengers on a stagecoach were overtaken by a blizzard and narrowly missed freezing to death. The stage was tipped over and the party had to spend 15 hours on the open plain in a "perfect gale and mercury at 42 below zero."

Brockway was appointed superintendent of the Cliff Mine, a position he held until 1895. That year, Daniel and Lucena retired to Lake Linden where they spent their final years. Lucena passed on March 3, 1899 with Daniel following a little over two months later.

CAPT. RICHARD EDWARDS (HOUGHTON COUNTY)

Richard Edwards was one of the earliest and most enterprising pioneers of the Copper Country. Born in Cornwall, England in 1809, Edwards was raised in mining work. He married Jane Pryor in 1834 and was later named a mining captain. He was eventually promoted to Superintendent and had charge of several mines in the region. Edwards immigrated to America in 1849 and made his home briefly in Brooklyn, New York.

In 1850, Edwards was hired by the Albion Mining Company to take charge of their copper mines near Eagle River. He moved his family to the site of present-day Houghton in 1853 where he ran the Albion (later the Sheldon and Columbia Mines). In 1854, Edwards purchased a sawmill in Houghton while dealing extensively in real estate. A year later, he resigned from active mining and devoted his energy to real estate.

Edwards worked with his son Thomas and together acquired some 20,000 acres in the Upper Peninsula. They also bought up a large amount of mining stock including 2,100 shares in the Calumet and 200 shares of the Hecla Mines.

Capt. Richard Edwards

His biography noted "probably no man in the Upper Peninsula had a better conception of or more correctly estimated the wonderful resources of this region; he was enterprising and public-spirited and commanded the respect and esteem of a large circle of friends and acquaintances. Capt. Richard Edwards died in Houghton in 1868.

CAPT. JAMES BENDRY (BARAGA COUNTY)

Capt. James Bendry was among the earliest mariners on Lake Superior and a pioneer of the village of Baraga. Bendry was born in England in 1822. At 12 years old, he went to sea as a cabin boy. In 1838, he shipped in the American merchant service and sailed between Liverpool, New Orleans and the West Indies. He also sailed to Africa and other foreign countries.

In 1845, Bendry began sailing the Great Lakes. He was shipwrecked off New Buffalo while on the brig *Indiana*. He was wheelsman of the *Independence*, the first steamer to sail on Lake Superior. He captained the schooner *Chippewa* and also sailed the schooners *Swallow* and *Siskowit*. In 1850, he relocated to Baraga where he operated a tug business. Bendry built a sawmill at Fall River near present-day L'Anse in 1851 and began lumbering. That mill burned down in 1878. He then built a steam saw mill in Baraga—the first of its kind in the area. Bendry's business interests also included a brickyard at L'Anse and a general towing business as owner and master of the steam tug *John Ely*. At the same time, he took on the duties of Supervisor of Baraga Township, a position he held for many years.

Biographers hailed Capt. James Bendry as "a man of much enterprise and public-spirit, taking an abiding interest in the general welfare of the community. [He was]…one of the most widely and favorably known men of this region." Bendry died in 1895 at the age of 73.

PETER CREBASSA (BARAGA COUNTY)

One of the earliest white settlers of L'Anse, Peter Crebassa was born in the Red River Country of Canada in 1807. He grew up in Montreal and became an agent for the American Fur Company. Crebassa came to Mackinac Island in 1829 and traveled extensively in the Lake Superior region up to the Canadian wilderness at Rainy Lake during his 25-year career with the fur trading company. He made his base of operation at L'Anse in 1837 and is considered the father of the town.

Crebassa was instrumental in bringing missionary Frederic Baraga to L'Anse, advising him the place would be a fertile ground for converts. Baraga visited the place in early 1843, using part of the Crebassa home as a chapel and school. During his three-week visit, Baraga baptized 30 new converts and returned later in the year to establish a permanent mission on the west side of Keweenaw Bay.

Crebassa became postmaster of L'Anse in 1852 and held that position for over 30 years.

PETER WHITE (MARQUETTE COUNTY)

Peter White was born in Rome, New York in 1830. Shortly afterwards, his family moved west to the village of Green Bay in the Wisconsin territory. White ran away from his Green Bay home in 1844 and headed north. He sought passage to the Copper Lands of the rugged Upper Peninsula, but was unsuccessful. Over the next several years, he worked as a mariner downstate and spent time in Detroit. He found his way north again and took a job as a clerk for the general store on Mackinac Island. In the spring of 1849, a Scotsman named Robert Gravereat came to the island recruiting men to work a claim in the newly discovered Iron

Hills of the central Upper Peninsula. White joined the Gravereat expedition and landed at an isolated trading post on the south-central shore of Lake Superior. He remained there for the rest of his life, helping to develop the little outpost into the City of Marquette.

White was a versatile and ambitious young man. Because he could read and write, abilities found in few U. P. frontiersmen, White was put in charge of Gravereat's general store and also supervised the construction of a sawmill and iron forge. By 1851 while not yet 21, Peter White was elected register of deeds and shortly afterward he was chosen as Marquette's Postmaster. He befriended a downstate lawyer who spent summers in the frontier village attending to legal matters of the town. Under the lawyer's counsel, White studied law and opened his own Marquette law office in 1854.

Peter White

Peter White, the lawyer, store clerk and postmaster began dabbling in real estate and banking. He eventually took over Gravereat's store and this venture contributed to his economic power in the town. Hard currency was scarce in the Upper Michigan wilderness and White took promissory notes and drafts on outside parties in exchange for goods. These drafts and notes were presented for collection in the banks of Cleveland, Detroit and New York. White developed a relationship and reputation with these large banks as a money broker. Eventually his bank, the First National Bank of Marquette, grew out of the general store.

White eventually opened an insurance firm. The Peter White Agency insured many of the business ventures of the area including mining, marine interests and the fledgling iron industry. White was a strong proponent of locally produced iron and though the effort was ultimately a failure, it contributed greatly to his wealth between 1860 and 1873.

An active Democrat until late in his life, Peter White worked his way up through the ranks starting as secretary of the local organization in 1852. Four years later, he was elected as state representative for his district. He undertook a 340-mile walk during the harsh winter of 1856-57 to make the legislative session in Lansing. His arrival at the meeting was greeted with a standing ovation. During his term, White worked for land grants for railroad construction in the Upper Peninsula among other issues. He had a moderate amount of success, hindered by the fact he was new to politics and a member of the minority party. He chose not to run for another term and remained politically inactive until after the Civil War.

In 1874, White ran for the state senate and scored an upset over his Republican opponent. When he arrived in Lansing for the 1875 legislative session, the *Detroit Free Press* described his career as colorful and varied with banking, manufacturing, mail-carrying and wood chopping among his pursuits. Already the reputation that was to define the frontier hero-entrepreneur was beginning to take shape. During this term, White's biggest success was passage of legislation that promoted railroad construction between Mackinac and Marquette Bay—a route that would, in effect, connect the Upper and Lower Peninsula for the first time. After the legislative session ended, Peter White was welcomed back to the Upper Peninsula by celebrations in a number of communities.

White switched party allegiance in 1896 when the Democrats chose William Jennings Bryant as their presidential nominee. As a Republican, he was elected to the University Of Michigan Board Of Regents in 1904.

Later in life, Peter White focused his energy on community involvement and philanthropy. He worked hard to bring a state institution of higher learning to the Upper Peninsula. The Northern Michigan Normal School, a teacher's college, was established in Marquette in 1899. White appealed directly to the U.S. Congress for federal land set aside for lighthouse construction northwest of Marquette. He asked that the land be given to the city for the establishment of a park. His efforts resulted in Presque Isle Park, a beautiful forested prominence jutting out into Lake Superior. The park remains essentially in its natural state and still draws residents and tourists today. He also established a library to which he donated thousands of books.

These philanthropic endeavors tended to ameliorate the reputation of a man who through most of his career amassed a fortune through the misfortune of others. His law office, in effect, became a collection agency. His bank operated a separate office the townspeople called the "shaving shop." In it, the "iron money" issued by local mining companies due to the lack of hard U.S. currency was exchanged—at a premium—for hard cash. It was the worker holding the substitute currency who was shaved.

Peter White was a man of his times. Through his banking business he gained recognition in the large metropolitan centers to the east. His renown as a frontier-entrepreneur who went from rags to riches in a harsh wilderness was encouraged and promoted by the man himself. He was a good story teller who told of the settling of the Lake Superior region from his perspective. Two notable books were published during Peter White's lifetime that drew heavily and uncritically from his tales. One, *A History of the Upper Peninsula*, was extracted directly from White's reminiscences of the founding of Marquette. In it, the clerk of the general store in town occupies the central role, while Robert Graveraet, Amos Harlow and Philo Everett barely receive a mention. Another book, *The Honorable Peter White, A Biographical Sketch of the Lake Superior Iron District*, was published in 1905. It portrayed White as the focal point and primary character in the settling and establishment of the Marquette Iron Range.

While Peter White's exploits and his significance to the region may have been exaggerated, there is no doubt his business, his charity and social behavior was a positive asset both to Marquette and the Upper Peninsula. The influence of Peter White is still seen in Marquette at Presque Isle, Northern Michigan University, St. Paul's Episcopal Church and the fine library that bears his name.

HENRY ROWE SCHOOLCRAFT (CHIPPEWA COUNTY)

Henry Rowe Schoolcraft, explorer, ethnologist and prominent figure in the first permanent American settlement in Upper Michigan was born near Albany, New York in 1793. He received a public school education, supplemented by outside studies in the classics, French, Hebrew and German. Upon graduation from public school, Schoolcraft planned to attend Union College in Schenectady, New York. However, his family was not able to finance his higher education. Undaunted, Schoolcraft took a job as superintendent of a glass factory in nearby Geneva, New York while continuing his studies at home with a tutor. Later, he accepted a similar position at a glass factory in Vermont. He wrote a treatise on glassmaking and might have stayed in the glass business if not for an influx of British glass on the U.S. market which forced the company he worked for into bankruptcy. In 1817 at the age of 24, Henry Rowe Schoolcraft, spurred by accounts of opportunities in the West, headed to the Missouri territory and began a new life.

He studied the lead mines of the Missouri Territory and wrote a book on his findings. *A View of the Lead Mines of Missouri* was published in 1819 and established his scientific reputation, while subsequently winning him a place on the Lewis Cass expedition to the ancient copper mines around Lake Superior in 1820. He wrote of this adventure in *Narrative Journal of Travels through the Northwestern Regions of the United States* published in 1821. The next year, Schoolcraft was ap-

Henry Rowe Schoolcraft

pointed first Indian agent in the Lake Superior region and so began another phase of his life.

Schoolcraft arrived with a contingent of American soldiers at the small trading post of Sault Ste. Marie in the summer of 1822. He immediately began studying the culture and customs of the Ojibwa Indians who occupied the territory around the Sault. In 1823, he married Jane Johnston, the daughter of a fur trader and full-blooded Ojibwa princess. During his 11 years in the Sault, he traveled along the shore of Lake Superior into the Minnesota territory and on several trips to the Wisconsin Territory to negotiate treaties with various Indian tribes. In 1833, Schoolcraft was given a larger territory and transferred to Mackinac Island. During his stay there he negotiated the Treaty of 1836, which gave the United States vast sections of land including roughly the eastern half of the Upper Peninsula. In return, the Ojibwa and Odawa received annuities paid individually to each tribal member. When the Whigs came to power in 1841, Schoolcraft lost his Indian agency appointment and returned to his native New York.

Henry Rowe Schoolcraft demonstrated an attitude toward Native Americans which was typical of the times. His negotiations deprived them of their land, yet he was sympathetic to their needs. He demonstrated a somewhat paternalistic attitude, believing it was necessary to "Christianize" them in order to educate them. To him, the Indian's loss of land was nothing more than "an interval of transition between the hunter and agricultural state." He also took a strong stand against alcohol.

Schoolcraft is remembered best as a scholar of ethnology. While at Mackinac Island, he finished his two volume set on Native American life and culture called *Algic Researches*. His *Personal Memoirs…of Thirty Years with the Indian Tribes* published in 1851 included journal entries from his 18 years in the Lake Superior region. His most renowned contribution provided the setting and character development for Henry Wadsworth Longfellow's poem "The Song of Hiawatha." From the time of publication in 1855, the poem was an immediate success and became part of the cultural background of every English-speaking school child. Longfellow later praised Schoolcraft's input: "…I have woven the curious Indian legends drawn chiefly from the various and valuable writings of Mr. Schoolcraft to whom the literary world is greatly indebted for his indefatigable zeal in rescuing from oblivion so much of the legendary lore of the Indians."

Henry Rowe Schoolcraft, writer, historian, scientist and educator died in Washington, D.C in 1864.

JACOB A.T. WENDELL (MACKINAC COUNTY)

Jacob A.T. Wendel

A prominent and nearly life-long resident of Mackinac Island, Jacob Wendell was born in Albany, New York in 1823. His family relocated to Mackinac Island when Jacob was three years old.

According to his biography, Wendell "received a good education by his own exertions, after which he turned his master mind in the direction of the commercial world. [He]…was largely instrumental in improving the Island and in developing the surrounding country."

Jacob Wendell served many terms in the state legislature, both in the House and Senate. At one point, he was chosen the democratic candidate for Lieutenant Governor but was defeated. Wendell's fortune was largely made in real estate. He left large tracts in Michigan, Indiana, Wisconsin and the Dakotas. At Mackinac, he was a Collector of Customs for several years as well as County Supervisor.

Wendell showed such generosity and kindness toward the Ottawa Indian tribe that the members elected him chief. He later went to Washington with a deputation of tribal members to help settle a dispute between the tribe and federal government. At another time, the Indians of Emmet County were afraid of losing their lands, so they deeded them to Wendell for safety.

In 1869, the 46-year-old Wendell married Annie Marie Hale of Washington, D.C. They had three daughters. Jacob A.T. Wendell died in 1879.

MARY L. TERRY (DELTA COUNTY)

Mary L. Terry, first keeper of the Escanaba Lighthouse was a native of Dartmouth, Massachusetts. She married Capt. John L. Terry of St. John's, Canada in 1845 and the couple settled in the Upper Peninsula in 1863. Capt. Terry worked on construction of the Chicago and Northwestern Railroad line and was one of the first men to do business on the dock at Escanaba.

In 1867, Capt. John Terry was appointed Light Keeper for the newly-built Escanaba Lighthouse at Sand Point. But before he could assume the position, he died of tuberculosis. Mary was eventually named his replacement despite "strong opposition" from government officials. She displayed the first light in May 1868.

Mary Terry served as lighthouse keeper for a bit less than 18 years. In March 1886, tragedy struck. A fire broke out in the lighthouse during the early morning hours. Before firemen arrived, much of the structure was engulfed in flames. Once daylight arrived, the community's worst fears were confirmed—Terry had perished in the blaze. Evidence suggested that foul play may have been involved and an inquest was held into her death. While there were some suspicious elements to the case, the investigation revealed no evidence that Terry had been robbed. The jurors who worked on the case ultimately ruled that the cause of death as "unknown."

After her death, Mary L. Terry was hailed in the local newspaper as "a methodical woman, very careful in the discharge of her duties and very particular in the care of the property in her charge." Even before her death in 1884, an editorial praised her as "a living illustration of the capacity of women to do honest, hard work." The editorial went on to state that she carried out her duties "in a manner not to be excelled by any masculine 'he' in the country."

Terry was one of only a handful of women employed as lighthouse keepers in the United States. Most, like Terry, came to the position with the death or disability of a husband who they replaced. According to the U.S. Coast Guard's Historian's Office, light keeping became one of the first non-clerical positions open to women. However, fewer than 3 percent of all lighthouse keepers or assistant keepers on the Great Lakes were women.

WILLIAM BONIFAS (DELTA COUNTY)

William "Big Bill" Bonifas was one of the toughest lumbermen of his era. Born the son of a blacksmith in Luxembourg in the 1860s, Bonifas immigrated to the United States as a young man. He intended on making the wheat fields of South Dakota his destination, but wound up on a train headed for the north woods instead. He made it to Green Bay and made his way north and was eventually offered a job in Upper Michigan's Delta County cutting railroad ties. It was exacting, hard work that paid by the number of ties cut. Bonifas excelled at the job. In time he saved enough money to start his own logging operation and bring his seven brothers and sisters from Luxembourg. He rounded out his family by marrying a chore-girl named Catherine.

William and Catherine Bonifas

He established a 40-man lumber camp in the Garden Peninsula east of Escanaba. His crew sent posts and ties south to Wisconsin, Illinois and the Lower Peninsula. When his jacks had stripped the swamps at Garden, Bonifas turned his attention westward, purchasing vast stands of hardwood north of Watersmeet. Eventually, he employed 350 men in six lumber camps.

Big Bill Bonifas became a substantial lumberman. However, he still operated his business like a struggling immigrant. He refused to quit work and relax. When he left on a business trip, he had his wife pack him a lunch. Bonifas caught the attention of author Edna Ferber when she was researching her novel "Come and Get It" about the life of a lumber baron. She drew heavily from the life of William Bonifas for the book's central character, Barney Glasgow—a less than scrupulous, aggressive man who rose from rags to riches like Bonifas.

As the U.P.'s timber reserves dwindled, Bonifas invested in automobile manufacturing, paper and oil amassing a substantial fortune. He withdrew from everyday lumber operations in the early 1930s. Thereafter, he spent a good deal of time warding off organizations and institutions looking for donations from his deep pockets. He made substantial gifts to the Catholic Church and gymnasium, now the Bonifas Art Center in Escanaba and to Marquette University in Milwaukee. However, when he died, much of his fortune was still intact. It was left to his wife, Catherine (the Bonifas's had no children) who dispersed large sums of money. She funded schools as well as city buildings and recreational facilities in and around Escanaba. When she died in 1948, it was reported she willed $2.5 million to charities, family members, schools and other projects.

RUEL O. PHILBROOK (DICKINSON COUNTY)

Born in 1843 at Freeport, Maine, Ruel O. Philbrook established the first store in Iron Mountain. He began his career as a teacher in Maine and then went into the mercantile business. Philbrook relocated his family to Peshtigo, Wisconsin in 1865 where he built a general store. He established a branch store in Iron Mountain in 1879 just as the western Menominee Range began producing iron ore. In addition, he got a post office built in Iron Mountain and was its first Postmaster, a position he held for two years.

Philbrook and his family were in Peshtigo and experienced the Great Fire of October 1871. He and his family escaped only with their lives. His store, it contents and his family's home were all completely destroyed in the fire.

SOLOMON S. CURRY (GOGEBIC COUNTY)

One of Ironwood's founders and earliest settlers, Curry was born in Lancaster, Ontario in 1839. He attended schools in that area and took on the blacksmith trade at age 20. He immigrated to the Upper Peninsula and spent much of his early life on the Marquette Iron Range where he was active in exploration of new mine sites in the area around Ishpeming.

At the age of 40, his life took a new turn when he became president of the Iron and Land Company. This company acquired the Norrie Mine in the newly established Gogebic Range on the western end of Upper Michigan in 1885. Later, the East Norrie, Pabst, Davis and Puritan Mines were added to the portfolio of Curry's company.

He made his home in Ironwood during this time and later became the first president of the First National Bank of Ironwood. Later, Curry established the People's Bank and was its first president. Among his contributions to Ironwood was a gift of an American flag—the first ever owned by the city.

Soloman Curry died in Ironwood on July 29, 1929. There is a beautiful monument erected in his memory on the family plot at the Ironwood Riverside Cemetery.

POPULATION

MICHIGAN POPULATION – BY COUNTY

		------ (Population estimates) ------			Percent of state
Rank	County	2007	2006	2005	population (2006)
1	Wayne	1,985,101	1,971,853	1,998,217	19.53
2	Oakland	1,206,089	1,214,255	1,214,361	12.03
3	Macomb	831,077	832,861	829,453	8.25
4	Kent	604,330	599,524	596,666	5.94
5	Genesee	434,715	441,996	443,883	4.38
6	Washtenaw	350,003	344,047	341,847	3.41

7	Ingham	279,295	276,898	278,592	2.74
8	Ottawa	259,206	257,671	255,406	2.55
9	Kalamazoo	245,333	240,720	240,536	2.38
10	Saginaw	202,268	206,300	208,356	2.04
11	Livingston	183,194	184,511	181,517	1.83
12	Muskegon	174,386	175,231	175,554	1.74
13	St. Clair	170,119	171,725	171,426	1.70
14	Jackson	163,006	163,851	163,629	1.62
15	Berrien	159,589	161,705	162,611	1.60
16	Monroe	153,608	155,035	153,935	1.54
17	Calhoun	136,615	137,991	139,191	1.37
18	Allegan	112,761	113,501	113,174	1.12
19	Bay	107,517	108,390	109,029	1.07
20	Eaton	107,390	107,237	107,394	1.06
21	Lenawee	101,243	102,191	102,033	1.01
22	Lapeer	92,012	93,761	93,361	.93
23	Grand Traverse	85,479	84,952	83,971	.84
24	Midland	82,818	83,792	84,064	.83
25	Van Buren	77,931	79,018	78,812	.78
26	Shiawassee	71,753	72,912	72,945	.72
27	Clinton	69,755	69,909	69,329	.69
28	Isabella	66,693	65,818	65,618	.65
29	Marquette	65,216	64,675	64,760	.64
30	Ionia	64,053	64,821	64,608	.64
31	Montcalm	62,950	63,977	63,893	.63
32	St. Joseph	62,449	62,777	62,984	.62
33	Barry	59,188	59,899	59,892	.59
34	Tuscola	56,805	57,878	58,428	.57
35	Cass	50,551	51,329	51,996	.51
36	Newaygo	49,171	49,840	50,019	.49
37	Hillsdale	46,781	47,206	47,066	.47
38	Branch	46,194	45,875	46,460	.45
39	Sanilac	43,640	44,448	44,752	.44
40	Mecosta	42,090	42,151	42,391	.42
41	Gratiot	42,141	42,107	42,345	.42
42	Chippewa	38,922	38,674	38,780	.38
43	Delta	37,367	38,156	38,347	.38
44	Houghton	35,201	35,334	35,705	.35
45	Emmet	33,393	33,607	33,580	.34
46	Huron	33,290	34,143	34,640	.33
47	Wexford	31,792	31,994	31,876	.32
48	Clare	30,697	31,307	31,653	.31
49	Alpena	29,707	30,067	30,428	.30
50	Mason	28,750	29,045	28,986	.29
51	Oceana	27,800	28,639	28,473	.28
52	Dickinson	26,937	27,447	28,032	.27
53	Cheboygan	26,768	27,282	27,643	.27
54	Gladwin	26,287	27,008	27,209	.27

55	Iosco	26,255	26,831	26,992	.27
56	Charlevoix	26,181	26,442	26,722	.26
57	Roscommon	25,517	26,064	26,079	.26
58	Manistee	24,803	25,067	25,226	.25
59	Menominee	24,249	24,696	24,996	.24
60	Antrim	24,299	24,463	24,422	.24
61	Otsego	24,223	24,711	24,665	.24
62	Osceola	23,148	23,584	23,750	.23
63	Leelanau	21,898	22,112	22,157	.22
64	Ogemaw	21,338	21,665	21,905	.21
65	Benzie	17,510	17,652	17,644	.17
66	Kalkaska	17,188	17,330	17,239	.17
67	Arenac	16,608	17,024	17,154	.17
68	Gogebic	16,287	16,524	16,861	.16
69	Missaukee	14,976	15,197	15,299	.15
70	Crawford	14,550	14,928	15,074	.15
71	Presque Isle	13,852	14,144	14,330	.14
72	Iron	12,151	12,377	12,299	.12
73	Alcona	11,538	11,759	11,653	.12
74	Lake	11,153	11,793	12,069	.12
75	Mackinac	10,877	11,050	11,331	.11
76	Montmorency	10,327	10,478	10,445	.10
77	Alger	9,612	9,665	9,662	.10
78	Oscoda	8,938	9,140	9,298	.09
79	Baraga	8,544	8,742	8,746	.09
80	Schoolcraft	8,518	8,744	8,819	.09
81	Ontonagaon	6,977	7,202	7,363	.07
82	Luce	6,728	6,684	6,789	.07
83	Keweenaw	2,151	2,183	2,195	.02
Michigan total	**10,071,822**	**10,095,643**	**10,120,860**	

The population of the 15 counties of the Upper Peninsula (309,737) make up 3.07% of the state's population.

POPULATION BY COUNTY: 1990 - 2005

Of Michigan's 83 counties, the five least populated lie in the U.P.

County	2005 (est.)	State rank	2000	% change 2000 - '05	1990	% change 1990 - 00
Marquette	65,760	29	64,634	0.2	70,887	-8.8
Chippewa	38,780	42	38,543	0.6	34,604	11.4
Delta	38,347	43	38,520	-0.4	37,780	2.0
Houghton	34,640	44	36,016	-0.9	35,446	1.6
Dickinson	28,032	52	24,472	2.0	26,831	2.4
Menominee	24,996	59	25,326	-1.3	24,920	1.6
Gogebic	16,861	68	17,370	-2.9	18,052	-3.8
Iron	12,299	72	13,138	-6.4	13,175	-0.3
Mackinac	11,331	75	11,943	-5.1	10,674	11.9
Alger	9,662	77	9,862	-2.0	8,972	9.9

Schoolcraft	8,819	79	8,782	-0.9	8,302	7.2
Baraga	8,746	80	8,746	0	7,954	10
Ontonagon	7,363	81	7,818	-5.8	8,854	-11.7
Luce	6,789	82	7,024	-3.3	5,763	21.9
Keweenaw	2,195	83	2,301	-4.6	1,701	35.3

POPULATION – BY COUNTY (1900 – 1990)

County	1900	1910	1920	1930	1940
Alger	5,868	7,675	9,983	9,327	10,167
Baraga	4,320	6,127	7,662	9,168	9,356
Chippewa	21,338	24,472	24,818	25,047	27,807
Delta	23,881	30,108	30,909	32,280	34,037
Dickinson	17,890	20,524	19,456	29,941	28,731
Gogebic	16,738	23,333	33,225	31,577	31,797
Houghton	66,063	88,098	71,930	52,851	47,631
Iron	8,990	15,164	22,107	20,805	20,243
Keweenaw	3,217	7,156	6,322	5,076	4,004
Luce	2,983	4,004	6,149	6,528	7,423
Mackinac	7,703	9,249	8,026	8,783	9,438
Marquette	41,239	46,739	45,786	44,076	47,144
Menominee	27,046	25,648	23,778	23,652	24,883
Ontonagon	6,197	8,650	12,428	11,114	11,359
Schoolcraft	7,889	8,681	9,977	8,451	9,524

County	1950	1960	1970	1980	1990
Alger	10,007	9,250	8,568	9,225	8,972
Baraga	8,037	7,151	7,789	8,484	7,954
Chippewa	29,06	32,655	32,412	29,029	34,604
Delta	32,913	34,298	35,924	38,947	37,780
Dickinson	24,844	23,917	23,753	23,341	26,831
Gogebic	27,053	24,370	20,676	19,686	18,052
Houghton	39,771	35,654	34,652	37,872	35,446
Iron	17,692	17,184	13,813	13,635	13,175
Keweenaw	2,918	2,417	2,264	1,963	1,701
Luce	8,147	7,827	6,789	6,659	5,763
Mackinac	9,287	10,853	9,660	10,178	10,674
Marquette	47,654	56,154	64,686	74,101	70,887
Menominee	25,299	24,685	24,587	26,201	24,920
Ontonagon	10,282	10,584	10,548	9,861	8,854
Schoolcraft	9,148	8,953	8,226	8,575	8,302

POPULATION PROJECTIONS – BY COUNTY

County	2005	2010	2015
Alger	10,100	10,200	10,200
Baraga	8,100	8,000	7,900
Chippewa	44,600	47,700	51,000
Delta	39,100	39,200	39,400
Dickinson	27,700	27,900	28,100
Gogebic	14,900	14,100	13,300
Houghton	37,500	38,100	38,600
Iron	11,900	11,600	11,200
Keweenaw	1,800	1,700	1,700
Luce	5,600	5,500	5,400
Mackinac	12,700	13,800	15,300
Marquette	68,400	67,600	66,700
Menominee	21,500	20,600	19,600
Ontonagon	7,700	7,400	7,000
Schoolcraft	8,900	9,000	8,900

Source: Michigan Dept. of Management and Budget, Office of the State Demographer, 1996

MOST POPULATED CITIES (2007)

City	Population	County
Marquette	20,780	Marquette
Sault Ste. Marie	16,695	Chippewa
Escanaba	12,297	Delta
Menominee	8,397	Menominee
Iron Mountain	7,816	Dickinson
Houghton	6,924	Houghton
Ishpeming	6,474	Marquette
Ironwood	5,808	Gogebic
Kingsford	5,549	Dickinson
Gladstone	5,103	Delta
Negaunee	4,451	Marquette
Hancock	4,149	Houghton
Manistique	3,368	Schoolcraft
Norway	2,841	Dickinson
West Ishpeming	2,818	Marquette
Newberry	2,579	Luce
St. Ignace	2,384	Mackinac
Munising	2,350	Alger
Laurium	1,999	Houghton
Gwinn	1,983	Marquette
L'Anse	1,888	Baraga
Bessemer	1,877	Gogebic
Wakefield	1,875	Gogebic
Iron River	1,787	Iron
Crystal Falls	1,616	Iron
Ontonagon	1,544	Ontonagon
Harvey	1,333	Marquette

Baraga	1,185	Baraga
Stambaugh	1,151	Iron
Quinnesec	1,163	Dickinson
Hubbell	1,081	Houghton
Lake Linden	1,048	Houghton
Caspian	895	Iron
Mackinac Island	843	Mackinac
Stephenson	808	Menominee
Calumet	798	Houghton
South Range	686	Houghton
Republic	619	Marquette
Palmer	453	Marquette
Powers	415	Menominee
De Tour Village	409	Chippewa
Gaastra	304	Iron
Michigamme	289	Marquette
Big Bay	267	Marquette
Daggett	254	Menominee
Garden	224	Delta
Chatham	215	Alger
Carney	212	Menominee
Mineral Hills	198	Iron
Copper City	193	Houghton

TOWNSHIPS – MOST POPULATED

Township	County	Population (2000)
Chocolay Charter	Marquette	7,148
Calumet Charter	Houghton	6,997
Breitung Charter	Dickinson	5,930
Kinross Charter	Chippewa	5,922
Wells	Delta	5,044
Forsyth	Marquette	4,824
McMillan	Luce	3,947
Menominee	Menominee	3,939
L'Anse	Baraga	3,926
Escanaba	Delta	3,587

TOWNSHIPS – LEAST POPULATED

Township	County	Population (2000)
Grand Island	Alger	45
Sherman	Keweenaw	60
West Branch	Dickinson	67
Bois Blanc	Mackinac	71
Bohemia	Ontonagon	77
Matchwood	Ontonagon	115
Turin	Marquette	131
Ewing	Marquette	159
Elm River	Houghton	169
Grant	Keweenaw	172

AGE CELLS - BY COUNTY (2005)

County	Under 5	Persons Under 18	Over 65
Alger	3.7%	17.8%	17.8%
Baraga	4.8%	20.2%	16.7%
Chippewa	4.6%	19.2%	**13.1%**
Delta	5.3%	21.6%	17.9%
Dickinson	4.8%	**21.9%**	20.2%
Gogebic	3.7%	17.9%	21.4%
Houghton	**5.4%**	19.8%	14.9%
Iron	3.7%	18.6%	22.8%
Keweenaw	4.7%	19.2%	21.7%
Luce	4.4%	19.4%	15.7%
Mackinac	4.6%	20.2%	20.6%
Marquette	4.7%	19.0%	14.0%
Menominee	5.1%	**21.9%**	17.4%
Ontonagon	**3.5%**	**17.4%**	**23.5%**
Schoolcraft	4.4%	20.5%	19.8%

*Highest and lowest percentage in each age group in **bold print**.*

BIRTHS-DEATHS – BY COUNTY

County	2002-03	2003-04	2004-05	2005-06	2006-07
Alger	75-105	87-132	66-111	75-122	77-136
Baraga	96-105	89-105	89-105	108-102	116-102
Chippewa	393-315	373-294	391-315	399-318	349-313
Delta	425-418	388-420	399-402	391-414	391-458
Dickinson	288-332	280-330	286-305	278-313	248-326
Gogebic	128-260	120-258	134-248	140-240	135-241
Houghton	390-374	385-395	407-362	388-381	395-418
Iron	87-199	93-233	97-198	106-186	117-177
Keweenaw	20 – 25	21 – 19	16 – 23	16 – 31	17 – 40
Luce	56 – 95	57 – 91	63 – 88	61 – 88	66 – 88
Mackinac	105-139	105-128	101-143	96-141	98-145
Marquette	633-641	613-646	634-618	612-627	589-654
Menominee	254-296	258-265	251-250	209-251	187-266
Ontonagon	49-110	50-115	38-133	41-120	56-107
Schoolcraft	89-108	66-124	79-107	79-124	77-139
U.P. Totals	**3,088-3,522**	**2,985-3,555**	**2,988-3,408**	**2,999-3,458**	**2,918-3,610**

Births and deaths statistics record between June 30 – July 1. Source: U.S. Census Bureau Estimated Population and Components of Population Change, 2000-2006 Source: Michigan Department of Community Health

LEADING CAUSE OF DEATH – BY COUNTY (2005)

Alger Cause	Deaths	Keweenaw Cause	Deaths
Heart Disease	29	Heart Disease	7
Cancer	25	Cancer	7
Chronic lower respiratory disease	8	Stroke	1
Stroke	5		
Diabetes	5		

Baraga

Cause	Deaths
Heart disease	42
Cancer	20
Stroke	10
Unintentional injury	6
Chronic lower Respiratory disease	4
Diabetes	4

Luce

Cause	Deaths
Cancer	16
Heart disease	14
Stroke	4
Chronic lower respiratory disease	4
Diabetes	4
Alzheimer's	4

Chippewa

Cause	Deaths
Heart disease	86
Cancer	66
Stroke	24
Chronic lower respiratory disease	14
Unintentional injury	14
Diabetes	14

Mackinac

Cause	Deaths
Cancer	43
Heart disease	32
Unintentional injury	7
Stroke	6
Pneumonia/Influenza	5
Chronic lower respiratory disease	5

Delta

Cause	Deaths
Cancer	115
Heart disease	113
Chronic lower respiratory disease	19
Pneumonia/Influenza	15
Unintentional injury	12

Marquette

Cause	Deaths
Heart disease	169
Cancer	133
Chronic lower respiratory disease	44
Stroke	36
Unintentional injury	34

Dickinson

Cause	Deaths
Heart disease	87
Cancer	76
Stroke	30
Diabetes	17
Chronic lower respiratory disease	15

Menominee

Cause	Deaths
Heart disease	73
Cancer	64
Diabetes	15
Chronic lower respiratory disease	14
Stroke	12

Gogebic

Cause	Deaths
Heart disease	79
Cancer	55
Stroke	20
Alzheimer's	13
Chronic lower respiratory disease	11
Pneumonia/Influenza	3

Ontonagon

Cause	Deaths
Heart disease	30
Cancer	25
Stoke	10
Chronic lower respiratory disease	4
Diabetes	3

Houghton

Cause	Deaths
Heart disease	119
Cancer	76
Stroke	37
Unintentional injury	17
Diabetes	16
Alzheimer's	16
Chronic lower respiratory disease	16

Schoolcraft

Cause	Deaths
Cancer	29
Heart disease	28
Stroke	15
Pneumonia/Influenza	11
Unintentional injury	6

Iron

Cause	Deaths
Heart disease	65
Cancer	39
Stroke	20
Chronic lower respiratory disease	11
Unintentional injury	10

Source: Michigan Department of Community Health

Photo S. Lake

MARRIAGE AND DIVORCE – BY COUNTY

The highest marriage rate in the U.P. is in Mackinac County, 44.3 marriages per 1,000 people (2007), more than twice the next highest rate. The likely reason for the high rate is the popularity of Mackinac Island as a wedding destination. The lowest rate of marriage occurs in Luce County where 9.6 people per 1,000 got married in 2007.

The highest divorce rate, 8.3 divorces per 1,000 people (2007), is in Delta County.

The toughest place for a divorce attorney to make a living is in Keweenaw County where there were only two divorces in 2005, seven in 2006, and eight in 2007.

2005

County	Marriages	Rate	Divorces	Rate
Alger	74	15.3	40	8.3
Baraga	36	8.2	16	3.7
Chippewa	235	12.1	106	5.5
Delta	256	13.4	130	6.8
Dickinson	211	15.1	119	8.5
Gogebic	109	12.9	61	7.2
Houghton	243	13.6	96	5.4
Iron	77	12.5	51	8.3
Keweenaw	22	20.0	2	--
Luce	45	13.3	16	14.7
Mackinac	228	40.2	44	7.8
Marquette	458	14.1	209	6.5
Menominee	190	15.2	85	6.8
Ontonagon	43	11.7	25	6.8
Schoolcraft	53	12.0	29	6.6

2006

County	Marriages	Rate	Divorces	Rate
Alger	44	9.1	38	7.9
Baraga	47	10.8	15	3.4
Chippewa	258	13.3	124	6.4
Delta	256	13.4	130	6.8
Dickinson	231	12.1	123	6.4
Gogebic	108	131	55	6.7

Houghton	221	12.5	80	4.5
Iron	91	14.7	46	7.4
Keweenaw	24	22.0	7	6.4
Luce	43	12.9	21	6.3
Mackinac	177	32.0	37	6.7
Marquette	464	14.3	215	6.6
Menominee	180	14.6	74	6.0
Ontonagon	27	7.5	23	6.4
Schoolcraft	49	7.5	23	6.4
Michigan	59,400	11.8	35,022	6.9

2007

County	Marriages	Rate	Divorces	Rate
Alger	59	12.2	31	6.4
Baraga	43	9.8	18	4.1
Chippewa	200	10.3	132	6.8
Delta	242	12.7	158	8.3
Dickinson	186	13.6	112	8.2
Gogebic	91	11.0	42	5.1
Houghton	241	13.6	90	5.1
Iron	66	10.7	45	7.3
Keweenaw	21	19.2	8	7.3
Luce	32	9.6	22	6.6
Mackinac	245	44.3	41	7.4
Marquette	483	14.9	206	6.4
Menominee	168	13.6	89	7.2
Ontonagon	44	12.2	15	4.2
Schoolcraft	55	12.6	27	6.2

Source: Michigan Department of Community Health.
Marriage and Divorce rates are persons per 1,000 population rather than events per population.

HOUSING UNITS PER COUNTY (2000 – '05)

County	2000	2001	2002	2003	2004	2005	rank '05
Marquette	32,940	33,200	33,345	33,503	33,828	34,080	29
Chippewa	19,430	19,485	19,710	19,941	20,234	20,530	46
Delta	19,282	19,523	19,765	19,769	19,889	20,045	48
Houghton	17,774	17,881	17,980	18,129	18,206	18,287	49
Menominee	13,675	13,825	13,935	14,053	14,140	14,226	63
Dickinson	13,726	13,825	13,879	13,928	14,000	14,038	65
Gogebic	10,849	10,892	10,932	10,981	11,012	11,025	70
Mackinac	9,446	9,580	9,690	9,774	9,956	10,135	72
Iron	8,783	8,828	8,892	8,932	8,972	8,999	77
Alger	5,987	6,080	6,133	6,195	6,267	6,458	78
Schoolcraft	5,716	5,775	5,834	5,885	5,943	5,995	79
Ontonagon	5,413	5,449	5,470	5,509	5,546	5,590	80
Baraga	4,646	4,708	4,747	4,765	4,797	4,821	81
Luce	4,016	4,051	4,102	4,150	4,200	4,250	82
Keweenaw	2,332	2,348	2,370	2,391	2,410	2,410	83

CRIME STATISTICS (2006), BY COUNTY

County	Murder	Rape	Robbery	Aggravated Assault	Burglary	Larceny	Auto Theft	Arson
Alger	0	5	0	2	34	63	2	2
Baraga	0	4	2	6	24	40	4	2
Chippewa	1	16	4	53	235	632	55	2
Delta	0	11	0	16	89	245	10	7
Dickinson	0	14	1	25	61	377	15	2
Gogebic	0	3	0	9	6	25	1	2
Houghton	0	9	2	43	119	471	22	6
Iron	0	11	1	13	47	127	23	3
Keweenaw	0	1	0	1	25	30	2	1
Luce	0	12	0	7	36	57	6	0
Mackinac	0	12	0	25	90	480	18	2
Marquette	1	45	7	58	273	1,118	94	8
Menominee	0	8	4	31	166	333	13	3
Ontonagon	0	3	0	9	15	30	5	0
Schoolcraft	0	3	0	7	47	53	9	3

Source: Michigan State Police

NATIVE AMERICANS OF UPPER MICHIGAN

According to tradition, the primary native people to occupy the region now known as Upper Michigan were part of the Algonquian body, which included the Chippewa (European corruption of Ojibwe or Ojibwa, which means "to roast until puckered up" referring to the moccasins they wore), Ottawa (Odawa) and Potawatomi. There was a time, according to Ojibwa lore, when their people lived near an ocean. This may have been at the mouth of the St. Lawrence River in eastern Canada, but it well may have been on the shore of Hudson Bay. About 1400, as the climate cooled leading into the Little Ice Age, the Algonquians began migrating southward to what is now the Upper Peninsula.

When Frenchman Etienne Brule visited the Lake Superior region in 1620, he left no written record of the Indians he encountered. A quarter-century later, Iroquois hostility in what is now eastern Ontario forced the Huron nation and other Ottawa tribes westward to Mackinac Island and eventually Green Bay. A contingent of Ottawa also moved northwest to Keweenaw Bay. There, Jesuit missionary Rene Menard unsuccessfully tried to establish a mission in 1660. The Indians who lived in the Straits area near present-day St. Ignace cultivated beans, corn, peas, squash, and melons and also took large quantities of whitefish. The Huron and Odawa villages at St. Ignace were separated by palisades and they communicated with each other through an interpreter, so different were their languages.

During this time, the Chippewa seasonally occupied the fertile fishing grounds at the entrance to Lake Superior. In 1641, two missionaries, Isaac Jogues and Charles Raymbault, visited these people and named the rapids near the entrance to Superior "Sault Ste. Marie" (Falls of St. Mary). By 1670, the Ojibwa population at the Sault grew from 150 to 550 after neighboring tribes were united.

Farther south, the Noquet Indians inhabited the area around present-day Escanaba. Their ranks were never very large (around 100 early in the 18th Century) since they were incorporated with other tribes, especially the Chippewa in the latter portion of the 17th Century. The

Menominee River was home to the Menominee or Wild Rice People. They numbered around 200 in 1721. The Huron permanently left the Upper Peninsula, settling in Detroit just after that southern Great Lakes outpost was formed by Cadillac around 1700. The Odawa gradually left the St. Ignace area for points south in an effort to find more fertile soil. By 1741, as most of them left, the Chippewa moved in.

As the 18th Century advanced, control of the Lake Superior region went from the French to the British and finally to the Americans with the Treaty of Paris in 1783. At this point, the Ojibwa became the primary Indian tribe along the south shore of Lake Superior, occupying small villages at the mouth of the Ontonagon, at the head of Keweenaw Bay, near present-day Marquette, on Grand Island and at the Sault. The Menominee remained along the Menominee River to the south.

With the dawn of the 19th Century, Indians in the territory remained openly pro-British. When the War of 1812 broke out, Fort Mackinac was attacked by a British-Indian force consisting of Chippewa, Ottawa and Menominee. Native tribes were slow to warm to American influence even after the war ended two years later. In 1820, Lewis Cass led the first official U.S. expedition into the Lake Superior territory. He held a council with area chiefs to discuss cessation of land at Sault Ste. Marie. One of the chiefs, Sessaba, walked out of the meeting in disgust and raised a British flag. Cass took the flag down and there was fear on both sides of a fight. With the help of Susan Johnston, (Ozha-guscoday-way-quay, wife of fur trader John Johnston, a full-blooded Ojibwa of high lineage) violence was averted and a treaty signed. The Indians ceded 16 square miles of land at the Sault to the Americans who constructed a fort on a portion of it near the St. Marys River at the Sault.

By the mid-1820s, the first Indian census showed a population of around 800 spread among villages in Sault Ste. Marie, at the Tahquamenon River, Grand Island, L'Anse, the Ontonagon River and along the Menominee River. The Chippewa were in constant warfare with the Sioux to the west. This continued to some extent until the middle of the century.

By the mid-1830s, Indian debt to traders had risen so high the debtors had only one option—sell their land. Indian agent Henry Rowe Schoolcraft viewed this situation as "an interval of transition between the hunter and agricultural state." G.W. Featherstonhaugh, an English travel writer touring the Lake Superior region in 1835, gave a more grim assessment of the "sad fate of the Indians." He observed that before the white man came, there was enough game to feed and clothe the native population. Then white traders offered them blankets instead of furs and fostered a need for firearms, tobacco and whiskey. Then, according to Featherstonhaugh, "The Indian must kill all the animals he meets with, not to subsist upon, but to carry the skins to the trader to discharge his debts." This practice brought a scarcity of game and soon the trader abandoned the Indians. "This state of things would cause their immediate extinction, but for the policy of the American government." The policy took the form of a treaty-bargain where the government seized Indian land and drove the previous owners "to a more distant region." Featherstonhaugh felt there was no alternative for the native people of the Great Lakes.

Susan Johnston

The Ojibwa and Menominee, the primary tribes of the Upper Peninsula, ceded all their land by 1842 (see below). As early as 1838, after the first major sell-off of land, the Sault Ste. Marie Chippewa met with Indian Agent Schoolcraft and strongly opposed removal to Missouri, objecting to the soil, climate and lack of forested land in that region. Over the next two decades there were periodic threats of removal. It went so far as a removal order signed by President Zachary Taylor in 1850. The order was held in suspension when Taylor died two days later. The sentiment of whites against Indian removal grew. Abner Sherman of Ontonagon fought for allowing the Indians to remain, pointing out that they carried out many necessary tasks for the whites and were seen to be "civilized." The next year, the Michigan legislature strongly requested that removal be halted. President Franklin Pierce finally veered away from removal later in 1853.

The Michigan legislature recognized the Ojibwa as full-qualified citizens of the state in 1867. The population was spread out among reservations and communities near L'Anse, Lac Vieux Desert along the Wisconsin border, Sault Ste. Marie, Marquette and in Mackinac County. A band of Potawatami Indians, with the aid of Methodist minister Peter Marksman, settled in the south-central Upper Peninsula west of Escanaba. This tribe today is known as the Hannahville Indian community.

In 1880, the Indian population of Upper Michigan was placed at 1,640. The next year, an Indian agent said the native population was "so…scattered among the whites…that it is almost impossible to get a correct enumeration." By 1885, another agent stated that "…the race will disappear in Michigan within fifty years."

That prophecy did not come to pass. Today, the various bands of native people exert their influence on all corners of the Upper Peninsula. From Watersmeet to L'Anse and Marquette; from Brimley to Sault Ste. Marie and Hannahville, Native Americans keep their rich Upper Michigan heritage alive.

TRIBAL TREATIES

In 1781, the Ojibwa and Odawa nations deeded over Mackinac Island to the British. There a fort was built at the height of the war against the Americans. Four years later, the Chippewa gifted Bois Blanc Island to the U.S. government for an annual payment of $1000. The first formal cessation of Upper Peninsula land by the Ojibwa nation to the United States occurred in 1820. A 16-square-mile tract of land was given to the United States government to build a fort on the St. Marys River. The fort came to be known as Fort Brady, named after the commander of the soldiers sent to establish the fort at Sault Ste. Marie—the first permanent American settlement in Upper Michigan.

On March 28, 1836, the Ojibwa and Odawa nations of the Michigan Territory ceded a large portion of their land to the United States. This huge tract included roughly the eastern half of the Upper Peninsula of Michigan west to the Chocolate (now Chocolay) River then south to the head of the Skonawba (now Escanaba) River to its mouth. At the same time in the Wisconsin Territory, the Menominee, residing on the Fox River in Wisconsin, cede their lands to the federal government. They also turned over their lands in portions of present-day Menominee and Delta Counties.

The rest of Upper Michigan was ceded by the Ojibwa of Lake Superior on October 4, 1842 at La Pointe. This treaty opened the mineral lands of the western U.P. to exploration and a copper rush occurred over the next several years.

Two treaties in the mid-1850s created permanent homelands for the Ojibwa in Upper Michigan. The Treaty of 1854 affirmed that the L'Anse tribe would "not be required to remove from the homes thereby set apart for them." And further, those that "reside in the territory hereby ceded, shall have the right to hunt and fish therein."

Local Ojibwa chiefs with Methodist missionary John Pitezel standing far left.
(Courtesy of Fred Rydholm from
"Superior Heartland, A Backwoods History")

After the treaty of 1854, the Ojibwa of Katikitegon (Lac Vieux Desert) left L'Anse and returned to their home along the Upper Michigan-Wisconsin line. When the ceded Indian lands were placed on public sale, the Katikitegon people pooled part of their winter hunting yield, took the furs to the Public Land Office in Marquette and purchased the land they were living on.

Out east, the Ojibwa residing around the Sault signed another treaty with the United States in 1855 allotting lands to Anishinabeg (Chippewa) families. The Treaty of 1836 gave the Indians 250,000 acres of land, but over the next two decades, the terms of the treaty were violated by white settlers moving into the area. This treaty was designed to affirm the Ojibwa claim to that land.

During the 20th Century, the original band of Chippewa Indians was given federal status as the Sault Ste. Marie Band of Chippewa Indians apart from the Bay Mills Indian Community. The Lac Vieux Desert tribe was officially recognized as a distinct tribe apart from the Keweenaw Bay Indian Community (L'Anse tribe).

In 2007, a hunting and fishing agreement was reached with the State of Michigan and five native tribes, among them the Sault Ste. Marie Chippewa. The decree recognizes and upholds tribal rights of the Treaty of 1836. The treaty gave Indians the right to hunt and fish on the land ceded. This new pact recognizes and clarifies these tribal rights, while providing a working relationship between the state and the tribes on issues of game management.

NATIVE AMERICAN COMMUNITIES OF THE U.P.

Bay Mills Indian Community (Ojibwa), Brimley

Established: 1854

Members: 1,758 (Membership by quarter blood quantum)

Reservation Size: 2,209 acres

Reservation established by Act of Congress June, 1837

Constitution and bylaws approved in 1837 as part of Indian Reorganization Act

Governing body is General Tribal Council which includes all members over 18 years of age. Chairman, vice-chair, treasurer and secretary elected by popular vote.

Hannahville Indian Community (Potawatomi), 26 miles west of Escanaba

Established: 1913 by Act of Congress

Members: 802

Living on reservation: 466

Reservation size: 5,200 acres

Constitution approved July 23, 1836 under Indian Reorganization Act

Governed by tribal council whose 12 members are elected annually.

Keweenaw Bay Indian Community, L'Anse

Established: 1854 (treaty)

Members: 3,159

Reservation size: 54,000 acres. The tribal community owns approximately 14,000 acres.

Constitution and bylaws approved December, 1836 under Indian Reorganization Act.

Governed by twelve-member tribal council elected to three year terms.

Lac Vieux Desert Band of Lake Superior Chippewa, Watersmeet

Established: Federally recognized in 1988

Members: 614

Living on reservation: 122

Reservation size: 300 acres

Sault Ste. Marie Tribe of Chippewa Indians, Sault Ste. Marie

Established: Formally recognized by Secretary of Interior, 1974

Members: 38,083

Reservation size: 400 acres total including land in Sault Ste. Marie, St. Ignace, Hessell-Cedarville, Manistique, Escanaba, Munising, and Marquette

Constitution and bylaws approved in November, 1975.

Governed by a board of ten directors elected to four-year terms.

MULTI-CULTURAL MELTING POT

The Copper Country of the Upper Peninsula became a melting pot of diversity with the growth of the copper and iron mining industries. By the mid-19th century, the industrial revolution was heating up in the United States and demand for raw materials was increasing, as was the need for labor. The opening of the Erie Canal in 1826 made it possible to sail the Great Lakes from New York to developing industrial port cities such as Buffalo, Cleveland, Detroit, Milwaukee, and Chicago. Immigrants from Europe were discovering freedom and jobs, which were in short supply in their countries of origin.

With the opening of the first copper mines around Houghton and Keweenaw counties in the 1840s, the "Help Wanted" signs went up around the new mining operations. The first groups of immigrants to answer the call were the Cornish and Welsh. They brought along the customs and culture of the Old Country, including a strong work ethic that led to long hours in the mines. Many of the Cornish immigrants were experienced miners, who brought with them the latest techniques in mine building and operations. Cornish miners heading underground for the day packed a warm half-moon shaped sandwich stuffed with meat, potatoes, and rutabagas. At mealtime they placed the enclosed sandwich

on a shovel and heated it over a fire. The Pasty lives on today in restaurants and kitchens across the U.P.

Although the English were the first large group of immigrants to arrive in the Copper Country, the Finns became the most influential. In the 1860s, letters recruiting mine workers were mailed to Finnish communities in northern Norway and Finland and agents of the mining companies were sent across the ocean on recruiting missions. The first Finnish immigrants from Norway arrived in Calumet in May of 1865. The first Finns lived in homes at "Swedetown" near the Quincy Mine. Eventually thousands of families from Finland, Norway and Sweden settled in the mining towns of the central and western U.P. They worked hard, raised families, and built homes, churches, schools and businesses. In 1896, the local Lutheran Finnish community founded Suomi College as a theological training school. In 1876, Hancock resident Antti Muikku published the first Finnish newspaper, *Amerikan Suomalainen Lehti* (America's Finnish Newspaper) in the United States.

Immigrants from Ireland, Italy, Germany, Poland, Czechoslovakia, and other European countries arrived in large numbers after the Civil War. They found work in the mines and became part of the melting pot alongside the Cornish, Scandinavians, French-Canadians and Native Americans. By 1870, two thirds of the mine workers in the U.P. were Cornish or Irish.

With the labor strikes of the early 20th century some of the Finnish workers took jobs in the lumber industry, and later farmed the land. By the turn of the century there were over 60,000 Finns living in the U.S., with 18,000 of them in the Upper Peninsula—the largest concentration of Finns in the U.S.

PERSONS BORN IN FINLAND LIVING IN THE U.P. (1900 U.S. CENSUS)

Alger	248	Keweenaw	710
Baraga	378	Luce	213
Chippewa	286	Mackinac	155
Delta	437	Marquette	3,871
Dickinson	372	Menominee	135
Gogebic	2,618	Ontonagon	251
Houghton	7,241	Schoolcraft	299
Iron	889	Total:	17,180

The Finnish culture was dominant, but not exclusive. There were strong communities of Italians, Germans, Hungarians, Poles, Swedes, and Norwegians. In 1910, Calumet schools showed students from 40 different nationalities on their enrollment records. In the early 1900's, there were six Catholic churches active in Calumet: Italian, Polish, Slovenian, Croatian, French, and one general. This multicultural society managed to protect, celebrate, and share their native customs and way of life, while adapting to the New World. Although there were cultural differences among the citizens of the bustling industrial towns, they all shared one thing in common: they were laborers who spent long hours involved in physically demanding and often dangerous work.

MOST COMMON FIRST ANCESTRIES, BY COUNTY

Alger County
- Finnish (15%)
- German (12%)
- French (except Basque) (10%)
- Polish (7%)
- United States or American (6%)
- English (6%)
- Irish (6%)

Baraga County
- Finnish (29%)
- German (10%)
- French (except Basque) (9%)
- French Canadian (5%)
- Irish (4%)
- Norwegian (3%)
- English (3%)

Chippewa County
- German (15%)
- English (10%)
- Irish (9%)
- French (except Basque) (7%)
- Polish (6%)
- United States or American (5%)
- Italian (4%)

Delta County
- French (except Basque) (16%)
- German (15%)
- Swedish (11%)
- French Canadian (11%)
- Irish (6%)
- English (5%)
- United States or American (4%)

Dickinson County
- Italian (17%)
- German (17%)
- Swedish (11%)
- French (except Basque) (8%)
- English (8%)
- Polish (6%)
- Irish (5%)

Gogebic County
- Finnish (23%)
- Italian (13%)
- German (13%)
- Polish (9%)
- Swedish (6%)
- English (6%)
- Irish (5%)

Houghton County
- Finnish (35%)
- German (12%)
- English (7%)
- French (except Basque) (7%)
- Italian (6%)
- Irish (4%)
- Polish (3%)

Iron County
- German (14%)
- Italian (13%)
- Finnish (13%)
- Polish (11%)
- Swedish (10%)
- English (7%)
- French (except Basque) (6%)

Keweenaw County
- Finnish (37%)
- German (10%)
- English (9%)
- Italian (7%)
- French (except Basque) (6%)
- Irish (4%)
- Polish (4%)

Luce County
- German (20%)
- English (10%)
- United States or American (10%)
- Irish (8%)
- French (except Basque) (8%)
- Finnish (5%)
- Swedish (4%)

Mackinac County
- German (19%)
- English (9%)
- Irish (8%)
- French (except Basque) (7%)
- United States or American (6%)
- Polish (6%)
- Swedish (4%)

Marquette County
- Finnish (21%)
- German (12%)
- English (11%)
- French (except Basque) (9%)
- Italian (8%)
- Irish (7%)
- Swedish (6%)

Menominee County
- German (27%)
- French (except Basque) (11%)
- Polish (10%)
- Swedish (8%)
- French Canadian (7%)
- Irish (5%)
- United States or American (5%)

Ontonagon County
- Finnish (33%)
- German (15%)
- Polish (7%)
- English (6%)
- Irish (5%)
- French (except Basque) (5%)
- United States or American (5%)

Schoolcraft County
- German (19%)
- French (except Basque) (11%)
- Swedish (9%)
- English (8%)
- French Canadian (7%)
- United States or American (7%)
- Irish (6%)

MOST COMMON PLACES OF BIRTH FOR FOREIGN-BORN RESIDENTS

Alger County
- Canada (19%)
- United Kingdom (13%)
- Philippines (13%)
- Germany (12%)
- Other Northern Europe (9%)
- Trinidad and Tobago (7%)
- Other Western Asia (6%)

Baraga County
- Other Northern Europe (20%)
- Germany (14%)
- Philippines (14%)
- Canada (14%)
- Italy (8%)
- Australia (8%)
- Haiti (8%)

Chippewa County
- Canada (63%)
- Germany (8%)
- United Kingdom (7%)
- Philippines (3%)
- Italy (2%)
- Japan (2%)
- Laos (2%)

Delta County
- Canada (20%)
- Other Northern Europe (13%)
- United Kingdom (10%)
- Korea (9%)
- Germany (9%)
- Philippines (4%)
- Italy (4%)

Dickinson County
- Italy (16%)
- Canada (12%)
- Korea (11%)
- Germany (9%)
- France (6%)
- India (6%)
- Philippines (6%)

Gogebic County
- Other Northern Europe (19%)
- Italy (19%)
- United Kingdom (14%)
- Germany (7%)
- Korea (6%)
- Canada (6%)
- Yugoslavia (4%)

Houghton County
- China, excluding Hong Kong and Taiwan (14%)
- Canada (9%)
- Germany (8%)
- India (8%)
- Other Northern Europe (7%)
- Other Western Africa (7%)
- Thailand (3%)

Iron County
- Canada (24%)
- Italy (13%)
- Germany (11%)
- United Kingdom (9%)
- Other Northern Europe (9%)
- Other Eastern Europe (5%)
- Vietnam (4%)

Keweenaw County
- Canada (33%)
- United Kingdom (21%)
- France (13%)
- Austria (8%)
- Other Western Europe (8%)
- Italy (8%)
- Born at sea (8%)

Luce County
- Canada (35%)
- Germany (24%)
- Mexico (12%)
- Chile (8%)
- Guatemala (7%)
- Philippines (5%)
- Sweden (3%)

Mackinac County
- Canada (40%)
- Germany (19%)
- Brazil (10%)
- United Kingdom (7%)
- Philippines (6%)
- Micronesia (5%)
- Russia (3%)

Marquette County
- Canada (18%)
- Germany (11%)
- United Kingdom (7%)
- Italy (6%)
- Korea (6%)
- China, excluding Hong Kong and Taiwan (5%)
- Other Northern Europe (3%)

Menominee County
- United Kingdom (18%)
- Canada (15%)
- Poland (15%)
- Germany (14%)
- Sweden (11%)
- Korea (7%)
- Jamaica (3%)

Ontonagon County
- Germany (29%)
- Canada (20%)
- United Kingdom (19%)
- Other Northern Europe (11%)
- Korea (5%)
- Poland (5%)
- Japan (4%)

Schoolcraft County
- Canada (34%)
- United Kingdom (18%)
- Germany (18%)
- Korea (11%)
- Poland (4%)
- Other Eastern Europe (4%)
- Vietnam (3%)

RELIGION

BISHOP FREDERIC BARAGA

The venerable "Snowshoe Priest," Frederic Baraga, was born June 29, 1797 in Slovenia in the northwest corner of what is now Yugoslavia. He grew up during a time of great upheaval in Europe but still had a normal boyhood. A normal childhood in Slovenia meant the study of multiple languages. By the time a youth left school, he was fluent in not only Slovene but German, French, Latin and Greek. This training in language would be an invaluable tool for Baraga's missionary work in America. Young Frederic also developed a talent in art and spent his holidays on long hikes—developing a skill that would serve him well in the Lake Superior wilderness.

Courtesy of Marquette Diocese

Baraga attended the University of Vienna with intentions of becoming a lawyer. During this time, he became engaged to a professor's daughter. Always devout and prayerful, Baraga joined a student group whose objective was personal sanctification through imitating the life of Jesus. It appears this experience led him to break his engagement, leave the University and enter the seminary. He was ordained in September of 1823.

Over the next several years, Baraga was as an assistant in various local parishes. He developed a large following and even wrote and edited devotional books for the common person. During this time, a Yugoslavian priest, an official in the Diocese of Cincinnati, came to Europe soliciting funds and clergy for the poor missions of the northern Midwest. This plea caught Baraga's attention and he decided to sign on as a missionary. He sold off his meager belongings, left his homeland and arrived in New York on New Year's Eve 1830.

Father Baraga's first assignment was at Arbre Croche near present-day Harbor Springs in northern Lower Michigan. There he studied and quickly learned the Ottawa and Chippewa languages. By 1832, he had already written the first of his many Indian language books. After a difficult stay at Grand River (now Grand Rapids), Baraga was transferred to the shores of Lake Superior where he would spend the rest of his life.

Baraga's first Lake Superior mission was at Indian Lake near Manistique. He visited the local Indians in the summer of 1832 and found they had already constructed a small chapel. Baraga dedicated the church to the Virgin Mary, fulfilling a vow he made that the first church he blessed among the Indians would be dedicated to her name.

Three years later, he arrived at La Pointe in the Apostle Islands at the site where the French Jesuits Allouez and Marquette had established a mission 165 years earlier. With only summer clothing and three dollars to his name, he arrived at La Pointe in late July 1835. He suffered much hardship that first severe winter reporting large blocks of ice still floating on Lake Superior in June 1836. La Pointe became Baraga's headquarters over the next several years. He traveled extensively, making trips on snowshoes to Fond du Lac (now Duluth), Grand Portage and Fort William (now Thunder Bay) on the west end of Lake Superior. Finally in 1843, at the urging of a fur trader named Crebassa, Baraga established a mission near present-day L'Anse

The Cross of Baraga's "Grand Traverse" near Shroeder, Minnesota.

on the shores of Keweenaw Bay in Upper Michigan.

The L'Anse mission became Baraga's base for the next decade. Rapid, irrevocable change came to the Lake Superior wilderness during this time. The Chippewa nation ceded the last of their holdings to the United States in 1842 and a mining boom immediately followed. While ministering to the Ojibwa, Baraga also served a growing population of white settlers. In 1853, he was elevated to Bishop of the newly-formed Sault Ste. Marie diocese. He moved to the Sault and made that his base of operation for most of the rest of his life.

Baraga's exploits quickly became a legend in the region. He was venerated for his faith and endurance, traveling many hundreds of miles throughout the Lake Superior region on snowshoes. On one occasion, Baraga undertook a 250-mile journey from L'Anse to near present-day Duluth to deliver medicine to a widow and her five sick children. On another, he was forced to walk for 24 hours straight to keep from freezing to death when he set out on a 30-mile "tramp" and only made it half way during daylight. His exploits were not confined to just winter. In the summer of 1846, he convinced a voyageur to take him across Lake Superior in a canoe. The 70-mile trip from the Apostle Islands to present-day Schroeder, Minnesota was safely completed and later, a wealthy fur trader on hearing of the miraculous voyage, set up a monument at the spot where they landed.

German travel writer Johann Georg Kohl, who traveled briefly with Baraga in the summer of 1855, wrote "Baraga is made of iron. Nothing holds him back and he lives even in places where an Indian would die of starvation." The privations and hardship did take their toll in later life. In 1865, the bishop admitted as much: "Now I first feel the results of my former mission hardships and physical exertions. I was told long ago that I would feel it in my old age, but at that time I did not believe it. Now I believe it, because I feel it."

Bishop Baraga moved to Marquette in 1866 where he spent the last of his life. He died in 1868 and was buried in a crypt at St. Peter's Cathedral. The Bishop Baraga Association, a member-funded organization headquartered in Marquette, preserves his extensive writings with the long-term goal of having the Catholic Church name him a Saint.

Baraga's residence in Marquette.

RELIGIOUS DENOMINATIONS – BY COUNTY (2000)

ALGER COUNTY

Catholic	3,150
Evangelical Protestant	1,176
Mainline Protestant	1,201
Other	3
Unclaimed	4,332

Religious Body	Theology	Congregations	Adherents
Assemblies of God	Evangelical Protestant	1	52
Association of Free Lutheran Congregation	Evangelical Protestant	1	180
Baha'I	Other Theology	0	3
Catholic Church	Catholic	4	3,150
Episcopal Church	Mainline Protestant	1	59
Evangelical Lutheran	Mainline Protestant	4	839
General Assoc. of Regular Baptist Churches	Evangelical Protestant	1	130
Lutheran Church –Missouri	Evangelical Protestant	2	543
Mennonite Church USA	Evangelical Protestant	1	25
Presbyterian Church USA	Mainline Protestant	1	89
Seventh-day Adventist	Evangelical Protestant	1	75
United Methodist Church	Mainline Protestant	3	214
Wesleyan Church	Evangelical Protestant	1	171
TOTAL		21	5,130

BARAGA COUNTY

Catholic	2,477
Mainline Protestant	1,908
Evangelical Protestant	389
Other	132
Unclaimed	3,840

Religious Body	Theology	Congregations	Adherents
Baha'I	Other Theology	0	1
Catholic Church	Catholic	3	2,477
Church of Jesus Christ of Latter-day Saints	Other Theology	1	131
Evangelical Lutheran	Mainline Protestant	5	1,664
General Association of Regular Baptist Churches	Evangelical Protestant	1	91
Lutheran Church-Missouri	Evangelical Protestant	1	277
Seventh-day Adventist	Evangelical Protestant	1	21
United Methodist	Mainline Protestant	2	244
TOTAL		14	4,906

CHIPPEWA COUNTY

Catholic	7,295
Evangelical Protestant	3,584
Mainline Protestant	2,845
Orthodox	69
Other	19
Unclaimed	24,731

Religious Body	Theology	Congregations	Adherents
American Baptist Churches	Mainline Protestant	1	93
Assemblies of God	Evangelical Protestant	3	178
Baha'I	Other Theology	0	19
Catholic Church	Catholic	12	7,295
Christian Churches and Churches of Christ	Evangelical Protestant	3	608
Christian Reformed Church	Evangelical Protestant	2	381
Church of the Nazarene	Evangelical Protestant	3	301
Church of Christ	Evangelical Protestant	1	26
Community of Christ	Evangelical Protestant	1	71
Episcopal Church	Mainline Protestant	4	216
Evangelical Lutheran	Mainline Protestant	2	676
Free Methodist Church	Evangelical Protestant	1	61
General Association of Regular Baptist Churches	Evangelical Protestant	1	97
Greek Orthodox	Orthodox	1	69
Lutheran Church-Missouri	Evangelical Protestant	4	234
Mennonite Church	Evangelical Protestant	1	31
Pentecostal Church of God	Evangelical Protestant	1	75
Presbyterian Church USA	Mainline Protestant	8	976
Reformed Baptist Churches	Evangelical Protestant	1	na
Salvation Army	Evangelical Protestant	1	261
Southern Baptist Convention	Evangelical Protestant	2	677
United Methodist Church	Mainline Protestant	5	884
Wesleyan Church	Evangelical Protestant	1	320
Wisconsin Evangelical Lutheran Synod	Evangelical Protestant	1	263
TOTAL		60	13,812

DELTA COUNTY

Catholic	20,547
Mainline Protestant	6,595
Evangelical Protestant	3,410
Other	157
Unclaimed	7,811

Religious Body	Theology	Congregations	Adherents
Assemblies of God	Evangelical Protestant	1	350
Association of Free Lutheran Congregations	Evangelical Protestant	1	38
Baha'I	Other Theology	0	27
Baptist General Conference	Evangelical Protestant	2	585
Catholic Church	Catholic	11	20,547
Christian Churches and Churches of Christ	Evangelical Protestant	1	155
Church of God (Cleveland, TN)	Evangelical Protestant	1	107
Church of Jesus Christ of Latter-day Saints	Other Theology	1	130
Church of the Nazarene	Evangelical Protestant	1	48
Churches of Christ	Evangelical Protestant	1	95
Community of Christ	Evangelical Protestant	1	91
Episcopal Church	Mainline Protestant	3	526
Evangelical Covenant	Evangelical Protestant	1	184
Evangelical Lutheran	Mainline Protestant	10	4,326
Free Methodist Church	Evangelical Protestant	1	38
General Association of Regular Baptist Churches	Evangelical Protestant	1	79
Lutheran Church-Missouri	Evangelical Protestant	1	388
Mennonite Church	Evangelical Protestant	1	38
Nat'l Association of Congregational Christian	Mainline Protestant	3	244
Presbyterian Church USA	Mainline Protestant	1	341
Salvation Army	Evangelical Protestant	1	431
Seventh-day Adventist	Evangelical Protestant	2	163
United Methodist Church	Mainline Protestant	4	1,158
Wisconsin Evangelical Lutheran Synod	Evangelical Protestant	4	620
TOTAL		55	30,709

DICKINSON COUNTY

Catholic	14,460
Mainline Protestant	5,315
Evangelical Protestant	2,817
Orthodox	96
Other	7
Unclaimed	4,777

Turrets of Society of St. John monastery near Eagle River, Keweenaw County

Religious Body	Theology	Congregations	Adherents
Antiochian Orthodox Christian Archdiocese	Orthodox	1	96
Assemblies of God	Evangelical Protestant	1	363
Baha'I	Other Theology	0	7
Baptist General Conference	Evangelical Protestant	3	541
Catholic Church	Catholic	8	14,460
Christian Churches and and Churches of Christ	Evangelical Protestant	1	147
Church of God (Cleveland, TN)	Evangelical Protestant	1	13
Episcopal Church	Mainline Protestant	1	377
Evangelical Covenant	Evangelical Protestant	3	620
Fellowship of Evangelical Bible Churches	Evangelical Protestant	1	25
General Association of Regular Baptist Churches	Evangelical Protestant	1	210
Lutheran Church-Missouri	Evangelical Protestant	1	612
Presbyterian Church USA	Mainline Protestant	2	664
Salvation Army	Evangelical Protestant	1	79
Seventh-day Adventist	Evangelical Protestant	1	61
Southern Baptist Convention	Evangelical Protestant	1	79
United Methodist Church	Mainline Protestant	4	1,088
Wisconsin Evangelical Lutheran Synod	Evangelical Protestant	1	136
TOTAL		37	22,695

GOGEBIC COUNTY

Catholic	5,588
Mainline Protestant	3,695
Evangelical Protestant	1,518
Orthodox	34
Other	1
Unclaimed	6,534

Religious Body	Theology	Congregations	Adherents
Antiochian Orthodox Christian Archdiocese	Orthodox	1	34
Assemblies of God	Evangelical Protestant	1	80
Baptist General Conference	Evangelical Protestant	1	78
Catholic Church	Catholic	5	5,588
Churches of Christ	Evangelical Protestant	1	8
Episcopal Church	Mainline Protestant	1	57
Evangelical Lutheran	Evangelical Protestant	6	3,236
General Association of Regular Baptist Churches	Evangelical Protestant	2	242
Lutheran Church-Missouri	Evangelical Protestant	4	1,083
Presbyterian Church USA	Mainline Protestant	3	109
Seventh-day Adventist	Evangelical Protestant	1	27
United Methodist Church	Mainline Protestant	2	293
TOTAL		28	10,836

HOUGHTON COUNTY

Catholic 9,810
Mainline Protestant 5,268
Evangelical Protestant 2,290
Other 386
Unclaimed 18,262

Religious Body	Theology	Congregations	Adherents
Assemblies of God	Evangelical Protestant	1	499
Association of Free Lutheran Congregations	Evangelical Protestant	2	113
Baha'I	Other Theology	0	19
Catholic Church	Catholic	11	9,810
Christian Churches and and Churches of Christ	Evangelical Protestant	1	90
Church of the Nazarene	Evangelical Protestant	1	11
Churches of Christ	Evangelical Protestant	1	29
Episcopal Church	Mainline Protestant	2	265
Evangelical Lutheran	Mainline Protestant	8	3,401
Friends (Quaker)	Mainline Protestant	2	108
General Association of Regular Baptist Churches	Evangelical Protestant	2	260
Jewish Estimate	Other Theology	1	150
Lutheran Church-Missouri	Evangelical Protestant	3	362
Menonite; Other Groups	Evangelical Protestant	1	51
Muslim Estimate	Other Theology	1	163
Presbyterian Church USA	Mainline Protestant	2	85
Russian Orthodox	Orthodox	1	na
Salvation Army	Evangelical Protestant	1	72
Seventh-day Adventist	Evangelical Protestant	1	80
Southern Baptist Convention	Evangelical Protestant	1	85
Unitarian Universalist	Other Theology	1	54
United Church of Christ	Mainline Protestant	2	146
United Methodist Church	Mainline Protestant	7	1,263
Wisconsin Evangelical Lutheran Synod	Evangelical Protestant	2	338
TOTAL		55	17,754

IRON COUNTY

Catholic 4,736
Mainline Protestant 2,377
Evangelical Protestant 887
Other 191
Unclaimed 4,947

The Most Holy Name of Jesus Church (later destroyed by fire) at Father Baraga's mission near Keweenaw Bay.

Religious Body	Theology	Congregations	Adherents
Assemblies of God	Evangelical Protestant	1	65
Baha'I	Other Theology	0	3
Baptist General Conference	Evangelical Protestant	2	150
Calvary Chapel Fellowship	Evangelical Protestant	1	na
Catholic Church	Catholic	3	4,736
Church of Jesus Christ Of Latter-day Saints	Evangelical Protestant	1	188
Church of the Nazarene	Evangelical Protestant	1	36
Episcopal Church	Mainline Protestant	2	59
Evangelical Covenant	Evangelical Protestant	1	272
Evangelical Lutheran	Mainline Protestant	4	1,815
General Association of Regular Baptist Churches	Evangelical Protestant	1	41
Lutheran Church-Missouri	Evangelical Protestant	2	214
Presbyterian Church USA	Mainline Protestant	1	152
Seventh-day Adventist	Evangelical Protestant	1	46
United Methodist Church	Mainline Protestant	3	351
Wisconsin Evangelical Lutheran Synod	Evangelical Protestant	1	63
TOTAL		25	8,191

KEWEENAW COUNTY

Mainline Protestant	583
Catholic	386
Other	2
Unclaimed	1,330

Religious Body	Theology	Congregations	Adherents
Baha'I	Other Theology	0	2
Catholic Church	Catholic	3	386
Episcopal Church	Mainline Protestant	1	43
Evangelical Lutheran	Mainline Protestant	1	506
United Methodist	Mainline Protestant	1	34
TOTAL		6	971

LUCE COUNTY

Mainline Protestant	776
Catholic	676
Evangelical Protestant	551
Unclaimed	5,022

Religious Body	Theology	Congregations	Adherents
Assemblies of God	Evangelical Protestant	1	106
Catholic Church	Catholic	1	675
Churches of Christ	Evangelical Protestant	1	30
Episcopal Church	Mainline Protestant	1	68
Evangelical Lutheran	Evangelical Protestant	1	364
General Association of	Evangelical Protestant	1	90

Regular Baptist Churches

Lutheran Church-Missouri	Evangelical Protestant	1	221
Pentecostal Church of God	Evangelical Protestant	1	38
Presbyterian Church USA	Mainline Protestant	1	133
Seventh-day Adventist	Evangelical Protestant	1	30
Southern Baptist Convention	Evangelical Protestant	1	36
United Methodist	Mainline Protestant	2	211
TOTAL		13	2,002

MACKINAC COUNTY

Catholic	2,572
Mainline Protestant	1,139
Evangelical Protestant	731
Other	2
Unclaimed	7,499

Religious Body	**Theology**	**Congregations**	**Adherents**
Assemblies of God	Evangelical Protestant	1	20
Baha'I	Other Theology	0	2
Catholic Church	Catholic	8	2,572
Episcopal Church	Mainline Protestant	4	136
Evangelical Free Church of America	Evangelical Protestant	1	52
Evangelical Lutheran	Evangelical Protestant	4	475
General Association of Regular Baptist Churches	Evangelical Protestant	2	265
Lutheran Church-Missouri	Evangelical Protestant	1	237
Mennonite Church USA	Evangelical Protestant	3	126
Presbyterian Church USA	Mainline Protestant	2	78
United Methodist	Mainline Protestant	2	378
Wisconsin Evangelical Lutheran Synod	Evangelical Protestant	1	21
TOTAL		30	4,444

MARQUETTE COUNTY

Catholic	19,217
Mainline Protestant	12,305
Evangelical Protestant	4,744
Other	541
Orthodox	12
Unclaimed	27,815

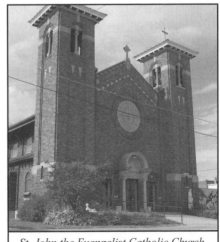

St. John the Evangelist Catholic Church, Ishpeming

Religious Body	Theology	Congregations	Adherents
American Baptist Church In the USA	Mainline Protestant	1	70
Assemblies of God	Evangelical Protestant	2	440
Association of Free Lutheran Congregations	Evangelical Protestant	1	201
Baha'I	Other Theology	1	57
Baptist General Conference	Evangelical Protestant	4	498
Catholic Church	Catholic	13	19,217
Christian Churches and and Churches of Christ	Evangelical Protestant	1	368
Christian Reformed Church	Evangelical Protestant	1	100
Church of God (Cleveland, TN)	Evangelical Protestant	1	9
Church of God General Conference	Evangelical Protestant	1	7
Church of Jesus Christ of Latter-day Saints	Evangelical Protestant	1	288
Churches of Christ	Evangelical Protestant	1	123
Episcopal Church	Mainline Protestant	5	694
Evangelical Covenant	Evangelical Protestant	2	189
Evangelical Lutheran	Mainline Protestant	15	8,490
Friends (Quaker)	Mainline Protestant	1	153
General Association of Regular Baptist Churches	Evangelical Protestant	1	72
Greek Orthodox Archdiocese	Orthodox	1	12
Jewish Estimate	Other Theology	1	150
Lutheran Church-Missouri	Evangelical Protestant	2	1,616
Missionary Church	Evangelical Protestant	1	87
Nat'l Association of Free Will Baptists	Evangelical Protestant	1	85
Presbyterian Church USA	Mainline Protestant	3	697
Salvation Army	Evangelical Protestant	2	478
Seventh-day Adventist	Evangelical Protestant	1	57
Southern Baptist Convention	Evangelical Protestant	3	235
Unitarian Universalist	Other Theology	1	46
United Methodist Church	Mainline Protestant	9	2,301
Wesleyan Church	Evangelical Protestant	1	30
Wisconsin Evangelical Lutheran Synod	Evangelical Protestant	2	149
TOTAL		80	36,819

MENOMINEE COUNTY

Catholic	11,072
Mainline Protestant	4,172
Evangelical Protestant	2,225
Other	3
Unclaimed	7,854

Religious Body	Theology	Congregations	Adherents
Assemblies of God	Evangelical Protestant	2	232
Baha'I	Other Theology	0	3
Baptist General Conference	Evangelical Protestant	1	228
Catholic Church	Catholic	6	11,072
Christian Churches and and Churches of Christ	Evangelical Protestant	1	368
Christian Reformed Church	Evangelical Protestant	1	100
Church of God (Cleveland, TN)	Evangelical Protestant	2	70
Churches of Christ	Evangelical Protestant	1	18
Episcopal Church	Mainline Protestant	2	107
Evangelical Covenant	Evangelical Protestant	4	288
Evangelical Free Church Of America	Evangelical Protestant	1	175
Evangelical Lutheran	Mainline Protestant	5	3,077
Moravian Church in In America	Mainline Protestant	1	66
Presbyterian Church USA	Mainline Protestant	1	387
Salvation Army	Evangelical Protestant	2	478
Seventh-day Adventist	Evangelical Protestant	2	336
Southern Baptist Convention	Evangelical Protestant	1	40
United Methodist Church	Mainline Protestant	4	535
Wisconsin Evangelical Lutheran Synod	Evangelical Protestant	4	838
TOTAL		37	17,472

ONTONAGON COUNTY

Catholic	1,751
Mainline Protestant	1,638
Evangelical Protestant	915
Unclaimed	3,514

Religious Body	Theology	Congregations	Adherents
Assemblies of God	Evangelical Protestant	2	107
Association of Free Lutheran Congregations	Evangelical Protestant	1	35
Catholic Church	Catholic	6	11,072
Episcopal Church	Mainline Protestant	2	26
Evangelical Lutheran	Mainline Protestant	7	1,236
General Association of Regular Baptist Churches	Evangelical Protestant	2	77
Lutheran Church-Missouri	Evangelical Protestant	2	499
Presbyterian Church USA	Mainline Protestant	1	19
Seventh-day Adventist	Evangelical Protestant	1	35
United Methodist Church	Mainline Protestant	6	357
Wisconsin Evangelical Lutheran Synod	Evangelical Protestant	1	162
TOTAL		30	4,304

SCHOOLCRAFT COUNTY

Catholic	1,959
Mainline Protestant	1,607
Evangelical Protestant	478
Other	53
Unclaimed	4,806

Religious Body	Theology	Congregations	Adherents
American Baptist Churches	Mainline Protestant	1	342
Baptist General Conference	Evangelical Protestant	1	33
Catholic Church	Catholic	4	1,959
Church of Jesus Christ of Latter-day Saints	Other Theology	1	53
Community of Christ	Evangelical Protestant	2	83
Episcopal Church	Mainline Protestant	1	57
Evangelical Lutheran	Mainline Protestant	1	774
International Church of Foursquare Gospel	Evangelical Protestant	1	75
Lutheran Church-Missouri	Evangelical Protestant	1	101
Mennonite Church USA	Evangelical Protestant	3	73
Mennonite; Other Groups	Evangelical Protestant	1	10
Nat'l Association of Congregational Christian	Mainline Protestant	1	143
Pentecostal Church of God	Evangelical Protestant	1	80
Presbyterian Church USA	Mainline Protestant	1	125
Seventh-day Adventist	Evangelical Protestant	1	23
United Methodist Church	Mainline Protestant	2	166
TOTAL	23		4,097

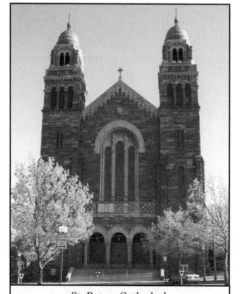

Source: Association of Religion Data Archives, www.TheARDA.com. Published in Religious Congregations and Membership in the United States 2000, Copyright 2002

St. Peters Cathedral, Marquette, MI

Chapter 6

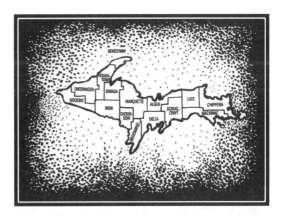

COUNTIES AND TOWNS

ALGER COUNTY   COUNTY SEAT: MUNISING

Organized: Set off from Schoolcraft County on March 17, 1885

Named after: Russell A. Alger, governor of Michigan at the time Alger County was organized.

Square miles (total): 5,049   **Land:** 918

Water: 4,131

With boundary lines stretching into Lake Superior, nearly 82% of Alger County is water.

Stats: (state rank out of 83 counties)
2007 est.: 9,612 (77)
2000: 9,862
Labor force: 4,517   (74)
Unemployment rate (2008): 9.8% (34)
Median household income: $37,825 (49)
Poverty rate: 13.4 (39)
Per capita income: $22,033 (71)
Avg. earnings per job: $32,965 (32)
Median age: 41
Male-to-female ratio (over 18): 120/100
Largest city: Munising 2,350
Early settlement

Russell A. Alger

There is evidence of ancient settlers in the Grand Marais region where artifacts have been discovered dating back 4,000 years ago. Chippewa Indians had camped or lived in the region for many years before French explorers discovered the big lake in the mid 1600s.

Until the 1600s the Pictured Rocks shore was known only to Native Americans of the region. By the mid 1600s French fur trappers and explorers had paddled the shore and probably camped on one of the bluffs.

The first industry in the U.P. was fur trapping and trading. It brought the first modern day settlement to the region in the mid-1820s when the American Fur Company opened a post on Grand Island. At that time, there was already a Chippewa village established at Sand Point.

By the middle of the 19th Century, fur trading was replaced by lumbering and mining, which brought more people and some of the first modern-day settlements to the U.P. In the early 1850s, settlers bought land and platted the Munising area. A post office opened in 1868

There is evidence that white men first settled in AuTrain in 1856 when William Cameron decided the hunting and trapping was good enough to lay down permanent roots.

Another early European settlement was recorded in the 1860s near Grand Marais, although the official origin of the town dates to 1879 when two lumber companies set up shop.

Munising Harbor

Township populations

Munising	3,125
Rock River	1,213
Au Train	1,172
Mathias	571
Burt	480
Limestone	407
Onota	310
Grand Island	45

CITIES

MUNISING   49862

Named after: Indian word *Minissing*, meaning island in the lake or near the island

Once known as: Minissing, Old Munising, East Munising

Incorporated as village: 1897   **Incorporated as city:** 1915

Slogan: *A Midwest Vacation Travel of Treasures*

Total area: 5.4 sq. miles   **Elevation:** 201 feet

Latitude: 4641 N,   **Longitude:** 8665 W

Population: 2,539 (2000)   2,350 (2007 est.)

Males: 1,105 (47%)   **Females:** 1,245 (53%)

Median age: 43.8 years

Races in Munising:
- White Non-Hispanic (93.3%)
- American Indian (4.9%)
- Two or more races (1.7%)
- Hispanic (1.0%)

Ancestries: French (14.7%), German (14.3%), Irish (12.9%), Polish (10.8%), Swedish (9.9%), French Canadian (7.4%). 0.6% Foreign born

Median household income: $33,700 (year 2005)

Median house value: $86,300 (year 2005)

Employment by industry
Educational, health and social services   24%
Manufacturing 20%
Arts, entertainment, recreation, 15%
Accommodations and food services

UNINCORPORATED VILLAGES

Christmas, Deerton, Diffon, Eben Junction, Forest Lake, Grand Marais, Limestone, Kiva, Melstrand, Rumely, Shingleton, Sundell, Traunik, Trenary, Wetmore

VILLAGES

CHATHAM 49816

Named after: Chatham, Ontario. Named by town founder, James Finn who started a lumber camp here in 1896.
Slogan: *Small town pride...big town conveniences.*
Total area: 2.7 miles   **Elevation:** 876 feet
Latitude: 46.35 N, **Longitude:** 86.93 W
Population: 231 (2000)   215 (2007 est.)
Males: 100 (47%)   **Females:** 115 (53%)
Median age: 40.8

Races in Chatham:
- White Non-Hispanic (94.4%)
- American Indian (5.6%)
- Two or more races (0.9%)

Ancestries: German (13.4%), Swedish (10.8%), French (9.1%), English (6.9%), Irish (6.9%), Polish (4.3%).   0.9% Foreign born

Median household income: $31,406 (2000)
Median house value: $60,800 (2000)

Employment by industry

Education, health and social services	17.9%
Retail trade	15.8%
Public administration	13.7%
Construction	11.6%
Manufacturing	10.5%

Early settlement: The first settler was G.A. Lindquist who arrived in 1896. About the same time, the Munising Railway Company, which later became the Lake Superior & Ishpeming railroad, laid track into the area. Also in 1896, the village was platted by the railroad and Sutherland Innis Company, a lumber operation with several camps in the area. One of the company's employees, Jim Finn, named the small U.P. settlement after Chatham, Ontario, the headquarters of Sutherland Innis.

The town produced telephone and telegraph poles, and later hardwood for the nearby charcoal plants. After the supply of mature trees was exhausted the land was sold for farming.

By 1899, the trees were harvested and the lumber camp was closed. The state opened the Experimental Agricultural Station in 1899 to help farmers develop the cutover land.

TOWNSHIPS

AU TRAIN   49806

Named after: French term *trainerant*, used by voyageurs to describe the act of dragging their canoes over the sandy shoal at the mouth of the river.

Once known as: Train River

Land area (twp): 165 square miles   **Elevation:** 974 feet

Population (twp): 1,154   (2006)

Early settlement: Whittley sawmill built in 1859. Larger commercial logging began around 1876, with a Detroit, Mackinaw & Marquette Railroad station established in 1882. Named as county seat in 1885 when Alger County was first organized.

GRAND ISLAND   49862

Named after: Kitchi Miniss the Chippewa phrase for Great Island.

Total area: 13,600 acres   **Elevation:** 689 feet

Population: 48 (2006)

Early settlement: Evidence of Native American activity dates back nearly 5,000 years. The Indians used the island for hunting, fishing and a source for quartzite, the rock used to make ancient tools.

Abraham H. Williams and family arrived in 1840. Williams built a home and farmed the land on Grand Island. He was invited by the Ojibwa Chief Omonomonee, whom he had previously met near Sault Ste. Marie.

Other early settlers were fur trapper Truman W. Powell, who settled on the island in the 1840s and John Murray, who built a home near the point of the bay which bears his name. He worked as a teacher for the island's few children, which included those of Abraham Williams.

GRAND MARAIS   49839

Named after: Named by voyageurs in the 17th century. In modern French language it translates to "great pond," or "great marsh." In the language of French voyageurs it meant *sheltered inlet*, or *harbor*.

Once known as: In the early 1880s the town was divided between *West Grand Marais* and *East Town*.

Slogan: *"Eastern Gateway to Pictured Rocks National Lakeshore"* and *"Nature in Abundance"*

Total area: **Elevation:** 838 ft.

Platted: 1884

Population: 350

Evidence of ancient Indians along the Lake Superior shore near Grand Marais dates back thousands of years. Chippewa Indians established fishing camps at Grand Marais long before the first French explorers and fur trappers arrived. Pierre Espirt Radisson and Sieur des Groseillers were two early explorers believed to have stopped at Grand Marais in 1658. Grand Marais was included on a French map in 1660.

Grand Marais was an important fur trading center in the 1700s, and in 1814 John Jacob Astor opened an outpost of his American Fur Company based on Mackinac Island.

The first permanent settlers arrived in the 1860s when a trading post was built by Peter Barbeau. After the fur trade diminished, Grand Marais became a fishing village with the establishment of the E.G. Endress Fish Co in 1872, and the building of a lighthouse in 1874. It was an important port during the lumber boom of the early 20th Century with a peak population of 2,500. Grand Marais was part of Schoolcraft County until Alger County was organized in 1885. It was the county seat of Alger County until 1902, when the seat was moved to Munising.

BARAGA COUNTY   COUNTY SEAT: L'ANSE

Organized: On February 19, 1875, Baraga County was formed after it split from Houghton County. At that time, present-day Houghton, Keweenaw and Baraga counties, were all part of Houghton County. Before 1875, Baraga was part of Ontonagon County, which was one of the original six counties of the Upper Peninsula. When Michigan was admitted to the Union in 1837, Ontonagon County included all of the land from Baraga, Keweenaw, Houghton and Ontonagon counties.

Named after: Father Frederic Baraga. "The Snowshoe Priest," who established a mission near L'Anse in 1843.

Square miles (total): 1,069   **Land:** 904   **Water:** 165

Stats: (state rank out of 83 counties)

Population 2007 (est): 8,544 (79)   **2000:** 8,746

Labor force: 4,378 (75)   **Unemployment rate (2008):** 14% (4)

Median household income: $37,283 (52)   **Poverty rate:** 13.1% (31)

Per capita income: $21,581 (76)   **Avg. earnings per job:** $30,652 (50)

Median age: 39   **Male-to-female ratio (over 18):** 114/100

Largest village: L'Anse – 1,888

Early settlement: The first European to visit Baraga County was Father Rene Menard who arrived in October of 1660 and spent the winter. He left on a trip south and disappeared during the summer of 1661. Chippewa families were the only inhabitants until 1842. That year, the Indians ceded their land to the United States as one of the provisions in the Treaty of LaPointe. The treaty also ordered the federal government to send a blacksmith, farmer and carpenter to work with the natives. Among the first settlers was blacksmith Daniel Brockway, who established a Methodist mission on the east side of the bay at L'Anse. A Catholic mission as established by Father Frederic Baraga at Assinins on the west side in 1843.

In the 1870s, after the railroad arrived in L'Anse the town became a major port on Lake Superior, boasting what some called the largest cargo dock in the world. Fire broke out in the L'Anse Lumber Company sawmill on May 9, 1896. The fire then spread through much of the town rendering hundreds of people homeless. The village was quickly rebuilt. The town of Baraga became an important lumber and shipbuilding town in the 1880s, led by the Nester family. In the 1920s, Henry Ford purchased the mills at Pequaming and L'anse, using the wood for his automobile manufacturing. He later built a mill at Alberta where he established a model community for his employees.

Township populations

L'Anse	3,926
Baraga	3,542
Covington	569
Arvon	482
Spurr	227

UNINCORPORATED VILLAGES

Alberta, Arnheim, Assinins, Aura, Covington, Herman, Keweenaw Bay, Nestoria, Pelkie, Pequaming, Skanee, Three Lakes, Watton

VILLAGES

L'ANSE   49946

Named after: *L'anse*, French name for bay

Incorporated as a village: 1873

Total area: 2.6 sq. miles   **Elevation:** 682 ft.

Latitude: 46.75 N   **Longitude:** 88.45 W

Population: 2,107 (2000)   1,888 (2007 est.)

Males: 887 (47%)

Females: 1,001 (53%)

Median age: 41.7

Races in L'Anse:
- White Non-Hispanic (90.9%)
- American Indian (7.8%)
- Two or more races (2.9%)
- Hispanic (0.6%)

Ancestries: French (15.8%), German (15.6%), English (9.5%), Norwegian (8.6%), Swedish (8.2%), Irish (7.3%). 0.9% Foreign born

Median household income: $31,200 (year 2005)

Median house value: $79,200 (year 2005)

Employment by industry:

Educational, health, and social services   23%
Manufacturing 15%
Arts, entertainment, recreation, food industry   13%
Public administration   13%
Retail   12%

Early settlement: In 1837, fur trader Peter Crebassa established the American Fur Trading Post. At the invitation of Crebassa, Father Frederic Baraga arrived in L'Anse in 1843. He established a Catholic mission on the west side of the bay.

BARAGA 49908

Named after: Reverend Baraga who, in 1843, opened Holy Name mission for local Native Americans

Once known as: Bristol
Incorporated as village: 1891
Total area: 2.3 sq. miles
Elevation: 614 ft.
Latitude: 46.78 N
Longitude: 88.49 W
Population: 1,285 (2000)
1,185 (2007 est.)
Males: 553 (47%)
Females: 632 (53%)
Median age: 36.9

Races in Baraga:
- White Non-Hispanic (68.7%)
- American Indian (29.8%)
- Two or more races (6.1%)
- Hispanic (0.9%)
- Other Asian (0.6%)

Ancestries: French (12.7%), German (12.2%), French Canadian (8.0%), Irish (5.2%), English (5.0%), Italian (4.0%), 0.4% Foreign born

Median household income: $26,100 (year 2005)
Median house value: $82,400 (year 2005)
Employment by industry:
Educational, health, and social services 19%
Arts, entertainment, recreation, food services 18%
Manufacturing 17%
Public administration 15%
Retail 13%

Early settlement: Father Frederic Baraga established a Catholic Mission for the Native Amerians at Assinins.

Assinins Community Cemetery

As far as anyone can remember, this burial ground has been here. We know that the Chippewa Nation was casting their nets in Keweenaw Bay in the 1600's. In our cultural tradition the circle is sacred. Some of the gravestones that are marked date back to the 1840's. These graves have the later stone grave marker.

Our ancient ancestors told the stories of how we are born in the East and enter the Spirit world at the west. At the time of death the deceased would be dressed in their finest clothing and the body removed from the wigwam or house from a westerly window. In the winter the body was placed on a scaffold or they were hung in a bag in the trees. Words were spoken in honor of the beloved. The bones were later collected and each year the Chippewa would travel and meet other bands for a feast of the dead. There these bones were buried in a communal ground. Spirit houses were put over the grave of the individual. The spirit houses were first built of birch bark, elm or cedar bark. Later they were built of lumber to provide a place to leave food and other necessary items such as arrows, bow, fishing equipment, beads, etc. to aid the deceased on his four day journey to the spirit world. Once a year some of the Chippewa people still celebrate the feast of the dead. They gather for a feast and honor their ancestors. Picnics even in recent years were held at this cemetery in memory of old customs. May our ancient ones rest well here on this sacred ground.

CHIPPEWA COUNTY
COUNTY SEAT: SAULT STE. MARIE

Organized: December 22, 1826 from part of Mackinac County. At this time, Chippewa covered what is now Luce, Schoolcraft, Baraga, Houghton, Keweenaw, part of Marquette and Ontonagon counties. In 1843, new counties were configured, leaving present-day Chippewa along with a good part of today's Luce County. In 1887, Luce County was formed by splitting from Chippewa.

Named after: The Native American tribe that lived near the Falls of St. Marys River for over 500 years. The word Chippewa comes from "otchipwa," an Algonquin word meaning "to pucker." The Algonquin's called the local tribe "people who wear puckered shoes," referring to the seams on the bottom of their moccasins.

Square miles (total): 2,698   **Land:** 1,561   **Water:** 1,136

Chippewa County is bordered by three of the Great Lakes: Lake Superior to the north, and Lakes Huron and Michigan to the south.

Stats: (state rank out of 83 counties)

Population 2007 (est): 38,922 (42)   **2000:** 38,543

Labor force: 17,502 (47)   **Unemployment rate (2008):** 9.8% (18)
Median household income: $35,329 (64)   **Poverty rate:** 14.8% (15)
Per capita income: $21,632 (75)   **Avg. earnings per job:** $30,708 (49)
Median age: 36   **Male-to-female ratio (over 18):** 132/100
Largest city: Sault Ste. Marie 16,695 (2007)

Early settlement Early settlement centered on Sault Ste. Marie, Michigan's oldest city and the point at which Lake Superior pours into Lake Huron via the St. Marys River. The town received its name, *Sault de Sainte Marie*, from the French missionaries Father Isaac Jogues and Charles Raymbault in about 1641. In 1668, Fathers Claude Dablon and Jacques Marquette established a mission at the Sault (Soo), making it the first permanent white settlement in Michigan and one of the first in the country.

The region around Sault Ste. Marie was "claimed" for Louis XIV in June of 1671 by Sieur de St. Lusson who was on a mission to find copper and a route to the Orient. An estimated two thousand Native Americans watched the ceremony led by St. Lusson.

The Soo region was the fur trading center of the Lake Superior region from the late 1700s through the early 1800s. One of the early fur traders was Irishman John Johnston who arrived in 1793. Johnston married the daughter of a Chippewa chief and built a home in 1815, which stands today as a museum.

In 1822, a fort was built at the Sault by a contingent of 250 soldiers. This became the first permanent American settlement in the Upper Peninsula of Michigan.

Bishop Baraga residence at Sault Ste. Marie

In 1827, the civilian population of newly formed Chippewa County was listed at less than 200. By the 1850s, the count was just under 2,000. The population jumped starting in 1852 when construction of the Soo Locks got underway, which made Sault Ste. Marie a major transportation center in the U.S.

Township populations
Kinross charter	5,922
Soo	2,652
Bruce	1,940
Pickford	1,584
Rudyard	1,385
Superior	1,329

Dafter	1,304
Bay Mills	1,214
Drummond Island	992
De Tour	894
Sugar Island	683
Raber	653
Whitefish	588
Trout Lake	465
Chippewa	238
Hulbert	211

CITIES

SAULT STE. MARIE   49783

Named after: Sault was a French word used by early fur traders and voyageurs meaning "the jump" or "the falls" of the rapids created by Lake Superior's drop into the St. Marys River. Named by French Jesuits Isaac Jogues and Charles Raymbault in 1641 to honor of the Virgin Mary.

Once known as: *Bahweting.* Native American word meaning, "The Gathering Place;" *Sault du Gastogne*; *Le Sault de Sainte Marie*; village of *St. Mary*

Slogan: *The Gathering Place*

Incorporated as a village: 1849 as village of St. Mary (changed to Sault Ste. Marie two years later)
Incorporated as a city: 1887
Land area: 14.8 sq. miles
Elevation: 613 feet
Latitude: 46.49 N   **Longitude:** 84.35 W
Population: 16,542 (2000) 14,272 (2006 est.)
Males: 9,174 (55%)
Females: 7,521 (45%)
Median age: 32.8

Races in Sault Ste. Marie:
- White Non-Hispanic (73.2%)
- American Indian (17.3%)
- Black (6.5%)
- Two or more races (4.6%)
- Hispanic (1.9%)

Ancestries: German (16.7%), Irish (13.5%), English (9.9%), French (9.2%), Polish (6.3%), Italian (5.7%). 4.1% Foreign born

John Johnston house in Sault Ste. Marie was purchased by the city in the 1940s is now a museum.

Median household income: $29,500 (year 2005)
Median house value: $87,900 (year 2000)
Employment by industry:
Educational, health and social services 28%
Arts, entertainment, rec., food service, hospitality 17%
Retail Trade   13%   Public administration   13%

Early settlement: Native Americans fished the waters of the St. Marys River at least as far back as two thousand years ago. They spent much of the year along the shores of the St. Marys River, moving south or inland for the winter months. In the 1600s, it was developed as a trading post for fur traders.

In 1641, French Jesuits Raymbault and Jogues created a mission for the Ojibwa Indians on Sugar Island. Then in 1668, Fathers Jacques Marquette and Claude Dablon built a Catholic mission at the Soo. The were joined by as many as 2,000 Ojibwa Indians on June 14, 1671 in a ceremony that claimed the region for France and created the first permanent European settlement in Michigan and the Midwest.

UNINCORPORATED TOWNSHIPS

Bay Mills, Barbeau, Brimley, Dafter, Drummond,   Keldon, Paradise, Stirlingville

VILLAGES

DE TOUR VILLAGE 49725

Named after: Named by Native Americans and early fur traders for the turn from the St. Marys River into Lake Huron leading to Mackinac Island and the Straits area.

Once known as: *Giwideonaning,* Ojibwa word meaning "point we go around in a canoe; *Warrenville*; *Detour*; *DeTour*

Slogan: *Gateway to the North Channel* and *Take a turn toward the Eastern U.P.*

Incorporated as a village: 1899

Incorporated as a city: 1887

Land area: 3.6 sq. miles

Elevation: 613 feet

Latitude: 45.99 N

Longitude: 83.90 W

Population: 421 (2000) 409 (2007 est.)

Males: 204 (50%)

Females: 205 (50%)

Median age: 53.3

Races in De Tour Village:

- White Non-Hispanic (82.2%)
- American Indian (17.1%)
- Two or more races (3.6%)
- Hispanic (2.4%)

Ancestries: English (16.4%), German (12.1%), Irish (10.5%), Polish (9.5%), United States (7.8%), French (5.5%). 3.1% Foreign born

Median household income: $31,100 (year 2005)

Median house value: $149,000 (year 2005)

Industries providing employment:

Educational, health and social services   19%

Arts, entertainment, rec., food services, hospitality   16%

Construction   12%

Early settlement: Located at the extreme eastern end of the U.P. where the St. Marys River turns into Lake Huron, DeTour has a rich maritime history. The first lighthouse was built here in 1847. Detour was an early wood fueling station for Great Lakes ships after the Soo Locks opened in 1855.

DELTA COUNTY   COUNTY SEAT: ESCANABA

Organized: In 1843 counties were reformed. Delta was set off from Mackinac, and at that time included the current Delta County, Menominee County and parts of Iron, Marquette and Dickinson Counties. Delta in its current form was officially organized in 1861.

Named after: The Greek letter, "Delta," which referred to the triangular shape of the original county.

Square miles (total): 1,991

Land: 1,170   **Water:**   821

Stats: (state rank out of 83 counties)

Population 2007 (est): 37,367 (43)   **2000:** 38,520

Labor force: 20,829 (77)   **Unemployment rate (2006):** 11% (4)

Median household income: $37,461 (51)   **Poverty rate:** 11.7% (41)

Per capita income: $26,799 (36)

Avg. earnings per job: 30,952 (45)   **Median age:** 40

Male-to-female ratio (over 18): 93/100

Largest city: Escanaba 12,297 (2007)

Early settlement

Noquet Indians lived near Fayette as far back as 500 A.D., as documented by the only Indian paintings ever discovered in Michigan.

Settlement began around Escanaba in the 1850s. The first post office opened in 1853, and the Chicago & Northwestern railroad built an iron ore dock in 1863. That same year the first home and hotel were built in Escanaba. A lighthouse was built in 1867.

Township Populations

Wells	5,044
Escanaba	3,587
Ford River	2,241
Masonville	1,877
Bark River	1,650
Brampton	1,090
Garden	817
Maple Ridge	808
Ensign	780
Baldwin	748
Cornell	557
Nahma	499
Bay De Noc	329
Fairbanks	321

Sand Point Lighthouse, Escanaba

CITIES

ESCANABA   49829

Named after: Ojibwa word Esconawba meaning either *flat rock*, describing the bed of the river, or *land of the red buck* referring to the many deer in the area

Once known as: Sandy Point; Esconawba; Flat Rock

Slogan: *The Heart of Upper Michigan*

Incorporated as a village: 1866

Incorporated as a city: 1883

Land area: 12.7 sq. miles

Elevation: 598 feet

Latitude: 45.75 N

Longitude: 87.07 W

Population: 13,140 (2000)   12,297 (2007 est.)

Males: 5746 (47%)

Females: 6551 (53%)

Median age: 40.1

Races in Escanaba:
- White Non-Hispanic (95.3%)
- American Indian (3.5%)
- Two or more races (1.1%)
- Hispanic (0.7%)

Ancestries: German (21.4%), French (20.2%), Swedish (11.1%), French Canadian (10.5%), Irish (9.2%), English (7.7%).

Median household income: $28,900 (year 2005)

Median house value: $98,400 (year 2005)

Industries providing employment:

Educational, health, and social services 21%

Manufacturing 15%

Arts, entertainment, rec., food services, hospitality 14%

Retail trade 14%

Early settlement: With its deep water harbor, Escanaba was the ideal place to establish a port to ship iron from the Marquette Range. In 1863, the Chicago and Northwestern Railroad built the first dock and connected Escanaba to Negaunee. A lighthouse was built in 1867. By the 1870s, Escanaba was connected by rail to the Marquette and Menominee Ranges as well as the rest of the United States when track was completed to the city from the south in 1872. It became a busy shipping port for iron and the growing lumber industry, as well as a welcome point for steamships full of summer vacationers.

GLADSTONE   49837

Named after: British Prime Minister William Ewart Gladstone. Local businessman William D. Washburn wanted to show appreciation to the British investment in the Soo Line railroad, which developed the port and built railroad engine repair stations in the town.

Once known as: Saunders Point; Minewasca (Sioux word for white water)

Incorporated as a village: 1887

Incorporated as a city: 1889

Land area: 5.0 sq. miles   **Elevation:** 601 feet

Latitude: 45.85 N   **Longitude:** 87.03 W

Population: 5,032 (2000) 5,103 (2007 est.)

Males: 2,392 (48%)   **Females:** 2,640 (52%)

Median age: 39.9

Races in Gladstone:
- White Non-Hispanic (96.4%)
- American Indian (2.5%)
- Two or more races (1.3%)

Ancestries: German (21.3%), French (18.8%), Swedish (14.0%), French Canadian (10.1%), Irish (9.7%), English (9.2%). 2.2% Foreign born

Median household income: $34,100 (year 2005)

Median house value: $88,900 (year 2005)

Industries providing employment:
Educational, health, and social services 20%
Manufacturing 19%
Retail trade   13%
Arts, entertainment, rec., food services, accommodations 11%

Early settlement: In 1877, the town was at the eastern end of the Soo Line railroad which extended from Minneapolis. Eventually the railroad ran farther east to Sault Ste. Marie. Investors from Minnesota opened a flour mill in 1887, and soon after the railroad developed the port connecting the deep harbor to the rail line.

UNINCORPORATED VILLAGES

Bark River, Fayette, Garden Corners, Isabella Schaffer

VILLAGES

GARDEN 49835

Named after: the fertility of the soil

Once known as: Haley's Bay; Garden Bay

Incorporated as a village: 1886

Land area: 0.8 sq. miles   **Elevation:** 618 feet

Latitude: 45.77 N   **Longitude:** 86.55 W

Population: 240 (2000) 224 (2007 est.)

Males: 110 (49%)   **Females:** 114 (51%)

Median age: 45.0

Races in Garden:
- White Non-Hispanic (80.4%)
- American Indian (19.6%)
- Two or more races (10.8%)

Ancestries: French (25.0%), German (15.4%), French Canadian (12.9%), Irish (8.8%), English (4.2%), Polish (4.2%).

Median household income: $36,000 (year 2005)

Median house value: $72,800 (year 2005)

Industries providing employment:
Manufacturing 18%
Educational, health, and social services 18%
Construction   17%
Transportation, warehousing and utilities 11%

Early settlement: First settler, Philomen Thompson, built cabin in 1850. Most early settlers were of French origin.

DICKINSON COUNTY
COUNTY SEAT: IRON MOUNTAIN

Organized: Michigan's "youngest" county was formed May 21, 1891 from parts of Dickinson, Iron and Marquette counties.

Named after: Donald M. Dickinson, Postmaster General under President Grover Cleveland.

Square miles (total): 777   **Land:**   766   **Water:** 11

Stats: (state rank out of 83 counties)

Population 2007 (est): 26,937 (52)   **2000:** 24,472

Labor force: 14,745 (51)

Unemployment rate (2008): 7.2% (71)

Dickinson County Courthouse
Iron Mountain

Median household income: $36,959 (51)

Poverty rate: 10.3% (63)

Per capita income: $29,869 (19)

Avg. earnings per job: $32,875 (33)

Median age: 40

Ratio of males to females (over 18): 92/100

Largest city: Iron Mountain 7,816

Early settlement: Much of the early settlement centered on the mining industry, specifically the Chapin Mine which opened in 1880 and operated until 1934.

Township populations

Breitung Charter	5,930
Norway	1,639
Sagola	1,169
Waucedah	800
Felch	726
Breen	479
West Branch	67

CITIES

IRON MOUNTAIN 49801

Named after: The iron deposits discovered in 1879

Slogan: *Proud Hometown of Tom Izzo and Steve Mariucci; Mindful of the past, secure in the future, driven to excellence*

Incorporated as a village: 1887

Incorporated as a city: 1889

Land area: 7.2 sq. miles   **Elevation:** 1,138 feet

Latitude: 45.82 N   **Longitude:** 88.06 W

Population: 8,154 (2000)   7,816 (2007 est.)

Males: 4,002 (49%)   **Females:** 4,152 (51%)

Median age: 39.4

Races in Iron Mountain:
- White Non-Hispanic (97.0%)
- Hispanic (1.1%)
- American Indian (0.8%)
- Two or more races (0.7%)

Ancestries: German (20.3%), Italian (19.5%), English (14.1%), Swedish (13.5%), French (13.0%), Irish (8.5%). 1.7% Foreign born

Median household income: $32,300 (year 2005)

Median house value: $81,000 (year 2005)

Industries providing employment:
Educational, health, and social services   24%
Manufacturing   16%
Retail trade   16%

Early settlement: Iron was discovered by geologist Dr. Nelson P. Hulst in 1879 and the town was laid out the same year. The Chapin Mine opened nearby and by the mid 1880s the population of the Iron Mountain area was near 8,000.

KINGSFORD 49802

Named after: Edward G. Kingsford, a Ford Motor Company dealer and real estate agent. He obtained land for Henry Ford to build a sawmill, manufacturing plant and chemical plant along with hundreds of homes for employees.

Slogan: *The Progressive City*

Incorporated as a village: 1924

Incorporated as a city: 1947

Land area: 4.3 sq. miles   **Elevation:** 1,099 ft.

Latitude: 45.80 N   **Longitude:** 88.08 W

Population: 5,549 (2000)   5,549 (2007 est.)

KINGSFORD CHARCOAL BRIQUETTES

One of the most popular brands of charcoal for back-yard barbecues is Kingsford. The briquettes were originally named Ford Charcoal Bri-quettes. The Kingsford plant where they were made was sold by Ford to local inves-tors who renamed the product Kingsford Charcoal Bri-quettes. The company moved out of the U.P. in 1961 and is now a division of the Clorox Company in California.

Males: 2,524 (47%) **Females:** 2,806 (53%)

Median age: 39.7

Races in Kingsford:
- White Non-Hispanic (97.5%)
- Two or more races (1.1%)
- American Indian (1.0%)
- Hispanic (0.5%)

Ancestries: German (25.7%), Swedish (17.0%), Italian (16.9%), French (13.2%), English (10.6%), Irish (8.6%). 0.7% Foreign born

Median household income: $33,000 (year 2005)

Median house value: $76,900 (year 2005)

Industries providing employment:
Educational, health, and social services 25%
Manufacturing 19%
Retail trade 11%

Early settlement: The town essentially built by Henry Ford as a base for mining and timber operations for his auto company. In 1920, a Ford parts plant and sawmill were built and the company acquired over 300,000 acres of land in the western Upper Peninsula. The land was chosen by real es-tate agent and Ford Motor auto dealer, Edward G. Kings-ford. Kingsford was part of the family, married to Henry Ford's cousin.

Ford provided well-built, affordable homes for his work-ers who numbered over 3,000 in the first year of operation. They worked in the mill, in a plant that manufactured bodies for the Ford Woody station wagon, and a chemical plant that made, among other products, charcoal briquettes.

NORWAY 49870

Named after: The home country of the town founder, Anton Odell, who sunk the first test pit of the Norway Mine in 1871. Another theory is that the town was named after the Norway Pine tree.

Once known as: Insglesdorf
Slogan: *City of Trails*
Incorporated as a village:
Incorporated as a city: 1891
Land area: 8.8 sq. miles
Elevation: 940 ft.
Latitude: 45.79 N

Longitude: 87.90 W

Population: 2,959 (2000) 2,841 (2007 est.)

Males: 1,350 (48%) **Females:** 1,491 (52%)

Median age: 38.6

Races in Norway:

- White Non-Hispanic (97.0%)
- American Indian (1.8%)
- Two or more races (1.1%)
- Hispanic (0.8%)

Ancestries: German (20.1%), Italian (20.0%), French (13.2%), Swedish (12.0%), Polish (10.9%), Irish (10.0%). 0.9% Foreign born

Estimated median household income: $30,900 (2005)

Estimated median house/condo value: $69,800 (2005)

QUINNESEC 49876

Named after: Indian word for smoky waters, referring to the mist over the Menominee River

Land area: 1.1 sq. miles   **Elevation:** 1,020 feet

Latitude: 45.80 N   **Longitude:** 87.99 W

Population: 1,187 (2000)   1,163 (2007 est.)

Males: 588 (51%)   **Females:** 575 (49%)

Median age: 37.9

Races in Quinnesec:

- White Non-Hispanic (98.3%)
- Two or more races (0.8%)
- American Indian (0.5%)

Ancestries: German (22.7%), Italian (18.4%), Swedish (14.6%), French (11.3%), English (11.1%), French Canadian (8.8%). 0.0% Foreign born

Median household income: $41,700 (year 2005)

Median house value: $84,900 (year 2005)

Industries providing employment:

Educational, health and social services   26%

Manufacturing 22%

Transportation and warehousing, and utilities   10%

Early settlement: Quinnesec Mine was discovered in 1871 by John L. Bell. He platted the village in 1876.

UNINCORPORATED VILLAGES

Alfred, Channing, East Kingsford, Felch, Felch Mountain, Floodwood, Foster City, Granite Bluff, Hardwood, Hylas, Loretto, Merriman, Metropolitan, Quinnesec, Ralph, Randville, Sagola, Skidmore, Theodore, Vulcan, Waucedah

GOGEBIC COUNTY   COUNTY SEAT: BESSEMER

Organized: In 1887, Gogebic County was formed from Ontonagon County.

Named after: Gogebic is from the Chippwa word, "Agogebic," which means either a "body of water hanging on high," or "where trout rising make rings of water."

Square miles (total): 1,476   **Land:**   1,102 **Water:** 374

Stats: (state rank out of 83 counties)

Population: 2007 (est): 16,287 (68)   **2000:** 17,370

Labor force: 7,616 (68)   **Unemployment rate (2008):** 8.9% (47)

Median household income: $27,835 (82)   **Poverty rate:** 15.3% (10)

Per capita income: $23,731 (56)   **Avg. earnings per job:** 27,083 (70)

Median age: 46   **Ratio of males to females (over 18):** 102/100

Largest city: Ironwood 5473

Early settlement: Early visitors included French explorers, fur trappers and Native Americans. In 1840, the Chippewa Copper Mining Company arrived, but failed to find any copper. Development began in the 1880s with the arrival of iron ore prospectors. The first iron was discovered at the Colby Hill Mine in Bessemer in 1884. By 1887, there were 184 mining company operations in Gogebic County.

Township populations

Ironwood Charter	2,330
Watersmeet	1,472
Bessemer	1,270
Marenisco	1,051
Wakefield	364
Erwin	357

CITIES

BESSEMER 49911

Named after: Railroad executive, F.H. Rhinelander named the town for Sir Henry Bessemer, the English inventor who discovered the smelting process that led to the first inexpensive means of manufacturing steel

Incorporated as a village: 1887

Incorporated as a city: 1889

Land area: 5.5 sq. miles   **Elevation:** 1,432 ft.

Latitude: 46.48 N   **Longitude:** 90.05 W

Population: 2,148 (2000)   1,909 (2006 est.)

Males: 920 (49%)   **Females:** 957 (51%)

Median age: 42.5

Races in Bessemer:
- White Non-Hispanic (96.6%)
- American Indian (1.8%)
- Two or more races (0.9%)
- Hispanic (0.7%)

Ancestries: Italian (24.3%), German (18.4%), Polish (15.0%), Swedish (10.1%), Irish (7.3%), French (6.9%). 1.6% Foreign born

Median household income: $27,500 (year 2005)

Median house value: $50,800 (year 2005)

Industries providing employment:

    Educational, health and social services   22%

    Arts, entertainment, accommodation and food services   14%

    Manufacturing 14%

    Retail trade   14%

Early settlement: Richard Langford discovered iron ore in 1880 leading to the establishment of the Colby Mine by 1884. The Milwaukee, Lake Shore & Western Railroad arrived that same year.

IRONWOOD 49938

Named after: Captain James R. "Iron" Wood prominent mining executive

Slogan: *Michigan's Western Gateway*

Incorporated as a village: 1887

Incorporated as a city: 1889

Land area: 6.6 sq. miles

Elevation: 1,503 ft.

Latitude: 46.46 N

Longitude: 90.16 W

Population: 6,293 (2000) 5,473 (2007 est.)

Males: 2,579 (47%)

Females: 2,894 (53%)

Median age: 42.2

Races in Ironwood:

- White Non-Hispanic (96.8%)
- American Indian (1.7%)
- Two or more races (1.3%)
- Hispanic (0.8%)

Ironwood's Carnegie Library was built in 1901 and still operates as the city's library

Ancestries: German (17.0%), Italian (14.8%), Polish (12.6%), English (10.4%), Swedish (9.5%), Irish (8.8%). 1.3% Foreign born

Median household income: $23,400 (year 2005)

Median house value: $46,100 (year 2005)

Industries providing employment:

    Educational, health and social services   23%

    Manufacturing 15%

    Arts, entertainment, rec., food services, accommodations 13%

    Retail trade   13%

Early settlement: The town formed as a result of Raphael Pumpelly's discovery of iron on Newport Hill in 1871. The Harvard geologist climbed to the top to view smoke coming from the historic Peshtigo Fire in Wisconsin. One of the rocks he picked up turned out to be iron ore and that led to the establishment of the Newport Mine in 1884, and later the Geneva Mine. The population of the mining town grew to 1,000 by 1887.

WAKEFIELD   49968

Named after: George M. Wakefield who co-owned the Brotherton Mine.

Incorporated as a village: 1887

Incorporated as a city: 1919

Land area: 8.0 sq. miles   **Elevation:** 1,550 ft.

Latitude: 46.48 N   **Longitude:** 89.94 W

Population: 2,085 (2000) 1,875 (2007 est.)

Males: 889 (47%)   **Females:** 986 (53%)

Median age: 48.3

Races in Wakefield:
- White Non-Hispanic (98.1%)
- American Indian (1.3%)
- Two or more races (1.2%)

Ancestries: German (12.0%), Italian (11.5%), Irish (10.0%), Swedish (9.4%), Polish (8.8%), English (6.8%). 1.7% Foreign born

Median household income: $25,200 (year 2005)

Median house value: $45,400 (year 2005)

Industries providing employment:

Educational, health and social services   30%

Arts, entertainment, accommodation and food services   13%

Manufacturing 10%

Early settlement: George M. Wakefield came to the area in search of iron ore and platted the town in 1886. He became one of the owners of the Brotherton Mine. The Chicago & Northwestern Railroad arrived in 1888.

UNINCORPORATED VILLAGES

Marenisco, Ramsay, Thomaston, Watersmeet

HOUGHTON COUNTY
COUNTY SEAT: HOUGHTON

Organized: On March 9, 1845 Houghton County was created from parts of Marquette, Schoolcraft, and Ontonagon counties. The county was officially organized on May 18, 1846. Houghton County included present-day Keweenaw County until 1861 when the new county was formed. Up to that point, Eagle River was the County seat.

Named after: Dr. Douglass Houghton, the state's first geologist, who also served as mayor of Detroit. Houghton was assigned the task of compiling a geological survey of the Upper Peninsula. It was Houghton who confirmed the existence of the first copper discovered in

Keeweenaw County. Dr. Houghton drowned in 1845 in Lake Superior near Eagle River.

Square miles (total): 1,501   **Land:**   1,011

Water: 490

Stats: (state rank out of 83 counties)

In the early 1900s due to the success of copper mining, Houghton County became one of the top five most populated counties in Michigan with 88,098 residents in the 1910 census.

Population: (2006 est.) 36,201 (44) **2000:** 36,016

Labor force: 17,695 (46)

Unemployment rate (2008): 8.0% (60)

Median household income: $30,739 (81)

Poverty rate: 14.8% (15)

Per capita income: $22,976 (65)

Avg. earnings per job: $29,0117 (60)

Median age: 34

Ratio of males to females (over 18): 115/100

Largest city: Houghton 6,924 (2007)

Monument in Eagle River to Douglass Houghton who drowned on Lake Superior near the village in 1845.

Early settlement: The rush to Copper Country began after the 1841 report from State Geologist Douglass Houghton that detailed large copper deposits on the Keweenaw Peninsula. Prospecting began in 1842 after the Lake Superior Chippewa ceded the western portion of the U.P. Eagle River became an early shipping port for mining companies and it was the first county seat of Houghton County before Keweenaw County was organized. By 1845, the Cliff mine was up and running—the first successful copper mine on the peninsula. By the 1870s, the Calumet and Hecla Mining Co. was producing 50% of nation's copper.

Township populations

Calumet Charter	6,997
Portage Charter	3,156
Adams	2,747
Osceola	1,908
Schoolcraft	1,863
Torch Lake	1,860
Chassell	1,822
Franklin	1,320
Stanton	1,268
Laird	634
Hancock	408
Duncan	280
Quincy	251
Elm River	169

CITIES

HOUGHTON 49921, 49931

Named after: State Geologist Douglass Houghton who, in 1840, discovered copper in the Keweenaw Peninsula

Slogan: *Gateway to the Keweenaw Peninsula*

Incorporated as a village: 1867

Incorporated as a city: 1919

Land area: 4.3 sq. miles   **Elevation:** 607 ft.

Latitude: 47.12 N   **Longitude:** 88.56 W

Population: 7,010 (2000)   6,924 (2007 est.)

Males: 4,267 (62%)   **Females:** 2,657 (38%)

Median age: 21.7

Races in Houghton:

- White Non-Hispanic (88.7%)
- Chinese (3.2%)
- Black (1.9%)
- Asian Indian (1.9%)
- Two or more races (1.4%)
- American Indian (0.8%)
- Hispanic (0.8%)
- Other Asian (0.7%)
- Korean (0.6%)

Ancestries: German (25.3%), Irish (11.5%), English (11.3%), Polish (8.5%), French (6.2%), Italian (5.4%). 8.4% Foreign born

Median household income: $21,100 (year 2005)

Median house value: $120,300 (year 2005)

Industries providing employment:

    Educational, health and social services   57%
    Arts, entertainment, accommodation and food services   14%
    Retail trade   10%

HANCOCK 49930

Named after: John Hancock, first signer of the Declaration of Independence

Slogan: *City of International Fellowship*

Incorporated as a village: 1875

Incorporated as a city: 1903

Land area: 2.5 sq. miles

Elevation: 686 ft.

Latitude: 47.13 N

Longitude: 88.60 W

Population: 4,323 (2000)
4,149 (2007 est.)

Males: 2,059 (50%)
Females: 2,090 (50%)

Median age: 38.6
Races in Hancock:
- White Non-Hispanic (95.4%)
- American Indian (1.2%)
- Two or more races (1.0%)
- Black (0.8%)
- Hispanic (0.8%)

Ancestries: German (21.8%), English (11.3%), French (7.1%), Irish (7.0%), Swedish (6.2%), Polish (5.6%). 2.3% Foreign born

Median household income: $27,900 (year 2005)
Median house value: $86,600 (year 2000)

Industries providing employment:
Educational, health and social services   43%
Retail trade   16%
Arts, entertainment, accommodation and food services   11%

Early settlement: In 1852, Christopher C. Douglas settled in a cabin built in 1846 to hold a mineral claim. Douglas, who owned the land, sold it to the Quincy Mining Company in 1859.

UNINCORPORATED VILLAGES

Atlantic Mine, Dakota Heights, Dodgeville, Dollar Bay, Dreamland, Franklin Mine, Hubbell, Hurontown, Jacobsville, Ripley, Senter

VILLAGES

CALUMET   49913

Named after: Calumet is the clay bowl of the Indian peace pipe

Once known as: Red Jacket (after a Native American Chief of the Seneca tribe)

Incorporated as a village: 1867

Land area: 0.2 sq. miles

Elevation: 1,208 ft.

Latitude: 47.25 N

Longitude: 88.45 W

Population: 879 (2000) 798 (2007 est.)

Males: 390 (49%)

Females: 408 (51%)

Median age: 28.7

Races in Calumet:
- White Non-Hispanic (98.5%)
- Hispanic (0.8%)
- Two or more races (0.8%)

Calumet Post Office Ironwork Detail.

Ancestries: German (16.2%), Irish (9.3%), French (8.4%), Italian (8.4%), United States (5.8%), English (5.5%). 0.3% Foreign born

Median household income: $17,300 (year 2005)

Median house value: $60,100 (year 2005)

Industries providing employment:
Educational, health and social services   28%
Retail trade   18%
Manufacturing   12%
Arts, entertainment, accommodation and food services   11%

COPPER CITY 49917
Incorporated as a village: 1917
Land area: 0.1 sq. miles   **Elevation:** 877 ft.
Latitude: 47.28 N   **Longitude:** 88.39 W
Population: 295 (2000) 193 (2007 est.)
Males: 95 (49%)   **Females:** 98 (51%)
Median age: 39.8

Races in Copper City:
- White Non-Hispanic (98.0%)
- Asian Indian (1.0%)
- Two or more races (1.0%)

Ancestries: German (13.2%), English (10.7%), United States (6.8%), Irish (6.3%), Italian (4.4%), French (3.9%). 1.0% Foreign born

Median household income: $24,300 (year 2005)
Median house value: $45,400 (year 2005)
Industries providing employment:
Educational, health and social services   27%
Manufacturing   21%
Construction   10%

Early settlement: Began as a train station on the KC railroad in the mining region of Calumet.

LAKE LINDEN 49945
Named after: After the linden trees lining Torch Lake
Once known as: Torch Lake
Incorporated as a village: 1885
Land area: 0.7 sq. miles   **Elevation:** 600 ft.
Latitude: 47.20 N   **Longitude:** 88.41 W
Population: 1,081 (2000) 1,048 (2007 est.)
Males: 503 (48%)   **Females:** 545 (52%)
Median age: 41.8

Races in Lake Linden:
- White Non-Hispanic (96.9%)
- American Indian (1.6%)
- Two or more races (1.2%)
- Hispanic (0.9%)

Ancestries: French (25.8%), German (19.3%), French Canadian (14.6%), English (13.8%), Italian (7.2%), Irish (5.8%). 0.6% Foreign born

Median household income: $24,100 (year 2005)

Median house value: $55,000 (year 2005)

Industries providing employment:

Educational, health and social services   37%

Retail trade   13%

LAURIUM 49913

Named after: Laureium, a well known silver mining site in the Attica district of ancient Greece

Once known as: Calumet

Slogan: *Maintaining Tradition While Embracing the Future*

Incorporated as village of Calumet: 1889

Reincorporated as Laurium: 1895

Land area: 0.7 sq. miles

Elevation: 1,246 ft.

Latitude: 47.24 N

Longitude: 88.44 W

Population: 2,126 (2000)   1,999 (2007 est.)

Males: 963 (48%)

Females: 1,036 (52%)

Median age: 39.5

Races in Laurium:

- White Non-Hispanic (97.9%)
- American Indian (1.0%)
- Two or more races (0.6%)
- Hispanic (0.5%)

Ancestries: German (16.6%), English (10.9%), Italian (10.8%), French (10.3%), Swedish (8.6%), Irish (6.4%). 0.6% Foreign born

Laurium Manor Bed and Breakfast

Median household income: $30,200 (year 2005)

Median house value: $65,700 (year 2005)

Industries providing employment:

Educational, health and social services   35%

Retail trade   15%

Arts, entertainment, accommodation and food services   11%

Manufacturing 10%

SOUTH RANGE 49963

Named after: Location at south end of county next to the Copper Range Mines

Incorporated as a village: 1906

Land area: 0.4 sq. miles   **Elevation:** 1,140 ft.

Latitude: 47.07 N   **Longitude:** 88.64 W

Population: 727 (2000)   686 (2007 est.)

Males: 354 (52%)   **Females:** 332 (48%)

Median age: 40.4

Races in South Range:

- White Non-Hispanic (96.8%) •Black (2.2%)

Ancestries: Italian (14.2%), English (11.7%), German (10.7%), French (7.2%), Irish (5.1%), Swedish (4.1%). 0.3% Foreign born

Median household income: $26,250 (year 2000)
Median house value: $42,000 (year 2000)

Industries providing employment:
    Educational, health and social services   23%
    Retail trade   22%
    Construction   11%

HUBBELL 49934

Named after: Hubbell's Mill, a sawmill and station on the Chicago, Milwaukee & St. Paul railroad
Once known as: Hubbell's Mill; South Lake Linden
Slogan:
Incorporated:
Land area: 0.7 sq. miles   **Elevation:** 1,246 ft.
Latitude: 47.17 N   **Longitude:** 88.43 W
Population: 1,105 (2000)   1,081 (2007 est.)
Males: 503 (47%)   **Females:** 578 (53%)
Median age: 40.7
Races in Hubbell:

- White Non-Hispanic (97.6%)
- American Indian (1.1%)
- Hispanic (1.0%)
- Two or more races (0.9%)

Ancestries: French (23.1%), German (16.2%), English (10.8%), French Canadian (10.7%), Italian (9.3%), Irish (6.2%). 1.6% Foreign born

Median household income: $29,400 (year 2005)

Median house value: $49,200 (year 2005)

Industries providing employment:
    Educational, health and social services   42%
    Retail trade   16%

IRON COUNTY   COUNTY SEAT: CRYSTAL FALLS*

Organized: On April 3, 1885 from Marquette and Menominee counties

Named after: Iron. In 1846 William Burt discovered iron ore in the region. Iron County is the only county in Michigan not named after a person, a geographical anomaly, or an Indian word.
Square miles (total): 1,211
Land: 1,166
Water: 45
Stats: (state rank out of 83 counties)
Population: 2007 (est) 12,151 (72) **2000:** 13,138

Labor force: 5,951 (71)
Unemployment rate (2008): 8.6%
Median household income: $31,163 (79)
Poverty rate: 12.9% (37)
Per capita income: $25,458 (45)
Avg. earnings per job: $28,095 (62)
Median age: 45
Ratio males to females (over 18): 96/100
Largest city: Iron River 1,789 (2007 est.)

Early settlement: Ojibwa Indians arrived from the east hundreds of years ago. They were attracted to the Iron County region by the excellent hunting and fishing.

White settlers began to arrive after the discovery of iron ore in 1846. Much of the early work involved clearing land and building rails for access to the mines. The railways were built in the 1870s. The first big company, Crystal Falls Iron Company, was formed in 1880. Eventually there were over 70 mines producing iron ore in Iron County.

IRON COUNTY

This county was set off in 1885 from Marquette and Menominee counties. Iron ore deposits which gave the new county its name were the first on the Menominee Iron Range to be discovered. Shipping of ores began in 1882 when the railroad came in. Iron River was the first county seat, but in 1889, after a celebrated struggle, the government was shifted to Crystal Falls. Logging, which began in 1875, has been second only to mining in Iron County's economy.

Iron County Historical Marker

*Iron River was chosen as the county seat, however residents in the eastern half of the county objected. Legend has it that the dispute was to be settled by a friendly game of poker. During the game, two key county commissioners said good night and went to bed...or so they said.

Supposedly, they went to the courthouse and removed all of the county business records, then hid them away in a mine shaft or hollow tree. On learning of the missing records, Iron River residents were mad and threatened violence if the records weren't returned. Instead a public vote was held with the Crystal Falls supporters winning by five votes, and the county seat was moved from Iron River.

Township populations

Crystal Falls	1,722
Iron River	1,585
Stambaugh	1,248
Bates	1,021
Mastodon	668
Hematite	352
Mansfield	243

CITIES

CASPIAN 49915

Named after: The Caspian Baltic and Fogarty Mines operated by the Veroner Mining Co. headquartered in Caspian.
Once known as: Spring Valley; Newtown; Palatka
Incorporated as a village: 1919
Land area: 1.4 sq. miles   **Elevation:** 1,492 ft.
Latitude: 46.06N   **Longitude:** 88.63 W

Population: 997 (2000)   895 (2007 est.)
Males: 435 (49%)   **Females:** 460 (51%)
Median age: 42.5

Races in Caspian:
- White Non-Hispanic (97.0%)
- American Indian (1.6%)
- Two or more races (0.5%)

Ancestries: Italian (27.9%), German (21.1%), Polish (13.7%), Swedish (12.0%), French (9.5%), Irish (7.1%). 2.6% Foreign born

Median household income: $24,400 (year 2005)
Median house value: $45,600 (year 2005)

Industries providing employment:
Retail trade   19%
Educational, health and social services   17%
Manufacturing   13%
Arts, entertainment, accommodation and food services   13%

CRYSTAL FALLS 49920

Named after: For the falls on the Paint River
Slogan: *Home of the Humongous Fungus*
Incorporated as a village: 1889
Incorporated as a city: 1899
Land area: 3.4 sq. miles   **Elevation:** 1,517 ft.
Latitude: 46.10 N   **Longitude:** 88.33 W

Population: 1,791 (2000)   1,616 (2007 est.)
Males: 766 (47%)   **Females:** 850 (53%)
Median age: 45.0
Races in Crystal Falls:
- White Non-Hispanic (97.3%)
- American Indian (1.3%)
- Hispanic (1.2%)
- Two or more races (0.8%)

Ancestries: German (15.9%), Swedish (15.0%), Italian (14.8%), English (11.9%), Polish (11.3%), Irish (7.7%). 1.9% Foreign born

Median household income: $26,500 (year 2005)
Median house value: $60,400 (year 2005)
Industries providing employment:
Educational, health and social services   33%
Retail trade   11%

GAASTRA 49927

Named after: Real estate speculator and builder, Douwe Gaastra who platted the town in 1908.
Incorporated as a village: 1919
Incorporated as a city: 1949
Land area: 1.65 sq. miles   **Elevation:** 1,620 ft.

Latitude: 46.06 N   **Longitude:** 88.61 W
Population: 339 (2000)   304 (2007 est.)
Males: 141 (47%)
Females: 163 (53%)
Median age: 44.1
Races in Gaastra

- White Non-Hispanic (97.1%)
- American Indian (1.5%)
- Two or more races (1.5%)
- Hispanic (0.9%)
- Other race (0.6%)

Ancestries: Polish (28.6%), Italian (19.2%), French (11.2%), Irish (6.5%), United States (6.5%), English (5.6%).
Median household income: $23,000 (year 2005)
Median house value: $44,800 (year 2005)

IRON RIVER 49935

Named after: Location in the iron region
Once known as: Nanaimo (after the mine of the same name)
Slogan: *Michigan's First Consolidated City*
Incorporated as a village: 1885
Incorporated as a city: 1926
Land area: 3.5 sq. miles
Elevation: 1,510 ft.
Latitude: 46.10 N
Longitude: 88.64 W
Population: 1,929 (2000)
            1,787 (2007 est.)
Males: 866 (45%) **Females:** 1,063 (55%)
Median age: 39.5
Races in Iron River:

- White Non-Hispanic (94.7%)
- American Indian (3.9%)
- Two or more races (2.3%)
- Hispanic (0.8%)

Ancestries: German (19.0%), Swedish (15.5%), Polish (11.9%), Italian (11.9%), English (10.7%), Irish (9.4%). 0.5% Foreign born

Median household income: $23,300 (year 2005)

Median house value: $56,000 (year 2005)

Industries providing employment:
    Educational, health and social services   27%
    Retail trade   12%
    Manufacturing 11%
    Arts, entertainment, accommodation and food services   11%

UNINCORPORATED VILLAGES

Amasa

TOWNSHIPS

STAMBAUGH 49964

Named after: John Stambaugh, president of the Todd, Stambaugh Co, owner of the Iron River Mine, or Stambaugh Mine;

Incorporated as a village: 1890

Incorporated as a city: 1923

Land area: 1.6 sq. miles   **Elevation:** 1,539 ft.

Latitude: 46.08 N   **Longitude:** 88.63 W

Population: 1,243 (2000) 1,151 (2007 est.)

Males: 522 (46%)   **Females:** 629 (54%)

Median age: 43.2

Races in Stambaugh:
- White Non-Hispanic (95.7%)
- American Indian (3.0%)
- Two or more races (1.4%)

Ancestries: German (21.3%), Swedish (13.8%), English (12.8%), Italian (11.1%), Polish (11.1%), French (10.4%). 0.9% Foreign born

Median household income: $23,500 (year 2005)

Median house value: $48,900 (year 2005)

Industries providing employment:
   Educational, health and social services   22%
   Arts, entertainment, accommodation and food services   12%
   Retail trade   10%

MINERAL HILLS 49935

Named after: The iron hills in the area.

Incorporated as a village: 1918

Land area: 1.4 sq. miles   **Elevation:** ft.

Latitude: 46.12N   **Longitude:** 88.65 W

Population: 214 (2000) 198 (2007 est.)

Males: 102 (52%)   **Females:** 96 (48%)

Median age: 35.8

Races in Mineral Hills:
- White Non-Hispanic (96.7%)
- American Indian (2.3%)
- Two or more races (2.3%)

Ancestries: English (13.1%), Italian (11.2%), German (10.3%), Irish (8.4%), French (7.9%), Polish (6.5%).

Median household income: $30,600 (year 2005)

Median house value: $46,500 (year 2005)

Industries providing employment:
   Educational, health and social services   21%
   Arts, entertainment, accommodation and food services 14%
   Public administration 14%
   Retail trade   11%

KEWEENAW COUNTY
COUNTY SEAT: EAGLE RIVER

Organized: March 11, 1861 set off from Houghton County.

Named after: From the Native American word "Kee-wi-wai-non-ing," meaning "place where portage is made."

Square miles (total): 5,966   **Land:** 541   **Water:** 5,425

Stats: (state rank out of 83 counties)

Population: 2007 (est) 2,151 (83)   **2000:** 2,301

Labor force: 1,068 (83)   **Unemployment rate (2008):** 11.3% (10)

Median household income: $31,391 (79)   **Poverty rate:** 12.8% (39)

Per capita income: $25,740 (43)   **Avg. earnings per job:** $19,235 (83)

Median age: 45   **Ratio of males to females (over 18):** 104/100

Early settlement: The first permits for copper mines were issued on the Keweenaw Peninsula and the first settlements of Copper Country were established. By the mid 1850s, the Central Mine was producing copper and providing a living for hundreds of newly arrived residents.

The first census of the county in 1870 counted 4,953 residents.

Eagle River Lighthouse

Township Populations

Allouez	1,584
Eagle Harbor	281
Houghton	204
Grant	172
Sherman	60

UNINCORPORATED VILLAGES

Copper Harbor, Eagle River, Lac La Belle

VILLAGES

AHMEEK 49901

*In 1875, **Isle Royale County** was created from Keweenaw County. The new county lasted until 1897, when the boundary lines were dissolved and the land and water area reverted back to Keweenaw County.*

LUCE COUNTY   COUNTY SEAT: NEWBERRY

Organized: March 1, 1887 from Chippewa County and a small portion of Mackinac County.

Named after: Cyrus Gray Luce who was Governor of Michigan (1887-1890) when the county was formed.

Square miles (total): 1,912

Land: 903
Water: 1,008
Stats: (state rank out of 83 counties)
Population: (2007 est.) 6,728 (82)   2000: 7,024
Labor force: 2,741 (82)
Unemployment rate (2006): 7.5% (44)   **Median household income:** $34,462 (68)
Poverty rate: 16.2% (6)
Per capita income: $19,115 (83)   **Avg. earnings per job:** $31,675 (40)
Median Age: 39   **Ratio males to females (over 18):** 132/100
Largest village: Newberry 2,579

Early settlement: There was little settlement in Luce County until 1881 when the Detroit, Mackinac & Marquette railroad built a line from St. Ignace to Marquette. After the rail was completed, Truman H. Newberry started the Vulcan Furnace Company. The area became a logging headquarters and the town of Newberry was established in 1882.

Township Populations

McMillan	3,947
Pentland	1,788
Lakefield	1,074
Columbus	215

VILLAGES

NEWBERRY 49868

Named after: Truman H. Newberry, industrialist from Detroit, who opened the Vulcan Furnace Company near the rail line.

Once known as: Grant's Corner

Slogan: *The Official Moose Capital of Michigan*

Incorporated as a village: 1885

Land area: 1.0 sq. miles

Elevation: 788 ft.

Latitude: 46.35 N

Longitude: 85.51 W

Population: 2,686 (2000)
                2579 (2007 est.)

Males: 1,661 (64%) **Females:** 918 (36%)

Median age: 33.9

Races in Newberry:
- White Non-Hispanic (69.1%)
- Black (19.3%)
- American Indian (7.2%)
- Two or more races (4.1%)
- Hispanic (3.7%)
- Other race (1.0%)

Ancestries: German (13.3%), Irish (8.8%), English (8.5%), French (7.2%), United States (4.5%), French Canadian (4.0%). 1.5% Foreign born

Median household income: $29,052 (year 2000)
Median house value: $53,900 (year 2000)
Industries providing employment:
    Educational, health and social services   25%
    Public administration   17%
    Arts, entertainment, accommodation and food services   14%
    Retail trade   11%

MACKINAC COUNTY
COUNTY SEAT: ST. IGNACE

Organized: First laid out as Michilimackinac County by order of Michigan Territories Governor Lewis Cass, it included most of the land in the lower and upper peninsulas. County government organized in 1849. The original county seat was Michilimackinac Island until 1882 when it was moved to St. Ignace.
  Named after: Michinimackinong, Chippewa word for place of the "Great Turtle."
  Square miles (total): 2,100   **Land:** 1,021 **Water:** 1,079
  Stats: (state rank out of 83 counties)
  Population: 2007 (est) 10,877 (75)   2000 11,943
  Labor force: 6,436 (71)   **Unemployment rate (2008):** 12.0%
  Median household income: $35,347 (62)   **Poverty rate:** 10.5% (61)
  Per capita income: $28,619 (25)   **Avg. earnings per job:** $25,905 (75)
  Median Age: 43   **Ratio of males to females (over 18):** 97/100

Largest city: St. Ignace 2,384 (2007)

Early settlement: Thousands of years ago ancient Indians fished the waters of the Straits, rowed handmade canoes to Mackinac Island and buried their dead in the island caves. The Straits region of Mackinac County was one of the earliest modern Native American settlements in Michigan.

Huron Indians, fleeing attacking Iroquois from the east, settled on Mackinac Island in 1651. Two years later, they moved west to the safety of present-day Green Bay, Wisconsin. By the mid 1650s, French fur traders and hundreds of local Ottawa and Huron Indians were engaging in trade and transportation of beaver pelts through the Straits.

In the mid 1600s, explorers, fur traders and missionaries from Montreal (New France) discovered the Mackinac region. It became a major center of commerce for the fur trade through the 1700s.

In 1671, the French claimed ownership of the Upper Peninsula and all lands west. That same year, Jesuit missionary Father Jacques Marquette established a mission at St. Ignace. About the same time, French soldiers established Fort DeBuade, later named Fort Mackinac.

The first French priest in the region was Father Claude Allouez who traveled from the LaPointe mission on Lake Superior to Sault Ste. Marie before traveling through the Straits in November of 1669. The Allouez party spent a week on a Lake Huron island he named St. Martin's Island he and his party departed the island on St. Martin's Day.

In 1670, St. Ignace was chosen as the site for a new Jesuit mission because of its location on the busy trade route. Father Claude Dablon spent the first winter (1670) there before Father Marquette arrived (1671) and built a temporary chapel. In 1673, Marquette and Joliet left St. Ignace in search of a passage to the West. Huron and Ottawa Indians numbered over one thousand in the 1670s. They built forts on the bays around St. Ignace.

The Straits served not only as a commercial passage but a strategic military outpost. The French ruled until 1760 when they were defeated in Canada by the British. The Brits moved into Forth Michilimackinac on the southern shore of the Straits where they suffered a massacre under a surprise attack by Indians from a number of tribes in the region. In 1780, they re-established the fort and moved it over the frozen water to Mackinac Island.

In 1783 following the Revolutionary War, the fort and Island were handed over to American control. In 1809, John Jacob Astor established the American Fur Company headquarters on Mackinac Island. Three years later during the War of 1812, the Island fort was captured by the British, who occupied it until 1815. It has remained under U.S. control since.

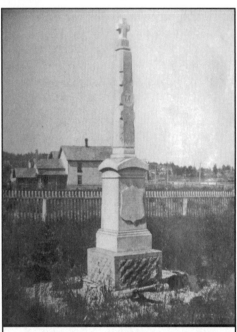

Father Marquette Memorial at St. Ignace

The American Fur Company left the island in 1854. By the 1880s, with the construction of the Grand Hotel on Mackinac Island and the growth of the railroad and steamship industry, the area became a vacation destination for wealthy city dwellers from Illinois, Lower Michigan and other southern points.

Township populations

Clark	2,200
Garfield	1,251
Moran	1,080
Portage	1,055
St. Ignace	1,024
Marquette	659
Brevort	649
Newton	356
Hudson	214
Hendricks	183
Bois Blanc	71

CITIES

ST. IGNACE 49781

Named after: St. Ignatius Loyola, founder of the Jesuits. Named by Father Jacques Marquette who founded a mission here in 1671.

Once known as: Mackinac; Ancient Fort Mackinac

Slogan: *Home of the Mackinac Bridge*

Incorporated as a village: 1882   **Incorporated as a city:** 1883

Land area: 2.7 sq. miles   **Elevation:** 788 ft.

Latitude: 45.87 N   **Longitude:** 84.73 W

Population: 2,678 (2000) 2,384 (2007 est.)

Males: 1,151 (48%)   **Females:** 1,233 (52%)

Median age: 38.9

Races in St. Ignace:
- White Non-Hispanic (71.5%)
- American Indian (26.6%)
- Two or more races (7.7%)
- Hispanic (0.9%)

Ancestries: German (19.8%), Irish (12.6%), French (10.9%), English (9.0%), Polish (7.8%), French Canadian (4.9%). 1.7% Foreign born

Median household income: $34,200 (year 2005)

Median house value: $112,200 (year 2005)

MACKINAC ISLAND 49757

Named after: Michilimackinac, French interpretation of Indian word. Was the county seat of Michilimackinac County in 1822.

Once known as: Michilimackinac

Incorporated as a village: 1882

Incorporated as a city: 1883

Land area: 4.4 sq. miles

Elevation: 590 ft.

Latitude: 45.85 N

Longitude: 84.62 W

Population: 523 (2000)   843 (2007 est.)

Males: 246 (52%)

Females: 227 (48%)

Median age: 41

Races in Mackinac Island:
- White Non-Hispanic (75.3%)
- American Indian (23.7%)
- Two or more races (5.4%)
- Hispanic (0.6%)

Mackinac County Court House. Photo by Ron Jolly

Ancestries: German (23.9%), Irish (16.6%), English (11.9%), French (8.8%), Polish (6.3%), Scottish (5.2%). 2.1% Foreign born

Median household income: $36,700 (year 2005)

Median house value: $220,700 (year 2005)

Industries providing employment:

Educational, health and social services   22%

Retail trade 16%

Arts, entertainment, accommodation and food services   16%

Professional, scientific, management, administrative services   13%

Transportation, warehousing, and utilities   10%

UNINCORPORATED VILLAGES

Brevort, Cedarville, Curtis, Hessel, Moran, Pointe aux Pins, Engadine, Naubinway

MARQUETTE COUNTY
COUNTY SEAT: MARQUETTE

Organized: In 1843 Marquette, Ontonagon and Schoolcraft counties were formed from Mackinac County. Until 1845 Marquette County included current day Houghton and Keweenaw counties. Marquette County was officially organized in 1851.

In 1867, the Michigan Supreme Court ruled against creation of a new county to be named Washington that would have contained some of the most valuable mining property in and around Ishpeming. The court ruling kept Marquette boundary lines as they were, and put an end to any idea of a Washington County in Michigan.

Named after: Father Jacques Marquette, Jesuit priest and explorer.

Square miles (total): 3,425   **Land:** 1,821 **Water:** 1,604

Stats: (state rank out of 83 counties)

Population: 2007 (est) 65,218 (30)   2000 64,634

Labor force: 35,753 (30)   **Unemployment rate (2008):** 7.1%

Median household income: $39,167 (43)   **Poverty rate:** 12.1% (47)

Per capita income: $26,506 (38)   **Avg. earnings per job:** $32,134 (35)

Median age: 38   **Ratio males to females (over 18):** 100/100

Largest city: Marquette 20,780 (2007 est.)

Early settlement: In 1820, Territorial Governor Lewis Cass stopped at present day Marquette during a federally sponsored expedition along the southern shore of Lake Superior. The governor hoped to confirm earlier reports of large copper deposits in the western U.P. and win cessation of land from Native Americans in order to attract settlers to the northern wilderness.

By 1842, the Lake Superior Ojibwe ceded their land in the western U.P., including Marquette County west of the Chocolay River (the land east of the Chocolay was ceded in 1836), to the federal government. In 1844, government surveyor William Burt discovered iron ore deposits near Negaunee after the needle on his magnetic compass began operating erratically. This led to the mining rush and settlement of Marquette County.

In 1845, a party led by Jackson, Michigan resident Philo M. Everett was led to a rich iron deposit near present-day Negaunee by Indian chief Marji Geesik. Two years later, the Cleveland Iron Company was formed to prospect for minerals in the wilderness. The Cleveland Mine opened near Ishpeming in 1853, and began producing commercial amounts of iron ore the next year. The company merged with the Iron Cliffs Company in 1891 and became the largest mining company in the Marquette range.

The mines offered hard work, dangerous conditions and long hours and attracted a work force that included immigrants from Finland, Ireland, Canada, Italy, France, England, Germany, and Sweden. The mining families learned to deal with the harsh winters and established strong communities in Negaunee, Ishpeming, Marquette, and later, by the end of the civil war, in towns like Forsyth, Champion, and Humboldt. By the end of the Civil War. By 1880, the county had already established its first hospital, churches and schools, roads, railroads and telephone service. It even had a baseball team.

Township populations

Chocolay Charter	7,148
Forsyth	4,824
Ishpeming	3,522
Marquette Charter	3,286
Negaunee	2,707
Sands	2,127
Ely	2,010
West Branch	1,648
Republic	1,106
Tilden	1,003
Richmond	974
Skandia	907
Powell	724
Humboldt	469
Michigamme	377
Champion	297
Wells	292
Ewing	159
Turin	131

View of the Marquette County Courthouse through the front gate.

CITIES

MARQUETTE 49855

Named after: Father Jacques Marquette the Jesuit missionary

Once known as: Worcester; Iron Bay; Carp River; White's Carp River

Slogan: *The Superior Location*; The *Premiere City in an All-American County*

Incorporated as a village: 1849

Incorporated as a city: 1871

Land area: 11.4 sq. miles   **Elevation:** 628 ft.

Latitude: 46.55 N   **Longitude:** 87.40 W

Population: 19,661 (2000)   20,780 (2007 est.)

Males: 10,091 (49%)   **Females:** 10,689 (51%)

Median age: 30.6

Races in Marquette:
- White Non-Hispanic (94.5%)
- American Indian (2.5%)
- Two or more races (1.3%)
- Black (0.8%)
- Hispanic (0.8%)

Ancestries: German (20.3%), French (12.9%), English (12.6%), Irish (11.7%), Swedish (8.6%), Italian (7.0%). 1.9% Foreign born

Median household income: $29,700 (year 2005)

Median house value: $112,200 (year 2005)

Industries providing employment:
Educational, health and social services 33%
Arts, entertainment, accommodation and food services   15%
Retail trade   14%

ISHPEMING 49849

"Old Ish" Downtown Ishpeming
Photo by S. Willey

Named after: Chippewa for *heaven or higher place.*
Once known as: Lake Superior
Slogan: *The Lake Superior Location*; *Home of the National Ski Hall of Fame*
Incorporated as a village: 1871
Incorporated as a city: 1873
Land area: 8.7 sq. miles
Elevation: 1,411 ft.
Latitude: 46.49 N
Longitude: 87.67 W
Population: 6,686 (2000) 6,474 (2007 est.)
Males: 3,158 (47%)
Females: 3,416 (53%)
Median age: 38.9

Races in Ishpeming:
- White Non-Hispanic (96.8%)
- American Indian (1.9%)
- Two or more races (1.0%)
- Hispanic (0.8%)

Ancestries: English (19.3%), French (18.6%), Italian (15.6%), German (11.0%), Swedish (9.4%), Irish (9.3%). 1.2% Foreign born

Median household income: $31,200 (year 2005)
Median house value: $67,600 (year 2005)
Industries providing employment:
Educational, health and social services   21%
Retail trade   12%
Arts, entertainment, accommodation and food services   11%

NEGAUNEE 49866

Named after: Chippewa for *pioneer*
Once known as: Neganee
Slogan: *Survey the past...explore the future!*
Incorporated as a village: 1865
Incorporated as a city: 1873
Land area: 13.8 sq. miles   **Elevation:** 1,375 ft.
Latitude: 46.50 N   **Longitude:** 87.60 W
Population: 4,576 (2000)   4,451 (2007 est.)
Males: 2,133 (48%)   **Females:** 2,313 (52%)
Median age: 40.4

Races in Negaunee:
- White Non-Hispanic (96.4%)
- American Indian (2.3%)
- Two or more races (1.4%)

Ancestries: English (18.8%), Italian (14.7%), Swedish (14.6%), German (13.4%), French (10.6%), Irish (5.9%). 1.0% Foreign born
Median household income: $32,900 (year 2005)
Median house value: $79,600 (year 2005)
Industries providing employment:

    Educational, health and social services   25%
    Retail trade   14%

BIG BAY 49808

Named after: Its location on Big Bay on Lake Superior
Slogan: *Your Destination for Adventure, Exploration and Relaxation*
Land area: 3.8 sq. miles   **Elevation:** 685 ft.
Latitude: 46.81 N   **Longitude:** 87.73 W
Population: 265 (2000)   267 (2007 est.)
Males: 137 (51%)   **Females:** 130 (49%)
Median age: 50.9

Races in Big Bay:
- White Non-Hispanic (96.2%)
- American Indian (3.8%)
- Two or more races (1.5%)

Ancestries: German (24.2%), French (18.9%), English (14.7%), Irish (14.0%), Swedish (9.4%), French Canadian (8.3%).

Median household income: $34,500 (year 2005)
Median house value: $106,100 (year 2005)
Industries providing employment:

    Educational, health and social services   29%
    Arts, entertainment, accommodation and food services 24%
    Retail trade   12%

GWINN 49841

Named after: William Gwinn Mather, president of Cleveland-Cliffs Iron Company, named the town after his mother's maiden name. Also named the company mine the Gwinn Mine.
Slogan: *A model town.*
Land area: 5.1 sq. miles   **Elevation:** 1,090 ft.
Latitude: 46.28 N   **Longitude:** 87.44 W
Population: 1,965 (2000) 1,983 (2007 est.)
Males: 976 (49%)   **Females:** 1,007 (51%)
Median age: 42.3
Races in Gwinn:
- White Non-Hispanic (94.4%)
- American Indian (2.5%)

- Two or more races (1.4%)
- Black (0.9%)
- Hispanic (0.9%)

Ancestries: Italian (17.4%), English (14.5%), French (13.4%), German (13.0%), Irish (9.8%), United States (6.8%). 1.5% Foreign born

Median household income: $30,600 (year 2005)

Median house value: $81,500 (year 2005)

Industries providing employment:
Educational, health and social services   26%
Retail trade   14%

HARVEY 49855

Named after: Charles T. Harvey, founder of the Northern Iron Co. and the town.

Once known as: Chocolay after the Chocolay Creek

Land area: 2.0 sq. miles   **Elevation:** 195 ft.

Latitude: 46.49 N   **Longitude:** 87.35 W

Population: 1,321 (2000)   1,333 (2007 est.)

Males: 679 (51%)   **Females:** 654 (49%)

Median age: 36.6

Races in Harvey:

- White Non-Hispanic (93.6%)
- American Indian (3.6%)
- Two or more races (1.7%)
- Black (1.1%)
- Hispanic (0.6%)

Ancestries: French (17.9%), German (14.7%), English (12.5%), Irish (9.9%), Swedish (7.8%), Italian (7.6%). 0.3% Foreign born

Median household income: $37,100 (year 2005)

Median house value: $125,900 (year 2005)

Industries providing employment:
Educational, health and social services   29%
Retail trade   20%

MICHIGAMME 49861

Named after: The Michigamme Mine discovered by Jacob Houghton in 1872.

Incorporated as a village: 1872

Land area: 2.5 sq. miles   **Elevation:** 1,620 ft.

Latitude: 46.34 N   **Longitude:** 87.10 W

Population: 287 (2000) 289 (2007 est.)

Males: 140 (49%)   **Females:** 149 (51%)

Median age: 50.5

Races in Michigamme:

- White Non-Hispanic (99.3%)
- American Indian (0.7%)

Ancestries: German (16.4%), French (13.2%), Irish (8.4%), Swedish (8.4%), English

(7.3%), Italian (7.3%). 1.7% Foreign born
Median household income: $26,900 (year 2005)
Median house value: $63,600 (year 2005)
Industries providing employment:

Agriculture, forestry, fishing and hunting, and mining   19%
Manufacturing   17%
Educational, health and social services   13%
Public administration   13%

PALMER 49871

Named after: Mining executive, L.C. Palmer
Land area: 0.6 sq. miles   **Elevation:** 1,298 ft.
Latitude: 46.44 N   **Longitude:** 87.59 W

Population: 449 (2000)   453 (2007 est.)
Males: 223 (49%)   **Females:** 230 (51%)
Median age: 43.9
Races in Palmer:

- White Non-Hispanic (96.4%)
- American Indian (3.1%)
- Two or more races (2.0%)

Ancestries: French (13.1%), English (10.5%), German (9.8%), Swedish (9.6%), Italian (8.0%), Irish (7.6%). 1.1% Foreign born
Median household income: $28,900 (year 2005)
Median house value: $49,600 (year 2005)
Industries providing employment:

Educational, health and social services   29%
Retail trade   16%

REPUBLIC 49879

Named after: Ed Breitung, founder of the Republic Mine renamed the town from Iron City to Republic for "the land of the free and the home of the brave."
Once known as: Iron City
Land area: 3.6 sq. miles   **Elevation:** 1,520 ft.
Latitude: 46.38 N   **Longitude:** 87.98 W

Population: 614 (2000)   619 (2007 est.)
Males: 294 (48%)   **Females:** 325 (52%)
Median age: 45.1
Races in Republic:

- White Non-Hispanic (98.0%)
- American Indian (2.0%)

Ancestries: German (10.7%), Swedish (9.9%), French (8.0%), English (6.7%), Irish (5.0%), Italian (3.7%). 0.3% Foreign born

Median household income: $24,400 (year 2005)
Median house value: $43,400 (year 2005)

Industries providing employment:
Educational, health and social services   15%
Agriculture, forestry, fishing and hunting, and mining   13%
Professional, scientific, management, administrative services   13%
Manufacturing 11%
Construction   10%

WEST ISHPEMING 49849
Land area: 3.0 sq. miles   **Elevation:** 1,440 ft.
Latitude: 46.48 N   **Longitude:** 87.71 W
Population: 2,792 (2000)   2,818 (2007 est.)
Males: 1,384 (48%)   **Females:** 1,464 (52%)
Median age: 41.9
Races in West Ishpeming:
• White Non-Hispanic (98.2%)
• American Indian (0.8%)
• Two or more races (0.8%)
• Hispanic (0.5%)

Ancestries: English (22.3%), Italian (13.7%), French (13.5%), Swedish (11.2%), German (8.7%), Irish (6.0%). 1.0% Foreign born

Median household income: $41,500 (year 2005)

Median house value: $95,000 (year 2005)

Industries providing employment:
Educational, health and social services   24%
Retail trade   19%
Agriculture, forestry, fishing and hunting, and mining   11%

UNINCORPORATED VILLAGES
Arnold, Big Bay, Gwinn, Harvey, Michigamme, Palmer, Republic, Trowbridge Park, West Ishpeming

MENOMINEE COUNTY
COUNTY SEAT: MENOMINEE
Organized: Formed as Bleeker County in 1861 from Delta County. Renamed Menominee in 1863.
Named after: Menominee County was named after a Native American Tribe that lived in the vicinity. By most accounts Menominee means, "rice men" or "wild rice gatherers."
Square miles (total): 1,338   **Land:** 1,044   **Water:** 294
Stats: (state rank out of 83 counties)
Population: 25,326 (2000) 24,249 (2007 est.)
Labor force: 13,479 (55)   **Unemployment rate (2008):** 6.4% (65)
Median household income: $36,507 (56)   **Poverty rate:** 11.8% (49)

Per capita income: $25,094 (48)   **Avg. earnings per job:** $28,157 (61)
Median age: 40   **Ratio of males to females (over 18):** 97/100
Largest city: Menominee   8,397 (2007 est.)

Early settlement: The Menominee tribe of Indians settled in the area at the mouth of the Menominee River. Menominee comes from the word meaning "rice people." These Indians harvested and grew wild rice in the marshy areas of the region.

In 1790, the French Canadian fur trader, Louis Chaput opened a trading post at present day Menominee. By the 1830s, the lumber industry was established in Menominee County with the first mill opening in 1832.

In 1852, Samuel Stephenson moved form Delta County to open the second mill on the Menominee River. He went on to become a U.S. Representative for the district and served in the U.S. Senate, while the Menominee region became one of the most successful lumbering regions in the country.

Fur traders were the first settlers to the area in the late 1700s but lumbering quickly shaped the area's economy. By 1890, the region ranked second in lumber production in the nation. By the early 20th Century, the supply of lumber was exhausted and residents turned to agriculture. The first school of agriculture in Michigan was established at Menomiee.

Township populations

Menominee	3,939
Harris	1,895
Spalding	1,761
Mellen	1,260
Nadeau	1,160
Ingallston	1,042
Meyer	1,036
Daggett	740
Stephenson	716
Lake	576
Gourley	409
Holmes	296
Cedarville	276
Faithorn	214

Menominee County Courthouse in Menominee

CITIES

MENOMINEE 49858

Named after: The Indian tribe that ceded control of their land to the United States in an 1836 treaty

Incorporated as a city: 1883
Land area: 5.2 sq. miles   **Elevation:** 590 ft.
Latitude: 45.12 N   **Longitude:** 87.62 W

Population: 9,131 (2000) 8,397 (2007 est.)
Males: 4,041 (48%) **Females:** 4,356 (52%)
Median age: 39.4

Races in Menominee:
- White Non-Hispanic (96.7%)
- American Indian (1.6%)
- Hispanic (1.1%)
- Two or more races (1.1%)

Ancestries: German (34.4%), French (14.1%), Polish (10.5%), Swedish (10.1%), Irish (9.2%), French Canadian (6.6%). 0.8% Foreign born

Estimated median household income: $30,300 (2005)
Estimated median house/condo value: $73,100 (2005)
Industries providing employment:
>Manufacturing 34%
>Educational, health and social services   18%

Menominee is the southernmost city in the Upper Peninsula.

STEPHENSON 49887
Named after: Samuel Stephenson, local civic leader and Congressman for the district
Once known as: Wacedah
Incorporated as a village: 1898
Land area: 1.1 sq. miles   **Elevation:** 670 ft.
Latitude: 45.41 N   **Longitude:** 87.61 W

Population: 875 (2000)   808 (2007 est.)
Males: 359 (45%)   **Females:** 449 (55%)
Median age: 47.6
Races in Stephenson:
- White Non-Hispanic (98.1%)
- American Indian (1.1%)
- Two or more races (1.1%)

Ancestries: German (32.6%), French (14.7%), Swedish (14.7%), Polish (9.6%), French Canadian (8.6%), Irish (6.5%). 0.3% Foreign born
Median household income: $25,200 (year 2005)
Median house value: $78,100 (year 2005)
Industries providing employment:
>Manufacturing 28%
>Educational, health and social services   18%
>Retail trade   11%

UNINCORPORATED VILLAGES

Cedar River, Wallace

VILLAGES

CARNEY   49812
Named after: Local land owner Fred Carney of Marinette, who logged in the area.
Land area: 1.0 sq. miles   **Elevation:** 790 ft.
Latitude: 45.59 N   **Longitude:** 87.55 W
Population: 225 (2000) 212 (2007 est.)

Males: 104 (49%)   **Females:** 108 (51%)
Median age: 40.1
Races in Carney:
- White Non-Hispanic (99.1%)
- Hispanic (0.9%)

Ancestries: German (30.2%), French (13.8%), Irish (8.4%), Italian (8.4%), Polish (8.4%), English (7.6%). 0.9% Foreign born
Median household income: $30,900 (year 2005)
Median house value: $58,400 (year 2005)
Industries providing employment:
    Educational, health and social services   29%
    Manufacturing   18%
    Retail trade   13%

DAGGETT 49821

Named after: The father-in-law of the town's founder, Thomas Faulkner. He married Clara Daggett who ran the the town's first post office from their kitchen.
Land area: 1.1 sq. miles   **Elevation:** 790 ft.
Latitude: 45.59 N   **Longitude:** 87.55 W
Population: 270 (2000) 254 (2007 est.)
Males: 118 (47%)   **Females:** 136 (53%)
Median age: 34.3
Races in Daggett:
- White Non-Hispanic (98.5%)
- Two or more races (1.1%)

Ancestries: German (35.9%), French (13.7%), Swedish (11.9%), Irish (6.7%), English (6.3%), French Canadian (6.3%).
Median household income: $24,400 (year 2005)
Median house value: $58,000 (year 2005)
Industries providing employment:
    Manufacturing   29%
    Educational, health and social services   27%
    Transportation and warehousing and utilities   22%

POWERS 49874

Named after: Chicago & Northwestern railroad civil engineer, Edward Powers, who began acquiring land in 1872
Land area: 1.0 sq. miles   **Elevation:** 869 ft.
Latitude: 45.69 N   **Longitude:** 87.53 W
Population: 430 (2000) 415 (2007 est.)
Males: 159 (39%)   **Females:** 256 (61%)
Median age: 68.3
Races in Powers:
- White Non-Hispanic (97.7%)
- American Indian (2.3%)
- Two or more races (1.9%)

Ancestries: French (23.0%), German (21.4%), Irish (12.6%), English (9.3%), Swedish (8.6%), Polish (6.5%).

Median household income: $20,100 (year 2005)
Median house value: $72,600 (year 2005)
Industries providing employment:
    Manufacturing 26%
    Educational, health and social services   25%
    Transportation and warehousing and utilities   11%

ONTONAGON COUNTY
COUNTY SEAT: ONTONAGON

Organized: Set off from Mackinac and Chippewa counties in 1843. When the county was organized on April 3, 1848, it included what is now Gogebic County until 1887.

Named after: Chippewa word (Nantaonagon) meaning "lost bowl," referring to an Indian story about a girl whose bowl was swept away in the current as she washed dishes. Also said to refer to the bowl-shaped mouth of the Ontonagon River. The name appeared on maps as early as 1672.

Square miles (total): 3,741   **Land:**   1,312   **Water:** 2,429
Stats: (state rank out of 83 counties)
Population 2007 (est): 6,977 (81)   **2000:** 7,818
Labor force: 3,445 (81)   **Unemployment rate (2008):** 9.3% (34)
Median household income: $34,896 (67)   **Poverty rate:** 11.8% (49)
Per capita income: $26,013 (42)   **Avg. earnings per job:** $29,742 (56)
Median age: 46   **Ratio of males to females (over 18):** 103/100
Largest village: Ontonagon 1,544

Early settlement: There are signs of copper-related activity dating back as far as 4,000 years ago. The first Europeans were probably the French fur trappers who discovered the area in the 1600s. English adventurer Alexander Henry developed the first documented mine at present-day Victoria in 1765. After area Indians showed him a five-ton copper boulder, Henry organized a mining expedition that failed. He concluded that it was impossible to extract and ship copper from the region. In 1843, James Kirk Paul was able to move the giant copper boulder from the woods to the mouth of the river, and ship it to Detroit. He was paid $1,800 for the boulder, funds he used to open the Deadfall Saloon. Kirk also operated the first store in town and later a hotel. By the 1850s, Ontonagon was a copper mining boomtown, and later a key lumbering region. A devastating fire destroyed most of the town in August 1896.

Ontonagon Boulder

Township populations

Ontonagon	2,954
Carp Lake	891
Greenland	870
Stannard	833
McMillan	601
Bergland	550
Interior	375
Rockland	324
Haight	228
Matchwood	115
Bohemia	77

Unincorporated Villages

Agate, Bergland, Bruce Crossing, Ewen, Matchwood, Paynesville, Trout Creek

VILLAGES

ONTONAGON 49953

Named after: From the Chippewa word Nan-ton-a-gon, meaning bowl, like the shape of the river's mouth. The name is found on maps dating as far back as 1672.

Incorporated as a village: 1885

Land area: 3.7 sq. miles

Elevation: 642 ft.

Latitude: 46.87 N **Longitude:** 89.31 W

Population: 1,769 (2000) 1,544 (2007 est.)

Males: 738 (48%)

Females: 806 (52%)

Median age: 46.7

Races in Ontonagon:
- White Non-Hispanic (97.2%)
- American Indian (1.6%)
- Two or more races (1.1%)
- Hispanic (0.8%)

Ancestries: German (26.8%), French (10.7%), English (10.4%), Irish (8.3%), Polish (8.0%), Swedish (6.8%). 1.6% Foreign born

Median household income: $28,100 (year 2005)

Median house value: $55,000 (year 2005)

Industries providing employment:

Educational, health and social services   27%

Manufacturing 16%

Retail trade   12%

WHAT'S IN A NAME?

The names of Upper Michigan towns were derived in a number of ways from a variety of sources and circumstances. Some names come via the traditional route—the city or town is named after a prominent citizen or historical figure. For instance, Houghton was named after Dr. Douglass Houghton, early Michigan State Geologist. Marquette was originally named Worcester for the Massachusetts hometown of one of its founders, Amos Harlow. The village's name was then changed to Marquette in honor of the Jesuit Missionary who legend says held worship service along the lakeshore at the present site of the lighthouse.

Other names come from both the native and European heritage of the region. Menominee

Douglass Houghton, Michigan's first State Geologist and namesake for Houghton city and county.

derives its name from its position at the delta of the U.P.'s largest river. The city and river draw their names from the "rice people" or Mnoomin nini. L'Anse, the village at the head of Keweenaw Bay, is a French word meaning cove. Munising comes from the Ojibwa word meaning island in a lake. Sault Ste. Marie got its name from the "Rapids of St. Mary"—the falls that run through the river that the French missionaries Jogues and Raymbault were said to have named in honor of the Virgin Mary in 1641.

Still other town names have less traditional or disputed origins. The Schoolcraft County town of Germfask was fashioned at its inception in 1881 by taking the first letter of eight of its founders: Grant, Edge, Robinson, Mead, French, Ackley, Shepard and Knaggs. Ontonagon is named after the river the village is situated on. However, the name's origin is in dispute. Popular legend says that "Ontonagon" is derived from the Ojibway word "nontounagon," which means "I lost my bowl." Supposedly a member of Chief O-Kun-De-Kun's band was washing bowls near the mouth of the river when she was startled by an unkempt European explorer in a canoe. The woman inadvertently dropped one of the bowls into the river and exclaimed "nontounagon". The white man took her declaration to be a reply to his

SCHOOLCRAFT COUNTY
COUNTY SEAT: MANISTIQUE

Organized: Created in 1843 when it was set off from Mackinac County and became part of Chippewa County. It was attached to Houghton County in 1846 and Marquette County in 1851. Schoolcraft County was officially organized in 1871, with Onota as the first County seat. Onota was settled in 1869 when the Bay Furnace Co. built a blast furnace on the lakeshore. It is now a ghost town in Alger County, which was created from Schoolcraft County in 1885. The County seat was moved to Manistique.

Named after: Henry Rowe Schoolcraft, first Indian Agent for the State of Michigan. Schoolcraft was an explorer who platted parts of the U.P., named many of Michigan's counties, and served as a liaison between the U.S. government and the Native Americans.

Square miles (total): 1,884

Land: 1,178

Water: 706

Stats: (state rank out of 83 counties)

Population 2007 (est): 8,518 (80) **2000:** 8,782

Labor force: 3,952 (80)

Unemployment rate (2008): 11.7% (6)

Median household income: $34,435 (69)

Poverty rate: 13.4% (27)

Per capita income: $23,837 (54)

Avg. earnings per job: $31,919 (38)

Median age:41

Ratio of males to females (over 18): 99/100

Early settlement: Artifacts suggest there were settlers here as far back as 500 B.C. Modern settlement began in the late 19th Century with the logging industry. Father Frederic Baraga established a mission in the region in 1832. A blast furnace was built in Onota in 1869, before it was split off as part of the newly created Alger County. Modern settlement began in Schoolcraft County during the late 19th Century with the logging industry. Several lumber operations were operating in the county by the 1880s and it became a major logging center by the turn of the century.

Largest city: Manistique   3,368 (2007 est.)

Township populations

Hiawatha	1,328
Manistique	1,053
Inwood	722
Thompson	671
Doyle	630
Germfask	491
Mueller	245
Seney	180

CITIES

MANISTIQUE   49854

Named after: The Ojibwa word, *Monistique*, meaning vermillion—a description of the reddish tint to the river. A spelling error was made when registering the name with the state and the name has remained Manistique.

Once known as: Epsport

Incorporated as a village: 1885

Incorporated as a city: 1901

Land area: 3.2 sq. miles

Elevation: 682 ft.

Latitude: 45.96 N

Longitude: 86.25 W

Population: 3,583 (2000)

3,368 (2007 est.)

Males: 1,632 (49%)

Females: 1,736 (51%)

Median age: 38.0

Races in Manistique:

- White Non-Hispanic (86.2%)
- American Indian (7.7%)
- Black (3.7%)
- Two or more races (3.1%)
- Hispanic (1.3%)
- Other Asian (0.5%)

Ancestries: German (21.6%), French (12.4%), Swedish (12.4%), Irish (11.2%), English (7.6%), French Canadian (7.2%). 0.7% Foreign born

Median household income: $24,100 (year 2005)

question about the name of the area. A more scholarly explanation claims the name comes from the native word "Nondon-organ" meaning "hunting river." Seney is either named after the railroad contractor who established a camp at the site in 1882 or from lumberjacks' mispronunciation of Mr. "Sheeney," a prominent town merchant.

The southwestern Baraga County community of Covington may have the most unusual source. The village sprang up quickly in the latter days of the 19th Century during the logging boom. The story goes that when it came time to name the frontier settlement, a name could not be decided upon. None of its first citizens wanted their name used. Finally, on the back of a whiskey bottle, someone spotted the name of the Kentucky town where the liquor was manufactured. The name had a certain ring to it and stuck—Covington!

Covington Town Hall: the town got its name from the back of a whiskey bottle.

MANISTIQUE'S PAST

Water was an integral part of the early history of Manistique. Up until the beginning of the 20th century, water was delivered in barrels by horse-drawn wagons to area hotels, homes and businesses. City authorities recognized the need for a more sophisticated water works. In 1906, a system was devised with Indian River as the water source. This first water and sewer system served the city for about 15 years.

The next upgrade was prompted by the lack of water to fight fires and supply industry. A tower with a pumping station was erected on land donated by the Consolidated Lumber Company. The project was completed in September 1922 and served the city until about 1951 when damage to the old wooden gravity mains forced the city to construct a new system.

The 137-foot water tower was used as city office space and Chamber of Commerce headquarters. However, deterioration of the structure due to time, weather and vandalism forced these entities to abandon the building. The Schoolcraft County Historical Society took over the structure in 1973 and has maintained it ever since.

It was declared a State Historical site in 1979.

Median house value: $60,400 (year 2005)

Industries providing employment:

Educational, health and social services   22%

Arts, entertainment, accommodation and food services 14%

Retail trade   14%

Manufacturing   13%

Manistique water tower now operated as a museum by the Schoolcraft County Historical Society

Remains of the Manistique limestone quarry

Chapter 7

ECONOMY

LABOR FORCE – BY COUNTY

County	2007 (# of workers over 16 years old)
Marquette	35,753
Delta	19,976
Houghton	17,694
Chippewa	17,502
Dickinson	14,462
Menominee	13,475
Gogebic	7,616
Mackinac	6,436
Iron	5,951
Alger	4,517
Baraga	4,312
Schoolcraft	3,952
Ontonagon	3,445
Luce	2,741
Keewenaw	1,068

Workers replacing the shingles on an Upper Peninsula home.

UNEMPLOYMENT RATE (2001-2008) – BY COUNTY

County	Unemployment rate (%)							
	2001	2002	2003	2004	2005	2006	2007	2008
Alger	6.1	7.0	7.7	7.9	7.3	7.8	8.3	9.8
Baraga	8.7	9.6	9.8	11.6	10.8	11.0	12.4	14.0
Chippewa	7.4	7.9	8.8	9.0	8.3	8.4	8.6	9.8
Delta	6.3	7.3	8.3	7.9	7.0	7.1	7.6	8.7
Dickinson	4.9	6.0	6.7	6.4	5.5	5.7	6.0	7.2
Gogebic	6.9	7.6	8.2	7.9	7.4	7.4	7.7	8.9

Houghton	5.9	6.7	6.9	6.4	6.2	6.8	7.1	8.0
Iron	6.2	6.9	7.2	7.5	7.1	7.1	7.3	8.6
Keweenaw	7.9	9.0	10.6	11.9	10.4	10.0	10.7	11.3
Luce	6.5	7.3	7.7	7.5	7.0	7.5	8.9	9.6
Mackinac	8.6	9.2	9.4	10.0	9.9	9.5	9.9	12.0
Marquette	5.4	6.6	6.5	6.1	5.6	6.0	6.1	7.1
Menominee	5.4	6.2	6.1	5.8	5.1	6.3	5.7	6.4
Ontonagon	7.3	7.3	7.7	7.7	7.0	7.8	8.3	9.3
Schoolcraft	8.8	9.9	10.8	11.0	10.3	10.4	10.7	11.7
Upper Peninsula	6.3	7.2	7.6	7.4	6.8			
Michigan	5.2	6.2	7.1	7.1	6.7	6.9	7.2	8.4

Source: Michigan Department of Labor and Growth

OUT OF COMMISSION

The Upper Peninsula was home to a number of U.S. Air Force facilities. These bases and stations are now closed. The closures hit the communities hard with loss of population and civilian jobs connected with the facilities. All three fields left behind are now regional airports:

Calumet Naval Air Station, now the Houghton County Airport (CMX)

K. I. Sawyer Air Force Base, now Sawyer International (SAW)

Kincheloe (Kinross) Air Force Base, now the Chippewa County International Airport

In addition to the airports, a prison and other industries have moved into the old Kincheloe base, while Sawyer is being developed as a community along with a growing industrial park.

MANUFACTURING IN THE U.P.

County	Number of manufacturers establishments	State rank
Delta	83	34
Menominee	69	43
Houghton	61	48
Dickinson	55	54
Marquette	54	55
Chippewa	44	61
Gogebic	35	67
Baraga	34	68
Schoolcraft	23	73
Iron	23	74
Mackinac	19	78
Alger	19	79
Luce	12	80
Ontonagon	12	82
Keweenaw	1	83
U.P. total	544	

MANUFACTURING EMPLOYEES

County	Employees	State rank
Delta	4,296	31
Menominee	3,197	38
Dickinson	2,305	48
Marquette	2,294	49
Alger	1,161	60
Chippewa	1,057	62
Houghton	972	64
Gogebic	781	66
Baraga	659	70
Ontonagon	490	72
Schoolcraft	442	75

Iron	432	76
Luce	280	80
Mackinac	233	81
Keweenaw	3	83
U.P. total	18,602	

Source: 2006 Harris Michigan Industrial Directory

AVERAGE MANUFACTURING WAGES

County	Manufacturing job ($)	State rank
Ontonagon	56,995	12
Schoolcraft	50,652	19
Delta	49,557	24
Dickinson	48,529	30
Alger	48,415	31
Menominee	39,149	46
Baraga	38,251	49
Marquette	36,224	61
Iron	34,499	67
Chippewa	33,415	68
Gogebic	29,127	77
Houghton	30,270	74
Mackinac	27,738	78
Luce	21,362	82
Keweenaw	N/A	

PERSONAL INCOME AND EARNINGS

County	Per capita income	Avg. earnings per job	(U.P. rank)
Dickinson	29,869	32,875	(2)
Mackinac	28,619	25,905	(14)
Delta	26,799	30,952	(6)
Marquette	26,506	32,134	(3)
Keweenaw	25,740	19,235	(15)
Iron	25,458	28,095	(12)
Ontonagon	26,013	29,742	(9)
Menominee	25,094	28,157	(11)
Schoolcraft	23,837	31,919	(4)
Gogebic	23,731	27,083	(13)
Houghton	22,976	29,017	(10)
Alger	20,919	32,965	(1)
Chippewa	21,632	30,708	(7)
Baraga	21,581	30,652	(8)
Luce	19,115	31,675	(5)

Bureau of Economic Analysis, US Department of Commerce., Issued May 2006

LARGEST EMPLOYERS – BY COUNTY
ALGER COUNTY

Company	City	Employees Full-time	Part-time
Neenah Paper Co.	Munising	340	
Alger Maximum Security Prison	Munising	279+16 in health care	
Timber Products Co.	Munising	235	
Kewadin Casino	Christmas	108	
Munising School District	Munising	107	
Tendercare	Munising	100	
Superior Central School District	Eben Junction	72	
Camp Cusino	Munising	61	
Munising Memorial Hospital	Munising	61.3 fte*	

BARAGA COUNTY

Company	City	Employees Full-time	Part-time
Ojibwa Baraga Casino	Baraga	600	
Baraga Maximum Security Prison	Baraga	358	
Baraga County Memorial Hospital	L'Anse	200	
CertainTeed Gypsum	L'Anse	120	
Pettibone Traverse Lift	Baraga	111	5
Bayside Village	L'Anse	100	
L'Anse Area Schools	L'Anse	91	
Baraga Area School District	Baraga	76	
Keweenaw Bay Indian Community	Baraga	75	
Baraga County Extended Care	Baraga	68	
Selkey Manufacturing Co.	Baraga	58	
Camp Kitwen	Baraga	54	

CHIPPEWA COUNTY

Company	City	Employees Full-time	Part-time
Kewadin Hotel and Convention Ctr.	Sault Ste. Marie	2,000	
Dept. of Corrections		978	
Chippewa Correctional Facility	Kincheloe		
Hiawatha Correctional Facility	Kincheloe		
Straits Correctional Facility	Kincheloe		
Bay Mills Resort and Casino and King's Club Casino	Brimley	725	
War Memorial Hospital	Sault Ste. Marie	655 emp/467 fte	
Lake Superior State University	Sault Ste. Marie	317	42
Sault Area Public Schools	Sault Ste. Marie	325	
Indian Health Service	Sault Ste. Marie	300	
Rudyard Area Schools	Rudyard	169*	

Bay Mills Indian Community	Brimley	150	
Wal-Mart Stores	Sault Ste. Marie	250	
Key Plastics	Sault Ste. Marie	66	
Catt's Realty	Sault Ste. Marie	190	
Sault Tribe of Chippewa Indians	Sault Ste. Marie	180	

DELTA COUNTY

Company	City	Full-time	Part-time
NewPage	Escanaba	1,140	
St Francis Hospital	Escanaba	535	
Island Resort & Casino	Harris	475	185
Engineered Machine Products	Escanaba	360	
Escanaba Area Schools	Escanaba	350	
Bay de Noc Community College	Escanaba	120	200
Gladstone Area Schools	Gladstone	176	
Wisconsin Central Transportation	Escanaba	200	
Wal-Mart	Escanaba	200	
Christian Park	Escanaba	180	
Community Action Agency	Escanaba	175	
Menards Hardware	Escanaba	150	

DICKINSON COUNTY

Company	City	Full-time	Part-time
Dickinson Memorial Hospital	Iron Mountain	832	
International Paper Co	Norway	580	
Cable Contractors	Iron Mountain	541	
Grede Foundries Inc	Iron Mountain	500	
Veterans Affairs Medical Center	Iron Mountain	350	
Wal-Mart	Iron Mountain	250	
Breitung Twp Schools	Kingsford	230	
TC Markets, Inc. (Econo Foods)	Iron Mountain	186	
L P Sagola	Sagola	150	
M J Electric Inc	Iron Mountain	150	
ShopKo Stores Inc	Kingsford	149	
Iron Mountain Pub School Dist	Iron Mountain	129	

GOGEBIC COUNTY

Company	City	Full-time	Part-time
Lac Vieux Desert Tribal Ent.	Watersmeet	530	
Grand View Hospital	Ironwood	400	
Ironwood School Dist.	Irownwood	228	
Gogebic Community College	Ironwood	175	
Jacquart Fabric Products Inc	Ironwood	200	

Gogebic Comm. Mental Health	Wakefield	160	
County Of Gogebic	Wakefield	150	
Gogebic-Ontonagon Community	Ironwood	150	
Gogebic Nursing Facility	Wakefield	148	
Ironwood Plastics Inc	Ironwood	165	

HOUGHTON COUNTY

		Employees	
Company	**City**	**Full-time**	**Part-time**
Michigan Technological Univ.	Houghton	1,137	81
Portage Health	Hancock	698 total 365	272 524 fte
Keweenaw Memorial Medical Ctr	Laurium	205	220
Copper Country Community Mntl	Houghton	220	
Gundlach Champion Inc	Houghton	200	
Wal-Mart Stores Inc	Houghton	165	
Houghton-Portage Twp Sch Dist	Houghton	150	
Northern Hardwoods	South Range	150	
EconoFoods	Houghton	150	

IRON COUNTY

		Employees	
Company	**City**	**Full-time**	**Part-time**
Iron County Community Hospital	Iron River	260	
Lake Shore Inc	Iron River	200	
Iron County Medical Care Fclty	Crystal Falls	190	
City of Crystal Falls	Crystal Falls	143	
West Iron School District	Iron River	140	
Hebert Construction Co	Iron River	125	
Connor Sports Flooring Corp	Amasa	100	
Angeli Foods	Iron River		100

KEWEENAW COUNTY

		Employees	
Company	**City**	**Full-time**	**Part-time**
Keweenaw Mountain Lodge	Copper Harbor	70 (seasonal)	
County of Keweenaw	Eagle River	20	
County Road Commission	Eagle River	19	
Lake Superior Bible Conference	Eagle River	21 (seasonal)	

LUCE COUNTY

		Employees	
Company	**City**	**Full-time**	**Part-time**
State of Michigan	Luce County	365	
Helen Newberry Joy Hospital	Newberry	217	34
Tahquamenon Area School Dist	Newberry	127	

Company	City	Full-time
Luce Mackinac Public Health	Newberry	125
LP Newberry	Newberry	124
Luce County/Village of Newberry	Newberry	65
Luce County Road Commission	Newberry	20

MACKINAC COUNTY

Company	City	Employees Full-time	Part-time
Kewadin Shores Casino	St. Ignace	500	
Grand Hotel	Mackinac Island	550 (seasonal)	
State of Michigan	Countywide	247	
Mac. Island Carriage Tours	Mackinac Island	210 (seasonal)	
MDOT		198	
Mackinac Straits Hospital	St. Ignace	190	
Shepler's Ferry	St. Ignace	150 (seasonal)	
Arnold's Ferry	St. Ignace	144 (seasonal)	
LMAS Health	St. Ignace	130	
St. Ignace Area School Dst	St. Ignace	104	
Michigan Limestone Operations	Cedarville	100	
MDOT (Mackinac Bridge)	St. Ignace	100	
Iroquois-On-The-Beach Hotel	Mackinac Island	100 (seasonal)	
Hessel Kewadin Slots	St. Ignace	70	

MARQUETTE COUNTY

Company	City	Employees Full-time	Part-time
Marquette General Health Sys.	Marquette	1,857	
Empire Iron Mining Partnership	Palmer	1,000	
Tilden Mining Co	Ishpeming	900	
Peninsula Medical	Marquette	619	
Marquette Area Public Schools	Marquette	455	
Michigan Dept Corrections	Marquette	479	
Bell Memorial Hospital	Ishpeming	334	
Marquette County	Marquette	300	
AMR-Regional Aircraft Maint.	Sawyer	237	
WE Energies	Marquette	205	
City of Marquette	Marquette	190	

MENOMINEE COUNTY

Company	City	Employees Full-time	Part-time
Chip Inn Island Resort/Casino	Harris	700	
Emerson Electric Co	Menominee	500	
Lloyd-Flanders Industries Inc	Menominee	400	
Menominee Area Public Schools	Menominee	325	
Angelis County Market	Menominee	300	

Pinecrest Medical Care	Powers	225	
L E Jones Co	Menominee	205	
Menominee Acquisition	Menominee	178	
Anchor Coupling Inc	Menominee	148	
Great Lakes Food	Menominee	130	

ONTONAGON COUNTY

	Employees		
Company	**City**	**Full-time**	**Part-time**
Stone Container Corp	Ontonagon	281	
Gogebic-Ontonagon ISD	Bergland	65	
Ontonagon County Road Commission	Ontonagon	63	
BHP Copper	White Pine	62	

SCHOOLCRAFT COUNTY

	Employees		
Company	**City**	**Full-time**	**Part-time**
Manistique Papers Inc	Manistique	150	
Manistique Schools	Manistique	150	
Schoolcraft Memorial Hospital	Manistique	126	
Specialty Minerals Inc	Gulliver	80	
Michigan Linestone Operations	Gulliver	80	
Schoolcraft County	Manistique	75	

*fte: Full-time equivalent (Part-time employees combined to create a "full-time" position)

TYPES OF EMPLOYMENT BY GENDER AND INDUSTRY

ALGER

Most common industries for males:

- Paper (16%)
- Public administration (14%)
- Construction (13%)
- Wood products (8%)
- Agriculture, forestry, fishing and hunting (7%)
- Accommodation and food services (5%)
- Educational services (4%)

Most common industries for females:

- Educational services (14%)
- Health care (14%)
- Accommodation and food services (13%)
- Public administration (8%)
- Finance and insurance (6%)
- Paper (4%)
- Social assistance (4%)

BARAGA

Most common industries for males:
- Public administration (16%)
- Construction (10%)
- Miscellaneous manufacturing (8%)
- Machinery (7%)
- Metal and metal products (6%)
- Educational services (5%)
- Arts, entertainment, and recreation (5%)

Most common industries for females:
- Health care (20%)
- Accommodation and food services (11%)
- Educational services (10%)
- Arts, entertainment, and recreation (9%)
- Social assistance (7%)
- Public administration (6%)
- Food and beverage stores (4%)

CHIPPEWA

Most common industries for males:
- Public administration (17%)
- Construction (12%)
- Educational services (10%)
- Arts, entertainment, and recreation (7%)
- Accommodation and food services (7%)
- Health care (3%)
- Professional, scientific, and technical services (3%)

Most common industries for females
- Educational services (16%)
- Health care (13%)
- Accommodation and food services (11%)
- Public administration (9%)
- Arts, entertainment, and recreation (9%)
- Social assistance (6%)
- Finance and insurance (4%)

DELTA

Most common industries for males:
- Paper (14%)
- Construction (10%)
- Accommodation and food services (5%)
- Public administration (5%)
- Educational services (5%)
- Agriculture, forestry, fishing and hunting (4%)
- Metal and metal products (4%)

Most common industries for females

LOUIS G. KAUFMAN – PIONEER BANKER

Louis Graveraet Kaufman hunting in the woods of Upper Michigan. (Courtesy of the Marquette County History Museum)

Louis Graveraet Kaufman was born in Marquette on November 13, 1870. His mother, Juliet, was the sister of Robert Graveraet, one of Marquette's founders. His father, Samuel, was born in Germany, arrived in Ontonagon and migrated east to Marquette a year later. Sam Kaufman initially made his living in the U.P. as a peddler. Later, he owned and operated a clothing store in Marquette.

One of eleven children, Louis graduated from Marquette High School at 17 and went to work as a laborer in one of his brother's iron mines. His original career goal was to become a mining engineer. He rose quickly through the ranks, becoming a superintendent at the mine, while occasionally helping out in his father's store.

At 23, he left the mine and went to work for another brother, Nathan, in his Marquette County Savings Bank. That is where Louis found his true calling. He started as an errand boy and within six years was named Vice President.

Around the turn of the century, there was a struggle for financial control of the City of Marquette. During this time, the Kaufman brothers bought controlling stock in Peter White's First National Bank. Besides Nathan's Savings Bank and First National, there was the Marquette Savings Bank. Then, the Marquette National Bank was organized by local businessmen to compete against the Kaufman financial institutions.

In 1906, Louis became president of the First National Bank. Soon after, he was named president of the Michigan Banker's Association. In this highly visible position, he caught the attention of powerful financial interests out east. He was chosen to be president of the Chatham National Bank in New York City in 1910. Federal laws had to be amended to allow one man to be president of banks in different states.

During his tenure at Chatham, he engineered a merger with Phoenix National Bank. The Chatham and Phoenix National bank became one of the largest in New York City with deposits of $300 million by 1914. He bought out a number of smaller financial institutions in the city and turned them into branch banks.

- Health care (17%)
- Educational services (12%)
- Accommodation and food services (11%)
- Social assistance (5%)
- Finance and insurance (4%)
- Arts, entertainment, and recreation (4%)
- Food and beverage stores (4%)

DICKINSON
Most common industries for males:
- Construction (11%)
- Paper (9%)
- Metal and metal products (6%)
- Accommodation and food services (5%)
- Public administration (4%)
- Educational services (4%)
- Health care (4%)
Most common occupations for females
- Health care (23%)
- Educational services (11%)
- Accommodation and food services (9%)
- Food and beverage stores (5%)
- Finance and insurance (5%)
- Social assistance (4%)
- Department other general merchandise stores (4%)

GOGEBIC
Most common industries for males:
- Construction (13%)
- Wood products (9%)
- Public administration (8%)
- Accommodation and food services (8%)
- Educational services (7%)
- Food and beverage stores (4%)
- Agriculture, forestry, fishing and hunting (4%)
Most common industries for females
- Health care (20%)
- Accommodation and food services (16%)
- Educational services (11%)
- Public administration (6%)
- Finance and insurance (4%)
- Department other general merchandise stores (4%)
- Food and beverage stores (3%)

HOUGHTON
Most common industries for males:
- Educational services (25%)
- Construction (10%)
- Accommodation and food services (7%)

- Health care (5%)
- Public administration (5%)
- Wood products (4%)
- Professional, scientific, and technical services (3%)

Most common industriesfor females

- Educational services (23%)
- Health care (23%)
- Accommodation and food services (10%)
- Finance and insurance (5%)
- Department and other general merchandise stores (5%)
- Social assistance (4%)
- Food and beverage stores (4%)

IRON

Most common industries for males:

- Construction (14%)
- Public administration (8%)
- Wood products (7%)
- Agriculture, forestry, fishing and hunting (7%)
- Accommodation and food services (6%)
- Educational services (5%)
- Food and beverage stores (4%)

Most common industries for females

- Health care (27%)
- Accommodation and food services (12%)
- Educational services (10%)
- Food and beverage stores (6%)
- Public administration (5%)
- Finance and insurance (5%)
- Social assistance (4%)

KEWEENAW

Most common industries for males:

- Construction (17%)
- Public administration (16%)
- Educational services (8%)
- Accommodation and food services (6%)
- Professional, scientific, and technical services (4%)
- Health care (4%)
- Agriculture, forestry, fishing and hunting (4%)

Entrance to Kaufman Auditorium at Graveraet Intermediate School, Marquette.

Kaufman is credited with developing the concept of branch banking as well as instituting the trust system into banking. He is also credited with providing the financing that helped get Chevrolet off the ground—the first serious competition for Henry Ford's Model T. A small group of investors headed by Kaufman funded the construction of the world's largest building at the time—New York City's Empire State Building. Louis Kaufman's fortune was estimated at $150 million during World War I. Just after the war he started work on a palatial "camp" north of Marquette. "Granot Loma" was constructed over a period of eight years with the involvement of 21 architects and 300 workers. The 20,000-square-foot lodge is set on over 5,000 acres with 3.64 miles of Lake Superior shoreline. A grand opening was held in 1927. Thereafter, the Kaufmans opened the doors of the lodge to the rich and famous from both coasts.

Composer/pianist George Gershwin played one of the grand pianos for guests, while dancer Irene Castle performed in the 80-foot Great Room. Silent film star Mary Pickford's visit is immortalized by an image of her set in a stone fireplace in one of the lodge's bathrooms.

Louis Kaufman gave back to the city of his birth. He provided land for construction of a new high school. The school was named "Graveraet" in honor of his mother. Kaufman funded a state-of-the-art auditorium in the school which bears his name. He then provided an endowment to the high school "to bring to the children and people of Marquette some of the finer things in the world of education, travel and art." He was the first person in the United States to endow a high school.

Louis G. Kaufman died in 1942. His remains are interred at Marquette's Park Cemetery in a mausoleum constructed to resemble the Greek Parthenon built at an estimated $3,000,000.

Most common industries for females

- Health care (23%)
- Educational services (15%)
- Accommodation and food services (15%)
- Finance and insurance (8%)
- Public administration (8%)
- Food and beverage stores (3%)
- Social assistance (3%)

LUCE

Most common industries for males:

- Public administration (19%)
- Construction (11%)
- Wood products (9%)
- Agriculture, forestry, fishing and hunting (7%)
- Accommodation and food services (5%)
- Educational services (5%)
- Arts, entertainment, and recreation (4%)

Most common industries for females

- Health care (20%)
- Accommodation and food services (17%)
- Educational services (12%)
- Public administration (10%)
- Social assistance (6%)
- Finance and insurance (5%)
- Food and beverage stores (4%)

MACKINAC

Most common industries for males:

- Construction (21%)
- Public administration (12%)
- Accommodation and food services (7%)
- Arts, entertainment, and recreation (6%)
- Educational services (5%)
- Agriculture, forestry, fishing and hunting (4%)
- Other transportation, and support activities, and couriers (3%)

Most common industries for females

- Accommodation and food services (15%)
- Health care (15%)
- Educational services (14%)
- Public administration (9%)
- Arts, entertainment, and recreation (6%)
- Finance and insurance (4%)
- Social assistance (4%)

Kaufman Mausoleum in Marquette's Park Cemetery

MARQUETTE

Most common industries for males:

- Construction (10%)
- Mining (8%)
- Educational services (8%)
- Public administration (8%)
- Accommodation and food services (7%)
- Health care (7%)
- Metal and metal products (3%)

Most common industries for females

- Health care (24%)
- Educational services (14%)
- Accommodation and food services (11%)
- Finance and insurance (6%)
- Public administration (4%)
- Department and other general merchandise stores (4%)
- Food and beverage stores (4%)

MENOMINEE

Most common industries for males:

- Metal and metal products (12%)
- Construction (10%)
- Transportation equipment (9%)
- Agriculture, forestry, fishing and hunting (6%)
- Machinery (5%)
- Truck transportation (4%)
- Wood products (4%)

Most common industries for females

- Health care (16%)
- Educational services (10%)
- Accommodation and food services (8%)
- Transportation equipment (4%)
- Public administration (4%)
- Social assistance (4%)
- Furniture and related products (4%)

ONTONAGON

Most common industries for males:

- Paper (15%)
- Construction (13%)
- Agriculture, forestry, fishing and hunting (10%)
- Educational services (6%)
- Accommodation and food services (6%)
- Public administration (6%)
- Arts, entertainment, and recreation (4%)

Most common industries for females

- Health care (21%)
- Accommodation and food services (15%)

- Educational services (9%)
- Food and beverage stores (7%)
- Public administration (5%)
- Finance and insurance (5%)
- Arts, entertainment, and recreation (4%)

SCHOOLCRAFT

Most common industries for males:

- Construction (14%)
- Paper (10%)
- Public administration (9%)
- Agriculture, forestry, fishing and hunting (9%)
- Wood products (5%)
- Educational services (4%)
- Mining (4%)

Most common industries for females

- Health care (22%)
- Accommodation and food services (12%)
- Educational services (11%)
- Public administration (6%)
- Social assistance (6%)
- Finance and insurance (5%)
- Arts, entertainment, and recreation (4%)

TYPES OF EMPLOYMENT BY GENDER AND OCCUPATION

ALGER

Most common occupations for males

- Other production occupations including supervisors (9%)
- Law enforcement workers including supervisors (8%)
- Laborers and material movers, hand (5%)
- Other management occupations except farmers and farm managers (5%)
- Electrical equipment mechanics and other installation, maintenance, and repair occupations including supervisors (4%)
- Carpenters (4%)
- Fishing and hunting, and forest and logging workers (3%)

Most common occupations for females

- Secretaries and administrative assistants (8%)
- Other management occupations except farmers and farm managers (5%)
- Cashiers (5%)
- Waiters and waitresses (5%)
- Preschool, kindergarten, elementary and middle school teachers (5%)
- Financial clerks except bookkeeping, accounting, and auditing clerks (4%)
- Nursing, psychiatric, and home health aides (4%)

BARAGA

Most common occupations for males

- Law enforcement workers including supervisors (10%)
- Metal workers and plastic workers (8%)

- Other production occupations including supervisors (5%)
- Driver/sales workers and truck drivers (5%)
- Laborers and material movers, hand (4%)
- Other sales and related workers including supervisors (4%)
- Building and grounds cleaning and maintenance occupations (4%)

Most common occupations for females

- Secretaries and administrative assistants (5%)
- Preschool, kindergarten, elementary and middle school teachers (5%)
- Cashiers (5%)
- Nursing, psychiatric, and home health aides (5%)
- Health technologists and technicians (5%)
- Information and record clerks except customer service representatives (4%)
- Supervisors and other personal care and service workers except personal appearance, transportation, and child care workers (4%)

CHIPPEWA

Most common occupations for males

- Law enforcement workers including supervisors (10%)
- Building and grounds cleaning and maintenance occupations (6%)
- Driver/sales workers and truck drivers (5%)
- Other management occupations except farmers and farm managers (4%)
- Electrical equipment mechanics and other installation, maintenance, and repair occupations including supervisors (4%)
- Other sales and related workers including supervisors (4%)
- Material recording, scheduling, dispatching, and distributing workers (3%)

Most common occupations for females

- Secretaries and administrative assistants (6%)
- Other office and administrative support workers including supervisors (5%)
- Cashiers (5%)
- Preschool, kindergarten, elementary and middle school teachers (4%)
- Building and grounds cleaning and maintenance occupations (4%)
- Waiters and waitresses (4%)
- Information and record clerks except customer service representatives (4%)

DELTA

Most common occupations for males

- Other production occupations including supervisors (9%)
- Metal workers and plastic workers (6%)
- Driver/sales workers and truck drivers (6%)
- Electrical equipment mechanics and other installation, maintenance, and repair occupations including supervisors (5%)
- Laborers and material movers, hand (4%)
- Vehicle and mobile equipment mechanics, installers, and repairers (4%)
- Other management occupations except farmers and farm managers (3%)

Most common occupations for females

- Secretaries and administrative assistants (7%)
- Retail sales workers except cashiers (5%)
- Preschool, kindergarten, elementary and middle school teachers (4%)

- Cashiers (4%)
- Building and grounds cleaning and maintenance occupations (4%)
- Other office and administrative support workers including supervisors (4%)
- Registered nurses (3%)

DICKINSON

Most common occupations for males

- Other production occupations including supervisors (6%)
- Electrical equipment mechanics and other installation, maintenance, and repair occupations including supervisors (6%)
- Metal workers and plastic workers (5%)
- Other management occupations except farmers and farm managers (5%)
- Driver/sales workers and truck drivers (5%)
- Vehicle and mobile equipment mechanics, installers, and repairers (4%)
- Laborers and material movers, hand (4%)

Most common occupations for females

- Other office and administrative support workers including supervisors (7%)
- Secretaries and administrative assistants (7%)
- Cashiers (5%)
- Health technologists and technicians (5%)
- Retail sales workers except cashiers (5%)
- Nursing, psychiatric, and home health aides (4%)
- Cooks and food preparation workers (4%)

GOGEBIC

Most common occupations for males

- Other production occupations including supervisors (5%)
- Laborers and material movers, hand (5%)
- Electrical equipment mechanics and other installation, maintenance, and repair occupations including supervisors (5%)
- Building and grounds cleaning and maintenance occupations (5%)
- Driver/sales workers and truck drivers (5%)
- Other management occupations except farmers and farm managers (4%)
- Vehicle and mobile equipment mechanics, installers, and repairers (4%

Most common occupations for females

- Secretaries and administrative assistants (6%)
- Other sales and related workers including supervisors (5%)
- Cooks and food preparation workers (5%)
- Nursing, psychiatric, and home health aides (5%)
- Preschool, kindergarten, elementary and middle school teachers (5%)
- Cashiers (5%)
- Building and grounds cleaning and maintenance occupations (4%)

HOUGHTON

Most common occupations for males

- Building and grounds cleaning and maintenance occupations (6%)
- Other management occupations except farmers and farm managers (6%)
- Postsecondary teachers (6%)
- Other sales and related workers including supervisors (4%)

- Material recording, scheduling, dispatching, and distributing workers (4%)
- Electrical equipment mechanics and other installation, maintenance, and repair occupations including supervisors (3%)
- Driver/sales workers and truck drivers (3%)

Most common occupations for females
- Secretaries and administrative assistants (8%)
- Other office and administrative support workers including supervisors (5%)
- Nursing, psychiatric, and home health aides (5%)
- Information and record clerks except customer service representatives (4%)
- Cooks and food preparation workers (4%)
- Registered nurses (4%)
- Other sales and related workers including supervisors (4%)

IRON

Most common occupations for males
- Building and grounds cleaning and maintenance occupations (5%)
- Vehicle and mobile equipment mechanics, installers, and repairers (5%)
- Electrical equipment mechanics and other installation, maintenance, and repair occupations including supervisors (5%)
- Other sales and related workers including supervisors (5%)
- Driver/sales workers and truck drivers (4%)
- Other production occupations including supervisors (4%)
- Other management occupations except farmers and farm managers (4%)

Most common occupations for females
- Nursing, psychiatric, and home health aides (9%)
- Secretaries and administrative assistants (5%)
- Preschool, kindergarten, elementary and middle school teachers (5%)
- Cooks and food preparation workers (5%)
- Other office and administrative support workers including supervisors (5%)
- Cashiers (4%)
- Registered nurses (4%)

KEWEENAW

Most common occupations for males
- Other management occupations except farmers and farm managers (7%)
- Driver/sales workers and truck drivers (6%)
- Building and grounds cleaning and maintenance occupations (5%)
- Other production occupations including supervisors (4%)
- Law enforcement workers including supervisors (4%)
- Construction trades workers except carpenters, electricians, painters, plumbers, and construction laborers (4%)
- Operations specialties managers except financial managers (4%)

Most common occupations for females
- Other office and administrative support workers including supervisors (7%)
- Secretaries and administrative assistants (7%)
- Other management occupations except farmers and farm managers (7%)
- Registered nurses (7%)
- Waiters and waitresses (6%)

- Nursing, psychiatric, and home health aides (5%)
- Preschool, kindergarten, elementary and middle school teachers (5%)

LUCE

Most common occupations for males

- Law enforcement workers including supervisors (10%)
- Building and grounds cleaning and maintenance occupations (6%)
- Driver/sales workers and truck drivers (6%)
- Other production occupations including supervisors (5%)
- Electrical equipment mechanics and other installation, maintenance, and repair occupations including supervisors (4%)
- Other management occupations except farmers and farm managers (4%)
- Carpenters (3%)

Most common occupations for females

- Cooks and food preparation workers (6%)
- Secretaries and administrative assistants (6%)
- Other office and administrative support workers including supervisors (6%)
- Building and grounds cleaning and maintenance occupations (5%)
- Preschool, kindergarten, elementary and middle school teachers (5%)
- Nursing, psychiatric, and home health aides (5%)
- Information and record clerks except customer service representatives (5%)

MACKINAC

Most common occupations for males

- Carpenters (7%)
- Other management occupations except farmers and farm managers (6%)
- Law enforcement workers including supervisors (6%)
- Other sales and related workers including supervisors (5%)
- Electrical equipment mechanics and other installation, maintenance, and repair occupations including supervisors (4%)
- Driver/sales workers and truck drivers (4%)
- Building and grounds cleaning and maintenance occupations (4%)

Most common occupations for females

- Secretaries and administrative assistants (8%)
- Preschool, kindergarten, elementary and middle school teachers (7%)
- Cashiers (5%)
- Other management occupations except farmers and farm managers (5%)
- Building and grounds cleaning and maintenance occupations (5%)
- Waiters and waitresses (4%)
- Other sales and related workers including supervisors (4%)

MARQUETTE

Most common occupations for males

- Electrical equipment mechanics and other installation, maintenance, and repair occupations including supervisors (6%)
- Vehicle and mobile equipment mechanics, installers, and repairers (6%)
- Driver/sales workers and truck drivers (4%)
- Other management occupations except farmers and farm managers (4%)
- Building and grounds cleaning and maintenance occupations (4%)

- Material recording, scheduling, dispatching, and distributing workers (4%)
- Law enforcement workers including supervisors (4%)
Most common occupations for females
- Secretaries and administrative assistants (6%)
- Other office and administrative support workers including supervisors (5%)
- Cashiers (5%)
- Health technologists and technicians (4%)
- Registered nurses (4%)
- Information and record clerks except customer service representatives (4%)
- Nursing, psychiatric, and home health aides (4%)

MENOMINEE

Most common occupations for males
- Metal workers and plastic workers (13%)
- Other production occupations including supervisors (10%)
- Driver/sales workers and truck drivers (8%)
- Laborers and material movers, hand (5%)
- Electrical equipment mechanics and other installation, maintenance, and repair occupations including supervisors (5%)
- Building and grounds cleaning and maintenance occupations (3%)
- Other management occupations except farmers and farm managers (3%)
Most common occupations for females
- Secretaries and administrative assistants (6%)
- Other office and administrative support workers including supervisors (5%)
- Other production occupations including supervisors (5%)
- Nursing, psychiatric, and home health aides (5%)
- Assemblers and fabricators (4%)
- Preschool, kindergarten, elementary and middle school teachers (4%)
- Building and grounds cleaning and maintenance occupations (4%)

ONTONAGON

Most common occupations for males
- Other production occupations including supervisors (9%)
- Driver/sales workers and truck drivers (7%)
- Electrical equipment mechanics and other installation, maintenance, and repair occupations including supervisors (6%)
- Carpenters (4%)
- Vehicle and mobile equipment mechanics, installers, and repairers (4%)
- Building and grounds cleaning and maintenance occupations (4%)
- Metal workers and plastic workers (3%)
Most common occupations for females
- Nursing, psychiatric, and home health aides (7%)
- Secretaries and administrative assistants (6%)
- Waiters and waitresses (5%)
- Building and grounds cleaning and maintenance occupations (5%)
- Cooks and food preparation workers (5%)
- Financial clerks except bookkeeping, accounting, and auditing clerks (4%)
- Cashiers (4%)

SCHOOLCRAFT

Most common occupations for males

- Electrical equipment mechanics and other installation, maintenance, and repair occupations including supervisors (7%)
- Other production occupations including supervisors (6%)
- Other management occupations except farmers and farm managers (5%)
- Driver/sales workers and truck drivers (4%)
- Vehicle and mobile equipment mechanics, installers, and repairers (4%)
- Building and grounds cleaning and maintenance occupations (4%)
- Law enforcement workers including supervisors (4%)

Most common occupations for females

- Nursing, psychiatric, and home health aides (7%)
- Preschool, kindergarten, elementary and middle school teachers (5%)
- Cashiers (5%)
- Secretaries and administrative assistants (5%)
- Other office and administrative support workers including supervisors (4%)
- Health technologists and technicians (4%)
- Other management occupations except farmers and farm managers (4%)

TRAVEL TIME TO WORK, BY COUNTY

County	Mean travel time to work (minutes)	Percent of county residents living and working in this county
Mackinac	22.5	75.6
Ontonagon	21.7	76.0
Keweenaw	21.3	**38.7**
Schoolcraft	20.8	85.8
Iron	20.2	82.6
Alger	19.8	83.7
Menominee	19.7	60.0
Delta	18.8	88.1
Luce	18.5	87.4
Baraga	17.8	87.8
Marquette	17.7	95.6
Chippewa	17.7	94.3
Gogebic	17.3	78.8
Dickinson	15.7	90.4
Houghton	15.6	**92.9** **Bold** (Highest-Lowest)

Motorcycling is one of the least used modes of transportation in Upper Michigan.

TRANSPORTATION TO WORK, BY COUNTY

Alger County
- Drove a car alone: 2,823 (76%)
- Carpooled: 444 (12%)
- Bus or trolley bus: 33 (1%)
- Taxi: 5 (0%)
- Motorcycle: 2 (0%)
- Bicycle: 5 (0%)
- Walked: 222 (6%)
- Other means: 25 (1%)
- Worked at home: 154 (4%)

Baraga County
- Drove a car alone: 2,587 (75%)
- Carpooled: 520 (15%)
- Bus or trolley bus: 13 (0%)
- Motorcycle: 2 (0%)
- Bicycle: 5 (0%)
- Walked: 138 (4%)
- Other means: 31 (1%)
- Worked at home: 144 (4%)

Chippewa County
- Drove a car alone: 11,109 (74%)
- Carpooled: 2,134 (14%)
- Bus or trolley bus: 184 (1%)
- Railroad: 12 (0%)
- Ferryboat: 15 (0%)
- Taxi: 49 (0%)
- Motorcycle: 10 (0%)
- Bicycle: 40 (0%)
- Walked: 733 (5%)
- Other means: 110 (1%)
- Worked at home: 522 (3%)

Delta County
- Drove a car alone: 14,283 (83%)
- Carpooled: 1,698 (10%)
- Bus or trolley bus: 90 (1%)
- Railroad: 2 (0%)
- Taxi: 41 (0%)
- Motorcycle: 19 (0%)
- Bicycle: 26 (0%)
- Walked: 419 (2%)
- Other means: 92 (1%)
- Worked at home: 446 (3%)

Dickinson County
- Drove a car alone: 9,810 (81%)
- Carpooled: 1,464 (12%)
- Bus or trolley bus: 13 (0%)
- Taxi: 2 (0%)
- Bicycle: 30 (0%)
- Walked: 356 (3%)

Pedal power is becoming more popular in this era of rising gas prices.

- Other means: 78 (1%)
- Worked at home: 285 (2%)

Gogebic County
- Drove a car alone: 5,077 (77%)
- Carpooled: 875 (13%)
- Bus or trolley bus: 24 (0%)
- Streetcar or trolley car: 3 (0%)
- Railroad: 2 (0%)
- Taxi: 3 (0%)
- Motorcycle: 3 (0%)
- Walked: 361 (5%)
- Other means: 20 (0%)
- Worked at home: 222 (3%)

Houghton County
- Drove a car alone: 10,814 (72%)
- Carpooled: 1,659 (11%)
- Bus or trolley bus: 76 (1%)
- Taxi: 39 (0%)
- Bicycle: 69 (0%)
- Walked: 1,631 (11%)
- Other means: 63 (0%)
- Worked at home: 567 (4%)

Iron County
- Drove a car alone: 3,827 (78%)
- Carpooled: 669 (14%)
- Bus or trolley bus: 12 (0%)
- Motorcycle: 4 (0%)
- Bicycle: 2 (0%)
- Walked: 219 (4%)
- Other means: 21 (0%)
- Worked at home: 162 (3%)

Keweenaw County
- Drove a car alone: 675 (76%)
- Carpooled: 97 (11%)
- Walked: 61 (7%)
- Other means: 2 (0%)
- Worked at home: 59 (7%)

Luce County
- Drove a car alone: 1,771 (76%)
- Carpooled: 307 (13%)
- Bus or trolley bus: 3 (0%)
- Railroad: 2 (0%)
- Walked: 88 (4%)
- Other means: 22 (1%)
- Worked at home: 148 (6%)

Mackinac County
- Drove a car alone: 3,279 (71%)
- Carpooled: 606 (13%)

- Bus or trolley bus: 8 (0%)
- Subway or elevated: 2 (0%)
- Ferryboat: 61 (1%)
- Taxi: 15 (0%)
- Bicycle: 154 (3%)
- Walked: 204 (4%)
- Other means: 43 (1%)
- Worked at home: 235 (5%)

Marquette County
- Drove a car alone: 24,127 (80%)
- Carpooled: 3,275 (11%)
- Bus or trolley bus: 169 (1%)
- Streetcar or trolley car: 1 (0%)
- Taxi: 8 (0%)
- Motorcycle: 16 (0%)
- Bicycle: 151 (1%)
- Walked: 1,515 (5%)
- Other means: 85 (0%)
- Worked at home: 698 (2%)

Menominee County
- Drove a car alone: 9,445 (81%)
- Carpooled: 1,240 (11%)
- Bus or trolley bus: 9 (0%)
- Streetcar or trolley car: 5 (0%)
- Taxi: 26 (0%)
- Motorcycle: 9 (0%)
- Bicycle: 56 (0%)
- Walked: 344 (3%)
- Other means: 97 (1%)
- Worked at home: 386 (3%)

Ontonagon County
- Drove a car alone: 2,268 (73%)
- Carpooled: 411 (13%)
- Bus or trolley bus: 31 (1%)
- Bicycle: 2 (0%)
- Walked: 190 (6%)
- Other means: 25 (1%)
- Worked at home: 163 (5%)

Schoolcraft County
- Drove a car alone: 2,384 (74%)
- Carpooled: 443 (14%)
- Bus or trolley bus: 24 (1%)
- Taxi: 2 (0%)
- Bicycle: 3 (0%)
- Walked: 153 (5%)
- Other means: 29 (1%)
- Worked at home: 166 (5%)

HOME OWNERSHIP AND RENTER STATISTICS

County	Owner-occupied houses and condos	Renter-occupied apartments	% of renters in county	average size household
Alger	3,120	665	18%	2.4 people
Baraga	2,605	748	22%	2.4 people
Chippewa	9,972	3,502	26%	2.4 people
Delta	12,599	3,237	20%	2.4 people
Dickinson	9,122	2,264	20%	2.4 people
Gogebic	5,842	1,583	21%	2.2 people
Houghton	9,865	3,928	28%	2.4 people
Iron	4,742	1,006	18%	2.2 people
Keweenaw	891	107	11%	2.1 people
Luce	1,974	507	20%	2.4 people
Mackinac	4,008	1,059	21%	2.3 people
Marquette	17,990	7,777	30%	2.4 people
Menominee	8,369	2,160	21%	2.4 people
Ontonagon	2,935	521	15%	2.2 people
Schoolcraft	2,948	658	18%	2.4 people

Percent of renters: 26% Average household size: 2.6 people

House and apartment values (2006), by county

County	Estimated median house/condo value ($)	Fair market value ($) 1-bedroom apt.	2-bedroom apt.
Alger	102,737	422	503
Baraga	90,825	422	503
Chippewa	104,632	418	516
Delta	108,286	415	503
Dickinson	87,441	397	503
Gogebic	53,737	415	503
Houghton	74,176	418	503
Iron	64,295	415	503
Keweenaw	59,693	415	503
Luce	91,773	424	503
Mackinac	124,259	418	517
Marquette	104,496	423	503
Menominee	85,817	419	503
Ontonagon	56,038	415	503
Schoolcraft	87,847	424	503

Est. median house/condo value: $149,300

Building permits (2006), by county

County	# of permits	Value of permits ($)
Marquette	286	32,462,000
Houghton	146	20,835,000
Gogebic	65	15,602,000
Mackinac	131	12,858,000
Delta	90	12,727,000
Chippewa	92	11,038,000
Menominee	115	8,628,000
Dickinson	74	8,346,000
Schoolcraft	45	6,212,000
Alger	53	5,969,000
Iron	34	5,068,000
Baraga	24	3,050,000
Keweenaw	23	2,408,000
Ontonagon	19	2,222,000
Luce	50	1,980,000
U.P. total	1,247	149,405,000

PRISONS

Marquette branch prison completed in 1889 at the cost of $200,000.

The first prison in the Upper Peninsula was approved by the State legislature in 1885 and opened four years later on the shores of Lake Superior in Marquette. It cost $200,000 to build the Marquette Branch Prison on land donated by the Marquette Businessmen's Association. In its early days, the Marquette Prison housed male and female inmates.

Up until the 1971 opening of Camp Ojibway in Marenisco, it was the only state prison in the U.P. Today the prison industry is one of the major employers in the U.P. with nine prisons and four prison camps.

The Upper Peninsula prison building boom has its roots in the 1977 closing of the Kincheloe Air Force Base in Chippewa County. After the base closed, the property was split up between local municipalities, a few private interests and the Michigan Department of Corrections. With the loss of thousands of jobs related to the base closure, a strategy was launched to use the land for state prisons.

By 1990, there were four new prisons and one prison camp on the former Air Force base property.

Total inmates in state corrections facilities in the U.P.   *11,091**

Total employees in state corrections facilities in the U.P.   *3,453**
*As of March 2007 – Michigan Department of Corrections

Marquette Branch Prison   Security Level: I and V (males 21 and older)
1960 U.S.Hwy. 41 South Marquette 49855 (Marquette County)
Warden: Gerald Hofbauer
Opened: 1889
Employees: 415
6 (Level V)   4 (Level I)
Inmate capacity: 1,216   Inmate population: 1,188*

Kinross Correctional Facility   Security Level: I and II (males, 17 and older)
16779 S. Watertower Dr. Kincheloe 49788 (Chippewa County)
Warden: Linda M. Metrish
Opened: 1978
Employees: 571
Inmate capacity: 1,817   Inmate population: 1,784*
Kinross Correctional Facility has the largest fenced in area, 113 acres, or any prison in Michigan.

Straits Correctional Facility Security Level: Secure Level I
4387 W. M-80 Kincheloe 49785 (Chippewa County)
Warden: Jeri-Ann Sherry
Opened: 1988
Employees: 593 (includes Chippewa Correctional Facility)
Housing units: 8 units in four buildings
Inmate capacity: 1,122   Inmate population: 1,116*

Chippewa Correctional Facility   Security Level: I, III, and IV
4269 W. M-80, Kincheloe 49784 (Chippewa County)
Warden: Jeri-Ann Sherry
Opened: 1989
Employees: 593 (includes Straits Correctional Facility)
Housing units: 1 (Level I)   3 (Level III)   1 (Level IV)
Inmate capacity: 1,150   Inmate population: 1,125*

Hiawatha Correctional Facility   Security Level: Secure Level I (males 17 and over
4533 W. Industrial Park Dr.,   not diagnosed as mentally ill)
Kincheloe 49786-0001 (Chippewa County)
Warden: Linda M. Metrish
Opened: 1989
Employees: 571 (includes Kinross Correctional Facility)
Housing units: 8 in four buildings
Inmate capacity: 1,122   Inmate population: 1,115*

Alger Maximum Correctional Facility   Security Level: V (Males, all ages)
Industrial Park Dr., Munising (Alger County)
Warden: David L. Bergh
Opened: 1990
Employees: 353 (includes Camp Cusino)
Housing units: 6
Inmate capacity: 536   Inmate population: 529*

Baraga Maximum Correctional Facility   Security level: I and V (males, all ages)
301 Wadaga Rd, Baraga 49908 (Baraga County)
Warden: Greg McQuiggin
Opened: 1993
Employees: 883 (includes Camp Kitwen)
Housing units: 1 (Level I)   7 (Level V, including four for segregation)
Inmate capacity: 896   Inmate population: 883*

Newberry Correctional Facility
Security Level: II (males, 17 and older)
3001 Newberry Ave. Newberry 49868
(Luce County)
Warden: Barry D. Davis
Opened: 1996
Employees: 308
Housing units: 12
Inmate capacity: 982
Inmate population: 979*
Formerly part of Newberry Regional
Mental Health Center.

Ojibway Correctional Facility   Security Levels: Secure Level I and II
N5705 Ojibway Rd.   (males, 17 and older)
Marenisco 49947-9771 (Gogebic County)
Warden: Jeff White
Opened: 2000 (re-opened after expanding to Level II prison; originally opened in 1971 as Camp Ojibway)
Employees: 281 (includes Camp Ottawa)
Housing units: 5
Inmate capacity: 1,090
Inmate population: 1,085*

PRISON CAMPS

Camp Kitwen
ADW: Evelyn E. Nicholls
M-26 South, P.O. Box 7 Painsedale, MI 49955 (Houghton County)
Built:
Employees:
Inmate capacity: 288   Inmate population: 284*
Under control of Baraga Maximum Correctional Facility

Camp Ottawa
ADW: Ken Tribley
216 Gendron Road Iron River, MI 49935 (Iron County)
Built: 1991
Employees: 50
Inmate capacity: 288
Inmate population: 286*
Employees: 48
Under control of Ojibway Correctional Facility
Includes a working sawmill operated by Michigan State Industries.

Entrance to the Ojibway Correctional Facility, Marenisco Township.

Camp Cusino
ADW Cathy Bauman
N5398 Percy Road Shingleton, MI 49884 (Alger County)
Built:
Employees: 50
Inmate capacity: 320   Inmate population: 319*
Under control of Alger Maximum Correctional Facility

Camp Manistique
401 North Maple Street Manistique MI, 49854 (Schoolcraft County)
Opened: 1993
Closed: October 2007

As of March 2007 – Michigan Department of Corrections

CASINOS

Fred Dakota

FRED DAKOTA: CASINO PIONEER

The first Indian-run gaming casino in the country opened for business on New Year's Eve 1983 in a two-car garage in Baraga County. Although licensed by the Keweenaw Bay Tribe Community (Lake Superior Band of Chippewa Indians), the business was started by and solely owned by tribal member Fred Dakota.

Dakota asked the tribal council to approve bingo games on reservation land, and during the discussion, a member of the council suggested they also permit other gambling. The Council agreed, but it was several years before Dakota followed through. He rented a two-car garage in Zeba, not far from the mission founded by the Father Baraga.

Opening night was New Year's Eve 1983. The casino featured one blackjack table and two video poker machines. Dakota said he barely broke even. A few weeks later, the profitable operation added several craps tables and a bar and was known as The Pines Bar and Casino.

Dakota borrowed $100,000 from a local bank and moved the operation about a mile north of Baraga on U.S. 41, where he built a new pole barn and added new poker and craps tables. The Tribal Council did not license the new location, limiting gaming operations to the garage in Zeba. However, Dakota ignored the elders and opened the new casino.

After a year in business at the new location, federal agents shut the operation down, claiming high-stakes bingo games must be regulated by the State. This led to a long legal battle, with the tribe defending its status as a sovereign nation not subject to State oversight.

While the lawsuit played out, other Michigan tribes opened mini-casinos featuring bingo and card games. In 1984, a ruling from the court permitted Indian tribes, but not individuals, to run gaming operations on tribal lands. Although there were still some questions about the extent of gaming that could be run, the court ruling opened the gates to tribal casinos across the country.

Another key ruling was the 1987 *California V. Cabazon Band of Mission Indians* which upheld the sovereignty of Native American tribes and excluded them from any State regulations or laws about gambling.

The next year Congress passed a bill that allowed States to regulate Indian-run gaming and required tribes to negotiate compacts with state governments. The first Indian-run casino to negotiate such a compact and open in Michigan was King's Club Casino in Brimley. The Bay Mills Tribe of Ojibwe Indians was the first tribal blackjack casino in the United States and later became the first casino in Michigan to offer slot machines and live Keno.

Today there are 345 tribal gaming facilities spread out over nearly 30 states in the country. The Indian gaming industry supports over 550,000 jobs with annual revenue approaching $20 billion dollars.

Dakota was convicted of tax evasion and accepting bribes from a slot machine vendor and was sentenced to federal prison in January of 1998. He left prison the following year declaring, "I was indicted by some foreign government," referring to the United States which does recognize the Keweenaw Bay Indian Community as a sovereign nation. Dakota was elected to the tribal council after leaving prison. He lost an election in 2006, but was elected back to the council in December 2007. He has served 32 years on the council, 21 of those as the chairman.

STATE COMPACTS

In 1993 seven Indian tribes signed a Compact with the State of Michigan that includes an agreement to share gaming profits with the state and with local municipalities. Of the seven original tribes, five are in the Upper Peninsula:

- Bay Mills Indian Community
- Hannahville Indian Community
- Keweenaw Bay Indian Community
- Lac Vieux Desert Band of Lake Superior Chippewa
- Sault Ste. Marie Tribe of Chippewa Indians

The tribes agreed to pay 10% of their profits to state and local governments—8% to the state and 2% to local municipalities.

Indian-run casinos in Michigan pay 2% of their profits from electronic video gaming and slot machines to local municipalities. The payments were based on the tribe's exclusive rights to run Class III gaming operations in Michigan. When the State approved a license for gaming in the City of Detroit, the tribes ended 8% payments to the State. The tribes continue to pay the State $25,000 per year towards oversight costs.

Tribal casino operations continue to pay 2% of gaming profits to local communities.

There are 11 Indian-owned casinos in the Upper Peninsula run by five Indian communities.

TRIBAL CASINO STATISTICS

Tribal community	Casinos	Year opened
Bay Mills Indian Community 11386 W. Lakeshore Dr. Brimley, MI 49715	Bay Mills Resort & Casino, Brimley Kings Club Casino, Brimley	1993
Hannahville Tribe of Potawatomi Indians PO Box 351 West 399 Hwy 2 & 41 Harris, MI 49845	Chip Inn Island Resort and Casino, Harris	1993
Keweenaw Bay Indian Community 797 Michigan Ave., Baraga, MI 49908 105 Acre Trail, Marquette MI 49855	Ojibwa Casino, Baraga Ojibwa II Casino, Marquette	1993
Lac Vieux Desert Band of Lake Superior Chippewa Indians P.O. Box 129 Watersmeet, MI 49969	Lac Vieux Desert Casino & Resort Watersmeet	1993

Tribal community	Casinos	Year opened
Sault Ste. Marie Tribe of Chippewa Indians 2186 Shunk Rd. Sault Ste. Marie, MI 49783	Kewadin Shores Casino St. Ignace	1993
	Kewadin Slots Christmas	
	Kewadin Slots Hessel	
	Kewadin Slots Manistique	
	Kewadin Vegas Casino Sault Ste. Marie	

Two percent payments to local municipalities

Since 1994 the five tribes operating casinos in the U.P. have paid over $46.5 million to local municipalities. That figure represents two percent of the profits earned which would be approximately $2.3 billion dollars since the first casinos opened in 1994.

Bay Mills Indian Community ($)

1994	1995	1996	1997	1998	1999
30,218	154,587	358,292	388,091	471,123	481,454

2000	2001	2002	2003	2004	2005
478,991	488,296	532,808	528,220	561,723	572,539

Total: $5,046,338

Hannahville Indian Community ($)

1994	1995	1996	1997	1998	1999
220,034*	263,201	334,616	353,091	347,643	554,543

2000	2001	2002	2003	2004	2005	2006
592,396	632,746	694,402	707,674	736,640	931,032	937,560

Total: $7,337,583

Keweenaw Bay Indian Community ($)

1994	1995	1996	1997	1998	1999
206,000*	360,407	391,578	510,128	467,177	503,556

2000	2001	2002	2003	2004	2005
555,265	326,968	594,197	624,866	627,799	673,471

Total: $5,840,816

Lac Vieux Desert Band of Lake Superior Chippewa ($)

1994	1995	1996	1997	1998	1999
94,965	131,946	152,551	282,521	308,392	307,166

2000	2001	2002	2003	2004	2005	2006
328,212	350,242	400,463	447,647	466,167**	504,478	221,173***

Total: $3,995,949

Sault Ste. Marie Tribe of Chippewa Indians ($)

1994	1995	1996	1997	1998	1999
984,320*	1,710,403	2,030,777	1,851,505	2,018,591	2,114,801

2000	2001	2002	2003	2004	2005	2006
1,978,515	2,004,083	1,932,657	1,913,192	1,926,099	1,980,728	1,982,290

Total: $24,407,968

* - based on revenue between August 20, 1993 – September 30, 1994

** - based on 14 months revenue, October 1, 2003 – December 31, 2004

*** - based on six months revenue, January 1, 2006 – June 30, 2006

Eight percent payments to State of Michigan

Since 1993 the five tribes operating casinos in the U.P. have paid the State over $84-million dollars.

Bay Mills Indian Community ($)

1993	1994	1995	1996	1997	1998	1999
13,347*	333,079	618,349	1,382,132	1,552,385	1,884,495	869,252**

Total: $6,653,022

Hannahville Indian Community ($)

1994	1995	1996	1997	1998	1999
880,138	1,172,804	1,338,464	1,412,364	1,390,580	1,532178

Total: $7,726,531

Keweenaw Bay Indian Community ($)

1994	1995	1996	1997	1998	1999
719,417	1,423,156	1,681,683	1,858,024	1,983,756	2,089,362

2000	2001	2002	2003	2004	2005	2006
2,221,060	2,236,740	2,478,915	2,496,798	2,511,199	1,970,641	1,143960

Total: $24,812,715

Lac Vieux Desert Band of Lake Superior Chippewa ($)

1994	1995	1996	1997	1998	1999
379,937	527,768	610,204	1,130,086	1,233,568	349,628***

Total: $4,231,193

Sault Ste. Marie Tribe of Chippewa Indians ($)

1994	1995	1996	1997	1998	1999
3,811,159	7,633,353	7,801,197	7,480,181	8,067,339	5,884,340****

Total: $40,677,571

* - based on revenues between August 20 – December 31 1993
** - based on revenue from January 1 – June 30, 1999
*** - based on revenue from October 1, 1998 – February 19, 1999
**** - based on revenue from October 1, 1998 – June 30, 1999

Number of slot machines – by Tribe (Upper Peninsula)

There are 11 tribal casinos in the Upper Peninsula with a combined 5,092 slot machines, a little over 30% of the total slots statewide.

Most machines (tribe): 1,604 Sault Ste. Marie Tribe of Chippewa Indians

Most machines (casino): 1,400 Chip Inn Island Resort Casino

Casino	# of slot machines
Sault Ste. Marie Tribe of Chippewa Indians	
Kewadin Shores (St. Ignace)	903
Kewadin Vegas (Sault Ste. Marie)	899
Kewadin Manistique	246
Kewadin Christmas	212
Kewadin Hessel	111
Total:	**2,371**

Hannahville Indian Community

Chip Inn Island Resort Casino	**1,400**

Bay Mills Indian Community

Bay Mills Resort Casino	695
Kings Club Casino	300
Total:	**995**

Keweenaw Bay Indian Community

Ojibwa Casino - Baraga	400
Ojibwa Casino II - Marquette	300
Total:	**700**

Lac Vieux Desert Bands of Lake Superior Chippewa Indians

Lac Vieux Desert Casino & Resort	**393**
Total slot machines in U.P.	**5,092**

Lower Peninsula casinos

Casino	# of slot machines
The Saginaw Chippewa Indian Tribe	
Soaring Eagle Casino & Resort	**4,400**

Grand Traverse Bay Bands of Ottawa and Chippewa Indians

Turtle Creek Casino	650
Leelanau Sands Casino	625
Total:	**1,275**

Little River Bands of Ottawa Indians

Little River Casino	**1,300**

Little Traverse Bay Bands of Odawa Indians

Victories Casino	**1,500**

Pokagon Band of Potawatomi Indians

Four Winds Casino	**3,000**

Total slot machines: Lower Peninsula	**12,275**
Total Slot Machines: Michigan	**17,067**

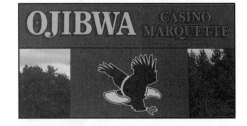

HEALTH CARE
HEALTH CARE EMPLOYMENT IN MICHIGAN

Helen Newberry Joy Hospital, Newberry

The health care industry is the largest private sector employer in Michigan, providing nearly 480,000 direct jobs and 260,000 indirect jobs. A total of $31.6 billion is pumped into the state's economy via wages and salaries from health care jobs.

Region	Direct Jobs	Indirect Jobs	Totals	Wages & Salaries Direct	Wages & Salaries Total
SE Mich.	245,379	120,408	365,787	$12.1 billion	$16.8 billion
W. Central	72,708	37,780	110,488	$3.2 billion	$4.3 billion
Mid Mich.	45,551	23,176	68,727	$2.1 billion	$2.9 billion
SW Mich.	40,237	19,919	60,156	$1.9 billion	$2.5 billion
E. Central	38,500	17,642	56,142	$1.6 billion	$2.1 billion
N. Central	20,776	10,188	68,727	$961 million	$1.24 billion
Upper Peninsula	**15,189**	**6,098**	**21,287**	**$670 million**	**$812 million**

Source: Michigan Health and Hospital Association, June 2006

ECONOMIC IMPACT OF HEALTH CARE – BY COUNTY

ALGER

Health Care Jobs			Salaries and wages		
Direct	**Indirect**	**Total**	**Direct ($)**	**Indirect ($)**	**Total ($)**
303	35.7	338.7	5,803,708	752,218	6,555,926

Federal, state, and local tax revenue generated: $1,850,544
Economic impact of Health Care sector: $11,283,777

CHIPPEWA

Health Care Jobs			Salaries and wages		
Direct	**Indirect**	**Total**	**Direct ($)**	**Indirect ($)**	**Total ($)**
1,156	385.4	1,541.4	53,023,547	9,589,791	62,613,338

Federal, state, and local tax revenue generated: $15,182,100
Economic impact of Health Care sector: $92,093,155

DELTA

Health Care Jobs			Salaries and wages		
Direct	**Indirect**	**Total**	**Direct ($)**	**Indirect ($)**	**Total ($)**
1,485	563.1	2,048.1	58,826,439	12,393,739	71,220,178

Federal, state, and local tax revenue generated: $18,616,870
Economic impact of Health Care sector: $105,042,606

GOGEBIC

Health Care Jobs			Salaries and wages		
Direct	Indirect	Total	Direct ($)	Indirect ($)	Total ($)
681	246.1	927.1	23,321,766	5,213,044	31,534,770

Federal, state, and local tax revenue generated: $ 8,219,509
Economic impact of Health Care sector: $51,781,619

HOUGHTON

Health Care Jobs			Salaries and wages		
Direct	Indirect	Total	Direct ($)	Indirect ($)	Total ($)
1,645	518.4	2,163.4	57,541,773	10,835,039	68,376,812

Federal, state, and local tax revenue generated: $17,122,771
Economic impact of Health Care sector: $ 102,750,110

IRON

Health Care Jobs			Salaries and wages		
Direct	Indirect	Total	Direct ($)	Indirect ($)	Total ($)
574	160.2	734.2	22,085,624	3,790,426	25,876,050

Federal, state, and local tax revenue generated: $6,529,434
Economic impact of Health Care sector: $ 39,697,271

KEWEENAW

Health Care Jobs			Salaries and wages		
Direct	Indirect	Total	Direct ($)	Indirect ($)	Total ($)
57	8.8	65.8	1,686,753	133,927	1,820,680

Federal, state, and local tax revenue generated: $450,578
Economic impact of Health Care sector: $2,680,226

LUCE

Health Care Jobs			Salaries and wages		
Direct	Indirect	Total	Direct ($)	Indirect ($)	Total ($)
323	69.8	392.8	14,269,073	1,438,782	15,707,855

Federal, state, and local tax revenue generated: $2,977,817
Economic impact of Health Care sector: $23,140,636

MACKINAC

Health Care Jobs				Salaries and wages	
Direct	Indirect	Total	Direct ($)	Indirect ($)	Total ($)
247	76.1	323.1	13,273,406	1,854,943	15,128,349

Federal, state, and local tax revenue generated: $ 3,470,218
Economic impact of Health Care sector: $19,912,216

MARQUETTE

Health Care Jobs	Salaries and wages				
Direct	Indirect	Total	Direct ($)	Indirect ($)	Total ($)
4,861	2,244.1	7,105.1	243,784,252	51,152,856	294,937,108

Federal, state, and local tax revenue generated: $ 76,382,479
Economic impact of Health Care sector: $416,131,733

MENOMINEE

Health Care Jobs		Salaries and wages			
Direct	Indirect	Total	Direct ($)	Indirect ($)	Total ($)
577	110.7	685.7	17,298,252	2,411,839	19,710,091

Federal, state, and local tax revenue generated: $4,857,719
Economic impact of Health Care sector: $29,413,537

ONTONAGON

Health Care Jobs		Salaries and wages			
Direct	Indirect	Total	Direct ($)	Indirect ($)	Total ($)
328	58.8	386.8	9,300,769	1,211,898	10,512,667

Federal, state, and local tax revenue generated: $2,623,584
Economic impact of Health Care sector: $16,467,362

SCHOOLCRAFT

Health Care Jobs		Salaries and wages			
Direct	Indirect	Total	Direct ($)	Indirect ($)	Total ($)
381	78	459	16,353,491	1,716,148	19,069,639

Federal, state, and local tax revenue generated: $3,934,884
Economic impact of Health Care sector: $26,663,630

Source: Michigan Health & Hospital Association and American Hospital Association 2004 annual survey

RETAIL

SALES TAX REVENUE (2006) – BY COUNTY

The largest source of revenue to the State of Michigan comes from sales and use taxes. In 2006, the State took in $6.5 billion dollars in sales and use taxes,

The 15 counties of the Upper Peninsula generated $157,862,000 dollars in sales tax, or just about 2.4% of statewide sales tax.

Marquette County generates the most sales tax revenue in the U.P., while the highest per-person sales tax is paid in Dickinson County.

County	Sales tax (000's)	State Rank	Sales tax ($ per capita)	State rank
Marquette	**34,771**	**29**	533	35
Delta	19,720	42	523	39
Chippewa	16,912	46	438	72
Houghton	16,250	48	460	63
Dickinson	16,187	49	**599**	**16**
Menominee	12,047	59	494	50
Gogebic	7,732	66	471	57
Iron	6,245	71	521	44
Mackinac	6,298	70	573	23
Alger	4,197	77	439	69
Schoolcraft	4,033	78	465	60
Baraga	3,776	79	438	71
Ontonagon	3,555	81	501	47
Luce	2,608	82	391	83
Keweenaw	1,118	83	521	40

THE LAST OF THE GREAT COPPER MINES

The White Pine Mine was the last copper mine to close in Upper Michigan after producing an enormous 4.2 billion pounds of copper and 47 million ounces of silver.

Early Mining in the Area

Prospectors swarmed the area around the Porcupine Mountains in the mid-19th Century hoping to strike it rich. Development in the region was slow. The Nonesuch Mine began mining operations around 1865, while close by, the White Pine Mine sunk a shaft in 1880. Milling techniques at the time could not recover the fine-particle copper in the Porcupine Mountain region. The mines in the area shut down before the turn of the century.

First Successful Operation

The Calumet and Hecla Mining Company (C & H) became interested in the property in the early years of the 20th Century. In 1907, it began exploratory drilling near the

MINING
MINING HISTORY OF UPPER MICHIGAN

The history of mining in Upper Michigan goes back thousands of years. A mysterious people mined copper on the Keweenaw Peninsula and especially on Isle Royale as long as 5,000 years ago. It is estimated that 1.5 billion pounds of pure copper was excavated from the region in ancient times.

The French Jesuits labored in the Lake Superior region in the latter part of the 17th Century. They brought back word of these ancient mining sites to the Old World. Later, when the English took control of the Old Northwest, the mineral reputation of the Lake Superior region was firmly established.

English adventurer Alexander Henry is credited with the first "modern" mining venture in what is now Upper Michigan. In the summer of 1771, Henry's nascent mining operation started excavating on a promising site up the Ontonagon River at the present site of the old Victoria Mine. The operation failed and Henry eventually went back into the fur trade.

A dozen years later, Great Britain rejected Benjamin Franklin's demands of cessation of Canada to the United States at the Treaty of Paris in 1783. Eventually, after months of hard bargaining, American independence and boundaries were accepted by the British. The American boundary through Lake Superior, which extends nearly to Canada on the west shore encompassing Isle Royale, was engineered by Franklin because of the stories he heard of numerous ancient mining pits on the island.

The U.S. territory adjacent to Lake Superior remained an isolated wilderness well into the 19th Century. Then in 1837 as a condition of Statehood, the Michigan Territory ceded a strip of land which included Toledo to Ohio. In exchange, Michigan was given the 16,500 square-mile of land bordering Lake Superior. State Geologist Douglass Houghton released a report to the State Legislature in 1841 that touted the potential mineral deposits of the northwestern portion of the Upper Peninsula. Finally in 1842, the Chippewa nation ceded the rest of their land holdings, which included the western half of Upper Michigan. The mineral rush began.

Pittsburgh pharmacist and adventurer John Hays is credited with establishing the first modern mine in the Upper Peninsula to yield pure native copper. He discovered what was to become the Cliff mine in the fall of 1844.

That same year, State Surveyor William Austin Burt discovered high grade iron ore in the rugged hills of the central Upper Peninsula. Two years later, the Jackson Mining Company established the first iron ore mine in the Lake Superior region near present-day Negaunee.

EARLY MINING

Life on the mining ranges of Upper Michigan was exceedingly difficult. To begin a mine, the company had to clear land for a farm to feed the workers, horses and mules. A blacksmith shop along with housing for the miners had to be constructed. Transportation was

Entrance to an underground mine on the Marquette Range. (Courtesy of Negaunee Public Library)

one of the main obstacles. Once the ore was hauled to a ship, the vessel had to pass through the obstacle of the St. Marys Rapids at Sault Ste. Marie.

OVERCOMING THE ST. MARYS RAPIDS

From the time Michigan was granted statehood, the state's congressional delegation unsuccessfully sought a federal land grant that would make the building of a canal and locks possible. The delegates had to overcome the perception that the location was a worthless wasteland. During one debate in the Senate, Henry Clay of Kentucky stated that a canal at the foot of Lake Superior was "a work quite beyond the remotest settlement of the United States, if not the moon." Finally, in 1852, Congress passed a bill that made the building of the locks possible. Construction of the first set of locks was completed in 1855. The locks led to increased shipping, which made for more immigration, commerce and cheaper transport of the ores.

old Nonesuch and eventually reached the site of the White Pine Mine. Favorable concentrations of copper were found and C & H moved in. It formed the White Pine Copper Company as a subsidiary to run the mine. The problem of salvaging the fine copper particles was solved and operations hit full throttle. By 1915, the mine was operating with a 300-man labor force producing copper at 12.6 cents-per-pound, while it was then sold on the open market at 25.3 cents-per-pound.

Bust Times

The mine operated at full capacity until after World War I. Then, a general recession lowered the price of copper and the production costs became prohibitive. The mine was closed in late 1920. The White Pine remained inactive during the next decade and its assets were finally sold off at an auction on the steps of the Ontonagon County Courthouse in May 1929. The winning bidder was Copper Range Company. The purchase price was $119,000.

During the depths of the depression, Copper Range acquired adjacent land around the mine and did some geological and metallurgical studies. Only in 1937 when economic conditions improved was serious exploration begun. Copper

Range came up against the same problem that the early miners faced—existing technology could not salvage enough copper out of the ore to make mining economically feasible. With the onset of World War II, exploration at the mine came to a virtual standstill.

Rejuvenation

After the war, an economical method of copper recovery was found. Then at the onset of the Korean War, the U.S. government became concerned that the country was importing too much copper. It approached Copper Range about the feasibility of reopening the mine and eventually produced a $68 million dollar grant to the company. Operations began in 1952, with construction of the mine and smelter. Eventually, a company town, White Pine, was built as well as a railroad spur leading to the mine. Mechanization made it possible to break up and transport up to 20,000 tons of ore per day.

In 1965, the billionth pound of copper was taken from the mine; in 1968, the White Pine produced 5 percent of the nation's copper. After the Vietnam War, copper prices again tumbled and operating costs went up. It was during this time that Louisiana Land and Exploration (LL & E) purchased the White Pine Mine

NEW TOWNS AND THE RAILROAD

In the Copper Country, settlement sprouted up quickly. Both Houghton and Hancock were platted around 1860. At the start of the Civil War, 33 companies with 3,700 employees produced 12 million pounds of copper annually. Communities grew all along the Copper Range from the tip of the Keweenaw to near Ontonagon. Railroads eventually connected these communities as well as the mines with the stamp mills. However, it was not until the 1870s that a railroad was built from the main Midwest lines to Upper Michigan. Only then did the isolation of winter cease.

C & H: THE LARGEST COPPER MINE

The Calumet and Hecla Mining Company Dredge 1913, Quincy Mill

In 1871, the Calumet Company and the Hecla Company merged to form the Calumet and Hecla Mining Company (C & H) near Red Jacket (now Calumet). This became the largest mine in the area and produced the most copper. If the C & H dividends paid were excluded from the total U.P. Copper Range dividends, investors would have just broke even. In the 1880s, Upper Michigan produced three-quarters of the nation's copper. By 1900, the area was booming, with a total population of around 70,000.

DECLINE OF THE COPPER MINING INDUSTRY

Copper production reached a peak in 1916, with 216 million pounds produced. Thereafter, production declined and the mines became less profitable. By the 1920s, copper mining in Upper Michigan was in decline. Every time the price of copper dropped, mining slowed and workers were laid off. The more marginal mining operations closed down. An exodus began as many workers headed downstate to work in the auto factories. The last mine on the range, the White Pine, closed in 1995 when the smelter could not reach environmental standards.

DEVELOPMENT OF IRON MINING INDUSTRY

On the Marquette Iron range, the five companies that

were formed before 1860 struggled for survival because of inadequate capital, poor transportation and high costs as well as the failure of early forges in the area. With the opening of the Sault locks and the arrival of the railroad, conditions slowly improved. In 1855, the year the Sault Locks opened, 1,500 tons of ore were shipped out. By 1860, 114,000 tons were shipped and by 1865, 236,000 tons passed through the locks. New technology such as power drills and dynamite also helped stimulate production. The railroad also helped open the interior wilderness along the Wisconsin State line. The Menominee range began production in the late 1870s, while the Gogebic Range mines commenced operation in the 1880s.

Initially, the mines were surface or "open pit" mines. Once the rich surface ore disappeared, the miners went underground. Mining costs went up, but so did production. During the 1890s, Upper Michigan Iron Ranges produced 80 percent of the nation's ore. Then around 1900, the Minnesota Iron Ranges were established and took the lead in iron production. U.P. mines still increased production right through both World Wars.

DECLINE OF IRON MINING

Iron mining peaked on the Menominee Range in about 1920. The last mine closed in 1978. In 1906, the Norrie Mine on the Gogebic Range was considered the greatest iron mine in the world. The Gogebic Range produced 255 million tons of iron ore until the last mine closed in 1967.

MINING TODAY

New methods that made the production of low-grade ores profitable saved the Marquette Range. Two open pit mines, the Empire and the Tilden, continue operations today. Several mining companies have found rich deposits of nickel and other minerals in north-central Upper Michigan. These minerals are located in sulfide-bearing rocks. Sulfide mining is controversial because of environmental problems brought on by this method of mining in some western states. As of this writing, tentative approval of a sulfide mining permit in northern Marquette County has been granted by the Michigan Department of Environmental Quality.

GOLD AND SILVER

The earliest European prospectors hoped to find gold and silver in the Lake Superior region. In 1771, Alex-

and Copper Range became a wholly owned subsidiary of LL & E. The company struggled under the pressure of labor strikes and lack of profitability and finally shut the mine and offered it for sale in 1982. An exodus began from White Pine as miners went to look for work elsewhere.

The Last Gasp

Ownership of the mine changed hands several times over the next decade as it continued marginal operations. In 1993, Copper Range Company was back and began research on solution mining. A dilute sulfuric acid solution was pumped into the mine to dissolve the chalcocite. The copper-rich solution was then pumped to a surface plant where the copper was extracted chemically. Finally in 1995, the White Pine Smelter was forced to shut down after a successful law suit led by an environmental group. The mine closed with the lay-off of 1,000 employees. Copper Range announced approval of a permit to begin solution mining again but opposition from environmental groups and native tribes in the area put the project on hold. In 1997, Copper Range abandoned its plan, sealing the fate of the White Pine.

Environmental Problems and New Life at the White Pine

The mine left considerable environmental problems in its

wake. The White Pine Mine is one enormous cavity nearly four square miles in area. It slopes downward from 800 to 2,800 feet below ground. The huge underground cavern has been gradually filling with brine. This brine would severely pollute Lake Superior if left unchecked. Prodded by the Michigan Department of Environmental Quality, the mine's owner has been pumping Lake Superior water into the cavity to suppress this brine water. In addition, the powdery tailings taken out of the mine are a source of pollution. To remedy this, the Mineral River has been diverted to create a pond at the 6,000 acre tailing site. The giant pond is gradually being replaced with vegetation.

Some economic activity continues at the White Pine Mine. A company called SubTerra is growing plants in the controlled climate of the deep mine. Using 50 1,000-watt growing lights, SubTerra occupies 3,000 square feet at the top of the big cavern. One of its contracts was for growing a certain modified tobacco plant whose extract is being used to treat cancer in Canada. The contained environment insures genetic containment and security from eco-terrorists, who seek to destroy genetically modified growing facilities.

One residual mining operation continues. The White Pine

ander Henry heard an Indian legend of an island in Lake Superior covered with heavy, yellow sand. Thinking the sand might be gold, Henry cast off in a 40-ton sloop in search of the mythic place. He found the island, but no gold or even heavy yellow sand, only a herd of stunted Caribou. The island is named in honor of this animal. Later that year, he began the first documented mine in the Upper Peninsula at a site up the Ontonagon River. The mine shaft collapsed the next spring and was abandoned.

State Geologist Douglass Houghton discovered some gold in rock specimens near present-day Negaunee in 1845. He kept his find a secret fearing his men would desert to prospect for gold. That fall, Houghton drowned in a canoe off Eagle Harbor and the location of his find went down with him.

Ropes Gold Mine, Ishpeming

While copper and iron were mined in profitable quantities beginning in the mid-19th Century, gold mining did not begin in Upper Michigan until the early 1880s. Julius Ropes opened the mine that bears his name north of Ishpeming. In its 14 years of operation, the Ropes Gold Mine produced gold bullion valued at $647,902 worth of the precious metal, but the mine was never able to pay its investors a dividend. In the following years, numerous prospects and mines were begun in Marquette County including the Michigan Gold Mine a few miles west of the Ropes. On the Gogebic Range in the far west, a number of gold mining ventures were begun about the time iron mining began, but none of the enterprises proved profitable.

A silver boom began in western Marquette County in 1864. Prospectors flooded the Silver Lake district northwest of Ishpeming but only a few mines were begun. These mines never found silver or gold in large enough quantities to be considered successful. The last of these mines closed down in 1868.

Silver was produced in some mines as a by-product of copper mining. The White Pine Copper mine produced 47-million ounces of the precious metal during its mid-to-late 20th Century run.

Occasional increases in the price of gold over the years

brought renewal of operations at the Ropes mine. During the depression, the mine was reopened but closed down during World War II. When the United States abandoned the gold standard in 1971 and the price of the metal sky-rocketed, prospecting began anew at the site. The Ropes reopened in 1985 and produced until 1989 when a combination of poor ore quality and a rock collapse forced its closure.

The Upper Peninsula has its share of "lost mine" stories. The most remarkable of these concerns a Keweenaw County mine operated by Alexander Henry's men after he abandoned mining in 1774. The group was said to have mined an incredibly rich vein of silver near present-day Kearsarge until an epidemic forced them to abandon the site. A prospector stumbled onto the mine about the time the depression began. He described the mine as a literal

Copper Refinery purifies copper shipped in from a mine in Flin Flon, Manitoba. The old power plant is now operating, which has created another company, White Pine Electric Power. It sells excess electricity generated to a major power company in the area. These operations are the last remnants of White Pine Mine—the last of the great copper mines in the Upper Peninsula of Michigan.

"wall" of silver and supposedly brought out large quantities of the precious metal, which he then smuggled to Chicago and traded for cash. He ceased mining the site and left the area after heavy pressure from some local residents to have him show them where the mine was. In the early 1970s, the man returned to the area and befriended a local bar owner. He took the bar owner to the mine and before he died, paid the bar owner to write a book about it. If the "Wall of Silver" mine exists, only the bar owner knows where it is.

No Upper Peninsula gold or silver mines are in operation at the present time, but as the price of these metals rise, it is conceivable that a gold and silver rush may begin again in the U.P.

HENRY FORD

"It is one of the prettiest places in the world," said automobile magnate Henry Ford to friends about the Upper Peninsula of Michigan. Ford loved Upper Michigan and spent a good deal of time in its forests and on its lakeshores. He also conducted business there on a large scale beginning about 1919. His company sold a million vehicles that year and he needed a ready-source of raw materials—steel for the frames and about 100 board-feet of wood for each car body.

With the help of Edward Kingsford, a U.P. native and relative of Ford through marriage, Henry Ford began the concept of industrial forestry. Up to this point, lumber barons were in business to log forests and then sell wood. Their product supplied the growing metropolitan areas of the Midwest. Henry Ford began logging to supply his manufacturing empire and as leverage against the high prices of other suppliers. Kingsford had experience as a logger and landlooker and Ford sent him into to the Upper Michigan woods to find forest land—lots of it. In 1920, Henry Ford paid the Michigan Iron and Land Company $2.5 million for 313,000 acres. By 1923, his land empire had grown to 400,000 acres over four counties.

When Ford went north to inspect his empire, he was treated like royalty. He sailed his yacht into Escanaba and was greeted by throngs of enthusiastic residents. The folks of Iron Mountain were ecstatic. Through heavy lobbying from Kingsford, the mining and lumber town became the center of the Ford Motor Company's activities in Upper Michigan. Ford spent

Ford Lumber Mill in Pequaming

millions there on construction of a large saw mill, and later, a dry kiln, an auto body parts mill and a wood chemical distillation plant.

He brought his entourage to Michigamme where school was dismissed for the day so children could line the streets and greet the industrial giant. The town built a new road on the possibility that Ford might reopen the old saw mill. He never did, but the town would do everything it could to promote and stimulate business. It, like many U.P. communities, was suffering as the 1920s began. A downturn in the economy after the conclusion of World War I closed area mines. The lumber supply was growing thin and demand dropped. Ford offered hope of a brighter future.

In Michigamme, it was iron Ford was after. He reopened the Imperial Mine in 1922. In its first year of operation after a shutdown of eight years, it shipped over 73,000 tons of ore. The next year, it turned out over 200,000 tons—nearly three times as much as the most productive mine in the Michigamme region ever produced. Later, he opened the Blueberry mine near Ishpeming. Both gave jobs to men who had been idle or underemployed in the iron mining district of the central U.P.

Ford's ultimate plan was to get a permanent source of timber, then farm the land that had been cleared with the objective of building a community. At the same time, he wanted to utilize the mineral rights on his property and turn the scrap wood into charcoal. His vision saw many small rural factories that would each turn out a part for his autos, which would then be shipped to a central plant for assembly.

Ford's activity in the Upper Peninsula had a profound affect in a short period of time. He immediately shook up the lumber industry by raising the wage of lumberjacks at his camps to between three and four dollars a day. The standard pay was $1.50. This incensed some lumbermen who felt Ford's pay scale would ruin the lumbering industry. Ford's aim was to bring wages of the area close to those he paid at his Detroit factories.

The Ford lumber camps also broke with U.P. tradition. The standard camp was a collection of shacks with limited washing facilities, shared bunks and a few kerosene lamps for light. Ford's camps were luxury facilities by comparison. They contained showers, iron-frame mattresses, electric lights and steam heat. Recreation rooms allowed workers a bit of reading or card playing after the evening meal.

Ford also attempted to apply scientific forestry practices to his logging operations. Foremen were ordered to clear the brush and slash left behind after a cut. Previously, loggers left the slash, which became a principal source of devastating forest fires in the late 19th and early 20th Centuries. In addition, old logging practice applied "clear-cutting" methods where all trees were taken down in a tract. Ford ordered selective cutting of his forests in keeping with new scientific management techniques which sought to promote the health of timberlands. This policy rankled some old lumbermen. By the mid-20s, with the big boss down in Detroit, supervisors ignored the selective cutting decree to a great extent. However, efforts were made to clear out the slash and debris after a cut. Early on this practice paid off. In the fall of 1923, fires raged across parts of northern Wisconsin and Upper Michigan. Millions of board-feet of lumber were burned all around the Ford holdings. While a few small fires began on his slash-cleared land, they were quickly extinguished.

Ford's luxury cottage in Pequaming north of L'Anse

The Ford Motor Company's U.P. business ventures never quite met the expectations of either Ford or the communities they touched. Only a small fraction of the iron needed for the Rouge Plant came from Henry Ford's iron mines. In the early 1930s after producing over 2 million tons of ore, the Imperial mine was closed for good. The shutdown left Michigamme in the same position it was a decade before. This led to bitterness and resentment toward the man that was once thought to be the savior of the town.

Ford developed the village of Alberta in rural Baraga County with the aim of making it the centerpiece of his rural factory vision. His concept included intermittent operation of a parts factory. When the factory was closed, the workers would farm the land around the town. In winter, men would participate in selective logging. This plan would insure a diverse economy that Ford felt would shield the area from resource depletion and economic depression. The plan failed, mainly due to the fact that the land around Alberta was not suitable for farming. In addition, there was little need for Alberta's saw mill production.

Ford was seen on one hand as an outsider—a cold, absentee landlord. On the other hand, sentiment rather than good business sense guided some of his decisions. Like Alberta, there was little need for the production of Big Bay's saw mill, but he bought it anyway—he did not want to see it sit idle.

Henry Ford's leisure life in the Upper Peninsula included a luxury cottage in Pequaming north of L'Anse and eventually membership in the exclusive Huron Mountain Club. At first, the northern Marquette County club denied membership to the upstart Ford. But he had some friends there and kept on good terms with the club. Eventually, he was voted in. He built a 16-room "rustic" cottage at the club with a price tag of about $100,000.

A worker at the Huron Mountain Club remembers his first encounter with Henry Ford. In the early 1940s, U.P. historian Fred Rydholm was a young man who had the job of delivering ice to the club residents. He would try to deliver as much as he could in the early morning before the heat of the day set in and people were out on the roads. On one particular morning, Rydholm loaded the truck and set out "maybe a little too fast" on the two-rut road behind the residents' cabins. He came around a curve and dip and there, sitting in the middle of the road, was a man with his back to Rydholm. The startled Rydholm slammed on the brakes about ten feet from the man. The man did not move for a time, but when he got up and made his way toward the truck, Rydholm recognized the trademark straw hat of Henry Ford in the morning twilight. The young man expected a bawling out from the old patriarch and the first words out of Ford's mouth seemed to be heading in that direction. "Weren't you going kind of fast young man?", Ford asked with a stern stare. Rydholm explained what he was doing and why and how surprised he was to see someone on the trail so early. Ford loosened up and explained he was looking for a four-leafed clover on the trail. What started out as a scolding turned into a pleasant chat. From then on, Ford addressed Rydholm as "Fred."

Rydholm explains that Henry Ford was very strict with his domestic help. The maids whispered and were quick to let him know if he was making too much noise putting ice in the ice box or slamming the door. On the other hand, Ford was not above creating a mess in his Huron Mountain household. At one point, Rydholm was told by Ford to bring the biggest spruce he could handle for planting near his cabin. A 4-to-5 foot tree was dug up and put in the back of a pick up truck and driven to the Ford cabin. Rydholm quietly knocked on the door and whispered to the maid that he had the tree out in the back of the truck. She went to inform the Fords and when she came back, she said Mr. and Mrs. Ford were in the main sitting room and would like to see the tree. Rydholm again said, "It's in back of the truck." The maid told him to bring it in so the Fords could see it. Rydholm explained it was large and very dirty. The maid insisted he bring it in anyway. Incredulous, Rydholm and his assistant lugged the spruce into the sitting room where the Fords inspected it. Rydholm relates that Mr. and Mrs. Ford examined it as if it were a Christmas tree. They took time to discuss where and how to plant it and Rydholm and his assistant completed the job while the maid must have had quite a task cleaning up the dirt left by the tree.

Henry Ford, the man who changed the way America lived and worked left a large footprint in the U.P. From the small lakeshore community of Big Bay to L'Anse and Pequaming over to Alberta and through the forests of the central and western Upper Peninsula south to the city of Kingsford, the model town he created adjacent to Iron Mountain, Ford did business and recreated in the Upper Peninsula for over two decades. His influence is still visible today.

HOWARD SHULTZ – COFFEE SHOP ENTREPRENEUR

Howard Shultz.

Howard Shultz, the founder of Starbucks, has ties to Upper Michigan. The entrepreneur was born in Brooklyn, New York in 1953. The oldest of three children, Shultz grew up in a government-subsidized housing project while his parents worked long hours to support the family. He excelled in sports and received a football scholarship to Northern Michigan University in Marquette. In 1975, Shultz became the first member of his family to graduate from college, receiving a bachelor's degree in business and marketing.

Shultz returned to New York and took a job with the Xerox Corporation. Later, he switched to working as a salesman for a Swedish housewares manufacturer. When he noticed he was selling a number of coffee percolators to a small company in Seattle, he flew out to see why. He met with the owners of Starbucks and fell in love with the company. Less than a year later, he was Director of Retail Sales for the coffee retailer.

In 1983, Shultz vacationed in Milan, Italy and became infatuated with the coffee shops in the city. He felt that the relaxed atmosphere of Milan's coffee bars could be transferred to the United States in a big way. However, the owners of Starbucks did not subscribe to Shultz's vision. When his idea was nixed by company officials, he resigned and opened II Giornale coffee bar in 1984. Three years later, he bought out Starbucks for $3.8 million and merged the company and II Giornale to form the Starbucks Corporation.

Shultz's concept—a coffee shop with a relaxed, comfortable atmosphere where a customer can not only enjoy a cup of coffee, but an entire experience—took off. After five years, Starbuck's went public and boasted 165 stores world-wide. Today, there are 10.000 Starbucks in over 30 countries. Howard Shultz has not forgotten the place that brought him academic and athletic success. The first Starbucks in Upper Michigan opened on the Northern Michigan University campus in 2003.

Chapter 8

TOURISM

TOURISM SPENDING RANKED BY COUNTY – 2000 (IN MILLIONS OF DOLLARS)

County	Motel	Camp	Seasonal Home	Visit F and R	Day Trips	State Total	Rank
Mackinac	117.1	4.6	19.9	3.0	30.7	175.2	11
Chippewa	43.7	6.4	24.1	9.8	13.9	97.9	19
Marquette	34.0	2.8	18.3	16.4	11.3	82.7	24
Houghton	31.6	0.9	13.3	9.1	7.0	62.0	36
Delta	16.8	1.5	11.8	9.8	7.0	46.9	44
Gogebic	23.1	2.7	11.4	4.4	3.7	45.3	47
Alger	9.1	2.5	9.3	2.5	4.7	28.1	68
Dickinson	6.9	1.4	7.9	7.0	3.4	26.6	70
Iron	5.4	2.2	12.0	3.3	1.2	24.1	74
Menominee	2.1	1.5	12.0	6.4	1.5	23.5	75
Keweenaw	8.9	1.7	5.9	0.6	0.7	17.8	80
Luce	5.7	2.3	6.3	1.8	1.6	17.7	81
Ontonagon	2.2	1.2	7.5	2.0	2.9	15.7	82
Baraga	4.8	0.8	5.1	2.2	1.1	14.1	83

Motel = hotels, motels, cabins, B&B's, and related lodging

Camp = public or private campgrounds

Seasonal home = private residence used as second, or seasonal home

Visit F & R = staying overnight at friends or relatives home

Day Trips = visitors from outside the immediate area (50 miles or more)

TOTAL TOURIST SPENDING IN U.P. (2000): $677,600,000
Michigan receives about 3% of the domestic travelers in U.S.

Region	2002 Person-trips	2002 Person-days
Michigan	94,800,000	189,080,000
Southeast	44,510,000	81,090,000
Northwest	11,130,000	22,890,000
Southwest	20,430,000	37,390,000
Northeast	11,970,000	30,690,000
Upper Peninsula	**6,760,000**	**17,020,000**

Person-trips – equal to number of travelers
Person-days – number of travelers *x* days spent visiting

Purpose of stay (%)

Region	General visit	Weekend visit	Special event	Other	Visit friends or relatives
U.S.	23	14	13	12	38
Michigan	21	17	13	10	39
Southeast	11	13	17	13	46
Northwest	28	23	8	9	32
Southwest	18	11	14	8	49
Northeast	30	27	8	5	30
Upper Peninsula	**34**	**14**	**13**	**17**	**22**

Purpose of stay, by region (2004, 2005, 2006)

Purpose for visit	Michigan	WUP	CUP	EUP
Touring, sightseeing	21.4%	34.1%	28.4%	33.9%
Dining	26.0%	22.9%	25.1%	42.6%
General entertainment	19.5%	18.5%	21.5%	42.2%
Shopping	23.1%	19.7%	25.4%	26.6%
National/State parks	9.5%	22.4%	20.4%	22.9%
Hunt, Fish	8.3%	18.6%	20.4%	14.9%
Gamble	7.4%	3.8%	11.6%	31.5%
Historic site	5.5%	8.3%	15.1%	16.7%
Beach/waterfront	13.9%	6.4%	7.3%	16.3%
Hike, Bike	6.4%	8.1%	11.0%	6.7%
Night life	5.6%	1.5%	3.2%	11.4%
Camping	7.3%	7.3%	8.0%	8.9%
Museum, art exhibit	5.3%	11.4%	4.4%	3.0%
Snow ski	1.5%	7.1%	4.7%	3.5%
Nature-eco travel	3.8%	4.3%	5.2%	6.4%
Shows (auto, boat, antique)	1.5%	10.0%	.4%	.8%
Watch sports event	4.9%	2.1%	5.3%	2.2%
Play golf	3.9%	2.6%	5.2%	0.4%
Boat/sail	5.2%	2.2%	1.9%	8.2%
Concert, Play, Dance	4.5%	4.0%	5.5%	3.5%
Other adventure sports	3.6%	8.0%	4.8%	3.4%

Type of accommodations, by region (2004, 2005,2006)

Accommodation type	Michigan	WUP	CUP	EUP
Hotel	33.8%	27.0%	45.2%	56.9%
Home/Apt./Condo	40.2%	46.2%	23.1%	22.6%
2nd (vacation) home/condo	5.2%	5.2%	7.3%	0.0%
Bed & Breakfast	0.8%	2.6%	0.0%	3.1%
Other	19.5%	19.1%	24.4%	17.4%

Season trip started, by region (2004, 2005, 2006)

Season	Michigan	WUP	CUP	EUP
Winter	18.5%	17.5%	15.0%	14.0%
Spring	17.8%	17.6%	17.7%	14.3%
Summer	43.4%	52.6%	42.5%	57.9%
Fall	20.3%	12.3%	24.8%	13.8%

Purpose of Stay and Personal Spending, by region (2004, 2005, 2006) per person

Purpose of stay	Michigan	WUP	CUP	EUP
Getaway weekend	94.96	139.25	85.27	122.08
General vacation	85.38	129.89	77.80	100.13
Visit friend/relative	73.54	78.24	77.66	136.93
Special event	91.05	77.69	67.62	94.66
Other personal	98.76	38.48	144.72	109.00

Length of stay, by region (2004, 2005, 2006)   Average days spent

Purpose of stay	Michigan	WUP	CUP	EUP
Getaway weekend	1.34	1.84	1.94	2.19
General vacation	3.88	4.02	4.46	5.85
Visit friend/relative	1.56	3.10	2.52	3.13
Special event	1.00	1.88	2.61	1.55
Other personal	0.45	1.75	0.33	0.56

Average age of visitors

Southeast	39
Northwest	39
Southwest	42
Northeast	40
Upper Peninsula	**44**

54% of UP visitors were 35-44 years old
26% were 55+
20% were 18-34 years old

Median Household Income of visitors

Northwest	$65,000
Northeast	$65,000
Michigan	*$61,000*
Southwest	$60,000
Southeast	$59,000
Upper Peninsula	**$57,000**

41% of visitors to UP have Median HH income of less than $50 k
22% of visitors to UP have Median HH income of $50-75 k
38% of visitors to UP have Median HH income of $75+k

Activity participation

U.P. led other regions with high participation in gambling, visits to state parks, adventure sports (ORV, canoe/kayak, etc.)

Source: Michigan 2002 Travel Summary for Travel Michigan Prepared by D.K. Shifflet & Associates

Mackinac Bridge Traffic – Monthly Crossings

Month	2006	%Change	2007	%Change	2008	%Change
JAN	212,007	(-1.5)	198,878	(-6.2)	180,895	(-9.0)
FEB	210,422	(-9.1)	204,068	(-3.0)	194,395	(-4.7)
MAR	241,322	(-1.8)	223,317	(-7.5)	217,800	(-2.5)
APR	255,784	(3.5)	234,249	(-8.4)	210,946	(-9.9)
MAY	334,103	(-4.6)	331,476	(-0.8)	309,549	(-6.6)
JUN	429,061	(-1.8)	413,485	(-3.6)	366,985	(-11.2)
JUL	579,192	(-8.0)	577,884	(-0.2)	504,818	(-12.6)
AUG	553,789	(-4.2)	574,968	(-3.8)	553,171	(-3.8)
SEP	440,179	(3.2)	442,156	(0.4)	365,919	(-17.2)
OCT	359,080	(-3.6)	360,835	(0.5)	340,071	(-5.8)
NOV	293,750	(4.2)	283,780	(-3.4)	263,126	(-7.3)
DEC	224,104	(1.5)	209,525	(-6.5)	188,083	(-10.2)
Total	4,132,810	(-2.4)	4,054,642	(-1.9)	3,520,802	(-13.1)

Mackinac Bridge Traffic – Monthly Fare Revenues

Month	2006 ($)	%Change	2007 ($)	%Change	2008 ($)	%Change
JAN	833,754	(-1.9)	763,991	(-8.4)	711,793	(-6.8)
FEB	823,514	(-7.9)	773,945	(-6.0)	757,109	(-2.2)
MAR	928,187	(-1.9)	829,402	(-10.6)	960,341	(15.8)
APR	933,521	(0.9)	848,249	(-9.1)	950,101	(12.0)
MAY	1,197,918	(-2.9)	1,168,064	(-2.5)	1,280,938	(9.7)
JUN	1,466,142	(-1.2)	1,371,481	(-6.5)	1,484,334	(8.2)
JUL	1,832,691	(-7.3)	1,799,740	(-1.8)	1,919,803	(6.7)
AUG	1,795,721	(-4.0)	1,808,543	(0.7)	2,055,049	(13.6)
SEP	1,460,340	(1.7)	1,427,874	(-2.2)	1,462,724	(2.4)
OCT	1,245,252	(-3.0)	1,224,441	(-1.7)	1,371,316	(12.0)
NOV	1,016,694	(1.9)	983,055	(-3.3)	1,034,948	(5.3)
DEC	769,766	(-4.5)	741,274	(-3.7)	758,026	(2.3)
Total	14,303,500	(-2.4)	13,740,059	(-4.0)	14,746,482	(7.3)

Tolls for crossing the Mackinac Bridge were increased in March of 2008 to $3.00 per passenger vehicle. Incremental toll increases are scheduled as follows: $3.50 per auto in 2010, $4.00 per auto in 2012, and $4.50 per auto in 2014. The Mackinac Bridge Authority voted unanimously for the increases to cover long-term maintenance and preservation programs, including a complete deck replacement project.

The "Mackinaw City," one of the state's fleet of ships that ferried cars across the Straits before the bridge was opened in 1957

MICHIGAN WELCOME CENTERS IN THE UPPER PENINSULA

The Upper Peninsula has six Department of Transportation Welcome Centers for visitors entering the U.P. from Canada, the Lower Peninsula, and Wisconsin.

IRON MOUNTAIN
Highway: US-2   **County:** Dickinson
Hours: 9-5 year round with expanded summer hours. Restrooms open 24 hours.
Parking: Cars – 14   Trucks and RVs - 5
GPS Coordinates: N 45° 49.0339' by W -88° 03.9259'

IRONWOOD
Highway: US-2 eastbound and westbound   **County:** Gogebic
Named for: Jack L. Gingross
Hours: 9-5 year round with expanded summer hours. Restrooms open 24 hours.
Parking: Cars – 34   Trucks and RVs - 7
GPS Coordinates: N 46° 27.792180' by W -90° 11.30904'

MARQUETTE
Highway: U.S.-41   **County:** Marquette
Named for: Carl Pellonpaa
Hours: 9-5 year round with expanded summer hours. Restrooms open 24 hours.
Parking: Cars – 30 spaces   Trucks and RVs – 6
GPS Coordinates: N 46° 30.2576' by W -87° 21.7623'
Visitors can enjoy a view of Lake Superior from the deck.

MENOMINEE
Highway: U.S.-41 northbound   **County:** Menominee
Named for: Claude Tobin, Highway Commissioner
Hours: 9-5 year round with extended summer hours. Restrooms open 24 hours
Parking: Cars – 18 spaces   RVs and Trucks – 0
GPS Coordinates: N 45° 06.23190' by W -87° 25.45386'
The log building was constructed in 1938 near the Michigan-Wisconsin border.
It features a stone floor, two stone fireplaces, and original wagon-wheel chandeliers.

SAULT STE. MARIE
Highway: I-75 northbound   **County:** Chippewa
Named for: James E. Brophy
Hours: 9-5 year round with expanded summer hours. Restrooms open 24 hours.
Parking: Cars – 52   Truck an RVs – 11
GPS Coordinates: N 46° 29.55774' by W -84° 22.28220'

ST. IGNACE
Highway: I-75 northbound, just past Mackinac Bridge toll booths   **County:** Mackinac
Named for: James Pitz
Hours: 9-5 year round with expanded summer hours. Restrooms open 24 hours
Parking: Cars – 88   Trucks and RVs – 15
GPS Coordinates: N 45° 50.9961' by W -84° 43.3441'

WELCOME CENTER VISITS 2002 - 2007

	Iron Mountain	Ironwood	Marquette	Menominee	Sault St. Marie	St. Ignace
2002	34,586	125,255	164,876	82,220	172,640	562,588
2003	44,160	120,889	161,612	87,300	173,529	551,378
2004	57,116	119,870	164,197	80,813	200,394	547,769
2005	59,256*	119,081	176,083	35,773*	178,456	546,777
2006	65,215	116,211	166,476	73,047	171,116	542,088
2007	73,270	122,033	174,502	33,777*	144,628	536,158

*The Menominee Welcome Center was closed for construction, November 2007

US-2 Highway in Iron Mountain was under construction, April 2005 through October 2005.

The bridge at Menominee was closed for reconstruction from November 2004, through November 2005.

NATIONAL PARK ATTENDANCE AND ECONOMIC IMPACT

Pictured Rocks National Lakeshore	(2005)	(2006)
Visits (recreational)	469,147	419,258
Overnight visits	27,475	26,256
Visitor spending (all):	$17,880,000	$16,660,000
Visitor spending (non-local)	$17,612,000	$16,406,000
Jobs:	420	368
Personal income:	$6,169,000	$5,745,000

Isle Royale National Park	(2005)	(2006)
Visits (recreational)	17,276	17,070
Overnight visits	52,236	51,816
Visitor spending (all):	$1,796,000	$1,851,000
Visitor spending (non-local):	$1,796,000	$1,851,000
Jobs:	43	37
Personal income	$629,000	$643,000

PICTURED ROCKS NATIONAL LAKESHORE

EARLY HISTORY

Henry Wadsworth Longfellow, with inspiration from the writings of Henry Rowe Schoolcraft, told of the legendary history of the Pictured Rocks. In "The Song of Hiawatha", the young brave was born and raised on Gitche Menesing (Grand Island). Hiawatha hunted among the cliffs and forests along Lake Superior.

Another Indian, Pau-Puk Keewis, the storm fool, wrecked Hiawatha's lodge and slaughtered his feathered friends. The storm fool then took shelter in the caves along the Pictured Rocks shores.

Hiawatha, wearing "magic mittens," sought vengeance for this belligerent act by smashing the sandstone cliffs where Pau- Puk was hiding. The warrior-hero also called upon the gods of Thunder and Lightning to aid him in his attack. The rocky caves and ruins represent Hiawatha's might and fury against his adversary, the storm fool.

Early Chippewa treated the Pictured Rocks as the dwelling place of various Indian Spirits. They would retreat to the rocks and caves for periods of fasting. After a time they were visited by these spirits in their dreams where they would receive important information.

Pictured Rocks

The first documented European visitor to Pictured Rocks was French fur trader Pierre Esprit Radisson in 1658. "We go along the coast, most delightful and wonderful," reflected Radisson. "Nature has made it pleasant to the eye, the spirit and the belly." A decade later, Jesuit missionaries marveled at the spectacular sandstone cliffs. Still later, when the English rose to prominence in the region, they named the sculptured cliffs Pictured Rocks. The British adventurer Alexander Henry's mineral expedition of 1771 stopped here to camp and search for mineral riches. In the summer of 1831, nine years after establishing the first permanent American settlement in the Lake Superior region, Henry Rowe Schoolcraft admired "the storm beaten and impressive horizontal coat of the Pictured Rocks."

While Pictured Rocks offers breath-taking beauty, it also comprises some of the most treacherous coastline on the lake owing to its shear rocky cliffs and full exposure to north and northwesterly gales. In late October 1856, the steamer *Superior* shipwrecked in a gale along the rocky shore with the loss of an estimated 50 lives, the greatest loss of life in a single Lake Superior shipping disaster.

MAKEUP

A half-billion years ago, shallow seas covered the Pictured Rocks area. Sediments deposited in this sea formed the red, yellow, light buff and brown sandstones that are seen in the cliffs today. Glaciers, owing to their advance and retreat along with frost and wave erosion, created the stacks, arches and caves along the shoreline.

NATIONAL LAKESHORE

The Pictured Rocks National Lakeshore was created by an Act of Congress in 1966 and was formally established in 1972. The area consists of a shoreline zone of 33,548 acres and a "buffer" zone of 37,849 acres. The shoreline zone is intended for recreational use; the buffer zone acts as stabilization and protection for the shoreline area. The National Park Service owns and operates the shoreline acreage, while the buffer zone is a mixture of public and private ownership.

The Pictured Rocks encompass around 38 miles of shoreline including sandstone cliffs, sandy beaches, dunes and waterfalls. The actual cliffs of Pictured Rocks run about 15 miles extending just northeast of Munising. The cliffs rise from 50 to 200 feet high. Farther east are sand dunes, the most prominent the Grand Sable Banks that rise 275 feet above lake level at a 35-degree angle.

VISITOR INFORMATION

There are two ways of viewing Pictured Rocks. The Park Service maintains hiking trails with camping allowed in designated areas. About six miles north of H-58, on County Road H-13, is the Miners Castle overlook complete with a picnic area and a walking trail to the Miners Castle formation (which just lost one of its two turrets in the spring of 2006).

Boat tours leaving Munising from spring to fall offer a panoramic view of the Pictured Rocks the way the early explorers saw them. Major attractions are Miners Castle, Indian Head Rock, Bridal Veil Falls, Battleship Row, Grand Portal Point and Chapel Rock.

Pictured Rocks National Headquarters is located just east of Munising at Sand Point. There are two visitor centers operated by the National Park Service. One is at Munising Falls on Sand Point Road in Munising; the other is on the east end of the National Lakeshore on H-58 just outside of Grand Marais.

STATE PARK ATTENDANCE (OCT. 1, 2006 – SEPT. 30, 2007)

Park	County	Campers	Day users
Baraga	Baraga	17,294	27,615
Bewabic	Iron	21,375	31,019
Brimley	Chippewa	30,608	9,394
Craig Lake	Baraga	2,741	9,878
Fayette	Delta	13,811	39,805
Fort Wilkins	Keweenaw	21,675	33,469
Indian Lake	Schoolcraft	41,242	5,791
Lake Gogebic	Gogebic	19,657	15,571
McLain	Houghton	32,896	96,972
Muskallonge Lake	Luce	31,256	15,571
Porcupine Mountains	Ontonagon/Gogebic	68,697	160,300
Straits	Mackinac	70,957	6,897
Tahquamenon Falls	Chippewa/Luce	89,672	176,090
Twin Lakes	Houghton	10,348	22,104
Van Riper	Marquette	34,297	50,733
Wells	Menominee	33,277	29,931

Most popular State Park for overnight camping (U.P.): Tahquamenon Falls

Most popular State Park for day visitors (U.P.): Tahquamenon Falls

STATE PARKS

PORCUPINE MOUNTAINS WILDERNESS STATE PARK

ESTABLISHED: 1945

Native Ojibwa Indians called the area *kaugabissing,* meaning place of the porcupine because the silhouette of the terrain resembles a porcupine profile.

Although there was some mining and lumbering conducted within the park boundaries, much of it was left untouched. In the 1930s, conservation advocates recognized the value of the natural wilderness, which led to its designation as a state park.

Porcupine Mountains

The park was established to preserve the last large stand of mixed hardwoods and hemlock in Michigan, and to establish a public site at and around the highest mountains in the Midwest.

County: Ontonagon/Gogebic

Size: 59,020 acres or 94 square miles

This largest state park in Michigan stretches 25 miles between Silver City and Presque Isle, and includes 26 miles of Lake Superior shoreline.

48,808 acres of the park were designated as the state's only Wilderness in 1972 to prohibit development.

Highlights: The Porcupine Mountains offer accessible hiking trails and stunning views. Summit Peak is 1,958 feet above sea level and features an observation tower.

Four lakes lie within the park including Lake of the Clouds, one of the most photographed lakes in Michigan. Within the park there are miles of wild rivers and streams and over 30 waterfalls.

Porcupine Mountains Ski Area features some of the finest skiing in the Midwest with a 640 foot vertical drop and runs as long as 5,800 feet, plus 42K of cross country trails.

25 miles of snowmobile trails

Over 90 miles of hiking trails

Almost 35,000 acres of the forest is old growth hardwoods, described by the Michigan Natural Features Inventory as the biggest and best tract of virgin northern hardwoods in North America.

Camping: 100 modern sites, 50 rustic, 3 yurts, 19 cabins

For more information: (906) 885-5275 or www.michigandnr.com/parksandtrails

TAHQUAMENON FALLS STATE PARK   ESTABLISHED: 1947

Tahquamenon Falls State Park - Lower Falls

Tahquamenon is believed to be an Ojibwa word used to describe the river's rust colored water. The river was highlighted by Henry Wadsworth Longfellow in his poem, The Song of Hiawatha.

Centuries ago Native Americans camped along the banks of this river that provided them with a bountiful supply of fish. Then in the late 1800s, the lumber industry set up shop. Logs were floated down the river to waiting mills and small towns or lumber camps sprang up along the river route.

Land for the park was donated to the state by Jack and Mimi Barrett of the Barrett Logging Company of Newberry. The couple, who loved canoeing and hiking to the falls, bought property next to the falls in the 1950s. They built a lodge on the rugged terrain and called it Camp 33. The property was reachable only by boat, but the couple worked out a deal with the DNR to have a road built through the wilderness ending three quarters of a mile shy of the falls. Of their 160 acres, they kept two for themselves and donated the rest to the state for a recreation area. That led to the establishment of the Tahquamenon Falls State Park.

County (s): Chippewa and Luce

Size: 46,179 acres or 72 square miles; 13 miles west from Whitefish Bay into Luce County

Highlights: The Tahquamenon Falls are the largest in Michigan and the second largest falls east of the Mississippi. Only Niagara Falls flows faster than the 50,000 gallons of water that passes over the Upper Falls of the Tahquamenon every second! The falls are 200 feet wide with a drop of 50 feet, third highest in the country. The Lower Falls are not as dramatic, but are a series of smaller falls split by an island in the river.

The Upper Falls are in Luce County, while the Lower Falls are within Chippewa County.

The final 16 miles of the 94 mile-long Tahquamenon River snake through the park and over the falls before draining into Whitefish Bay.

The water rushing over the falls appears to be rusty. The tea color comes from tannic acid in the cedar, spruce and hemlock swamps that the river flows through.

Tours of the falls include a combination train and guided riverboat ride and the Toonerville Trolley, the longest 24-inch gauge rail in the country.

There are over 12 lakes within the park and 25 miles of hiking trails, including a section of the North County Trail.

The park is a paradise for birders and viewing of other wildlife. It is one of the best known breeding sites in Michigan for the palm warbler and scarce rusty blackbird. Visitors can also spot moose, bears and river otters along with other wildlife.

Camping: 241 modern sites, 36 semi-modern

For information call: (800) 447-2757 or www.michigandnr.com/parksandtrails

CRAIG LAKE STATE PARK   ESTABLISHED: 1967

Frederick Miller of the Miller Brewing Company of Milwaukee built a lodge and small cabin on Craig Lake in the 1950s. He bought the land as a getaway for hunting and fishing and later sold it to a logging company, which in turn sold it to the state.

County: Baraga

Size: 6,983 acres or about 11 square miles

Described as the most remote state park in Michigan, the park is completely undeveloped except for the cabins and lodge built by the Miller family. Access to the park is limited to old rocky lumber roads. Vehicles with high ground clearance are recommended.

Highlights:

374-acre Craig Lake is the largest of the six lakes in the park. The lake features high granite cliffs and six islands.

Motorized vehicles are not allowed on the lake or in the park.

Wildlife viewing includes moose, black bear, loons and beaver.

Camping: Two rustic cabins, and backcountry camping

Call (906) 339-4461 or www.michigandnr.com/parksandtrails.com on the web.

VAN RIPER STATE PARK

Named after Dr. Paul Van Riper, the physician for the Champion Mine in the early 1900s. Van Riper went on to become a pioneering expert in the field speech pathology. He wrote over a dozen books about growing up in the Champion area under the name of Cully Gage. (*The Northwoods Reader, Tales of the Old U.P.*, etc.)

County: Marquette

The park is in the Marquette Iron Range where the first iron ore discovery was made in 1845. Evidence of iron mining activity can be seen along some of the hiking trails.

Size: 1,044 acres

Highlights: The park includes one half-mile of sandy beach on Lake Michigamme and a mile-and-a-half of frontage along the Peshekee River.

Beach Area at Van Riper State Park

Photo S. Willey

The 59 moose transplanted near the park from Canada in the mid 1980s have grown to a much larger herd. There is a good chance of spotting one while spending any time in the park. There is an information center in the park with details on the moose transplant. 4.5 miles of trails for hiking or cross country skiing

Camping: 150 modern, 40 rustic, 2 mini-cabins and one rustic cabin that overlooks the Peshekee River For information: (906) 339-4461 orwww.michigandnr.com/parksandtrails on the web.

LAUGHING WHITEFISH FALLS SCENIC SITE

County: Alger

Size: 960 acres

INDIAN LAKE STATE PARK   ESTABLISHED: 1932 AND 1939

There are two separate units located three miles apart. The south shore property was acquired in 1932 with CCC and WPA labor used for development. The West shore land was acquired in 1939, but not developed until 1965.

County: Schoolcraft

Size: 847 acres, six miles long, three miles wide

Highlights:

One mile of sandy beach on Indian Lake

Camping: 145 modern, 72 semi-modern

For information: (906) 341-2355 or www.michigandnr.com/parksandtrails on the web.

FAYETTE HISTORIC STATE PARK   ESTABLISHED: 1959

County: Delta

Size: 711 acres

Besides the beautiful shoreline setting amidst limestone cliffs, Fayette Historic State Park features the Historic Townsite of Fayette, a bustling 19th Century industrial town that had a life-span of 25 years.

The town was named after Fayette Brown, the general manager of the nearby Jackson Iron Company. Brown decided he wanted ore from the Jackson mine smelted into iron before shipping it south to the steel towns. He settled on this site because there was a natural harbor and plenty of hardwood trees nearby to fuel his blast furnaces.

Fayette Historic State Park

The town's population peaked around 500 in the 1880s. Eventually better methods of smelting ore were developed out East, making it expensive and inefficient to continue the operation in Fayette. By 1890, Fayette was a ghost town and remained so until 1959 when the State took possession of the property and began to restore the remaining buildings.

Today over 20 of the former

homes, offices and stores are preserved as a living museum.

Highlights: Three miles of shoreline on Big Bay De Noc with campground

300 feet of dockage in Snail Shell Harbor for overnight or day usage by boaters

7 miles of hiking trails

Camping: 61 semi-modern sites

Call (906) 644-2603 or www.michigandnr.com/parksandtrails on the web.

FORT WILKINS STATE HISTORIC PARK   ESTABLISHED: 1923

County: Keweenaw

Size: 700 acres

Tense times were at hand at the tip of the Keweenaw in the 1840s. The copper rush was on, which drew some surly characters, and the local Native Americans were not happy with all of these people on what used to be their land. Secretary of War William Wilkins sent troops to build the fort and keep the peace in 1844. In less than two years soldiers from the fort were sent to the Mexican-American conflict, and the fort was abandoned. Fort Wilkins was temporarily re-garrisoned in the 1860s and then permanently closed down.

Highlights: 1840s fort and outbuildings entirely restored and open for tours

Copper Harbor Lighthouse Museum has exhibit and information on Lake Superior shipping, shipwrecks and lighthouse living.

Four miles of hiking trails. Two miles of shoreline on Lake Superior and Lake Fanny Hooe

Camping: 160 modern sites with one mini-cabin

Call (906) 289-4215 or www.michigandnr.com/parksandtrails on the web.

J.W. WELLS STATE PARK   ESTABLISHED: 1925

County: Menominee

Size: 678 acres, a three-mile long strip along the Green Bay waterfront

The land was donated to the State by the children of John Walter Wells, a pioneer lumberman and former mayor of Menominee.

The Civilian Conservation Corps did most of the landscaping and built most of the cabins and shelters in the park.

Highlights: Sandy swimming beach and large picnic area on Green Bay

Trails for biking, hiking and cross country skiing

Camping: 150 modern sites and 5 rustic cabins

Call (906) 863-9747 or www.michigandnr.com/parksandtrails on the web.

F. J. MCLAIN STATE PARK

Named after Houghton County commissioner from the 1880s

County: Houghton

Size: 443 acres

Highlights: Two miles of scenic Lake Superior shoreline

Large swimming and sunbathing beach

Trails for hiking and cross country skiing

Excellent sunset views from the sandy dunes.

Camping: 103 modern sites with six mini-cabins and one rustic cabin

Call (906) 482-0278 or www.michigandnr.com/parksandtrails on the web.

PALMS BOOK STATE PARK   ESTABLISHED: 1926

Kitch-iti-kipi hand-pulled barge

County: Schoolcraft

Size: 388 acres

The State purchased the spring and the land from the Palms Book Land Company for $10.00 in 1926.

The attraction here is not camping, but Kitchitikipi—Michigan's largest spring. The 40-foot deep spring is 200 feet from shore-to-shore, featuring crystal clear water.

Kitchitikipi is a Chippewa word meaning *big, cold water* or *big spring.*

Over 10,000 gallons of water per minute is pumped out from beneath the limestone.

Visitors can cross over the surface in a hand-pulled barge that holds up to 40 people.

Call (906) 341-2355 or www.michigandnr.com/parksandtrails on the web.

LAKE GOGEBIC STATE PARK   ESTABLISHED: 1930

Gogebic County Parks officials obtained land on the lake in 1926 with the intent of preserving it as a public park. The county donated the land to the State and adjacent acreage was deeded to the state by E.J. Stickley and W. Bonifas. Lake Gogebic State Park opened in 1930.

County: Gogebic   **Size:** 360 acres

Highlights: Located on the west shore of the largest lake in the U.P

Sandy swimming beach and good fishing.

Two miles of trails for hiking and cross country skiing

Camping: 105 modern sites, 22 semi-modern sites.

Call (906) 842-3341 or www.michigandnr.com/parksandtrails on the web.

BEWABIC STATE PARK   ESTABLISHED: 1966

Bewabic State Park is sometimes referred to as Fortune Lake State Park after the four Fortune Lakes. The land was purchased in the 1920s by Iron County upon the urging of local highway engineer, Herb Larson. Larson, who created the first roadside park in the country, wanted to preserve the forested land which was almost sold to a lumber company. The county sold the property to the State, which established the State Park in 1966.

County: Iron

Size: 315 Acres

Highlights: Only State Park in Michigan to offer tennis courts, which were built in the 1940s when the park was owned by Iron County.

Features a chain of five small lakes, Fortune 1, Fortune 2, Fortune 3, Fortune 4, and Mud Lake

Over two miles of trails including a small bridge leading to an island on Fortune Lake 1

Several structures, including a stone pavilion, were built in the 1930s by the Civilian Conservation Corps

Popular with anglers and canoeists

Camping: 135 modern sites

Call (906) 875-3324 or www.michigandnr.com/parksandtrails on the web.

MUSKALLONGE LAKE STATE PARK

The park is on land once known as Deer Park, a former lumbering town. Timber was brought by rail to Muskallonge Lake which was used as a mill pond. The mill closed in 1900. Before the lumber era, the land served Native Americans as a fishing encampment and during the heyday of shipping, a Coast Guard Life Saving Station was situated here.

County: Luce

Size: 217 acres

Highlights: Frontage on Lake Superior and Muskallonge Lake

Park is over a mile in length

Good swimming on Muskallonge Lake

Quiet and out of the way

Good rock and agate hunting on Lake Superior shore

1.5 mile trail connects to North Country Trail

Camping: 159 modern campsites

Call (906) 658-3338 or www.michigandnr.com/parksandtrails on the web.

STRAITS STATE PARK   ESTABLISHED: 1924

County: Mackinac

Size: 181 Acres

Highlights:

Good views of the Mackinac Bridge and ship traffic through the Straits

Father Marquette National Historic Site

This site is located near several popular visitor sites including Colonial Fort Michilimackinac, Mackinac Island, Seney Wildlife Refuge, Soo Locks and Tahquamenon Falls.

800 feet of shoreline on the Straits

Camping: 255 modern, 15 semi-modern

Call (906) 643-8620 or www.michigandnr.com/parksandtrails on the web.

FATHER MARQUETTE MEMORIAL STATE PARK   ESTABLISHED: 1974

County: Mackinac

Size: 58 acres

Highlights: The national memorial honoring Father Jacques Marquette was dedicated here

in 1980 to honor the Catholic priest and explorer credited with discovering the Mississippi River in 1673. In 1668, Marquette established a mission for Native Americans at modern day Sault Ste. Marie, which became Michigan's first settlement. He also founded St. Ignace.

The park features grand views of the Straits of Mackinac, a picnic area and an interpretive trail.

TWIN LAKES STATE PARK   ESTABLISHED: 1964

Houghton County Commissioner of the 1880s, F.J. McClain, who has a State Park named after him, fought to have land set aside for a state park at this location in the Copper Country.

County: Houghton

Size: 175 acres

Highlights: Excellent swimming, boating and water skiing on Lake Roland with sandy bottom and shallow water 500 foot long swimming beach

Quiet! Least visited State Park in Michigan

1.5 mile hiking trail and five miles of cross country ski trails

Bill Nichols ORV and snowmobile trail cuts through park property

Camping: 62 modern sites including one mini-cabin

Call (906) 482-0278 or www.michigandnr.com/parksandtrails on the web.

BRIMLEY STATE PARK   ESTABLISHED: 1923

The Village of Brimley donated 38 acres to the State in 1923 making this one of the oldest State Parks in Michigan. Over time other parcels were acquired through purchase or trade.

County: Chippewa

Size: 160 acres

Highlights: Nearly a mile of Lake Superior shoreline on Whitefish Bay featuring sandbars and warmer water that allows for swimming in the big lake

Views of Canadian highlands across Lake Superior

Near Soo Locks, Tahquamenon Falls and Whitefish Point

Camping: 237 modern sites and a mini-cabin

Call (906) 248-3422 or www.michigandnr.com/parksandtrails on the web.

BARAGA STATE PARK

County: Baraga

Size: 56 acres

Highlights: Kitchigami Tepee on the shoreline sleeps 4-6 people and offers campers the opportunity to learn the culture of the native Ojibwa.

Great views of Keweenaw Bay

Shady camping sites Sandy beach

Nearby attractions include Bishop Baraga Shrine, Sturgeon River gorge, Mt. Arvon (highest point in Michigan), and Copper Harbor

Camping: 96 modern sites, 10 semi-modern sites, one mini-cabin and a teepee

Call (906) 353-6558 or www.michigandnr.com/parksandtrails on the web.

WAGNER FALLS SCENIC SITE

One of the smallest State Parks in Michigan

County: Alger

Size: 22 acres

Highlights: The 20-foot falls and the footpath along Wagner Creek

Call (906) 341-2355 orwww.michigandnr.com/parksandtrails on the web.

Michigan Department of Natural Resources

Michigan State Parks: A Complete Recreation Guide for Campers, Boaters, Anglers, Hikers & Skiers, Jim DuFresne in cooperation with the DNR, 1989

Michigan State and National Parks: A Complete Guide, Fourth Edition, Tom Powers, copyright 2007, Thunder Bay Press

SENEY NATIONAL WILDLIFE REFUGE   ESTABLISHED: 1935

Mission: Protect migratory birds and other wildlife

Area: 95,212 acres including 7,000 acres of water

Location: Schoolcraft County , 5 miles south of Seney, two miles north of Germfask on M-77

Animals: deer moose, geese, loons, eagles, Trumpeter swans, osprey, turtles

Viewing: 7-mile Marshland Wildlife Drive for automobiles or bicycles includes observation decks

Attracts over 88,000 visitors per year

TOURISM ATTRACTIONS, BY COUNTY

ALGER

Alger County Historical Society Heritage Center Museum occupies the site of the old Washington School

Pictured Rocks National Lakeshore –70,000 acres of public land

Miners Castle

Pictured Rocks Cruises – Munising

Grand Sable Banks sand dunes – Grand Marais

Miners Beach

Sand Point

North Country National Scenic Trail (42 miles through the National Lakeshore)

Hiawatha National Forest (five campgrounds: Bay Furnace, Wide Waters, Island Lake, AuTrain Lake, and Pete's Lake)

Grand Island National Recreation Area – Grand Island/Munising

Laughing Whitefish Falls Scenic Site, Wagner Falls Scenic Site and 22 other waterfalls

Lake Superior recreational harbors at Grand Marais and Munising

Grand Sable Lake – Grand Marais

Alger Underwater Preserve – Munising Bay

Coast Guard Point historical and maritime museums – Grand Marais

Tyoga Historical Pathway - Deerton

Lake Superior beaches: agate and rock hunting

Glass bottom boat tours

Alger Heritage Museum

Teenie Weenies Pickle Barrel house – Grand Marais

Kewadin Casino – Christmas

LIGHTHOUSES

Au Sable Light between Munisng and Grand Marais

Grand Island East Channel Light- Grand Island

Grand Island Harbor Range Front Light – Grand Island

Grand Island Harbor Range Rear Light – Grand Island

Grand Island North Light – Grand Island

Grand Marais Harbor of Refuge Inner Light

Munising Rear Range Light – Munising

Munising Front Range Light – Munising

Snowmobiling: miles of marked trails, and permitted on county roads

ORV/ATV trail system in Hiawatha National Forest and permitted on county roads Cross-country skiing: miles of marked trails

Mountain biking

Hunting and fishing (stream and lake)

Hiking, camping, birdwatching

Grand Marais Fly-In (September) – Grand Marais

BARAGA

Craig Lake State Park

Baraga State Park

Mt. Arvon – Michigan's highest point – 12 miles east of L'Anse

Lake Superior recreational harbor at L'Anse

Shrine to Father Baraga, the Showshoe Priest – L'Anse

Ojibwa Casino and Resort – Baraga

Canyon Falls "The Grand Canyon of the U.P." – 9 miles south of L'Anse

41 other waterfalls

Canyon Falls Nature Trail – L'Anse

L'Anse to Anderson Corner snowmobile trail (38 miles);

Baraga County Historical Museum – Baraga

Alberta Village Museum – Alberta

"The Grand Canyon of the U.P."

The Ford Motor Company insignia at the Alberta Village Museum was recently removed

Hanka Homestead Museum – Baraga (restored 1920s Finnish farm)

Historic Pelkie Grade School – Pelkie

Lake Superior recreational harbor at L'Anse

Baraga County Historical Museum – Baraga

Alberta Village Museum – Alberta

Indian Cemetery – L'Anse

Henry Ford Alberta Village Museum – Alberta

EVENTS

Fiddler's Jamboree (July) – Aura

Baraga County Fair (2nd wk of August) – Pelkie

Keweenaw Indian Community Pow-Wow (4th weekend of July) - Baraga

Baraga County Lumberjack Days (4th of July)

CHIPPEWA

Soo Locks - world's largest and busiest locks system

Soo Locks Boat Tours

Tahquamenon Falls State Park

Lower Tahquamenon Falls near Paradise

Lake Superior recreational harbor at Whitefish Point and Sault Ste. Marie

Whitefish Point Underwater Preserve

Lake Superior agate and rock hunting

Vegas Kewadin Casino – Sault Ste. Marie

Bay Mills Resort and Casino - Brimley

DeTour Lighthouse

Great Lakes Shipwreck Museum – Whitefish Point

DeTour Passage Historical Museum and Marine Park

Valley Camp Museum Ship – Sault Ste.Marie ina a stem-powered freighter)

Tower of History – Sault Ste. Marie

River of History Museum – Sault Ste. Marie

Iroquois Pt. Lighthouse – Brimley (Historical site and museum)

DeTour Point Lighthouse – DeTour

Lake Superior State University (Old Fort Brady) – Sault Ste. Marie

Drummond Island

Fort Drummond Memorial Plaque

Harbor Island National Wildlife Refuge

Whitefish Point Bird Observatory

Freighter watching – Sugar Island, Sault Ste. Marie
Fishing: stream, lake and ice
Groomed snowmobile and cross country ski trails
Mountain biking, hiking
Hunting

EVENTS

International Bridge Walk (June)
Soo Locks Festival (late June-early July)
DeTour Winterfest – Antique snowmobile show and race, parade, snow sculptures, etc.
I-500 Snowmobile Classic – Sault Ste. Marie (February)

DELTA

Fayette Historic State Park featuring restored iron smelting town
Hiawatha National Forest
Recreational harbors and marinas at Escanaba and Gladstone on Lake Michigan
Lake Michigan recreational harbors at Escanaba and Gladstone

Bays de Noc – 211 miles of shoreline (white sand) the most of any county in continental U.S.

Island Resort and Casino – Harris
Sand Point Lighthouse – Escanaba
Point Peninsula Lighthouse Tower (1870) – Rapid River
Delta County Historical Museum
Bay de Noc Grand Island Trail
Fishing on Little and Big Bay de Noc and inland lakes; ice fishing, kayaking, scuba diving, snowmobiling, cross country skiing, mountain biking, hiking and hunting
Bonifas Fine Arts Center – Escanaba

Jackson Iron Company Blast Furnace (1867), Fayette Township

EVENTS

Great Lakes Championship Rodeo, Escanaba (June)
Civil War Encampment with battle recreations and exhibits, Escanaba (June)
Walleye tournament, Gladstone (June)
Blessing of the Fleet, Fayette Historic State Park (July)
Upper Peninsula State Fair, Escanaba (August)
Outdoor Channel/Optima Pro Am Walleye Tournament, Escanaba (August)
Peninsula Pt. Lighthouse (site of annual monarch butterfly migration in October)
Bay de Noc Classic Walleye Tournament Escanaba (October)
Krusin Klassics Fun Run parade and car show, Escanaba)
MWC Escanaba Waterfront Art Festival

Antique Steam and Gas Engine Show
Great Lakes Log Rolling Championship (July) - Gladstone

DICKINSON

Furnee Lake Natural Area – between Quinnesec and Norway (mountain biking, hiking, birdwatching)
Fumee Falls – Quinnesec
Piers Gorge – Norway (whitewater rafting, kayaking, rock hunting, hiking)
Norway Lake – Norway

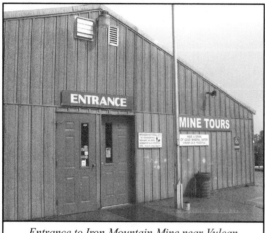

Entrance to Iron Mountain Mine near Vulcan

Pine Mountain Resort (skiing, golf)
Pine Mountain Ski Jump – Iron Mountain
Norway Mountain – Norway
Downhill and cross-country skiing
Canoeing, whitewater rafting on several rivers
Fishing, deer and small game hunting
ORV/ATV and snowmobile trails (120 miles of trails)
Millie Mine Bat Cave – Iron Mountain
Iron Mountain Iron Mine Tour – Vulcan
Menominee Range Historical Museum
Ardis Furnace

Cornish Pump and Mining Museum – Iron Mountain
Jake Menghini Historical Museum – Norway

EVENTS

Dickinson County Fair (Labor Day weekend)
Dickinson County Festival of the Arts
U.P. Triathlon, Lake Antoine (June)
Pine Mountain Music Festival, Iron Mountain (June)
Pine Mountain Music Jam, Iron Mountain (July)
Wonders in Wood Carving (October)
Leif Ericson Days , Norway (October)
Pine Mountain Ski Jumping Tournament, Iron Mountain (February)

GOGEBIC

Porcupine Mountains Wilderness State Park
Lake Gogebic State Park
Lake Superior recreational harbor at Black River
Black River Parkway and Park (waterfalls, camping)
Ottawa National Forest – Ironwood
Sylvania Wilderness and Recreation Area (19,000 acres within Ottawa National Forest)
Cisco Chain of Lakes (15 interconnected lakes)

Waterfalls
- Slate River Falls
- Yondota Falls
- Gabbro Falls, 120 foot drop
- Bond Falls
- Presque Isle Waterfalls
- and 30 others

Big Snow Country – receives 300 inches of snowfall per year

Blackjack Ski Resort Bessemer

Copper Peak Ski Resort – north of Bessemer (only ski flying facility in the Western Hemisphere, 18 stories high)

Bond Falls near Paulding, Baraga County

Indianhead Mountain Resort and Mt. Zion – Wakefield

Big Powderhorn Mountain – Bessemer

Johnson Nordic Ski System – Wakefield

Lac Vieux Desert Casino – Watersmeet

Open Pit Lake – former Wakefield Iron & Plymouth open pit iron mines

Hiawatha, World's Tallest Indian (53 feet tall) – Ironwood

Wakefield Historical Museum

Wood carving of Nee-gaw-nee-gaw-bow (Leading Man) by acclaimed Hungarian sculptor, Peter Toth – Wakefield (one of the 50 carvings presented by Toth to every state in honor the Chippewa Indians)

Hundreds of miles of trout streams and lakes, canoe trips

EVENTS

Gogebic County Fair (August) – Ironwood

Stock Outboard and Modified Boat Races every two years – Sunday Lake

"Home of the Nimrods" (Watersmeet)

HOUGHTON

Isle Royale National Park (headquarters and ferry service)

Keweenaw Historic National Park (16 sites on the Keweenaw Peninsula related to history and heritage of copper mining)

Keweenaw Water Trail

J.F. McLain State Park

Twin Lakes State Park – Toivola

Copper Country State Forest

Wyandotte Falls – 1.5 mile south of Twin Lakes State Park

Emily Lake State Forest Campground

Keweenaw Star Excursions Boat Tours

Swedetown X-country and snowshoe trails – Calumet

Indian totem at the Wakefield Chamber of Commerce Visitor's Center on Sunday Lake

Mont Ripley Ski Area – Houghton (Michigan Tech)

Fishing, boating, camping, hiking and hunting

Snowmobiling (five major trails, 250 miles); skiing

Many Lake Superior agate beaches

Finnish American Heritage Center

Calumet with Calumet Theatre, Quincy Mine and Steam Hoist

Quincy Mine Tours - Calumet

Coppertown USA Museum

A.E. Seaman Mineral Museum – Houghton (Official Mineral Museum of Michigan)

Copper Range Historical Museum – South Range

Chassell Heritage Center

George Gipp Memorial – Laurium

Michigan Tech Nordic Training Center

EVENTS

Great Bear Chase cross country ski race – Calumet (2nd Sunday in March)

Great Deef Chase (August)

Heritage Celebration (August)

PastyFest (June)

Pine Mountain Music Festival

Sibelius Academy Music Festival – Calumet 3 consecutive, nightly concerts by world-class student musicians from the Sibelius Academy in Helsinki, Finland at the Calumet Theatre

Copper Island Classic Cross-Country Ski Race   (January) – Chassell

Strawberry Festival (July)

Keweenaw Chain Drive Mountain Bike Festival (mid-June) – Houghton/Hancock

MTU Winter Carnival – early February

Houghton County Fair (August) – Hancock

Keweenaw Trail Running Festival (July)

Keweenaw Chain Drive Festival (mid-June)

Seafood Fest (mid-June) – Houghton

Bridgefest (mid-June) – Houghton and Hancock

Heikinpäivä Hiihto Festival and cross country ski race (mid-January) – Hancock

Greenlight Resort Ice Fishing Derby – Chassell (mid-January)

IRON

Ottawa National Forest (300+ lakes, miles of rivers including the Paint, the Iron, the Brule and the Michigamme)

Copper Country State Forest

Bewabic State Park

Iron County Courthouse, Crystal Falls (National Historic Site)

Iron County Museum Park

Fishing canoeing, hunting, camping, snowmobiling and skiing

Iron County Museum – Caspian (one of the top historical sites in Michigan with its 25 buildings that make up Heritage Village)

Ski Brule

Crystella Ski Hill – Crystall Falls

Indian Village – Stambaugh Twp. (Ojibwa village and cemetery preserved in honor of the native inhabitants)

EVENTS

Father's Day Antique Car Show

Upper Peninsula Championship Rodeo (July)

Iron County Fair – Iron River

Lions Club Bass Festival

Humoungus Fungus Fest – Crystal Falls

Remains of a mining structure at the Iron County Museum Park, Caspian

KEWEENAW

Isle Royale National Park

Keweenaw National Park, Brockway Mountain Drive, and Summit lookout – Copper Harbor

Ft. Wilkins State Park (19th century military post) – Copper Harbor

Rock and mineral hunting – numerous agate beaches and old mine sites

Lady of the Pines Church

Gratiot River Recreation Area – Lake Superior shoreline near Ahmeek

Delaware Copper Mine Tours – Delaware

Estvant Pines nature sanctuary (600 year old giant pines)

Fanny Hoe Resort

Manganese Falls

Montreal Falls

Fishing, skiing, snowmobiling and scuba diving

Cross-country skiing and snowmobiling

Excellent fishing – inland lakes and Lake Superior

Kayaking & canoeing

Copper Harbor Lighthouse

Historic Lighthouse Boat Tour

Eagle Harbor Lighthouse

Keweenaw County Historical Museum

Rathbone One-Room Schoolhouse – Eagle River

Astor House Antique Doll & Indian Museum – Copper Harbor

EVENTS

Copper Harbor Fat Tire Festival (Labor Day Weekend)   13 & 23 mile cross country mountain bike races

Copperman Triathlon (August)

Keweenaw Trail Running Festival (July)

LUCE

Tahquamenon Falls, Tahquamenon River Boat Tour, and Toonerville Trolley Wilderness Train Ride

Tahquamenon Logging Museum just north of Newberry on M-123

Lake Superior recreational harbor at Little Lake

Crisp Point Lighthouse

Muskallonge Lake Area

Two Hearted River Canoe trips

Luce County Historical Museum

Tahquamenon Falls Logging Museum

Hemingway's Big Two-Hearted River, 31 miles of Lake Superior shoreline

Snowmobiling and sking

EVENTS

Tahquamenon Falls Nordic Invitational (X-country Ski Race)

Superior Circle Sled Dog Race

Polka Festival

Old Time Music Jamboree

Lumberjack Days

Original Michigan Fiddler's Jamboree

Luce-West Mackinac County Fair

Cardboard Classic at Big Valley Ski Area

Woodchopper's Ball, Newberry (March)

Antique Car Show and Parade, Newberry (August)

MACKINAC

Mackinac Island (Grand Hotel, Ft. Mackinac, Lilac Fetival)

Mackinac Island State Park

Straits State Park

Father Marquette National Memorial

Les Cheneaux Islands

The Mystery Spot – St. Ignace

Kewadin Casino – Hessell

Kewadin Casino and Hotel – St. Ignace

Big Knob State Forest Campground

Black River State Forest Campground

Island Point State Forest Campground

Straits of Mackinac Underwater Preserve – St. Ignace

Sand dunes along Lake Michigan, US-2 scenic highway (Pt. Aux Chenes)

Top of the Lake Roadside Park – Naubinway northern-most point of Lake Michigan

Garlyn Zoological Park – Naubinway

Marquette Mission Park and Museum of Ojibwa Culture

Les Cheneaux Island Historical Museum

Les Cheneaux Islands Maritime Museum

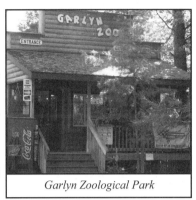
Garlyn Zoological Park

EVENTS

Mackinac Bridge Labor Day Walk

Straits Area Antique Auto Show

Les Cheneaux Islands, Antique boat Show, 4th of July

Dockside Arts Fair

Sled Dog Enduro

MIRA Pro-Enduro snowmobile races, MSDRA Pro national Snowmobile Drag Races

MACKINAC ISLAND TOURISM

The big draw on Mackinac Island, besides the natural beauty of its setting in the Straits, is the lack of automobiles. Mackinac is known around the world as the island where cars are not allowed. Visitors experience today much what late 19th Century tourists experienced: travel by horse and buggy or bicycle, beautiful Victorian cottages, and the smell of fresh lake breezes mixed with the fresh byproduct of the large horse population.

Motorized vehicles were banned from the island in 1896. Carriage operators, who had been providing transportation and tours on the island for over 25 years, complained that the loud road machines spooked their horses. It was the carriage operators, led by Thomas Chambers, who convinced the village council to ban motorized transportation from the island.

Today, fourth and fifth generation members of the Chambers family run Mackinac Island Carriage Tours, Inc. It is the world's largest, oldest and continually operated horse and buggy livery.

Number of horses on the island: 600 – summer, 30 – winter.

Number of carriages: approximately 100.

Where they go in the winter: The horses are ferried off the island and stabled near Pickford in the Upper Peninsula. Horses raised by Mackinac Island Carriage Tours are trained specifically for their work on the island.

Motor vehicles permitted on island: snowmobiles, construction equipment, and police and fire vehicles. All other motorized vehicles are by permit only, and only if the work at hand cannot be handled by horse drawn cart or wagon.

Annual visitors: 850,000 – 1,000,000 between May and October

Busiest day: 2nd Tuesday of August is historically the most crowded on the island. Saturdays tend to be the busiest overall, and Thursdays the slowest.

Number of hotels and inns: 46

Number of guest rooms: 3,000 est.

Oldest continuously operated hotel: Lake View Hotel opened in 1858

Oldest building housing a hotel: Part of the Harbour View Inn dates back to 1820, when it was built by a fur trader.

Hotel Iroquois has made Conde Nast Traveler Magazine's *"Gold List" on three occasions, 1997, 2000, and 2005.*

Number of bicycles available for rent on typical day: 1,325

Most popular tourist sites: Tie between Fort Mackinac, Marquette Park, Arch Rock and Grand Hotel.

Fort Mackinac includes the oldest standing structures in Michigan—the Officers' Stone Quarters was built in 1780.

The 4th of July celebration held at Fort Mackinac every year includes 38-gun salute. The 38 represents the number of states in the Union when the fort was occupied by the U.S. 23rd Regiment, 1884-1890.

Number of weddings performed on island per year: about 1,500

Oldest church: Mission Church, built in 1829, is **the oldest surviving church building in Michigan**. A Protestant church built by the early settlers of the island. It has been restored, and is a Michigan registered Historic site.

The Mission Church was used for Catholic services while St. Anne's Catholic Church was under construction.

Mackinac Island is home to Michigan's first and oldest continuously played

9-hole golf course. Designed by Alex Smith in 1898, *Wawashkamo*, meaning walk a crooked path, was named by the Ojibwe Chief Eagle Eye. The Course is built on a battlefield from the War of 1812, and is now a National Landmark.

AWARDS AND RECOGNITION

- One of the Top Ten Islands in the World by *Conde Naste Traveler* in 2002.
- National Historic Landmark by National Trust for Historic Preservation.
- Lilac Festival one of Top 100 Events by American Bus Association.
- Marquette Park-One of Top 10 Lawns by Briggs and Stratton.

MARQUETTE

Huron Mountains

Van Riper State Park, Lake Michigamme - Champion

Presque Isle Park, 323 acre natural park offers hiking, biking or cross country skiing, all with views of Lake Superior.

Escanaba River State Forest

McCormick and Donnelly Wilderness Areas, 16,850 acres, 18 small lakes and Yellow Dog National Wild and Scenic River

Lake Superior recreational harbor at Big Bay

Teal Lake

Mt. Marquette and Sugarloaf lookout points: Mount Marquette is located right in Marquette's city limits and has panoramic views of both harbors, the city and hills to the northwest and Gobbler's Knob scenic lookout and rock climbing. Sugarloaf Mountain is a few miles northwest of town and has stairs to the top of its summit.

Blueberry Ridge Pathway

Al Quaal Recreation Area – Ishpeming, hiking trails, baseball field, tennis, cross-country and downhill skiing and toboggan slide

Lake Superior lighthouses

Marquette Underwater Preserve

Greenwood Reservoir – Ishpeming

Scenic waterfalls: Alder, Little Garlic, Bushy Creek, Black River

Over 80 miles of public access beaches, five lighthouses, 24 miles of underwater preserve, wilderness areas, downhill and cross-country skiing, snowmobiling (over 200 miles of groomed trails), fishing and hunting, kayaking, dog-sledding, snowshoeing, golfing, canoeing, hiking, and mountain biking.

Ojibwa Casino – Harvey

Anatomy of a Murder Tours

Suicide Bowl Ski Jump – Ishpeming

U.S. Olympic Education Center   One of four Olympic Training Centers in the U.S

Negaunee Naturbahn Luge Track

Superior Dome – Marquette, World's largest wooden dome.

U.S. National Ski Hall of Fame and Museum

Tilden Mine Tour – Ishpeming

Marquette Maritime Museum – Marquette

Marquette County History Museum – Marquette

Cliffs Shaft Mine Museum – Ishpeming

U.P. Children's Museum, Marquette

Michigan Iron Industry Museum – Negaunee

Iron Ore Monument – Negaunee, marks discovery of iron ore in Marquette County

Michigamme Historical Museum – Michigamme

John Burt House – oldest home in Marquette

John Burt House – oldest home in Marquette

EVENTS

Art on the Rocks (late July) – Presque Isle Park

Hiawatha Music Festival (July) – Marquette Tourist Park

International Food Fest (4th of July) – Marquette

Seafood Festival (late August) - Marquette Lower Harbor

U.P. 200 Dog Sled race (February) – Marquette

Noquemanon Ski Marathon – Ishpeming, Michigan's largest point-to-point cross country ski marathon.

MENOMINEE

J.W. Wells State Park – Cedar River

Lake Michigan recreational harbors at Cedar River and Menominee

Green Bay shoreline

Henes Park, Menominee

Menominee River Lighthouse and Pier

Snowmobiling, camping, cross-country skiing, hiking, hunting, fishing and mountain biking

Menominee County Historical Museum (formerly St. John's Catholic Church)

IXL Historical Museum (in 1882 building once serving as headquarters for Wisconsin Land & Lumber Co.) – Hermansville   (State Historic Site)

Stevenson Island Logging Museum

EVENTS

Menominee County Fair (July)

Montongator County Music Festival (July)

Waterfront Festival, Menominee (August)

Brown Trout Fishing Derby, Menominee

ONTONAGON

Porcupine Mountains Wilderness State Park (Lake of the Clouds, downhill skiing and historic sites, 80 miles of hiking trails, waterfalls)

Ottawa National Forest with rustic camping

Ontonagon Harbor with marina and lighthouse

Ontonagon River fishing and canoeing

Lake Superior recreational harbor

Lake Gogebic Area and Ontonagon County Park

Bond Falls flowage

Agate Falls and over 20 other waterfalls;

One of the structures of the oldest standing log home village in the United States at Old Victoria, Ontonagon County

Adventure Mining Company – Greenland

Ontonagon County Historical Museum

Old Victoria Restoration (historic cabins from 1890s used to house miners at Victoria Copper Mine) Rockland

Adventure Mountain Sports Area and ski hill – Greenland

Porcupine Mountains Ski Area – Ontonagon

Over 200 miles of snowmobiling on five trails;

Paulding Mystery Light – Four miles south of Pauldin on Robbins Pond Road. Strange lights appear on the horizon!

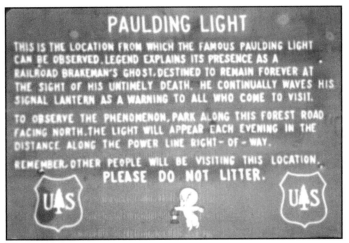

EVENTS

Snowmobile Radar Run race (February)

Ontonagon River Festival (June)

Snowburst (Feb)

County Fair (August)

Log Jam-Boree (September)

Porkie Festival (September)

Ontonagon Labor Day Festival

SCHOOLCRAFT

Indian Lake State Park with museum featuring Ojibwa life exhibits – Manistique

Big Spring Kitchitikipi at Palm Brook State Park – Thompson

Seney National Wildlife refuge – Germfask, 96,000 acres of wetland habitat with hiking trails, public fishing and bald eagle viewing

Thompson Fish Hatchery – Manistique

Seul Choix Pt. Lighthouse (1895)   A Michigan and National Historic site

Kewadin Casino – Manistique

Lakeview Park, Manistique

Manistique Marina and Boardwalk

Rogers Park on Lake Michigan – Manistique

Siphon Bridge (the bridge is below the water level and supported, in part, by the water; once featured in *Ripley's Believe It or Not*) – Manistique

Schoolcraft County Historical Museum and Water Tower – Manistique

Pioneer Park historical complex

Bishop Baraga Shrine and Chapel – Indian Lake

Mackinac Trail Winery – Manistique

EVENTS

Folk Fest (July)

Schoolcraft County Fair, Manistique (August)

Manistique Merchants Car and Antique Snowmobile Show (Sept)

TOP TEN WINTER GETAWAY

In January 2008 The Weather Channel included the Upper Peninsula in the *Top Ten Family Winter Getaways* list. The U.P. was ranked sixth between Taos, New Mexico and Snowshoe, West Virginia. Other locations include: Methow Valley, Washington, Lake Tahoe, Nevada, Joshua Tree National Park, California, Rocky Mountain National Park, Colorado, Kiawah Island, S. Carolina, Sanibel Island, Florida, and Waterville Valley, New Hampshire.

The Weather Channel labeled the U.P. as a "can't miss destination for your family…but, only the hearty and adventurous need apply. But if zero crowds, mile after mile of near-virgin snow and family time in a rustic cabin by a roaring fire sound good to you, then look no further."

SNOWMOBILE REGISTRATIONS – BY COUNTY

County	Registered Snowmobiles (as of May 1, 2007)
Marquette	6,010
Chippewa	5,523
Delta	3,484
Houghton	3,197
Mackinac	2,930
Gogebic	2,364
Dickinson	1,971
Alger	1,882
Luce	1,813
Menominee	1,592
Ontonagon	1,478
Schoolcraft	1,417
Iron	1,358
Baraga	922
Keweenaw	299
U.P.	36,240
Michigan	365,498

DOWNHILL SKI VOLUME IN THE UPPER PENINSULA

Day pass lift tickets sold 2001-2002		Day pass lift tickets sold 2002-2003	
U.P	172,480 (*17%*)	U.P.	156,262 (*14%*)
Northern lower	782,710 (*75%*)	Northern lower	821,447 (*71%*)
Southern lower	80,637 (*8%*)	Southern lower	167,855 (*15%*)
Michigan total	1,035,827	Michigan total	1,145,564

From the 2001-02 season to the 2002-03 season attendance increased at Michigan ski slopes however, the Upper Peninsula saw a decrease in the number of skiers and a smaller share of the ski pie.

Region	2001-02	2002-03	+/-	% Change
U.P.	172,480	156,262	-16,218	-9.4
Northern lower	782,710	821,447	+38,737	+4.9
Southern lower	80,637	102,855	+22,218	+27.6

Source: Travel, Tourism and Recreation Resource Center, Michigan State University, July 2003
(based on information provided by 5 Upper Peninsula ski resorts, 8 ski resorts in northern lower Michigan)

HISTORIC MUSEUMS

A number of local historical societies and private companies are preserving the history of their regions and communities by setting up museums at the sites of old mines, mills and lighthouses. Here is a survey of these historic sites from west to east across the Peninsula.

BESSEMER AREA HERITAGE CENTER

Located on Sophie Street adjacent to city hall, the Bessemer Area Heritage Center has a growing display depicting the logging and mining history of the area. The Bessemer Historical Society was established in 2001 and the Heritage Center was renovated and opened in 2003. Contact the Society for more information at P.O. Box 148 Bessemer, MI 49911 or email: BAHS@mattsonworks.com

OLD DEPOT MUSEUM IRONWOOD

Operated by the Ironwood Historical Society, the Old Depot Museum is the renovated railroad depot constructed in 1892. It was operational during the iron mining boom days of the Gogebic Range which ended in 1966. The beautiful structure is built of sandstone and brick in Romanesque style. This museum features iron mining displays and railroad memorabilia along with other artifacts. The museum, located at 150 Lowell St. off Business US-2 just before the center of town, is open daily Memorial Day through Labor Day from 10 a.m.-5 p.m..

WAKEFIELD HISTORICAL SOCIETY

This house features memorabilia from old Wakefield and the history of area mining and lumbering. Located at 306 Sunday Lake Street in Wakefield, the museum is open from June through September 1-4 p.m. daily. Admission is free with donations accepted.

ONTONAGON HISTORICAL SOCIETY MUSEUM AND LIGHTHOUSE

The museum, located downtown on River Street, contains numerous displays depicting the rich history of the Ontonagon region. There are room displays of 18th, 19th and early 20th Century life including numerous old photos and artifacts along with a replica of the famous "Ontonagon Boulder" that helped ignite the copper rush of the mid-1840s. The fully-accessible museum is open Monday through Friday from 10 a.m. to 5 p.m. and Saturdays 10 a.m. to 4 p.m.

Ontonagon was the site of one of the first five lighthouses on Lake Superior established at the mouth of the Ontonagon River, the largest river emptying into the lake on its south shore. The first wooden structure was built in 1851-52 and was replaced by the existing brick building in 1866. It was placed on the National Register of Historic Places in 1975. The Ontonagon Historical Society acquired the structure in 2003 and offer tours which include a climb up the stairs into the lantern room where visitors can get a panoramic view of the lake, harbor and distant Porcupine Mountains. Tours are offered during the summer months Monday through Saturday at 11 a.m., 2 p.m. and 4 p.m. and by appointment.

This existing brick Ontonagon lighthouse was built in 1866, to replace the original wooden structure that was built in 1851-52.

ROCKLAND MUSEUM

The Rockland Museum is located on US-45 in Rockland. Enjoy photographs, antiques, and attractive displays. Also on the same grounds is the Ontonagon County Veterans' Memorial, a tribute to those who have served our country in the military services.

OLD VICTORIA MINE SITE

Located in the rugged high country of Ontonagon County, Old Victoria is the restored remains of the village that served the Victoria Copper Mine over 100 years ago. Wander through hand-hewn log cabins and hear stories of the hardships endured by 19th Century mining pioneers. Guided tours 9 a.m. to 6 p.m. daily from Memorial Day through the fall color season. A small admission fee is required with family and group rates available. The historic site is operated by the Society for the Restoration of Old Victoria, Inc. and can be reached from U.S.-45 just outside of Rockland to Victoria Dam Road. Take the road 4 miles southwest.

ADVENTURE MINING COMPANY

This is a privately owned mine that offers tours of one of the first copper mines in the Ontonagon region. A variety of experiences are available from surface tours to underground copper mine walking tours to more challenging underground hiking excursions that involve rappelling to lower mine levels with a rope and harness. The Adventure Mine is located 12 miles east of Ontonagon off M-38. For admission fees and other information visit: http://www.exploringthenorth.com/mine/venture.html

CHASSELL HERITAGE CENTER

Home of the Chassell Township Museum and Friends of Fashion Vintage Clothing Collection, the building is located on Hancock Street in Chassell. The museum contains permanent exhibits on lumbering in the region to strawberry farming, which began near the turn of the century and continues today. The Chassell historic organization runs the museum which is open in July and August on Tuesdays from 1 to 4 p.m. and Thursdays from 4 to 9 p.m.

A.E. SEAMAN MINERAL MUSEUM

Located on the campus of Michigan Technological University, this museum is recognized as having the world's finest collection and display of minerals from Michigan and the Lake Superior Region. The museum has over 5,000 mineral specimens on display.

The A.E. Seaman Mineral Museum is in the heart of campus on the fifth floor of the Electrical Engineering Resources Center (EERC) at 1400 Townsend Street. Hours are Monday through Friday from 9 a.m. to 4:30 p.m. and Saturdays and Sundays from Noon to 5 p.m. from July to September. Donations are requested with children under 12 free.

CARNEGIE CULTURAL MUSEUM

Located in Houghton, the museum is now open to the public featuring the Raffaelli Historical Photo collection as well as other exhibits. Hours: Tuesday and Thursday 3 p.m. to 8 p.m. and Saturday Noon to 4 p.m. For more information call 906-482-7140.

KENNER RUOHONEN MEMORIAL HISTORY ROOM

This exhibit at Dee Stadium on Lakeshore Drive in Houghton contains a photographic history of Houghton/Hancock along with a history of the birthplace of professional hockey. Open Monday thru Saturday 9 a.m. to 5 p.m. or by appointment. Call 906-482-7760.

FINNISH-AMERICAN HERITAGE CENTER

The Heritage Center and Historical Archive is located on the campus of Finlandia University. It houses a museum, art gallery, a theater and the Finnish- American Family Center along with the Finnish-American Reporter newspaper. The building and gallery are open Monday thru Saturday from 8 a.m. to 4 p.m. For more information call 906-487-7437.

QUINCY MINE

Located just outside the city of Hancock on U.S.-41, the Quincy Mine offers a number of tour options to visitors. There are exhibits in a museum on site including the world's largest steam-powered hoist, plus a full underground mine tour and a ride on a cog-rail tram car. Operated by the Quincy Mine Hoist Association, the mine is open 9:30 a.m. to 5 p.m. daily from mid-June to late-October and Friday and Saturday from the end of April until mid-June. For admission prices or to request group tours, call 906-482-3101.

HOUGHTON COUNTY HISTORICAL MUSEUM

This 15-acre complex, located in Lake Linden on the site of the Calumet and Hecla millsite, houses a museum containing a variety of copper mining heritage exhibits as well as the Lake Linden and Torch Lake Railroad—a working railroad with track laid on the museum complex. The museum and gift are open daily June through September from 10 a.m. to 4:30 p.m.

LAURIUM MANOR INN

Built in Laurium at the height of the Copper Boom in 1908, this 13,000 sq. ft. mansion now serves as a Bed and Breakfast. 30 to 60-minute tours of the Inn are given everyday between 11 a.m. and 5 p.m.

COPPER RANGE HISTORICAL SOCIETY MUSEUM

This museum preserves the historical heritage of the mines and surrounding communities. Located on Main Street in South Range in the South Range State Bank building, the museum is open from June to September with hours from noon to 3 p.m. Tuesday through Saturday. Open Monday as well in July and August.

COPPERTOWN U.S.A. MINING MUSEUM

Located in the historic copper boomtown of Calumet, Coppertown U.S.A. houses a variety of exhibits from the copper mining era. The museum is open from June through mid-October from 10 a.m. to 5 p.m. and on Sundays in July and August from 12:30 p.m. to 4 p.m. Admission is $3.00 for adults and $1.00 for children with children under 12 free.

UPPER PENINSULA FIREFIGHTER'S MEMORIAL MUSEUM

Housed in the Red Jacket Fire Station on Sixth Street in historic Calumet, it contains memorabilia and exhibits from nearly a century of fire fighting. Open June through September daily from Noon to 3 p.m.

DELAWARE COPPER MINE

Delaware Copper Mine Stope

This mine operated from 1847 until 1887. Take a walking tour 100 feet below ground to explore one of the earliest working mines to operate during the country's first major copper mining boom. You'll see pure veins of copper exposed in the walls of the mine, along with other geological interests. Open mid-May to mid-October with hours from 10 a.m. to 5 p.m. in May, June, September and October and 10 a.m. to 6 p.m. in July and August. The site is on Delaware Mine Road in Delaware. For more information, call 906-289-4688.

EAGLE HARBOR LIGHT STATION MUSEUM COMPLEX

Operated by the Keweenaw County Historical Society, this complex features the lighthouse in Eagle Harbor, the Rathbone School, Central Mine and the Phoenix Church of the Assumption. All sites are open from mid-June to early October.

ASTOR HOUSE MUSEUM

This privately owned museum in Copper Harbor houses a fine collection of antique dolls, toys and American Indian artifacts as well as a collection of mining materials of the early copper rush days along with a mineral display. Admission: $2.00 for adults with children under 12 free.

THE HISTORIC PELKIE GRADE SCHOOL

Pelkie Grade School was erected in 1909 to replace the original 1905 structure destroyed in a forest fire. It served as a one-room school house until 1932, then as town hall. In 1979, the Sturgeon Valley Historical Society began renovation. It now serves as local museum. Take M-38 approximately 9 miles past the junction of M-38 and U.S.-41. A half-mile past the Sturgeon River Bridge turn right on Pelkie Road and drive 3 miles until reaching the town of Pelkie. Continue driving a half-mile past Pelkie until reaching the school at the corner of Pelkie and Mantila Road. The museum is open Sundays and holidays 1 to 4 p.m. between Memorial Day through the end of September.

BISHOP BARAGA SHRINE

Located between L'Anse and Baraga this 60-foot brass likeness of the "Snowshoe Priest" is set on a cloud of pewter and can be seen for miles. At the shrine you will also find a gift shop and restaurant along with the Red Rock Lodge, a condo unit available for rent that sleeps 8-12. On U.S. 41 take Lambert Road up the Red Rocks bluff overlooking Keweenaw Bay.

BARAGA COUNTY HISTORICAL MUSEUM

This museum contains photos and displays of local history including a number of artifacts from Captain James Bendry, the founder of Baraga Village. A complete record of births and deaths are available for family research. The museum, located on U.S.-41 along the shore of Keweenaw Bay just outside of Baraga, is barrier-free and open to the public from June until the end of September. Hours are 11 a.m. to 3 p.m. Tuesday through Saturday. Admission is $2 for adults, $1 for teens, while children under 12 are free when accompanied by an adult. To arrange tours or for special hours call 906-353-6810

COVINGTON TOWNSHIP HISTORICAL MUSEUM

This museum contains artifacts from the village and township of Covington, which was first settled after the arrival of the railroad in 1888. The museum is located in the township hall just off U.S.-141 in Covington on Elm Street, one block west of the post office. Hours of operation are from Memorial Day to Labor Day, on Friday and Saturday from 10 a.m.-2 p.m. or by appointment. Call either 906-3552573 or 906-355-2413.

ALBERTA VILLAGE MUSEUM

The museum contains many displays which tell the story of Henry Ford's historic model sawmill town. Hear the story of this special village and the people who lived here. Tour the sawmill and learn about its fully operational machinery. See a reconstructed 1925 "Woodie" Model T and much more. Hours of operation are Tuesday through Saturday 9:30 a.m. to 3:30 p.m. from mid-June through the fall color season. On U.S.-41 8 miles south of L'Anse

AMASA MUSEUM

Amasa served as a mining town and a major hub for logging and rail transportation. The museum, located in the old township hall, is a fine example of late-1800s balloon-style architecture. The main floor has many pictorial displays of the mining and logging industries of the area as well as memorabilia from Amasa School and Triangle Ranch. The second floor has been developed into a replica of "The Streets of Old Amasa." Located 12 miles north of U.S.-2 just off Hwy-141 on Pine Street in Amasa. Open from Memorial Day on during the summer months. Winter tours can be made by appointment. Free Admission.

IRON MINING MUSEUM

Located on the north side of the city of Iron Mountain, the mine contains the Cornish Pumping Engine. This pump was used to keep water out of the Chapin Mine, part of which was located under a cedar swamp. The pump was featured on the History Channel's Modern Marvels series on the world's biggest machines. In addition to the pump, the museum contains the largest collection of underground mining equipment on display in the state of Michigan. The Iron Mining Museum, located on Kent Street in Iron Mountain, is open 9 a.m. to 5 p.m. Monday through Saturday and noon to 4 p.m. on Sundays from Memorial Day through Labor Day. Other times are available by appointment.

Cornish Pumping Engine

IRON COUNTY MUSEUM

The complex comprises 22 buildings including a Cultural Center and the Lee LeBlanc Art Gallery. Tour the outdoor buildings which include the Homestead, reflecting pioneer life circa 1890 to 1900, the Lumber Camp, the Mining Area and more. The museum is located in Caspian, 2 miles off U.S.-2. Open daily May to October from 9 a.m. to 5 p.m. and Sundays 1 p.m. to 5 p.m. Admission charged with special group tours welcome.

HARBOUR HOUSE

This Queen Anne Colonial Revival home was built in 1900 and now serves as a museum as well as an antique and gift shop. On the first floor are furnishings and decorations of the period. The second floor holds Ojibwe, logging and mining artifacts. Located on North 4th Street in Crystal Falls, Harbour House is open Tuesday through Saturday 11 a.m. to 4 p.m. from June 1 to September 1 or by appointment. For guided tours call 906-875-4341 or 906-875-6026.

IRON MOUNTAIN MINE

Take a guided underground mine tour by train through a half-mile of subterranean shafts and tunnels to 400 feet below the surface. The largest rock shop in Upper Michigan is also on the premises. Located on U.S.-2 in Vulcan just east of Iron Mountain, the mine is open 9 a.m.-5 p.m. daily from Memorial Day through October 15. Group rates and tours are available by appointment.

Photo Courtesy Hunts' Guide

MILLIE MINE BAT CAVE

This abandoned mine shaft contains one of the largest hibernating bat colonies in North America. A specially designed cage allows the bats free passage and keeps everything else out. Best viewing times are late April and then from the latter part of August to September. Located on Park Ave. North off East A St. in Iron Mountain, the cave has a parking lot adjacent, walking paths and informational plaques. Admission is free.

HOUSE OF YESTERYEAR MUSEUM

A one-man collection of 30 1910-to-1939 cars in mint condition are housed in this museum. There is also a collection of guns, skates, license plates and more. On U.S.-2 Iron Mountain; call 906-774-0789 for more information.

MENOMINEE RANGE HISTORICAL MUSEUM

The museum houses over 100 exhibits that depict the rich heritage of the Menominee Iron Range boom days that began in the late 1800s. It is housed in the former Carnegie Library on Ludington Street in downtown Iron Mountain. Call 906-774-4276 for hours of operation and admission information.

MICHIGAMME HISTORICAL MUSEUM

This museum, resting on the hills overlooking Lake Michigamme, has over 125 years of history displayed in artifacts, memorabilia and antiques. It is open daily from May through September. Free admission

CLIFF SHAFT MINE MUSEUM

Walk the grounds that the miners walked and stand beside 9-story headframes that were used to lower miners 1250 feet below the surface. Take a guided tour of the tunnels the miners walked and listen to the history of mining from those who worked underground. The museum and Cliff Shaft Mine Gift Shop are open Tuesday through Saturday 10 a.m.-4 p.m. from late May through September. A nominal admission fee is charged. Located on Euclid Street in Ishpeming

U.S. NATIONAL SKI HALL OF FAME

Ishpeming is the birthplace of organized skiing in the United States. The Ski Hall of Fame pays tribute to Olympic skiers and offers a historical perspective of the sport. This is the only national sports hall of fame in Michigan. Open daily year-round with a nominal admission fee.

MICHIGAN IRON INDUSTRY MUSEUM

Nestled overlooking the Carp River in the rugged, forested Marquette Iron Range, this museum is located at the site of the first iron forge in Michigan. It contains extensive exhibits, audio-visual programs and outdoor interpretive paths that depict the large-scale capital and human investment that made Michigan an industrial leader. The museum and gift shop are open daily 9:30 a.m. to 4:30 p.m. from May through October. Admission is free.

NEGAUNEE HISTORICAL MUSEUM

In 1844, surveyors made the first discovery of iron ore in the Lake Superior region here. Two years later, the first iron mine was established within the city limits of present-day Negaunee. The city's rich history is preserved in this four-story museum located near the central business district. Open daily from May 29 to Labor Day with a nominal admission fee.

FORSYTH TOWNSHIP HISTORICAL SOCIETY

This historical society maintains a small but comprehensive museum on the 2nd floor of the Forsyth Township office building in Gwinn. It features exhibits, photographs, maps and artifacts depicting the rich mining history of Gwinn a Model Town built by Cleveland-Cliffs Iron Company in the early 20th Century. Open from July 4 through Labor Day on Monday through Friday 10 a.m.-2 p.m. and Wednesdays from 5 p.m. to 7 p.m. Admission is free.

MARQUETTE COUNTY HISTORY MUSEUM

Established in 1918, the Marquette County historical society maintains this immaculate multi-story museum which includes permanent exhibits depicting the founding of Marquette County as well as a special new exhibit every year. The John M. Longyear Research Library is also housed in the facility. The museum, located on Front St. next to the Peter White Public Library, is open Mon. through Fri. from 10 a.m. to 5 p.m., Saturdays (Jun.-Aug.) 11 a.m. to 4 p.m. and every third Thursday from 10 a.m. to 9 p.m. Admission is $3 for adults, $1 for students 12 and over, children and school groups are free.

MARQUETTE MARITIME MUSEUM

Located on the shore of Lake Superior in the old historic Waterworks building, the Marquette Maritime museum offers permanent displays depicting local maritime history along with the best lighthouse lens collection on the Great Lakes. The museum also offers tours of the historic Marquette Point Lighthouse and grounds. Open daily from late May to late October 10 a.m. to 5 p.m. with special openings by request. Admission for adults is $4 for either the museum or lighthouse, $7 for both. Children 12 and under are $3 for either the museum or lighthouse and $5 for both.

UPPER PENINSULA CHILDREN'S MUSEUM

Located on Baraga Street in the heart of Marquette, this museum contains floors of interactive, hands-on exhibits for children designed by the youth of Upper Michigan. Open 7 days a week with hours varying seasonally, closed some holidays. A nominal admission fee is charged with family rates available.

BISHOP BARAGA ASSOCIATION—DIOCESE OF MARQUETTE

This museum contains collections of artifacts, books and photos that pertain to the life and work of the legendary "Snowshoe Priest." The original home of Bishop Baraga is located near the museum. Hours are Monday through Friday from 8:30 a.m. to Noon and from 1 p.m. to 4:30 p.m. Admission is free.

WEST SHORE FISHING MUSEUM

This museum is situated on the property of fisherman Charles T. Bailey on M-35 about 15 miles north of Menominee. Bailey operated a commercial fishery from 1893 until the end of the 1940s. Four properties on the house have been made ready for public viewing including the family home. View early commercial fishing as well as Native American fishing exhibits. The museum is open Saturday and Sunday 1 to 4 p.m. from Memorial Day through Labor Day. To enter the museum, look for the signs on M-35 at the north end of Bailey Park.

MENOMINEE COUNTY HERITAGE MUSEUM

Get the complete story on how Menominee County was built since its inception in 1863. History is on display in pictures, words and artifacts. The museum is located in the former St. John's Catholic Church on 11th Avenue in Menominee. It is open Monday through Saturday from 10 a.m. to 4:30 p.m. Memorial Day through Labor Day. For group tours, call 906-863-9000.

IXL MUSEUM

Constructed in 1881-82, the building that houses this museum preceded the building of the community of Hermansville itself. Once the offices of the Wisconsin Land and Lumber Company, the building stands essentially as it was built. The museum is a richly preserved memorial to the lumber era of the northern Great Lakes. Located on River Street in Hermansville. For hours of operation, call 906-498-2181.

SAND POINT LIGHTHOUSE

This light in Escanaba served mariners continuously from 1868 until 1939. It has now been restored as authentically as possible with 19th Century furnishings and decoration. The museum also contains photographs, books, newspaper articles and other memorabilia. Open to the public from June 1 to September 1 from 9 a.m. to 4 p.m. and in September from 1 to 4 p.m. at Ludington Park.

DELTA COUNTY HISTORICAL MUSEUM AND ARCHIVES

The museum houses 50 years of memorabilia including vintage costumes, furniture, a blacksmith shop, bank and post office displays. The archives contain a wealth of documents and photographs including newspapers, city directories, yearbooks, family scrapbooks and oral histories. It is open daily June 1 to September 1.

U.P. STEAM AND GAS ENGINE MUSEUM

Housed on the U.P. State Fair grounds in Escanaba, this museum contains steam-powered tractors and other agricultural equipment as well as operating steam and gas engines. The village next to the museum has a steam-powered sawmill. Open U.P. State Fair week—the third week of August—and Labor Day weekend.

GARDEN PENINSULA HISTORICAL MUSEUM

Located in the village of Garden on Delta County's Garden Peninsula, this former one-room schoolhouse offers community history on logging and fishing as well as a classroom display. A genealogy library is also available. Open June through Labor Day or by appointment. Directions: from U.S.-2 take Hwy. 183 to Garden about 21 miles from Rapid River.

PAULSON HOUSE MUSEUM

This cedar log house was built in the 1880s by Swedish pioneer Charles Paulson. It was the original site of the first schoolrooms in the Au Train area. The museum contains exhibits that are changed constantly along with a historic garden on the grounds and a gift shop. On Forest Lake Road in Au Train; m28lakehouse@aol.com for more information.

ONE OF AMERICA'S BEST BEACHES

Sand Point Beach was named as one of the Top Five Summer Beaches in America by Stephen Leatherman, aka "Dr. Beach." Each year Leatherman is featured on morning television shows and The Weather Channel talking about the best beaches in the world. In 2007, he appeared on The Weather Channel naming his Top Five Beaches in America: Ocracoke Beach at Cape Hatteras National Seashore in North Carolina, and beaches in Maine, California, Oregon and Sand Point Beach, part of the Pictured Rocks National Lakeshore in Alger County. Leatherman described the water at Sand Point, in a Detroit News interview, as "perfectly clean and clear," and called the setting, "idyllic." The white sand beach offers views of Munising Bay, Grand Island and the East Channel Lighthouse.

Sand Point Beach

ALGER COUNTY HERITAGE CENTER MUSEUM

The museum holds numerous photographic displays and donated Alger County memorabilia as well as Grand Island artifacts. There is also a collection of taped interviews and Munising News bound originals and microfiche. Located on Washington St. in Munising; email algerchs@up.net for more information.

GRAND MARAIS LIGHTHOUSE KEEPER'S HOUSE AND MUSEUM

The Grand Marais Historical Society has restored this building and uses it as their home. Tour the house that was the home of the sentinels who kept the light burning along the storm-tossed south shore of Lake Superior. The Museum is open seasonally—July and August daily from 1 to 4 p.m., in June and September weekends from 1 to 4 p.m. For tour information, call 906-494-2404.

GITCHE GUMEE AGATE AND HISTORY MUSEUM

This is "a small, profound and very different museum." In it, you will find a diverse mineral display featuring a wide variety of Lake Superior agates as well as a collection of lumbering and fishing artifacts. On Lake Superior in Grand Marais, the museum is open year round. Call 906-494-2590 for hours of operation.

LUCE COUNTY HISTORICAL MUSEUM

Built in 1894 of Jacobsville Sandstone, this museum is set in the old sheriff's residence and jail in a building. It features a glass and china collection, many historic photographs, original furnishings along with a renovated jail cell. It is open 2-4 p.m. Tuesday, Wednesday and Thursday from late June until Labor Day or by appointment. Admission is free, but donations are greatly appreciated. Located at 411 W. Harrie Street in Newberry.

TAHQUAMENON LOGGING MUSEUM

Explore original buildings full of memorabilia from lumberjack days of the past. Located 1 ½ miles north of Newberry on M-123, the museum grounds has a nature trail and boardwalk nestled along the famous Tahquamenon River. For information, including hours of operation, call 906-293-3700 or email newberry@sault.com.

GREAT LAKES SHIPWRECK MUSEUM

Take a trip back in time on a guided tour through a refurbished 1861 lighthouse—the oldest active light on Lake Superior. Then tour the main museum containing artifacts from 13 local shipwrecks and a special tribute to the Edmund Fitzgerald, which sank roughly 15 miles north of the lighthouse and museum site. The grounds contain a large gift shop along with accommodations for overnight guests in the fully restored Crews Quarters. Located on Whitefish Point north of Paradise off M-123, the museum is open daily 10 a.m. to 6 p.m. from mid-May until October 31. Admission prices are $10 for adults, $7 for children 6-17, under 5 free; full-family admission is $28.00. For more information call the museum store at 888-492-3747.

WHEELS OF HISTORY MUSEUM

Get a glimpse of early life in Brimley, which includes the history of rail traffic through the area, logging and milling of lumber, commercial fishing and early telephone and telegraph communication. The museum is located in Superior Township Park at the corner of Depot St. and M-221 in Brimley. Hours are 10 a.m. to 4 p.m. Wednesday through Sunday from June

20-Labor Day and Saturday and Sunday only from May 15 to June 20. Admission is free but donations are gratefully accepted.

VALLEY CAMP MUSEUM

A 1917 steam powered freighter is now the world's largest Great Lakes Maritime museum. Explore the old ship from bow to stern, engine room to pilot house. It is filled with exhibits including aquariums and shipwreck artifacts including a recovered lifeboat from the Edmund Fitzgerald. Located on Water Street in Sault Ste. Marie. For information on hours and admission, call toll-free 888-744-7867.

SOO LOCKS VISITORS CENTER

Experience the engineering marvel of the Soo Locks. You would have to sign on as a ship crew member to get any closer than this. There are numerous displays including a 30-minute movie that chronicles the construction of the canal and locks. Located within the Soo Locks on Portage Avenue, the center is open daily from mid May to mid October.

RIVER OF HISTORY MUSEUM

This museum contains 8,000 years of history and culture with a sound system that tells the stories of the past. Exhibits include glacial history, Ojibwa culture, French fur-trader cabins as well as British influence, 19th Century expansion and the history of the Soo locks. The River of History Museum is located on Portage Street in historic Sault Ste. Marie. For hours and admission information call 906-632-3658 or email sues@sault.com.

TOWER OF HISTORY

This 21-story structure offers a panoramic view of historic St. Marys River, the Rapids, Sault Locks and the International Bridge. The lower level contains a mini-museum featuring an exhibit of Native American culture as well as a video of the early history of the area. Open mid-May through mid-October from 10 a.m. to 6 p.m. daily.

THE JOHN JOHNSTON HOME

John Johnston made his way to Sault Ste. Marie in1793. He made his fortune in fur trading, and took a native wife, the daughter of one of the revered chiefs of the region. The couple eventually had eight children and built one of the most regal structures in the Sault, part of which serves as the museum today. The home is Monday through Saturday from June 15-September 4. Hours may vary.

KINROSS HERITAGE SOCIETY

This museum contains artifacts from life at the turn of the century in the area including farming, logging and household exhibits. Rooms are set up to represent a barber shop, one-room schoolhouse and a blacksmith shop. Located in Kinross on Tone Road across from Kinross Community Center. Open from June through August on Thursdays through Saturdays from 1-5:30 p.m. Free admission. Call 906-678-3761.

SCHOOLCRAFT COUNTY HISTORIC VILLAGE AND MUSEUM

Visit the Post House museum located in an early 1900s home as well as a log cabin from the 1880s and a restored water tower constructed in 1922. Exhibits change annually. Located in Pioneer Park on Deer St. in Manistique, the museum is open from the last weekend in June through Labor Day. Hours are Tuesday through Saturday from Noon-4 p.m. Admission is $1.00 for adults and $0.50 for children. Guided tours are available; call 906-341-5045.

FORT DEBAUDE INDIAN MUSEUM

Watch history come alive with the largest collection of artifacts in the region including military and Indian weapons. Located in St. Ignace, this is the newest of the fort museums covering pre-contact French, English and American periods as well as the Indians of the area. For information, call 906-643-6622.

MARQUETTE MISSION PARK AND MUSEUM OF OJIBWA CULTURE

A national historic landmark, this St. Ignace museum interprets the rich archaeological history of a 17th Century Huron Indian village as well as Ojibwa traditions and contemporary culture. View exhibits, continuous videos and live demonstrations by nature interpreters. For more information call 906-643-9161 or email mmperry@up.net.

Souvenir shop at the Museum of Ojibwa Culture, St. Ignace

TOTEM VILLAGE

This museum of Indian lore contains an outstanding display of Indian folk art, artifacts and lumbering relics. Indian crafts and gifts are available. Open daily 2 ½ miles west of the bridge on U.S.-2 in St. Ignace.

FORT MACKINAC

The fort is located on Mackinac Island. Stroll through some of the oldest buildings in Michigan at this 200-year old fortress. Open May through October.

MACKINAC ISLAND'S HISTORIC DOWNTOWN BUILDINGS

Go back in time and experience 19th Century life recreated on Market and Huron Streets in the Biddle House, Benjamin Blacksmith Shop, Dr. Beaumont Museum and others. Historic house interpreters stitch quilts, create meals over cook fires and provide insight into the lives of early Mackinac Island settlers.

LES CHENEAUX MARITIME MUSEUM AND HISTORICAL MUSEUM

Take a self-guided tour of a model lumber camp. View photos along with artifacts from the past including Indian crafts and tools from the logging era in the Historical Museum. The nearby O.M. Reif Boathouse is home to displays of vintage boats, marine artifacts, antique outboard motors, as well as historic photos of the area's maritime past and a gift shop. These two Cedarville museums are operated by the Les Cheneaux Historical Society. Open from Memorial Day weekend to early September with hours from Tues.-Sat. 10 a.m.-4 p.m. and on Sundays 1-4 p.m. An admission of $5 allows visitors access to both museums. Call 906-484-2821; http//lchistorical.org

U.P. IS TOPS FOR FALL COLORS - THE TODAY SHOW

Lake of the Clouds, Porcupine Mountains State Park

The Upper Peninsula is one of the best places in the country to view fall colors according to The Today Show Travel Editor, Peter Greenberg. In September 2007, Greenberg shared his suggestions on the network and the MSNBC website. Of the Upper Peninsula, he praised the availability of hiking and biking trails through public parks and forests. He specifically mentioned the rugged trails of the Porcupine Mountains Wilderness State Park and Brockway Mountain on the Keweenaw Peninsula.

The Upper Peninsula was ranked first in Greenberg's column followed by Glacier National Park in Montana; Cherokee Foothills National Scenic Highway and Mountain Bridge Wilderness Area in South Carolina; Great Smoky Mountains National Park in Tennessee; Aspen, Colorado; Cedar Breaks National Monument in southern Utah; Yakima and Leavenworth in Washington, and Sonoma County, California.

"Nowhere, probably on the continent, is fall foliage more beautiful in brilliancy or contrasting colors". —George Shiras, *National Geographic*, August 1921

Presque Isle River

Brockway Mountain, Keweenaw County

GREAT LAKES SHORELINE MILES

Alger
Great Lakes shoreline: 120 miles
Number of lakes over 50 acres in size: 51
Miles of rivers and streams: 709
Miles of trails (hike/bike/cross-country ski): 230
Miles of state-funded snowmobile trails: 112
Total no. acres of legislatively protected
sand dunes 3,987

Baraga
Great Lakes shoreline: 70
Number of lakes over 50 acres in size: 38
Miles of rivers and streams: 696
Miles of trails (hike/bike/cross-country ski): 26
Miles of state-funded snowmobile trails: 100

Chippewa
Great Lakes shoreline: 456
Number of lakes over 50 acres in size: 34
Miles of rivers and streams: 800
Miles of trails (hike/bike/cross-country ski): 145
Miles of state-funded snowmobile trails: 220

Delta
Great Lakes shoreline: 199
Number of lakes over 50 acres in size: 20
Miles of rivers and streams: 514
Miles of trails (hike/bike/cross-country ski): 82
Miles of state-funded snowmobile trails: 54

Dickinson
Great Lakes shoreline: 0
Number of lakes over 50 acres in size: 30
Miles of rivers and streams: 645
Miles of trails (hike/bike/cross-country ski): 45
Miles of state-funded snowmobile trails: 111

Gogebic
Great Lakes shoreline: 30
Number of lakes over 50 acres in size: 78
Miles of rivers and streams: 1,208
Miles of trails (hike/bike/cross-country ski): 289
Miles of state-funded snowmobile trails: 176

Houghton
Great Lakes shoreline: 51
Number of lakes over 50 acres in size: 25

Miles of rivers and streams: 923
Miles of trails (hike/bike/cross-country ski): 1444
Miles of state-funded snowmobile trails: 157

Iron
Great Lakes shoreline: 0
Number of lakes over 50 acres in size: 87
Miles of rivers and streams: 902
Miles of trails (hike/bike/cross-country ski): 131
Miles of state-funded snowmobile trails: 123

Keweenaw
Great Lakes shoreline: 424
Number of lakes over 50 acres in size: 14
Miles of rivers and streams: 271
Miles of trails (hike/bike/cross-country ski): 249
Miles of state-funded snowmobile trails: 87

Luce
Great Lakes shoreline: 31
Number of lakes over 50 acres in size: 29
Miles of rivers and streams: 658
Miles of trails (hike/bike/cross-country ski): 63
Miles of state-funded snowmobile trails: 117

Mackinac
Great Lakes shoreline: 298
Number of lakes over 50 acres in size: 34
Miles of rivers and streams: 347
Miles of trails (hike/bike/cross-country ski): 193
Miles of state-funded snowmobile trails: 158

Marquette
Great Lakes shoreline: 79
Number of lakes over 50 acres in size: 87
Miles of rivers and streams: 1,906
Miles of trails (hike/bike/cross-country): 164
Miles of state-funded snowmobile trails: 191

Menominee
Great Lakes shoreline: 41
Number of lakes over 50 acres in size: 17
Miles of rivers and streams: 815
Miles of trails (hike/bike/cross-country ski): 31
Miles of state-funded snowmobile trails: 53

Ontonagon
Great Lakes shoreline: 56
Number of lakes over 50 acres in size: 9
Miles of rivers and streams: 1,282
Miles of trails (hike/bike/cross-country ski): 153
Miles of state-funded snowmobile trails: 201

Schoolcraft
Great Lakes shoreline: 46
Number of lakes over 50 acres in size: 79
Miles of rivers and streams: 734
Miles of trails (hike/bike/cross-country ski): 135
Miles of state-funded snowmobile trails: 89

Chapter 9

TRANSPORTATION

MILES OF ROADS, BRIDGES, AIRPORTS, RAILS AND SHIPPING

MILES OF ROADS – BY COUNTY

County	State Trunkline	County	City	Federal	Total
Chippewa	225	1,259	98	230	1,813
Marquette	174	1,243	168	10	1,595
Delta	134	864	128	210	1,336
Menominee	115	1,110	86	17	1,328
Houghton	122	805	99	90	1,117
Gogebic	112	597	133	170	1,012
Iron	97	605	91	161	964
Mackinac	166	637	30	117	950
Ontonagon	162	566	22	101	851
Dickinson	84	540	153	0	777
Alger	105	483	24	156	768
Schoolcraft	136	431	23	81	671
Baraga	77	487	28	31	623
Luce	64	390	14	0	468
Keweenaw	57	171	2	0	230
U.P. total	1,830	10,188	1,099	1,364	14,481
Michigan	9,695	88,960	20,914	1,887	121,456

The Upper Peninsula contains 12% of the roads and highways in the state of Michigan. However, 72% of the federally owned roads are in the U.P.

HIGHWAYS

I-75: Only Interstate highway in the Upper Peninsula

Length: 51 miles from the International Bridge at Sault Ste. Marie to the Mackinac Bridge at St. Ignace. The highway continues south over the Mackinac Bridge to the Ohio border. Total length of I-75 in Michigan is 395 miles.

- The state's longest highway, I-75 runs through Michigan's two oldest cities: Detroit and Sault Ste. Marie

- Only three highways have ever been designated to cross the Straits of Mackinac. In the 1930s, U.S.-31 crossed the Straits on the state ferries. In the late 1950s after the Mackinac Bridge opened, U.S.-27 was the designated highway that linked the two peninsulas via the bridge until 1960 when it was changed to I-75.

U.S. HIGHWAYS

U.S.-2

Length: At 305 miles, U.S.-2 is the longest highway in the U.P. running from Ironwood at the Wisconsin border to St. Ignace. The highway is split into two segments. The western segment extends from Crystal Falls to Ironwood, while the eastern segment runs from Iron Mountain to St. Ignace. Between Iron Mountain and Crystal Falls is the dual highway U.S.-141 and U.S.-2.

U.S.-2 East runs 196 miles from I-75 near St. Ignace to the Wisconsin State line four miles northwest of Iron Mountain in Dickinson County.

U.S.-2 West runs 109 miles from the Wisconsin state border ten miles south of Crystal Falls in Iron County northwestward to the state border at Ironwood.

- A combination of old logging roads and early automobile dirt roads that connected the east and west ends of the U.P. were known collectively as M-12 until 1926 when the U.S. Highway system was created. The U.S.-2 designation replaced M-12 at this time.

- The U.S.-2 designation runs along I-75 between St. Ignace and Sault Ste. Marie on some maps, although in 1983 that 54 mile route was removed from U.S.-2 and designated exclusively as I-75.

- The final stretch of U.S.-2 to be paved was in 1941 near Watersmeet.

U.S.-41

Length: 279 miles between Menominee north to Copper Harbor

Actually, U.S.-41 begins at a cul-de-sac a couple of miles east of Copper Harbor. There is a sign that marks the beginning of this U.S. highway that leads drivers through eight states and 1,992 miles to Miami, Florida!

- U.S.-41 is considered a north-south highway, although it snakes east and west through a good portion of its course through the U.P.

- U.S.-41 runs through some of the largest towns in the U.P. Houghton, Hancock, Marquette, Escanaba and Menominee.

- The highway was originally named M-15 between 1918-1925, then in 1926 the U.S. Highway System was formed and it was renamed U.S.-41.

- The final sections of U.S.-41 were paved in 1952. This included a stretch in Keweenaw County and a short segment in Baraga County.

- In 1994, U.S.-41 between Copper Harbor and Central in Keweenaw County was named as Michigan's first Scenic Heritage Route.

- By 2004, much of the remainder of U.S.-41 was added to the Scenic Heritage Route.

- In 2005, U.S.-41 between Houghton and Copper Harbor is named as a National Scenic Byway.

U.S.-45

Length: 55 miles from the Wisconsin border eight miles south of Watersmeet to Ontonagon.

- U.S.-45 was designated in 1934 replacing M-26 and M-35

U.S.-141

Length: U.S.-141 runs 58 miles between the Wisconsin border near Iron Mountain, north to Baraga County where it ends at the M-28/U.S.-41 south of L'Anse.

The south segment runs 8 miles from the Wisconsin line southeast of Iron Mountain to about four miles northwest of downtown Iron Mountain

The North segment runs 50 miles Wisconsin state line (with U.S.-2) to the M-28/U.S.-41 highway in Baraga County.

- The northern section of U.S.-141 replaced U.S.-102 in 1928. U.S.-102 became the first US highway ever to be decommissioned.

U.S.-8

Length: 2.3 miles

U.S.-8 is the shortest U.S. highway in Michigan. It runs from the Wisconsin line north into Norway.

- There were plans to extend U.S.-8 eastward to Hermansville, but that plan was abandoned in the 1960s.

MICHIGAN HIGHWAYS

M-28

Length: The U.P.'s longest state highway is 290 miles long running between Sault Ste. Marie in Chippewa County and Wakefield in Gogebic County.

- M-28 passes through Munising, Marquette, Negaunee, Ishpeming and Wakefield

- The beginning of M-28 dates to 1919 when it ran from Wakefield east to souther Baraga County.

M-35

Length: 125 miles

This state highway runs from U.S.-41 two miles north of Menominee, to M-28/U.S.-41 eight miles west of Marquette.

- Originally M-35 was supposed to run through the Huron Mountains northwest of Marquette, then on to Skaney and L'Anse, and westward to Ontonagon.

- M-35 is sometimes referred to as The Highway Henry Ford Stopped because the auto pioneer fought to prevent the road from extending into the Huron Mountains.

In the 1930s, Ford was trying to gain membership into the exclusive Huron Mountain Club. To gain favor with the members, he purchased more land adjacent to the club property and fought to prevent extension of the highway through their private wilderness area.

- In the plans that ran M-35 through the Huron Mountains, there were two segments of highway: one running southeast from Marquette and Negaunee and another that approached the mountains from L'Anse and Skanee on the west side.

- M-35 passes through Menominee, Gladstone, Escanaba, Marquette and Negaunee.

NAMED ROADS AND HIGHWAYS

Blue Water Trail: Designed in 1940 as a 1,000-mile scenic drive along the water to attract tourists. The Blue Water Trail ran from Port Huron to Detroit and up through Bay City to Mackinac City. In the U.P., the Blue Water Trail ran ran from St. Ignace to The Soo, and from St. Ignace to Escanaba on U.S.-2, and from Escanaba to Menominee along M-35. Plans were never fully implemented due to World War II.

Bohn Highway: In 1924 when U.S.-2 was known as trunkline No. 12, it was named for Frank Probasco Bohn, president of the Newberry State Bank. Bohn served in the state senate and the U.S. House of Representatives.

Brockway Mountain Drive: The 9.5 mile highway between Copper Harbor and Eagle River rises 735 feet above the surface of Lake Superior. It was built as a public works project during the Great Depression at a cost of $30,000. Some 300 men were paid 25 cents-an-hour for their labor. It is named after Daniel D. Brockway, who built the first permanent home and hotel in Copper Harbor. Brockway served as a mining agent, Copper Harbor postmaster and state road commissioner in the U.P. Brockway Mountain Drive is reached via M-26 from Copper Harbor or Eagle River.

Cloverland Trail: U.S.-2 between Ironwood and Iron River was lined with clover when the road was completed in 1915. The following year 1,500 people turned out for a ceremony dedicating the new highway as Cloverland Trail. Signs with the Cloverland logo were posted along the route, and later stretched from Ironwood to Escanaba. Tourism promoters later decided to designate all state highways in the U.P. as part of the Cloverland Trail. In 1927, promoters dropped the Cloverland name, opting for Hiawatha Land as a new theme.

Courtesy of the Marquette County History Museum

Coolidge Trail: U.S.-2 between Crystal Falls and Brule, Wisconsin was named after Calvin Coolidge, the 30th President of the United States. In 1928, Coolidge announced his plans to go fishing on the Brule River during his final summer in the White House. Tourism increased after the announcement, and a merchants group in Iron River hoped to capitalize by drawing traffic from the Green Bay area up through Dickinson County and west along U.S.-2 to Brule. Besides the U.S.-2 route, U.S.-141 between

Green Bay and Crystal Falls was part of the Coolidge Trail. In 2001, the state designated U.S.-2 between Crystal Falls and Iron River as an Historic Heritage Route.

Curley Lewis Memorial Highway: Federal Forest Highway 42, 18 miles of highway winding through the forest along Whitefish Bay, was named after Curley Lewis, advocate for better roads in the U.P. Irwin L. Lewis owned a bar in Paradise, and served as Chippewa County Supervisor. In 1981, the state designated the stretch of highway the Curley Lewis Memorial Highway, and two years later the Chippewa County Road Commission expanded the name to the Curley Lewis Memorial Highway Scenic Lakeshore Drive.

Isle Royale Trail: U.S.-141 between Crystal Falls and U.S.-41 was named Isle Royale Trail in 1932 by the Crystal Falls Businessmen's Association. After Isle Royale was named a national park, they hoped draw more business to town by luring visitors to U.S.-141 as the main route to the ferry docks on Lake Superior. The route name was never officially adopted by the State, as business interests in Wisconsin and in the U.P. along U.S.-41 objected.

Jacobetti Highway: The portion of M-28 between Negaunee and M-123 was named after the legendary legislator, Dominic Jacobetti, who traveled the roadway frequently during his trips to and from Lansing. Jacobetti holds the record for longest service in the legislature, serving 42 years from 1954 to 1986. Upon his retirement, his colleagues designated the stretch of highway in his honor.

Joseph Meagher Memorial Highway: M-38 between the city of Ontonagon and the Houghton County line is named after Joseph Meagher, a longtime public official in Ontonagon. The Bessemer native died in 1991, and one year late the state designated the highway in his name.

King's International Highway: U.S.-2 from Ironwood to St. Ignace to Sault Ste. Marie was part of the King's International Highway from 1920 to 1960. The highway was part of Canada's transcontinental highway that ran from Vancouver to Halifax. Because a road could not be built on the north shore of Lake Superior, the road dipped south and ran through the U.P. By 1960, Canadian road builders were able to blast through the rocky landscape along Lake Superior, to form the final connector for the Canadian highway, which negated the need for the Michigan portion.

Leif Erickson Highway: M-95 between Kingsford and Champion was named after the Viking explorer in 1951. The Norse Civic Association of Detroit requested official recognition for Erickson, whom they believe was the first white man to set foot on North American soil.

MEMORIAL HIGHWAYS

I-75 is the only interstate highway in the U.P. In 1969, the state legislature designated it as the **American Legion Memorial Highway** from Sault Ste. Marie to St. Ignace. At 395 miles, I-75 is Michigan's longest highway, running through the state's two oldest cities: Sault Ste. Marie and Detroit.

Memorial Drive (Iron Mountain): U.S.-2 between Iron Mountain and Quinnesec is dedicated to deceased veterans of Dickinson County. It was dedicated in 1931 by the Kiwanis Club of Iron Mountain. Over one hundred apple and cherry trees were planted – one for each veteran. None has survived the test of time and weather.

Memorial Highway (Ishpeming-Negaunee): County Road 480, formerly M-15 between Ishpeming and Negaunee, was dedicated by the Women's Service Club of Ishpeming in memory of 20 local men who died in World War I. Elm trees donated by the Cliffs Iron Co. were planted along the roadside in 1920, but none survived.

Memorial Road (Houghton): M-26 (Sheldon Street) west of the Houghton-Hancock Bridge was dedicated to 16 local men who died in World War I. In 1921, the Houghton City Council approved naming the road Memorial Road, and one Dutch Elm tree was planted for each soldier. The trees eventually died or were uprooted when the road was widened.

Memory Lane (Baraga): U.S.-41 from the north side of Baraga to the Baraga State Park was dedicated in 1947 to the men and women who served in both World Wars. Members of the local Lions Club planted 100 red maple trees along both sides of the road. The trees are gone, victims of weather and development.

Memory Lane (Bessemer): U.S.-2 between Bessemer and Ramsay is dedicated to the men and women who served the United State in all wars prior to the highway dedication in 1949. The Bessemer Women's Club planted 140 elm trees and 1,840 evergreens, flowering trees and shrubs.

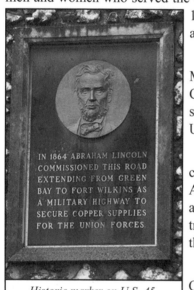

IN 1864 ABRAHAM LINCOLN
COMMISSIONED THIS ROAD
EXTENDING FROM GREEN
BAY TO FORT WILKINS AS
A MILITARY HIGHWAY TO
SECURE COPPER SUPPLIES
FOR THE UNION FORCES

Historic marker on U.S.-45, Ontonagon County

Memory Lane (Crystal Falls): U.S.-141 from Amasa to M-69 is dedicated to veterans of World War I. In 1931, the Crystal Falls American Legion planted pine trees along the stretch of highway and had a stone monument erected at the U.S.-2 and U.S.-141 intersection.

Memory Lane (Escanaba): U.S.-2 on the west end of Escanaba is dedicated to the honor of World War I veterans. In April 1929, American Legion volunteers planted 200 maple and elm trees along U.S. 2 and U.S. 41. Unfortunately, the trees did not survive the spread of disease and expansion of the highways.

107th Engineers Memorial Road: M-107 from Silver City to the Porcupine Mountains Wilderness State Park is named after the 107th Engineers Combat Battalion which shares number 107, and was formed in Calumet. The unit served in the Spanish-American War and both World Wars. Highway Commissioner Charles Ziegler designated the road in the 107th's honor in 1954. The dedication ceremony attracted 1,200 people. In 2001, the state legislature officially designated the road for the 107th Engineers.

117th Quartermaster Battalion Highway: M-117 between U.S.-2 and M-28 is named for the Michigan Army National Guard battalion that shares number 117. The short-lived battalion was headquartered in Kingsford in 1987, with companies in Munising, Marquette and Manistique. Their mission was to deliver petroleum supplies to the front lines. The battalion was deactivated in 1992 and moved to Detroit. The state legislature passed a Resolution urging the Transportation Department to dedicate the highway to the 117th. Because supporters did not raise the $1,500 needed for signage the highway was never formally dedicated.

Oscar G. Johnson Memorial Highway: M-69 from Randville to U.S.-2 is named for the only U.P. native to earn the Congressional Medal of Honor. Oscar Johnson was born in 1921 in Foster City. In a World War II battle, Private Johnson was the last man in his position not killed or wounded. Over two days he managed to kill 20 Nazi soldiers, take another 25 prisoner, and rescue two American soldiers. For his heroics, he was one of only 463 Americans to earn the Congressional Medal of Honor. After the war, he returned to the U.P. to help out on the family dairy farm. In 2002, the legislature passed a bill dedicating the highway in Johnson's name.

Prentiss M. Brown Memorial Highway: I-75 from the Mackinac Bridge to Sault Ste. Marie is named for the man known as "The Father of the Mackinac Bridge." Prentiss served as Chairman of the Mackinac Bridge Authority when it finally gained funding for construction. The St. Ignace native also served in the U.S. House of Representatives and U.S. Senate. In 1976, the state Senate voted to recognize Brown by naming the U.P. portion of I-75 in his honor. In 2001, the Prentiss M. Brown Memorial Highway designation was extended southward across the bridge into Cheboygan County.

Road of Remembrance (Sault Ste. Marie): In 1921, the Chicago Tribune started a national effort to plant trees along U.S. highways in honor of all soldiers who served in World War I. Five years later, Sault Ste. Marie city officials dedicated 19 miles of M-129 from The Soo through Pickford as their portion of the Road of Remembrance. Groups were organized to plant trees every year until all 19 miles were covered. After two years, participation fell off and the project came to an end.

Sheridan Road: U.S.-41 from Menominee to the tip of the Keweenaw Peninsula is named for the Civil War major general, Philip Henry Sheridan, a cavalry commander who never lost a battle. Sheridan was born in Albany, New York and has no ties to the U.P. Upon his death a fort was named in his honor north of Chicago where he served after the Civil War. The road connecting the fort to the city of Chicago was named Sheridan. After World War I, the Greater Sheridan Road Association moved to expand the road name from St. Louis, Missouri all the way to the Keweenaw Peninsula. Only a few signs remain along the route indicating that it was once named Sheridan Road.

Tahquamenon Falls Memorial Highway: M-123 from St. Ignace to Whitefish Pt. was once a dirt road. In 1947, interested parties agreed to promote the road as the best route to the new Tahquamenon Falls State Park. Ultimately, they wanted the road paved and their best hope was to attract more traffic so that the state highway department would take it over. In 1954, the state took over the road, naming it M-123, at which time it ceased to be called Tahquamenon Falls Memorial Highway.

Theodore Roosevelt International Highway: Following the death of the 26th President in 1919, supporters set out to lay out a transcontinental highway to be named in his honor. The highway ran from Portland Maine, to Portland, Oregon, crossing into Canada between Buffalo and Detroit, hence the international designation. In Michigan, it covered the current day route of I-75, and in the U.P. included U.S.-2 and M-28.

Townsend National Highway: Designed to run from Lake Superior to the Gulf of Mexico and named in honor of Charles Townsend, a native of Concord, Michigan. Townsend served in the U.S. House of Representatives and U.S. Senate where he introduced the federal highway bill in 1919. This provided the financial means to begin work on a national network of roads. In 1920, the Good Roads Association set out to create the Townsend National Highway from Mobile, Alabama to the U.P. From St. Ignace the route ran north to Sault Ste. Marie, along M-28 to Marquette; U.S.-41 from Marquette to Calumet, and all of U.S.-141. The Townsend National Highway name never caught on.

Veterans Memorial Highway: M-28 from Ishpeming to U.S.-2 became the sixth Veterans Memorial Highway in Michigan. Former soldiers from the western U.P. noted that the five existing memorial highways honoring veterans were all in the Lower Peninsula. These veterans appealed to the state for a U.P. designation, and the legislature obliged. This stretch of highway was dedicated in Wakefield on Memorial Day 2004.

William Howard Taft Memorial Highway: Following the death of the 27th President, a group from his home state of Ohio proposed a national highway be named in his honor. The route was to run from Fort Myers, Florida to Sault Ste. Marie. The idea was approved in every state along the route including Michigan in 1933. In the Upper Peninsula, the route follows I-75 from The Soo to the Mackinac Bridge. From there it follows U.S.-127. Although there is no signage along the route, by law the highway remains the William Howard Taft Memorial Highway.

Source: *A Drive Down Memory Lane: The Named State and Federal Highways of Michigan*, by LeRoy Barnett,Phd., copyright 2004, The Priscilla Press, Allegan Forest, Michigan

HISTORIC HERITAGE ROUTES

There are three types of Heritage Route designations created by the legislature in 1993: Scenic, Historic and Recreational. Scenic routes feature outstanding natural beauty; Historic routes feature historic buildings and resources along its path, and Recreational routes capture the recreational setting of the area.

FIRST SCENIC ROUTE IN MICHIGAN

U.S. 41 between Delaware and Copper Harbor in Keweenaw County is noted for the canopy of trees along most of its 18-mile length, and attractions such as Lake Superior beaches, Ft. Wilkins State Park and fall color touring. In addition, U.S.-41 from Houghton to Copper Harbor received National Scenic Byway status in 2005. The Copper Country Trail tells the story of the nation's first mineral rush, combining scenic beauty with many landmarks of historical significance.

M-123 between Paradise and County Road 500 is the other Scenic Heritage Route in the U.P. Most of the 27-mile route runs through or near the Tahquamenon Falls State Park and features views of the falls and the Lake Superior State Forest.

A 16-mile section of U.S.-2 in Iron County features a connection to the iron mining history of Michigan.

AVERAGE VEHICLE MILES DRIVEN (2005) – BY COUNTY

County	Miles driven
Marquette	621,616
Delta	412,066
Chippewa	354,031
Mackinac	287,808
Menominee	245,772
Houghton	225,500
Dickinson	217,939
Gogebic	172,380
Schoolcraft	150,986
Iron	141,827
Ontonagon	117,748
Alger	117,359
Baraga	105,683
Luce	67,502
Keweenaw	34,430
U.P. total	**3,272,647**
Michigan	103,159,310

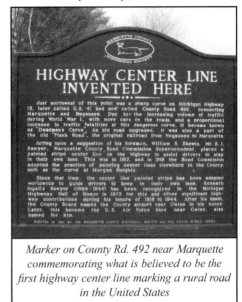

Marker on County Rd. 492 near Marquette commemorating what is believed to be the first highway center line marking a rural road in the United States

NUMBER OF CRASHES – BY COUNTY 2005-2007

County	# of crashes			fatalities		
	2005	2006	2007	2005	2006	2007
Marquette	2,051	2,122	2,113	6	6	4
Delta	1,994	1,724	1,778	2	3	1
Menominee	1,358	1,218	1,276	3	4	1
Chippewa	1,197	1,240	1,256	1	5	4
Houghton	1,127	1,147	1,218	6	5	7
Dickinson	1,147	1,058	1,077	3	4	2
Iron	739	680	629	1	3	2
Mackinac	743	636	609	5	0	2
Schoolcraft	493	415	507	4	3	3
Ontonagon	409	412	418	0	5	2
Baraga	390	398	407	1	1	0
Alger	355	340	378	3	0	2
Gogebic	372	353	333	0	0	2
Luce	245	213	228	1	4	2
Keweenaw	80	107	102	0	0	4
TOTAL:	**12,700**	**12,063**	**12,329**	**36**	**43**	**37**

Source: Michigan State Police

CAR-DEER ACCIDENTS – BY COUNTY

County	2007	2006	2005	2004
Delta	932	875*	1,068	1,075
Menominee	783	749	799	911
Dickinson	598	548	589	598
Marquette	495	452	379*	459
Chippewa	446	428	409	458
Iron	394	420	476	500
Houghton	324	313	240	296
Mackinac	316	352	401	413
Schoolcraft	313	248	285	314
Ontonagon	311	256*	275	281
Baraga	251	236	224	239
Alger	163	145	145	182
Luce	125	117	131	135
Gogebic	118	123	119	143
Keweenaw	43	47	21	31
U.P. Total	**5,612**	**5,309**	**5,561**	**6,035**

* - one fatality

AUTOMOBILE REGISTRATIONS – BY COUNTY (AS OF MAY 13, 2007)

County	Vehicles registered
Marquette	66,898
Delta	45,797
Chippewa	35,813
Dickinson	32,552
Houghton	32,106
Menominee	27,009
Gogebic	16,134
Iron	14,723
Mackinac	13,306
Schoolcraft	10,604
Alger	10,388
Ontonagon	8,989
Baraga	7,726
Luce	7,386
Keweenaw	2,234
U.P.	331,665
Michigan	9,472,629

BRIDGES

THE MACKINAC BRIDGE – MACKINAC COUNTY

The Mighty Mac has come to symbolize the state of Michigan as much as the Great Lakes that define the State. But The Bridge belongs solely to Michigan, and stands as one of the great achievements in the states engineering, labor, and political history.

From the time it was built in 1957 until 1998 it stood as the world's longest suspension bridge. It now ranks as the longest suspension bridge in the western hemisphere, and the 3rd longest in the world, based on total suspension, or the length between anchorages.

Bridge	Total suspension	Main span(between towers)
Akashi Kaikyo Bridge, Japan	12,826 ft.	6,529 ft.
Great Belt Bridge, Halsskov-Sprogoe, Denmark	8,921 ft	5,328
Mackinac Bridge	8,614	3,800

LARGEST BRIDGES BASED ON MAIN SPAN (DISTANCE BETWEEN TOWERS)

Bridge	Main Span
Akashi Kaikyo Bridge, Japan	6,529
Izmit Bay, Turkey	5,472
Great Belt Bridge, Denmark	5,328
Humber, England	4,626
Jiaangyin, China	4,543
Tsing Ma, Hong Kong	4,518
Verrazzano-Narrows, New York	4,260
Golden Gate, San Francisco	4,200
Hoga Kusten, Sweden	3,969
Mackinac Bridge, Michigan	3,800

Construction of the Mackinac Bridge

In 1999, the Michigan Section of the American Society of Civil Engineers named the Mackinac Bridge as the state's number one civil engineering achievement. The Soo Locks finished 2nd ahead of the Detroit-Windsor Tunnel. Rounding out the top 10 were: the Ambassador Bridge, Ford Motor Commpany Rouge complex, Detroit's Wastewater Treatment Plant, the Ludington Pumped Storage facility and the St. Clair River Railroad Tunnel.

HISTORY

The first public expression of the need for a bridge across the Straits was in 1884, when the *Grand Traverse Herald* newspaper wrote that ferry service was a failure, and that a bridge or tunnel was necessary.

That same year, a St. Ignace shop owner took out a print ad with a drawing of the just completed Brooklyn Bridge and labeled it as the "proposed bridge across the Straits of Mackinac."

In 1888, Cornelius Vanderbilt, the railroad and shipping magnate who also had a hand in founding the Grand Hotel, called for a bridge across the Straits.

The idea wasn't approached seriously until 1934 when the legislature created the Mackinac Bridge Authority to investigate the feasibility of building and financing a bridge.

Bridge alternatives

- Former State Highway Commissioner, Horatio Earle, in 1920, suggested a floating tunnel.
- He later proposed a system of bridges, causeways and island roads that would lead from St. Ignace to Mackinac Island, to Round Island, to Bois Blanc Island, across two island lakes, and finally to Cheboygan.
- Charles Fowler, a civil engineer, refined the plan and submitted it as a federal public works project, but was denied.

- The State Highway Department started a ferry service for automobiles in 1923, but demand for service quickly outgrew ferry capacity.

The initial report of the Mackinac Bridge authority found it was feasible to build a two-lane highway and one-track railroad bridge across the Straits at an estimated cost of $32,400,000. The federal government again denied funding.

Studies continued and in the late 1930s, a 4,200-foot causeway was built over the water in St. Ignace. World War II brought an end to the pursuit of a bridge across the Straits, and in 1947 the legislature abolished the Bridge Authority.

Bridge promoters managed to convince lawmakers to approve a second version of the Mackinac Bridge Authority in 1950, and there next report stated the bridge could be built for $86,000,000. Several attempts to sell bonds to investor failed, but in 1953 $99,800,000 worth of bonds were purchased, and the Authority began awarding engineering and construction contracts.

Contracts

Firm	Project	Contract
David B. Steinman	Architect	$3,500,000
US Steel, American Bridge Division	Steel superstructure including towers, cables and truss spans	$43,927,806
Merritt-Chapman and Scott Corp.	Underwater and land foundations	$26,335,000
Louis Garavaglia, Centerline, MI and Johnson-Greene, Ann Arbor, MI	Paving of bridge superstructure	$2,181,093

Construction
Start date: May 7, 1954
Finish date: November 1, 1957
Men employed at bridge site: 3,500
Men employed at quarries, shops, mills, etc: 7,500
Number of engineers: 350
Number of steel rivets: 4,851,700
Number of steel bolts: 1,016,600

Five men died while building the bridge: Frank Pepper, September 16, 1954; James R. LeSarge, October 10, 1954, Albert Abbot, October 25, 1954, Jack C. Baker, June 6, 1956, and Robert Koppen, June 6, 1956. Their names are engraved on a plaque that hangs in their honor on a bridge pillar near Colonial Michilimackinac.

Two of the men fell approximately 550 feet from a catwalk that snapped; one man fell into a caisson while welding, one fell a few feet into the water and drowned and one died in a diving accident. All but the body of one of the men who fell from the catwalk were recovered. Contrary to urban legend, there are no bodies buried in the concrete foundations beneath the water.

Mackinac Bridge stats
Total length: 26,372 ft. (5 miles)
Width of roadway: 54 feet / 68 feet at suspended span
Length of main span (between towers): 3,800 ft.
Height of main towers (above water): 552 ft.

Height of roadway above water: 199 ft.

Max depth of tower piers below water: 210 ft.

Max. depth of water at midspan: 295 ft.

Total length of wire in cables: 42,000 miles

Diameter of each wire: 0.196 inches

Number of wires in each cable: 12,580

Diameter of cables: 24 ½ inches

Weight of cables: 11,480 tons

Total concrete in bridge; 466,300 cu. yds.

Total weight of concrete: 931,000 tons

Total weight of Bridge: 1,024,500 tons

Design: The bridge is specially designed to withstand the high winds, stiff currents and moving ice in the Straits. Architect David B. Steinman designed the middle two lanes to be open grids instead of solid concrete, which gives the bridge added resistance to strong winds. At the center span of the bridge it is possible for it to sway as much as 35 feet in one direction under severe wind conditions.

In Lawrence Rubin's book, "Mighty Mac," Steinman wrote: "The Mackinac Bridge represents the triumph of the new science of suspension bridge aerodynamics. It represents the achievement of a new goal of perfect aerodynamic stability, never before attained or approximated in any prior suspension bridge design."

First citizen to cross the bridge: Al Carter, a Chicago jazz musician who looked for opportunities to get his name in the news by being "the first" to do something. Carter drove a 1951 station wagon across the span when it opened at 2:00 pm, November 1, 1957.

First snowmobile crossing: February 14, 1970. One lane of the bridge was shut down so that members of the Pathfinders snowmobile club could continue their trip from Marquette to Cadillac.

First birth on the bridge: On May 11, 1983, Kim Shuman of Eckerman was about to give birth to her first baby. At the time, she was in a Kinross Ambulance speeding over the Mackinac Bridge towards Northern Michigan Hospital in Petoskey. Halfway across the bridge, they realized there wasn't enough time to make it to Petoskey, so they turned around on the bridge and raced toward Straits Area Hospital. The baby didn't wait. The 4 lb. boy was born in the ambulance on the north end of the bridge at 5:10 p.m. The next day a banner proclaiming "It's A Boy!" hung from the bridge office *Thanks to Karen Gould, St. Ignace News.* In March of 2007 Shawn Shuman was reunited with Cathy Flores, the paramedic who helped deliver him into the world on the Mackinac Bridge on May 11, 1983.

In 1997, Yvette Johnson gave birth to her fourth child, a baby girl, halfway across the bridge as she was returning from a winning day at the Kewadin Casino in St. Ignace.

First marriage proposal: Andrew Nelson proposed to Julie Engel on the bridge in 1995. His truck stalled on the bridge, and he had to pull over—it is illegal to stop on the bridge. State troopers pulled up as he was down on one knee popping the question.

First suicide: A Royal Oak man jumped to his death from mid-bridge on April 22, 1974.

First vehicle off the bridge: During a blizzard in September of 1989, Leslie Pluhar's 1987 Yugo went over the side rail and plunged 150 feet into the frigid Straits below. High winds contributed to the tragedy, and in 1990 the state Senate recommended side rails be raised from 36 to 48 inches.

A sport utility vehicle drove off the bridge in March of 1997, but investigators believe it was a suicide.

First buggy crossing: It took an Amish family with horse and buggy one hour to cross the bridge on June 30, 1973. Bridge officials agreed to shut down one lane for the crossing.

First Bridge Walk: September 7, 1959. It took Governor G. Mennen Williams 65 minutes to walk from St. Ignace to Mackinaw City. An estimated 15,000 walkers joined the Governor.

First plane crash: Three off-duty National Guard officers were killed on September 10, 1978, when their small plane crashed into suspension wires near the north tower during foggy conditions. The crash left an oil slick in the Straits and pieces of the plane scattered on the bridge roadway.

The man who flew under the bridge: Muskegon native John Lappo was a decorated Air Force Captain who made his last flight for the military over northern Michigian. He flew 28 bombing runs over North Korea, and led spy missions over the Soviet Union during the early years of the Cold War. However, he is best remembered for a flight over northern Michigan on April 24, 1959.

Early on a Friday afternoon while returning from a simulated bombing run and navigation mission, Lappo was flying a $3.5 million RB-47E Stratojet over northern Lake Michigan when he decided to fulfill a longtime desire: to fly a plane under a bridge. He had told friends he thought it would be the Golden Gate, but on this clear day he saw only two cars on the bridge, and away he went. The huge bomber descended rapidly, leveled off less than two hundred feet over the water, and flew under the deck of the Mighty Mac. Mission accomplished.

Lappo later told reporters that only one crew member objected to the stunt, "Of course, I had no idea at the time that he was the general's son and that he was going to go rat on me once we got back to Lockbourne."

Lappo was charged at a general court-martial in August of that year. In his defense, several officers testified to his superior piloting skills, proven integrity and unquestioned courage. He was found guilty of violating an Air Force regulation that prohibited flying lower than 500 feet except during takeoffs and landings. Lappo was ordered to pay $50 a month for six months.

Lappo and his wife moved to Alaska, where he piloted his own small plane until his death in November of 2003.

Highest wind gust recorded at Mackinac Bridge

128 mph on May 9, 2003

Most crossings – year: 4,936,417 in 1999

Most crossings – month: 726,400 crossings in July, 1999

Most crossings – day: 37,846 on June 29, 1996 during Straits Area Antique Auto Show

Crossings first year: 140,518 (November and December of 1957)

Crossings first full year (1958): 1,390,390

First year with over two million crossings: 1971 with 2,090,492

First year with over three million crossings: 1987 with 3,032,547

First year with over four million crossings: 1994 with 4,333,185

50 millionth crossing: September 25, 1984

100 millionth crossing: June 25, 1998

Current Rates

Passenger cars	$3.00	
	($1.50 per axle with trailer)	
Commuters	$1.60	
Motorcycles	$2.50	
Motor Homes	$3.50	
	per axle	
Trucks and all others	$3.50	
	per axle	

Commuters can buy 24 tokens for $30.00

Bicycles, pedestrians and snowmobiles are not permitted on the bridge, but for a fee can be carried over by the Bridge Authority.

Bikes and persons	$2.00
Snowmobile and one person	$10.00

History of Fares for Passenger Cars

1957 –1960	$3.25
1/01/60 - 4/30/60	$3.50
5/01/60 - 12/31/68	$3.75
1/01/69 - 5/01/03	$1.50
5/01/03 - 2/29/08	$2.50
3/01/08 – present	$3.00

In December of 2007 the Mackinac Bridge Authority approved an incremental rate increase that started in March of 2008. The increased tolls are intended to cover major bridge maintenance and improvement projects scheduled to start in 2017.

Before the days of the Bridge, long lines of vehicles waited to cross the Straits by ferry

The scheduled toll increases are as follows:

	Passenger cars	Passenger vehicle with trailer	Motor home and trucks
2010	$3.50	$1.75 per axle	$4.50 per axle
2012	$4.00	$2.00 per axle	$5.00 per axle
2014	$4.50	$2.25 per axle	$6.00 per axle

In addition, commuter tolls will increase by 10 cents per year beginning in 2009 through 2014.

INTERNATIONAL BRIDGE

Each year since 1987 the International Bridge Walk is held in late June. Walkers gather on the campus of Lake Superior State University. Those from the Canadian side are bussed over. Besides the festive atmosphere and international fellowship, the walk offers tremendous views of the Sault Locks and surrounding landscape.

SAULT STE. MARIE INTERNATIONAL BRIDGE – CHIPPEWA COUNTY

Built: Construction started on September 16, 1960

Opened: October 31, 1962

Cost: $20,000,000

Designer: Dr. Carl Gronquist of Steinman, Boynton, Gronquist and Birdsall.

Length: 2.8 miles

Width: 28 feet of roadway between curbs provides 14-foot traffic lanes in each direction

Height: Road surface is 145 feet above ground level at highest point

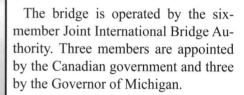

The bridge is operated by the six-member Joint International Bridge Authority. Three members are appointed by the Canadian government and three by the Governor of Michigan.

The need for the bridge was recognized long before construction began in 1960. Until then the only available crossings were by car ferry or a railroad bridge dating back to 1880. The State of Michigan in 1935 created the International Bridge Authority, and in 1940 Congress approved the concept of an international crossing at Sault Ste. Marie. By 1955, the Ontario government created a company to work with Michigan toward financing and building an international bridge.

Construction costs were shared by the Michigan and Ontario governments. The Province of Ontario used revenue from bridge tolls to pay off $7.85 million in bonds by the year 2000. Michigan sold $8.4 million to private investors. Michigan's debt was paid off in 1983. Today the bridge is self sufficient, with operating costs covered mainly by toll revenue. Annual average toll revenue is $4.5 million (U.S), of which approximately $3.4 million is used for bridge maintenance. The rest is set aside for future capital projects.

In 2007, the Bridge Authority raised rates from $1.50 per passenger car each way to $2.00 per vehicle. Tolls for trucks and buses are $3.00 per axle. Traffic volume averages 7,000 vehicles per day and over 10,000 vehicles on a busy day.

Houghton-Hancock Portage Lake Bridge – Houghton County

Built: 1959

Opened: December of 1959. Official dedication ceremony was held June 25, 1960.

Location: Connects Houghton and Hancock in Houghton County

Length: 1,310 ft.

Height: Lift towers are 180 feet above the water. Maximum clearance between the main span when it is lifted to the water is 100 feet.

Designer: Hazelet and Erdal, consulting engineers based in Chicago

Cost: $13,000,000

The Houghton-Hancock Bridge is the only double-deck vertical lift bridge in Michigan and at time of construction, it was the heaviest lift bridge ever built.

Designed to accommodate railroad and vehicular traffic as well as shipping traffic below, the bridge features two decks. The upper deck features four lanes for highway traffic, while the lower deck is designed for freight or passenger trains, although it could also accommodate vehicle traffic.

The middle section of the bridge spans 268 feet between the lift towers. Before the end of railroad traffic over the bridge in 1982, the operator would leave the bridge in its low position with the trains using the lower level and vehicles on top. This left a seven foot clearance between the water and bridge.

When the railroads were not operating, the bridge was left in the intermediate position, leaving a 35-foot clearance for shipping traffic. Vehicular traffic uses the lower deck, now raised, and the upper deck is unused. On the rare occasion that ship needs more than 35 feet to pass through, the bridge is raised to high position which disrupts vehicle traffic to create a 100-foot clearance. After the ship passes, the bridge is lowered back to intermediate position.

For nine months of the year the bridge operates from the intermediate position, however it is lowered in the winter allowing snowmobiles to use the lower deck.

The current bridge replaced a steel swing bridge built in 1905. The first rail bridge over the Portage Lake channel was made of wood. It opened in 1885.

HOUGHTON-HANCOCK PORTAGE LAKE BRIDGE DEDICATION

On the day before the official dedication ceremony, the steamer J.F. Schoellkopf almost hit the bridge. The captain said he sounded the whistle to raise the mid-span, but the bridge didn't rise. The Captain reversed engines and dropped anchor to avoid the collision, however the anchors ensnared telephone cables at the bottom of the channel leaving about 1,000 customers without phone service. Meanwhile the steamer ran aground in shallow water.

Cut River Bridge – Mackinac County

Built: 1947

Location: U.S.-2 over the Cut River between Epoufette and Brevort

Length: 641 feet

New Ontonagon River Bridge on M-64

Height: 147 feet above the surface of the river

Designer: State Highway Department

The Cut River Bridge is one of only two cantilevered deck truss bridges in Michigan. It's been called "the million dollar bridge over a two-bit creek."

There is a State Roadside Park featuring picnic tables and stairways down to the river and a sandy beach area.

The Siphon Bridge (U.S.-2 & M-94) Schoolcraft County

The only bridge in the world lower than the water around it! The 296-foot bridge was built in 1919 to carry traffic across the Manistique River. The bridge sits within a concrete system of walls that create artificial river banks. It was designed as part of a dam for the Manistique Pulp and Paper Company. The "Siphon Bridge" was once featured in Ripley's Believe-It-Or-Not.

NEW BRIDGES

The U.S.-41 Bridge between Menominee and Marinette, Wisconsin opened in December of 2005. The previous bridge, built in 1929, was removed. During the opening ceremony on December 3, 2005, the ribbon was cut by Mrs. Catherine (VanCamp) Anderson, who at the age of 12, was the ribbon-cutter for the previous bridge.

A new bridge to carry traffic on M-64 over the Ontonagon River opened in October of 2006. It replaced the Ontonagon River Swing Bridge built in 1939. The first bridge at this location was a swing bridge built in 1891 next to the Diamond Match Company. Five years later it was damaged in a fire that destroyed the match factory and most of the town. It was rebuilt and lasted until 1939 when it was replaced.

The new bridge features 13 spans and measures nearly 1,700 feet long. It includes two lanes of traffic and a 12-foot-wide lane for pedestrians and snowmobiles. The new M-64 bridge over the Ontonagon River cost $27-million.

AVIATION

U.P. AIRPORTS

Airport	Call sign	County	Length of longest runway (ft.)
Sawyer International	SAW	Marquette	12,370 asphalt/concrete
Chippewa County International	CIU	Chippewa	7,201 conc.
Delta County	ESC	Delta	6,501 asphalt
Houghton County Memorial	CMX	Houghton	6,501 asphalt
Gogebic-Iron County	IWD	Iron	6,501 asphalt
Ford (Kingsford)	IMT	Dickinson	6,500
Menominee-Marinette	MNM	Menominee	6,000 asphalt
Sault Ste. Marie Municipal/ Sanderson Field	ANJ	Chippewa	5,235 asphalt
Schoolcraft County (Manistique)	ISQ	Schoolcraft	5,000 asphalt
Luce County Airport (Newberry)	ERY	Luce	4,300
Drummond Island	DRM	Mackinac	4,000 asphalt
Hanley Field (Munising)	5Y7	Alger	4,000 turf
Mackinac County Airport	83D	Mackinac	3,800 conc.
Iron County (Crystal Falls)	50D	Iron	3,700 asphalt
Albert J. Lindberg (Hessel)	5Y1	Mackinac	3,700 asphalt
Mackinac Island	MCD	Mackinac	3,501 asphalt
Ontonagon County	OGM	Ontonagon	3,500 asphalt
Bois Blanc Airport	6Y1	Mackinac	3,500 asphalt
West Gladstone	9C9	Delta	3,000 turf
Grand Marais	Y98	Alger	2,800 turf
Bonnie Field (Rock)	6Y4	Marquette	2,600 turf
Baraga Airport	2P4	Baraga	2,200 turf
Edward F. Johnson (Ishpeming)	M61	Marquette	2,200 turf
Stambaugh (Iron River)	Y73	Iron	2,000 asphalt
Prickett-Grooms Field	6Y9	Houghton	2,000

U.P. AIRPORTS: TOTAL SCHEDULED PASSENGERS (2006)

Months with highest volume of passenger air traffic are August followed by May, July, June, October, and March

Month	Delta County	Sawyer Internat'l	Houghton County	Ford	Gogebic	Chippewa County	U.P. TOTAL
JAN	1,344	8,982	3,979	1,029	468	1,890	**17,692**
FEB	1,430	9,065	3,876	1,251	471	1,556	**17,469**
MAR	1,794	11,449	4,419	1,395	566	2,011	**21,634**
APR	1,516	10,626	4,329	1,335	598	1,867	**20,271**
MAY	1,436	11,636	6,966	1,364	543	2,602	**24,547**
JUN	1,690	11,645	4,678	1,339	604	2,490	**22,446**
JUL	1,735	13,267	5,306	1,541	527	2,529	**24,905**
AUG	1,754	13,295	5,861	1,565	580	2,662	**25,717**
SEP	1,427	10,543	4,369	1,152	559	2,224	**20,294**
OCT	1,431	11,188	5,002	1,234	589	2,436	**21,880**
NOV	1,440	10,249	4,696	1,147	535	2,154	**20,221**
DEC	1,488	10,224	4,308	1,133	582	1,987	**19,722**
	18,485	**132,169**	**57,789**	**15,485**	**6,622**	**26,428**	**256,978**
	Delta County	**Sawyer Internat'l**	**Houghton County**	**Ford**	**Gogebic**	**Chippewa County**	**UP Total**

COMMERCIAL AIRLINE SERVICE

AIRLINE	DESTINATIONS

Marquette: Sawyer International Airport (SAW)

Mesaba/Northwest Airlink	Detroit, MI
	Minneapolis-St. Paul, MN
American Eagle	Chicago IL
	Madison, WI
	Green Bay, WI

Sault Ste. Marie: Chippewa County International Airport (CIU),

Mesaba Airlines/Northwest Airlink	Detroit, MI

Kingsford/Iron Mountain: Ford Airport (IMT)

Mesaba Airlines/Northwest Airlink	Detroit, MI
Superior Aviation	Lansing

Houghton: Houghton County Memorial Airport (CMX)

Mesaba Airlines/Northwest Airlink	Minneapolis-St. Paul, MN
Royale Air Service	Isle Royale, MI

Ironwood: Gogebic Iron County Airport (IWD)

Great Lakes Airlines	Milwaukee, WI

RAILROADS

RAILROAD TIMELINE

1842 The Ojibwa cede the western half of the Upper Peninsula to the U.S. government.

1843 Copper mining rush begins.

1846 First iron mining operations begin.

1855 *Iron Mountain Railroad* begins work on a 14-mile line from Marquette to the Jackson and Cleveland iron mines.

Soo Locks completed, opening Lake Superior to the other Great Lakes.

1856 First steam powered locomotive in the U.P. arrives by boat at Marquette. The "Sebastopol" is bound for the *Iron Mountain Railroad*.

Quincy Mine opens near the site of present-day Hancock.

1857 The first railroad, the *Marquette and Iron Mountain Railroad*, is completed from Lake Superior to the Superior Mine near present-day Ishpeming. The cars hauling ore were moved by mules and oxen.

1864 Escanaba to Negaunee line completed by *Peninsula Railroad*. It is consolidated with *Chicago and Northwestern* the next year.

1865 *Marquette & Ontonagon Railroad* opens Ishpeming-Champion line and Winthrop Junction-Lake Michigamme line.

First Escanaba ore dock built.

Calumet Mine and Hecla Mine open.

1867 *Hecla & Torch Lake Railroad* built between Calumet Mine and stamp mill.

1870 *Chicago and Northwestern* open line between Negaunee and Ishpeming.

Calumet to Kale Linden railroad is built.

1871 *Chicago and Northwestern* reaches from Green Bay to the Menominee River.

1872 *Chicago and Northwestern* opens line between Escanaba and Powers.

First passenger train reaches from Escanaba to Green Bay.

Marquette, Houghton and Ontonagon Railroad opens line between Champion and L'Anse.

Old Railroad depot at Gladstone

Line between Escanaba and Norway opens.

Hancock and Calumet connected by the *Mineral Range Railroad*.

1873 Lake Superior Ship Canal opens allowing ships to cross the Keweenaw Peninsula at Houghton and Hancock.

Mineral Range Railroad connects Houghton and Hancock by ferry.

1875 First bridge between Houghton and Hancock is built.

1877 *Menominee Range Railroad* connects Quinnesec to Powers.

First railroad reaches the Breen Mine near Iron Mountain.

1880 *Detroit, Mackinac and Marquette* railroad opens line between Marquette and Onota, near AuTrain.

1881 Munising and Marquette connected by the *Detroit, Mackinac & Marquette*.

Detroit, Mackinac & Marquette finishes work on line connecting Marquette to the Straits.

Detroit, Mackinac & Marquette joins *Michigan Central* and the *Grand Rapids & Indiana* in the Lower Peninsula to form the Mackinac Transportation Company with the purpose of starting a rail ferry service across the Straits of Mackinac.

1882 Iron Mountain route to Iron River/Crystal Falls line opened by *Chicago & Northwestern*.

1883 *Marquette, Houghton & Ontonagon* line connects L'Anse with Houghton.

1884 Menominee to Green Bay route completed by *Menominee Branch Railroad*.

Line opened between Watersmeet and Iron wood by the *Milwaukee, Lake Shore & Western*

Gogebic Range opens for iron mining.

1885 Wooden bridge built connecting Hancock to Houghton.

1886 First passenger train crosses Portage Canal Bridge between Hancock and Houghton

Seney and Grand Marais connected by *Manistique Railway* line.

1887 Passenger trains begin running between Ironwood and Bessemer.

Grand Hotel opens on Mackinac Island. Built by Cleveland Steamship Co., and two Lower Peninsula railroads, *Michigan Central* and *Grand Rapids & Indiana*.

A rail bridge over the St. Marys River at Sault Ste. Marie opens becoming the only international railroad bridge in Michigan.

Soo Line completes route from Sault Ste. Marie to Minneapolis.

1888 The first railroad finally reaches Sault Ste. Marie in January.

1888 St. Ignace ferry becomes first ship to offer rail connection between Michigan's two peninsulas.

1889 Michigan Lt. Governor James H. MacDonald and one of his associates are killed when their railroad car overturns 18 miles west of Iron River.

1895 New steel swing bridge built between Hancock and Houghton.

1896 Presque Isle near Marquette and Ishpeming connected by new *Lake Superior & Ishpeming Railroad*.

1897 Railroad car ferry service between Manistique and the Lower Peninsula begins with the arrival of Ann Arbor No. 1 at the Manistique harbor.

1899 Menominee line extended to Wisconsin state border.

Copper Range RR completes line between Houghton and Mass City.

1900 *Copper Range RR* builds hoist on Portage Lake for unloading coal.

The expanding Copper Range RR builds 60-foot turntable at Houghton, purchases more Pullman Passenger cars and connects to four more mines in the region.

L, S & I locomotive on display at the Upper Harbor, Marquette

1901 Streetcars begin running in Calumet.

1902 Car ferry service begins between Manistique and Elberta/Frankfort with launch of *Manistique, Marquette & Northern* car ferry No. 1.

1903 Copper Range RR completes line from McKeever to Calumet.

1904 Rail ferry service between Manistique and Northport begins.

1905 Houghton-Hancock Bridge damaged by steamer ship. An average of 50 railcars a day that cross on the bridge are now backed up. A temporary pontoon bridge and car ferry are put into service for the next year.

1906 Houghton-Hancock Bridge reopens to rail traffic after year long shutdown.

The new Keweenaw Central RR opens line from Calumet to Lac LaBelle.

1907 Keweenaw Central completes line to Mandan, a mining area about 12 miles south of Copper Harbor, making it the most northern railroad in Michigan.

1909 Steam railroads run an average of 9,059 miles per day in Michigan and employ over 81,000 people, a high point for the steam railroad era.

1910 Copper Range RR unveils the Copper Range Limited, a new passenger line with sleeper cars and dining service.

1912 Copper miners go on strike, demanding owners recognize Western Federation of Miners union. Mining activity stops, violence escalates and 2,000 Michigan National Guard troops are sent to region.

1913 Another strike erupts, this one lasting 10 months, resulting in miners winning a shorter workday.

The new International Bridge over the St. Marys River is completed replacing the one built in 1887.

Construction on the second International Bridge begun in 1960. (Photo courtesy of Marian Strahl Boyer)

1914 Line between Crystal Falls and Iron River extended by *Milwaukee RR*.

1916 The large *Pere Marquette RR* and other Michigan railroads declare bankruptcy.

1918 *Keweenaw Central* line between Calumet and Manden is abandoned.

1921 Service discontinued between Mineral Hills, Iron River, Stambaugh, Caspian and Gaastra by the *Iron River, Stambaugh and Crystal Falls St. RR.*

1924 Cleveland Cliffs Iron Co. abandons 60 miles of track in Alger County.

1925 Copper Range RR buys a bus line between Painesdale and Lake Linden.

1928 Soo Line discontinues regular passenger service between Bessemer, Ironwood and Wisconsin.

Many railroads operate at a loss for the first time.

Greyhound Bus service begins in the U.P..

1934 Diesel locomotives first used for passenger trains.

1937 The new air-conditioned *Chippewa* begins passenger service between Chicago and Iron Mountain.

1942 Track between Escanaba and Negaunee improved to accommodate new *Chicago & Northwestern* passenger diesel trains.

1945 Quincy Copper mine closes.

1948 Last logging railroad in Michigan, the *Nahma & Northern*, is abandoned.

1955 *Soo Line* retires its last steam locomotive.

Ferry service of passenger cars over the Straits ends.

1956 *Escanaba and Lake Superior* discontinues passenger service.

1957 Mackinac Bridge opens to vehicle traffic.

Last year that *Copper Range RR* earns a profit.

1958 *Duluth, South Shore & Atlantic* ends passenger service between St. Ignace and Marquette.

1959 Vertical lift bridge between Houghton and Hancock completed. It carries four lanes of vehicle traffic on the upper span, and one railroad track on the lower span.

1964 *Copper Range RR* discontinues one third of its lines.

1967 Gogebic iron range closes.

1968 *Manistique & Lake Superior RR* is abandoned.

Calumet and Hecla mine closes.

1969 The last remaining passenger train in the U.P., the *Peninsula 400* makes its final run between Ishpeming and Chicago.

1973 *Copper Range RR* abandons all operations.

1978 Menominee iron range closes it last mine.

1979 *Lake Superior and Ishpeming* abandons remaining lines east of Marquette except for short connection near Munising.

1980 *Escanaba & Lake Superior RR* takes over the Ontonagon to Green Bay route from *Milwaukee RR*.

1982 Last train crosses over the Houghton-Hancock Bridge.

2003 *Lake Superior & Ishpeming RR* becomes a division of Cleveland Cliffs.

RAILROAD TO NOWHERE

Millions of dollars were spent and millions of man hours expended to build 42 miles of rail that never carried a train.

In 1890 at the peak of the iron mining industry, investors were convinced that a new ore dock near L'Anse in Baraga County could successfully compete with the big docks in Marquette and Escanaba. There were rich deposits of ore and other mineral resources in the Huron Mountains west of Marquette. The plan was to build a 42- mile rail bed to haul the ore from the Champion Mine near Michigamme to the ore dock on Huron Bay in Baraga County for loading on to freighters.

On June 27, 1890 seven investors from the Lower Peninsula started the Iron Range and Huron Bay Railroad (IR&HB), and the work began. The hilly and rocky terrain presented an immediate challenge. The 500-man work crew tripled within a year. There were cost over-runs, but by 1893, the line was completed and the 1,000-foot ore dock was built. However by then, activity at the mines near Michigamme had peaked and was declining; the remaining iron ore was difficult to mine and demand had decreased with the economic Panic of 1893.

The IR&HB purchased two locomotives but only one of them ever made it onto the tracks, and that didn't turn out well. The caretaker of the locomotives managed to get twenty yards before a rotted rail bed gave way, sending the engine into a ditch.

Ten years and two-million dollars after starting the IR&HB, investors sold it to the Detroit Construction Company for $110,000. The rails were sold and used in downstate railroads, the locomotives were sold to Algoma Central Railroad and the iron ore dock was taken apart and shipped to Detroit. The State took over the railway, selling the part within Marquette to the city for $1,600. The chief engineer, Milo Davis, is said to have fled to Mexico to avoid arrest on allegations of fraud.

HUMOROUS RAILROAD NICKNAMES

Duluth, South Shore & Atlantic (DSS&A)

Damn Small Salary & Abuse, Damn Slow Service & Abuse, Dead Slow Service & Agony, Delayed Short-Steamed & Antiquated, Damn Slow and Sure Awful

Escanaba & Lake Superior (E&LS)

Easy, Lazy & Slow

Lake Superior & Ishpeming (LS&I)

Lazy, Slow & Independent

Manistique & Lake Superior (M&LS)

The Haywire
(from www.michiganrailrods.com)

RAILROAD CAR FERRIES

Postcard commemorating Chief Wawatam railroad ferry, Mackinaw City

In 1894 the Ann Arbor & North Michigan railroad established ferry service between Frankfort in northwest Lower Michigan and Menominee via the Sturgeon Bay ship canal.

The following year, reorganized under the name Ann Arbor Railroad, the company opened lines between Frankfort and Gladstone with a stop in Escanaba. In 1897, the line ran from Frankfort to Menominee to Gladstone. In 1898, a line was opened between Frankfort and Manistique.

In 1902, the Manistique, Marquette & Northern Railroad launched ferry service between Manistique and Northport situated at the tip of the Leelanau Peninsula in Lower Michigan. The 75-mile trip took about seven hours in good weather.

In 1908 the *Manistique, Marquette & Northern 1* sunk near the Chicago Lumber Company dock in Manistique. Attempting to stay in business, the company chartered the *Ann Arbor I* and *Ann Arbor II*. However, it closed for good later that year.

The first ferry to run between St. Ignace and Mackinaw City was the *Algomah*, a bulk steamer, which began service in 1881. Copper and other cargo was unloaded from rail cars onto the ferry, and once across the Straits it would be reloaded to waiting rail cars. The ferry was jointly owned by three railroads: the Duluth South Shore & Atlantic in the U.P., and two railroads from the Lower Peninsula: the Grand Rapids & Indiana and Michigan Central.

The following year the company added a barge, the *Betsy*, which carried four rail cars. The *Algomah* towed the *Betsy*, but was insufficient when it came to ice breaking. So in 1888, the *St. Ignace* was added to the fleet. It became the first car ferry ever equipped with a bow propeller, as well as the aft propeller. This prevented the ferry from becoming stuck in the thick lake ice.

In 1893, another ferry with bow and aft props the *Sainte Marie I* was added to the fleet. Later the *Chief Wawatam* (1911) and *Sainte Marie II* (1913) were added.

In 1923, the state formed Michigan State Ferries to provide affordable automobile crossings of the Straits. The few auto owners who had crossed on the rail ferries complained of high prices—up to $40—for one trip.

The first state-run automobile ferry was the *Arial*, which carried 20 cars. In 1924 two 40-car ferries were added, the *Sainte Ignace* and the *Mackinaw City*.

Four years later the *Straits of Mackinac* was added to the fleet. The 35-car ferry was expanded to a capacity of 90 cars and 400 passengers.

The *City of Cheboygan*, a former rail ferry was converted to carry 85 autos and joined the fleet in 1935. The following year the *City of Munising*, 105-car ferry was added.

In 1940, the 105-car *City of Petoskey* replaced the *Sainte Ignace* and *Mackinaw City,* which were sold to the federal government.

In 1952, the *Vacationland* which held 150 cars and trucks became the eighth and final ferry in the Michigan State Ferries fleet. The five ferries remained active until November 1, 1957 when the Mackinac Bridge opened to traffic.

LIGHTHOUSES

FIRST LIGHTHOUSES ON LAKE SUPERIOR

Whitefish Point and Copper Harbor Light both opened in early 1849. Congress approved funding for both lights in March of 1847. Both original lighthouses have been replaced: Whitefish Point in 1861 and Copper Harbor in 1866. The original 1849 Copper Harbor lighthouse keepers' residence remains standing near the current light.

Big Bay Point Light is serving as a Bed and Breakfast (B & B).

Sand Hills Light serves as a B & B.

Manitou Island Light is the oldest iron skeletal light tower on the Great Lakes.

Rock of Ages Light and Isle Royale (Menagerie Island) Light are part of the Isle Royale National Park.

Copper Harbor Light serves as a museum.

Whitefish Point lighthouse

Rock Harbor Light serves as a museum.

Eagle Harbor Light serves as a museum and is active.

Copper Harbor Rear Range Light used as residence for manager of Ft. Wilkins State Park.

Fourteen Mile Point Light was burned down by vandals in 1984.

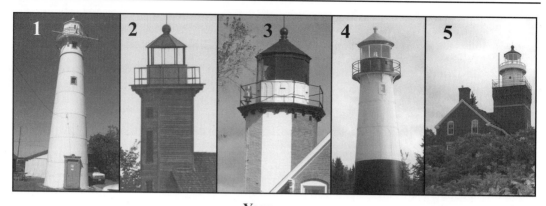

Lighthouse	Year Built	Height	Status
Frying Pan Island	1887		Inactive
Pipe Island	1888		Active
Round Island	1895	53 ft.	Inactive
Point Iroquois	1870	65 ft.	Inactive
Whitefish Point	1861	80 ft.	Active
Crisp Point	1904	58 ft.	Inactive
Grand Marais Front Range	1895	34 ft.	Active
Grand Marais Rear Range	1898	47 ft.	Active
Au Sable Point	1873	87 ft.	Active
Grand Island Old North	1867	25 ft.	Inactive
2) Grand Island East Channel	1868	45 ft.	Inactive
1) Munising Range – Front	1908	30 ft.	Active
4) Munising Range – Rear	1908	58 ft.	Active
Grand Island Harbor West Channel	1914		Inactive
Marquette Harbor	1866	39 ft.	Active
Presque Isle Harbor Breakwater	1941		Active
Granite Island	1868	40 ft.	Inactive
Stannard's Rock	1882	87 ft.	Active
5) Big Bay Point	1896	65 ft.	Active
Huron Island	1868	39 ft.	Active
Sand Point	1878	30 ft.	Inactive
Portage Lake Lower Entrance	1920	31 ft.	Active
Portage River	1870	65 ft.	Inactive
Keweenaw Waterway	1920		Active
Mendota (Bete Grise)	1895	40 ft.	Inactive
Gull Rock	1867	46 ft.	Active
Manitou Island	1861	80 ft.	Active
Copper Harbor Light	1866	62 ft.	Inactive
Copper Harbor Rear Range	1964		Inactive
Copper Harbor Front Range	1927	60 ft.	Inactive
3) Eagle Harbor	1871	40 ft.	Active
Eagle River	1855	40 ft.	Inactive
Sand Hills	1919	50 ft.	Inactive
Keweenaw Waterway Entrance	1950	50 ft.	Active
Fourteen Mile Point	1894		Inactive

Ontonagon	1867	34 ft.	Inactive
Ontonagon West Pierhead	1915	20 ft.	Active
Rock of Ages	1908	130 ft.	Active
Isle Royale (Menagerie Island)	1875	61 ft.	Active
Rock Harbor	1855	50 ft.	Inactive
Passage island	1882	44 ft.	Active

SHIPPING ON LAKE SUPERIOR

The rapids of St. Marys at Sault Ste. Marie provided an almost insurmountable obstacle to navigation on Lake Superior in the early days of the 19th Century. For that reason, commerce developed much slower than on the Lower Great Lakes.

In 1809, the sloop *Otter* was one of the first vessels of any size on Lake Superior. The schooners *Fur Trader*, *Recovery* and *Invincible* were sailing

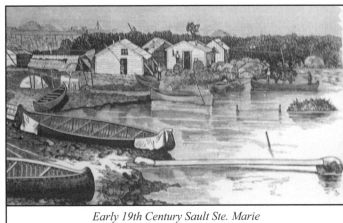

Early 19th Century Sault Ste. Marie

Lake Superior in the service of the fur trade in 1812. A short time later, the *Fur Trader* was damaged beyond repair while being hauled across the rapids at the Sault.

The War of 1812 saw several British fur trading company vessels captured by the Americans on Lake Superior. To avoid capture, the company hid the *Recovery* in a deep-water canyon on the northeast side of Isle Royale. Finally in the fall of 1816, the *Invincible* met her demise in a furious northwest gale at Whitefish Point. The 30-ton *Exmouth* then became the first vessel successfully hauled over the rapids at the Sault in 1817, pressed into service to offset the loss of the *Invincible*. The *Exmouth* was scrapped in 1821. Then in 1828, the *Recovery* was sent down to the Lower Lakes. This left nothing but canoes and small Mackinaw boats on Lake Superior the next seven years. Finally in 1834, the American Fur Company began construction on the *John Jacob Astor*, named after the company's owner.

FIRST AMERICAN VESSEL

The *Astor* became the first American vessel launched on Lake Superior in 1835. Its commander at the time, Captain Charles Stannard, discovered the rocky shoal in central Lake Superior later that season. Stannard Rock bears the captain's name today. A manned lighthouse was eventually built on the rock to protect marine interests. The *Astor* failed to receive protection from an early autumn storm off Copper Harbor and was dashed to pieces on the rocks at that location on September 19, 1844.

THE MINERAL RUSH

After the Chippewa ceded the last of their land holdings over the western U.P. in 1842, mineral exploration began in earnest. With the copper rush came a rapid increase in the Lake Superior fleet. By 1845, the sails on the lake consisted of nine schooners led by the 70-ton vessels *Algonquin*, *Swallow* and *Merchant*. That same year the *Independence* became the first steam craft to navigate the lake. The *Napoleon* and *Julia Palmer* soon followed. A good crew of voyageurs in canoes could easily outdistance these early steamers, which achieved a maximum speed of around four miles-an-hour.

There was always the obstacle of the St. Marys Rapids at the Sault. To navigate this barrier, the cargo would have to be shipped off the vessel; the vessel would then be transported over the portage by a system of rollers and reloaded. The freight was initially handled by an old gray horse and cart. Over the next several years, the operation became the Chippewa Portage Company, which employed a number of teams working day and night to transport goods as well as iron ore at the Sault. This cumbersome method of transportation continued until the locks opened in 1855.

THE LOCKS AT SAULT STE. MARIE

No other action helped stimulate the growth of Michigan's Upper Peninsula more than the building of the locks and canal at Sault Ste. Marie. Congress appropriated 750,000 acres of land to the State of Michigan, which would be paid to a concern that successfully completed construction of a lock and canal system by the rapids. A group of wealthy eastern businessmen organized the St. Mary's Falls Ship Canal Company. With much difficulty, the project was finished in the spring of 1855. The first steamer, *Illinois*, passed through the locks on June 18, 1855.

The first year, some 116,000 tons of cargo, including copper and iron ore along with just over 4,000 passengers passed through the locks. Ten years later, over 400,000 tons of cargo passed through along with nearly 20,000 passengers. These figures grew exponentially so that by the end of the century nearly 19 million tons of freight and over 43,000 passengers moved through the locks annually.

DEVELOPMENT OF LAKE SUPERIOR PORTS

The development of ports on Lake Superior accelerated following the building of the Sault locks.

Eagle Harbor, 16 miles west of Copper Harbor, was the first port established in 1844. It became a harbor of refuge on the western side of the Keweenaw but traffic was never large.

Copper Harbor was settled a bit later. During the mining excitement of the mid-1880s, Copper Harbor was filled with adventurers and would-be entrepreneurs. Most of the mines failed in the northern region of the Keweenaw Peninsula and the town fell into decay. Today Copper Harbor is a year-round tourist town and serves as one of the ferry ports to Isle Royale.

In 1847-48, **Ontonagon** came to prominence when the mines 14 miles up river began producing mass copper. The village at the mouth of the Ontonagon River grew rapidly and, for a time, was the largest community on Lake Superior. Improvements to the harbor, which originally was only seven feet deep, were slow and did not progress satisfactorily until the government took over the project in 1867. Mining slowed late in the 19th Century but Ontonagon found new life as a lumber town. Then in 1896, a disastrous fire consumed most of the town and completely wiped out the Diamond Match Company, which was the town's major employer. Diamond chose not to rebuild and the village never fully recovered. Today Ontonagon has an active historical society that runs the museum in town and is working to refurbish the lighthouse. Ontonagon serves as the northern gateway to the Ottawa National Forest and Porcupine Mountain State Park.

L'Anse was the site of various Indian villages and missions through the middle of the 19th Century. The village was platted in 1871 and went through a speculative boom until the panic of 1873. It became the center of a large lumbering district in the western U.P. during the late 1800s. Just like Ontonagon, L'Anse suffered a major fire in 1896. Its fire was in May and destroyed a large portion of the town. Today its economic base includes lumber, lumber-related industry and tourism.

Marquette became established on what was then called Iron Bay in the summer of 1849. Its founders came to exploit the newly-discovered iron deposits in the hills west of the settlement. Development was slow until the locks opened at Sault Ste. Marie. The harbor was originally totally unprotected from northeast storms. In 1866, a project was approved to build a 2,000 foot breakwater. It was completed in 1875 but was soon found to be inadequate due to increased volume of shipping. The breakwater extension was completed at about the turn of the century. The city soon became the largest U.P. metropolis with immense ore docks and railroad connections to the Marquette and Gogebic Range iron mines. Marquette still serves as an iron port for the still-operating open pit mines west of the city. It has become a regional center of commerce with a medical center and a state university.

Munising, derived from the Ojibwa word meaning island in a lake, was originally occupied about 1850. The village was platted at its current location in 1895. It became a lumbering center in the latter days of the 19th Century into the early 20th Century. Its harbor, formed by Grand Island just off shore, is considered one of the finest on the lake. Today Munising is a tourist town and serves as a gateway community to the Pictured Rocks, just east of the village.

Grand Marais is a picturesque town east of the Pictured Rocks. It was settled as a lumbering and fishing village in 1879. Russell Alexander Alger brought boom times to Grand Marais in the 1890s when he extended his Manistique Railroad to the sleepy village. Quickly, the village population rose to 3,000. The port was always a refuge on this dangerous section of Lake Superior shoreline. During the boom time, the harbor was dredged and improved to accept large ships. Then about the turn of the century, Alger turned his attention to his forest holding in Minnesota. In 1911, he tore up the track leading to Grand Marais and the town withered to a tenth of its former size. Today Grand Marais is a tourist village and safe harbor for recreational vessels.

Sault Ste. Marie is the oldest settlement in Michigan. Native tribes gathered for generations along the St. Marys to take advantage of the excellent fishery. French Jesuits established a mission at the site in about 1669. It remained a fur trading post during the 18th Century after the French lost influence in the area and the Jesuits left. In 1822, Indian Agent Henry Rowe Schoolcraft and a contingent of U.S. soldiers established the first permanent American settle-

ment here.

Sault Ste. Marie became the focal point of activity and the gateway to the mineral lands to the west. Everyone had to pass through the city as they traveled west. When the first locks were opened in 1855, irrevocable change came to the Sault. Now passengers and freight could pass the through the locks without staying in the city. Eventually, the cities to the west in the iron and copper mining districts became more prominent. Railroads reached these settlements first in the 1860s. The Sault remained isolated in the winter except by sled or horse-drawn sleigh through the 1870s into the 1880s. The railroad finally reached this city on the rapids in January 1888.

Today Sault Ste. Marie is the largest city and center of commerce for the eastern Upper Peninsula.

MAJOR SHIPPING PORTS OF THE UPPER PENINSULA

City/County	Receives	Ships
Ontonagon/Ontonagon	Coal	
Houghton/Houghton	Coal	
Hancock/Houghton	Coal, lime	Iron Ore
Marquette/Marquette	Coal, lime	
Menominee/Menominee	Coal	
Escanaba/Delta	Coal, lime	Iron Ore
Gladstone/Delta	Liquid Bulk	
Munising/Alger	Coal	
Port Inland/Schoolcraft		Lime
Brevort		Sand/Gravel
Drummond Island		Limestone

IRON ORE SHIPMENTS FROM LAKE SUPERIOR (NET TONS IN MILLIONS)

About 75% of iron ore moved on the Great Lakes is shipped from Lake Superior.

2000	2001	2002	2003	2004	2005
50.84	40.90	46.25	41.32	48.1	45.2

COAL SHIPMENTS FROM LAKE SUPERIOR (NET TONS IN MILLIONS)

2000	2001	2002	2003	2004	2005
17.0	18.7	20.0	19.5	20.1	22.0

About 50% of coal moved on the Great Lakes is shipped from Lake Superior.

SAULT CANAL AND LOCKS

The last ice age covered the area now known as the Upper Great Lakes with a glacier around a mile thick. After the ice receded the Great Lakes were formed. Several thousand years ago, Lakes Superior, Michigan and Huron were on the same level. A constant process of uplift, caused by the rebounding of the land from the weight of the glacier, raised the Superior basin by about six feet. This raising of the land also caused greater outflow of Huron and Michigan lowering them by 16 feet. Most of that 22-foot difference in elevation occurs in one mile at the Falls of St. Mary at Sault Ste. Marie. The falls, in effect, cut off Lake Superior from the rest of the Great Lakes. This proved to be an obstacle to settlement of the Upper Peninsula of Michigan.

The first canal built to by-pass the rapids and falls was constructed in 1797 by the Northwest Company, a British fur-trading concern. The canal was merely a ditch with a tiny, crude lock. It served its purpose by ferrying canoes and small company-supply boats by the rapids for years. Then during the War of 1812, an armed band of Americans destroyed the canal.

The next serious attempt to construct a Sault canal began soon after Michigan was granted statehood. In 1838, the State legislature appropriated $25,000 to begin construction and a Buffalo firm entered into a contract to build the canal. The project was never completed and barely even started. The engineering plan called for the canal to intersect, and thus destroy, the army's millrace at Fort Brady. The race provided power for the Fort's sawmill and under orders from Washington, the canal workers were evicted.

The Michigan congressional delegation tried getting land appropriation for the building of a canal in 1840. The role of the federal government in "internal" state improvements was viewed much differently than it is today. Cash appropriations or grants from the United States government to states were rare. The states of the Old Northwest, of which Michigan was a part, had large reserves of public land owned by the government. Appropriations of land could be made by Congress to a state. A state would then use the land to pay a company for making internal improvements like a canal. The company would then shoulder the entire financial burden of canal construction.

Michigan's Congressional delegation was met with frustration in its attempt to get government support for the Sault canal. While neighboring states saw the canal as a "community-of-interest" project that would eventually benefit commerce in their states, states more removed from the region rejected this notion. Senator Henry Clay of Tennessee stated that a canal at Sault Ste. Marie would be about as useful as "a canal on the moon." South Carolina's Senator called the Upper Peninsula "terra incognita" fearing a revival of vast, costly internal improvements. President James K. Polk summed up the prevailing attitude toward state aid in the mid-1800s: "The Constitution has not, in my judgment, conferred upon the Federal Government the power to construct works of internal improvement within the states, or to appropriate money from the Treasury for that purpose."

Meanwhile, Douglass Houghton, Michigan's State Geologist, released a report containing information on large copper deposits in parts of the western Upper Peninsula. Then in 1842, the Ojibwa nation ceded the last of their land in the Great Lakes to the United States. A mining boom soon followed along with increased nation-wide attention to Michigan's Lake Superior wilderness. A newspaper, *The Lake Superior News and Miners Journal*, was begun at Copper Harbor in 1846 by John Ingersoll, a protégé of eastern newspaper magnate Horace Greeley. The Journal's stories in support of the canal were often printed in Greeley's news-

papers back east. Greeley took an interest in the region and even invested in one of the early Keweenaw mining ventures. A more favorable picture began to emerge concerning investment in improved transportation to and from the region.

It took until late summer 1852 for the land-bill appropriation to pass the House. The bill granted the State of Michigan 750,000 acres of land for construction of a ship canal around the Falls of the St. Marys River. Now a company had to be found that was willing and able to take on the immense project. Within a few months, a young salesman named Charles T. Harvey arrived at the Sault to set up outlets for his employer's product, the Fairbanks platform scale. The 23-year-old Harvey, though not an engineer, saw the potential of the canal project for his employer. Erastus Fairbanks realized the project would be too large for one man to finance, so he approached Erastus Corning, a railroad man and one of the most powerful financiers in New York. The St. Mary's Falls Ship Canal Company was formed by these men and their associates and after much political maneuvering, the company was given a contract to construct the canal and locks within two years for a payment of 750,000 acres of land in the State of Michigan.

A comparison was made between the Sault Canal project and the construction of the Erie Canal. The Erie Canal, constructed in 101 months between 1817 and 1825, ran 363 miles across several rivers from the Hudson River to Lake Erie. The cost of the project was $7.1 million dollars. Planners for the roughly one-mile Sault Canal thought it reasonable to assume their venture would take less than one-fifth the time and cost no more than one-eighth the Erie model. It would be easy!

Their project was anything but easy. First, the inexperienced Harvey was put in charge of it. His skills were in promoting and selling ideas, not engineering. Poor planning got construction off to a slow start. He failed to secure the services of a bookkeeper before it was too late. Once one arrived from back east, the books were in such disarray the bookkeeper could not vouch for their accuracy. Despite the confusion and poor progress, Harvey always sent enthusiastic, optimistic reports to the board of directors.

Labor shortage was one of the biggest problems for the Canal Company. Low wages and poor morale were chief deterrents in building an adequate work force. Harvey paid the standard laborers who boarded with the company at the work site $20 per month. They had to work 11-and-a-half hour days compared to the standard work day of ten hours. At the end of a month of back-breaking work the men had nothing to spend their wages on except whiskey. When winter arrived in December 1853, about 400 men remained. No more miserable conditions existed than working on a canal during the Sault winter. Often, the men had to search for their tools in deep snow before work began in the morning. Always they had to chop away at up to two feet of ice before excavation of the rock could begin.

The next year an epidemic of cholera hit the work site. Conventional wisdom, or wishful thinking, held that the Sault's vigorous climate was immune from the scourge. Further, it was assumed the disease was a by-product of "sinful or vicious living." Today it is known that poor

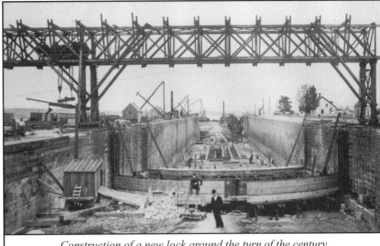

Construction of a new lock around the turn of the century

sanitation, rife in the shanty village of the workers, is the chief cause of cholera. Eventually, 10-percent of the work force succumbed to the illness.

The Canal Company's board of directors demoted Harvey, though he retained his title, and replaced him with John W. Brooks, one of Corning's railroad men. Brooks inherited an operation beset by problems of coordination between carpenters, who had to wait for timber that arrived late and was in short supply, for stone that had to be shipped at much cost and delay from the Detroit area, as well as a unique set of difficulties encountered while building a structure adjacent to a rapidly moving river. Despite the obstacles, the canal and locks were completed on time. The steamer *Illinois* was the first boat to pass through the structure on June 18, 1855.

The Falls of St. Mary's Ship Canal Company turned the structure over to the State of Michigan and, except for minor finishing work, was through with it. Today, companies specialize in areas like marine construction. Back in the mid-1800s, this company was really involved in land speculation and canal construction was a means to an end. The land was paid for by the building of a mile-long canal along with two locks 70-feet wide and 350-feet long. The entire cost of the venture was just under $1 million, substantially more than the original estimate.

The State of Michigan then appointed a series of superintendents who were responsible for running and maintaining the locks and collecting user fees to offset costs. Boats passing through the lock were charged a toll of 4 cents per ton. In 1877, the toll was lowered to 3 cents. There was no great rush of traffic the first year. The *Illinois* took 28 days to reach the canal again with cargo and passengers bound for the Lake Superior region. A few more steamers followed. Only $4,474.66 was collected in tolls the first year on about 109,000 tons.

Traffic built slowly and unevenly into the 1860s. It took an innovation in technology—the conversion of iron into steel, perfected late in the 1860s—for a surge in activity. The schooner *Columbia* brought the first load of red iron ore, 132 tons strewn on her deck, in 1855. A century later, 100 million tons of ore passed through the locks annually. As traffic increased, the need for a new set of locks was apparent. Michigan was not financially capable of undertaking this project and in 1881, the locks were turned over to the U.S. Army Corps of Engineers. This agency has operated the locks toll-free ever since.

SAULT LOCKS: TRAFFIC AND TONNAGE (2005 SEASON)

Lock	Total passages	Net tonnage (millions)	Vessel Flag passages		
			U.S.	Canadian	Foreign
Poe	3,732	64,608,208	2,620	712	185
MacArthur	4,033	17,270,623	1,915	1,282	297
Davis	13	4,120	2	3	0

SAULT LOCKS: OPERATING SEASON (2005)

Lock	Opening Day	Closing Day	Days	Passages
Poe	3/25/05	1/16/06	297	3,732
MacArthur	4/03/05	12/25/05	266	4,033
Davis	Occasional use		3	13

SAULT LOCKS: TEN YEAR TRAFFIC RECORD

Year	Passages	Year	Passages
1996	4,439	2001	4,309
1997	4,836	2002	4,543
1998	4,648	2003	4,205
1999	4,595	2004	4,189
2000	4,845	2005	4,312

SAULT LOCKS: LAKE COMMERCE (NET TONNAGE)

Commodity	Eastbound	Westbound	Net Tons
Iron Ore	42,810,643	0	42,810,643
Coal	18,670,168	2,844,571	21,514,739
Wheat	6,922,497	0	6,922,497
Limestone	0	4,077,560	4,077,560
Vegetable Products	949,704	9,304	959,008
Oilseeds	856,391	0	856,391
Salt	0	656,021	656,021
Slag	577,774	21,966	599,740
Cement/Concrete	506	518,464	518,970
Potassic fertilizer	477,655	0	477,655

Source: Lake Carrier's Association

SHIPWRECKS

"Lake Superior, they say, never gives up her dead," go the words to a song about the most famous and last fatal shipwreck on the big lake. While the words are only partially true, they illustrate the mystery and peril of a lake that has haunted sailors from the earliest days of shipping in the 18th Century. The aura of danger connected with traveling on Lake Superior goes back further. The Ojibwa offered sacrifices to the evil spirit of the lake before launching their canoes and would only mention its name during winter when the creature was safely locked beneath the ice.

Lake Superior is not the deadliest Great Lake. The shipwreck annals show more losses and fatalities on the lakes below. Lake Superior accounts for only 10 percent of the total losses from shipwrecks on the Great Lakes, while Lakes Huron, Michigan and Erie are each responsible for about a quarter of shipping losses. The higher totals on the Lower Lakes were due to heavier traffic. But Lake Superior's light traffic and isolation added to its danger. A good deal of Superior's shoreline is rugged and rocky. Through the early portion of the 20th Century, much of its coast remained uninhabited and desolate. This fact made shipwreck all the more terrifying; if sailors were washed up on shore and survived, it could mean being stranded in the wilderness and dying of exposure. It's this feature that sets Lake Superior apart. Winter comes to its shores earlier, while spring arrives later than on the lakes farther south and east. Mid-lake temperatures stay in the 30s into early summer; washing overboard could lead to hypothermia and death in minutes.

Geography also set Lake Superior apart. It is more than 20 feet higher than Lakes Michigan and Huron. Most of the elevation drop occurs in a mile-long section of the St. Marys River at Sault Ste. Marie. The rapids there created a barrier that prevented large ships from sailing to Lake Superior from the Lower Great Lakes. One of the first marine disasters connected with Superior occurred in 1812 when a fur-trading company attempted to send a schooner over the rapids. It was damaged beyond repair during the passage. A shipyard on Lake Superior near the Sault turned out a number of schooners that were used exclusively on the lake in the early 19th Century. It was not until the completion of the canal and locks at Sault Ste. Marie in 1855 that ships were free to pass from Lakes Michigan and Huron into Lake Superior.

Shipwrecks on the Superior have claimed around 350 vessels and 1,000 lives. Here are ten of the most notable wrecks near or along the Upper Peninsula shoreline.

Invincible, 1816: This 60-foot British-Canadian schooner, part of the Northwest Company fleet, met her end when one of the company's leaders made a rash decision to sail across the lake in stormy November. The ship only made it to Whitefish Point where it was hurled ashore during a furious gale. Those aboard made it safely to dry land, but the *Invincible* was dashed to pieces—the first documented shipwreck on Lake Superior.

John Jacob Astor, 1844: This 78-foot, 112-ton schooner was the first American vessel launched on Lake Superior in 1835. She was a work-horse for the next nine years, hauling supplies from the Sault to wilderness outposts on the Keweenaw Peninsula. On September 19, 1844, Captain Ben Stannard brought the *Astor* into presumed safe harbor at Copper Harbor. At intense "equinoctial" storm proved him wrong—he watched from land as his ship parted her cables and collided with the rocky shore. The *Astor's* crew and soldiers from nearby Fort Wilkins were able to salvage much of the cargo, but not the ship. The *John Jacob Astor* was the first documented American shipwreck on the lake.

Merchant, 1847: This 80-ton schooner's last voyage got off to an ominous start before even leaving port. Robert Moore, the ship's captain, broke his leg the day before sailing and tried to induce another skipper to take his place. Moore wound up sailing the vessel out of the Sault anyway with 14 passengers and crew on June 11, 1847. The *Merchant* was never heard from again. Months later, some wreckage from the ship was recovered on the north shore of the lake. Five years later, some explorers off Grand Island spotted the top masts of a schooner about 30 feet below the surface. It is here where she met her fate—the first disappearance with all hands on Lake Superior.

A side note: A 15-year-old runaway from Wisconsin attempted to get passage to the Copper Lands on the *Merchant* but was turned down because the ship was filled to capacity. Fate was kind to the young man, Peter White, who later became one of the founders of the city of Marquette.

Superior, 1856: This is among the most tragic Lake Superior shipwrecks. The 184-foot, 646-ton wooden side-wheeler was captained by veteran lake-master Hiram J. Jones on October 29, 1856 when it hit a northerly gale just west of Whitefish Point. Captain Jones made a run for the shelter of Grand Island when his ship lost her rudder while approaching Pictured Rocks. Jones could not keep the *Superior* from crashing broadside into the rocky ledge. The side-wheeler disintegrated quickly. An estimated 18 passengers and crew managed to float on debris to the rocks. They then watched as Captain Jones and eight of his crew went under one by one.

A couple of crew members took a patched up lifeboat to the home of a fur trader near present-day Munising, while the rest of the survivors were forced to walk through snow along the shoreline to reach shelter. Two more victims were claimed by exposure and exhaustion bringing the toll of the *Superior* shipwreck to an estimated 50—the worst loss of life in a single accident on Lake Superior.

W.W. Arnold 1869: This shipwreck illustrates the utter desolation of the south shore of Lake Superior in the 19th Century. The schooner *Arnold*, under the command of Captain Beardsley with a crew of nine and two passenger, left Marquette bound for the Sault on November 4. A few hours later a tremendous northwest gale set in. It raged a full 24 hours leading the light keeper at Whitefish Point to pronounce the storm "the most terrific of all others in his recollection." Days later, when no ships reported any sign of the *Arnold*, and she had not gone through the Sault locks, it seemed her fate was sealed. Over a month later, a mail carrier passing along the deserted, lonely shoreline of the eastern Upper Peninsula spotted the hull of a vessel near the Two Hearted River, about 35 miles east of Munising. He was prevented from getting closer by a pack of wolves. Later, a search party discovered the remains of the ship with some of the dead crew members encased in ice. The bodies were recovered and buried on a bank above the lake the next spring.

Ice blockade in Marquette Harbor, June 1873
(Courtesy of Superior View Studio, Marquette)

Saturn and Jupiter, Griswold and W.O. Brown 1872: These schooners all met their ends during one of the worst storms to ever hit the lake in late November 1872. The wooden side-wheel steamer *John A. Dix* towed the schooner barges *Saturn* and *Jupiter* out of Marquette the morning of November 27. That evening the three ships were overtaken by huge waves just off Vermillion Point. The *Jupiter* broke her towline and a short time later, the *Saturn* did the same. The *Dix* took a run for Whitefish Bay in a desperate attempt to save herself. The *Dix* succeeded, but the two schooners were cast ashore on the eastern end of the Upper Peninsula and the entire crews of both vessels including 14 men and a woman died, either by drowning or exposure.

The *Griswold* was likely overwhelmed over southern Whitefish Bay with all hands. Masts protruding from deep water in the area are presumed to be hers. The *W.O. Brown* was flung ashore north of the Sault. The *Brown's* captain and several crew members were washed over-board, while three crew members survived, clinging to the remains of the ship for two hours. They then made a dash for the beach, jumping from rock to rock. Their ordeal had only begun; an intense cold wave set in at the tail-end of the storm. The three survived along the beach by building a fire without matches in the remains of the ship's cabin. They were able to keep from starving by boiling the raw wheat the *Brown* was carrying into a kind of porridge. When the lake finally calmed ten days later, they recovered the ship's yawl boat, patched it the best they could and paddled southeast for help. They eventually made it to a Canadian logging camp where they were fed and nursed back to health. At Christmas, an Indian guide led them to the Sault. Later, the Sault Canal superintendent took them to a railhead in the Lower Peninsula where they eventually made it to their homes a full two months after the disaster. The wreck of the *W.O. Brown* provided the most unique story of survival and rescue on Lake Superior, while the tragedy that befell the *Saturn* and *Jupiter* provided the impetus to construct four Life-saving stations along the Upper Peninsula's eastern shore.

Manistee, 1883: The Ontonagon lighthouse keeper put out the light for the season on December 3, 1883. He wrote later that day in his journal he was "not sorry" to close the shipping season after a fall "fraught with disaster to shipping and life."

Several storms hit during the fall. The mid-November blow brought "genuine Christmas weather" to Ontonagon and later, great anxiety about the fate of the steamer *Manistee*. The venerable 184-foot, 677-ton vessel left Duluth with supplies for western Upper Michigan ports and drove straight into the teeth of the tremendous storm. Days later, when no word came from the ship, a search was made by other vessels. Finally on November 21, a tug came into Ontonagon with a pail and part of the cabin of the *Manistee* confirming the loss of the ship and its 38 passengers and crew. This was the first major disappearance on the western end of Lake Superior.

Iosco and Olive Jeanette 1905: The steamer *Iosco,* with the schooner *Olive Jeanette* in tow, left Duluth on August 30 laden with iron ore. On September 2, a captain of another steamer spotted the two wooden ships 20 miles east of the Huron Islands. Something must have gone wrong, which forced the captain of the *Iosco* to turn back west, probably for the shelter of the Keweenaw Bay. The ships never made it. Presumably, the *Olive Jeanette's* cable broke loose. The next day, the keeper of the light on one of the Huron Islands reported only a schooner about four miles north of the islands. He then watched in horror as the vessel sank. By September 5, the bodies of sailors in life preservers began washing up on shore from Keweenaw Bay all the way east to the Huron Mountains. The bodies—15 in all—were identified as crew members of the *Iosco* and her consort, *Olive Jeanette*. These two vessels were among the 21 total wrecks of the 1905 shipping season—by far, the worst single-season toll on Lake Superior.

L.C. Waldo and Henry B. Smith 1913: The granddaddy of all November storms claimed two vessels off Upper Peninsula shores with very different outcomes. The ore carrier *L.C.*

Waldo left Two Harbors, Minnesota on November 7. By the early hours of the 8th, she was hit full-force by the storm. A huge wave ripped the pilot house off the 451-foot, 4,466-ton steel steamer and nearly washed overboard the captain, John Duddleston. Later, a mountainous wave broke into the cabin containing the rest of the crew. The 22 men and two women barely escaped with their lives, taking refuge in the forward portion of the ship. Then disaster struck. Duddleston, navigating with an oil lamp and lifeboat compass, tried to thread the needle between Keweenaw Point and Manitou Island. The *Waldo* rammed Gull Rock between the two points and split in half. The captain and crew stayed alive for three days by burning the interior cabin, furniture and anything else that would ignite. Finally, on the early morning of November 11, Life-saving crews from two stations on the Keweenaw Peninsula converged on the vessel and took all the crew members to safety. The mangled *L.C. Waldo*, however, was left to the mercy of the lake.

The 25-man *Henry B. Smith* crew was not as fortunate. Captain Jimmy Owen decided to run the 525-foot, 6,631-ton steel steamer to the Sault late Sunday afternoon November 9 when the storm showed signs of easing. He had not even moved out of sight of observers at Marquette Harbor when the storm re-intensified with howling northwest winds and blinding snow. One Lake Captain on shore swore he saw the *Smith* turn around less than a half hour after leaving the harbor, presumably for the shelter of Keweenaw Bay.

When the storm finally eased and telegraph service was restored, it was discovered that the *Smith* never passed through the Sault locks. Fears that the *Smith* was lost turned to certainty when a landlooker returned from a nine-mile walk down the deserted beach east of Marquette with an ore marked "*Henry B. Smith*." Other wreckage also floated to the beach and a body of one crew member was recovered two weeks later 50 miles west of Whitefish Point. The next spring, another crew member was found encased in a chunk of ice at Michipicoten Island, far to the northeast of where the *Smith* was thought to have gone down. Twenty-three crew members including Captain Owen were never recovered. The *Henry B. Smith* remains missing. Several attempts have been made over the years to locate the ship in waters off Marquette. To this day the whereabouts of the *Smith* remains a mystery.

Edmund Fitzgerald 1975: This is the most famous Lake Superior shipwreck. The sinking of a modern steel freighter on a fresh water lake shocked the marine world and captured the attention of the nation.

The 729-foot *Fitzgerald* was the pride of the Oglebay Norton fleet. She set shipping records for years. On Sunday morning November 9, she was loaded with 26,000 tons of iron at Superior, Wisconsin in mild weather with a light southeast wind. However, off to the southwest a low-pressure system was forming over the Southern Plains— a familiar, dangerous spot for November storms on the Great Lakes. The U.S. Weather Bureau issued gale warnings in anticipation the storm would move close enough to affect Lake Superior. Captain Ernest McSorley decided to take the normal Lake Carrier's shipping route across the lake despite the warnings. About the same time the *Fitz* left Superior, the *Ar-*

Edmund Fitzgerald lifeboat on display at Valley Camp Museum, Sault Ste. Marie

thur M. Anderson, captained by Lake Master Bernie Cooper, took off with a load of ore from Two Harbors. The two captains communicated by radio and decided to travel closely in case the storm got as bad as the forecast suggested. This way they could monitor each other's progress and decide in tandem what to do if the seas got rough.

As the Plains low-pressure area approached from the southwest, northeast winds increased. McSorley reported 52-knot winds and 10-foot seas during the night. As morning approached, the winds eased and it appeared that the worst of the storm was over. Nothing could have been further from the truth. The storm center drifted near Marquette and then shot northeastward while continually deepening. The *Fitzgerald* and *Anderson* sailed into a hell of wind and mountainous waves. West to northwesterly winds increased all afternoon as the ships moved into the eastern end of the lake. The wind now had over 200 miles of open water to churn before reaching the two ships.

During the late afternoon, McSorley reported to Cooper that he had lost his radar and sustained some top-side damage. More ominous, the *Fitzgerald* was taking on water and had developed a list. Cooper, as close to an eye witness to the tragedy as anyone, felt McSorley had sailed too close to a dangerous shoal off Caribou Island. He felt that the Fitzgerald shoaled and received hull damage—explaining why the ship was taking on water. About 6:30 that evening, Cooper observed two immense waves hit his ship. The second one put green water over the *Anderson's* bridge deck 35 feet above the waterline. Downstream, the listing *Fitzgerald* likely caught these waves about 7 p.m. When a heavy snow squall diminished and the *Anderson's* radar image sharpened, the *Fitzgerald* shadow did not appear on the screen. There were no lights observed in the distance where the *Fitz* was supposed to be. No reply came from repeated attempts to reach the ship by radio. The *Edmund Fitzgerald* had disappeared.

An all-out search was conducted by the Coast Guard and other ships in the area including the *Anderson*. The next morning, enough flotsam was washed up on the Canadian shore to fill a three-ton truck, including life boats, life rings and preservers as well as fully-inflated life rafts. However, no trace of the 29 men aboard the ship was found.

The next year, Gordon Lightfoot's "Wreck of the *Edmund Fitzgerald*" became one of the top pop hits of the year. The haunting ballad etched the tragic last voyage of the ore boat into the nation's consciousness and immortalized the infamous "Gales of November."

UNDERWATER PRESERVES: The tragedy of years past brings opportunities for adventure today. The Whitefish Point Underwater Diving Preserve offers deep-diving experiences to a variety of shipwrecks over 376 square miles. Farther west, the Alger Underwater Preserve boasts several unusual diving attractions including shipwrecks, and "sea caves," protected from Lake Superior's fury by the shelter of Grand Island. For those who prefer to stay out of the water, there are glass-bottom boat tours of several wrecks in Munising Bay. Farther up the coast, the Marquette Underwater Preserve offers opportunities to dive for wrecks in the harbor adjacent to the city and in another area off the Huron Islands. Finally, the Keweenaw Underwater Preserve hosts 40 discovered shipwrecks and many more still undiscovered from Keweenaw Bay to the Portage Entry up to Copper Harbor and west to Eagle Harbor. The Straits of Mackinac Underwater Preserve covers 148 square miles where Lake Michigan and Lake Huron meet. There are about a dozen accessible shipwrecks in the Preserve as well as the "Rock Maze," an unusual formation of rock a few hundred yards east of Mackinac Island that resembles an underwater maze.

All these sites help keep the history and secrets of the Great Lakes maritime past alive.

FIRST OUTBOARD MOTOR?

Nels Flodin (Courtesy of Fred Rydholm, from "Superior Heartland")

Boating magazines and history books give conflicting reports on the inventor of the first outboard motor. One consistent element running through all of the stories and reports is the absence of Nels Flodin's name.

Flodin was born in Sweden in 1862, and emigrated to the U.S. in 1883. He worked in the building industry in Duluth, Minnesota until 1892 when he moved to Marquette and signed on as foreman at the Lake Shore Engine Works company.

There was a report in *The Mining Journal* that referred to Lake Shore Engine Works as the birthplace of the world's first gas-driven outboard motor. The Marquette County website features Flodin in its timeline, noting that he invented the outboard motor in Marquette in 1896.

Flodin had a background as a pattern maker and has been cited for upgrading an underground shovel system used in the mining industry. If he indeed was the first to invent an outboard motor powered by gas, he did not apply for a patent or record the feat in any official manner.

Historians credit another Swede with the invention. Ole Evinrude received a patent in 1907 for an outboard motor, and in 1909 he built ten of them by hand and sold all of them. Evinrude is credited with building the first commercially successful outboard motor.

In 1957, *Yachting Magazine* reported that the American Motor Co. of Long Island, New York built an outboard motor as early as 1896.

Cameron Waterman has been credited with building the first outboard, but the Yale Law School student only adapted his motorcycle engine to power a propeller. Somebody had already patented the idea. Waterman was the first to actually put it together. He is credited with coming up with the name, "outboard motor," which he patented. It is a bit ironic that a fellow named *Waterman* is involved in developing the outboard motor.

The story cited in *The Mining Journal* states Flodin's outboard motor was likely built in 1897 or 1898, with assistance form Carl Blomstrom. This and the Marquette County timeline remain the only written record staking a claim for the birthplace of the outboard motor.

Chapter 10

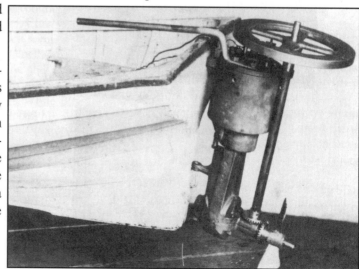

EDUCATION
UPPER MICHIGAN SCHOOLS AND EDUCATION
SCHOOL ENROLLMENT (2005)

School	Students	District	County
Munising High School	345	Munising Public	Alger
William G. Mather School (5-8)	148	Munising Public	Alger
Central Elementary (K-4)	383	Munising Public	Alger
Munising SDA School (2-10)	*14*		*Alger*
Superior Central School (K-12)	376	Superior Central Schools	Alger
Arvon Township School (K-3)	12	Arvon Twp	Baraga
Baraga Area High School	305	Baraga Area Schools	Baraga
Philip Latendresse School (K-6)	152	Baraga Area Schools	Baraga
Pelkie Elementary School	113	Baraga Area Schools	Baraga
L'Anse High School	239	L'Anse Area Schools	Baraga
L'Anse Middle School	224	L'Anse Area Schools	Baraga
Sullivan Elementary	358	L'Anse Area Schools	Baraga
Brimley Elementary School	234	Brimley Area Schools	Chippewa
Brimley Jr./Sr. High	242	Brimley Area Schools	Chippewa

Photo Courtesy B. Polkinghorne

Photo Courtesy R. Gauthier

School	Enrollment	District	County
DeTour High School	106	DeTour Area Schools	Chippewa
DeTour Elementary School	68	DeTour Area Schools	Chippewa
Pickford High School (9-12)	135	Pickford Public	Chippewa
Pickford Elementary (K-12)	288	Pickford Public	Chippewa
Rudyard High School	336	Rudyard Area Schools	Chippewa
Rudyard Middle School	265	Rudyard Area Schools	Chippewa
Turner-Howson Elementary	224	Rudyard Area Schools	Chippewa
R.J. Wallis Elementary	208	Rudyard Area Schools	Chippewa
Sault Area High School	978	Sault Ste. Marie Area Schools	Chippewa
Alternative High School	99	Sault Ste. Marie Area Schools	Chippewa
Sault Area Middle School	670	Sault Ste. Marie Area Schools	Chippewa
Lincoln School (K-5)	488	Sault Ste. Marie Area Schools	Chippewa
Soo Township School (K-5)	281	Sault Ste. Marie Area Schools	Chippewa
Bruce Township School (K-5)	132	Sault Ste. Marie Area Schools	Chippewa
Washington Elementary (3-5)	282	Sault Ste. Marie Area Schools	Chippewa
Bahweting Anishnabe PSA	431	Bahweting Anishnabe	Chippewa
Whitefish Township School	64	Whitefish Twp. Schools	Chippewa
Big Bay De Noc School	286	Big Bay De Noc	Delta
Powell Township Elementary	57	Powell Township	Delta
Escanaba Area Public High School	1,116	Escanaba Area Public	Delta
Escanaba Junior High School	518	Escanaba Area Public	Delta
John Lemmer School	411	Escanaba Area Public	Delta
Soo Hill School	398	Escanaba Area Public	Delta
Webster School	335	Escanaba Area Public	Delta
Franklin Elementary School	195	Escanaba Area Public	Delta
Holy Name School (Pre-8)	*325*		*Delta*
Escanaba SDA School	*10*		*Delta*
Bay De Noc Christian School (K-8)	*7*		*Delta*
Gladstone Area High School	563	Gladstone Area Schools	Delta
Gladstone Area Middle School	366	Gladstone Area Schools	Delta
Cameron Elementary School	418	Gladstone Area Schools	Delta
James T. Jones Elementary	370	Gladstone Area Schools	Delta
Mid Peninsula School (K-12)	287	Mid Peninsula Sch. Dist.	Delta
Tri-Township School (K-12)	452	Rapid River Schools	Delta
Kingsford High School	677	Breitung Township	Dickinson
Woodland Elementary	775	Breitung Township	Dickinson
Kingsford Middle School	503	Breitung Township	Dickinson
Iron Mountain High School	440	Iron Mt. Schools	Dickinson
Central Middle School	332	Iron Mt. Schools	Dickinson
Central Elementary	204	Iron Mt. Schools	Dickinson
East Elementary	157	Iron Mt. Schools	Dickinson

Photo Courtesy S. (Stewart) Gronvall

North Elementary	177	Iron Mt. Schools	Dickinson
Dickinson Area Catholic (Pre-8)	*192*		*Dickinson*
Pine Mountain Christian (K-8)	*30*		*Dickinson*
North Dickinson School (K-12)	391	N. Dickinson County	Dickinson
Norway-Vulcan School (K-12)	894	Norway-Vulcan Schools	Dickinson
A.D. Johnston Jr./Sr. High	253	Bessemer Area	Gogebic
Washington School (Pre-6)	191	Bessemer Area	Gogebic
St. Sebastian School (Pre-8)	67	Private	Gogebic
Luther L. Wright High School	666	Ironwood Area Schools	Gogebic
Norrie Elementary School	198	Ironwood Area Schools	Gogebic
Sleight Elementary School	266	Ironwood Area Schools	Gogebic
Our Lady of Peace Catholic GRA	92		Gogebic
Wakefield School (Pre-12)	333	Wakefield School Dist.	Gogebic
Chassell K-12 School	314	Chassell Township	Houghton
Jeffers High School	212	Adams Twp	Houghton
South Range Elementary	238	Adams Twp	Houghton
Calumet High School	521	*CLK Public Schools	Houghton
C.L.K. Elementary School	692	*CLK Public Schools	Houghton
Washington Middle School	371	*CLK Public Schools	Houghton
Copper Country Christian School	*76*		*Houghton*
* - Calumet-Laurium-Keweenaw Public Schools			
Dollar Bay High School	134	Dollar Bay-Tamarack City Area Schools	Houghton
T.R. Davis Elementary School	153	Dollar Bay-Tamarack City Area Schools	Houghton
Elm River Township School (K, 2-6)	13	Elm River Township	Houghton
Hancock Central High School	343	Hancock Public	Houghton
Hancock Middle School	215	Hancock Public	Houghton
Hancock Elementary School	414	Hancock Public	Houghton
Houghton Central High School	506	Houghton-Portage Township Schools	Houghton
Houghton Middle Schools	286	Houghton-Portage Township Schools	Houghton
Houghton Elementary School	475	Houghton-Portage Township Schools	Houghton

Lake Linden-Hubbell High (7-12)	267	Lake Linden-Hubbell	Houghton
Lake Linden-Hubbell Elementary	291	Lake Linden-Hubbell	Houghton
E. B. Holman Elementary	139	Stanton Twp. Public Sch.	Houghton
Forest Park School	597	Forest Park Schools	Iron
West Iron County High School	416	West Iron County Public Schools	Iron
Stambaugh Elementary	384	West Iron County Public Schools	Iron
West Iron County Middle School	340	West Iron County Public Schools	Iron
Developmental Kindergarten	32	West Iron County Public Schools	Iron
Iron River Christian Academy	*18*		*Iron*
Grant Township School (K, 3-4)	3	Grant Township	Keweenaw
Newberry High School (9-12)	358	Tahquamenon Area Sch.	Luce
Newberry Middle School (6-8)	267	Tahquamenon Area Sch.	Luce
Newberry Elementary	376	Tahquamenon Area Sch.	Luce
Curtis Elementary	107	Tahquamenon Area Sch.	Luce
Bois Blanc Pines School	2	Bois Blanc Pines	Mackinac
Engadine Elementary School	136	Engadine Consolidated	Mackinac
Engadine High School	140	Engadine Consolidated	Mackinac
Cedarville High School	148	Les Cheneaux Community Schools	Mackinac
Cedarville Middle School	108	Les Cheneaux Community Schools	Mackinac
Cedarville Elementary School	161	Les Cheneaux Community Schools	Mackinac
Mackinac Island School (K-12)	70	Mackinac Island Public Schools	Mackinac
LaSalle High School	302	St. Ignace Area Sch.	Mackinac
St. Ignace Middle School (5-8)	252	St. Ignace Area Sch.	Mackinac
St. Ignace Elementary (K-4)	255	St. Ignace Area Sch.	Mackinac
Gros Cap School (K-8)	92	Moran Twp. Schools	Mackinac
Gwinn High School	436	Gwinn Area Community Schools	Marquette
K.I. Sawyer Elementary	471	Gwinn Area Community Schools	Marquette
George D. Gilbert Elementary	313	Gwinn Area Community Schools	Marquette
Gwinn Middle School	237	Gwinn Area Community Schools	Marquette
Ventura Head Start	64	Gwinn Area Community Schools	Marquette
Ishpeming High School	383	Ishpeming Public School District	Marquette
C.L. Phelps School (K-8)	293	Ishpeming Public School District	Marquette

Birchview School (K-4)	271	Ishpeming Public School District	Marquette
Central School (1-4)	109	Ishpeming Public School District	Marquette
North Star Academy (7-12)	55	North Star Academy	Marquette
Westwood High School	397	N.I.C.E. Community Schools	Marquette
Aspen Ridge Elementary (Pre-12)	610	N.I.C.E. Community Schools	Marquette
Aspen Ridge Middle School (6-8)	286	N.I.C.E. Community Schools	Marquette
Marquette Sr. High School	1,311	Marquette Area Public	Marquette
Bothwell Middle School	767	Marquette Area Public	Marquette
Graveraet Intermediate (4-5)	438	Marquette Area Public	Marquette
Cherry Creek Elementary	321	Marquette Area Public	Marquette
Sandy Knoll School (K-3)	257	Marquette Area Public	Marquette
Superior Hills Elementary (K-3)	231	Marquette Area Public	Marquette
Vandenboom Elementary (K-3)	168	Marquette Area Public	Marquette
Father Marquette Catholic (Pre-8)	*365*		*Marquette*
Father Marquette Middle (5-8)	*125*		*Marquette*
Negaunee High School (9-12)	502	Negaunee Public	Marquette
Negaunee Middle School (6-8)	357	Negaunee Public	Marquette
Lakeview School (Pre-5)	644	Negaunee Public	Marquette
Powell Township Elementary (K-8)	57	Powell Township	Marquette
Republic-Michigamme School (Pr-12)	156	Republic-Michigamme	Marquette
Bark River-Harris Elementary	374	Bark River-Harris	Menominee
Bark River-Harris Jr./Sr. High	292	Bark River-Harris	Menominee
Carney-Nadeau School (K-12)	256	Carney-Nadeau	Menominee
Menominee High School (9-12)	641	Menominee Area Pub.	Menominee
Menominee Middle School (6-8)	278	Menominee Area Pub.	Menominee
Central Elementary School	328	Menominee Area Pub.	Menominee
Lincoln Elementary School	268	Menominee Area Pub.	Menominee
Blesch Intermediate School (4-6)	418	Menominee Area Pub.	Menominee
Menominee Community Ed. (9-12)	34	Menominee Area Pub.	Menominee
Menominee Catholic Central (K-8)	*168*		*Menominee*
North Central Elementary	230	North Central Area Schools	Menominee

School	Students	District	County
North Central Area Jr./Sr. (7-12)	282	North Central Area Schools	Menominee
Stephenson High School (K-12)	428	Stephenson Area Pub.	Menominee
Daggett Elementary School (K-3)	101	Stephenson Area Pub.	Menominee
Stephenson Elementary (4-6)	248	Stephenson Area Pub.	Menominee
Mellen Elementary School (K-2)	115	Stephenson Area Pub.	Menominee
Ewen-Trout Creek Cons. (K-12)	337	Ewen-Trout Creek Consolidated	Ontonagon
Ontonagon Area Jr./Sr. High (7-12)	298	Ontonagon Area Sch.	Ontonagon
Ontonagon Area Elementary (Pre-6)	287	Ontonagon Area Sch.	Ontonagon
Superior School of Opportunity (9-12)	17	Ontonagon Area Sch.	Ontonagon
Manistique Middle and High (6-12)	662	Manistique Area Sch.	Schoolcraft
Lakeside School (K-5)	166	Manistique Area Sch.	Schoolcraft
Lincoln School (K-5)	178	Manistique Area Sch.	Schoolcraft
Fairview School (K-5)	105	Manistique Area Sch.	Schoolcraft
Manistique Alternative Ed. (9-12)	21	Manistique Area Sch.	Schoolcraft
St. Francis DeSales School (K-8)	*121*		*Schoolcraft*
Bethel Baptist Christian (1-11)	*12*		*Schoolcraft*

Italics: Private school   Source: Standard & Poor's School Matters

LARGEST SCHOOLS IN THE U.P. (STUDENT POPULATION)

School	Students	District	County
Marquette Sr. High School	1,311	Marquette Area Public	Marquette
Escanaba Area Public High School	1,116	Escanaba Area Public	Delta
Sault Area High School	978	Sault Ste. Marie Area Schools	Chippewa
Norway-Vulcan School (K-12)	894	Norway-Vulcan Schools	Dickinson
Woodland Elementary	775	Breitung Township	Dickinson
Bothwell Middle School	767	Marquette Area Public	Marquette
C.L.K. Elementary School	692	*CLK Public Schools	Houghton
Kingsford High School	677	Breitung Township	Dickinson
Sault Area Middle School	670	Sault Ste. Marie Area Schools	Chippewa
Luther L. Wright High School	666	Ironwood Area Schools	Gogebic

OPERATING DOLLARS AND STUDENTS PER TEACHER 2006

Adams Township Schools – Houghton County

Students	Students per Teacher	Operating $ per student	Instructional $ per student	Instruction $ % of operating $
450	14.6	7,542	4,228	65

Arvon Township School District

Students	Students per Teacher	Operating $ per student	Instructional $ per student	Instruction $ % of operating $

Baraga Area Schools - Baraga

Students	Students per Teacher	Operating $ per student	Instructional $ per student	Instruction $ % of operating $
570	16	9,085	4,747	64.6

Bark River Harris Schools – Delta County

Students	Students per Teacher	Operating $ per student	Instructional $ per student	Instruction $ % of operating $
666	17	7,436	4,746	72.8

Big Bay De Noc School District – Delta County

Students	Students per Teacher	Operating $ per student	Instructional $ per student	Instruction $ % of operating $
286	15.9	9,352	4,803	64.5

Bois Blanc Pines Schools – Mackinac County

Students	Students per Teacher	Operating $ per student	Instructional $ per student	Instruction $ % of operating $
2	2	n/a	n/a	n/a

Bessemer Area School District – Gogebic County

Students	Students per Teacher	Operating $ per student	Instructional $ per student	Instruction $ % of operating $
444	12.5	7,701	5,041	76.2

Breitung Township Schools – Dickinson

Students	Students per Teacher	Operating $ per student	Instructional $ per student	Instruction $ % of operating $
1,955	18.4	7,620	4,595	70.5

Brimley Area Schools – Chippewa County

Students	Students per Teacher	Operating $ per student	Instructional $ per student	Instruction $ % of operating $
476	12.5	10,835	6,434	69.9%

Calumet-Laurium-Keweenaw Public Schools – Houghton County

Students	Students per Teacher	Operating $ per student	Instructional $ per student	Instruction $ % of operating $
1,584	17.6	7,727	4,416	68

Carney-Nadeau Public Schools – Menominee County

Students	Students per Teacher	Operating $ per student	Instructional $ per student	Instruction $ % of operating $
256	14.4	8,287	4,669	76

Chassell Township Schools – Houghton County

Students	Students per Teacher	Operating $ per student	Instructional $ per student	Instruction $ % of operating $
314	15.8	7,867	4,367	68

Detour Area Schools – Chippewa County

Students	Students per Teacher	Operating $ per student	Instructional $ per student	Instruction $ % of operating $
219	12.7	9,732	4,937	63.3%

Dollar Bay-Tamarack City Area Schools – Houghton County

Students	Students per Teacher	Operating $ per student	Instructional $ per student	Instruction $ % of operating $
287	15.8	7,629	4,465	74.6

Elm River Township School District – Houghton

Students	Students per Teacher	Operating $ per student	Instructional $ per student	Instruction $ % of operating $
13	7.6	n/a	n/a	n/a

Engadine Schools – Mackinac County

Students	Students per Teacher	Operating $ per student	Instructional $ per student	Instruction $ % of operating $
276	14.9	9,507	5,037	67%

Escanaba Area Public Schools – Delta County

Students	Students per Teacher	Operating $ per student	Instructional $ per student	Instruction $ % of operating $
2,973	20.2	7,808	4,656	68.3

Ewen-Trout Creek Consolidated Schools – Ontonagon County

Students	Students per Teacher	Operating $ per student	Instructional $ per student	Instruction $ % of operating $
337	12.6	9,642	5,681	68.2

Forest Park School District – Iron County

Students	Students per Teacher	Operating $ per student	Instructional $ per student	Instruction $ % of operating $
597	16.2	7,982	4,938	74

Gladstone Area Schools – Delta County

Students	Students per Teacher	Operating $ per student	Instructional $ per student	Instruction $ % of operating $
1,717	18	7,067	4,424	70.3

Grant Township Schools District #2 – Keweenaw County

Students	Students per Teacher	Operating $ per student	Instructional $ per student	Instruction $ % of operating $
3	1	n/a	n/a	n/a

Gwinn Area Community Schools – Marquette County

Students	Students per Teacher	Operating $ per student	Instructional $ per student	Instruction $ % of operating $
1,521	15.8	7,867	4,400	66

Hancock Public Schools – Houghton County

Students	Students per Teacher	Operating $ per student	Instructional $ per student	Instruction $ % of operating $
972	17.5	7,945	4,927	72.1

Houghton-Portage Township Schools – Hougton County

Students	Students per Teacher	Operating $ per student	Instructional $ per student	Instruction $ % of operating $
1,267	17.9	7,375	4,403	70.5

Iron Mountain Public Schools – Dickinson County

Students	Students per Teacher	Operating $ per student	Instructional $ per student	Instruction $ % of operating $
1,410	16.2	6,618	4,074	72.1

Ironwood Area Schools – Gogebic County

Students	Students per Teacher	Operating $ per student	Instructional $ per student	Instruction $ % of operating $
1,184	17.7	7,913	4,851	72.6

Ishpeming Public Schools – Marquette County

Students	Students per Teacher	Operating $ per student	Instructional $ per student	Instruction $ % of operating $
980	15.4	8,634	5,026	70

N.I.C.E Community Schools – Marquette County

Students	Students per Teacher	Operating $ per student	Instructional $ per student	Instruction $ % of operating $
1,322	16.3	7,573	4,476	68.9

L'Anse Area Schools – Baraga County

Students	Students per Teacher	Operating $ per student	Instructional $ per student	Instruction $ % of operating $
821	16.5	7,999	4,951	70.9

Lake Linden-Hubbell School District – Houghton County

Students	Students per Teacher	Operating $ per student	Instructional $ per student	Instruction $ % of operating $
558	16.5	7,455	4,066	65.3

Les Cheneaux Schools

Students	Students per Teacher	Operating $ per student	Instructional $ per student	Instruction $ % of operating $
417	15.4	8,782	4.654	63%

Mackinac Island Public Schools – Mackinac County

Students	Students per Teacher	Operating $ per student	Instructional $ per student	Instruction $ % of operating $
70	8.8	n/a	n/a	n/a

Manistique Area Schools – Schoolcraft County

Students	Students per Teacher	Operating $ per student	Instructional $ per student	Instruction $ % of operating $
1,132	17.3	9,548	4,318	64.1

Bird's eye view of Ishpeming High School

Photo by S. Willey

Marquette Area School District – Marquette County

Students	Students per Teacher	Operating $ per student	Instructional $ per student	Instruction $ % of operating $
3,572	18.2	7,429	4,338	68.5

Menominee Area Public Schools – Menominee County

Students	Students per Teacher	Operating $ per student	Instructional $ per student	Instruction $ % of operating $
1,967	17.6	7,281	4,405	70.2

Mid Peninsula School District – Delta County

Students	Students per Teacher	Operating $ per student	Instructional $ per student	Instruction $ % of operating $
287	14.4	8,129	4,861	69.4

Moran Twp Schools - Mackinac County (2004)

Students	Students per Teacher	Operating $ per student	Instructional $ per student	Instruction $ % of operating $
92	13.1	9,914	5,895	72%

Munisng Public Schools – Alger County

Students	Students per Teacher	Operating $ per student	Instructional $ per student	Instruction $ % of operating $
876	13.6	7,722	4,246	65

Negaunee Public Schools – Marquette County

Students	Students per Teacher	Operating $ per student	Instructional $ per student	Instruction $ % of operating $
1,503	18	7,717	4,777	69.6

North Central Area Schools – Menominee County

Students	Students per Teacher	Operating $ per student	Instructional $ per student	Instruction $ % of operating $
230	35.4	n/a	n/a	n/a

North Dickinson County Schools – Dickinson County

Students	Students per Teacher	Operating $ per student	Instructional $ per student	Instruction $ % of operating $
391	16.9	7,610	4,123	66.6

Norway-Vulcan Area Schools – Dickinson County

Students	Students per Teacher	Operating $ per student	Instructional $ per student	Instruction $ % of operating $
894	17	7,423	4,841	76.3

Ontonagon Area Schools – Ontonagon County

Students	Students per Teacher	Operating $ per student	Instructional $ per student	Instruction $ % of operating $
602	14.2	8,602	4,967	69

Pickford Public Schools - Chippewa County

Students	Students per Teacher	Operating $ per student	Instructional $ per student	Instruction $ % of operating $
533	20.5	7,069	4,073	71.1%

Powell Township Schools – Marquette County

Students	Students per Teacher	Operating $ per student	Instructional $ per student	Instruction $ % of operating $
57	9.5	14,018	8,357	72.9

Rapid River Public Schools – Delta County

Students	Students per Teacher	Operating $ per student	Instructional $ per student	Instruction $ % of operating $
452	18.3	8,144	4,552	66.4

Republic-Michigamme Schools – Marquette County

Students	Students per Teacher	Operating $ per student	Instructional $ per student	Instruction $ % of operating $
156	12.8	10,137	5,607	66.6

Rudyard Area Schools - Chippewa

Students	Students per Teacher	Operating $ per student	Instructional $ per student	Instruction $ % of operating $
1,033	14.8	8,723	4,851	67%

Sault Ste. Marie Schools – Chippewa County

Students	Students per Teacher	Operating $ per student	Instructional $ per student	Instruction $ % of operating $
2,930	17.6	8,662	4,942	65.5

Stanton Township Public Schools – Houghton County

Students	Students per Teacher	Operating $ per student	Instructional $ per student	Instruction $ % of operating $
139	15.3	8,570	4,831	71.4

St. Ignace Schools – Mackinac County

Students	Students per Teacher	Operating $ per student	Instructional $ per student	Instruction $ % of operating $
827	16.8	8,746	5,021	67.6

Stephenson Area Public Schools – Menominee County

Students	Students per Teacher	Operating $ per student	Instructional $ per student	Instruction $ % of operating $
892	17.7	7,775	4,570	68.5

Superior Central Schools – Alger County

Students	Students per Teacher	Operating $ per student	Instructional $ per student	Instruction $ % of operating $
376	16.1	8,054	4,848	71

Tahquamenon Area Schools – Luce County

Students	Students per Teacher	Operating $ per student	Instructional $ per student	Instruction $ % of operating $
1,108	15.9	8,192	5,065	73.8

Wakefield School District – Gogebic County

Students	Students per Teacher	Operating $ per student	Instructional $ per student	Instruction $ % of operating $
333	14.5	9,517	5,608	66.9

West Iron County Schools – Iron

Students	Students per Teacher	Operating $ per student	Instructional $ per student	Instruction $ % of operating $
1,186	16.6	8,715	5,348	70.9

Whitefish Township Schools – Chippewa County

Students	Students per Teacher	Operating $ per student	Instructional $ per student	Instruction $ % of operating $
64	10.7	n/a	n/a	n/a

Escanaba Area Public Schools – Delta County

Students	Students per Teacher	Operating $ per student	Instructional $ per student	Instruction $ % of operating $
2,973	20.2	7,808	4,656	68.3

ONE ROOM SCHOOL-HOUSE

The Elm River Township School is one of the last surviving one-room school-houses in Michigan. In 2006, students, teachers and alumni celebrated the school's Cen-

tennial. When the school opened in 1906, the town of Winona was a busy mining and lumber town. The Winona School, as it was known, accommodated 300 students at its peak and provided living quarters for the superintendent. Today there is one teacher and an average of 15 students in the K-6 school located in Toivola, about 30 miles south of Houghton.

Educational attainment (2000), by county

People 25 years or older

County	with high school degree or higher (%)	with bachelor's degree or higher (%)
Alger	81.5	14.7
Baraga	80.6	10.9
Chippewa	82.4	15.0
Delta	86.1	17.1
Dickinson	**88.8**	16.7
Gogebic	85.5	15.8
Houghton	84.6	23.0
Iron	84.8	13.7
Keweenaw	83.7	19.1
Luce	75.5	11.8
Mackinac	82.5	14.9
Marquette	88.5	**23.7**
Menominee	83.5	11.0
Ontonagon	83.8	13.0
Schoolcraft	79.4	11.3

GLENN T. SEABORG – ISHPEMING'S NOBEL LAUREATE

This Ishpeming native lived in poverty for much of his youth but went on to win a Nobel Prize and became the first living person ever to have an element named after him.

Seaborg was born on April 19, 1912 in Ishpeming, where he attended elementary school. Teachers remember him as an average student. When he was ten, his family moved to California. His parents struggled to put food on the table, while young Glenn dreamed of someday attending college. He wanted to study literature and become a writer. The family had no hopes of paying for a college education, but in California there was no tuition for residents who could win acceptance at a State university. Part of the admissions criteria was a passing grade in high school science.

In 11th grade, Seaborg enrolled in a chemistry class that changed his life. His teacher tapped into the young Seaborg's imagination and encouraged his natural scientific abilities. Seaborg was admitted to UCLA, where he studied physics and in 1934 earned a degree in chemistry. In 1937, he earned a Ph.D from the University of California – Berkeley.

On February 23, 1941, Seaborg and his team of researchers at Berkeley discovered element 94, which he called plutonium, after the planet Pluto. During his years of research at Berkeley and the University of Chicago he is credited with discovering ten transuranium elements, those man-made elements beyond uranium (element 92)—the heaviest naturally occurring element.

In 1951, he shared the Nobel Prize in chemistry with colleague Edwin McMillan for "their discoveries in the chemistry of the transuranium elements." In 1994, he became the only living person to have an element named after him. Although Seaborg did not discover element 106, it was named seaborgium (Sg) in his honor.

In 1998, he returned to the Upper Peninsula for the groundbreaking of the Seaborg Science Complex at Northern Michigan University in Marquette. The campus is also home to the Glenn T. Seaborg Center for Teaching and Learning Science and Mathematics. He counted the naming of these learning centers among his highest honors, right up there with the Nobel Prize and the naming of seaborgium.

Glenn T. Seaborg
Ishpeming's Nobel Laureate

Seaborg is featured in the "Legends of the Upper Peninsula" exhibit in the U.P. Heritage Center inside the Superior Dome.

Although Seaborg's academic path swerved from writing to science he did manage to write numerous books and more than 500 scientific articles. He has been awarded 50 honorary doctoral degrees, and holds more than 40 patents.

Seaborg passed away February 25, 1999 at his California home.

COLLEGES AND UNIVERSITIES: ENROLLMENT

College/University	Location	Student enrollment
Northern Mich. University	Marquette	9400+
Michigan Technological Univ.	Houghton	6,500+
*Bay De Noc Community	Escanaba	4,723
Lake Superior State Univ.	Sault Ste. Marie	3,392
*Gogebic Community	Ironwood	1400+
Finlandia College	Hancock	550
*Bay Mills Community College	Brimley	500
*Ojibwa Community College	Baraga	

* - 2 year community college

COMMUNITY COLLEGES

Bay College Founded: 1963

Bay de Noc Community College - Escanaba

Campus: 160 acres in Escanaba (Delta County)

Although a two-year community college, Bay College partners with universities including Ferris and Lake Superior State, to offer four-year and master degree programs on its Escanaba campus. With relatively low tuition and on-campus housing, the college provides a viable option for newly graduated local high school students.

The average age of a Bay College student is 26, with the median age listed as 23 years old, an indication that older students utilize Bay College to update their career skills. Typically, Bay College serves over five-thousand credit students each year.

Bay College maintains a West Campus in Iron Mountain on 25 acres donated by Dr. Theodore and Eleanor Forntti. The new $12 million facility, funded by the State of Michigan and citizens of Dickinson County, opened in the fall of 2007 with 535 students enrolled.

Bay College is also the home of the first Michigan Technical Education Center (M-TEC), which provides technical skill training for working adults across the U.P.

Bay College hosts more than 40,000 visitors each year for conferences and meetings.

Gogebic Community College – Ironwood founded: 1932

Campus: 260 acres in Ironwood (Gogebic County). The former Ironwood Community College opened to 188 students in 1932 on the third floor of the L.L. Wright High School. Tuition that first year was $25.00 per semester. (Current rate is $74.00 per semester hour.) The first graduating class in 1934 produced 74 students. In 1938 the name was changed to Gogebic Junior College, reflecting the financial support of the county. In 1953, the name was changed in accordance with state law to Gogebic Community College. In 1965, the college officially separated from the Ironwood School System, becoming its own entity as a Gogebic County college district. Gogebic Community College offers on-campus housing. Its academic programs are designed to serve students who intend to pursue a four-year degree, and those who intend to enter the labor force upon graduation from G.C.C. Today the school serves about 1,400 students per year.

Campus facilities include the Rutger Erickson Liberal Arts Center, the Carl Kleimola Technical Center, the Jacob Solin Center for Business Education and Computer Science, and the Daid G. Lindquist Student Center.

Bay Mills Community College – Brimley Founded: 1981

In 1981 the U.S. Department of Education funded vocational programs that attracted eleven students to the classrooms on the reservation of the Bay Mills Indian Community (BMIC). In 1984 the school was officially chartered by the BMIC, and today attracts over 400 students to its campus and online classes.

Bay Mills Community College is the only fully accredited Tribal College in Michigan. The academic program is designed to serve Native Americans, who make up 60% of the student body, but it is open to all interested students.

The school has an updated technological center which allows it to offer classes around the world, via the Internet.

With a philosophy of making quality education widely available for low-income and minority students, the college became an authorized charter school institution in 2000. Since then 30 schools have been chartered by the college, providing education for over 7,400 students, 53% of which are minority and 47% of which are low-income. The tribe operates the Ojibwe Charter School on the Bay Mills Reservation.

UNIVERSITIES

Lake Superior State University

Sault Ste. Marie   Founded: 1946

Campus: 115 acres

Enrollment: approximately 3,000 students

Faculty: 111 full-time

In 1946 the Michigan College of Mining and Technology (Michigan Tech) opened a branch in Sault Ste. Marie to serve students in the eastern U.P. These students could take class and earn credits, but had to move to Houghton to complete the four year programs. The school expanded its offerings and by 1967 was offering four-year degrees. During the 1960s, it was known as Lake Superior State College of Michigan Technological University. It became independent in 1970 with the name changing to Lake Superior State University (LSSU).

LSSU is situated on the site of the U.S. Army's former Fort Brady. Many of the dorms are in former army barracks, and several campus buildings are noted in architectural and historic registers. From its hilltop setting students can see the International Bridge, the Soo Locks, the St. Marys River and the city of Sault Ste. Marie.

LSSU offers undergraduate degrees in 45 areas of study. Michigan students make up 68% of the student population, and come from every county in the state. Seventeen percent of students are from other states, and 15% come from Ontario.

Lake State was the first college in the U.S. to offer a four-year degree in Fire Science. The school's List of Banished Words receives international news attention every New Year's Day. (see *The Unicorn Hunters* page 412)

Michigan Technological University

Houghton - Founded: 1885

Campus: 925 acres-Main campus, 4,000 acres-Ford Forestry Center

Enrollment: 6,500+

Faculty: 437 (2007)

Michigan Technological University (Michigan Tech or MTU) is recognized as one of the top four research universities in Michigan, and was ranked number 124 in *U.S. News & World Report* America's Best Colleges report in February 2008.

MTU was established in 1861 by the State of Michigan, however due to the Civil War it did not open until 1885. The state saw the necessity to

address the growing mining industry and the need for better trained engineers and workers. In 1886, the institution opened under the name Michigan Mining School, opened in the Houghton Fire Hall to 23 students and four instructors. By the 1890s, it was the largest mining school in the United States.

With the growth of the school the name changed to the Michigan College of Mines and in the early 20th Century, to the Michigan College of Mining and Technology. Through its hallways passed some of the most talented mining engineers of that century.

As the mining industry faded in the 1920s, the school began offering new programs such as chemical, civil and mechanical engineering and degree programs in forestry management. In the 1940s an eastern branch was opened in Sault Ste. Marie at what is now Lake Superior State University. The school also obtained the 4,000 acre forest and sawmill in Alberta from the Ford Motor Company.

By 1963 enrollment was at 2,700 with only 44 students in the mining program, so the name was changed in 1964 to Michigan Technological University. During the 1960s and 70's, the campus grew with the addition of high-rise buildings for the engineering and chemistry-metallurgy programs, administration, and student services. The upper campus on the hill was created on the south side of the campus. New programs added during this period include bioengineering, computer science, and forest engineering.

Campus additions since the 1980s include the 1,100-seat Rozsa Center for the Performing Arts, the $47-million dollar Minerals and Materials Engineering Building, and the $44-million Dow Environmental Sciences and Engineering Building.

Today Michigan Tech attracts nearly 900 students to its Graduate School, and another 5,600 students are enrolled in four-year programs. Ninety percent of the faculty hold the highest degree in their field.

Northern Michigan University

Marquette Founded: 1899

Campus: 350 acres

Enrollment: 9,400+

Faculty: 300+

Northern Michigan University first opened its doors as a school to train teachers. In 1875 while serving in the state legislature, Peter White proposed funding for a Normal School to serve the U.P. from Marquette. The legislation was not passed until 1899, and the school opened as the Northern State Normal School, also called Marquette Normal. The first class attracted 32 students and six instructors.

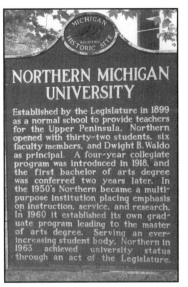

NORTHERN MICHIGAN UNIVERSITY

Established by the Legislature in 1899 as a normal school to provide teachers for the Upper Peninsula. Northern opened with thirty-two students, six faculty members, and Dwight B. Waldo as principal. A four-year collegiate program was introduced in 1918, and the first bachelor of arts degree was conferred two years later. In the 1950's Northern became a multipurpose institution placing emphasis on instruction, service, and research. In 1960 it established its own graduate program leading to the master of arts degree. Serving an ever-increasing student body, Northern in 1963 achieved university status through an act of the Legislature.

The school began offering four-year degrees in 1920, and in 1927 the name changed to Northern State Teachers College. In 1941 the name was changed to the Northern Michigan College of Education to reflect an expanding curriculum.

During the 1950s, the college began offering more programs leading to rapid growth. In 1963, it became Northern Michigan University (NMU).

Today Northern offers 180 degree programs and 80 percent of faculty have doctorates of the highest degree in their fields. The campus includes the Center for Upper Peninsula Studies and Center for Native American Studies, and the Bureau of Business and Economic Research.

There are 52 buildings on campus including the Superior Dome, the world's largest wooden dome. The campus features an award-winning library, university center, two art galleries and the United State Olympic Education Center—one of four Olympic training centers designated to offer academic education.

Newer facilities include the state-of-the-art Seaborg Science Complex and a renovated Thomas Fine Arts and Art and Design buildings.

Finlandia University

Hancock   Founded: 1896

Campus: situated on a few city blocks in the hills overlooking Portage Canal

Enrollment: 550

Faculty: 40+

The only private college in the Upper Peninsula, Finlandia's history dates back to 1896 when the mining industry was attracting a growing population of Finnish immigrants. The Finnish communities developed their own schools, associations and churches including the Finnish Evangelical Church – Suomi Synod. The church was established in 1890 and with a need for more clergy, church leaders established Suomi College in 1896 as a religious training college. It is the only college or university in the U.S. to be founded by Finns.

There were only eleven students in the first classes. Although the college was designed by and for Finns to develop and preserve their religious and cultural heritage, it began to admit non-Finns in the 1920s when it began to offer additional courses outside of its theological training.

The school has gained regional accreditation and now offers four-year degrees in nine academic programs including Art and Design, Nursing, Business Administration, Elementary Education and Rural Human Services.

BANISHED WORDS 1976

*The first-ever **List of Words Banished from the Queen's English for Mis-Use, Over-Use and General Uselessness** from the LSSU Unicorn Hunters:*

At This Point in Time - *Why not say "now," or "today?" Typical Delay-by-Elongation, giving subject at press conference time to think up plausible lie, e.g. "At this point in time we are, err, mmmmm, unaware of the allegation that the earth is round." -Queen Isabella.*

Meaningful - *Has lost all of its meaningfulness.*

Input - *Has unfortunately replaced "contribution." Of-*

Since 1990, the campus has been home to the Finnish American Heritage Center which includes a theatre, art gallery and the Finnish American Historical Archive. The Center has hosted Finland's President Tarja Halonen and former Finnish Prime Minister Paavo Lipponen.

Today Finlandia University is one of 28 colleges and universities in the U.S. affiliated with the Evangelical Lutheran Church. The University has established a Campus Ministry to reflect the school's Lutheran and Christian heritage, and to encourage spiritual growth among students, faculty and staff.

The LSSU Unicorn Hunters

After splitting off from Michigan Tech in 1970, officials with the new Lake Superior State College needed to raise awareness of the school. They turned to former Detroit public relations wiz William (Bill) Rabe. In his role as Director of Public Relations, Rabe not only made fellow Michiganians familiar with the small college in the eastern U.P., he made it as famous as the Rose Bowl.

When Rabe moved north, the eastern U.P. was better known among hunters than college-bound students. As an alternative to the annual deer hunting season Rabe and some of the school's English Professors organized the Unicorn Hunters, created a Unicorn Questing Season and offered Unicorn Questing Licenses. Rabe alerted the press and before long newspaper readers across the state knew about Lake Superior State College in Sault Ste. Marie.

Rabe's shrewd PR skills attracted international recognition to LSSU and created the image of a fun-loving, magical atmosphere for learning. His stunt-oriented style never diminished the academic integrity of the school. One of the first efforts of the Unicorn Hunters was the creation and launching of *The Woods-Runner*, a quarterly literary magazine that put the work of LSSU students in the hands of readers around the world.

For potential students and faculty deterred by thoughts

of a cold, snowy and barren region, Rabe created the annual Snowman Burning held on the first day of spring each year. Since 1971, students, professors, and local residents gather around a snowman made of paper, lumber and other flammables. They recite poems to bid farewell to winter, and then torch the snowman. The event caught the attention of media around the country year after year.

In 1992, the event was cancelled. A campus environmental group objected to the burning, concerned that it released toxins into the atmosphere. The post-Rabe PR office wanted to avoid any negative publicity, so the event was cancelled. But then reporters from news organizations around the country familiar with the event began to call for their annual "First Day of Spring" story. The local business community and even local politicians demanded the Snowman Burning continue. More negative publicity was created by cancelling the event, so it returned the following year and continues today.

The *International Stone Skipping Tournament* held every Fourth of July on Mackinac Island was a creation of the Unicorn Hunters. The widespread media attention generated by the event generally brings more benefit to the island economy than to LSSU.

Rabe's most well-known creation is the annual *List of Words Banished from the Queen's English for Mis-Use, Over-Use and General Uselessness*. The first list of banished words was devised by Rabe and friends at a party in 1975 and released to the news media the following New Year's Day. Rabe figured January 1st was a traditionally slow news day, so it was decided to announce the list then and give the college a better chance at national exposure. The playful list attracted widespread coverage, and people from around the country began to mail their own submissions. After Rabe retired and the Unicorn Hunters disbanded in 1987, the University copyrighted the concept and continues to accept submissions and publishes the list each New Year's Day.

ten used in combination; as "meaningful input."

Scenario - Spread like wildfire after Watergate. It can be roughly translated as "I don't know what had happened (or will happen) but this is a scenario." Means: "I'm making this up." Also used when reporter doesn't want to use "according to unimpeachable source."

Detente - Invented by Henry Kissinger. Nobody else knows what it means, and now even Kissinger has forgotten. [Before the year was out the president of the United States also banished "detente." Later, voters banished Kissinger and the president.]

Dialogue - and its other form Meaningful Dialogue. Neither has meaning remaining in it.

Macho - Seldom pronounced properly and therefore lacks meaningfulness.

Implement and Viable - Gobbledygook disguised as intelligence: as in "that is not a viable alternative which we can implement." Meaning: "We don't want to do it and think you have a crazy idea here."

Call for Resignation - Of all sports reporters who fail to state clearly in the lead: The winner and the score.

LIBRARY COLLECTIONS – BY COUNTY

Library	County	Books	Audio/Video Materials	Operating Income
Munising School-Public	Alger	21,083	742 / 863	$72,715
L'anse School-Public	Baraga	18,759	528 / 354	$128,706
Bayliss Public	Chippewa	123,603	5,341 /8,509	$549,463
Gladstone Area School and Public Library	Delta	31,083	322/ 651	$90,319
Garden City Public	Delta	61,456	2,046 /2,103	$309,297
Escanaba Public	Delta	70,605	1,166 / 453	$501,673
Dickinson County	Dickinson	83,337	2,027 /3,819	$896,298
Wakefield Public	Gogebic	20,457	15 / 271	$53,767
Ironwood Carnegie	Gogebic	28,344	911 /1,160	$142,443
Bessemer Public	Gogebic	16,976	602 / 889	$64,800
Portage Lake District	Houghton	41,195	2,461 / 853	$278,183
Hancock School Public	Houghton	18,359	101 / 202	$80,480
Lake Linden-Hubbell Public School	Houghton	15,020	28 / 112	$91,313
Calumet Public-School	Houghton	28,719	593 / 732	$170,074
Crystal Falls District	Iron	17,423	1,032 / 221	$129,392
West Iron District	Iron	34,863	2,095 / 750	$247,493
Tahquamenon Area	Luce	17,242	156 / 180	$59,888
St. Ignace Public	Mackinac	21,727	572 / 553	$104,170
Mackinac Island Public	Mackinac	10,731	475 / 479	$54,411
Rudyard School-Public	Mackinac	20,533	938 /1,936	$66,087
Ishpeming Carnegie	Marquette	72,545	2,593 / 408	$209,910
Peter White Public	Marquette	124,128	9,658 /4,993	$1,051,954
Forsyth Towhship Public	Marquette	12,000	370 / 322	$90,539
Negaunee Public	Marquette	25,479	155 / 52	$140,184
Richmond Township	Marquette	8,953	31 / 387	$36,069
Republic-Michigamme	Marquette	9,630	60 / 6	$17,024
Spies Public	Menominee	57,235	1,180 /1,421	$368,782
Menominee County	Menominee	58,137	2,000 / 437	$226,985
Ontonagon Township	Ontonagon	37,188	1,270 / 157	$70,220
Manistique School-Public	Schoolcraft	29,105	1,100 / 395	$147,119

L: Spies Public Library, Menominee
R: One-time Carnegie Library now the Carnegie Museum on Huron St. in Houghton

Chapter 11

GOVERNMENT

SUPERIOR: THE 51ST STATE

There have been a few serious, and not-so-serious, attempts to make the Upper Peninsula and adjacent portions of Wisconsin the 51st State.

The concept originally got legs in the late 19th Century when the Upper Peninsula, of Michigan and the northern portion of Wisconsin, from the mouth of the Menominee River west, talked of ceding from their respective states. Both entities felt over-taxed, under funded and appreciated by their home states to the south.

In 1962, five years after the Mackinac Bridge opened connecting Michigan's two Peninsulas, the U. P. Independence Association was formed. It failed in its mission to secede from Michigan to form the new State of Superior.

In the 1970's, legendary Upper Peninsula legislator, Dominic Jacobetti, introduced bills calling for the 15 counties of the U.P. to secede and form Superior, the 51st state. Although popular with many residents of the U.P., the bills failed in the legislature.

From 1983-85, a petition drive to put secession to a vote gathered about 20,000 signatures. That effort fell short by about 16,000 signatures.

A less formal attempt to declare U.P. independence was launched in the 1970s when Mr. Joe Zimmer constructed a billboard outside his mobile home on Highway 28 in Bruce Crossing (Ontonagon County) proclaiming it the "Governor's Mansion" of the 51st State.

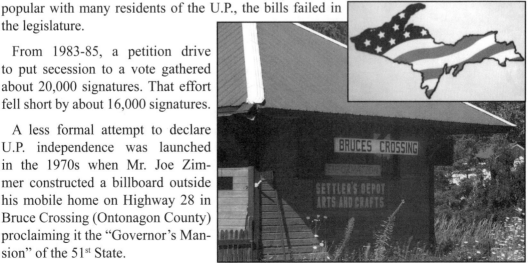

FEDERAL GOVERNMENT SPENDING (2004), BY COUNTY

County	Federal gov't. expenditures ($)	Per capita	Salaries and wages	Retirement and disability payments to individuals ($)
Alger	63,211,000	$6,477	$3,962,000	30,571,000
Baraga	64,815,000	$7,426	$2,311,000	25,444,000
Chippewa	259,401,000	$6,687	$24,826,000	99,896,000
Delta	246,370,000	$6,419	$13,763,000	123,587,000
Dickinson	198,502,000	$7,259	$33,976,000	91,184,000
Gogebic	141,306,000	$8,298	$11,331,000	61,873,000
Houghton	223,554,000	$6,285	$12,560,000	87,053,000
Iron	93,651,000	$7,440	$3,651,000	48,037,000
Keweenaw	14,929,000	$6,774	$412,000	7,701,000
Luce	44,161,000	$6,447	$1,068,000	19,045,000
Mackinac	77,161,000	$6,779	$5,568,000	35,081,000
Marquette	355,954,000	$5,487	$20,458,000	180,408,000
Menominee	132,834,000	$5,277	$4,384,000	67,514,000
Ontonagon	63,395,000	$8,410	$3,598,000	29,423,000
Schoolcraft	65,737,000	$7,408	$3,545,000	30,084,000

NOTABLE POLITICIANS

DOMINIC JACOBETTI

LONGEST SERVING LEGISLATOR IN MICHIGAN

Born: Negaunee, MI July 20, 1920

Died: November 29, 1994

Married: 1942 to Marie Burnette, three children: Judith, Colin and Dominic, Jr.

Office: State Representative for the 108th district 1955-1992

State Representative for the 109th district 1992-1994

Dominic Jacobetti served nearly forty years in the state legislature, longer than any other Michigan lawmaker. With term limits in place that record will probably never be broken.

Jacobetti won twenty elections, often going unchallenged.

Jacobetti was a native of his district. He was born in Negaunee to Italian immigrant parents. He graduated from St. Paul's High School, where he set an Upper Michigan record for most points scored during a high school basketball career. He then went on to play four years at Northern Michigan University.

While attending college, Jacobetti worked at the Athens Mine. He went on to become president of the United

Steel Workers union local. His interest in politics blossomed during the 1940s, eventually leading him to the state legislature.

Jacobetti's legislative career was marked by 18 years as the powerful Chairman of the Appropriations Committee, a position he used to steer dollars not only to his district, but to the entire U.P. Jacobetti used his influence to improve educational and employment opportunities, services for the low-income and elderly, roads and just about anything that would benefit the quality of life in his beloved Upper Peninsula.

Jacobetti's work on behalf of veterans is honored in the hospital that bears his name. He fought to have Michigan's second veterans hospital located in the Upper Peninsula. In 1979, the federal government purchased the former St. Mary's Hospital in Marquette for that purpose. In 1981, it was officially named the Dominic J. Jacobetti Veterans Facility. After that, Jacobetti secured funding to have the center expanded, from 152 beds to over 250 beds, with the addition of an Alzheimer's treatment center for Veterans.

Jacobetti also led the charge to prevent construction of a nuclear waste site in the U.P., and to prevent the U.S. Navy from moving forward with Project ELF, an underground network of extremely low frequency antenna designed to work with submarine communications.

One area Jacobetti did not succeed was in establishing the Upper Peninsula as the 51st State. He introduced secession bills in the 1970s, with the new state to be named Superior, but they failed to win much support in Lansing.

Among his awards and recognitions, he was named as one of the Ten Outstanding State Legislators in the United States in 1978; Upper Peninsula Person of the Year; Distinguished Citizen Award from Lake Superior State University, and an Honorary Doctorate of Law degree from Northern Michigan University.

Jacobetti was known to his friends and colleagues as *Jake*, and sometimes as *The Godfather*.

On November 29, 1994, Jacobetti died shortly after winning re-election to the State House. The following day, Congressman Bart Stupak of Menominee went to the floor of the U.S. House of Representatives to memorialize his political mentor. Among his remarks: "Some joke that the former chairman of the House Appropriations Committee had a heart as big as the State treasury because of Jake's unyielding desire to steer tax dollars to the Upper Peninsula. But, in my mind, that is a downstate view. I believe Jake had a heart as big as the Upper Peninsula--because that is who he worked for. He worked for us. Jake always believed that the powers-that-be in Lansing overlooked the Upper Peninsula, and he was determined to do everything he could to help the people who live in our region of Michigan."

JOE MACK – THE LAST OF A BREED

Born: May 8, 1919

Died: April 20, 1995, Wausau, Wisconsin, cause: heart attack

Office: State Representative 1961-1964

State Senator, 38th district, 1965-1990

Upon his death in 1995, the *Ironwood Daily Globe* said of Joe Mack, "The last true giant of Upper Michigan politics is gone." Mack was a politician who knew how and when to twist arms, and when to cut a deal – whatever it took to bring the bacon home to his beloved Upper Peninsula.

Joseph S. Mack was born May 8, 1919 in Ironwood, the son of a miner, and one of ten children. He graduated from Luther L. Wright High School and went on to study steel fabrication at the Milwaukee Vocational School. During World War II, Mack worked on the Manhattan Project which developed the atom bomb.

After the war, Mack worked as a car salesman, restaurant owner, and local businessman before entering local politics. He was elected to the state house in 1961, serving two terms before winning election to the state senate. Mack would wind up serving 25 years in the state senate, building power and influence which he used to benefit the western U.P.

Mack built up seniority on the influential Appropriations Committee which held the purse strings to the budget. He also sat on the Economic Affairs Committee. Mack and fellow U.P. legislators, Rep. Dominic Jacobetti of Negaunee and Russell Hellman of Dollar Bay were known as the U.P. Mafia for their ability to cut deals in Lansing to benefit their home districts.

He earned a reputation as a strong advocate for the local mining and timber industries and fought to bring home money for new and improved roads. In the process, he also earned a reputation as an anti-environmentalist. He butted heads with conservation groups and environmental activists. Regarding the nature lovers from the Lower Peninsula who wanted to create policy in the U.P., Mack was quoted by the *Ironwood Daily Globe* to have said: "…these kids with beards and backpacks, who bring in one set of underwear and a five dollar bill don't change either one." Bill Ballenger, publisher of Inside Michigan Politics and former State Senator who served with Mack said, "He always wanted to be on the conservation committee so he could kill environmental bills and protect the mining and other commercial interests in his district."

He fought to protect a way of life in the U.P., while also improving the quality of life through economic development. Besides his support for the mining and timber industries, Mack was also instrumental in legislation that led to the growth of Northern Michigan University and Michigan Tech. He supported early efforts in the gaming industry, including a 1988 proposal for a casino near the Gogebic Country Club.

Mack's long and successful legislative career ended on a down note when he was accused of submitting travel vouchers for trips he did not take. He pleaded no contest, agreeing to resign from the Senate, pay a $100 fine, and reimburse the state $6,200 for the alleged false claims. Mack claims his opponents singled him out for political reasons.

He is fondly remembered by colleagues for his colorful sport coats, colorful language, and colorful office with red shag carpeting and mirrored walls. Upon his death the Senate adopted a resolution honoring Mack that stated in part, "Whereas, It is with the utmost sorrow that the members of the Michigan Senate mourn the sudden passing of Joe Mack, an individual who in every way exemplified the heart and soul of the Upper Peninsula. Indeed, as they say in the U.P., Joe Mack had "Sisu." It marked every aspect of his life and will be a lasting testimony to his strength of character. He will be missed;

Mack died after collapsing at an airport in Wausau, Wisconsin while traveling home to Ironwood form Florida.

CHASE OSBORN

THE ONLY GOVERNOR FROM THE UPPER PENINSULA

Born: January 22, 1860, Huntington County, Indiana

Died: April 12, 1949 at Possum Poke, his winter cabin in Poulan, Georgia

Office: 27th Governor of the State of Michigan 1911-1912

Although he served as Governor of Michigan and was named after Salmon P. Chase, a former Governor and U.S. Senator from Ohio, Chase Osborn did not make a career out of politics. Osborn's interests and passions were numerous: he was a successful iron prospector and metallurgist; a journalist and newspaper publisher; the author or co-author of 13 books; and a conservationist, outdoors man and explorer.

Born in Indiana, Osborn attended Purdue University for three years, but did not graduate. His career as a newspaperman began with a reporting job for the Chicago Tribune, and led to jobs with smaller newspapers in Wisconsin. His energy and enthusiasm was enough to gain needed financing to buy his own newspaper in Florence, Wisconsin near the Michigan border. The young newspaperman moved to northern Wisconsin with his new bride, Lillian Jones of Milwaukee, and their first child. Osborn expanded the newspaper into Crystal Falls and other mining towns in Michigan, and began to spend more time studying the geology of the region. During this period of the early 1880s, he developed a lifelong passion for prospecting iron.

He moved permanently to the Upper Peninsula in 1887 when he purchased the Sault Evening News. In his autobiography, *The Iron Hunter*, Osborn said of his first visit to the Soo, "it was to me a passage into paradise. I had never breathed such air nor drunk such water. Pure as nature was the entire Northland."

Much of Osborn's time was filled by exploring and traveling, mostly looking for iron. He discovered the Moose Mountain Iron Range in Canada and other iron deposits in Latin American, Africa, the Orient and Sweden. The discoveries made Osborn a wealthy man but hardly selfish. From the proceeds of the Moose Mountain discovery he insured that his mother and two invalid brothers would be comfortable for life. He gave away much of his fortune to relatives and friends, schools, churches, his adopted hometown of Sault Ste. Marie, and even strangers. Osborn told Time magazine, in 1940, "It just happened that I was a money maker... Why shouldn't I give it away?"

His interest in politics began as he became more involved in the business community of Sault Ste. Marie. He was appointed local postmaster in 1890. His first statewide office was an

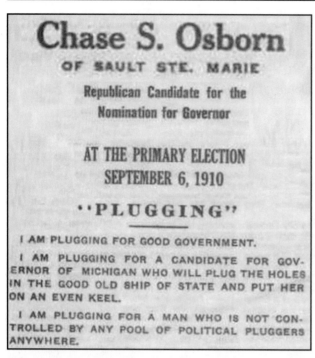

Chase S. Osborn

OF SAULT STE. MARIE

Republican Candidate for the
Nomination for Governor

AT THE PRIMARY ELECTION
SEPTEMBER 6, 1910

"PLUGGING"

I AM PLUGGING FOR GOOD GOVERNMENT.

I AM PLUGGING FOR A CANDIDATE FOR GOVERNOR OF MICHIGAN WHO WILL PLUG THE HOLES IN THE GOOD OLD SHIP OF STATE AND PUT HER ON AN EVEN KEEL.

I AM PLUGGING FOR A MAN WHO IS NOT CONTROLLED BY ANY POOL OF POLITICAL PLUGGERS ANYWHERE.

appointment as the Michigan Game and Fish Warden (1895-1899). He ran an unsuccessful campaign for Congress in 1896.

In 1899 Osborn was appointed Commissioner of Michigan Railroads. He believed strongly that the government should own and operate the rail system, a controversial opinion within the Republican Party. Osborn ran unsuccessfully for governor in 1900. In 1908 he was selected as Chair of the Michigan delegation to the National Republican Party convention, and as a regent for the University of Michigan. Two years later he ran for governor, this time beating Democrat Lawton Hermans, 209,803 – 159,770.

During his one two-year term Osborn turned a half million dollar deficit into a half million dollar surplus by cutting state jobs and offices he deemed unnecessary. He devoted more resources to improving Michigan roads, and signed into law a bill that allowed the state to use prisoner labor on such projects. The first workers compensation bill and bills to protect women and children laborers were promoted and signed by Governor Osborn.

He did not succeed in establishing a State Department of Agriculture, but did help establish a curriculum for teaching agriculture in public schools. His efforts to win voters rights for women failed during his administration, however women's suffrage laws passed in Michigan six years later.

During the Osborn administration the state gained more authority over railroads but never took ownership, a stance Osborn passionately supported, but one that left him in the minority of his party. Some historians believe he could have been a serious Presidential contender were it not for his advocacy of government-owned railroads.

Osborn signed a bill that prohibited distributors of liquor to own saloons, and he eventually advocated prohibition, believing that easy access to alcohol was the primary problem behind the social problems of the country.

True to his word Osborn did not run for a second term. He did run for governor again two years later, but lost the 1914 election to Woodbridge Ferris. Osborn also had unsuccessful campaigns for U.S. Senate in 1918 and 1930.

Out of office he continued his travels, studies of animals, plants and geology, and writing. He maintained political contacts and lobbied them on behalf of his beloved U.P. Osborn was successful in promoting Isle Royale as a national park, but struck out on two other ideas: naming Sugar Island as the home of the newly established United Nations, and gaining support to build a bridge over the Mackinac Straits. The U.N. did not choose the U.P., but Osborn's vision of the bridge did materialize, ten years after his death.

Time Magazine featured Osborn on his 80th birthday. He was described as "blind in one eye and weak in the other, but still a voracious reader." Time reported that Osborn awakened at three o'clock every morning and shaved while standing on one foot to practice poise. The article noted that the former governor was still fighting for Michigan, having won a battle against the U.S. Census Bureau the year before. The Bureau had pegged Michigan as the 22nd largest state based on size, but Osborn successfully argued that Michigan's borders stretched into the Great Lakes thereby increasing its size by nearly 40,000 acres, and boosting it to status of 8th largest state in the nation.

Osborn's marriage to Lillian produced seven children, but the couple eventually grew apart, separating in 1923. The following year, the 71-year old former governor, while conducting research at the University of Michigan, met Stella Lee Brunt, a writer and student 41 years his junior. The two had common interests when it came to travel, politics and writing. Osborn hired Brunt as his secretary and, in 1931, legally adopted her. Brunt later explained that they wanted to marry but could not, as Osborn remained legally married to Lillian. On the day after Lillian Osborn passed away in 1949, Osborn had the adoption to Brunt annulled, and the couple, he 89 and she 48, was legally married. Osborn died two days later at Possum Poke, his summer home in Georgia.

Funeral services were held in Lansing and Sault Ste. Marie. He is buried on Duck Island in the St. Marys River.

CONNIE BINSFELD
LIEUTENANT GOVERNOR

The only U.P. native to serve as Lt. Governor is Connie Binsfeld, born in 1924 in Munising.

Binsfeld was the daughter of Omer and Elsie Beube. He was an electrician and she was a schoolteacher. Binsfeld would eventually became a schoolteacher and marry an electrical engineer.

Binsfeld attended Sacred Heart Catholic Grade School before graduating from Munising High School in 1941. She earned her teaching certificate from Siena Heights College in Adrian. she went on to teach in the Pontiac and Berkley school systems in Oakland County.

In 1947 she married John Binsfeld, an electrical engineer. They produced five children and eventually moved north to Leelanau County.

Binsfeld entered politics in 1970 when she became the first woman elected to the Leelanau County Commission. Four years later she was elected to the State House of Representatives. She became the Republican leader in the House in 1979, but elected to run for the State Senate three years later. Her winning streak continued as she won election to the Senate, serving eight years, including six years as assistant majority leader.

Binsfeld retired from politics to enjoy time with family split between her Leelanau County home and the family home on Lake Superior in Munising. In 1990, she received a call from

John Engler whom she served with in the State Senate. Engler had just won the Republican nomination for governor and was calling to invite Binsfeld to be his running mate.

She accepted, and at age 66 hit the campaign trail. The Engler-Binsfeld ticket was successful, ousting two-term Governor Jim Blanchard. They won again in 1994 her second four-year term, Binsfeld retired again; this time for good.

She is recognized and remembered best for her legislation protecting children. Binsfeld crafted legislation that banned surrogate parenthood for profit in Michigan. She updated and improved legislation affecting adoptions, foster care and child abuse. In 1988, she was elected to the Michigan Women's Hall of Fame.

During her career she sat next to President Ronald Reagan at a White House Dinner and rode on Air Force One with President George H.W. Bush, and met President Clinton in the Oval office of the White House.

Today she splits her time between her lake front home in Leelanau County and her home in Munising where she spent the first 17 years of her distinguished life.

BART STUPAK: 1ST CONGRESSIONAL DISTRICT

Since 1992 Bart Stupak has represented the 1st Congressional District which includes all 15 counties in the Upper Peninsula and 16 counties in northern Lower Michigan.

Prior to his election to the U.S. House of Representatives Stupak served in the state legislature representing Menominee, Delta and Dickinson counties between 1989-90.

Stupak was a leap year baby, born February 29, 1952 in Milwaukee, Wisconsin. He was raised in Delta County and graduated from Gladstone High School. He attended Northwestern Michigan College in Traverse City where he earned an Associate's degree in 1972. He earned a Bachelor's degree in Criminal Justice from Saginaw Valley State University in 1977, and a Juris Doctorate degree from Cooley Law School in Lansing.

Before politics, Stupak worked in law enforcement serving as an Escanaba police officer in 1972, and a Michigan State Trooper from 1973 -1984. He was injured in the line of duty and medically retired in 1984. He worked as an attorney before entering politics as a State representative in 1989.

In Congress, Stupak is a member of the House Energy and Commerce Committee. Within the Committee, he chairs the Oversight and Investigation Subcommittee. He also sits on the Telecommunications and the Internet Subcommittee and the Environment and Hazardous Waste Subcommittee.

He founded and is co-chair of the Congressional Law Enforcement Caucus which includes over 100 house members.

The 1st Congressional district contains more shoreline within the continental U.S. than any other district. Stupak is recognized as a leader on issues affecting the Great Lakes, he has successfully fought against diversion of Great Lakes water, oil and gas drilling under the lakes, and against Coast Guard proposals to hold live-fire training exercises on the Great Lakes.

Stupak lives in Menominee with his wife, Laurie who served as the town's mayor from 1996 – 2003. His son Ken is a graduate of the Pepperdine University School of Law and lives in California. The Stupak's other son, Bart Jr., died in May of 2000.

First Congressional District

With 24,875 square miles, the 1st District is the 2nd largest congressional district east of the Mississippi River. It makes up 44% of the land mass of the entire state of Michigan.

The 1st District has more shoreline than any other district in the continental U.S.

The district includes all 15 of the counties in the Upper Peninsula as well as 15 and-a-half counties in north central and northeastern Lower Michigan.

Largest counties in the 1st Congressional District.
1) Marquette   64,634
2) Chippewa   38,543
3) Delta   38,520
4) Houghton   36,016
5) Emmet   31,433 (LP)
6) Alpena   31,314 (LP)
7) Dickinson   27,472
8) Iosco   27,339 (LP)
9) Cheboygan   26,448 (LP)
10) Charlevoix 26,090 (LP)

(Population numbers from the 2000 U.S. Census)

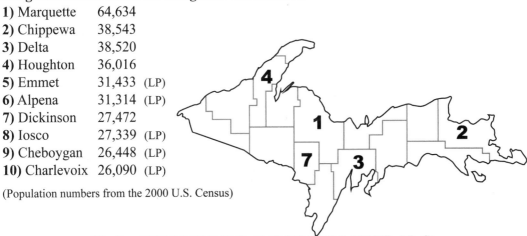

U.S. SENATORS BORN IN THE U.P.

Prentiss Marsh Brown (D) Born: 6/18/1889 in St. Ignace, Mackinac County

Served in the U.S. Senate 1936-43; U.S. Representative (11th District) 1933-36;

Ran unsuccessfully for Michigan State Supreme Court in 1928; prosecuting attorney, Mackinac County, 1914-26; first chairman, Mackinac Bridge Authority 1950 until his death, December 19, 1973. Interred at Lakeside Cemetery, St. Ignace.

Thomas White Ferry (R) Born: 6/10/1827 in Astor Fur Co. mission house on Mackinac Island, Mackinac County

Served in U.S. Senate 1871-83. Grew up in Grand Haven; Michigan House of Representatives, 1850-52; Michigan Senate 1857-58; U.S. Representative (4th District), 1865-71; Died in Grand Haven, 10/13/1896; interred Lake Forest Cemetery, Grand Haven.

U.S. REPRESENTATIVES BORN IN THE U.P.

Frank Eugene Hook (D)   Born: 5/26/1893, L'Anse, Baraga County

U.S. Representative, 12th District, 1935-43 and 1945-47; served in U.S. Army during WW I; started political career on the board of supervisors for Gogebic County, 1921-23; Wakefield city commissioner, 1921-23; municipal judge in Wakefield, 1924-25; died 6/21/82; interred in Fort Snelling National Cemetery.

Alfred Victor Knox (R) Born: 1/13/1899, Sault Ste. Marie, Chippewa County

Served in U.S. House (11th District) 1953-65; Chippewa County supervisor, 1925-31; Michigan State House, 1937-52; Speaker of the Michigan State House, 1947-52; died 12/13/76 in Petoskey, MI; interred at Oaklawn Chapel Gardens near Sault Ste. Marie

John Frederick Luecke (D)   Born: 7/4/1889 in Escanaba, Delta County

Served in U.S. House (11th District) 1937-39; served in U.S. Army during WW I; Escanaba City Council, 1934-36; Michigan State Senate, 1935-36; died 3/21/52 in Escanaba; interred in Lakeview Cemetery, Escanaba.

John Bonifas Bennet (R)   Born: 1/10/04 in Garden, Delta County

Served in U.S. House (12th District) 1943-45 and 1947-64; prosecuting attorney for Ontonagon, 1929-34; died 8/9/64 in Chevy Chase, MD; interred in Gate of Heaven Cemetery, Silver Spring, MD.

James Harvey (R)   Born: 7/4/22 in Iron Mountain, Dickinson County

Served in U.S. House (8th District) 1961-74; served in U.S. Army Air Corps during WW II; practiced law in Saginaw after the war; mayor of Saginaw 1957-59; appointed by President Richard Nixon as U.S. District Court judge for the Eastern district of Michigan, 1974; served on federal bench through 2002; resides in Port Huron.

Philip Edward Ruppe (R)   Born 9/29/26 in Laurium, Houghton County

Served in U.S. House (11th District) 1967-79; served in U.S. Navy during Korean War; resides in Houghton. Was married to the late Loret Ruppe, former Ambassador to Norway.

Robert (Bob) William Davis (R)   Born: 7/31/32 in Marquette, Marquette County

Served in U.S. House (11th District) 1979-93; grew up in St. Ignace; Michigan State House 1967-70; Michigan State Senate, 1971-78; resides in Gaylord

U.S. REPRESENTATIVES FROM OTHER STATES, BORN IN THE UPPER PENINSULA

Roger Herschel Zion (R)   Born 9/17/21 in Escanaba, Delta County

Served in U.S. House representing Indiana (8th District) 1967-75

Walter Albin Norblad (R)   Born: 9/12/08 in Escanaba, Delta County

Served in U.S. House representing Oregon (1st District) 1946-64

Robert John Cornell (D)   Born: 12/16/19 in Gladstone, Delta County

Served in U.S. House representing Wisconsin (8th District) 1975-79.

Jay W. Johnson (D)   Born: 9/30/43 in Bessemer, Gogebic County

Served in U.S. House representing Wisconsin (ith District) 1997-99.

Raymond Joseph Cannon (D)   Born: 8/26/1894 in Ironwood, Gogebic County

Served in U.S. House representing Wisconsin (4th District), 1933-39.

Thomas Hall (R)   Born: 6/6/1869 in Cliff Mine, Keweenaw County

Served in U.S. House representing North Dakota (2nd District), 1924-33.

Daniel Patrick Norton (R)   Born: 5/17/1876 in Ishpeming, Marquette County

Served in U.S. House representing North Dakota (3rd District), 1913-19.

AMBASSADOR

Loret Miller Ruppe (R)   Born: 1936, Houghton, Houghton County

Served as Ambassador to Norway, 1989-93; married to Philip E. Ruppe; died in 1996.

ELECTED STATE OFFICIALS FROM THE U.P:

Connie Berube Binsfeld (R) Born: 1924, Munising, Alger County

Served in State House (104th District) representing Leelanau County, 1975-82; Michigan state senate (36th district), 1983-90; **Lieutenant Governor** of Michigan, 1991-98.

Victor Alfred Knox   (R)   Born: 1/13/1899, Sault Ste. Marie, Chippewa County

Michigan State House representing Chippewa County, 1937-52; served as **Speaker of the Michigan House**, 1947-52; U.S. Representative (11th district), 1953-65 (defeated in 1947 and 1964); died 12/13/76 in Petoskey, MI; interred at Oaklawn Chapel Gardens near Sault Ste. Marie

Martin R. Bradley (D)   Born: 4/1/1888, Newberry, Luce County

Michigan State House representing Menominee County, 1923-24 and 1927-34; **Speaker of the Michigan House**, 1933-34; died in 1976. Burial location unknown.

Paul Lincoln Adams (D)   Born: 4/9/08, Sault Ste. Marie, Chippewa County

Mayor of Sault Ste. Marie, 1938-42; University of Michigan Board of Regents, 1956-57; **Attorney General of Michigan**, 1958-61; Justice, Michigan State Supreme Court: appointed in 1962, defeated that year in election bid; elected in 1964, served until 1972; died in Lansing, MI, November 23, 1990. Burial location unknown.

Patrick Henry O'Brien (D) Born: 3/15/1868, Phoenix, Keweenaw County

Ran unsuccessfully for Michigan state senate in 1900, and for U.S. Representative in 1908 (12th District) and 1930 (6th District); served as circuit judge (12th Circuit), 1912-22; unsuccessful candidacies for Michigan State Supreme Court in 1919 and 1925, and for Governor of Michigan in 1932. Served as **Attorney General** of Michigan 1933-34.

John Donaldson Voelker (D) Born 6/29/03, Ishpeming, Marquette County

Ran unsuccessfully for U.S. Representative (12th District) in Democratic primary of 1954; Appointed justice of Michigan State Supreme Court, 1956. Elected to **State Supreme Court** that same year, resigned in 1960 to pursue writing career. Best know for writing *Anatomy of a Murder*, a bestseller which was made into a movie filmed in the Upper Peninsula; died of heart attack, March 18, 1991. Interment at Ishpeming Cemetery.

Michael D. O'Hara (R) Born 9/19/10, Menominee, Menominee County

Justice of Michigan State Supreme Court, 1963-68; died in 1978. Burial location unknown.

PRESIDENTIAL VISITS TO THE UPPER PENINSULA

First President to visit the U.P.

William R. Taft, as the sitting President, campaigned in Marquette for re-election in the fall of 1911. He would lose his bid for a second term to Woodrow Wilson. Taft spent four days in Michigan starting with a train from Detroit to Mackinaw City where he took the ferry to Mackinac Island. He later took a tug ride through the Soo Locks before continuing by train to Marquette.

First Former President to visit the U.P.

President Taft visited Marquette in the fall of 1911.

Like Taft, Theodore Roosevelt lost the 1912 election to Woodrow Wilson. He campaigned through the U.P. as a candidate for the Bull Moose Party. Roosevelt spoke at the Amphidrome in Houghton on October 10, 1912, and had stops in Calumet, Trout Lake, Soo Junction, Newberry, Seney, Munising, Marquette, Ishpeming, Negaunee, Michigamme, L'Anse, and Baraga. It was Roosevelt's bid for a third non-consecutive term.

One year later (May 13 1913), he came to Marquette to defend his reputation. An article in The *Iron Ore*, based in Ishpeming, called the former President a drunk. Roosevelt sued the publisher, George Newett, and came to Marquette for the five-day trial. He won the suit and a token award of six cents – equal to the price of a newspaper – the amount requested by Roosevelt.

George H. W. Bush: Bridgewalker

In 1992, President Bush became the first and only President to take part in the annual Labor Day Bridge Walk. He and First Lady Barbara Bush landed at the airport in Kinross and spent the night at the Ojibway Hotel in Sault Ste. Marie. The President took a helicopter to Mackinaw City the next morning where he officially led the walk across the Mackinac Bridge.

George W. Bush: 2nd Sitting President to visit Marquette

President George W. Bush campaigned in Marquette in the summer of 2004. On a hot, humid and rainy July 13th, Air Force One landed at Sawyer International Airport, about 20 miles from Marquette. The President was greeted by Grace McCarthy, a local volunteer in the RSVP program. The presidential motorcade drove to the Superior Dome on the campus of Northern Michigan University where the President was greeted by a packed house of approximately 11,000 people. He was introduced by Iron Mountain native, Steve Mariucci, who was head coach of the Detroit Lions at that time. The President's daughter, Barbara Bush accompanied him on the trip to Marquette, which was the first by a sitting President since Howard Taft in 1911.

GRAND HOTEL: PRESIDENTIAL MAGNET

The jumbo jet used for Air Force One can not get near Mackinac Island, but that doesn't stop Presidents from visiting the Grand Hotel. Since 1955, the Grand has hosted five Presidents:

Harry S. Truman

Truman visited Sault Ste. Marie and Mackinac Island two years after he left the White House. He took part in the 1955 Centennial celebration at the Soo Locks, and visited St. Ignace on his way to Mackinac Island where he spoke at a Democratic Party gathering and spent the night in the Stewart Woodfill house.

John F. Kennedy

JFK campaigned on the island in 1959 and in 1960 when he met with Governor G. Mennen Williams. After winning the presidency, Kennedy returned to the island for another visit with Governor Williams.

GOVERNOR'S SUMMER RESIDENCE

One of the great perks of being Governor of Michigan is the Summer Residence on Mackinac Island. The three-story arts-and-crafts style cottage was built in 1902 for a Chicago family, and later owned by a Detroit family. It was sold in 1944 for $15,000 to the Mackinac Island State Parks Commission. Since then the 11 bedroom, 9 ½ bath home has served as a summer residence for nine Michigan governors. In 1997, it was named to the National Register of Historical Places.

The Governor's Summer Residence is open for public tours on Wednesday mornings during the summer. Boy and Girl Scouts from around the state who are members of the Mackinac Island Scout Service Camp act as tour guides. You can tell if the Governor is in—the Michigan flag will be raised.

President Gerald Ford visiting the Ski Hall of Fame with Ray Leverton.

Gerald Ford

The only President from Michigan was a guest of Governor William Milliken during the summer of 1976. President Ford spent time at the Governor's summer residence and at the Grand Hotel, enjoying the tennis courts and other amenities.

George H. W. Bush

The 41st President visited the Grand Hotel in 1976 while serving as Director of the CIA.

Bill Clinton

The former President and his wife, Senator Hilary Clinton, stayed at the Grand Hotel in July of 1987 while he was still the governor of Arkansas.

OTHER PRESIDENTIAL VISITS

After leaving the White House, President Gerald Ford spoke to students at Northern Michigan University in 1978.

As vice-President, Richard Nixon spoke at a rally in Negaunee in 1954. In 1956, he and future First Lady Pat Nixon stayed at the Mather Inn in Ishpeming after he addressed a Republican gathering.

George H.W. Bush gave a commencement address at Northern Michigan University in Marquette in 1973, three year before he became Ronald Reagan's vice-president.

As Secretary of Commerce, future President Herbert Hoover visited Ontonagon in the early 1920s.

After his presidency, Dwight Eisenhower vacationed on Snap Jack Lake for 13 days in 1961. He stayed in a lodge owned by Lawrence Fisher of Fisher Body.

PRESIDENTIAL ELECTION RESULTS

1840

Alger	*
Baraga	*
Chippewa	Van Buren (D)
Delta	*
Dickinson	*
Gogebic	*
Houghton	*
Iron	*
Keweenaw	*
Luce	Van Buren (D)
Mackinac	**Harrison (W)**
Marquette	*
Menominee	*
Ontonagon	*
Schoolcraft	*

* - No returns, unsettled

(W) – Whig, William Henry Harrison

(D) – Democrat, Martin Van Buren

1844

Alger	*
Baraga	*
Chippewa	Clay (W)
Delta	*
Dickinson	*
Gogebic	*
Houghton	*
Iron	*
Keweenaw	*
Luce	Clay (W)
Mackinac	**Polk (D)**
Marquette	*
Menominee	*
Ontonagon	*
Schoolcraft	*

* - No returns, unsettled

(D) – Democrat, James Knox Polk

(W) – Whig, Henry Clay

1848

Alger	*
Baraga	*
Chippewa	**Taylor (W)**
Delta	*
Dickinson	*
Gogebic	*
Houghton	*
Iron	*
Keweenaw	*
Luce	**Taylor (W)**
Mackinac	Cass (D)
Marquette	*
Menominee	*
Ontonagon	*
Schoolcraft	*

* - No returns, unsettled
(W) – Whig, Zachary Taylor
(D) Lewis Cass

1852

Alger	*
Baraga	*
Chippewa	*
Delta	*
Dickinson	*
Gogebic	*
Houghton	*
Iron	*
Keweenaw	*
Luce	*
Mackinac	**Pierce (D)**
Marquette	*
Menominee	*
Ontonagon	*
Schoolcraft	*

* - No returns, unsettled
(D) Democrat, Franklin Pierce

1856

Alger	*
Baraga	**Buchanan (D)**
Chippewa	*
Delta	*
Dickinson	Fremont (R)
Gogebic	*
Houghton	**Buchanan (D)**
Iron	Fremont (R)
Keweenaw	**Buchanan (D)**
Luce	*
Mackinac	*
Marquette	Fremont (R)
Menominee	*
Ontonagon	*
Schoolcraft	*

* - No returns, unsettled
(D) – Democrat, James Buchanan
(R) – John C. Fremont

1860

Alger	*
Baraga	*
Chippewa	Douglas (D)
Delta	*
Dickinson	*
Gogebic	**Lincoln (R)**
Houghton	*
Iron	*
Keweenaw	*
Luce	Douglas (D)
Mackinac	Douglas (D)
Marquette	*
Menominee	*
Ontonagon	**Lincoln (R)**
Schoolcraft	*

* - No returns, unsettled
(R) – Republican, Abraham Lincoln
(D) – Stephen A. Douglas

1864

Alger	*
Baraga	McClellan (D)
Chippewa	McClellan (D)
Delta	McClellan (D)
Dickinson	**Lincoln (R)**
Gogebic	McClellan (D)
Houghton	McClellan (D)
Iron	**Lincoln (R)**
Keweenaw	McClellan (D)
Luce	McClellan (D)
Mackinac	McClellan (D)
Marquette	**Lincoln (R)**
Menominee	**Lincoln (R)**
Ontonagon	McClellan (D)
Schoolcraft	**Lincoln (R)**

(R) – Republican, Abraham Lincoln
(D) – Democrat, George B. McClellan

1868

Alger	*
Baraga	Seymour (D)
Chippewa	*
Delta	Seymour (D)
Dickinson	**Grant (R)**
Gogebic	Seymour (D)
Houghton	Seymour (D)
Iron	**Grant (R)**
Keweenaw	Seymour (D)
Luce	*
Mackinac	Seymour (D)
Marquette	**Grant (R)**
Menominee	**Grant (R)**
Ontonagon	Seymour (D)
Shoolcraft	**Grant (R)**

(R) – Ulysses S. Grant
(D) - Horatio Seymour

1872

Alger	**Grant (R)**
Baraga	**Grant (R)**
Chippewa	**Grant (R)**
Delta	**Grant (R)**
Dickinson	**Grant (R)**
Gogebic	**Grant (R)**
Houghton	**Grant (R)**
Iron	**Grant (R)**
Keweenaw	**Grant (R)**
Luce	**Grant (R)**
Mackinac	Greely (D)
Marquette	**Grant (R)**
Menominee	**Grant (R)**
Ontonagon	**Grant (R)**
Schoolcraft	**Grant (R)**

(R) – Republican, Ulysses S. Grant

(D) – Democrat, Horace Greeley

1876

Alger	**Hayes (R)**
Baraga	**Hayes (R)**
Chippewa	Tilden (D)
Delta	**Hayes (R)**
Dickinson	**Hayes (R)**
Gogebic	Tilden (D)
Houghton	**Hayes (R)**
Iron	**Hayes (R)**
Keweenaw	**Hayes (R)**
Luce	Tilden (D)
Mackinac	Tilden (D)
Marquette	**Hayes (R)**
Menominee	**Hayes (R)**
Ontonagon	Tilden (D)
Schoolcraft	**Hayes (R)**

(R) – Republican, Rutherford B. Hayes

(D) – Democrat, Samuel J. Tilden

1880

Alger	**Garfield (R)**
Baraga	Hancock (D)
Chippewa	**Garfield (R)**
Delta	**Garfield (R)**
Dickinson	**Garfield (R)**
Gogebic	**Garfield (R)**
Houghton	**Garfield (R)**
Iron	**Garfield (R)**
Keweenaw	**Garfield (R)**
Luce	**Garfield (R)**
Mackinac	Hancock (D)
Marquette	**Garfield (R)**
Menominee	**Garfield (R)**
Ontonagon	**Garfield (R)**
Schoolcraft	**Garfield (R)**

(R) – Republican, James Garfield

(D) – Democrat, Winfield S. Hancock

1884

Alger	Blaine (R)
Baraga	Blaine (R)
Chippewa	Blaine (R)
Delta	Blaine (R)
Dickinson	Blaine (R)
Gogebic	Blaine (R)
Houghton	Blaine (R)
Iron	Blaine (R)
Keweenaw	Blaine (R)
Luce	Blaine (R)
Mackinac	**Cleveland (D)**
Marquette	Blaine (R)
Menominee	Blaine (R)
Ontonagon	Blaine (R)
Schoolcraft	Blaine (R)

(D) – Democrat, Grover Cleveland

(R) – James G. Blaine

1888

Alger	**Harrison (R)**
Baraga	Cleveland (D)
Chippewa	**Harrison (R)**
Delta	**Harrison (R)**
Dickinson	**Harrison (R)**
Gogebic	**Harrison (R)**
Houghton	**Harrison (R)**
Iron	**Harrison (R)**
Keweenaw	**Harrison (R)**
Luce	**Harrison (R)**
Mackinac	Cleveland (D)
Marquette	**Harrison (R)**
Menominee	**Harrison (R)**
Ontonagon	Cleveland (D)
Schoolcraft	**Harrison (R)**

(R) – Republican, Benjamin Harrison

(D) – Democrat, Grover Cleveland

1892

Alger	Harrison (R)
Baraga	**Cleveland (D)**
Chippewa	Harrison (R)
Delta	Harrison (R)
Dickinson	Harrison (R)
Gogebic	Harrison (R)
Houghton	Harrison (R)
Iron	Harrison (R)
Keweenaw	Harrison (R)
Luce	Harrison (R)
Mackinac	**Cleveland (D)**
Marquette	Harrison (R)
Menominee	Harrison (R)
Ontonagon	**Cleveland (D)**
Schoolcraft	**Cleveland (D)**

(D) – Democrat, Grover Cleveland

(R) – Republican, Benjamin Harrison

1896

All 15 Upper Peninsula counties voted for the **Republican, William McKinley** over Democrat William Jennings Bryan in both 1896 and 1900.

1900

1904

All 15 Upper Peninsula counties voted for Republican Theodore Roosevelt over Democrat Alton B. Parker

1908

All 15 Upper Peninsula counties voted for **Republican William Howard Taft** over Democrat William Jennings Bryan.

1912

Alger	Roosevelt (P)
Baraga	Roosevelt (P)
Chippewa	Roosevelt (P)
Delta	Roosevelt (P)
Dickinson	Taft (R)
Gogebic	Roosevelt (P)
Houghton	Roosevelt (P)
Iron	Taft (R)
Keweenaw	Roosevelt (P)
Luce	Taft (R)
Mackinac	**Wilson (D)**
Marquette	Roosevelt (P)
Menominee	Roosevelt (P)
Ontonagon	Taft (R)
Schoolcraft	Taft (R)

(P) – Progressive, Theodore Roosevelt

(R) – Republican , William Howard Taft

(D) – Democrat, Woodrow Wilson

1916

All 15 Upper Peninsula counties voted for **Republican Woodrow Wilson** over Democrat Charles Hughes.

1920

No returns, unsettled.

1924

All 15 Upper Peninsula counties voted for **Republican Calvin Coolidge**, over Democrat John W. Davis.

1928

All Upper Peninsula counties voted for **Republican Herbert Hoover** over Democrat Alfred E. Smith.

1932

Alger	**Roosevelt (D)**
Baraga	**Roosevelt (D)**
Chippewa	Hoover (R)
Delta	**Roosevelt (D)**
Dickinson	**Roosevelt (D)**
Gogebic	**Roosevelt (D)**
Houghton	Hoover (R)
Iron	Hoover (R)
Keweenaw	Hoover (R)
Luce	Hoover (R)
Mackinac	**Roosevelt (D)**
Marquette	Hoover (R)
Menominee	**Roosevelt (D)**
Ontonagon	**Roosevelt (D)**
Schoolcraft	Hoover (R)

(D) – Democrat, Franklin D. Roosevelt

(R) – Herbert Hoover

1936

All Upper Peninsula counties *except Keweenaw* voted for **Democrat, Franklin D. Roosevelt*** over Alf M. Landon

Feminist Suffrage Parade Circa 1912

1940

Alger	**Roosevelt (D)**
Baraga	Willkie (R)
Chippewa	Willkie (R)
Delta	**Roosevelt (D)**
Dickinson	**Roosevelt (D)**
Gogebic	**Roosevelt (D)**
Houghton	Willkie (R)
Iron	Roosevelt (D)
Keweenaw	Willkie (R)
Luce	Willkie (R)
Mackinac	Willkie (R)
Marquette	**Roosevelt (D)**
Menominee	**Roosevelt (D)**
Ontonagon	**Roosevelt (D)**
Schoolcraft	**Roosevelt (D)**

(D) – Democrat, Franklin D. Roosevelt*

(R) – Republican, Wendell Willkie

1944

Alger	**Roosevelt (D)**
Baraga	**Roosevelt (D)**
Chippewa	Dewey (R)
Delta	**Roosevelt (D)**
Dickinson	**Roosevelt (D)**
Gogebic	**Roosevelt (D)**
Houghton	**Roosevelt (D)**
Iron	**Roosevelt (D)**
Keweenaw	**Roosevelt (D)**
Luce	Dewey (R)
Mackinac	Dewey (R)
Marquette	**Roosevelt (D)**
Menominee	Dewey (R)
Ontonagon	**Roosevelt (D)**
Schoolcraft	**Roosevelt (D)**

(D) – Democrat, Franklin D. Roosevelt*

(R) – Republican, Thomas Dewey

1948

Alger	**Truman (D)**
Baraga	Dewey (R)
Chippewa	Dewey (R)
Delta	**Truman (D)**
Dickinson	**Truman (D)**
Gogebic	Dewey (R)
Houghton	Dewey (R)
Iron	**Truman (D)**
Keweenaw	Dewey (R)
Luce	Dewey (R)
Mackinac	Dewey (R)
Marquette	**Truman (D)**
Menominee	**Truman (D)**
Ontonagon	Dewey (R)
Schoolcraft	Dewey (R)

(D) – Democrat, Harry S. Truman

(R) – Republican, Thomas Dewey

1952

Alger	**Eisenhower (R)**
Baraga	**Eisenhower (R)**
Chippewa	**Eisenhower (R)**
Delta	**Eisenhower (R)**
Dickinson	**Eisenhower (R)**
Gogebic	Stevenson (D)
Houghton	**Eisenhower (R)**
Iron	Stevenson (D)
Keweenaw	**Eisenhower (R)**
Luce	**Eisenhower (R)**
Mackinac	**Eisenhower (R)**
Marquette	**Eisenhower (R)**
Menominee	**Eisenhower (R)**
Ontonagon	**Eisenhower (R)**
Schoolcraft	**Eisenhower (R)**

(R) – Republican, Eisenhower

(D) – Democrat, Adlai Stevenson

1956

All counties in the Upper Peninsula *except Alger* voted for **Republican, Dwight D. Eisenhower***, over Democrat Adlai Stevenson.

1960

Alger	**Kennedy (D)**
Baraga	**Kennedy (D)**
Chippewa	Nixon (R)
Delta	**Kennedy (D)**
Dickinson	Kennedy (D)
Gogebic	Nixon (R)
Houghton	**Kennedy (D)**
Iron	**Kennedy (D)**
Keweenaw	Nixon (R)
Luce	Nixon (R)
Mackinac	Nixon (R)
Marquette	**Kennedy (D)**
Menominee	**Kennedy (D)**
Ontonagon	Nixon (R)
Schoolcraft	Nixon (R)

(D) – Democrat, John F. Kennedy

(R) – Richard M. Nixon

1964

All 15 Upper Peninsula counties voted for **Democrat Lyndon B. Johnson*** over Republican, Barry Goldwater.

1968

Alger	Humphrey (D)
Baraga	Humphrey (D)
Chippewa	**Nixon (R)**
Delta	Humphrey (D)
Gogebic	Humphrey (D)
Houghton	Humphrey (D)
Iron	Humphrey (D)
Keweenaw	Humphrey (D)
Luce	**Nixon (R)**
Mackinac	**Nixon (R)**
Marquette	Humphrey (D)
Menominee	Humphrey (D)
Ontonagon	Humphrey (D)
Schoolcraft	Humphrey (D)

(R) – Republican, Richard M. Nixon

(D) – Democrat, Hubert H. Humphrey

1972

Alger	**Nixon (R)**
Baraga	**Nixon (R)**
Chippewa	**Nixon (R)**
Delta	McGovern (D)
Gogebic	**Nixon (R)**
Houghton	**Nixon (R)**
Iron	**Nixon (R)**
Keweenaw	**Nixon (R)**
Luce	**Nixon (R)**
Mackinac	**Nixon (R)**
Marquette	**Nixon (R)**
Menominee	**Nixon (R)**
Ontonagon	**Nixon (R)**
Schoolcraft	**Nixon (R)**

(R) – Republican, Richard M. Nixon*

(D) – George McGovern

1976

Alger	**Carter (D)**
Baraga	Ford (R)
Chippewa	Ford (R)
Delta	**Carter (D)**
Dickinson	**Carter (D)**
Gogebic	**Carter (D)**
Houghton	Ford (R)
Iron	**Carter (D)**
Keweenaw	**Carter (D)**
Luce	Ford (R)
Mackinac	Ford (R)
Marquette	Ford (R)
Menominee	Ford (R)
Ontonagon	**Carter (D)**
Schoolcraft	**Carter (D)**

(D) – Democrat, Jimmy Carter

(R) – Republican, Gerald Ford

1980

Alger	Carter (D)
Baraga	**Reagan (R)**
Chippewa	**Reagan (R)**
Delta	Carter(D)
Dickinson	**Reagan (R)**
Gogebic	**Reagan (R)**
Houghton	**Reagan (R)**
Iron	Carter (D)
Keweenaw	**Reagan (R)**
Luce	**Reagan (R)**
Mackinac	**Reagan (R)**
Marquette	Carter (D)
Menominee	**Reagan (R)**
Ontonagon	**Reagan (R)**
Schoolcraft	**Reagan (R)**

(R) – Republican, Ronald Reagan

(D) – Democrat, Jimmy Carter

1984

Alger	**Reagan (R)**
Baraga	**Reagan (R)**
Chippewa	**Reagan (R)**
Delta	**Reagan (R)**
Dickinson	**Reagan (R)**
Gogebic	Mondale (D)
Houghton	**Reagan (R)**
Iron	Mondale (D)
Keweenaw	Mondale (D)
Luce	**Reagan (R)**
Mackinac	**Reagan (R)**
Marquette	**Reagan (R)**
Menominee	**Reagan (R)**
Ontonagon	**Reagan (R)**
Schoolcraft	**Reagan (R)**

(R) – Republican, Ronald Reagan*
(D) – Democrat, Walter Mondale

1992

All Upper Peninsula counties *except* *Chippewa* voted for **Democrat Bill Clinton** over Republican George H.W. Bush.

2000

Alger	**Bush (R)**
Baraga	**Bush (R)**
Chippewa	**Bush (R)**
Delta	**Bush (R)**
Dickinson	**Bush (R)**
Gogebic	Gore (D)
Houghton	**Bush (R)**
Iron	Gore (D)
Keweenaw	**Bush (R)**
Mackinac	**Bush (R)**
Marquette	Gore (D)
Menominee	**Bush (R)**
Ontonagon	**Bush (R)**
Schoolcraft	**Bush (R)**

(R) – Republican, George W. Bush
(D) – Democrat, Albert Gore, Jr.
Bold – General Election winner

1988

Alger	Dukakis (D)
Baraga	Dukakis (D)
Chippewa	**Bush (R)**
Delta	Dukakis (D)
Dickinson	**Bush (R)**
Gogebic	Dukakis (D)
Houghton	**Bush (R)**
Iron	Dukakis (D)
Keweenaw	Dukakis (D)
Luce	**Bush (R)**
Mackinac	**Bush (R)**
Marquette	Dukakis (D)
Menominee	**Bush (R)**
Ontonagon	Dukakis (D)
Schoolcraft	Dukakis (D)

(R) – Republican, George H.W. Bush
(D) – Democrat, Michael Dukakis

1996

All 15 Upper Peninsula counties voted for **Democrat Bill Clinton*** over Republican Bob Dole.

2004

Alger	Kerry (D)
Baraga	**Bush (R)**
Chippewa	**Bush (R)**
Delta	**Bush (R)**
Dickinson	**Bush (R)**
Gogebic	Kerry (D)
Houghton	**Bush (R)**
Iron	**Bush (R)**
Keweenaw	**Bush (R)**
Mackinac	**Bush (R)**
Marquette	Kerry (D)
Menominee	**Bush (R)**
Ontonagon	**Bush (R)**
Schoolcraft	**Bush (R)**

(R) – Republican, George W. Bush*
(D) – Democrat, John Kerry
* - incumbent

2008

Alger	Obama (D)	Keweenaw	McCain (R)
Baraga	McCain (R)	Luce	McCain (R)
Chippewa	McCain (R)	Mackinac	McCain (R)
Delta	Obama (D)	Marquette	Obama (D)
Dickinson	McCain (R)	Menominee	Obama (D)
Gogebic	Obama (D)	Ontonagon	Obama (D)
Houghton	McCain (R)	Schoolcraft	Obama (D)
Iron	Obama (D)		

SALARIES: ELECTED OFFICIALS, BY COUNTY

County	Sheriff	Prosecutor	Clerk	Treasurer	Register of Deeds
Alger	48,302	65,000	40,170*	42,174	
Baraga	47,393	74,629	45,179*	42,929	
Chippewa	67,466	83,926	59,232	59,232	59,232
Delta	66,175	92,700	56,838*	60,215	
Dickinson	57,000	105,511	54,346*	52,346	
Gogebic	49,537	68,011	42,204*	38,600	
Houghton	57,336	71,211	52,121*	44,030	
Iron	50,481	70,063	40,233	40,233	41,713
Keweenaw	41,900	34,700	36,000*	33,920	
Luce	34,942	48,572	35,452*	34,942	
Mackinac	51,825	76,213	47,481	43,254	44,929
Marquette	75,825	118,931	63,488	61,090	58,272
Menominee	55,076	82,001	48,956*	46,509	
Ontonagon	43,276	61,898	38,734*	38,734**	See below
Schoolcraft	46,710	57,832	43,552*	48,637	

Clerk and Register of Deeds is one position

**The Clerk receives $6,965 additional administrative pay and the Treasurer receives $4,715 additional administrative pay for duties that would normally be performed by a County Controller or Administrator. If the County were to hire a Controller or Administrator then the Clerk and Treasurer would not receive this pay.*

COUNTY COMMISSION, COMPENSATION

Alger

Commissioners: 5 — Catherine Kilgore (1), Joseph VanLandschoot (2), Pete Benson (3), Don Sandstrom (4), Edward Lindstrom (5)

Compensation: — $140 monthly salary ($175 for Chairman, $160 for Vice-Chair), $30 per meeting, mileage reimbursement, and $10,000 life insurance

Baraga

Commissioners: 5 — Gale Eilola (1), Mike Koskinen (2), Daune Smith (3), William Menge (4), Larry Menard (5)

Compensation: — $250 per month, $30 per diem per meeting, health insurance if over 25 years of service

Chippewa

Commissioners: 7 — Don Cooper (1), Earl Kay (2), Scott Shackleton (3), Bernard LaJoie (4), Ted Postula (5), Jim Moore (6), Richard Timmer (7)

Compensation: — $450 per month ($530 for Chairman), $45 per meeting up to two meetings per day, eligible for health insurance, mileage reimbursement

Delta

Commissioners: 5 — Thomas Elegeert (1), Leslie Ruohomaki (2), David Schultz (3), Darrel Bengry (4), David Rivard (5)

Compensation: — $607 per month, ($675 for Chairman) plus per diem of $20 per meeting less than 3 hours, $35 per meeting 3-6 hours, $50 per meeting over 5 hours (maximum $50 per day) and mileage reimbursement

Dickinson

Commissioners: 5 Joe Stevens (1), Ann Martin (2), Frank Smith (3), Henry Wender (4), John Degenaer Jr. (5)

Compensation: $300 per month ($400 for Chairman), $35 per meeting under two hours, $50 per meeting over two hours ($100 daily maximum), gas mileage reimbursement

Gogebic

Commissioners: 9 Bob Morin (1), James Oliver(2), Dan Siirila (3), Thomas Gerovac (4), Leroy Kangas (5), Dennis Jacobson (6), Joe Bonovetz (7), William Anonich (8), George Peterson III (9)

Compensation: $300 monthly salary ($425 for Chairman, $375 for Finance Chair), and $20 per committee meeting

Houghton

Commissioners: 5 Edward Jenich (1), Dennis Barrette (2), Anton Pintar (3), Scott Ala (4), Paul Luoma (5)

Compensation: $3,000 per year ($3,600 for Board Chairman), $30 per diem per Meeting, mileage reimbursement, $3,000 term life insurance ($4,000 for Chairman), BC/BS health insurance available – four options available with premium co-pay

Iron

Commissioners: 5 George Brunswick (1), Francis A. Wills (2), Rosalie King (3) Lawrence Harrington (4), Robert T. Black (5)

Compensation: $225 per month ($250 for chairman), $25 per meeting or $40 for extended meeting or two meetings in one day, gas mileage reimbursement

Keweenaw

Commissioners: 5 Randy Eckloff (1), Donald Keith (2), Alfred Gunnari (3), Frank Stubenrauch (4), Joe Langdon (5)

Compensation: $1,956 annual salary ($2,340 for chairman), $25 per diem per meeting, mileage reimbursement

Luce

Commissioners: 5 Nancy Morrison (1), Terry Stark (2), Rita Lemanek (3), Jill Maki (4), Phyllis French (5)

Compensation: $2,100 per year ($2,400 for Chair), $35 per meeting, $20 for commissioners on bill-approving committee, BC/BS health insurance, or $1,000 in place of health insurance

Mackinac

Commissioners: 5 Dawn Nelson, Carl Frazier, Mike Patrick, Calvin McPhee, Lawrence Leveille

Compensation: $4,222 per year ($5,049 for chairman), $60 per meeting, $50 for second meeting on same day, health and life insurance

Marquette

Commissioners: 9 Gerald Corkin, Debbie Pellow, Jim Cihak, Harvey Wallace, Bruce Heikkila, Nick Joseph, Paul Arsenault, Bob Struck, Charles Bergdahl

Compensation: $8,000 per year ($(9,006 for chairman), health insurance including dental and vision, life insurance 1.5 times salary, MERSDefined

Benefit or Defined Contribution Retirement w/2% contribution, can opt out of health insurance for $2,400 per year, mileage reimbursement

Menominee

Commissioners: 5

Bernie Lang (1), Greg Furmanski (2), Bill Kakuk (3), Jim Lynch (4), Floyd Berger (5)

Compensation:

$4,000 per year ($4,500 for Chairman), $50 per meeting, not to exceed $100 per day, $75 per day plus expenses when attending Michigan or Upper Peninsula Association Counties conferences. gas mileage reimbursement

Ontonagon

Commissioners: 5

Robert Schulz (1), Hubert Lukkari (2), John Pelkola (3), Dale Parent (5). Louis Paulman – District 4 who was also the Chair just passed away on May 2nd so the seat is currently vacant. We expect to make the appointment on May 29th or 30th.

Compensation:

$150 per month ($175 for Chair), $30 per diem for partial days or $60 for a full day. Mileage at the rate of 35¢ per mile. $300 per month in lieu of health insurance.

Schoolcraft

Commissioners: 5

Lindsley B. Frenette (1), Dan McKinney (2), Keith P. Aldrich (3), Doug Erickson (4), Dale Dufour (5)

Compensation:

$3,200 per year ($3,500 for Chair), $30 per meeting, or $60 per out-of-town meeting, retirement benefits

COUNTY BUDGETS

County	2008 general fund budget ($)
Marquette	19,742,559
Chippewa	15.700,000
Delta	9,267,955
Dickinson	8,554,751
Houghton	7,870,909
Menominee	6,404,354
Gogebic	5,878,757
Mackinac	5,509,619
Iron	4,776,362
Schoolcraft	3,524,875
Alger	3,169,712
Ontonagon	3,081,594
Baraga	2,978,007
Luce	2,017,618
Keweenaw	1,603,766

Chapter 12

CULTURE

UPPER MICHIGAN MEDIA

The following is a survey of Upper Peninsula media—newspapers, radio and television. Included are profiles of a few of the personalities who pioneered or spent their careers in these U.P. communication mediums. Care was taken to present men and women from all ends of the Peninsula who have entertained, informed and served their communities over the years. Space restraints and not neglect are the reason why your favorite personality might be omitted.

NEWSPAPERS

Early Upper Peninsula Newspapers

The first Upper Peninsula newspaper grew out of the early mining ventures on the Keweenaw Peninsula. John Ingersoll, an associate of eastern newspaper magnate Horace Greeley, published the *Lake Superior News and Miners' Journal* in Copper Harbor starting in 1846. The paper was moved to Sault Ste. Marie the next year. A number of articles advocating the building of a canal and locks at the

Finnish Printing Office found in the Copper Country at the turn of the Century. Donated from a private collection.

Sault made it into Greeley's newspapers back East. These articles drew attention to the mineral potential of the Lake Superior region as well as the need for a canal. The *Lake Superior News and Miners' Journal* was moved to Marquette as the *Lake Superior Journal* in 1855.

The bustling copper mining town of Ontonagon acquired a newspaper that same year. *The Lake Superior Miner* was published for four decades beginning in 1855, and starting in 1881, it competed for readers with another paper, the *Ontonagon Herald*. The *Miner* eventually folded and was printed for the last time in 1895. The *Herald* continues as a weekly publication today.

Soon after a settlement began, a town newspaper followed. The City of Houghton was platted in 1859, the same year the *Portage Lake Mining Gazette* appeared. Iron mining on the Menominee Range was in its infancy during the early 1870s. Shipment of ore had to wait for the arrival of the railroad from Escanaba in 1877. Soon after, Iron Mountain sprang up and became the primary commerce center on the Range. Its first paper, the *Menominee Range,* began publication in 1879. The railroad finally reached the Gogebic Range during the next decade and a mining boom ensued. Ironwood grew as a village soon after. While a devastating fire virtually destroyed the town in 1887, the next year it was rebuilt and the *Ironwood Times* started publication.

The railroad from the iron mines in Negaunee did not reach Escanaba until 1864. Yet in 1859, the diminutive outpost acquired its first newspaper appropriately named *Medborgaren,* Swedish for "small town." Foreign immigrants began newspapers in other communities as well. Lake Linden was home to two French papers, the *L'Union Franco American* (1889-1891) and the *Le Courier Du Michigan* (1912-1957). An Italian paper, *Minatore Italiano* began publishing at Laurium in 1895 and continued until 1938. A twice weekly Finnish language paper, *Amerikan Suomalainen Lehti* made its first appearance in Hancock in 1876. It was the first Finnish-language newspaper published in the United States. Nearly three dozen Finnish papers started up from the later 19th through the early 20th Centuries, mostly in the Copper Country. *Amerikan Suometar*, began in Hancock in 1899, is one of the few surviving Finnish-language newspapers in existence. It appears as a tri-weekly under the auspices of the Suomi Synod (Lutheran) Church.

Many papers changed names as well as owners over time. The previous example of the *Lake Superior News and Miners' Journal* is a good case in point. The publication morphed into the *Lake Superior Journal* in its move to Marquette. Eventually it became the *Lake Superior Mining Journal*, then the *Mining Journal*. The paper became the first daily publication in Upper Michigan and the name was changed to the *Daily Mining Journal* in 1884. That title continued for seven decades until 1954 when it reverted back to the *Mining Journal*, the name that continues today.

Here is a selected list of U.P. newspapers still in existence today and the evolution of their present names.

Ironwood Daily Globe: Began publication in 1919 under its present name.

Ontonagon Herald: Began publication in 1881 under its present name.

Houghton: *Daily Mining Gazette* began publication under the name *Portage Lake Mining Gazette* in 1859.

L'Anse Sentinel: Began publication in 1880 under its present name.

Marquette: *Mining Journal*

Munising News: Began publication in 1898 under its present name.

Newberry News: Began publication in 1886 under its present name.

Sault Sainte Marie Evening News: Began publication under the name *Sault Sainte Marie News* in 1879. The title and frequency of publication changed in 1903.

St. Ignace News: Formed out of the merger of the *Saint Ignace Republican* (1880) with the *Saint Ignace News* (1883) to form the *Saint Ignace Republican News* in 1900. The paper merged with the *Saint Ignace Enterprise* to form the *Saint Ignace Republican News and Enterprise* in 1933. The title was subsequently shortened to its present title and continues publishing as a weekly.

Manistique Pioneer-Tribune: Began publication as the *Schoolcraft County Pioneer* (1880) then changed to the *Manistique Pioneer* (1884) then merged with the *Manistique Tribune* (1896) to form *Manistique Pioneer-Tribune*.

Escanaba: The *Escanaba Morning Press* (1909) changed to *Escanaba Daily Press* (1922)

Iron Mountain: *Iron Mountain News* (1921) changed name to current title *The Daily News*.

Iron River: *Iron County Reporter* (1884)

A. P. Swineford

A pioneer Upper Peninsula journalist, A.P. Swineford was one of the more colorful newspapermen of his time. The long-time editor and publisher of the Marquette *Mining Journal* was eulogized as an "old school editor" on his passing in 1909. He was described as a man "whose joy it was to gird up his loins, seize a club and wade in, laying on right and left."

Born in Ashland, Ohio in 1834, he earned a law degree in Wisconsin but never practiced. He drifted into journalism and in 1855 began work at the *Milwaukee Free Democrat*. Intensely pro-Southern in his views, this stance embroiled him in "savage newspaper controversies almost from the start."

In 1868, he moved to the Upper Peninsula and took up publishing Negaunee's short lived *Lake Superior Mining and Manufacturing News*. Swineford eventually took charge of Marquette's *Mining Journal* where he "speedily made his paper the recognized authority on the copper and iron mining industries of northern Michigan." Newspapers of the day squabbled amongst each other and Swineford's publications led the charge. For example in 1875 during one of the coldest winters on record, a Duluth newspaper proposed building a railroad across the thick, solid ice of Lake Superior.

Swineford's newspaper responded to the idea with "what awful long drunks those fellows… must be in the habit of indulging in." Another tiff during his tenure at the *Mining Journal* was with the head of the *Ontonagon Miner* over which newspaper was the oldest.

While he built a large circulation with the *Mining Journal*, he was often "hampered financially." His eulogist stated "he lacked the financial trait to enable him to keep acquainted with a bank account." The story goes that he was actually happy in debt. After his interest in the *Mining Journal* was cleared from debt, he studied the paper work for a time and reportedly said he would go buy a house. Then he could, "mortgage it up to the eaves without any damned business partner…insisting on paying off the mortgages."

Swineford is remembered as a spokesman for the resources of the Upper Peninsula. He was appointed the commissioner of mining statistics in Michigan and published "The Mineral Resources of Lake Superior" in 1874. He drew national attention when, as commissioner, he was in charge of the state mineral exhibit at the New Orleans Exposition in 1884. The next year President Grover Cleveland appointed Swineford governor of the Alaska territory. There he founded the first newspaper published at Sitka. He also started a newspaper in Juneau and still another in Ketchikan. When Benjamin Harrison succeeded Cleveland in 1889, Swineford resigned his post as governor. In Cleveland's second term, he was appointed as special agent of the United States land office. He made visits to the Upper Peninsula, but remained a resident of Alaska until his death in Juneau in late October 1909.

Wesley H. Mauer

Wesley H. Mauer, journalism professor at the University of Michigan, became a "country" editor in 1957 after he asked the University to buy the *Town Crier* of Mackinac Island and staff it with student interns. Procedures at the University changed and Mauer found himself the sole owner and publisher of the paper. He kept the innovative student laboratory newspaper going and expanded his operations, purchasing the *St. Ignace News* in 1975. He later bought the *Les Cheneaux Islands Weekly Wave* and eventually merged the two papers.

Mauer founded the first teacher's union in Michigan, the Michigan Federation of Teachers and served as its president from 1963-67. He retired from the U. of M. in 1966 and then spent nearly 30 more years publishing the *News*. At the time of his death at age 98 in 1995, Wesley H. Mauer was the oldest active newspaper publisher in the United States. He was elected to the Michigan Journalism Hall of Fame in 1987.

Marion Strahl Boyer

One of America's earliest female photojournalists, Marian Strahl wanted to be a journalist from day one. However in the 1930s, women were relegated to basically two professions—teaching and nursing. So when Strahl went to college, she studied to be a teacher at the University of Wisconsin. After attending the University for two years, she went to live with her father in Escanaba and began working at the *Daily Press* at the height of the Great Depression in 1935. At first she sold advertising to pay her salary. Then in her second year at the paper, she took over the photography department at a salary of $10 a week for 48 hours. While she headed the department, she came upon a new magazine called *Life*. She looked at the cover photo (taken by a woman) and determined that she was going to work for the publication. To that end, she furthered her studies by attending a photography school in Los Angeles. While there, she met and studied for a year under Ansel Adams.

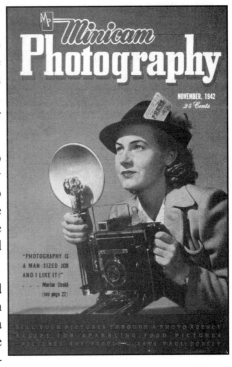

Finally, her connections and skills got her the job she longed for at *Life Magazine*. She moved to New York and was sent to various parts of the country to photograph events like natural disasters or to take pictures of celebrities. She found that life on the road as a magazine photographer was not for her and after about a year, she returned to Escanaba.

Strahl went back to work for the *Daily Press* and eventually married a long-time boy friend, John Boyer. After the war, John went to work in Panama and Marian eventually joined him there. After the birth of their first child, they moved back to the Upper Peninsula. They eventually settled in Sault Ste. Marie and Marian became a photographer and reporter at the *Sault Evening News*.

Her experience in journalism finally brought her to the teaching profession she studied but never pursued. At age 55, she determined that students going into journalism were coming out of school ill-prepared for their profession. So Marian changed careers and moved into the classroom where she taught English for ten years and put together a nationally honored high school newspaper.

Jean Worth

Menominee native Jean Worth was long considered the dean of Upper Peninsula journalism. In 1922 at age 18, he began his career at the *Menominee Herald-Leader*. A year later he moved on to the *Detroit Times*.

Worth had ambitions as an actor, and to that end, enrolled in the American Academy of Dramatic Arts in New York. He was forced off Broadway and back to journalism by an automobile accident. He returned to the Herald-Leader in 1930 and was named the editor in 1943. In 1955, he moved north to Escanaba and took on the same position at the *Daily Press*. During his tenure there, he turned the paper into the most influential voice of the Upper Peninsula. After he stepped down from the *Daily Press* in 1969, Worth stayed active as a contributing writer and columnist.

Jean Worth received such notable acknowledgements as Upper Peninsula Person of the Year, Michigan Ambassador of Tourism and a posthumous induction into the Michigan Journalism Hall of Fame in 1989.

David Rood

Marquette native David Rood received Michigan Journalism's highest honor for a stand he took to uphold the integrity of his profession.

Born in 1926, Rood began work at the *Mining Journal* while still in high school. He spent two years in the service and then attended Michigan State University, graduating with a journalism degree in 1950. He worked at various newspapers across the state as a reporter, editor and publisher. In 1971, he found himself back in the Upper Peninsula where he was named managing editor and finally editor at Escanaba's *Daily Press*. Six years later, Rood was asked by Panax Corporation, the publisher of the paper, to run two stories on President Jimmy Carter. Rood refused to comply, maintaining the stories were shoddy journalism. He was fired for his insubordination and the ensuing battle gained national attention as a struggle between an absentee owner and a local editor.

"When he took his courageous stand in 1977 against those whose ideas of journalism ran counter to all he believed in," said former publisher of the *Detroit Free Press* Neal Shine, "he took that stand for all of us who cherish the same principles. His contributions to the industry, as well as his stand for journalistic integrity, will long endear him to all in the field."

David Rood was inducted into the Michigan Journalism Broadcast Hall of Fame in 1997.

RADIO

U.P. RADIO STATIONS BY LOCATION

Ironwood
99.7 WIMI - Hot adult contemporary (AC) "99.7 The Storm"
106.9 WUPM - Contemporary Hits Radio (CHR) "106.9 WUPM"
WHRY 1450 AM - Oldies
WJMS AM 590 - Country

Ontonagon
101.1 WUPY - Country "Y-101"
88.5 WOAS - Ontonagon area schools, non-commercial student radio

Houghton-Hancock/Keweenaw area
91.9 WMTU - Michigan Tech University, College/mixed variety
93.5 WKMJ - Hot AC
97.7 WOLV - Classic Rock "The Wolf"
98.7 WGLI - Classic Rock, "The Rockin' Eagle"
102.3 WHKB - Country
105.7 WCUP - Country "Eagle Country"
AM 920 WMPL - Sports/Talk
AM 1400 WCCY - ESPN Sports affiliate/Nostalgia

Iron River/Crystal Falls
99.1 WIKB - AC, "99.1 The Breeze"
100.7 WOBE - Classic Hits, "Classic Hits 100.7
AM 1230 WIKB - Adult standards/Memories

Iron Mountain/Kingsford
91.5 WVCM - Christian-WVCY, Milwaukee
93.1 WIMK (WUPK 94.1 Marquette) - Classic Rock "The Bear"
94.3 WZNL - Adult Contemporary "Star 94.3"

98.1 WEUL (WHWL Marquette) - Christian
101.5 WJNR - Country "Frog Country 101.5"
AM 1450 WMIQ - Talk/Sports
Escanaba
97.1 WGLQ - Contemporary Hit Radio "Magic 97"
102.5 WCMM - Country
104.7 WYKX - Country "KX-104.7"
105.5 WGKL - Oldies "Kool 105.5"
AM 600 WCHT - News/Talk "News Talk 600"
AM 680 WDBC - Nostalgia
Menominee/Marinette
95.1 WLST - Country
96.3 WSFQ - Rock
103.7 WHYB - Adult Contemporary "103.7 The Wave"
106.3/106.7 WMXG - Classic Hits/Rock (Dayparted) "Mix 106"
AM 1340 WAGN - Oldies
Manistique
99.9 WPIQ - Talk
AM 1490 WTIQ - Oldies
St. Ignace
102.9 WMKC - Country
AM 940 WIDG - Sports
Sault Ste. Marie
90.1 WLSO - College/Mixed Lake Superior State University Radio
99.5 WYSS - Top 40
101.3 WSUE - Rock "Rock 101"
102.3 WTHN - Religious
AM 1230 WSOO - News/Talk
AM 1400 WKNW - Talk
Newberry
93.9 WNBY - Oldies "Oldies 93"
97.9 WIHC - Classic Rock "The Bear"
AM 1450 WNBY - Country
Munising
98.3 WRUP - Classic Rock
AM 1400 WQXO - Oldies

Marquette
90.1 WNMU - News/Classical—Northern Michigan University Radio
91.5 WUPX - College/Mixed "Radio X"
92.3 WJPD - Country "Big Country"
95.7 WHWL - Christian
99.5 WNGE - Oldies
101.9 WKQS - Adult Contemporary "Sunny 101.9"
103.3 WFXD - Country
107.7 WMQT - Contemporary Hit Radio "Q-107"
AM 970 WZAM - Sports—ESPN Radio sports network affiliate
AM 1240/1320 WIAN/WDMJ - Talk/Sports

THE FIRST UPPER PENINSULA RADIO STATIONS

On May 20, 1920, Detroit's WWJ (then called 8MK) signed on the air. It was the first Michigan radio station to broadcast after the invention of radio around the turn of the century. The problem at that time was there was no one to listen; no one except a few hundred technophiles with home-made receivers. During the early 1920s, the technology developed rapidly and soon radio receiving sets were being sold.

The first station in Upper Michigan appears to be WRAK in Escanaba. The station was licensed to broadcast in March 1923 with a power of 100 Watts at 1170 on the AM dial. Later, the station's power was lowered to 50 Watts and the frequency moved to 1060. It is not known how much broadcasting WRAK did. It likely was not a resounding success because it was no longer licensed after 1927. Similarly, stations WFLB in Menominee (1210, 50 Watts) and WLBY in Iron Mountain (1410, 50 Watts) were licensed for a couple of years and then went silent. WLBY probably was in the list of 162 stations the Federal Radio Commission's (FRC) ordered off the air in 1928 to minimize interference on the already crowded AM dial.

Radio really took a foothold in the Upper Peninsula around 1930. A year earlier, the Upper Michigan Broadcasting Corporation received a license for 1370 WHDF in Calumet. It later became WCCY and in 1934 was broadcasting on 250 Watts daytime and 100 Watts at night.

In 1931, Marquette's 1310 WBEO was licensed to the Lake Superior Broadcasting Company. It broadcasted on the FRC's "special hours" schedule at 100 Watts. Also in November of that year, WJMS in Ironwood signed on the air. Originally owned by Marius Johnson, the station was licensed to broadcast at 1420 with unlimited hours at 100 Watts of power (In 1938, WJMS was moved to 1450 on the dial, and then in 1947 to 630 AM. Finally in 1968 it was moved to its present position of 590 on the AM dial.). By 1942, WBEO became WDMJ (*Daily Mining Journal*), named for the paper owned by the station's proprietor, Frank Russell.

On the east end, 1230 WSOO signed on the air in 1940. About that time, 1490 WDBC in Escanaba began broadcasting.

Through all the changes in technology, ownership and radio formats, WCCY, WDMJ, WJMS, WSOO and WDBC remain on the air today.

LEGENDARY U.P. RADIO PERSONALITIES

Bill Thorne—WSOO Broadcast Legend

Bill Thorne may have the record for the longest continuous broadcast stint of anyone in Upper Michigan radio.

In 1948 at age 16, Thorne applied for a job at WSOO radio in Sault Ste. Marie. He was turned down. Not to be deterred, Thorne visited the station for the next 30 days asking for a job. Persistence paid off when he was finally offered the 4 p.m. to midnight show.

Thorne has been on the air ever since. In the early days, he got out of school at 3:30 and ran as fast as he could to make it to the station in time for his 4 p.m. shift. Later, he signed on at a Canadian station at 6 a.m. He then caught a ferry back to Sault, Michigan to begin his day job as a Chippewa County Juvenile Officer. When that job ended at 5 p.m. he had a short break before his WSOO shift began at 6.

One of Thorne's proudest professional moments was being crowned "Mr. Deejay USA" in 1959 at an annual competition held in Nashville. There he had a chance to interview some of Country Music's biggest stars including Johnny Cash and Patsy Cline. Thorne even enjoyed a steak dinner with Elvis.

In 1972, Thorne was selected from a pool of 50 reporters for a one-on-one interview with President Richard Nixon. On the same Washington trip he also had the chance to interview Chief Justice of the Supreme Court Warren Burger.

After sixty years, Thorne is still on the air. His weekly show "The Four Horsemen" is broadcast live on Saturday mornings from a local car dealership. He also hosts the Sunday "Hymn Time" show.

Dick Storm—U.P. Radio News Pioneer

Richard Tuisku, better known as radio news man Dick Storm, began his Keweenaw broadcasting career at WMPL in Houghton in 1964.

Storm attended the Michigan School for the Blind in Lansing through the sixth grade. He then returned home to attend Houghton High school where he graduated with honors in 1960. He attended the Brown Institute of Broadcasting in Minneapolis and got his first radio announcing job in Platteville, Wisconsin.

While working at WMPL, Storm continued his education at Suomi College. He later enrolled at Michigan Tech where he earned a BS in Business administration in 1968. That same year he began his career in radio news. The news director at WMPL quit and he stepped into the position. "He was making more money than me," Storm says, explaining his decision to change careers from mere announcing to news.

Over the years, Storm learned the news business while developing his "own rules and codes of ethics by trial and error." In addition to news, he produced a weekly public affairs program called "Copper Country Today." His business acumen led him to co- found "Tu-Mar Broadcasting" which owned and operated three Copper Country radio stations.

Dick Storm was elected to the Michigan Association of Broadcasters Hall of Fame in 2002 and was named U.P. Person of the Year in 1991. Storm and his associates sold their radio stations in 2004 and he gave his last broadcast on December 31, 2004. After his last broadcast, the self-confessed "political junkie" received a surprise phone call from Governor Jennifer Granholm. The governor reportedly told him "Please don't run against me."

Radio is still in Storm's blood. He now hosts a two-hour Saturday morning show called "The Eagle Country Hall of Fame" on 105.7 WCUP.

America's Longest-running Radio Talk Show

Iron River's WIKB boasts the longest-running radio talk show in America and a native son has been the host from day one.

"We started on January 5, 1965," says Jay Barry. "It started as a half-hour talk show, call-in show and now it's three hours." After over 40 years hosting Telephone Time, Barry still finds the show interesting. "Everyday is a memorable moment because you don't know what's

going to happen for three hours," he explains. "We broadcast live on the internet, so we're all over the world. And because we have a watts line, we can get calls from all over."

Telephone Time has no rules or guidelines except that nothing malicious or profane is allowed. "If people want to buy something, if they are looking for something or if they want to wish grandpa a happy birthday or whatever," Barry explains. "Participants can almost do whatever they want."

Over the years, Barry has talked to a number of celebrities on the show. One of his most memorable celebrity interviews was with General Norman Schwarzkopf. The general was at a hunting camp in Wyoming when Barry chatted with him. "He was so personable," recalls Barry. "Of all the celebrities we've talked to, Schwarzkopf was a guy that really impressed me."

What really gives him a sense of pride are the good things the show has accomplished. Barry cites as an example a call he received on the very first day of the show: "A lady called in and kind of blasted the road commission for not plowing the fishing spots on Lac Vieux Desert—a good 25 miles west of Iron River. The next day they were plowed."

After 45 years on the air, Barry turned off the microphone for the last time on September 30, 2009.

Jan Tucker—Western U.P. Broadcast Icon

Ontonagon's Jan Tucker began her radio broadcasting career on Ironwood's AM 590 WJMS in 1964. "They set the receiver up in the house," she says. "I had five small children then and I balanced between getting them ready for school and being on the air."

At first Tucker played some music and did a few features. Then one fateful day her co-host asked what she had done over the weekend. She said she spent it trying to get a Kool Aid stain out of her kitchen counter. The phone started ringing off the hook with listeners calling to give advice on how to remove the stain. "It went so well," she recalls, "I thought I would try it the next day with a different problem and wham, the program changed dramatically from that day on."

One day a woman called about a recipe she had lost. The audience responded with that recipe and more and thus was born the recipe-of-the-day feature. Along with household advice and recipes, Tucker covered local news.

Tucker was originally hired by Joe Blake (a U.P. radio legend in his own right). When WJMS was sold, the new owners fired Blake and Tucker quit. Around 1970, Blake and an associate, Bob Olsen, bought WMPL in Houghton. They approached Tucker about renewing her show on their new station. "I can't," she remembers telling them, "I'm going to have a baby. The guys said that's OK and I literally had her on the air. The morning after she was born, I had my show from the hospital bed!"

Tucker broadcasted on WMPL for the next three decades until Blake and Olsen sold the station in 2001. Tucker stayed on for a while after the sale, but her show was switched to the AM dial. Reception was poor in her hometown of Ontonagon and brought her to another broadcasting crossroads. She left WMPL. "It was a tough decision," she says, "but I agreed to join WUPY 101...[in]...Ontonagon."

She marks four years at her new station at the end of 2008 and now has the added bonus of also broadcasting on her old station. The owners of WMPL took over management of WUPY and the Jan Tucker Show is now simulcast on both WUPY and WMPL. After over four decades on the air, Tucker says she is "still hooked on work." When asked how long before she retires, she answers "When it's no longer fun!"

TELEVISION

UPPER MICHIGAN'S FIRST TELEVISION STATION

On April 28, 1956, WDMJ-TV (TV6) officially signed on the air. The brainchild of U.P. media mogul Frank Russell, WDMJ (*Daily Mining Journal*) first broadcast from a make-shift studio set up at the top floor of the *Daily Mining Journal* Building in downtown  Marquette. "With an Eye for Upper Michigan" was the early motto of the station, tying into the station's affiliation with the CBS television network.

Some of the earliest local programs featured a local band "Ray Adamini and his Hiawatha Ramblers," "The Double O Ranch" along with a local news show. Later, the station added "Darby O'Six," a children's show hosted by Roy Peterson, an NMU student from Ishpeming. Another popular show in those days was "At Home with Ingrid," a cooking show featuring Michigan State Extension Service's Ingrid Bartelli. 1962 saw the start of the only Finnish language program in the United States—"Suomi Kutsuu" (Finland Calling). Host Carl Pellonpaa has hosted the show since and was named a Knight of the Order of the Lion—White Rose, Finland's highest civilian honor.

Many changes have come to the station over the years, including a name change. In 1960, Russell sold WDMJ-TV to M & M Broadcasting, owner of WLUK-TV in Green Bay. In keeping with the "luck" theme, WDMJ became WLUC. Ownership of the station has changed hands seven times. The Post Corporation of Appleton, Wisconsin owned the station the longest—from 1962 to 1984. The current owner is Barrington Broadcasting out of the Chicago area.

TV6 quickly outgrew its downtown Marquette studio. In 1959, the station moved to a new facility on Airport Road a few miles east of Negaunee. The building was expanded to its present size in 1978. When TV6 signed on in 1956, the station had a staff of less than 20. Today, there are more than 60 employees, including an 18-person news department.

Television markets are based on population size. WLUC-TV is in the Marquette, Michigan television market, one of the smallest in the country. As such, TV6 is a training ground for young broadcast journalists who hone their skills and move on to bigger markets. Over the years, many reporters, producers and anchors have passed through TV6. A few have remained, imparting a stability and identity that few stations its size enjoy. Steve Asplund is the station's longest tenured news anchor. The Milwaukee area native arrived at WLUC in 1979 and after leaving for a brief stint as a producer at a Milwaukee station, came back to the U.P. and made it his home. Along with anchoring duties, Asplund also serves as assistant news director.

WLUC-TV6, the Upper Peninsula's first TV station, has changed names, owners, personnel and technology during its five decades on the air. One constant is the station's loyal viewers who turn to TV6 for the most local news and feature programming of any television station in Upper Michigan.

Carl Pellonpaa

Born and raised in Ishpeming, Carl Pellonpaa began his career in broadcasting after completion of high school in 1948. He worked at WJPD radio for 15 months, and then left for a two-year tour of duty in the army. After the military, Pellonpaa moved back to the Upper Peninsula and went to work for Cleveland Cliffs. When layoffs hit the mining industry, he left the area and lived and worked in Chicago for a time. In 1958, Pellonpaa returned to the U.P. and re-joined the staff of WJPD.

In 1961, Pellonpaa began his television career at WLUC. He filled a variety of roles at the station, including weatherman during the local evening news. The next year, station management was approached by an area travel agency with an idea to produce a Finnish language show that would encourage travel to Finland by Upper Michigan's large population of first and second-generation Finns. The show, "Finland Calling", was approved and second-generation Finn Carl Pellonpaa was chosen as host.

The first half-hour show aired on March 25, 1962. The show proved popular and was extended to an hour and briefly to two hours. During the early years every show was completely live. Occasionally the Finnish records that were played on the turntable in the studio would jump off track. Outside of Pellonpaa, none of the station personnel spoke or understood Finn, so they were left guessing as to what was going on. The staff learned quickly that "levy" meant record, so each time Pellonpaa spoke the word during an interview, it was a cue for a song to be played.

The show accomplished its aim of promoting travel to Finland and Scandinavia. The first tour, hosted by Pellonpaa and his wife, was in 1962. Since then there have been over two dozen tours, most of them led by Pellonpaa. In 1988, he was recognized by the Finnish government for his promotion of Finnish tourism with the "Knight of the Order of the White Rose," their highest civilian honor.

After 46 years in production, the show continues. Pellonpaa retired from full-time work at WLUC-TV in 1995, but still hosts the show. The passion he brings for his Finnish heritage to the show makes it one of the longest-running success stories in television.

Buck LeVasseur

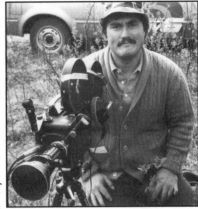

Born and raised in Bay City, David "Buck" LeVasseur developed an interest in broadcasting at an early age. He studied broadcasting for two years at Delta College near Bay City and then took a job with Gerity Broadcasting. LeVasseur did some pioneering work with the company, doing live broadcasts of various events on a local cable channel.

He moved to the U.P. in 1974 and started as a photographer/reporter at WLUC two years later. Finally in 1981, he took on the role as producer and host of the show "Discovering". "Discovering" explores the great outdoors of Upper Michigan including some of the region's unique characters through the award-winning photography of LeVasseur. It is the longest running outdoor-related television program in the history of Michigan broadcasting.

Steve Asplund

A native of the Milwaukee area, Steve Asplund started as a reporter at WLUC in 1979.

He has held positions as news anchor, weather anchor, morning news anchor, newscast producer, assignment editor and news director. Asplund has been the primary anchor for the TV6 Early News since 1985. In addition to anchoring, he also serves as assistant news director.

Asplund is married with two grown children and resides in Negaunee. He is active in the community, volunteering as a firefighter with the City of Negaunee Fire Department since 1989. He is a past President of the Upper Peninsula Firefighters Association. In his free time he and his family enjoy movies and television, camping, travel and the outdoors.

Ed Kearney—Hall of Fame Broadcaster

Ed Kearney, the long-time news director of WLUC-TV in Marquette was inducted into the Michigan Journalism Hall of Fame in 2005. He is one of less than a handful of U.P. journalists to receive the honor and the first from the television industry.

Kearney came to the Upper Peninsula from Washington D.C. during the late 1960s to attend Suomi College (now Finlandia University) in Hancock. He received an associate's degree there and then transferred to Northern Michigan University (NMU) in Marquette where he received a BS in English in 1972. While attending NMU, Kearney took a part-time job as camera operator at WLUC-TV. After graduation, he became a full-time reporter at the station rising to the rank of assistant news director in 1975. Kearney assumed the news director position in 1981, a position he held for the next 24 years except for a brief stint as operation manager in the 1990s.

Kearney caught the wider attention of news colleagues in the 1980s when he took cameras into local courtrooms as part of his news department's "Paying the Price" series. The series revolved around drunken driving—an issue that reached the national forefront at that time. His reporters brought their cameras into the courtrooms and helped generate more lively interviews with victims and perpetrators.

Kearney watched as his news department grew from a staff of four when he started to 24. During his tenure he hired more than 110 reporters, producers, meteorologists and videographers. For many, it was their first experience in broadcast journalism.

In addition to the Hall of Fame recognition, Kearney won broadcast excellence awards from the Michigan Association of Broadcasters in 2001, 2002 and 2003 along with honors for community involvement, breaking news, features and special interest programs. After 34 years in television news, Ed Kearney retired from WLUC-TV in late August 2004.

New Kids on the Block

There are 210 television markets in the United States divided by size or number of households. The largest is New York City with over 7 million households. The smallest is Glendive, Montana with 3,890. The Marquette television market (covering most of the Upper Peninsula except Chippewa and Mackinac Counties in the far east, Gogebic County in the west and Menominee County to the south) is market 179 with around 89,000 households. This small size and low population density has historically been a deterrent to the development of more television stations in the U.P. WLUC-TV was the only television station for 16 years until WNMU, a non-commercial education and PBS station signed on the air in 1972.

Recently, several new stations have fired up transmitters and begun broadcasting. WBKP in Calumet signed on in October 1996 as an ABC affiliate. A year later, the station began airing local news. That same year, the station set up a repeater station in Marquette in an attempt to reach the most densely populated portion of the Peninsula. The station's main broadcast facility was moved to Marquette in 2001. However in March of 2002, the station dropped its local newscast because of low ratings and budget cuts. A year later, the station replaced its low-power repeater with a full power satellite, WBUP Channel 10 in Ishpeming. The stations then took on the brand-name "ABC 5 and 10."

The stations changed hands in 2004 when the original owner, Tom Scanlon, sold to Lake Superior Community Broadcasting owned by Stephan Marks of Maryland. Shortly afterward, a new newscast, UGN news (Upper Great Lakes News Network), debuted originating from both WBUP and WBKB in Alpena, another Marks-owned station. UGN covers news from the entire Upper Peninsula and northern portions of the Lower Peninsula.

In July 2007, the stations split. WBKP Calumet switched affiliation to the CW Network, while WBUP Ishpeming retained its ABC affiliation.

Most recently, WMQF Channel 19 Marquette joined the list of TV stations in the U.P. WMQF signed on in February 2003 as a FOX and UPN affiliate.

MEDIA CELEBRITIES FROM THE U.P.

Terry O'Quinn

Born: Newberry, Michigan July 15, 1952 as Terrance Quinn. He later added the *O* to his last name to avoid confusion with the actor Terry Quinn.

Best known as: John Locke on ABC Television's hit drama, *Lost.* Received 2005 Emmy nomination for best supporting actor

O'Quinn caught the acting bug at age 15 when he saw Franco Zeffirelli's Romeo and Juliet, and acted in his first play at Newberry High School.

He performed in many plays while attending Central Michigan University and University of Iowa. Upon graduation he is quoted as saying "I didn't want to look for a real job. So, I decided to see if I could make it as an actor." He worked on stage in New York for about ten years before landing his first movie role in *Heaven's Gate*, an epic western from director Michael Cimino. The film became notorious for its delays, budget overruns, and ultimate flop at the box office.

That first movie role did have an upside. O'Quinn required riding lessons for the role, and eventually married his instructor. Terry and Laurie O'Quinn have been married for over 25 years, have raised two sons, and now live in Hawaii where ABC's *Lost* is shot.

Other notable television roles: Captain Thomas Boone on *JAG*; Nicholas Alexander on *The West Wing*; Gordon Buchanan on *Law & Order: Criminal Intent*; Asst. Director of the FBI on *Alias*; Col. Will Ryan on *Navy NCIS: Naval Criminal Investigative Service.* Also seen on *The X Files* and *Millennium*.

TV movies: *Murder in a Small Town* (1999), *Roe vs. Wade* (1989), and *Guts and Glory: The Rise and Fall of Oliver North*

Movies: *Ghosts of the Mississippi* (1996), *Primal Fear* (1996), *Young Guns* (1988), lead role in *The Stepfather* (1987), and *Heaven's Gate* (1980), *Old School* (2003)

• While at CMU O'Quinn wrote and directed the play *Orchestrina*. At that time (mid 1970s) he cast a young actor, another Michigan resident, who went on to attend CMU before launching a successful career in Hollywood. His name: Jeff Daniels

• O'Quinn is said to be a talented singer and guitar player who does a great impersonation of one of his favorite performers, Neil Young.

Doris Packer

Born: Menominee, Michigan May 30, 1904

Best known as: Mrs. Rayburn, the principal of Grant Avenue Grammar School on *Leave it to Beaver*

Packer's family moved from Menominee to California when she was a young girl. She began acting in high school productions of Shakespeare, and continued acting while attending

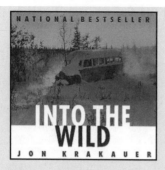

The mother of Christopher McCandless, the subject of the book and movie Into the Wild, was born in Iron Mountain to Mr. and Mrs. Loren Johnson. Wilhelmina "Billie" McCandless and her husband Walt would bring their kids to visit her parents at Iron Mountain. During these visits Grandpa Loren Johnson's love of nature rubbed off on young Christopher. Several of Chris McCandless' aunts and uncles still reside near Iron Mountain.

UCLA. From L.A. she went east to study acting under Evelyn Thomas at The Drama School in New York. She landed roles on Broadway and appeared on radio programs including *Henry Aldrich* and *Mr. & Mrs. Smith.* In 1928, while working in New York she met and married the famed stage actor, Rowland G. Edwards. After her husband's death in 1952 she moved back to southern California where she began her TV career by working on *The Burns and Allen Show.*

Notable television roles: Mrs. Rayburn on *Leave it to Beaver*; Mrs. Chatsworth Osborne, Sr. on *The Many Loves of Dobie Gillis;* Mrs. Fenwick on *The Beverly Hillbillies;* also enjoyed roles on many of the popular sitcoms of the 1960s such as: *Petticoat Junction, The Dick Van Dyke Show, The Andy Griffith Show, Green Acres,* and *Mr. Ed.*

Movies: Mrs. Swaile in *Meet Me at the Fair* (1953); Helen Abernathy in *Annette* (1958); Mrs. Henderson in *Bon Voyage* (1962); Mrs. Barrington in *Paradise, Hawaiian Style* (1966); Mrs. Carruthers in *The Perils of Pauline* (1967), and as Rosalind in *Shampoo* (1975)

Doris Packer died of natural causes in Glendale, California at age 74 on March 20, 1979.

Bill Jamerson

Born: March 3, 1955, Washington D.C.

Jamerson has produced ten documentaries on Michigan history which have been broadcast on Michigan Public Television. Subjects include the history of the cherry-growing industry and the National Cherry Festival in Traverse City; the furniture industry of Grand Rapids; the cereal industry in Battle Creek; the golden age of downhill skiing in Michigan; chemical pioneer, Herbert H. Dow; General Motors founder, William Durant, and the Civilian Conservation Corp.

Jamerson spent 37 years in Michigan before his first trip to the U.P. He grew up in metro Detroit where he enjoyed reading biographies and listening to his grandfather's stories about life as a lumberjack and as a soldier in World War I. Jamerson studied history at the University of Michigan and worked in the advertising business in Traverse City. After seeing Ken Burns Civil War documentary, he devoted his talents to chronicling highlights of Michigan history on film, in song, and in books. His first trip to the U.P. was in 1992 while producing *Camp Forgotten-The Civilian Conservation Corps in Michigan*, and *Winter Wonderland – The Golden Age of Skiing in Michigan.* Jamerson spent hundreds of hours in the backwoods looking for old CCC camps and interviewing former CCC "boys." His research also brought him to Pine Mountain, Porcupine Mountain Wilderness State Park, and Ishpeming and other important sites related to the history of Michigan's ski industry.

In November of 1999, Jamerson was in the middle of filming a documentary on William Durant, founder of General Motors, when he decided to move to Escanaba. During his earlier travels to the U.P. he began to learn of the rich iron and copper mining heritage, a history he was anxious to portray on film, however the funding never materialized. Jamerson said at this point he did not want to leave the U.P., so he had to figure out how to earn a living.

Jamerson used his newfound knowledge of Upper Peninsula history to compose dozens of songs about lumberjacks, the mining industry and the CCC. He put together a multi-media show that combined music, video and storytelling and hit the road, performing at festivals, libraries, and schools around Michigan and Wisconsin.

In October 2007 he published his first book, *Big Shoulders;* the novel, set during the Great Depression, follows a Detroit youth sent to Camp Raco in the U.P. The story is based on the real life experiences of a former CCC enrollee who Jamerson interviewed extensively for his documentary on the same subject. All of the characters in his book are based on real life veterans of the CCC camps Jamerson has interviewed.

The Civilian Conservation Corps was created by President Franklin Roosevelt to make jobs during the Depression and conserve natural resources. There were 80 CCC camps in the U.P. and northern Lower Michigan. Through the efforts of CCC members, 480 million trees were planted in northern and Upper Michigan, more than in any other state.

Jamerson spends most of his time promoting the book, and sharing his love of Michigan history with audiences around Michigan and Wisconsin. For more information: www.billjamerson.com

MOVIES FILMED AND ABOUT THE U.P.

Anatomy of a Murder (1959)

The movie, starring Jimmy Stewart and Lee Remick, was shot in Marquette County and featured a Grammy-winning score by Duke Ellington. Like the book, the movie was critically acclaimed and to this day is considered one of Hollywood's best courtroom dramas. Some of the language used in the courtroom scenes, though technical, managed to cause scandal.

Jimmy Stewart at the Roosevelt Supper Club in Ishpeming, autographing "The Wall".

Photo courtesy Gigs Gagliardi

The story is based on the 1957 book of the same title written by Robert Traver, pen name of the beloved Ishpeming native, John Voelker. It bears close resemblance to a case in which Voelker defended a local army officer charged with murdering a bartender who allegedly raped the man's wife. Voelker won the case and five years later his book was published.

The movie was directed by Otto Preminger and starred Stewart as the defense attorney, Remick as the wife of the defendant played by Ben Gazzara and Michigan native George C. Scott as the prosecutor. Preminger used about 300 local residents as movie extras: those with speaking parts earned $90 a day; others earned $10 a day. The murder victim was played by

Otto Preminger and film crew from "Anatomy of a Murder"
Photo courtesy Paul Richards of Ishpeming

Ishpeming businessman Robert B. Brebner.

The cast and crew numbered about 150, and the six-week production injected about $300,000 into the local economy.

The courtroom scenes were filmed at the Marquette County Courthouse. Other locations included: the Bay View Inn and Big Bay Inn in Marquette; Ishpeming Public Library and Ishpeming Rail Depot; Tripoli Bar and Main Street in Ishpeming; Lumberjack Tavern and Thunder Bay Inn in Big Bay; Mt. Shasta Lodge in Michigamme; and various outdoor locations around Marquette.

The movie premiered at United Artists Theatre in Detroit on July 1, 1959. Among those in attendance: Mr. and Mrs. John Voelker, Governor and Mrs. G. Mennen Williams, Lee Remick, George C. Scott and the director, Otto Preminger.

Police in Chicago tried to ban the movie, demanding that certain language was offensive and should be removed. Courtroom scenes included the first-ever use in a Hollywood movie of the words, "contraceptive," "sexual climax," "rape," "slut," and "sperm." Objections by the police were overruled by a federal judge.

Stewart's father was so offended by the movie that he purchased newspaper ads calling the film a "dirty picture."

The movie was nominated for seven Academy Awards including Best Picture, Best Actor (Stewart), Best Supporting Actor (Scott and Arthur O'Connell), and Best Cinematography. Duke Ellington won Grammy Awards for his score in the categories of Best Sound track Album, Background Score from Motion Picture or Television.

Escanaba in da Moonlight (2001)

The original play, *Escanaba in da Moonlight*, was written by Michigan actor Jeff Daniels and performed at his Purple Rose Theater in Chelsea, Michigan. Daniels wrote the screenplay, directed it, and played the lead role of Reuben Soady, the "buckless yooper."

As Daniels explains the plot, "If Reuben doesn't get one this year, he will be the oldest person in the Soady family to not have bagged a buck, except for an uncle who is missing a few screws... I've described it as 'Jeremiah Johnson' meets 'Dumb and Dumber'...Reuben is guided by his Indian wife, 'Hawk Moon,' who is a better shot."

His wife is played by Kimberly Norris Guerrero who has

appeared in several movies and on episodes of *The Soprano's*. Albert Soady, Reuben's father was played by Harve Presnell, best known for his work in *Saving Private Ryan*, *Fargo*, and *Patch Adams*.

Music for the film was composed by Alto Reed, former member of Bob Seger's Silver Bullet Band, and Michigan rocker, Ted Nugent supplied a few realistic props for the deer camp scenes.

The film's budget was over $1 million dollars, much of it spent in Escanaba. Daniels could have saved half of that amount by filming in Canada, but as a Michigan resident and business owner he opted to keep it in-state. Original plans called for filming most of the scenes in Traverse City, and using Escanaba for some exterior shots. After a scouting mission to the U.P., Daniels and crew instead chose to film the entire movie in and around Escanaba.

The hunting camp scenes were filmed at an actual hunting camp owned by Reinhold and Gladys Bittner of Bark River. Bar scenes were filmed at The Swallow Inn in Rapid River.

Three dozen residents were given roles as named extras — Escanaba waitress Rosy Cox plays a restaurant patron, and former City Manager Mike Uskiewicz is featured in a bar scene — and hundreds of locals appeared as fans in a scene shot at the Escanaba High athletic field. During that scene Reuben, played by Daniels, dreams he's standing in front of hundreds of fans wearing nothing but his underwear. The fans taunt him with chants of "Buckless! Buckless!"

Daniels said he was inspired to write the story after spending time with the hunters in his wife's family, and by the stories of Robert Traver (John Voelker) in the book, *Danny and the Boys*.

Escanaba in da Moonlight premiered at the Fox Theatre in Detroit on October 22, 2001 before a sold out crowd. One week later it had its Upper Peninsula premier at the Chip Inn Resort, where the 760 seats sold out for two shows.

Watersmeet Goes Hollywood

An eight-part documentary carried on the Sundance Channel follows the Watersmeet Nimrod basketball team through its 2005-06 season. The documentary was directed by Brett Morgan, who also directed the ESPN commercials that brought the Nimrods national attention. Morgen said he had always wanted to capture the rhythm and flow of small town life, and his experience filming the ESPN commercials inspired him to return to Watersmeet.

The film premiered at the 2007 Sundance Film Festival and in July of 2007, it had its Michigan premiere at the Traverse City Film Festival. Several students, players and parents were invited to Traverse City to answer audience questions after the film was shown. The series received generally favorable reviews. With its focus on a small town drawn together by high school sports, it was compared several times to the TV show, "Friday Night Lights."

Several reviewers from large city newspapers mentioned, as highlights of the series, the ice-cold, snowy landscape, the prominence of hunting including scenes of skinning a deer and shooting a pig between the eyes; racial tension after the mother of Brian Aimsback questions why he didn't get his picture in the local paper after scoring his 1,000[th] career point as did George Peterson IV, the son of the coach; the old timers, former Nimrod athletes now in their 70's and 80's who gather at a local diner to access the current team; the fight to prevent a housing development at Bond Falls and the scenes of contented family life centered around bonfires and ice-fishing.

"Nimrod Nation" first aired on the Sundance Channel on November 26, 2007. Two half-hour episodes were aired every Monday night over four weeks.

MOVIES FILMED ON MACKINAC ISLAND

This Time for Keeps

In 1947 the film *This Time for Keeps* was filmed at the Grand Hotel and other island locations. The film starred Jimmy Durante and Esther Williams for whom the Grand Hotel swimming pool was built and named after.

In the film a soldier, the son of an opera singer, is brought to the island by his father where he falls in love with Esther Williams the swimming pool showgirl.

The film includes rare footage of the island in the winter time as well as footage from the Grand Hotel pool and and surroundings.

Somewhere In Time

The film starring Christopher Reeve and Jane Seymour was filmed entirely on Mackinac Island, with the exception of a few scenes filmed in Chicago. Filming took place over seven weeks in June and July of 1979. The film was released the following year to mixed reviews.

In the movie, Christopher Reeve plays a Chicago playwright who meets an elderly lady who whispers to him, "come back to me." Later while vacationing he becomes obsessed with a portrait of a woman hanging in the Grand Hotel. The portrait is of Elise McKenna, an early 20th century actress, and the same woman who whispered "come back to me."

Reeve's character, Richard Collier, uses self-hypnosis to travel back in time where he meets and falls in love with the young actress.

The movie was not a big hit at the box office but was highly rated when shown on cable television and remains a popular video rental. It is one of three films with a dedicated fan club, the other two being *The Wizard of Oz*, and *Gone With the Wind*. *Somewhere in Time* was nominated for one Academy Award, for Best Costumes, but lost to the movie *Tess*.

The owner of the Grand Hotel, R.D. "Dan" Musser agreed to allow Universal to film on location for no charge as long as the famous hotel was portrayed in a positive light. Filming was done at the peak of the tourist season, with the crew and actors working around the hotel guests. Many of the dining room scenes were filmed late at night after the dinner hour when the room could be transformed to look as it may have in the early 1900s.

Large trucks hauling the necessary lighting equipment, costumes, set designs and other production equipment were allowed on the island with the stipulation that they drive no faster than a man can walk. The trucks were moved around primarily in the overnight hours, and frequently behind a walking man, so as not to violate the rules laid down by the State Parks Commission.

Most of the scenes were filmed in and around the Grand Hotel, and many were filmed at the Mission Resort, site of an old movie soundstage. The production crew did not know about the soundstage until they arrived at the island to scout locations. They used the soundstage for most of the interior shots, such as those in the hotel rooms. The soundstage was built in the 1940s by the Moral Re-Armament Movement and used to film propaganda movies. The Mission Resort was once a college with several dormitory buildings, all of which fit the needs for the production of *Somewhere in Time* (SIT).

Since 1990 the Grand Hotel has hosted a Somewhere in Time weekend featuring a show-ing of the film, tours of movie locations, and a chance to meet members of the cast and crew.

Christopher Reeve came back for the 1994 SIT weekend, and seven months later became paralyzed after a fall from his horse; injuries which led to his death in October of 2004.

Jane Seymour starred at the 2002 SIT weekend where she accepted a surprise phone call from Reeve during the dinner event. The approximately 850 people in attendance listened in on the phone call, which drew cheers and tears. Seymour also performed the "Man of My Dreams" soliloquy on stage that night.

Mr. Art Critic

In September of 2007, Traverse City film maker-screenwriter-director Rich Brauer shot much of the movie Mr. Art Critic on Mackinac Island. The star of the film is Bronson Pinchot, best known for his role as Serge in the movie *Beverly Hills Cop*, and for his Emmy-nominated character performance as cousin Balki Bartokomous in the TV sitcom, *Perfect Strangers*. Pinchot plays a snooty Chicago art critic known for his mean-spirited reviews. While vaca-tioning at his cottage on Mackinac Island he meets up with one of the artists whose work he has ripped. After a few drinks Pinchot's character proclaims that any idiot can make art. He winds up entering the island's art festival contest using somebody else's work. Eventually he discovers that he was not born with the gift of artistry.

The Mackinac Island scenes were shot in less than three weeks in and around Main Street and the Mission Point Resort. Many of the paintings used in the art festival scenes are the work of local artists who also worked as extras in some scenes.

Brauer has seven other films to his credit. He worked as director of photography for two of Jeff Daniels' films: *Escanaba in da Moonlight* and *Super Sucker*. He's written and produced three films starring Ernest Borgnine, including *Frozen Stupid* and *Barn Red*.

Mr. Art Critic was released in 2008.

MUSICAL GROUPS

Da Yoopers Ambassadors of Da U.P.

The most famous musical act to come out of the Upper Peninsula is Da Yoopers. The group's humorous songs poke fun and celebrate the unique traditions and people of the U.P.

Da Yoopers is an offshoot of The Night Beats, a band started up in the 1960s by Jim De-Caire and the late Joe Potila. The wedding band morphed into Da Yoopers and by the early

1980s they hit their stride as the plaid-shirted, wise cracking band from the U.P.

Their first hit was *Smelting U.S.A.*, followed by *Rusty Chevrolet* (sung to the tune of Jingle Bells), which sold 3,000 copies in its first year. Their comic songs were a hit with radio dee-jays around Michigan and Wisconsin. As more people heard their songs, sales went up as did demand for Da Yoopers to perform live.

Their breakthrough hit was *Second Week of Deer Camp,* which sold 70,000 copies in its first year of release. Today the band performs over 100 concerts a year.

In 1991, DeCaire opened the Da Yoopers Tourist Trap and Museum on U.S.-41 outside of Ishpeming. The store is stocked with U.P. memorabilia and souvenirs, Da Yoopers CD's, hats, t-shirts, coffee cups, and a complete Fart Section. The museum includes such items as the largest working chainsaw and largest working rifle in the world!

The group has produced 11 CD's including: *One Can Short of a Sixpack*, *Turdy Point Buck*, and *Songs for Fart Lovers.*

Da Yoopers are: Jim "Hoolie" DeCaire, Lynn "Too-Burger" Coffey, Jim "Schween-Bel-la-Budda-Elmo" Bellmore, Bobby "No one calls me Bob" Symons, Reggie "Reggae-De-Sardine" Lusardi, Richard "Danglin-Dickling-Dick-e-Bird" Bunce, and Robert "Dill-Dere-Dough" Nebel.

Co-founder Joe Potila, passed away in 2001 after a bout with cancer.

White Water

The White Water string band is a family affair. Founders Dean and Bette Premo have been making music together for over a quarter century. They added their children, Laurel and

Evan, to the group early on. At the ages of three and five they were dancing, demonstrating traditional folk dances like clogging and schottische. It wasn't long before they joined the group as full-fledged musicians and singers.

The band plays traditional and contemporary folk music with an emphasis on the history and stories of the people who settled the Great Lakes. All members sing, while Dean plays guitar, Bette the fiddle and Evan bass. Laurel is considered the "Swiss Army Knife" of the group because of her abilities on several instruments including banjo, mandolin, fiddle as well as finger style and flatpick guitar.

Amasa's White Water is known for its musicianship, four-part harmonies and endearing stage presence. It plays at a variety of venues across Upper Michigan and northern Wisconsin including the annual Fortune Lake Festival held at the Fortune Lake Lutheran Camp each spring and the Aura Jamboree in the Baraga County village of Aura each summer.

These days, the band is often reduced to a trio because Evan is studying at the University Of Michigan School Of Music. Evan has teamed up with soprano Mary Bonhag to form Duo Borealis. The duo occasionally shares the stage with White Water. For more information on the band's concert schedule and to sample their music, go to http://www.white-water-associates.com/music.htm.

Flat Broke Blues Band

"North Country Blues" is how a *Blues Revue* critic describes the music of Marquette's Flat Broke Blues Band (FBBB). The band has been playing clubs, festivals and concerts throughout the Upper Great Lakes for well over a decade. The band features founders Walt Lindala on guitar and vocals and bassist/vocalist Mark Johnson along with guitarist/vocalist Mike Letts, drummer Jim Cohen and lead vocalist/harmonica player Lorrie Hayes.

Mark Johnson   Walt Lindala   Lorrie Hayes   Mike Letts   Jim Cohen

FBBB takes the influences of blues, rock, soul and R&B to create a sound that respects the tradition of the blues but also pushes its contemporary bounds. The band brings a play list of over 80 songs to its stage shows, which are filled with an entertaining and danceable mix of blues and R&B classics along with a variety of original songs. Over the years, FBBB has performed with the likes of such blues greats as Koko Taylor, Tab Benoit, Shemekia Copeland, Lonnie Brooks and most recently as the opening act for Johnny Winter at the historic Calumet Theater.

The band has received glowing reviews outside of the Upper Peninsula. A reviewer writing for *BluesWax E-zine* described FBBB as "one of the regions most promising bands" and "an act to watch for." Its album *Worth the Weight* was released in 2004. Flat Broke Blues Band is currently road testing" songs for a future release.

Conga Se Menne

Founded in 1994, this Marquette-based group bills itself as a Finnish Reggae band. The name of the band is a play on the Finnish-American phrase "Kuinka Se Menne" (How is it going?). Bandleader Derrell Syria listened to his grandfather's old traditional Finnish folk music records. He eventually realized the basic beat of the music parallels tropical reggae music. His first tune of the new genre was *Come Take a Sauna.* The blending of Finnish marches and schottisches with reggae worked and band has become a local and regional favorite.

While their lyrics are geared for fun, the band is made up of competent musicians. Some of the music is difficult to play, but the band members pull it off with ease. They navigate the parallel styles of reggae and traditional Finnish music mixed with rock, blues, funk and Latin influences. Current products include their third album *Living Inna Northern Paradise* and the CD *Finnish Reggae and Other Sauna Beats,* which is a compilation of the band's first two albums. Their 2008 summer season consisted of performances in such varied geographical venues as Ely and Duluth, Minnesota as well as Menominee and St. Ignace in the Upper Peninsula.

MUSIC FESTIVALS

Aura Jamboree

The tiny town of Aura on the Pointe Abbaye in Baraga County boasts the longest-running annual music festival in the Upper Peninsula. The Aura Jamboree celebrated its 32nd anniversary in 2008 with ethnic Finnish-based music, bluegrass, folk, country and rock. The two-day weekend festival is held both indoors on the Community Hall stage and outdoors under trees and tents around the village.

Fortune Lake Festival

Fortune Lake Festival celebrated its 5th annual event in May 2008. The folk and traditional music celebration is held on the campus of Fortune Lake Lutheran Camp located between Crystal Falls and Iron River on U.S.-2. Besides live musical acts, the one-day festival includes a dance, music classes and a jam session. For more information, go to http://www.white-water-associates.com/fortunefest.htm.

Grand Marais Music and Arts Festival

The sleepy lakeshore village of Grand Marais comes alive with music each summer during the second weekend in August. The Grand Marais Music and Arts Festival features an eclectic blend of country, rock, folk and bluegrass. In 2008, the festival celebrated its 27th season.

Hiawatha Music Festival

The Hiawatha Music Festival began its run in the western Marquette County village of Champion in 1979. Now the three-day event draws around 3500 people from throughout the region to Marquette's Tourist Park. The event features acoustic traditional-music styles including bluegrass, old-time, Celtic, Cajun, folk and dance. The festival also has a special area for children and teens with organized activities and performances for these age groups.

Run by the non-profit Hiawatha Music Co-op, the festival received the Governor's Art Award in 1993 and in 2006 received a community arts award from the Marquette Arts and Culture Center. In addition to the annual festival, the Co-op strives to keep traditional music alive all year by sponsoring dances, concerts and workshops.

Pine Mountain Music Festival

This yearly summer festival was organized in Iron Mountain back in 1991 by cellist Laura Demming, a member of the orchestra of the Lyric Opera of Chicago. The Pine Mountain Music Festival (PMMF) was originally a week-long chamber music series. It expanded over the ensuing years to include opera and then grew into other cities of the western and central Upper Peninsula. The festival has grown from 5 or 6 events in one city to more than 40 performances and workshops in various cities.

The PMMF has won numerous awards over the years including the coveted Governor's award for Arts and Culture and the Great Lakes Community Arts Award. Its orchestra has been graced by musicians from such prestigious orchestras as the Chicago Symphony Orchestra, Detroit Symphony Orchestra, Lyric Opera of Chicago, Washington National Opera and many more. The organization initiated OPERAtion Imagination, a free educational outreach program that brings opera to students throughout the U.P.

Economic conditions have challenged the Festival recently. However, the PMMF still brought opera and classical music to 18 venues in 10 different U.P. cities in 2008.

Porcupine Mountain Music Festival

Friends of the Porkies organized this late-summer festival in 2005. Since then it has grown to include audience members and performers from all over the country and even abroad.

The festival is held at the Winter Sports Complex located within the park. Temporary canopy-covered stages are erected and several acres of open slope are mowed for audience members' blankets and lawn chairs. In addition to the main stages, a third "busking" stage is erected where amateurs and professionals can play and jam for tips.

The fourth annual festival in 2008 featured an eclectic mix of rock, blues, folk and traditional music forms. For more information, visit www.porkiesfestival.org.

Marquette Area Blues Fest

The idea for a Marquette Blues festival grew out of an idea born on the Fourth of July 2003. Since then, the Labor Day Weekend festival has continued to grow. It is held in Marquette's Lower Harbor Park and runs through Saturday and Sunday of the holiday weekend.

Some of the featured headliners of past concerts include blues guitarist Tinsley Ellis, soul singer Bettye LaVette, Blues legend Magic Slim and Marquette's own Flat Broke Blues Band. The 5th Annual Marquette Area Blues Fest was held in 2008.

Woodtick Music Festival

This home-grown U.P. tradition got its start in the garage of Hermansville's Bill Martin in 1994. Martin called friends and local musicians to a jam session and cookout. A local bartender commented that it sounded like a regular "Woodstock" was planned and that since it was taking place in the Upper Peninsula, it should be called the "Woodtick."

The name stuck and the country-rock festival grew. The inaugural event drew a crowd of 100 and attendance has grown each year. In 2000, the Woodtick moved to the park at the lake in downtown Hermansville. Bands were actually hired and scheduled and the next year, admission was charged for the first time. In 2003, the events 10th season, the venue moved again to its present location, which includes camping facilities on County Road 338 between Hermansville and Powers. Originally begun as a Labor Day event (to coincide with the first Packer game of the season), the 2008 festival was held from July 31-August 3.

The Day the Rolling Stones Came to Marquette

One of the world's most famous rock-and-roll bands came to Marquette on July 24, 2002. They performed only one song – no vocals – before a small audience that offered no applause. There were no photographs, no autographs. The occasion was not about the Rolling Stones, it was about their beloved road manager, Chuch Magee.

Magee died of a heart attack in Toronto on July 18th while helping the Stones prepare for a world tour. Royden W. "Chuch" Magee was 54 and had been a member of the Rolling Stones family for 27 years.

Magee was born in Utica, Michigan and met Stones guitarist Ron Wood at the old Grande Ballroom in Detroit when he was with the group Faces. Magee began working with the Faces in the early 70s after reconnecting with Wood in London. When Wood joined the Rolling Stones in 1975, Magee went with him.

Magee and his wife, Claire, lived in her hometown of Marquette when he was not touring with the band. He was active in the Messiah Lutheran Church which is where his funeral was held and where the Stones performed in his honor.

Band members Mick Jagger, Keith Richards, Ron Wood, Charlie Watts, new bassist Daryl Jones, and about two dozen members of the Stone's support team interrupted their rehearsals to fly to Marquette. After arriving at Sawyer International Airport on the afternoon of July 24, 2002, band members drank coffee at the Northland Bar inside the Landmark Hotel, and visited the Peter White Library as well as the Marquette County History Museum before heading to the church.

They sat in the front pew before performing "Amazing Grace," with Richards on acoustic guitar, Woods on dobro, and Jagger on harmonica. Photographer Tom Wright said, "When they finished they walked back to their seats. You could have heard a pin drop except that everybody was crying. To see Keith Richards playing guitar with tears coming down his face is a whole different take on that band and what they're all about."

After the service, the band was driven back to Sawyer where they boarded their private jet and flew away long before most Marquette residents realized the Rolling Stones were there.

Steven Wiig – Metal Man

Born: December 30, 1972   Negaunee, MI

Wiig plays drums in *Papa Wheelie*, the band started by former *Metallica* member Jason Newsted. He is also a friend and assistant to *Metallica* drummer Lars Ulrich. Wiig can be seen in the documentary *Metallica: Some Kind of Monster* (2004), which followed the heavy metal band through the recording of the album, *St. Anger.*

He's also appeared on the big screen in the movie, *Into the Wild* (2007) directed by Academy Award winner Sean Penn. The film is based on the John Krakauer book of the same title that tells the true story of Christopher McCandless, the 22-year old college graduate who gave everything he owned and hiked into the Alaskan wilderness. He survived for three months on game and edible plants, but was found dead in an abandoned bus, probably of starvation or plant poisoning. In the movie, Wiig portrays Park Ranger Steve Koehler.

Wiig is also recognized for his talents as a graphic artist. He designs logos, t-shirts and CD cover designs for the bands he works with.

He was born in Negaunee, the son of schoolteachers Ray and Judy Wiig. His father taught at Westwood High, and his mother at Negaunee High School. His grandmother, Alice Arbelius lives in Palmer. Wiig graduated from Negaunee High School where he played basketball, football and tennis, and was voted "Most Artistic" by his graduating class in 1991.

Wiig lives in California with his wife Patricia and a son, Magnus. He returns the U.P. frequently to visit his mother and grandmother. In an October 2007 interview with *The Mining Journal*, Wiig said after traveling around the world he appreciates the U.P. more than ever. When he does return to the U.P., he said he makes sure he gets "each of the four basic U.P. food groups: Villa Capri pizza, Thunder Bay Inn cudighi, Lawry's pasties and Togo's No. 16 sub."

THE UPPER PENINSULA IN SONG

1913 Massacre – Woody Guthrie

Guthrie's song is based on the Italian Hall tragedy of Christmas Eve 1913. At that time, a miners strike was in its fifth month. The striking miners and their families planned a holiday celebration on the second floor of the Italian Hall in downtown Calumet. As parents and children took part in the festivities somebody yelled "Fire!" There was only one way out: down the narrow stairwell and out the front door. In the ensuing panic to escape 74 people, including 59 children, were trampled to death. There was no fire.

It was never proven who yelled "fire," and there were no arrests or convictions.

Twenty-eight years later, Woody Guthrie wrote his song singing of the "copper thugs" who "screamed, there's a fire!" He was not the first or the last person to theorize that the mining companies and scab workers were behind the tragedy. Guthrie first read of the Italian Hall disaster in *We Are Many*, the autobiography of Mother Bloor, a socialist and labor organizer who witnessed the events of that Christmas Eve.

The song never became a folk hit, but was recorded by Guthrie and included on two albums. The song was performed by his son, Arlo Guthrie and by Bob Dylan, who sang it at Carnegie Hall.

Wreck of the Edmund Fitzgerald – Gordon Lightfoot

The largest freighter to sink on the Great Lakes and its crew has been immortalized by the Canadian songwriter and singer, Gordon Lightfoot. His 1976 hit, *Wreck of the Edmund Fitzgerald,* rose to #2 on the Billboard pop charts in November, one year after the iron ore carrier sank in Lake Superior.

The *Fitzgerald* and its crew of 29 men went down in a fierce windstorm on November 10, 1975. At that time the 729-foot long freighter was the largest boat to sail the Great Lakes. It had left Superior, Wisconsin with 26,000 tons of iron ore bound for Detroit. Facing 60 mile-an-hour winds and waves over 20 feet, Captain Ernest McSorley sought the shelter of Whitefish Bay, but never made it. The *Fitzgerald's* image was lost from radar at 7:25 p.m., 15 minutes after McSorley reported, "We're holding our own."

Newsweek magazine carried a report about the sinking later that month, a story that caught Lightfoot's eye and heart. He said he wrote the song as a tribute to the ship, the sea, and the men who lost their lives that night. He has called the song his most significant contribution to music.

Specific references to the U.P. include the opening lines,

The legend lives on from the Chippewa on down Of the big lake they called 'Gitche Gumee' and later after "The Wreck," *The searches all say they'd have made Whitefish Bay If they'd put fifteen more miles behind her.*

The Wreck of the Edmund Fitzgerald remains Lightfoot's most popular song, and is played on hundreds of radio stations around the U.S. and Canada every year on November 10th.

Greetings from Michigan: The Great Lakes State – Sufjan Stevens

The Detroit-born songwriter-singer-musician crafted a conceptual album based on his home state, after the meager success of two earlier albums. While living in New York City he collected his various writings and crafted them into songs about Michigan. The result: a 15-song set of ethereal and unusual songs ranging in content from unemployment and poverty to Sleeping Bear and an estranged mother. Several of the songs are instrumental.

Those songs about or mentioning the U.P includes:

For the Widows in Paradise, for the Fatherless in Ypsilanti

The Upper Peninsula

Tahquamenon Falls

Sleeping Bear, Sault Ste. Marie

Oh God, Where Are You Now? (In Pickeral Lake? Pigeon? Marquette? ...)

Stevens' Michigan album is the first in his plan to record an album for each of the fifty states. He has since recorded a collection of 21 songs entitled, *The Avalanche: Outtakes and Extras from the Illinois Album.*

WRITERS AND AUTHORS

Robert Traver (John Voelker)

Born: June 19, 1903 in Ishpeming, MI (youngest of six boys)

Died: March 19, 1990

John Voelker authored ten books under the pen name of Robert Traver. The fourth book, *Anatomy of a Murder* (1957), was his best known. Hollywood took notice of the best seller set in the woods of Upper Michigan and shot the movie version in Marquette County. It starred Jimmy Stewart, Lee Remick, and fellow Michigan native George C. Scott.

Voelker grew up exploring the woods and waters of Marquette County and developed an appreciation for reading and writing from his schoolteacher mother. As a teenager, his academic talent was nurtured by a local attorney who also served as the boy's Sunday school teacher. He attended Northern Michigan University in the mid-1920s, then known as Northern Michigan Normal School, before heading to Ann Arbor. In 1928, he graduated with a law degree from the University of Michigan, where he also met his future wife, Grace Taylor.

After college, Voelker moved to Marquette where he served as assistant prosecutor before moving to Chicago to marry Grace and work in a large law firm. After three years, he had had enough of the big city bustle and moved back to the U.P. In 1934, Voelker ran as a Democrat and was elected prosecuting attorney of Marquette County.

While serving in this post he began to dabble in writing and chose the pen name of Robert Traver so voters wouldn't think that he was writing books on taxpayer time. The name came from an older brother who died of influenza while serving in the Navy during World War I, and his mother's maiden name. His first book, *Trouble Shooter: Story of a Northwoods Prosecutor* (1943) shared stories of odd characters and cases handled by his office.

In 1950, Voelker lost his bid for re-election by 36 votes to Republican Edmund J. Thomas. He went into private practice which allowed him more time with Grace and their three daughters. It also freed up time to fish at his beloved Frenchman's Pond, play cribbage at Polly's Rainbow Bar, and focus on writing.

In 1952, he represented U.S. Army officer Coleman A. Peterson who was charged with murder. He allegedly killed local bartender Mike Chenoweth after Chenoweth allegedly raped his wife. Defense attorney Traver went up against prosecutor Edmund Thomas, the man who defeated him two years earlier for that post.

Voelker had the satisfaction of defeating his nemesis in a case widely covered in the press. But the story wasn't over when the trial ended. In 1956, Voelker spent three months writing a fictitious account of the trial which was published the following year. *Anatomy of a Murder* was chosen as a Book-of-the-Month Club selection and spent over a year on the N.Y. Times best-seller list.

About this time he was appointed by Governor G. Mennen Williams to fill an open seat on the Michigan State Supreme Court. He ran for and was elected to an eight year term on the

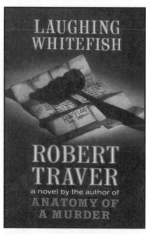

high court in 1958, and shortly after that Hollywood called. Renowned director Otto Preminger purchased film rights to *Anatomy of a Murder,* and in 1959, brought film crews and movie stars to Marquette County. The movie won six Academy Awards and featured a sound track by Duke Ellington.

After less than two years on the bench Voelker resigned, writing to Governor Williams; "Other people can write my opinions, but none can write my books. I have learned that I can't do both so regretfully I must quit the court."

He now engaged full time in fishing, cribbage, writing and family. He turned out books about trout fishing and trout fishermen that established his reputation as an outdoorsman and icon of the Upper Peninsula. During this period he befriended Charles Kurault, host of the popular *On the Road* series on CBS. The well-traveled television personality is quoted as saying Voelker "was really about the nearest thing to a great man I've ever known…one of the most graceful writers on the American literary scene."

Voelker died of a heart attack on the morning of March 8, 1991 while driving his car on a snowy road near his home. His wife Grace survived him by eight years.

Bibliography

Troubleshooter (1943)	Danny and the Boys (1951)
Smalltown D.A. (1954)	Anatomy of a Murder (1957)
Trout Madness (1960)	Hornstein's Boy (1962)
Laughing Whitefish (1965)	Jealous Mistress (1967)
Trout Magic (1974)	People vs. Kirk (1981)

Courage Burning: Incredible Stories about Incredible People, by Sonny Longtine
Copyright 2006, Sunnyside Publications, Marquette, MI
Michigan History Magazine Nov. /Dec. 2001

Charlotte Armstrong

Born: 1905 in Vulcan, Michigan (Dickinson County)

Armstrong was an author of popular mysteries in the middle 20th century. Several of her books were adapted to the movie screen.

The daughter of a mining engineer, Armstrong attended local schools and graduated from Vulcan High School in 1921. She received a liberal arts education at Ferry Hall, a "finishing school" in Lake Forest, Illinois, then attended the University of Wisconsin.

Armstrong began her writing career in the classified ads department of the *New York Times*. She went on to work as a fashion reporter for a smaller publication and then moved to Chicago where she married Jack Lewi. The marriage produced two boys and a girl and kept Armstrong busy at home.

During this period she dabbled in writing plays and then switched to writing mysteries after reading several "whodunits" while suffering from the flu. Her first mystery accepted for publication was *Lay on McDuff* which was well received. This encouraged her to continue as a mystery writer.

Her fourth mystery novel, *The Unsuspected*, was a big success, while her fifth book, *Mischief*, was made into the movie *Don't Bother to Knock* starring Marilyn Monroe and Richard Widmark.

Armstrong had 27 mysteries published between 1940 and 1970, and in 1957 her book, *A Dram of Poison*, won the prestigious Edgar Award for best mystery novel of the year.

Armstrong died on July 19, 1969.

Screenplays "Incident at a Corner", episode of Startime, dir. Alfred Hitchcock, 1959, "The Summer Hero," episode of The Chevy Mystery Show, 1960, Three episodes of Alfred Hitchcock Presents: "Sybilla" (dir. Ida Lupino), "The Five-Forty-Eight," "Across the Threshold" (1960)

Films The following films were adapted from Armstrong's novels and stories. *Merci pour le Chocolat,* 2000 (from the novel The Chocolate Cobweb) (dir. Claude Chabrol), *The Sitter,* 1991 (from the novel Mischief) (dir. Rick Berger), *La Rupture,* 1970 (from the novel The Balloon Man) (dir. Claude Chabrol), *Talk About a Stranger,* 1952 (from the short story, "The Enemy"), *Don't Bother to Knock,* 1952 (from the novel Mischief), *The Three Weird Sisters,* 1948 (from the novel The Case of the Weird Sisters) (dir. Daniel Birt), *The Unsuspected*, 1947.

Tom Bissell

Born: Escanaba, Michigan 1974

The Escanaba native has gone from Peace Corp dropout to accomplished author, referred to as a "rising star of American literature" by *Publisher's Weekly*. During that period, Bissell has authored three books of non-fiction, co-authored two others and contributed to several books including *Best American Travel Writing, 2003.*

He began writing poetry in junior high, and short stories in high school. While enrolled at Bay de Noc Community College, Bissel attended the Bennington Summer Writing Workshop in Vermont. While at Michigan State University, Bissell was co-editor of the *Red Cedar Review*, the literary magazine founded by Thomas McGuane, one of the writers whom Bissell admired.

Upon graduation from MSU in 1996, Bissell entered the Peace Corps, assigned to teach English in the former Soviet republic of Uzbekistan. He returned home early, after only eight months, depressed, confused about his future, and struggling to make sense of his life. He applied for a job at the local paper mill, but his application was not accepted.

Since high school, he had been reading *Harper's*, and knew about the magazine's intern program in their New York offices. He sent in an application, not expecting a response, but he got one. Bissell says after receiving the phone call inviting him in for an interview he may have set a world record for driving from Michigan to New York.

He landed the internship which, after four months, led to a job as an editorial assistant at the publisher Henry Holt. After arriving in New York he continued to write short stories and worked on a novel, but failed to get anything published. In early 2000, he heard that director-actor Jeff Daniels was filming the movie *Escanaba in da Moonlight* in Bissell's hometown. He proposed an article to *Harper's*, which was accepted and published in September 2000.

That Mitten Hand Thing

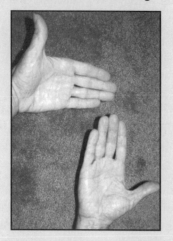

Many people don't even know it (the Upper Peninsula) exists. When you say you are from Michigan a lot of people do that irritating mitten hand thing, when you point. Well, I'm not on the mitten. [laughs] I'm off the mitten. I am from a part of Michigan that's attached to Wisconsin.

-Tom Bissell, The Morning News (online magazine) with Robert Birnbaum

The article, *Escanaba's Magic Hour*, led to Bissell's first book deal.

He revisited Uzbekistan and wrote *Chasing the Sea: Lost Among the Ghosts of the Empire in Central Asia* (Pantheon, 2003), a well received cross-country travelogue and account of the death of the Aral Sea.

His first book of fiction, *God Lives in St. Petersburg: and Other Stories* (Pantheon, 2005), was met with strong reviews, including one from *Outside* magazine which called it "a stunning fictional debut by a wildly talented young writer."

His most recent book resulted from an assignment for GQ. The magazine sent Bissell and his father to Vietnam, where the elder had served as a Marine in 1965 and '66. Bissell tried to capture his father's experience as a young man at war, and the effects on his life and his family's life upon his return home. After reading the article GQ editors chose not to publish it.

However, *Harper's* published it in December 2004 and it was later included in *The Best American Travel Writing 2005*, and was read on NPR's *Selected Shorts*. The exposure led to the publishing of *The Father of All Things* (Pantheon, 2007), which includes a history of the war and is recognized as the first book about the war and its effects written by a child of a Vietnam veteran.

Bissell has also written, with Webster Younce, *The Bellybutton Fiasco* (Xlibris, 2001); with Jeff Alexander *Speak, Commentary* (McSweeney's, 2003); and is a contributing writer to *A Galaxy Not So Far Away* (Holt, 2002), *Wild East* (Justin Charles, 2003), and *The Best American Travel Writing* (Houghton Mifflin, 2003 and 2005)

Lon Emerick

Lon Emerick is a fifth-generation descendant of Cornish copper miners who came to the Upper Peninsula of Michigan in the mid-1800s. As a disciple of Henry David Thoreau, he explores and writes about the woods and waters of the Superior Peninsula.

In a prior lifetime, Emerick was a professor of speech pathology at several universities, with the longest and most satisfying years at Northern Michigan University. Although he is the author of several university textbooks and numerous professional articles in speech pathology, he is most pleased to be identified with his later books about his ancestral land — the Upper Peninsula of Michigan. These include *With Stick and String — Adventures with Bow and Arrow; The Superior Peninsula — Seasons in the Upper Peninsula of*

Michigan; Sharing the Journey — Lessons from my Students and Clients with Tangled Tongues; Going Back to Central (Mine) — On the Road in Search of the Past; You Wouldn't Like it Here — A Guide to the Real Upper Peninsula; You STILL Wouldn't Like it Here — The Sequel.

Lon Emerick has two daughters who grew up exploring the wilds of the Upper Peninsula. One is now a wilderness ranger in the Tongass National Forest, based in Sitka, Alaska and the other a helitack manager for wildland fire with the Kootenai National Forest in Libby Montana.

Lon Emerick lives now in a log home in the woods of Marquette County with his wife Lynn, who is the co-editor, with her sister, of the book *Lumberjack — Inside an Era in the Upper Peninsula of Michigan.*

Steve Hamilton

Born: Detroit area

Hamilton is the author of seven mystery novels starring Alex McKnight a former minor league baseball player and Detroit cop, who lives by himself in a cabin in Paradise. The first book in the series, *A Cold Day in Paradise*, was published in 1998 and went on to win the Shamus Award from the Private Eye Writers of America and the Edgar Award from the Mystery Writers of America. Hamilton is the only author whose first book won both of those prestigious awards. In 2006, he won the Michigan Author Award from the Michigan Center for the Book.

Hamilton is a native of the Detroit area who spent a lot of vacation time in Upper Michigan. The desire to be a writer goes back to childhood when Hamilton submitted a short story to Ellery Queen Mystery Magazine (it was rejected), and continued through college where he won the prestigious Hopwood Award from the University of Michigan. However, after surveying the job market of the 1980s, Hamilton chose to pursue a more prudent path majoring in computer science.

After college he took a position with IBM, started a family and writing took a back seat. About ten years later, a friend invited him to a writers group that met every Thursday at a local library. Before long he read about a contest for Best First Private Eye Novel sponsored by St. Martin's Press. He wrote *A Cold Day in Paradise* and won the contest that launched his writing career.

He followed up with *Winter of the Wolf Moon* (2000), and *The Hunting Wind* (2001). In each book Alex McKnight struggles to lead an uncomplicated life as he recovers from a broken marriage and the shooting death of his police partner. In that incident Alex took a bullet but survived, which may explain why he can't seem to say no when called on to put his police detective skills to work. Each book features his pal Jackie, owner of the Glasgow Inn where Alex spends a good amount of time by the fire nursing an ice cold Molson's; Vinnie, his Ojibwe friend; Leon the wannabe private eye from the Soo, and in later books a love interest Natalie Reynaud an officer with the Ontario Provincial Police.

The settings and weather of the eastern U.P. and Canada are prominently featured in all seven of his books.

In 2006 a short story of Hamilton's was adapted to film by producer/director Nick Childs. The result was *The Shovel* starring David Stathairn who played newsman Edward Murrow in the movie, *Good Night and Good Luck.* The 15 minute short co-written by Hamilton earned awards at the Tribeca Film Festival, the USA Film Festival and a handful of other awards.

That same year Hamilton took Childs on a tour of Alex McKnight's stomping grounds in the eastern U.P. as the pair began work on a film production of *Winter of the Wolf Moon.*

Upon accepting his Michigan Author Award in 2006 Hamilton said, "I'm still a Michigan boy at heart. I can't even tell you what this award means to me. It feels like the whole state is calling me back home, to let me know I did something worth celebrating. It's overwhelming." He maintains his day job at IBM in New York's Hudson Valley, but says he would like to someday become a full-time writer.

Jerry Harju

Born: Ishpeming, Michigan, 1933

Jerry Harju's career as a humor writer began in an unlikely way. The Ishpeming native received a degree in engineering mechanics at the University of Michigan in 1957 and completed his formal education with a Master's of Science degree from Southern Cal in 1985. He

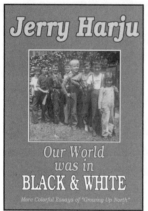

spent 30 years as a manager in the aerospace industry in California before he began his second career as a writer.

Jerry's novel, *Cold Cash* won a Midwest Independent Publisher's Book Achievement award in 1999. In all, he has written ten books, all with humor as an overriding theme, *Northern Reflections, Northern D'Lights, Northern Passages, Northern Memories, Northern Tales No. 5, The Class of '57, Cold Cash, Here's what I think..., Way Back When,* and *Our World Was in Black & White.* Some of his works are autobiographical, including *Class of '57* which details his six years at U. of M. 1950's University life was much different than it is today particularly in the attitudes towards morals, world affairs and women's roles in society. These attitudes provide plenty of fodder for Harju's humorous style.

In addition to writing, publishing and promoting his work, Harju has ventured into publishing other authors' work. Larry Chabot's *The U.P. Goes to War* was successfully released by Harju's company North Harbor Publishing in 2006. His latest work, *Northern Tales #5,* was released in February 2009.

Jim Harrison

Born: Grayling, Michigan December 11, 1937

Harrison is one of the great writers of the 20th century whose published works have been translated into dozens of languages, and made into several major motion pictures. Most of Harrison's novels are set in rural America, including the Upper Peninsula where, for many years, the author found a peaceful escape from the rest of the world.

Harrison was raised in the rural setting of Reed City south of Cadillac, Michigan. His family moved there from Grayling when he was three. At age seven he lost sight in his left eye after a young playmate injured him with a glass laboratory beaker. Now scarred and half blind, the young boy found hope and comfort in the woods.

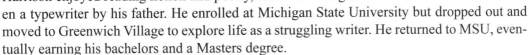

His father built a cabin on a lake deep in the woods where the family spent most of their summers. Harrison's curiosity was sparked by nature. He loved observing wildlife, swimming in the lake, wandering the forest, and sleeping outdoors. Later in life he bought a cabin near Grand Marais because it reminded him of his family's cabin in the woods.

Nature sparked his curiosity which fueled his desire to learn. Harrison enjoyed reading fiction and poetry, and at 17 was given a typewriter by his father. He enrolled at Michigan State University but dropped out and moved to Greenwich Village to explore life as a struggling writer. He returned to MSU, eventually earning his bachelors and a Masters degree.

While in East Lansing he met and married Linda May King and forged friendships with fellow writers Thomas McGuane and Dan Gerber. His first daughter, Jamie Louise was born 1960, the year he earned his bachelors degree. While attending MSU in 1962 he received news that his father and younger sister Judith had died in an automobile accident.

Harrison was living and working in Kingsley, Michigan near Traverse City in 1965 when his first book of poetry, *Plain Song*, was published. Over the next few years he taught at SUNY in Stony Brook, New York, continued to write and, with Dan Gerber, started the literary magazine *Sumac*.

In 1969, Harrison injured his back after falling from a cliff while hunting. During his lay up he began work on his first novel, *Wolf: A False Memoir* (partially set in the U.P.). The book was published in 1971 along with a collection of poetry, *Outlyers and Ghazals*. Also during this year the Harrison's welcomed their second daughter, Anna Severin.

Through the early 1970s Harrison traveled with Dan Gerber, dabbled in screenwriting and had three more books published: *A Good Day to Die* (1973), *Letters to Yesinen* (1973), and *Farmer* (1976).

His friendship with Thomas McGuane lead Harrison to meet actor Jack Nicholson who was impressed enough to bankroll Harrison's writing for one year. This resulted in *Legends of the Fall* (1978), a collection of three novellas: *Revenge, The Man Who Gave Up His Name*, and *Legends of the Fall*. This brought commercial success as film rights for all three novellas were sold and Harrison signed on as a contracted screenwriter in Hollywood.

The boy who loved the woods did not find the cut-throat, glitzy Hollywood life to his liking. In 1980 he bought a cabin on 50 acres near Grand Marais. When he wasn't writing in the cabin or walking through the woods near the Sucker River, he could be found at the Lake Superior Brewing Co. and Dunes Saloon in Grand Marais.

Harrison followed *Legends of the Fall* with *Warlock* (1981) and *Sundog* (1984), both with scenes set in the U.P. He also had two collections of poems published in the 1980s: *Selected and New Poems* (1981) and *The Theory and Practice of Rivers, and Other Poems* (1986).

In 1990, Harrison introduced readers to Brown Dog (B.D.) a half Finn, half Chippewa Indian who wishes to be left alone to live in the woods. B.D. manages to survive on the land

and a string of temporary odd jobs, and attracts a good number of females and odd characters to his orbit. Brown Dog appeared in *The Woman Lit by Fireflies* (1990), a collection of three novellas and again in *Julip* (1994).

Harrison also made his mark in Hollywood during the 1990s. He co-wrote the movie *Wolf* (1994), starring Jack Nicholson; he co-wrote the screen version of *Legends of the Fall* (1995) that starred Anthony Hopkins and Brad Pitt; and the movie *Carried Away* (1996), based on his book *Farmer*, starring Dennis Hopper and Amy Irving.

In 2000, Harrison revisited Brown Dog and the U.P. in *The Beast That God Forgot to Invent*, another collection of three novellas, and Harrison's first children's book, *The Boy Who Ran into the Woods*, was published. The autobiographical story recounts Harrison's eye injury and discovery of the great outdoors as a young boy.

In 2004, Harrison sold his remote cabin near Grand Marais and moved to Montana to be closer to his daughter and grandchildren. That same year Harrison's *True North* was published. The story features guilt-riddled David Burkett, part of a fourth generation pioneer lumbering family that earned its fortune ravaging the forests of the Upper Peninsula.

The U.P. family saga continued in *Returning to Earth* (2007) which found Burkett's brother-in-law dying of Lou Gehrig's disease. On death's doorstep he recounts his family history in the U.P. to his wife. The story includes a good bit of logging history and Chippewa legend from the Upper Peninsula.

Harrison has delivered his version of the Upper Peninsula's people, places and history to readers around the world. His books have been translated into 22 languages. He has won numerous writing awards including: a Guggenheim Award, Michigan Foundation for the Arts Award, Detroit News Michiganian of the Year (1983), Mark Twain Award from M.S.U., Michigan Author Award from the Michigan Library Association, Pushcart Prize, L.A. Times Book Prize, Mountains & Plains Booksellers Association Spirit of the West award, and PEN American/International PEN Award.

His personal and professional papers are now open to the public for research at Grand Valley State University Special Collections in Allendale, Michigan.

Harrison splits his time between homes in Montana and Arizona.

Joseph Heywood

Born: Oct 18, 1943 Rhinebeck, NY

Former resident and frequent visitor to the U.P., Joseph Heywood has written five books in the "Woods Cop" series that stars conservation officer Grady Service.

The son of a career U.S. Air Force officer, Heywood and family moved frequently, eventually settling in Chippewa County. Heywood attended Rudyard High School, playing on the football, baseball, and basketball teams before graduating in 1961. At Michigan State University, Heywood starred on the lacrosse team and in 1965 earned a degree in journalism. He studied English Literature in graduate school at Western Michigan University.

In 1965, Heywood married Sandra V. Heywood (1943-2002). The marriage produced five children.

Heywood followed in his father's footsteps by serving in the Air Force. As a navigator, he flew missions in Vietnam and achieved the rank of Captain before his honorable discharge in 1970. His post-military career path included stints as a high school coach, university professor, rent-a-cop, forest fighter with the US. Forest Service and from 1970-1998 he worked for Upjohn Pharmaceutical, retiring as the Vice President for Worldwide Public Relations.

All of the "Woods Cop" books are centered on Grady Service, a former Marine and son of a conservation officer. Service lives in a shack in the woods, risks his life protecting the natural resources of the rugged country, and detests the bureaucracy of the DNR in Lansing.

Heywood has professed his respect for the talents of the men and women of the DNR conservation corps, and spends up to 30 days a year shadowing them as part of his research for each book.

The "Woods Cop" series includes: Ice Hunter (2001), Blue Wolf in Green Fire (2002) Chasing a Blond Moon (2003), Running Dark (2005), Strike Dog (2007), and Death Roe (2008), all published by the Lyons Press.

In 2003 he wrote *Covered Waters: Tempests of a Nomadic Trouter (Lyons Press),* more a memoir than a book about trout fishing. As Heywood says, "If it's true that five percent of the fishermen catch 90 percent of the fish, then I have something to say to the ninety-five percent of us who subsist on the ten percent."

Heywood is retired and lives in Portage, Michigan. He spents lots of time in the forests of the Upper Peninsula.

Sue Harrison

Born: August 29, 1950, Lansing, Michigan

In 1990, after 13 years of research, writing, re-writing, soliciting agents, and numerous rejections Sue Harrison became an internationally known author when her first book, *Mother Earth Father Sky*, was published by Doubleday. The novel sold hundreds of thousands of copies in 20 countries. The success led to a follow up book, and eventually a trilogy.

Harrison was born in Lansing and raised in the Chippewa County town of Pickford. She was the oldest of five children; her father was a teacher, and her mother a musician. She became hooked on reading at age ten when given a copy of Laura Ingalls Wilder's *Little House in the Big Woods*. The book had an immediate and lasting impact as Harrison later recalled; "The words seemed to sing, and I could see the whole book in my mind as if I were watching a movie. I was fascinated with the idea that words could "make pictures" in the mind, and decided that I, too, wanted to write books, and that I would write novels."

She graduated from Pickford High School in 1968 and from Lake Superior State University in 1971 with a degree in English Language and Literature. Before graduating from college she married Neil Harrison, whom she knew since elementary school. Their first child, a daughter, died of meningitis. Two more children, a boy and girl, followed. During this time they ran a sporting goods store, but were forced to close after the Kincheloe Air Force Base shut down.

After reading *Roots* by Alex Haley, Harrison was inspired to learn about the native peo-

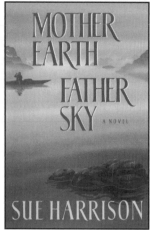

ple of Michigan. Her research led to books and stories about the land bridge that once connected North America to Siberia. Many anthropologists theorize that North American natives arrived by crossing over this land bridge thousands of years ago into what is now Alaska. She was fascinated by the stories of these ancient peoples who learned to hunt whales, endure frigid weather and survive occasional volcanoes.

She began research in 1977, completed a rough draft by 1984, and after several unsuccessful attempts, landed an agent in 1989. Later that year *Mother Earth Father Sky* was purchased by Doubleday; Harrison received a $407,000 advance and a commitment for two more books in what has become the Ivory Carver Trilogy.

Mother Earth Father Sky was published in 1990 and named a Main Selection by the Literary Guild in 1991. Harrison followed up with *My Sister the Moon* in 1992, and completed the trilogy with *Brother Wind* (1994).

Her stories of the ancient people on the frozen land continued with the Storyteller Trilogy: *Song of the River* (1997), *Cry of the Wind* (1998) and *Call Down the Stars* (2001).

Harrison also authored *SISU* (1997), a young adult novel about a boy with diabetes who runs away from a hospital to hide in the woods of the Upper Peninsula.

She continues to write and live in Pickford where her husband is principal of the local high school. In the works: perhaps a suspense novel or a historical novel set in the eastern U.P.

Stellanova Osborn

Born: July 31, 1894. Hamilton, Ontario

Stella Lee Brunt was a writer and student at the University of Michigan in 1924 when she met Chase S. Osborn, former governor of Michigan. The pair shared an interest in writing and hit it off even though Osborn, at 71, was forty years her senior. She became his secretary, and in 1931 he adopted her as his daughter. At the time Osborn was separated from his wife Lillian, but would remain married in the interests of the couple's children.

"The adoption principally was for appearances…I wanted to marry him, but that was not possible," she later explained. She changed her name to Stellanova, meaning "new star" as the request of Osborn.

Osborn attended the Collegiate Night School in Hamilton, Ontario prior to her studies at the University of Michigan. In 1922, she earned her Bachelor of Arts degree and in 1930 her Masters degree.

She became active in the International Movement or Atlantic Union which advocated for world government to avoid war. She served as secretary for several years and traveled extensively throughout Europe.

Osborn acted as editor for her first book, compiling and arranging the written tributes to her husband in *An Accolade for Chase S. Osborn. Home, State, and National Tributes on the Occasion of Chase S. Osborn Day, October 4, 1939.*

She and the former Governor co-authored her second book, *The Conquest of a Continent*, also published in 1939. The book detailed border disputes and how boundary lines were negotiated in Michigan and Alaska. The couple also co-authored *Schoolcraft-Longfellow-Hiawatha* in 1942, a detailed account of the writings of Indian agent Henry Schoolcraft and his influence on the epic Longfellow poem, *Song of Hiawatha*.

The couple would co-author three more books together including another look at the Schoolcraft-Longfellow connection in *Hiawatha with Its Original Indian Legends* (1945).

Stellanova authored *Some Sidelights on the Battle of Tippecanoe* (1943); *A Tale of Possum Poke in Possum Lane* (1946); and several books of poems including: *Balsam Boughs* (1949); *Jasmine Springs* (1953); *Polly Cadote* (1955); *Beside the Cabin* (1957); *Iron and Arbutus* (1962) and *Summer Songs on the St. Mary's* (1982)

In 1949, upon the death of Osborn's wife Lillian, the adoption of Stellanova was annulled and the couple was married. Osborn, who was 89 and in poor health, died two days later. Stellanova moved to the campus of Lake Superior State University and continued to write.

Stellanova Brunt Osborn passed away in 1988 at the age of 94. She and the governor are buried near their cabin on Duck Island off the southeastern shore of Sugar Island. Their graves are surrounded by 3,000 acres of wilderness donated by the Osborn's to the University of Michigan.

Carroll Watson Rankin

Born: May 11, 1864 in Marquette

The Marquette native is best known for her book, *The Dandelion Cottage* published in 1904. Set in Marquette, it is the story about four girls who spend a summer using a local cottage as their own playhouse after ridding the front lawn of all dandelions. The small home in the story was modeled after the sexton's house used by St. Paul's Episcopal Church in Marquette.

Rankin had two sequels to *The Dandelion Cottage* published in 1908 and in 1911 by Henry Holt and Company.

Her writing career began when the *Daily Mining Journal* hired her, at the age of sixteen, as a reporter. After she was married, Rankin wrote articles for *Ladies Home Journal* and the children's magazine, *Youth's Companion*. Her stories caught the eye of editors from Henry Holt and Company requesting that she write a children's book.

Rankin gathered up seven chapters of stories, written for daughter Eleanor and her friends and submitted them to the publisher. Within a year, *The Dandelion Cottage* was published and became a widely popular children's book.

First editions of the book are highly collectible, but scarce. Newer editions are available from the Marquette County Historical Museum. Carroll Watson Rankin died in 1945 while living in Marquette.

Fred Rydholm

Born: 1924 in Marquette - Died: April 4, 2009

Rydholm may hold the record for writing the largest book ever on U.P. history. For 35 years he collected stories and researched the history of the central Upper Peninsula. The result: *Superior Heartland, A Backwoods History,* a two-volume hardcover set that comes in at 1,600 pages.

His interest in local history goes back to his boyhood when he listened to his traveling salesman father spin tales about the people and places in his U.P. territory. His first official research and writing project would come in 1950 as a history student at Western Michigan University (WMU). By that time, Rydholm had graduated from Gravaraet High School and Albion College, started his teaching career, served in the U.S. Navy and for several years, studied the history of the Bentley Trail. At WMU, he wrote a 68-page history of the trail that runs 25 miles between the Huron Mountain Club and the McCormick camp on White Deer Lake.

His professor was so impressed with the paper that he visited the Bentley Trail, and encouraged Rydholm to write more of the region's history, as little had been recorded.

In 1953, Rydholm began a 35 year stint as a teacher in the Marquette school system. Two years later, he began a research project that ended in 1989 and resulted in his 1,600 page book, *Superior Heartland.* In 1952, he married fellow schoolteacher June Beltrame, a marriage that produced two children.

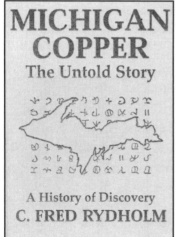

In 1949, Rydholm was able to purchase the old Bentley halfway cabin that he discovered while researching the trail. He now owns adjacent property that he has developed into a 1,000-acre tree farm. He planted 2,000 trees a year on the property for 40 years.

His latest book, *Michigan Copper: The Untold Story* was published in 2006. In it, he presents research to support his claim that explorers of European origin, dating back to 1700 BC, were the first to mine copper from the Keweenaw Peninsula and Isle Royale.

He lived in the family home where he had been raised, a Lake Superior cabin that his parents acquired in 1917. While the original structure still stands, it has had several additions.

Rydholms website is www.superiorheartland.com.

Richard P. Smith

Born: March 9, 1949 in Bremerton, Washington

The Marquette resident has authored 22 books, mostly related to deer and bear hunting. He is a regular contributor to *Michigan Sportsman Magazine, Woods-N-Water News* and *The Porcupine Press.* His writing and his photography have appeared in such national magazines as *Buckmasters, North American Whitetail, Deer & Deer Hunting, Outdoor Life* and *North American Hunter.*

In 1997, he received the Ben East Prize from the Michigan United Conservation Clubs for conservation journalism about bear management. That same year he was also named Outdoor Journalist of the Year by the Flint, Michigan chapter of the Safari Club.

Smith was born into an outdoor family. Both parents were natives of the U.P. He was introduced to hunting and fishing by his father and his uncle, George. While his father finished a tour of duty overseas with the U.S. Navy, Uncle George would frequently take Richard and his brother hunting or fishing. Smith's relatives from his mother's side of the family also shared their knowledge of the outdoors with young Richard.

While attending Marquette High School, Smith walked into the offices of *The Mining Journal,* the town's daily newspaper, and offered to contribute a few articles. Editor, Kenneth S. Lowe encouraged the teen, which led to Smith writing a weekly outdoor column for the paper.

After high school Smith earned a degree in Biology and Conservation from Northern Michigan University. He worked on, but did not complete a Masters program in wildlife and fisheries management due to the demands of his full-time career as a writer.

When Lowe took over as editor of *Michigan Out-of-Doors* magazine published by the Michigan United Conservation Clubs, he hired Smith as a regular contributor. That job led to Smith contributing articles to other outdoors magazines and to the first of his many books.

Smith has firsthand knowledge of his subject gained from over forty years of hunting deer and black bear.

In November 2000, Smith became only the second person in Michigan to achieve the CBM Grand Slam by shooting a deer, bear, elk and turkey that qualify for listing in state records maintained by Commemorative Bucks of Michigan (CBM).

One of his trophy bear is on display at the Cabela's Store in Hamburg, Pennsylvania. Smith used a .45 caliber Knight Super Disc Muzzleloader to take the bear in Saskatchewan in 2002, the second highest scoring black bear in national muzzleloading records.

His most famous bear was not a record-setter. The snarling bear shows up at the beginning of the movie Escanaba in da Moonlight, filmed in 2000 in Escanaba. The bear head fills the screen at the beginning of the movie and shows up in later scenes. Smith took the bear in 1974 using a bow and arrow.

His 22nd book, *Black Bear Hunting* was published in August 2007. The 350-page hardcover book is packed with Smith's knowledge and photographs of bear and bear hunting.

Ten of Smith's nearly two dozen books have been published by Smith Publications, with his wife as publisher. He credits her for much of the success he has enjoyed in his writing and publishing career.

John Smolens

Smolens has authored five critically acclaimed novels, a collection of short stories, and in 2008 his sixth novel, *The Anarchist*, will be published by Shaye Areheart/Random House. Critics have praised his ability to bring alive the natural surroundings and small towns where his stories unfold. Two of his books, Cold (2001) and Fire Point (2004), are set in the Upper Peninsula.

A professor of English who teaches at Northern Michigan University, Smolens is the former director of NMU's MFA Program in Creative Writing. He moved north to Marquette in 1996 in time to experience a record-setting winter of snowfall. Before NMU, Smolens taught at Michigan State University and Western Michigan University.

Long, severe winters were nothing new to Smolens who grew up in Wellesley, Massachusetts. He spent a lot of time playing hockey and other sports, and as a boy dreamed of becoming a goaltender for the Boston Bruins. Among early influences on his life he cites the Sisters of Charity of Halifax, who taught at St. Paul's Parochial School in Wellesley.

Smolens earned a hockey scholarship to Boston College, where he earned his Bachelor of Arts in English. He received an MA at the University of New Hampshire, and an MFA from the Writers' Workshop at the University of Iowa.

While attending Boston College he shared an apartment with the late Andre Dubus, nationally acclaimed author. From Dubus, Smolens learned the discipline required to be a good writer. His first book, *Winter by Degrees* (E.P. Dutton, 1987) was well-received by reviewers in major newspapers who praised his ability to capture life in a small seacoast town where surviving the harsh winters is a source of pride for the locals.

His next book, *Angel's Head* (Countryman's Press, 1994), was a novel of suspense set on an isolated island near Cape Cod (his mother lived on Cape Cod for many years). It was also well received by critics. Later, Smolens and his wife Reesha were living in Marquette near the prison that was built decades before their 100-year old house. He heard tales from neighbors about escaped inmates who turned themselves in rather than endure the harsh winter weather. This provided inspiration for his next book, *Cold* (Shaye Areheart Books, 2001), of which fellow writer Jim Harrison said: "a finely crafted, wild yarn set in the great north. John Smolens gives us a suspenseful tale in a style somewhere between Jack London and Raymond Chandler. A fine read."

In *The Invisible World* (Shaye Areheart Books, 2002) set in and around Boston, Smolen's alludes to the various conspiracy theories associated with the JFK assassination in a story described by The Boston Globe as "more than a first-rate political thriller."

His book, *Fire Point* (Shaye Areheart Books, 2004) is set in the Upper Peninsula. A young woman and her lover are stalked by her former boyfriend, a local police officer who is also the police chief's son. In 2004, it was named by the *Detroit Free Press* as the best book by a Michigan author.

Smolens next novel, *The Anarchist,* is his second novel to create a story and characters from the events surrounding a Presidential assassination. This time it's the 25th President, William McKinley, who was shot in 1901 by Leon Czolgosz, an anarchist who worked the lumber camps near Seney in the U.P.

Frederick Stonehouse

Born: 1948, New Brunswick, New Jersey

When scholars and historians need an expert opinion or bottom line answer on the history of the Great Lakes they turn to Frederick Stonehouse. The Marquette resident has authored thirty books, many of them focusing on Great Lakes Maritime history and lore. He is regarded as an authority on the subject and has served as an on-air consultant for television productions on the *History Channel*, *National Geographic* and *Fox Family.* His book, *Wreck Ashore: the United States Life-Saving Service on the Great Lakes* won a national award and is regarded as the preeminent work on the topic.

His interest in maritime history began at an early age. He was raised in Seaside Park, New Jersey, a small town on the Atlantic Ocean. In 1966, he moved to the Marquette to study at Northern Michigan University. With the largest Great Lake in his backyard Stonehouse began research on historic shipwrecks. His knowledge of local maritime history caught the attention of George and Bettey Tomasi, his scuba instructors at the time.

After college Stonehouse left Marquette to serve in the U.S. Army in Vietnam. While there, he continued to write about Lake Superior shipwreck history, sending his work back to the Tomasi's, who formed a company specifically to publish his first book, *Great Wrecks of the Great Lake: A Directory of the Shipwrecks of Lake* Superior (Harboridge Press, 1973).

Returning from Vietnam, Stonehouse continued his research and writing and produced *Isle Royale Shipwrecks*, and *Marquette Shipwrecks,* both published in 1974. He married and settled in Marquette pursuing his interests in Great Lakes history. To date, he has authored 30 books along with dozens of magazine articles. Stonehouse has received many awards for his writing and his achievements as a historian as well as his accomplishments in diving and underwater exploration of the Great Lakes.

Stonehouse holds a Master of Arts degree in history from Northern Michigan University (NMU), where he now serves as an Adjunct Instructor. He has developed courses on Great Lakes maritime history for NMU and Central Michigan University, where he also works as an Adjunct Instructor.

He serves on the boards of Northern Michigan University Alumni, Marquette Harbor Advisory Committee, Marquette

County Economic Club, DeVos Art Museum Advisory Board, and several others.

Of his thirty books, Stonehouse is most proud of *Wreck Ashore: the United States Live-Saving Service on the Great Lakes* (originally published in 1994, updated in 2003), the first book to detail the heroic deeds of the men who risked their lives to save others on the Great Lakes from the 1870s through 1915.

Below is a partial list of the books authored by the preeminent Great Lakes scholar Frederick Stonehouse.

They Had to Go Out (2007) (Contributor)   *Haunted Lake Michigan* (2006)
Shipwrecks of Lake Superior (2005)   *The Wreck of the Edmund Fitzgerald* (1999)
Great Lakes Lighthouse Tales (1998)   *Went Missing* (1993)
Keweenaw Shipwrecks (1988) *Lake Superior's Shipwreck Coast* (1985)
Munising Shipwrecks (1983)   *Isle Royale Shipwrecks* (1977)
Marquette Shipwrecks (1977)
Great Lakes Crime II, More Murder, Mayhem, Booze and Broads (2007)
Steel on the Bottom, Great Lakes Steel Shipwrecks (2006)
Cooking Lighthouse Style, Favorite Recipes From Coast to Coast (2003)
Women and the Lakes: Untold Great Lakes Maritime Tales (2001)
Haunted Lakes, Great Lakes Maritime Ghost Stories, Superstitions and Sea Serpents (1997)
Children's books
Final Passage, True Shipwreck Adventures (2002)
My Summer at the Lighthouse, A Boy's Journal (2003)

Betty Sodders

Outdoor writer Betty Sodders began her writing career later in life. She states that she and her husband Bill "retired at the early age of 46 and basically lived in the wilderness on love instead of dollars." At age 80, she is still enjoying her profession.

Sodders first book, *Michigan Prehistory Mysteries* was published in 1991. Her best known work, *Michigan on Fire* came out in 1997. It chronicles Michigan wildfires through eye-witness accounts and newspaper articles dating back to the disastrous Peshtigo Fire of 1871 that jumped the Menominee River into the Upper Peninsula. Both books were followed by sequels.

Sodders still contributes 100-200 articles annually in such publications as *Whitetails Unlimited, Outdoor Times* and *Wood-N-Water News*. She lives in the Chippewa County community of Goetzville.

John Walker

Born: June 21, 1943   Ontonagon, Michigan

The former DNR Game Warden has written nine books, most of them humorous accounts of his adventures in the field. He has started a scholarship fund using profits from book sales. Walker has donated $60,000 to the fund, and handed out over $20,000 so far, mostly in amounts of $500 or less.

Walker's boyhood was spent playing in the great outdoors around Ontonagon. He learned to appreciate a good story from his grandfather, and later enjoyed stories swapped between fellow DNR officers. He considers himself more a storyteller than writer.

After graduating from Ontonagon High in 1967, he served three years in the U.S. Army. He then married Eunie Brown who he met in Missouri. The couple moved to the U.P. so Walker could study forestry at Michigan Tech. Upon graduation, he was hired by the DNR as a fire agent in Caro, Michigan where he spent eight years.

In the mid-70s, the Walker's moved to Manistique where he served as a conservation officer until retiring in 1991. During this time Walker began his writing career, although he had no intention of ever becoming an author. He wrote a weekly column for the *Manistique Pioneer Tribune* describing some of his experiences as a conservation officer, which resulted in his first and most popular book, *A Deer Gets Revenge*, which has sold 25,000 copies.

Once Walker retired, he had more time to scour his memory banks for more book material. The result was his second book, *A Bucket of Bones*, which was followed by *From the Land Where BIG Fish Live*. All of Walker's books are self-published and sub-titled "*Tales from a Game Warden*." He strives to keep all of the stories positive, humorous and G-rated.

The Walker's, who raised four children, are active members of the Bethel Baptist Church near their home in Manistique. Most of his scholarship donations have gone to members of the church, but he also provides money for students who study at any Christian college or university.

Walker's books are not widely available, mostly sold in small stores throughout the Upper Peninsula, but they remain wildly popular. His ninth book, *Remember! Someone's Watching You!*, was published in 2008.

Cully Gage (Charles Van Riper)

"Cully Gage" was the pen name of Charles Van Riper born in the western Marquette County town of Champion in 1905. The son of an Upper Peninsula family doctor, "Cully" (Finnish derivative of Carl or Charles) spent his years exploring the forests of the central U.P. He also listened intently to the stories of the miners and loggers of early 20th Century Upper Michigan and developed a love of the local history.

Van Riper left his rural Marquette County home to attend Northern State Teachers College (NMU) where he studied for two years. He then transferred to the University of Michigan earning a bachelor's and master's degree. After college, he taught at the high school level in both Saline and Champion.

Van Riper was plagued with severe stuttering all his life. It was a major impediment that caused him much distress and even led him to contemplate suicide. Determined to conquer the problem, he enrolled in graduate psychology courses at the University of Iowa. He eventually completed his PhD and went back to his home state to accept a teaching position at Western Michigan University. There he set up a speech clinic and wrote a number of text books and papers on the subject of speech pathology.

In his other life, Cully Gage wrote a series of "Northwoods

Readers" spinning yarns about what it was like to live in the Upper Peninsula at the turn of the 20th Century. His bibliography includes eight books published between 1978 and 1994 and numerous articles in various Upper Michigan publications. Charles Van Riper died in 1994.

THE U.P. IN LITERATURE

Two of the most recognized names in American literature used the natural terrain of the Upper Peninsula as settings for their work. Nobel Prize winning author Ernest Hemingway likely fished the Fox River upon his return from service in the World War I. Henry Wadsworth Longfellow never set foot in the U.P., but relied on the writings of Indian agent Henry Rowe Schoolcraft as inspiration for his poem, *Song of Hiawatha*.

Hemingway and the Big Two-Hearted River

Hemingway was born in Oak Park, Illinois on July 21, 1899. He made his first visit to the family's summer home near Petoskey before his first birthday. He spent every summer in northern Lower Michigan, learning to fish, camp, and hunt.

While serving as an ambulance driver in the war, Hemingway was hit in the legs by mortar and machine gun fire. He returned to the family cottage on Walloon Lake to recuperate. Around 1919 or 1920, Hemingway took a fishing trip to the U.P., riding the rails to St. Ignace, where he boarded another bound for Seney. By the end of 1920, he had moved to Toronto, taking a job as a reporter with the *Toronto Star Weekly*.

The following year he married Hadley Richardson in the town of Horton Bay near the Hemingway cottage. The couple lived a short time in Toronto before moving to Paris, where Hemingway pursued his writing career. Some of his early stories featuring the character Nick Adams were set in northern Lower Michigan. In his story, *Big Two Hearted River: Part I and II* Nick rides the train to St. Ignace and sets off on a fishing adventure, just as Hemingway did three years earlier.

Big Two Hearted River is actually set on the Fox River that runs through Seney in Schoolcraft County. In the story, Nick grabs a sandwich at the St. Ignace train station before catching another train to Seney. Hemingway describes the town as burned out from fire. Nick hikes until reaching a point where the river runs through a forest of small pine trees. There he builds a camp and fishes for trout in the Fox River.

In writing about Seney, Hemingway also mentions the 13 saloons that once lined its main street, and the burned out Mansion House hotel (probably a reference to the old White House Hotel). For years, scholars thought the story was set on the Two Hearted River in the U.P., but Hemingway confirmed in a letter to his father that the story was set on the Fox.

It first appeared in 1925 in *This Quarter*, published in Paris. Later it was included in his book of short stories, *In Our Time*.

Source: Hemingway in Michigan, by Constance, Cappel Montgomery, copyright 1966, Fleet Publishing Corporation

Song of Hiawatha

One of the most popular poems of the 19th Century is set in the Upper Peninsula, the land of Hiawatha. Henry Wadsworth Longfellow (1807-1882) retired from his position of professor at Harvard in 1854 with the goal of writing an epic poem dedicated to the American Indian. Research led him to the writings of Henry Rowe Schoolcraft, who recorded Ojibwe words and customs during his tenure as federal Indian Agent Sault Ste. Marie and later Mackinac Island. After a year-and-a-half of writing, the result was *The Song of Hiawatha*.

The character Hiawatha is born to Wenonah and the god of the West Wind, Mudjekeewis. Hiawatha's mother dies after she is abandoned by Mudjkeewis, so the boy is raised by his grandmother Nokomis. When Hiawatha learns the truth about his mother's death, he seeks to kill his father. Because Mudjekeewis is immortal, young Hiawatha cannot kill him, but the father is impressed with his son's strength and determination. Mudjekeewis tells Hiawatha he will someday became the ruler of the West Wind after he learns to lead his people.

Hiawatha earns the respect of the Ojibwe by disposing of evil spirits, demonstrating superior strength, sharing powers to heal and teaching kindness. He eventually marries Minnehaha of the Dakota tribe, bringing peace to the two tribes. Hiawatha predicts the coming of the "pale face," teaching his people not to fear the "black robes," but to welcome their presence and message. After his wife dies, Hiawatha sails off after her to the land of the west wind as promised by his father.

Longfellow never set foot in the Upper Peninsula, but managed to capture the feel of the land of Gitche Gumee (big water), or Lake Superior. Longfellow writes of Hiawatha building a canoe from the "white skin wrappers" of the birch trees to paddle down the "rushing Taquamenaw, Sailed through all its bends and windings, Sailed through all its deeps and shallows…"

The poem is based on legends and words taken from Schoolcraft's *Algic Researches: Comprising Inquiries Respecting the Mental Characteristics of the North American Indians* published in 1839. The character of Hiawatha was based on the Algonquin legend, Manabazho; the name, Hiawatha, is taken from a legendary Iroquois chief.

Indian Country, by Philip Caputo

In *Indian Country*, the Pulitzer Prize-winning journalist and author, best known for his best-selling Vietnam memoir, *A Rumor of War* (1977), examines the effects of post-traumatic stress disorder on a veteran who returns home to the Upper Peninsula.

Christian Starkmann volunteers for the military partly to defy his pacifist father and to follow his boyhood friend, Boniface, a Native American. Boniface dies in the war and Christian returns to the U.P., battling the memories of war, and the creeping onset of mental health issues.

Caputo served in the war with Jack Bissell of Escanaba, who is mentioned in *A Rumor of War*. The two remained friends with Caputo serving as a mentor to Bissell's son Tom, author of the critically acclaimed book, *The Father of All Things: A Marine, His Son, and the Legacy of Vietnam.*

Ursula, Under, by Ingrid Hill

A two-and-a-half year old girl, Ursula Wong, falls down an old mine shaft near Copper Harbor, and the world watches. Ursula is the daughter of Justin Wong, half-Chinese/half-Polish, and Annie Maki a Finnish librarian. They live in Sault Ste. Marie and are spending the day on the Keweenaw researching Annie's roots, which includes a grandfather who died in a 1926 mine collapse near Houghton. The author traces Ursula's ancestry back to ancient China, through 8th Century Finland, the gold rush in California, and the mining boom on the Keweenaw Peninsula.

Ursula, Under, the first novel for Hill, was well-received by critics. It was written after her husband walked out on her and their 11 children. She is now remarried and the mother of 12 children.

Other notable books set in the U.P. include several by **Jim Harrison**: *Wolf: A False Memoir* (1969), *Warlock* (1981), *Sundog* (1984), *A Woman Lit By Fireflies* (1990), *Julip* (1994), *The Beast That God Forgot To Invent* (2000), the epic *True North* in 2004 and its continuation *Returning to Earth* (2007).

All ten of **Robert Traver's** (John Voelker) books are set in the U.P. including the best-seller made into a movie, *Anatomy of a Murder* (1958).

LITERARY TOWNS

Two small towns of the Upper Peninsula are named for the literary giant Rudyard Kipling. His best known works include *Kim, The Jungle Book* and the poem *Gunga Din*. In 1907 he became the youngest person ever to win the Nobel Prize for literature. There is no clear evidence that Kipling ever visited the U.P., and he had never written about Michigan prior to the naming of the towns in his honor.

Until the 1890s Rudyard was known as Pine River, a common name for towns in Michigan. Kipling was a station on the Soo Line outside Gladstone. The general manager of the railroad, Frederick D. Underwood, was an admirer of Kipling and requested that Pine River be changed to Rudyard, and that the station next to Gladstone be given the name Kipling. The local residents agreed and the news eventually found its way to the author.

Kipling learned of his namesake towns from Edward Kay Robinson, his former editor and friend at the *Lahore Civil and Military Gazette* in India. Robinson traveled from Minneapolis, presumably through the Upper Peninsula to visit Kipling in Vermont. Upon receiving the news, Kipling wrote to Underwood noting that Robinson had shown him "a folder of your R.R. in which appear the stations 'Rudyard' and 'Kipling! Robinson tells me too that "Kipling" may some day have a great future before it in the iron ore way. This immensely flatters my vanity: and I write to beg you to send me a photograph if possible, of either 'Rudyard' or 'Kipling' or preferentially both. I shall take a deep interest in their little welfares. 'Rudyard' I gather is already a post office, but I have not heard of Kipling"

Kipling penned this poem, written on the back of an envelope, and mailed it to Underwood:

'Wise is the child who knows his sire,'
The ancient proverb ran,
But wiser far the man who knows
How, where and when his offspring grows,
For who the mischief would suppose
I've sons in Michigan?
Yet I am saved from midnight ills,
That warp the soul of man,
They do not make me walk the floor,
Nor hammer at the doctor's door;
They deal in wheat and iron ore,
My sons in Michigan.
O, tourist in the Pullman car
(By Cook's or Raymond's plan),
Forgive a parent's partial view;
But maybe you have children too—
So let me introduce to you
My sons in Michigan.
—Rudyard Kipling

Rudyard Kipling

There is no record of Kipling visiting the U.P., although in 1923 after receiving a copy of the history of Rudyard compiled by the town's residents, he wrote back:

"I have not been in Michigan since a trifle more than thirty years ago, and in those days big stretches of the State were hardly settled up, and the trade at the small stores in Schoolcraft county, if I recollect aright, was nearly all barter. There certainly did not seem to be any prospect of hay for export in those days and it is hard to realize that all the lumber round you must be cleared by now."

In *Hunt's Guide To Michigan's Upper Peninsula* the authors write that financial backers of the Soo Line hosted Kipling on a tour of the U.P. in which he passed through both towns. It was, they report, at that time that the towns were named after the British author.

MICHIGAN NOTABLE BOOKS

The annual Michigan Notable Book awards started in 1991 as part of Michigan Week. Originally the list of books was named Read Michigan. Books chosen for the annual recognition are by Michigan authors or about Michigan or the Great Lakes. The books, both fiction and non-fiction, highlight cultural heritage of the state and region.

Selections are chosen by judges from the following organizations: Library of Michigan, the Michigan Library Association, the Michigan Historical Center, the Grand Rapids Press, the Detroit News, Schuler Books & Music, Archives/Curious Book Shop, the Northland Library Cooperative, Capital Area District Library and Michigan Center for the Book.

Following are Notable Books about or related to the Upper Peninsula.

2000 Read Michigan

A Sailor's Logbook: A Season Aboard Great Lakes Freighters, by Mark Thompson, Wayne State University Press.

Hemingway in Michigan, by Dr. Constance Cappel, Little Traverse Historical Society, republished in 1999.

Keepers of Valor: Lakes of Vengeance, Lakeboats, Lifesavers & Lighthouses, by Wes Oleszewski.

Winter of the Wolf Moon, by Steve Hamilton, Thomas Dunne Books.

2001 Read Michigan

Canoeing Michigan Rivers: A Comprehensive Guide to 45 Rivers, Jerry Dennis and Craig Date, Friede Publications.

Mail By the Pail, by Colin Bergel, illustrated by Mark Koenig, Wayne State University Press.

The Place of the Pike (Gnoozhekaaning): A History of the Bay Mills Indian Community, by Charles E. Cleland, University of Michigan Press.

Views of Mackinac Island, by Thomas Kachadurian, Sleeping Bear Press.

Women and the Lakes: Untold Great Lakes Maritime Tales, by Frederick Stonehouse, Avery Color Studios.

2002 Read Michigan

Historic Cottages of Mackinac Island, by Susan Stites and Lea Ann Sterling, photography by Lanny Sterling and Lea Ann Sterling, Arbutus Press.

Schooner, Skiffs & Steamships: Stories Along Lake Superior's Water Trails, by Howard Sivertson, Lake Superior Port Cities.

Traver on Fishing: A Treasury of Robert Traver's Finest Stories and Essays About Fishing for Trout, by Robert Traver, edited by Nick Lyons, Lyons Press.

2003 Read Michigan

A Good Boat Speaks for Itself: Isle Royale Fishermen and Their Boats, by Timothy Cochrane and Hawk Tolson, University of Minnesota Press.

Lake Michigan Passenger Steamers, by George W. Hilton, Stanford University Press

Off to the Side: A Memoir, by Jim Harrison, Atlantic Monthly Press.

White Hurricane: A Great Lakes November Gale and America's Deadliest Maritime Disaster, by David G. Brown, International Marine.

Windjammers: Songs of the Great Lakes Sailors, by Ivan H. Walton with Joe Grimm, Wayne State University Press.

2004 MICHIGAN NOTABLE BOOKS

The Edmund Fitzgerald: The Song of the Bell, by Kathy-jo Wargin, illustrated by Gijsbert van Frankenhuyzen, Sleeping Bear Press

The Forests of Michigan, by Donald I. Dickmann and Larry A. Leefers, University of Michigan Press.

Going Back to Central: On the Road in Search of the Past in Michigan's Upper Peninsula, by Lon L. Emerick, North Country Publishing.

The Living Great Lakes: Searching for the Heart of the Inland Seas, by Jerry Dennis, Thomas Dunne Books.

Voelker's Pond: A Robert Traver Legacy, by Ed Wargin and James McCullought, Huron River Press.

2005 MICHIGAN NOTABLE BOOKS

Eight Steamboats: Sailing Through the Sixties, by Patrick Livingston, Wayne State University Press.

True North: A Novel, by Jim Harrison, Grove Press.

Ursula, Under: A Novel, by Ingrid Hill, Algonquin Books of Chapel Hill.

2006 MICHIGAN NOTABLE BOOKS

Mighty Fitz: The Sinking of the Edmund Fitzgerald, by Michael Schumacher, Bloomsbury.

Soapy: A Biography of G. Mennen Williams, by Thomas J. Noer, University of Michigan Press.

The Summer He Didn't Die, by Jim Harrison, Atlantic Monthly Press.

2007 MICHIGAN NOTABLE BOOKS

Death's Door: The Truth Behind Michigan's Largest Mass Murder, by Steve Lehto. Momentum Books.

Mackinac Bridge: The Story of the Five-Mile Poem, by Gloria Whelan. Illustrated by Gijsbert van Frankenhuyzen. Sleeping Bear Press.

Saving Daylight, by Jim Harrison. Copper Canyon Press.

So Cold a Sky: Upper Michigan Weather Stories, by Karl Bohnak. Cold Sky Publishing.

2008 MICHIGAN NOTABLE BOOKS

The Father of All Things: A Marine, His Son, and the Legacy of Vietnam, by Tom Bissell, Pantheon Books

Mackinac Bridge: A 50-Year Chronicle, 1957-2007, by Mike Fornes, Cheboygan Tribune Printing Co.

Returning to Earth, by Jim Harrison Grove Press.

The Sound the Stars Make Rushing Through the Sky: The Writings of Jane Johnston Schoolcraft, edited by Robert D. Parker University of Pennsylvania.

2009 MICHIGAN NOTABLE BOOKS

The Expeditions: A Novel, by Karl Iagnemma, Dial Press

A Picturesque Situation: Mackinac Before Photography, 1615-1860, by Brian Leigh Dunnigan, Wayne State University Press.

The Toledo War: The First Michigan-Ohio Rivalry, by Don Faber, University of Michigan Press.

FOOD AND TRADITIONS
The Pasty

This pastry is a unique Upper Michigan tradition. Originally introduced by Cornish immigrants who came to work in the underground iron and copper mines of the Upper Peninsula, the pasty (PAH-stee) is a half-moon shaped meat pie these miners took to work. There was no need to come back up the shaft for a lunch break. The miners took their pasties underground and then warmed them by placing them on a shovel and putting the shovel over a lantern light.

The pie is traditionally made from pork, beef, potatoes, and rutabagas, though the modern version has more vegetables such as carrots. The ingredients are then wrapped in a rather heavy crust made from lard and suet. There are a number of specialty shops in the Upper Peninsula that make and sell pasties exclusively. Some of these shops concentrate on catering to today's preferences and tastes. Pasties can be made without salt or meat, with chicken instead of beef and pork and a wider variety of vegetables. Many of these shops ship frozen pasties all over the United States to expatriate residents who long for a taste of home.

Trenary Toast

The sweet and crusty cinnamon toast is a form of *korpu*, a traditional Finnish toast. The Hallinen family and a staff of 18 turn out 3,000 to 4,000 bags of Trenary Toast each week.

The cinnamon and sugar are added to the bread before toasting and results in a hard crusty toast with a shelf life of six months—all that with zero preservatives!

Trenary Toast has put the town of Trenary, about 25 miles southeast of Marquette, on the map. The simple treat is packed in brown paper bags that are recognizable to thousands of fans. Its taste is not the only reason for the popularity of Trenary Toast. Knowing that its part of the rich Finnish heritage of the U.P., and produced by the Hallinen family is part of the draw. Hans and Esther bought the bakery from the Siiranen family in 1950. Today most of the work is done by their son Bruce along with his son and daughter-in-law. Go to www.trenary-toast.us or call 1-800-TOAST-01

Hilltop Sweet Rolls

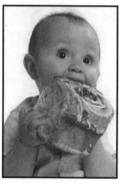

L'Anse's Hilltop Restaurant has served breakfast, lunch and dinner for over 60 years. However, this 60-year-old family-run business is most famous for its humungous sweet roll. Tipping the scale at over a pound, the pastry is credited to the aunt of one of the owners.

Hilltop Sweet Rolls are made fresh daily from scratch. On a typical busy weekend, Hilltop bakers go through 3,000 pounds of flour, 150 pounds of sugar, 60 pounds of apples and cinnamon that comes to the kitchen 100 pounds at a time. The Hilltop current record is 204 dozen sweet rolls baked in one day. Hilltop Sweet Rolls can be ordered on the web at: http://www.sweetroll.com/order.html.

Cudighi

A popular sausage among the Italian-American population of the Upper Peninsula of Michigan. The word "cudighi" refers to a spicy Italian sausage patty specific to the region.

Cudighi consist of a spicy sausage, made from ground pork, garlic salt, black and red pepper, and a few secret spices, served on a chewy Italian roll or bun. The first cudighis were sold in Ishpeming by Mr. Felix Barbiere in 1951 out of a take-out door installed in his home.

This sandwich is rarely encountered in the United States except in the Marquette, Ishpeming, Gwinn, and Negaunee areas of the Upper Peninsula of Michigan. Retrieved from "http://en.wikipedia.org/wiki/Cudighi"

Chapter 13

SPORTS AND RECREATION

U.P. SPORTS CELEBRITIES

The Gipper

The most successful and widely followed college athletic program in history is Notre Dame football. No other athlete in the school's glorious history typified that success better than George Gipp. Raised in Laurium on the Keweenaw Peninsula, George Gipp never played high school football, but was an avid participant in track, hockey, sandlot football, and organized baseball.

The beginning of Gipp's college football career is clouded in mystery, but nothing is mysterious about the numbers he produced once on the gridiron. Over a 4-year career, the Gipper scored 21 touchdowns en route to Notre Dame's amazing 27 wins, 2 losses, and 3 ties. On the defensive end, not a single pass was completed against his protective zone during his four years with the Irish.

On November 20, 1920, during a game against Illinois, Gipp contracted a serious streptococci infection of the throat which later worsened in his final game at Northwestern. As the story is told, Notre Dame coach Knute Rockne visited his superstar player in the hospital. Gipp supposedly told Rockne that when the breaks are beating the boys, I tell them to "win one for the Gipper."

George Gipp died on December 14, 1920. Eight years later, with Notre Dame trailing to Army at half time, Rockne supposedly told the story of his dying star player. Not a single eye was dry, and when the speech was concluded, the Irish went out and won one for the Gipper. In the 1940 movie, *Knute Rockne: All American*, the role of George Gipp was played by Ronald Reagan.

- Played football at Notre Dame for four years.
- Inducted into the Michigan Football Hall of Fame, National Football Hall of Fame, and Upper Peninsula Sports Hall of Fame.
- Gipp was Notre Dame's first member of the All-American team.
- Died from pneumonia and strep infection.
- The George Gipp Award is awarded to an outstanding senior athlete. It was started at his alma mater, Calumet High School, in 1934.

In October of 2007 as cameras for the ESPN cable sports network rolled, the body of George Gipp was exhumed from a cemetery near his hometown of Laurium. The grandson of Gipp's sister, Rick Frueh, gave the okay for the exhumation to determine if The Gipper had fathered an illegitimate child.

An author writing a biography on Gipp had heard that a woman claimed to be the football great's granddaughter. She claimed that her mother, Eva Bright of South Bend, Indiana, had dated Gipp for about a year before his death. The author put her in touch with Frueh, who authorized the exhumation.

ESPN had been preparing a special program on Gipp when it heard about the plans to exhume the body.

Gipps's right femur bone was removed, and the rest of his remains were reburied. DNA testing proved negative–Gipp had not fathered a daughter illegitimately.

In early 2008, some descendants angry about the exhumation of Gipp were planning a lawsuit against Frueh who said he did not regret the incident, as it proved Gipp had not fathered the Bright girl.

Hunk Anderson
The Man Who Blocked for The Gipper
Born: September 22, 1898   **Birthplace:** Hancock, MI

Hunk Anderson graduated from Calumet High School before moving on to play football for coach Knute Rockne at Notre Dame. During the 1918 season, he blocked for his good friend, George Gipp. Anderson went on to become a four-year starter for the Fighting Irish.

After leading the way for The Gipper, Anderson enjoyed an outstanding college career. The Irish went undefeated in 1919 and 1920, winning 20 straight games before losing to Iowa in a 1921 upset. Anderson was an All-American in his senior year, and in a game against Purdue, he blocked two punts, recovering them in the end zone to become the first guard ever to score two touchdowns in a game.

Anderson went on to the NFL playing four seasons with the Chicago Bears. He returned to Notre Dame as a line coach for Rockne and became the head coach in 1931 upon Rockne's death. During his three years as coach the Irish went 16-9-2.

Anderson also coached at the University of St. Louis, North Carolina State, Cincinnati, and Michigan. He was an assistant coach with Chicago Bears until his retirement in 1951.

Sportswriter Grantland Rice wrote of Hunk, "pound for pound Anderson was the toughest man I have ever known."

Steve Mariucci

Born: November 4, 1955
From: Iron Mountain, MI

Career: The native son of Iron Mountain, who slept with a football as a child, went on to become an All-American quarterback in college and a head coach in the NFL.

Mariucci played football and basketball at Iron Mountain High School with another Iron Mountain native, Tom Izzo. After graduating in 1973, the two attended Northern Michigan University together. At NMU Mariucci was a three-time Division II All-American quarterback and a three-time MVP.

After graduating, he began his coaching career at NMU during the 1978-79 season as a quarterback and running back coach. The stint at his alma mater was brief, and Mariucci moved to California State Fullerton from 1980 through 1982. During the 1983-84 season Mariucci worked for Louisville.

He accepted his first pro position and joined the Orlando Renegades of the USFL. Later, Mariucci had a short stint with the LA Rams. In 1986, he returned to the college ranks at the University of Southern California where he was named receivers coach and special teams coordinator. The next year he moved to the University of California as an assistant until 1992 when he was hired as quarterback coach for the Green Bay Packers. One of his players was future Hall-of-Famer Brett Favre, who on one occasion filled the role of babysitter for Mariucci's children.

In 1996, "Mooch" was hired as head coach of the University of California Golden Bears. He led them to a 6-6 record and an appearance in the Aloha Bowl. Before he could build on that success, he was back to the NFL with the San Francisco 49'ers.

During six seasons with the 49'ers he compiled a 60-43 record and went to the playoffs four times over five years.

Despite his record of success in San Francisco, Mariucci was fired by the team after the 2002 season. The next team that came calling was closer to home. On February 4, 2003 the Detroit Lions named Mariucci as their 22nd head coach. During two-and-a-half seasons with the struggling Lions, Mooch compiled a 15-28 record and was fired on November 28, 2005 after a Thanksgiving Day loss to Atlanta. Some teachers chose to let students at Iron Mountain High watch the ensuing press conference on classroom televisions.

During his NFL coaching career, Mariucci set a record for most consecutive wins (11) by a rookie head coach, and became one of 13 head coaches to lead his team to a division title in his first season.

His name is brought up almost anytime a coaching position becomes available in the NFL or college ranks. He interviewed for the Washington Redskins head coaching job in early 2008. The Skins went with former quarterback Jim Zorn. In 2006, he was rumored to have been considered for the head coaching job at Michigan State University, where his boyhood friend Tom Izzo coaches the basketball team.

After leaving the NFL, Mariucci signed on as an analyst and commentator with the NFL Network for the game day broadcasts.

Mariucci remains loyal to the town where he was raised and where his parents, Ray and Dee, still live. He and Izzo held an annual fundraising golf tournament every summer for ten years, donating the proceeds for local projects such as scholarships and the $2-million Izzo-Mariucci Fitness Center. The 17,000-square foot addition to the Iron Mountain High gymnasium opened in 2004 and houses a weight training room, wrestling rooms, offices, conference rooms, and a concession/meeting area.

Mariucci is partners with local businessman, Bruce Varda in Mariucci Ventures LLC. In late 2007, the pair proposed building a convention center in Iron Mountain that would include a 1,200-seat conference center, hotel, retail center and possible retirement home and assisted living home. The proposed three-phase project is estimated to cost over $20-million.

Family: Wife, Gail, and four children - Tyler, Adam, Stephen, and Brielle.

Mariucci's father, Ray is considered "the father of Upper Peninsula wrestling." Each year the top wrestling team in the U.P. is awarded the Ray Mariucci trophy.

Tom Izzo

Born: January 30, 1955 **From:** Iron Mountain, MI

Career: Tom Izzo was raised in Iron Mountain, Michigan. He played on the Iron Mountain High School football and basketball teams with close friend, Steve Mariucci; former coach of the Detroit Loins. They also attended the same college, rooming together at Northern Michigan University. Izzo went to NMU from 1973-1977. During college, he played guard for the NMU Wildcats basketball team. Izzo set a school record for minutes played during his senior season. That same season he was named a Division II All-American. In 1977, he was NMU's basketball MVP.

After earning his degree, Izzo was head coach at Ishpeming High School. He worked there for one season before returning to NMU. He was hired as an assistant coach until 1983 when Izzo joined the staff at Michigan State University as an assistant coach under Jud Heathcoate. In 1995, Heathcoate retired and named Izzo as his replacement.

Izzo is credited with returning the MSU basketball program to its glory days of the late 1970s. During his tenure as head coach, Izzo has led the Spartans to an NCAA National Championship (1999-2000), four Big Ten Chamionships and two Big Ten Tournament titles along with four appearances in the NCAA Final Four.

After twelve seasons at the helm of the Spartan basketball program, Izzo has compiled a record of 278-121, and has earned four National Coach of the Year awards. He is recognized for his talents as coach, mentor, leader and teacher. Of his players who complete their eligibility, 82 percent leave with a degree in hand.

Assistant coaches serving under Izzo have also fared well. Five of the current head coaches at Division I schools are former assistants under Izzo: Stan Joplin (Toledo), Tom Crean (formerly Marquette now Indiana), Stan Heath (Arkansas), Brian Gregory (Dayton), and Doug Wojcik (Tulsa).

Ten of Izzo's players have been selected in the NBA Draft, six of them in the first round since 2000. First rounders include: Mateen Cleaves-2000, Morris Peterson-2000, Jason Richardson-2001, Zach Randolph-2001, Shannon Brown-2006, and Maurice Ager-2006.

There have been career highlights off the court as well. In 2005, Izzo golfed with Tiger Woods at the Buick Pro-Am. He took part in Operation Hardwood in 2005 and 2006. The program took college coaches to Kuwait military camps to coach basketball teams of service members. Izzo's team won the tournament in 2005.

Izzo has been with the Spartan basketball program for 26 years, 13 as head coach. He has received offers from other universities and the NBA, but has said he's committed to bringing another NCAA Championship to East Lansing. Among the offers he's turned down: the Atlanta Hawks offered him a job after the NCAA Championship season of 2000; he was contacted by the Toronto Raptors in 2004, and was rumored to be a candidate for the head coaching job at Kentucky in 2007. Izzo was even rumored to be a candidate to coach the Spartan football team after John L. Smith was fired in 2007.

Izzo and his friend Steve Mariucci have raised millions of dollars for charitable projects in their hometown by holding a fundraising golf tournament, which ended in 2007 after ten years. Money raised from the event was spent on community projects such as scholarships and the $2-million Izzo-Mariucci Fitness Center. The 17,000-square foot addition to the Iron Mountain High gymnasium that opened in 2004 houses a weight training room, wrestling rooms, offices, conference rooms, and a concession/meeting area.

Family: Wife Lupe, 13-year old daughter Raquel, and 7-year old Steven.

The Izzo's named their son Steven Thomas Mateen Izzo after his friend Steve Mariucci and the captain of the 2000 NCAA Championship team, Mateen Cleaves.

Kevin Tapani

World Series Pitcher

Kevin Tapani was born in Des Moines, Iowa and raised in Escanaba. He graduated from Escanaba High School and went on to play baseball for Central Michigan University.

The 6'1" right-hander was selected by Oakland in the second round of the 1986 draft. He was then traded to the N.Y. Mets the following year. Tapani made his major league debut on July 4, 1989 against the Houston Astros.

He was traded to Minnesota that year and spent the next six seasons with the Twins. During that period, he was a regular in the starting rotation and enjoyed his best year in 1991 with a 16-9 record, 2.99 ERA, and gave up only 40 walks in 244 innings.

In 1995, he was traded to the L.A. Dodgers, and the following year he signed as a free agent with the Chicago White Sox. Despite a finger injury he went 13-10 for the Sox.

In the off season he signed with the Cubs where he pitched for five seasons before retiring at the end of 2001. With the Cubs, Tapani had his career best record when he went 19-9 in 1998. He finished his 13-year major league career with a record of 143-125, a 4.35 ERA and 1,482 strikeouts. He was in double digits in the win column for eight of those thirteen seasons. He finished with career earnings of $34,209,500.

Mike Bordick

Major League All-Star Shortstop

Mike Bordick was born in Marquette on July 21, 1965, but spent most of his childhood in Presque Isle, Maine. After graduating from the University of Maine, he signed with the Oakland A's. Bordick went on to play for four different teams over 14 seasons in the major leagues: Oakland, the Baltimore Orioles, New York Mets and the Toronto Blue Jays.

His first game in the majors was April 11, 1990 with Oakland. In 1992, he played his first full season, batting .300—10th best average in the league.

His most productive years were with Baltimore (1997-2000) when he played shortstop for the best infield in baseball that included Cal Ripken at third, Roberto Alomar at second and Rafael Palmeiro at first. In 2000, he batted .297 with Baltimore and .260 with the Mets while hitting 20 home runs and 70 RBI; good enough to make the American League All Star team and play in the World Series.

In 2002, Bordick set a major league record by fielding 428 consecutive chances without an error. By the end of the season, Bordick would go 543 straight chances without an error over 110 consecutive games – both major league records. However, he lost out to Alex Rodriquez for the Gold Glove award, even though A-Rod committed 10 errors that season.

Bordick finished his career with a .260 average, 91 homers and 626 RBI. Career earnings: over $27 million. Today Bordick is the head baseball coach at his Presque Isle High School in Maine.

Becky Iverson

LPGA

Becky Iverson was born October 12, 1967 in Escanaba and started playing golf eight years later. Iverson went on to play golf for Michigan State University (1985-88) and become the Michigan Junior Amateur Champion in 1986 and the Michigan Women's Junior Amateur Champion in 1987.

On the LPGA tour, Iverson has carded three hole-in-ones. She has two victories—the Friendly's Golf Classic in 1995 and the Solheim Cup in 2000. In 2007, she ranked 94th with career earnings of $1,535,292.

Her LPGA bio lists her hobbies as gambling, sports card collecting and going to Disney World with her daughter, Emma, born in 2003.

John Gilmore (Jr.)

National Football League

Marquette native plays tight end for the Chicago Bears.

Attended high school in Pennsylvania before attending Penn State (1998 – 2001), where he lettered all four years.

Drafted in the sixth round by New Orleans in 2002.

Waived by Saints and signed with Chicago Bears in 2002.

Appeared with the Bears in 2007 Super Bowl, which they lost to Indianapolis.

Chris Thorpe

World Champion –Luge

Thorpe was born October 29, 1970 in Waukegan, Illinois and moved to Marquette at a young age. He learned the sport on a homemade luge course near his home. Chris graduated from Marquette High School in 1988, and went on to compete in the 1992, 1994, 1998 and 2002 Winter Olympics.

He was the first American to win a World Cup Championship and his Silver Medal at Nagano in 1998 made him the first American ever to win a medal in luge. Thorpe and his luge partner, Gordy Sheer, also won a Bronze Medal in the Winter Olympics.

Thorpe has won over 30 international luge medals – the most ever by an American.

Bruce Martyn

Red Wings announcer

The voice of Detroit Red Wing hockey over four decades has earned a place in the heart of Red Wing fans. He is a member of the NHL Hockey Hall of Fame and Michigan Sports Hall of Fame.

The Sault Ste. Marie native started his broadcasting career at hometown WSOO radio in 1950. He began broadcasting Red Wing play-by-play in 1964 and continued through his retirement in 1995. Martyn also called a few games over the radio for the Detroit Pistons and Michigan State University.

He moved to Gaylord upon his retirement in 1995, and now lives in Venice, Florida.

BIRTHPLACE OF PROFESSIONAL HOCKEY

There was a time when it was frowned upon to pay athletes for playing what many considered to be children's games. Playing hockey, baseball, and football was for kids or young men who had finished all of their chores and work. As far as hockey goes, all of that changed in 1904 when hockey enthusiasts in Houghton formed the International Hockey League.

The league included the Portage Lakes, Calumet Laurium Miners, the Sault Ste. Marie Indians, a team from Soo, Ontario and a team from Pittsburgh, PA. The Portage Lakes played in the Amphidrome, built in Houghton in 1902. The Calumet team played at the Palastra (1904) in Laurium, believed to be the first hockey-only facility built in the United States. The Sault Ste. Marie Indians played at the Ice-A-Torium.

The league attracted the best players from the Upper Peninsula and Canada. Players were paid for their time and talent, thus making Houghton the birthplace of professional hockey. The International Hockey League lasted only three years until 1907. That year, many of the Canadian players left their U.S. teams to play in the newly established Canadian professional league.

The first championship was won by Calumet. The Portage Lakes won the next two championships in the International Hockey League.

In 2004, a Centennial celebration was held at Dee Stadium in Houghton. Mr. Hockey, Gordie Howe, was a special guest as was *the* Stanley Cup.

CHAMPIONSHIP FLOOR MANUFACTURER

The best college and professional basketball players in the world run and jump all over the floors produced by Connor Floor in the town of Amasa (Iron County). The company designed and manufactured the floor for the 2008 NBA All Star game in New Orleans, and has been providing the floors for the NCAA Final Four for several years.

The company dates back to 1872 and the early stages of the Upper Peninsula lumber industry. In 1974 the company began producing portable gymnasium floors from local hardwood maple trees. The trees are milled in the company's Amasa plant, and the basketball courts they design are actually built there before being taken apart and shipped to their intended location. It takes about two-and-a-half weeks to build one court, which measures 120 by 63 feet and weigh about 23 tons.

Connor Floors has made floors for 14 NBA teams. Their business began to boom in 1999 after they manufactured the floor for the Fleet Center, the homecourt for the Boston Celtics now known as Banknorth Garden. Since then they have become the official provider of basketball floors for the NCAA Men's and Women's Final Four. The company's QuickLock Portable Court System can be assembled in five hours by ten people. When the games are over, the winning team keeps the floor. Some customers have them installed in their home arenas and gymnasiums, while others have cut them up and sold the pieces as souvenirs.

Connor supplies the flooring for the Final Four as well as the Division I Regional Tournament sites, and NCAA Men's and Women's Volleyball championship sites. Connor Floors produced 17 floors for the NCAA basketball playoffs in 2006. That number increased to 30 floors in 2007 and to 40 floors for the 2008 tournament.

U.S. NATIONAL SKI & SNOWBOARD HALL OF FAME

The idea for a national ski museum dates back to 1941 when journalist and ski historian, Harold Grinden of Duluth, MN raised the idea at a National Ski Association convention in Milwaukee. Grinden said a place was needed to store and display national trophies and related paperwork. He suggested the national ski museum be built in the town where organized skiing began in the U.S., Ishpeming, Michigan.

Skiing began around Ishpeming in the 1880s as Norwegian immigrants, and later Finns, moved to the region to work the iron mines. They brought along with them a strong work ethic and a penchant for ski jumping. The earliest ski jumps were formed using piled and packed snow and lumber. The first ski jump tournament was held on February 25, 1888. It was organized by the Norden Ski Club (renamed the Ishpeming Ski Club in 1901).

In 1891, four similar ski clubs in Wisconsin and Minnesota joined the Ishpeming club to form the Central Ski Association of the Northwest, the first regional organization of ski clubs in the country. The association's first tournament was held on Ishpeming's Superior Hill that same year.

Norden Ski Club, Courtesy Ishpeming Ski Club

The Ishpeming Ski Club sponsored annual tournaments beginning in 1904 and called the winner of the 1905 tournament, Ole Westgard of Ishpeming, the "national champion." Proclaiming a national championship led to formation of the National Ski Association in Ishpeming that winter; hence Ishpeming's title, "Birthplace of Organized Skiing."

With that heritage in mind, Grinden's idea of a national ski museum was raised in 1944 by National Ski Association (NSA) President, Roger Langley, during an NSA dinner in Ishpeming. Official fund-raising began in 1949 with sizable donations from local mining companies, regional ski clubs, citizen fund-raising drives and an interest-free loan from the city of Ishpeming. Construction began in 1953 and the newly named U.S. National Ski Hall of Fame & Museum opened on February 19, 1954.

The first four inductees, known as Honored Members, were named in 1956; Carl Tellefsen, Aksel Holter, Arthur J. Barth and Edward F. Taylor were all selected for their efforts to establish the National Ski Association. There are now 349 Honored Members in the Hall of Fame.

In 1989, skiing enthusiasts and local citizens helped raise $2.7 million for construction of a new and larger building. The new building is five times larger than the original two-story cinder block structure, and features a soaring and sloped roof line that resembles the ramp of a ski jump.

The 15,000 square feet of exhibit space includes a history of skiing from Stone Age carvings of ancient skis to early rope tows, chair lifts and gondolas. The Roland Palmedo Ski Library features 1,300 books, magazines, videos and films; photographs and bios of the 300+ Hall of Fame members; national ski trophies, and a gift shop. Admission is free. www.skihall.com

SUICIDE HILL

The community of Negaunee is home to one of the best ski jumps in the country, one that has produced Olympic champions and hosted some of the finest competitions in the U.S.A. Suicide Bowl is actually a group of five jumps between Negaunee and Ishpeming. Although Suicide Bowl has a rich heritage among the international ski jumping community, its name can be a deterrent to skiers.

The jump was built in 1925 as a replacement to other hills that limited jumping distances. Peter Handberg and Leonard Flaa, officers with the Ishpeming Ski Club are credited with finding the location. The property was owned by Cleveland Cliffs Iron Company which agreed to lease it to the club. Volunteers from the club and other groups worked to build the jump and scaffolding, which towers 140 feet above the surrounding pine forest. The first meet was held on February 26, 1926. During that first winter one skier was injured, leading a newspaper reporter, Ted Butler, to describe the jump as Suicide Hill. The name stuck.

Since the first meet in 1926 Suicide Hill has attracted competitive skiers from European and Scandinavian countries as well as Japan and Australia. It has produced Olympians and serves as a training ground for students at the Olympic Education Center. In February 2008, it hosted the 121st Invitational Ski Jumping competition, attracting over 1,000 spectators.

Since 1953 Suicide Hill has hosted the Paul Bietila Memorial Tournament in honor of one of the most promising young skiers in the history of the Ishpeming Ski Club. Paul was member of the "Flying Bietilas," six ski jumping brothers: Walter, Roy, Ralph, Leonard, Anselm and Paul. All of them displayed talent but Walter was the most accomplished, competing in three Olympics and coaching the 1962 Olympic team.

Paul Bietila was only ten years old in 1928 when he first launched himself from Suicide Hill. At 15, he set the boys world record jumping 196 feet. He set over one dozen records in the next few years, establishing himself as the best upcoming skier in the country. He was headed toward the 1940 Olympics, but the games were cancelled when war broke out between Finland and Russia.

On February 5, 1939, while competing in the Nationals in St. Paul, Minnesota Paul Bietila hit ice and crashed into a restraining post and later died of his injuries. He was twenty years old.

Suicide Hill also hosts the annual Troy Gravedoni Memorial Tournament in honor of another talented skier who died before reaching his full potential. Gravedoni, a popular member of the Ishpeming Ski Club died in an auto accident on June 3, 1998 after qualifying for the Junior Olympics National Championships.

The annual competitions and tournaments continue at Suicide Hill which has been nominated for National Historic Designation. In February of 2008, the Ishpeming Ski Club hosted the USSA Chevrolet Junior Olympics Ski Jumping and Nordic Combined.

PINE MOUNTAIN SKI JUMP

Iron Mountain is home to the Pine Mountain Ski Jump, one of the highest artificial ski jumps in the world. Each year it hosts an international competition attracting the best jumpers from twelve countries. At the 2006 Continental Cup Competition, Austrian Stefan Kaiser broke the hill record with a jump of 468 feet.

Pine Mountain Ski Jump was built in 1938 as a WPA project. It was started by local volunteers, turned over to a non-profit parks group, which applied for the WPA help. The Kiwanis Ski Club is the host organization.

Pine Mountain specs:
Scaffold Height, 176 feet
Scaffold Length, 380 feet
Length of Underhill (end of take off to outrun), 632 feet
Length of Underhill (end of scaffold to end of outrun), 1032 feet
Critical point (K-point) of landing hill, 394 feet
Pitch of Landing Hill, 39 degrees
Estimated speed of skiers at takeoff, 55 mph
Pine Mountain attracts about 20,000 spectators each winter, most of them attending the annual Pine Mountain Tournament in February.

U.P. SPORTS HALL OF FAME

The idea for a U.P. Sports Hall of Fame dates back to the 1960s, but it did not become a reality until 1971 when local supporters including NMU sports officials and sportswriters organized the first Council. Since then the Council inducts ten new members each year. Anybody can nominate a candidate for the Hall.

The stated purpose of the U.P. Sports Hall of Fame is to honor outstanding men and women from the U.P. "whose achievements in sports have brought distinction to themselves and enduring pride and inspiration to the entire U.P. community."

MEMBERS OF THE INAUGURAL CLASS OF 1972

GEORGE "The Gipper" GIPP, Laurium

an all-around Calumet High athlete and the legendary halfback who was Notre Dame's first All-American in 1920 under coach Knute Rockne. "The Gipper" scored 83 touchdowns in 32 college games and is enshrined in the National Football Foundation Hall of Fame.

TAFFY ABEL, Sault Ste. Marie

a member of the U.S. ice hockey team in the 1924 Olympic Games and the U.S. flag bearer for the opening ceremonies. He played for the New York Rangers and the Chicago Blackhawks of the NHL and on Stanley Cup championship teams in 1928 and 1934.

HEARTLEY "Hunk" ANDERSON, Calumet

an All-American at Notre Dame and an All-Pro with the Chicago Bears. He coached at Notre Dame as Knute Rockne's successor, at four other schools, and with the NFL Lions and Bears. He is a member of the National Football Foundation Hall of Fame.

JOHN L. "Doc" GIBSON, Houghton

was the Captain of the Worlds first Professional Hockey Team in Houghton, Michigan, the Portage Lake Hockey Team. Born in Berlin (Kitchener), Ontario, Doc is in the Hockey Hall of Fame. He was instrumental in establishing hockey in the United States. Gibson was the leading scorer on the 1904 Portage Lakers, winners of the American Championship over Pittsburgh and the World Championship over the Montreal Wanderers.

JOHN MACINNES, Houghton

was a legendary ice hockey coach at Michigan Tech. His teams won 555 games and NCAA championships in 1962, 1965 and 1975. Named the NCAA Coach of the Year in 1970 and 1976, he received the NHL's Lester Patrick Award for service to hockey in the U.S. in 1986.

FRED NORCROSS, Menominee

the 150-pound quarterback and captain of three of Coach Fielding H. Yost's greatest Michigan football teams. These teams had a record of 33-1-2 and out scored their opponents 1,627 to 30 during the 1903-04-05 seasons. He later coached two seasons at Oregon.

GENE RONZANI, Iron Mountain

a running back for the Chicago Bears for eight seasons beginning in 1933 and the head coach of the Green Bay Packers in 1950-53. He was on a state championship basketball team at Iron Mountain High and was the first nine-letter athlete at Marquette University.

GUS SONNENBERG, Marquette

world heavyweight wrestling champion in 1929 and NMU Sports Hall of Famer. He played on the 1915-16 U.P. champion basketball and football teams at Marquette High, college football at NMU and Dartmouth where he was an All-American, and pro football with Portsmouth and Detroit.

C.C. WATSON, Ishpeming

who coached Ishpeming High basketball teams to a 444-206 record in 37 seasons and captured 18 district and eight U.P. titles. He was state coach of the year in 1950 when his team won the state title. His 1934-36 clubs won 42 in a row.

BILLY WELLS, Menominee

the Outstanding Player in the 1954 Rose Bowl when he scored two touchdowns for Michigan State. An all-around Menominee High athlete, he scored 17 touchdowns at MSU in 1951-52-53 and played five years in the NFL.

OTHER NOTABLE MEMBERS... PROFESSIONAL FOOTBALL

RAY BRAY, Caspian/Vulcan (1973)

All-Pro guard (1946-49) with the Chicago Bears. 11 seasons in the NFL.

HERMAN "Winks" GUNDLACH, Houghton (1973)

From Houghton High to Harvard. First Harvard player in the NFL. Played with old Boston Redskins as two-way guard. The "Iron Man."

WALTER NIEMANN, Menominee (1974)

Menominee High grad played three years for the Green Bay Packers (1922-24).

DICK DESCHAINE, Menominee (1976)

All around athlete at Menominee High. Second leading punter in the NFL during two seasons with the Green Bay Packers (1955-56).

RAY EBLI, Ironwood (1978)

Played with old Chicago Cardinals, Buffalo Bills and Cleveland Browns in 1940s.

JOEL MASON, Stambaugh (1979)

Played with old Chicago Cardinals and Green Bay Packers. Coached basketball at Wayne State University.

RUDOLPH ROSATTI, Norway (1979)

Norway High grad went on to play with the Green Bay Packers and NY Giants in 1920s.

DAVE MANDERS, Kingsford (1980)

Kingsford High grad who set U.P. shot put record. Ten years in the NFL with Dallas Cowboys. Played in 1970 and 1972 Super Bowls.

JOHN BIOLO, Iron Mountain (1982)

Played guard for the 1939 NFL champion Green Bay Packers.

BILL RADEMACHER, Menominee/Marquette (1983)

Played with Broadway Joe Namath on 1969 Super Bowl champion NY Jets.

GEORGE ZORICH, Wakefield (1987)

Wakefield High grad played guard for the 1946 world champion Chicago Bears.

TOM DOMRES, Gladstone (1988)

All-stater from Gladstone High played for Houston and Denver in the NFL (1960s).

TIM KEARNEY, Kingsford (1990)

Ten years in the NFL as linebacker for the St. Louis Cardinals. Member of the NMU Hall of Fame.

ROB RUBICK, Newberry (1995)

Seven years as receiver with the Detroit Lions in the 1980s. Newberry native.

BOB LANDSEE, Iron Mountain (1996)

Iron Mountain High All-Stater, drafted by Philadelphia Eagles in 1986. Played three years in the NFL.

CHUCK KLINGBEIL, Houghton (2002)

Defensive lineman for Miami Dolphins (1991-95). Recovered a fumble and scored aTD during Coach Don Shula's 300th game. Houghton High School hockey and football standout. Four years at NMU.

ROMANUS "Peaches" NADOLNEY, Ironwood (2003)

Ironwood High football star recruited by Knute Rockne to play at Notre Dame where he roomed with Earl "Curly" Lambeau. Played for the Green Bay Packers in 1922.

CLAY WILLMAN, Kingsford (2004)

Kingsford High and Michigan Tech grad drafted by Minnesota in the NFL. Was runner-up to Fran Tarkenton as Viking's quarterback before injuries ended his career. Member of Michigan Sports Hall of Fame.

BOB JURASIN, Bessemer (2005)

Spent 12 years in the Canadian Football League where he is ranked 2nd in career sacks and career tackles. Spent four years at NMU where he returned to coach after CFL career. Member of NMU Sports Hall of Fame.

PROFESSIONAL HOCKEY

WILLIAM "Pud" HAMILTON, Sault Ste. Marie (1974)

Played in first pro hockey league in U.S. and Canada. Also played pro football and lacrosse, and was an accomplished rugby player.

CHARLES UKSILA, Calumet (1974)

First American-born hockey player to compete in the Stanley Cup playoffs. Played with Detroit, Portland, Seattle and Vancouver.

VICTOR DESJARDINS, Sault Ste. Marie (1976)

Played with Chicago Blackhawks and NY Rangers. Elected to U.S. Hockey Hall of Fame in 1974.

EDDIE OLSON, Marquette (1979)

1953 MVP in the American Hockey League. Olson Rink at Marquette Lakeview Arena named for his family, which included nine boys.

JOHN SHERF, Calumet (1979)

First American-born player on a Stanley Cup team. Played with Detroit Red Wings from 1935-36, and with the NY Rangers.

ERNEST "Ike" KLINGBEIL, Hancock (2000)

Known for playing entire games without a rest. Played on the Chicago Blackhawks in 1938.

OLYMPIANS

The Flying Bietila Brothers L-R: Roy, Ralph, Leonard & Walter (A History of the Ishpeming Ski Club)

WALTER BIETILA, Ishpeming/Iron Mountain (1973)

Ski jumper in three Olympics, 1936, 1940 and 1948. Member of the "Flying Bietila" family.

PAUL COPPO, Hancock (1982)

Leading scorer for U.S. hockey team in 1964 Olympics.

WELDON "Weldy" OLSON, Marquette (1984)

Won Olympic Gold in 1960, and Silver Medal in 1956 with U.S. ice hockey teams.

PAUL "Joe" PERRAULT, Ishpeming (1984)

Was on two U.S. Olympic ski jumping teams. Set North American distance record of 297 feet in 1949.

ROD PAAVOLA, Hancock (1985)

Won a Gold Medal in 1960 on the U.S. ice hockey team. Set U.P. pole vault record and was a football player at Hancock High.

RALPH BIETILA, Ishpeming (1987)

Ski jumper in 1948 and 1952 Olympics. Youngest brother in the "Flying Bietila" family.

DICK RAHOI, Iron Mountain (1991)

Captain of the 1960 U.S. Olympic ski jumping team. Member of 1956 Olympic team.

BUTCH WEDIN, Iron Mountain (1995)

Member of the 1960 Olympic ski jump team.

WILLIE ERICKSON, Kingsford (1998)

Member of ski jump team in 1960 Olympics. Three-time ski jump champion at U.S. Nationals.

STEN FJELDHEIM, Marquette (2001)

On the U.S. Olympic ski team coaching staff at Lillehammer, Norway in 1994.

MARK KONOPACKE, Kingsford (2006)

Highest placing U.S ski jumper at 1988 Olympics in Calgary.

MAJOR LEAGUE BASEBALL

DICK POLE, Trout Creek (1988)

Trout Creek High grad pitched for the Boston Red Sox and appeared in the 1975 World Series. Pitching coach for the Chicago Cubs.

DAN DOBBEK, Ontonagon (1991)

Played with the Washington Senators and was a charter member of the Minnesota Twins when the team moved there in 1961.

GEORGE BRUNET, Houghton (1993)

Signed by the Detroit Tigers in 1953 and played Major League ball for 18 seasons.

NELLO "Fungo" TEDESCHI, Iron Mountain (1993)

Signed by Chicago White Sox but was let go in 1919 when the team released most of its minor league players.

JOHN GOETZ, Sault Ste. Marie (2001)

Relief pitcher for Chicago Cubs. Struck out Willie Mays and Orlando Cepeda in his first Major League appearance.

PROFESSIONAL GOLF

MARY AGNES WALL, Menominee (1973)

Greatest woman golfer from the U.P. Won three Michigan championships in the 1940s and 1950s.

JOHNNY REVOLTA, Menominee (1987)

Won 41 major tournaments and was leading money winner in 1935 when he was the PGA national champion. Member of PGA Hall of Fame.

BOB ERICKSON, Norway (1993)

Joined the PGA Tour in 1968 and played for seven years before joining the Senior Tour in 1980. Won the U.S. National Senior PGA title in 1982.

SUSIE FOX, Iron Mountain (2001)

Joined LPGA's Futures Tour in 1988 and played in the U.S. Open in 1993. Serves as golf pro at Timberstone Golf Course in Iron Mountain. Led Iron Mountain High to state ski championship in 1979.

COACHES

LYMAN FRIMODIG, Calumet (1973)

Coached basketball at MSU in 1921-22, as student lettered ten times in basketball, baseball and football. Wrote the book, *Spartan Saga: A History of MSU Athletics*, and was elected mayor of East Lansing.

BILL GAPPY, Houghton (2005)

Won 146 games over 12 seasons, more victories than any other Michigan Tech basketball coach. After leaving in 1985 he's worked for Horner Flooring, the Dollar Bay company which produces wood basketball floors for NCAA Final Four tournaments and NBA teams.

C.B. HEDGECOCK, Marquette (1974)

NMU field house named for Hedgecock, the former coach of all sports at the school. Charter member of the NMU Sports Hall of Fame.

STAN ALBECK, Marquette (1985)

Before coaching in the NBA with San Antonio, New Jersey, Cleveland and Los Angeles, Albeck coached Northern Michigan University to 178 wins.

TOM IZZO, Iron Mountain (1997)

Head coach for Michigan State University named NCAA Division 1 Coach of the Year in 1998 as he led team to NCAA Championship.

MISCELLANEOUS

BARBARA DESCHEPPER, Norway (1976)

Only speed skater to simultaneously hold the "Big Four," skating titles: National Indoor and Outdoor and North American Indoor and Outdoor. Established 11 major speed skating titles in the 1950s.

CLIFFORD "Kip" CRASE, Rockland (1979)

1969 National Wheelchair Athlete of the Year.

PAUL BIETILA, Ishpeming (1996)

Member of the U.S. National Ski Hall of Fame. Member of the "Flying Bietilas" family of ski jumpers. Died in 1939 at age of 21 from injuries suffered during ski meet.

WALTER "Huns" ANDERSON, Ishpeming (1988)

Pioneer U.P. ski jumper. Made first jump at Ishpeming's Suicide Hill.

CHARLES POLICH, Caspian (1987)

Professional bowler was ranked 12th nationally in 1951 by National Bowling writers Association. Bowled a 716 series at age 74.

RAY "Dude" RANGUETTE, Nahma (1987)

Said to have officiated more U.P. high school basketball and football games in his 35-year career than anyone. Member of NMU Sports Hall of Fame.

DOMINIC JACOBETTI JR., Negaunee (1990)

Highest scoring high school basketball player in U.P. history with 2,140 points scored over four seasons with Negaunee St. Paul High. Went on to become powerful State Senator.

BRUCE MARTYN, Sault Ste. Marie (1998)

Detroit Red Wings radio announcer for 31 years, 1964-1995. Started career at WSOO in 1950. Member of NHL Hockey Hall of Fame and Michigan Sports Hall of Fame.

RAY HILL, Wakefield (2003)

Two-time world champion horseshoe pitcher in senior division, 187 and 1989

ROSEMARY STEVENSON, Stalwart (1990)

Member of the Grand Rapids Chicks of the American Girls Professional Baseball League in the 1950s. Honored in 1988 at Women in Baseball ceremony at Baseball Hall of Fame.

CHERYL CLARK, Wetmore (2001)

Member of the All American Red Heads, a barnstorming women's basketball team featured in permanent exhibit at Women's Basketball Hall of Fame in Knoxville, Tennessee.

UNITED STATES OLYMPIC EDUCATION CENTER (USOEC)

The only Olympic Education Center in the U.S. is located on the campus of Northern Michigan University (NMU) in Marquette. The center opened in 1985 as the country's third Olympic Training Center, following Colorado Springs, CO and Lake Placid, NY. It is the only Olympic Training Center located on a college campus. In 1989 it was named as the first and only Olympic Education Center.

Northern Michigan University's Superior Dome

Young athletes live on campus in Meyland Hall, eat in campus dining halls, attend class at NMU or Marquette Sr. High School and use university training facilities in the Berry Events Center and the Superior Dome. Student athletes approved for the program by the Olympic Education Committee and NMU pay lower in-state tuition, and can qualify for the B.J. Stupak Scholarship to help with expenses.

Since 1985 over 25,000 athletes from more than 40 countries have trained and studied at the center. They have won over 70 Olympic medals and earned more than 100 high school diplomas and college degrees.

Current training programs at the USOEC include: boxing, Greco-Roman wrestling, short track speed skating, weight lifting and women's freestyle wrestling.

With approximately 100 resident athletes, coaches and trainers the USOEC in Marquette is the second largest Olympic Training Center behind Colorado Springs, CO and ahead of Lake Placid, NY and Cula Vista, CA.

Training Facilities

Superior Dome	football/soccer field
(Enclosed stadium	three basketball courts
With 8,000 seats)	Two tennis courts
	200-meter eight-lane rubberized running track
	Locker rooms
	Boxing training gymnasium
	Wrestling room
	Strength and conditioning weight room
	Olympic weightlifting facility
	Sports medicine clinic
PEIF Athletic Complex	Six basketball courts
	Volleyball arena
	Seven racquetball courts
	Weight room
	Indoor tennis court
	Eight-lane swimming pool and diving tank
	Rock-climbing wall
Berry Events Center	Olympic-sized ice rink
(3,800 seats)	Dedicated locker rooms for USOEC short track speedskaters
	Six other locker rooms for visitors

Two short track speedskating world records were set in this facility at the 2003 World Cup and it was the site of the 2006 U.S. Short Track Championships, which determined the 2006 Olympic team.

THE WATERSMEET NIMRODS

Thanks to ESPN, the Watersmeet Nimrods is one of the most famous high school sports nicknames in the world. In 2004, the sports network began broadcasting a series of promotional commercials as part of a campaign titled, "Without Sports." ESPN shot video of local fans praising their home team and of 81-year old Dale Jenkins singing the Nimrod fight song. Jenkins played for the Watersmeet team in the 1930s. At the end of the commercials the announcer asks, "Without sports, who would cheer for the Nimrods?"

Soon after the promo spots began to air, the phone began to ring at the Watersmeet High School offices. People from around country wanted to order Nimrod hats and sweatshirts.

In modern day slang "nimrod" can be used as a derogatory term. But the true meaning from the Old Testament, means "mighty hunter before the Lord." The high school came up with the nickname in 1904 because the area was, and still is prime hunting land.

The Nimrods may have been the butt of some jokes over the years, but the ESPN commercials have been a plus. The school has sold over $600,000 worth of Nimrod logo-wear since 2004. The school has received vast news coverage including an appearance by the principal and coach, George Peterson and Dale Jenkins on "The Tonight Show with Jay Leno."

In November 2007 "Nimrod Nation," an eight-part documentary that followed the 2005-06 season in Watersmeet debuted on the Sundance Channel. (see Culture chapter)

TOP TEN NICKNAMES FOR HIGH SCHOOL SPORTS TEAMS

ESPN came up with this list in 1986 that included the Watersmeet Nimrods and the Kingsford Flivvers.

1) Syrupmakers of Cairo, Ga.
2) Beetdiggers of Brush, Co.
3) **NIMRODS of Watersmeet, MI**
4) Imps of Cary, NC
5) Atomsmashers
   of Johnson Prep in Savannah, Ga.
6) Angoras of Clarkston, Ga.
7) **FLIVVERS of Kingsford, Mi.**
8) Squirrels of Winslow, Az.
9) Peglegs of Stuyvesant in NYC
10) Dots of Poca, W. Va.

MICHIGAN HIGH SCHOOL RECORDS
FOOTBALL

Some of the longest running school rivalries in Michigan are based in the U.P., including an annual interstate game that dates back over 100 years.

OLDEST SCHOOL RIVALRY

1) 1893 - Battle Creek Central vs. Kalamazoo Central (1893-2005, 102 games)
2) **1894 - Negaunee vs. Marquette (1894-2005, 130 games)**
3) **1894 - Menominee, Michigan vs. Marinette, Wisconsin (99 games, 1894-2005)**

LONGEST RUNNING SCHOOL RIVALRY (INTERSTATE)

99 years- Menominee, Michigan vs. Marinette, Wisconsin
(99 games, 1894 - 2005)

TOTAL NUMBER OF GAMES PLAYED, * = SERIES ACTIVE

1) 134 - * Negaunee vs. Ishpeming (1895-2007, 132 games, Negaunee leads the series 63-59-12 through 2007) (Ishpeming 28, Negaunee 14 in 2007)
2) 132 - * Negaunee vs. Marquette (1894-2007 132 games, Negaunee leads the series 67-54-11 through 2007) (Marquette 22, Negaunee 14 in 2007)
3) 111 - * Escanaba vs. Menominee (1897-2007, 111 games, Menominee leads the series, 57-51-3 through 2007) (Menominee 53, Escanaba 14 in 2007)

VICTORIES:ALL-TIME

1) 716 - Muskegon (1895-2006) (716-254-43), 14-0-0 in 2006
2) 667 - Ann Arbor Pioneer (1891, 1896-2006) (667-389-38), 7-4-0 in 2006
3) **564 - Escanaba (1897-2006) (564-276-37), 7-4-0 in 2006**
3) 564 - Lansing Central/Sexton (1893-1909, 1913-2006: 564-345-46), 3-6-0 in 2006
4) 558 - Battle Creek Central (1893-2006) (558-368-48), 6-4-0 in 2006
5) 556 - Traverse City Central (1896-2006) (556-297-50), 0-9-0 in 2006
6) **552 - Menominee (1894-2006) (552-264-40), 14-0-0, in 2006**

MOST OVERTIME PERIODS IN A GAME

1) 9 - Detroit Southeastern 42, Detroit Northeastern 36 (1977)
2) **6 - Marquette 42, Gwinn 36 (1981)**
Two others tied with 6.

MOST POINTS SCORED IN A GAME

1) 216 - Muskegon 216, Hastings 0 (1912)
2) 160 - Detroit University School 160, East Bay City 0 (1908)
3) **150 - Menominee 150, Kingsford 0 (1929)**

MOST CAREER COACHING VICTORIES (MINIMUM 200) * = ACTIVE

1) 374 - * Al Fracassa, Royal Oak Shrine; Birmingham Brother Rice (1960-07, 374-98-7)
2) 351 - * John Herrington, Farmington Hills Harrison (1970-07, 351-74-1)
3) 315 - * Mike Boyd, Waterford Our Lady of the Lakes (1965-68, 1970-07; 324-100-1)
4) 308 - Leo "Smokey" Boyd, Standish-Sterling; Saginaw SS Peter & Paul; Saginaw Nouvel (1953, 1956-99; 308-116-4)
5) 304 - * Jack Pratt, Flint St. Matthew; Grand Blanc; Flint Kearsley; Flint Powers Catholic (1958-76, 1980-06; 304-129-7)
6) 300 - Walt Braun, Marysville (1956-1998, 300-98-2)
7) 293 - Jeff Smith, East Lansing (1966-03, 293-93-2)
8) 283 - * Tom Mach, Detroit Catholic Central (1976-07, 283-68-0) 10-3-0 in 2007
9) **281 - * Ken Hofer, Stephenson; Menominee (1964-71, 1975-07; 281-122-2) 14-0-0 in 2007**
10) 271 - * Bob Lantzy, Utica Eisenhower (1971-07; 271-102-1) 6-4-0 in 2007
11) 273 - Bill Maskill, Galesburg-Augusta (1951-91, 273-84-2)
12) 271 - * Bob Lantzy, Utica Eisenhower (1971-07; 271-102-1) 6-4-0 in 2007
13) 250 - * James Reynolds, Detroit Martin Luther King (1974-2007, 250-106) 14-0-0 in 2007
14) 245 - Mel Skillman, Saginaw MacArthur; Merrill (1963-03, 245-130-6)
14) 245 - * Herb Brogan, Jackson Lumen Christi (1980-07, 245-58-0) 12-1-0 in 2007
14) 245 - * Rick Bye, Sterling Heights Stevenson (1975-07; 245-91-0) 2-7-0 in 2007
15) 243 - Jack Ver Duin, Wyoming Park (1962-01, 243-112-6)
15) 243 - * Rick Bye, Sterling Heights Stevenson (1975-06; 243-84-0)
16) **239 - Richard Mettlach, Crystal Falls-Forest Park (1956-89, 239-73-6)**

INDIVIDUAL RECORDS: REGULAR SEASON

Points Scored: Game

66 - Cecil Hardy, Flint Central (Flint Central 106, Lapeer 0), 11 TDs (9-26-14)
66 - Duke Christie, Escanaba (Escanaba 102, Ishpeming 0) 10 TDs, 6 PATs (1920)
60 - Herb Dunphy, Lansing Central (Lansing Central 111, Lapeer 0) 10 TDs (1917)
54 - Fred Jacks, Muskegon (Muskegon 216, Hastings 0) 9 TDs (1912)
54 - Francis Tallent, Menominee (Menominee 150, Kingsford 0) 9 TDs (1929)
50 - Tony Ceccacci, Rudyard (Rudyard 52, Cheboygan Catholic 0) 7 TDs, 4 PATs (1982)

TOUCHDOWNS: GAME (MINIMUM 7)

11 - Cecil Hardy, Flint Central (Flint Central 106, Lapeer 0) (9-26-1914)
10 - Herb Dunphy, Lansing Central (Lansing Central 111, Lapeer 0) (1917)
10 - Floyd Brown, Saginaw (Saginaw 82, Alma 0) (1918)
10 - Duke Christie, Escanaba (Escanaba 102, Ishpeming 0) (1920)

TOUCHDOWNS SCORED: QUARTER (MINIMUM 5)

5 - Chris Zablocki, Lake Linden-Hubbell vs. Baraga (1st Qtr.) (10-10-1997)

RUSHING YARDS: GAME (MINIMUM 400)

529 - Dwain Koscielniak, Gaylord St. Mary (35 carries) (1990)
527 - Francis Tallent, Menominee (1928)

RUSHING: CONSECUTIVE 100-YARD GAMES

24 - Kevin Grady, Jr., East Grand Rapids (10-18-02 thru 09-10-04)

23 - Dean Arcand, Crystal Falls-Forest Park (1981-83)

RUSHING: ATTEMPTS SEASON

374 - Jamie Sundberg, Ishpeming (9 games) (1997)

RUSHING: ATTEMPTS GAME (MINIMUM 40)

55 - Jamie Sundberg, Ishpeming vs. Stephenson (10-16-1998)

53 - Matt O'Connor, Grand Ledge vs. Lansing Sexton (11-7-1997)

52 - Robert Bills, Jackson vs. Lansing Eastern (9-17-1993)

51 - Lee Dorchak, Harper Woods vs. Hamtramck (10-17-1997)

51 - Mark Koski, Baraga vs Wakefield (10-26-2002)

RUSHING ATTEMPTS CAREER (MINIMUM 700) * = ACTIVE

1,154 - Kevin Grady, Jr., East Grand Rapids (51 games) (2002-04)

931 - Benny Clark Jr., Ravenna (46) (1993-96)

849 - Tom Tyson, Whittemore-Prescott (36) (1992-95)

788 - Ryan Cunningham, Middleton Fulton (36) (1992-95)

735 - Joe Patovisti, Baraga (37) (2002-05)

RECEIVING: YARDS GAME (MINIMUM 220)

341 - Matt LaFreniere, Burton Bendle vs Genesee (13 receptions) (9-23-2005)

305 - Shannon Harper, Vassar vs. Millington (3 receptions) (9-30-2002)*

300 - Brant Athey, Decatur vs. Marcellus (10) (10-8-1999)

290 - Jason Hofer, Menominee vs. Green Bay Southwest (7) (9-5-2003)

KICK RETURNS FOR TOUCHDOWS - SEASON

6 - Josh Tarbox, Menominee (1998)

FUMBLE RETURN FOR TOUCHDOWN - LONGEST

100 - Justin Hubbard, Gwinn vs. Manistique (9-19-98)

Two others tied with 100

QUARTERBACK SACKS: GAME (MINIMUM 5)

7 - Ben Baragrey, Gaylord vs. Ogemaw Heights (8-29-2003)

5 - Tim Wadaga, Baraga vs. Wakefield (10-22-05)

Twelve others tied with 5

MHSAA CHAMPIONSHIP GAME RECORDS: INDIVIDUALS

MOST APPEARANCES IN MHSAA FOOTBALL FINALS (TEAM)

1) 16 - Farmington Hills Harrison (12 State titles)

2) 13 - Detroit St Martin dePorres (12 State titles)

3) 12 - Detroit Catholic Central (9 State titles)

3) 12 - Crystal Falls-Forest Park (State titles in 1975, 1976, and 2007)

MOST RUSHING ATTEMPTS

64 - Crystal Falls-Forest Park vs. Flint Holy Rosary, 1977 Class D (175 yards)

LOWEST RUSHING TOTAL ALLOWED BY DEFENSE

(-32) - Crystal Falls-Forest Park vs. Flint Holy Rosary, 1975 Class D

LOWEST TOTAL YARDS ALLOWED BY DEFENSE

46 - Crystal Falls-Forest Park vs. Flint Holy Rosary, 1975 Class D (-32 Rushing, +78 Passing)

MARGIN OF VICTORY (PTS.)

50 - Crystal Falls-Forest Park (50) vs. Flint Holy Rosary (0),1975 Class D

UNSCORED UPON DEFENSE - NO POINTS ALLOWED IN PLAYOFFS:

0 - Crystal Falls, Two games, 117 points to opponent's zero. (D-1975)
Three others tied with 0 points allowed.

MOST POINTS SCORED IN MHSSA CHAMPIONSHIP GAME (INDIVIDUAL)

1) 24 - Bill Santilli, Crystal Falls Forest Park vs. Flint Holy Rosary, 1975 Class D (4 TDs)
Nine others tied with 24

FOOTBALL CHAMPIONS 1975-2007

Year	Champion (coach),score, opponent	Division or Class
1975	Ishpeming (*Mike Mileski*) 38-22 Hudson	Class C
1975	Crystal Falls-Forest Park 50-0 Flint Holy Rosary (Richard Mettlach)	Class D
1976	Crystal Falls-Forest Park (Richard Mettlach)	
1979	Ishpeming (John Croze) 13-0 Watervliet	Class C
1979	Norway (Robert Giannunzio) 21-6 Schoolcraft	Class D
1980	Munising (Terry Sayen) 19-7 White Pigeon	Class C
1980	Norway (Robert Giannunzio) 25-0 Fowler	Class D
1981	Escanaba (Jerry Cvengros) 16-6 Fraser	Class A
1983	St. Ignace (Barry Pierson) 15-12 Mendon	Class D
1993	Kingsford (Chris Hofer 35-14 Imlay City	Class B
1993	Iron Mountain (Thomas Wender) 28-8 Manchester	Class C
1998	Menominee (Ken Hofer) 42-6 Haslett	Class BB
2000	Iron Mountain (Tom Wender) 25-23 Gobles	Division 7
2002	Negaunee (Paul Jacobson) 28-20 (OT) Hopkins	Division 6
2006	Menominee (Ken Hofer) 41-6 Madison Heights Madison	Division 5
2007	Menominee (Ken Hofer) 21-7 Jackson Lumen Christi	Division 5
2007	Crystal Falls Forest Park (Bill Santilli) 22-14 Fulton-Middleton	Division 8

BASKETBALL

MOST CAREER COACHING VICTORIES (MINIMUM 500) * = ACTIVE

1) 739 - Lofton Greene, Center, Kentucky, New Buffalo, & River Rouge (739-231, 1941-84)
2) 635 - Paul Cook, Lansing Resurrection & Lansing Eastern (635-243, 1949-91)
3) 612 - Bernie Holowicki, Detroit St. Hedwig, Detroit St. Gregory, Detroit DeLaSalle, & Detroit Catholic Central (612-216, 1953, 1956-1994)
4) 589 - * Dave Soules, Detroit East Catholic, Riverview Gabriel Richard (589-279, 1964-69 & 1972-05, 2006-07)

5) 571 - * Ray Lauwers, Monroe St. Mary (571-270, 1967-05) 6) 565 - Chuck Turner, Willow Run & Battle Creek Central (565-207, 1965-00)

6) 565 - Chuck Turner, Willow Run & Battle Creek Central (565-207, 1965-00)

7) 555 - * Irv Dieterle, Merritt, Gaylord St. Mary, Alpena, Remus Chippewa Hills, & Ishpeming Westwood (555-260, 1965-67 & 1969-03, 2007) (12-10 in 2007)

8) 547 - Warren (Whitey) Wilson, Calumet & Frankenmuth (547-222, 1960-96)

8) 545 - Russell (Lefty) Franz, Bay City St. Stanislaus, Bay City All Saints, & Pinconning (545-215, 1953-82 & 1984-91)

9) 544 - Bill Zabonick, Bronson (544-241, retired 1992)

10) 543 - * Irv Dieterle, Merritt, Gaylord St. Mary, Alpena, Remus Chippewa Hills, & Ishpeming Westwood (543-250, 1965-67 & 1969-03, 2007)

11) 540 - Jim Barker, Utica Ford, Centerline St. Clement, Warren Zoe Christian, Sterling Heights Parkway Christian (540-216, 1972-06) (13-10 in 2005-06)

12) 537 - *Roy Johnson, Montrose, Yale, Howell and Beaverton (533-193, 1971-06)

13) 526 - Leo (Sam) Franz, Saginaw St. Mary, Saginaw St. Stephen, & Merrill

14) 524 - Don Miller, Maple City Glen Lake (524-207, 1973-04)

15) 518 - Grover Kirkland, Flint Northwestern (518-148, 1973-00)

16) 513 - * Tom Caudill, Ewen-Trout Creek (513-145, 1977-06) (12-8 in 2005-06)

LONGEST WIN STREAK

65 - Chassell (2-1-56 - 11-23-58)

MOST POINTS SCORED IN A QUARTER – ONE TEAM

48 - Engadine vs. Grand Marais (4th quarter) (1-28-66)

MOST POINTS SCORED IN A HALF – ONE TEAM

83 - Engadine vs. Grand Marais (second half) (1-28-66)

MOST POINTS SCORED IN A GAME – ONE TEAM

1) 171 - Glen Arbor-Leelanau vs. Freesoil (171-94) (2-17-89)

2) 155 - Trout Creek vs. Mercer, Wis. (155-42) (1966-67)

3) 154 - Engadine vs. Grand Marais (154-51) (1-28-66)

AVERAGE POINTS PER GAME – SEASON

97.8 - Trout Creek (1966-67)

When it comes to shooting three-pointers Carney dominates the record books!

MOST THREE-POINT FIELD GOALS SCORED: GAME

1) 23 - Waterford Mt. Zion vs. Saginaw Arts & Science Academy (23 of 82) (1-21-04)

2) 20 - Carney-Nadeau vs. Big Bay deNoc (20 of 39) (2-13-01)

3) 19 - Carney-Nadeau vs. Rapid River (19 of 41) (1-27-98)

MOST THREE-POINT FIELD GOALS SCORED: SEASON

1) 253 - St. Ignace (253 of 587) (2000-01)
2) 225 - Carney-Nadeau (225 of 628) (1998-99)
3) 224 - Carney-Nadeau (224 of 630) (1999-00)
4) 215 - Carney-Nadeau (215 of 596) (1996-97)
5) 212 - Marine City (212 of 578) (1993-94)
6) 209 - Wyoming Tri-unity Christian (209 of 547) (1996-97)
7) 208 - Carney-Nadeau (208 of 544) (2000-01)
8) 193 - Wyoming Tri-unity Christian (193 of 500) (1997-98)
9) 190 - Carney-Nadeau (190 of 567) (1997-98)
10) 189 - Carney-Nadeau (189 of 574) (2001-02)

MOST FREE THROW ATTEMPTS IN A SEASON

758 - St. Ignace (461 of 758) (1982-83)
645 - St. Ignace (432 of 645) (1997-98)
621 - St. Ignace (379 of 621) (2001-02)
596 - Rockford (1968-69)
582 - St. Ignace (387 of 582) (2002-03)

MOST FREE THROW SHOTS MADE: SEASON

461 - St. Ignace (461 of 758) (1982-83)
432 - St. Ignace (432 of 645) (1997-98)
415 - Allegan (415 of 559) (1997-98)
387 - St. Ignace (387 of 582) (2002-03)

INDIVIDUAL RECORDS

MOST POINTS IN A GAME

97 - Ed Burling, Crystal Falls (107) vs. Iron River (27) (1910-11)

HIGHEST SEASON AVERAGE: POINTS PER GAME

1) 44.4 - Richie Jordan, Fennville (20/888) (1964-65)
2) 39.5 - Todd Bayle, Walkerville (22/869) (1985-86)
3) 38.6 - Jim Sobolewski, Ironwood Catholic (21/810) (1978-79)

MOST TWO-POINT FIELD GOALS MADE: GAME

1) 31 - Roger Roell, Channing vs. Michigamme (1-5-60)
2) 29 - Jim Manning, Trout Creek vs. Amasa (2-26-60)
3) 27 - Dirk Dunbar, Cadillac vs. Remus Chippewa Hills (27 of 47) (12-10-71)
4) 26 - Keith Cutler, Cooks vs. Grand Marais (1-22-50)
5) 26 - Norbert Purol, Ironwood St. Ambrose vs Mass (2-21-52)

MOST THREE-POINT FIELD GOALS MADE: SEASON

1) 143 - Brad Redford, Frankenmuth (2007-08)
2) 116 - Ben Liedel, Monroe St. Mary Catholic Central (2005-06)
3) 103 - Jon Mills, Auburn Hills Oakland Christian (206 att.) (1996-97)
4) 102 - Brad Gray, Adrian Lenawee Christian (260 att.) (1995-96)
5) 100 - Brad Redford, Frankenmuth (240 att.) (2006-07)
6) 97 - Nate Meyers, Benzie Central (239 att.) (1996-97)
7) 96 - Ryan Wallace, Freeland (239 att.) (1994-95)
7) 96 - Matt Bennett, Erie-Mason (1997-98)
7) 96 - Steve MacDonald, St. Ignace (186 att.) (2000-01)

MOST THREE-POINT FIELD GOALS MADE: CAREER

1) 340 - Matt Kitchen, Mayville-Unionville-Sebewaing (1999-03)
2) 314 - Brad Gray, Adrian Lenawee Christian (835 att.) (1994-98)
2) 314 - Brad Redford, Frankenmuth (2005-08)
3) 254 - Zach Ingles, Greenville (638 att.) (1999-02)
4) 244 - Jon Mills, Auburn Hills Oakland Christian (525 att.) (1994-97)
5) 234 - Brad Noll, Parma Western (1995-99)
6) 233 - Jacob Polfus, Carney-Nadeau (543 att.) (1996-99)
7) 229 - Tyler Laser, Hillsdale (569 att.) (2004-2007)
8) 227 - Drew Neitzel, Wyoming Park (2001-04)
9) 218 - Anthony Hamo, Flint Powers Catholic (2000-02)
10) 217 - Mike Polfus, Carney-Nadeau (588 att.) (2000-03)
11) 216 - Alex Fleck, Munising (601 att.) (2003-06)
12) 212 - Brian Foltice, Wyoming Tri-unity Christian (1996-99)
13) 210 - Steve MacDonald, St. Ignace (484 att.) (1997-01)

MOST FREE THROWS MADE: SEASON

255 - Dustin Orns, Tekonsha (323 att.) (2007-08)
226 - Dave Archer, Manistique (274 attempts) (1984-85)

MOST FREE THROWS MADE: CAREER

1) 629 - Dustin Orns, Tekonsha (830 att.) (2005-08)
2) 572 - Austin Thornton, Cedar Springs (2004-07)
3) 518 - Zach Ingles, Greenville (616 attempts) (1999-02)
4) 493 - Marcus Taylor, Lansing Waverly (1997-00)
5) 478 - Steve MacDonald, St. Ignace (582) (1997-01)

MOST ASSISTS: SEASON

1) 341 - Eric Turner, Flint Central (1980-81)
2) 240 - Drew Neitzel, Wyoming Park (2003-04)
3) 238 - Anthony Crater, Flint Southwestern Academy (2005-06)
4) 227 - Mark Kraatz, Allen Park Inter-City Baptist (1984-85)
5) 222 - Doug Ingalls, Gladstone (1985-86)

MOST ASSISTS: CAREER

1) 726 - Eric Turner, Flint Central (1979-81)
2) 692 - Drew Neitzel, Wyoming Park (2001-04)
3) 679 - Mark Kraatz, Allen Park Inter-City Baptist (1981-85)
4) 581 - Steve MacDonald, St. Ignace (1997-01)

MOST STEALS: SEASON

1) 131 - Troy Boehm, Kent City (2004-05)
1) 131 - Eric Bialczyk, Hanover-Horton (1993-94)
1) 131 - Matt Taylor, Pinckney (21 games) (1999-00)
2) 129 - John Wekwert, Posen (1981-82)
3) 119 - Matt Taylor, Pinckney (21) (1997-98)
4) 117 - Anthony Acho, Walled Lake Western (2003-04)
5) 115 - Jake Suardini, Gwinn (2002-03)

MOST STEALS: CAREER

1) 363 - Matt Taylor, Pinckney (62) (1997-00)
2) 337 - Mark Kraatz, Allen Park Inter-City Baptist (1981-85)
3) 300 - Mike Leifeld, Battle Creek St. Philip (1999-03)
4) 288 - Steve MacDonald, St. Ignace (1997-01)

MHSAA CHAMPIONSHIP GAME: TEAM RECORDS

HIGHEST SCORE–LOSING TEAM
94 - Ewen-Trout Creek vs. Covert (105), 1982 Class D

LARGEST MARGIN OF VICTORY
43 - Brimley 74 – 31 Dimondale 1951 Class D

MHSAA CHAMPIONSHIP GAME: INDIVIDUAL RECORDS

MOST POINTS
1) 47 - Antoine Joubert, Detroit Southwestern vs. Flint Central, 1983 Class A
2) 44 - Mark Harris, Flint Central vs. Detroit Murray-Wright, 1981 Class A
3) 43 - Ralph Simpson, Detroit Pershing vs. Flint Central, 1967 Class A
4) 43 - David Kool, Grand Rapids South Christian vs. Muskegon Heights, 2005 (B)
5) 42 - Ernie Thompson, Saginaw vs. Benton Harbor, 1962 Class A
6) 40 - Bob Gale, Trout Creek vs. Covert, 1966 Class D

BLOCKED SHOTS

8 - Tony Vaught, Iron River West Iron County vs. Saginaw Nouvel, 1991 Class C
Two others tied with 8.

STATE BASKETBALL CHAMPIONS: CLASS B

Year	Champion (coach), score, opponent
1967	Menominee (Bob Krysiak) 63-59 Ypsilanti Willow Run
1957	Negaunee (Jack Taylor) 68-66 Harper Woods
1956	Stephenson (Duane Lord) 73-71 (2 OT) Detroit St. Andrew
1950	Ishpeming (C. C. Watson) 43-37 Grand Rapids Godwin
*1947	Bessemer (Helge Pukema) 46-45 Lake Linden
*1946	Escanaba (George Ruwitch/Jim Rouman) 52-38 Sault Ste. Marie
*1945	Marquette (James Soli) 36-28 Ironwood
*1944	Escanaba (George Ruwitch) 54-45 Negaunee
1943	No Championship games
*1942	Iron River (James Crummey) 41-30 Hancock
*1941	Sault Ste. Marie (Dave Ripley) 30-27 Stambaugh
*1940	Marquette Graveraet (Roger Keast) 28-27 Escanaba
*1939	Iron Mountain (George Mason) 32-30 Iron River
*1938	Ishpeming (Clairmont Watson) 20-12 Lake Linden
*1937	Ironwood (Al Treado) 17-15 (4 OT) Ishpeming
*1936	Iron River (Edward Morcombe) 51-34 Calumet
*1935	Ishpeming (Clairmont Watson) 25-23 Ironwood
*1934	Ishpeming (Clairmont Watson) 25-23 Crystal Falls
*1933	Iron Mountain (Leonard Thune) 22-18 Stambaugh
*1932	Ishpeming (Clairmont Watson) vs. Escanaba

1932- 1947 Separate champions for Lower and Upper Peninsula

STATE BASKETBALL CHAMPIONS: CLASS C

Year	Champion (coach),score, opponent
1930	Negaunee (Ed Shadford) 31-25 Orchard Lake St. Mary
1928	Iron Mountain (Lars Thune) 23-17 Dearborn Fordson
2001	Negaunee (Tom Russo) 52-45 Merrill
1995	Ishpeming (Gerald Racine) 69-61 Lakeview

1981   Stephenson (Paul Miller) 64-48 Three Oaks-River Valley
1966   L'Anse (Bill Popp) 89-70 Flint Holy Redeemer
1956   Crystal Falls (Bob Boldt) 71-69 Berrien Springs
1955   Houghton (John Gafney) 65-62 Wayland
*1947   Norway (Alan Ronberg) 55-54 Gwinn
*1946   Norway (Alan Ronberg) 48-44 Newberry
*1945   L'Anse (Joe Hampton) 39-33 Norway
*1944   Crystal Falls (Eddie Chambers) 32-31 Gladstone
1943   No championship tournament
*1942   Crystal Falls (Eddie Chambers) 35-27 Norway
*1941   Crystal Falls (Eddie Chambers) 37-26 Felch
*1940   Crystal Falls (Eddie Chambers) 36-23 L'Anse
*1939   Crystal Falls (Eddie Chambers) 41-26 Marquette Baraga
*1938   Crystal Falls (Eddie Chambers) 32-22 Laurium Sacred Heart
*1937   Newberry 24-16 Crystal Falls
*1936   Norway (Alan Ronberg) 28-27 Crystal Falls
*1935   Gwinn (E. L. Miller) 34-13 Ewen
*1934   Gwinn (E. L. Miller) 32-25 Vulcan
*1933   Newberry 44-16 Amasa
*1932   Lake Linden (Henry Anerle) beat Escanaba St. Joseph
1932- 1947 Separate champions for Lower and Upper Peninsula
1926   Newberry (Ogden Johnson) 31-14 Bay City St.James

STATE BASKETBALL CHAMPIONS: CLASS D

Year	Champion (coach), score, opponent
2007	Cedarville 77-74 Wyoming Tri-unity Christian
1972	Ewen-Trout Creek (Rudy Perhalla) 74-62 Flint Holy Rosary
1969	Marquette Baraga (Gordon LeDuc) 68-53 Detroit St. Martin
1961	Marquette Pierce (Vic Hurst) 68-61 Freesoil
1958	Chassell (Ed Helakowski) 66-61 Owosso St. Paul
1957	Chassell (Ed Helakowski) 58-50 Stevensville
1956	Chassell (Ed Helakowski) 71-68 Portland St. Patrick
1951	Brimley (Karl Parker) 74-31 Dimondale
1950	Brimley (Karl Parker) 37-30 Fowler
*1947	Mass (John D. Wilson) 63-48 Vulcan
*1946	Rock (George Kulack) 41-36 Cedarville
*1945	Vulcan (Tim Barry) 43-20 Rudyard
*1944	Channing (Einar Eckholm) 39-36 Rock
1943	No Championship game
*1942	Hermansville (Jack Kleimola) 51-27 Pequaming
*1941	Stevensville (Marshall Shearer) 42-25 Hanover
*1940	Hermansville (Jack Kleimola) 24-23 National Mine
*1939	Bergland (Glenn Johnson) 31-16 Pequaming
*1938	Bergland (Glenn Johnson) 41-23 Negaunee St. Paul
*1937	Trout Creek (Al Kircher) 42-20 Trenary
*1936	Channing (Arleigh Mautner) 37-20 Trenary
*1935	Trout Creek (Al Kircher) 25-24 Champion

*1934   Alpha (Ballard Damschroeder) 34-9 Michigamme
*1933   Alpha (Ballard Damschroeder) 29-28 Bergland
*1932   Palmer beat Daggett
1932-1947 Separate champions for Lower and Upper Peninsula
1926   Michigamme (C. C. Walters) 27-15 Alpena St. Bernard

STATE BASKETBALL CHAMPIONS: CLASS E

Year	Champion (coach), score, opponent
1960	Hermansville 72-50 Perkins
1959	Nahma 55-45 Trout Creek
1958	Trout Creek (Bruce Warren) 61-41 Perkins
1957	Hermansville 77-51 Michigamme
1956	Trout Creek (Bruce Warren) 86-68 Trout Creek
1955	Trout Creek (Bruce Warren) 84-83 Alpha
1954	Alpha (Gerhardt Gollackner) 52-48 Perkins
1953	Nahma (Harold Anderson) 67-64 Maranisco
1952	Nahma (Harold Anderson) 64-44 Maranisco
1951	Michigamme 59-48 Nahma
1950	Alpha (Gerhardt Gollackner) 52-28 Michigamme
1949	Alpha (Gerhardt Gollackner) 50-34 National Mine
1948	Hermansville 58-38 Rockville
1947	Bergland (Al Londo) 40-37 Perkins
1946	Alpha (Gerhardt Gollackner) 48-28 Champion
1945	Bergland (Al Londo) 49-39 Trenary
1944	Amasa (Gerhardt Gollackner) 51-43 Cedarville
1943	No Championship game
1942	Palmer (Elvin Niemi) 37-31 Bergland
1941	Palmer (Joseph Miheve) 39-29 Hulbert

SKIING: TEAM CHAMPIONSHIPS

BOYS	Year	Champion (coach)	Runner Up	Class
	1997	Marquette (Derek Anderson)	Traverse City	A
	2000	Marquette (Derek Anderson)	Traverse City Central	A
	2001	Marquette (Derek Anderson)	Traverse City West	A
	2002	Marquette (Derek Anderson)	Lake Orion	A
	2003	Marquette (Derek Anderson)	Petoskey	A
	2006	Marquette (Derek Anderson)	Traverse City West	A
	2009	Marquette	Waterford U	Div. 1
GIRLS	Year	Champion (coach)	Runner Up	Class
	1979	Iron Mountain (Linda Vren)	Marquette	Open
	1999	Marquette (Derek Anderson)	Traverse City Central	A
	2000	Marquette (Derek Anderson)	Traverse City Central	A
	2001	Marquette (Derek Anderson)	Cadillac	A
	2002	Marquette (Derek Anderson)	Traverse City Central	A
	2003	Marquette (Derek Anderson)	Petoskey	A
	2004	Marquette (Derek Anderson)	Traverse City Central	A
	2008	Marquette (Christy Salonen)	Traverse City Central	Div. 1
	2009	Marquette	Traverse City Central	Div. 1

SKIING: INDIVIDUAL RECORDS

Boys **Giant Slalom: Three-Time MHSAA Champion**
Greg Kyle, Houghton (1985-87)
Girls **Slalom: Two-Time MHSAA Champion**
Susie Fox, Iron Mountain (1978-79)
Giant Slalom: Four-Time MHSAA Champion
Christy Salonen, Stambaugh West Iron County (Class B-C-D) (1993-96)
Two-Time MHSAA Champion
Susie Fox, Iron Mountain (1978-79)

HOCKEY

MOST CAREER COACHING VICTORIES

1) 598 - * Ron Baum, East Kentwood (598-214-31, (1973-2006)
2) 458 - * Mike Turner, Trenton (458-79-36, 1974-1981, 1995-2006)
3) 427 - Chris Christensen, Flint Kearsley (427-221-45, 1975 -2002), Retired
4) 411 - * Jim Crawford- Calumet (411-168-14, 1984-present)
5) 381 - Don Miller- Houghton (381-260-19, 1969-1997), Retired
6) 357 - Rick Miller- Hancock (357-239-22, 1981-2004), Retired
7) 312 - Jerry Sullivan, Marquette (312-158-13, 1975-1994), Retired

MHSAA CHAMPIONSHIP GAME RECORDS

FASTEST TWO GOALS BY SAME TEAM

1) :08 - Calumet vs. Bloomfield Hills Cranbrook-Kinwood, 1998, Class B-C- D
(3rd period, 5:07 & 5:15)
2) :09 - Trenton vs. Flint Kearsley, 1986 Class A (3rd period, 12:32 & 12:41)
3) :09 - Allen Park Cabrini vs. Marysville, 1994 Class B-C-D (2nd period, 1:31 & 1:40)
4) :16 - Calumet vs. Flint Powers Catholic, 1993 Class B-C-D (3rd period, 2:33 & 2:49)

MOST POINTS IN A GAME: INDIVIDUAL

6 - Todd Mapes, Sault Ste. Marie vs. Detroit Country Day, 1989 Class B-C-D
(2 goals, 4 assists)
6 - Marc Pomroy, Calumet vs. Flint Powers Catholic, 1993 Class B (4 goals, 2 assists)
Two others tied with 6

STATE HOCKEY CHAMPIONS

Year	Champion (coach), score, opponent	Class/Division
2008	Orchard Lake St. Mary's (Brian Klanow) / Marquette (Joe Papin) *	DIV. 1
Co-Champions: Determined by tournament administration after no winner was decided in 8 overtimes		
2008	Calumet (Jim Crawford) 1-0 (OT) Flint Powers Catholic	DIV 3
2003	Calumet (Jim Crawford) 3-1 Riverview Gabriel Richard	DIV 3
1999	Hancock (Rick Miller) 7-3 Big Rapids	B-C-D
1998	Calumet (Jim Crawford) 6-3 Bloomfield Hills Cranbrook-Kingswood	B-C-D
1996	Calumet (Jim Crawford) 2-1 Bloomfield Hills Cranbrook-Kingswood	B-C-D
1995	Marquette (Mike L'Huillier) 2-0 Trenton	CLASS A
1993	Calumet (Jim Crawford) 13-0 Flint Powers Catholic	B-C-D
1992	Calumet (Jim Crawford) 8-0 Riverview Gabriel Richard	B-C-D

1989	Sault Ste. Marie (Fred DeVuono) 8-0 Detroit Country Day	B-C-D
1988	Marquette (Gerry Sullivan) 6-5 (OT) Ann Arbor Pioneer	CLASS A
1984	Sault Ste. Marie (Fred DeVuono) 5-2 Allen Park Cabrini	B-C-D
1982	Houghton (Don Miller) 6-2 Flint Powers Catholic	B-C-D
1977	Marquette (Gerry Sullivan) 3-2 Trenton	TIER 1

STATE CHAMPIONS: GIRLS BASKETBALL

Year	Champion, score, opponent Class	
1976	Marquette (Barb Crill) 68-41 Farmington Our Lady of Mercy	A
1999	St. Ignace (Dorene Ingalls) 65-40 Sandusky	C
2000	St. Ignace (Dorene Ingalls) 74-56 Detroit Commercial and Media Arts	C
2003	Ishpeming (Dave Mann) 74-51 St. Ignace	C
2005	Houghton (Julie Filpus) 50-44 Michigan Center	C
1973	Ewen-Trout Creek (Betty Neilsen) 57-48 N. Muskegon	D
1979	Norway (Barbara Perry) 62-61 Maple City Glen Lake	D
1983	DeTour (David Miller) 49-37 Wyandotte Mt. Carmel	D
1989	Carney-Nadeau (Paul Polfus) 73-59 Potterville	D
1990	Carney-Nadeau (Paul Polfus) 56-31 Fowler	D
2001	Carney-Nadeau (Paul Polfus) 54-32 McBain NMC	D

MOST CAREER VICTORIES: COACHES
1) 599 - *Kathy McGee, Flint Powers Catholic (1976-06, 599-153)
2) 574 - *Nancy Osier, Ewen-Trout Creek (1973-06, 574-172) (13-10 in 2006)
3) 543 - *William Winfield, Detroit Southeastern, Detroit Martin Luther King
4) 539 - *Diane Laffey, Harper Woods Regina (1962-05, 539-306)
5) 509 - *Frank Orlando, Detroit Country Day (1981-05, 509-92) (25-1 in 2005)
6) 502 - *Paul Polfus, Carney-Nadeau (1979-05, 502-124) (20-4 in 2005)

LONGEST TEAM WINNING STREAK
78 - Carney-Nadeau (1989-91)

BEST TEAM FREE THROW AVERAGE: SEASON
.734 - Ishpeming Westwood (301-410) 2003

MOST POINTS IN A GAME: INDIVIDUAL
1) 63 - Debra Walker, Detroit Mumford vs. Detroit Central (1979)
2) 61 - Beth Blake, Marquette vs. Negaunee (11-7-89)
3) 60 - Leah Abla, Manistee vs. Remus-Chippewa Hills (1980)
4) 59 - Shelly Chapman, Marquette vs. Ironwood (1977)

MOST POINTS IN A SEASON: INDIVIDUAL
1) 846 - Stephanie Hass, Harbor Springs Harbor Light Christian
2) 812 - Julie Polakowski, Leland (28/29.0) (1981)
3) 812 - Cheri Swarthout, Climax-Scotts (28/29.0) (1986)
4) 804 - Evelyn Johnson, Lansing Everett (23/36.0) (1978)
5) 775 - Lisa Roell, Iron Mountain North Dickinson (23/33.7) (1990)

HIGHEST FREE THROW PERCENTAGE – SEASON: INDIVIDUAL
1) .915 - Marissa DeMott, Sandusky (118 of 129) (2007-08)
2) .909 - Lindsey Neal, Charlotte (50 of 55) (1998)
3) .881 - Hayley Purdy, Swartz Creek (52 fo 59) (2003)
4) .882 - Debra Frisk, Ishpeming Westwood (75 of 85) (1996)

MOST ASSISTS IN A SEASON: INDIVIDUAL

1) 217 - Jackie Stoor, Crystal Falls Forest Park (1995)

2) 201 - Krista Clement, St. Ignace (2002)

3) 198 - Ann Roys, Grand Rapids West Catholic (1999)

4) 189 - Randi Johnson, St. Ignace (1998)

MOST GAMES PLAYED IN CAREER: INDIVIDUAL

1) 111 - Aiysha Smith, Redford Bishop Borgess (1994-97)

2) 106 - Erika Ledy, DeTour (1980-83)

CHRONOLOGY OF UPPER PENINSULA GOLF COURSES

1898

Les Cheneaux Club & Golf Link (Public) Cedarville

Wawashkamo Golf Club (Semi-Private) Mackinac Island. Designed by Alex Smith

1901

Grand Hotel Golf Course (Resort), Mackinac Island. Back nine designed by Jerry Matthews

1902

Pine Grove Country Club (Semi-Private), Iron Mountain. Larry Packard/back nine-1962

1903

Sault Ste. Marie Country Club (Semi-Private) Sault Sainte Marie. Re-designed by Jerry Matthews

1920

Crystal View Golf Course, Crystal Falls

1922

Gogebic Country Club, Ironwood

Nahma Golf Course, Nahma

1924

Escanaba Country Club, Escanaba-(Semi-Private)

1925

Calumet Golf Club, Calumet-(Semi-Private)

1926

St. Ignace Golf and Country Club, St. Ignace

Oak Crest Golf Course, Norway

1927

Marquette Golf & Country Club, Marquette-(Semi-Private) Designed by William Langford & Theodore J. Moreau

1930

Highland Golf Club, Escanaba (expanded to 18 holes in 1968

1932

Arthur Hills Iron River Country Club (Semi-Private), Iron River

1935

Keweenaw Mountain Lodge, 9 holes

1936

Gladstone Golf Course (Public), Gladstone Designed by A. H. Jolly.

1959

Ontonagon GC, Ontonagon

1961

Wyandotte Hills Golf Club, Toivola

1963

Drummond Island GC, Drummond Island; designed by Jerold R. Gabel

1965

Munoscong Golf Club, Pickford

1966

Red Fox Run Golf Club, Gwinn

L'Anse Golf Course, L'Anse (semi-private)

1967

Wawonowin CC, Champion

Pictured Rocks Golf and Country Club, Munising (semi-private)

1970

Perttu's Big Spruce Golf Course (9 holes), Bruce Crossing

1972

Terrace Bluff Golf Club, Gladstone

Indianhead Mountain Resort (9 holes), Wakefield

1973

Country Meadows GC, Escanaba. Designed by Leo Degrand

1978

Indian Hills Golf Course, Stephenson

1983

Pine Mountain GC - Iron Mountain.

William Newcomb designed the back nine 1986

1984

George Young Recreation - Gaastra

Designed by George Young

Sault Ste.Marie CC - Sault Ste. Marie

Jerry Matthews Renovation 1996

1987

Kincheloe Memorial GC - Kincheloe

Rock at Woodmoor - Drummond Island, designed by Harry Bowers

1993

Chocolay Downs - Marquette

Designed by Jerry Matthews and Bruce Matthews III. Now named the **NMU Golf Course.** In 2007, Chocolay Downs owners Joe and Patsy Gibbs donated the course, valued at $1.6 million, to the NMU Foundation.

1994

Tri-Valley Golf and Country Club (public),-Garden Designed by John Lucas

1997

Timberstone GC, Iron Mountain; designed by Jerry Matthews

Hessel Ridge Golf Course, Hessel; designed by Jeff Gorney

1998

Tanglewood Marsh, Sault Ste. Marie; designed by Dr. Richard Zelbecka

1999

Newberry (new nine); designed by Mike Husby

Wild Bluff GC, Brimley Mike Husby

2000

Indian Lake, Manistique (new nine); designed by Mike Husby

2002

Irish Oaks Golf Club, Gladstone

2005

Greywalls GC, Marquette

Source: www.michigangolfer.com, Art McCafferty

Photos by R. Poutanen

STATE RECORD FISH CAUGHT IN THE U.P.

Species	Lake	County	Year	Wgt/lgth	Caught by
Black Bullhead	Milakokia Lake	Mackinac	1998	2.5/15.5"	Harry Wayne Fisher
Brook Trout	Clear Lake	Houghton	1996	9.5/28.10"	Dennis Nevins
Burbot	St. Mary's River-Munuscong Bay	Chippewa	1980	18.25/40"	Thomas Courtemanche
Lake Trout	Lake Superior		1997	61.5/49"	Lucas Lanczy
Lake Whitefish	Lake Superior	Ontonagon	1993	14.28/31.75"	Robert J.Majurin
Muskellunge	Thousand Island Lake	Gogebic	1980	45/51.5"	William Pivar
Northern Pike	Dodge Lake	Schoolcraft	1961	39/51.5"	Larry Clough
Pink Salmon	Carp River	Mackinac	1987	8.56/28"	Ron Karasek
Sauger	Torch Lake	Houghton	1976	6.56/25.5"	Gary Frederick
Smelt	Lake Superior	Houghton	1996	12"	John Watson (family)
Tiger Musky	Lac Vieux Desert	Gogebic	1919	51/54"	John Knoble
Yellow Perch	Lake Independence	Marquette	1947	3.75/21"	George E. Slutter

DEER HUNTING - ARCHERY

	Antlerless deer harvested			Antlered Bucks harvested		
Region	2006	2007	Change from 2006 to 2007 (%)	2006	2007	Change from 2006 to 2007 (%)
Western U.P.	3,690	4,736	28.4	3,665	3,888	6.1
Eastern U.P.	1,050	960	-8.6	948	909	-4.0
NE lower	5,323	4,893	-8.1	5,982	6,249	4.5
NW lower	7,615	7,611	0.0	11,746	10,948	-6.8
Saginaw Bay	8,553	9,236	8.0	12,652	12,170	-3.8
SW lower	7,949	8,243	3.7	13,604	14,228	4.6
SC lower	11,251	11,744	4.4	19,030	17,512	-8.0
SE lower	4,409	5,242	18.9	7,568	7,625	0.8

Both sexes Region	2006	2007	Change from 2006 to 2007
Western UP	7,356	8,626	17.3
Eastern UP	1,997	1,869	-6.4
NE lower	11,306	11,142	-1.4
NW lower	19,361	18,560	-4.1
Saginaw Bay	21,204	21,406	1.0
SW lower	21,553	22,470	4.3
SC lower	30,280	29,256	-3.4
SE lower	11,976	12,867	7.4
Statewide	125,035	126,197	0.9

DEER HUNTING – REGULAR FIREARM

Region	Antlerless deer harvested 2006	2007	Change from 2006 to 2007 (%)	Antlered Bucks harvested 2006	2007	Change from 2006 to 2007 (%)
Western UP	6,263	7,441	18.8	22,110	26,496	19.8*
Eastern UP	1,042	876	-15.9	4,982	6,605	32.6*
NE lower	9,981	11,229	12.5	26,082	25,948	-0.5
NW lower	7,729	9,542	23.5*	28.028	26,706	-4.7
Saginaw Bay	16,034	19,787	23.4*	25,545	25,839	1.2
SW lower	19,914	19,370	-2.7	23,835	22,872	-4.0
SC lower	26,358	27,159	4.4	30,186	28,689	-5.0
SE lower	5,519	6,009	8.9	8,282	8,255	-0.3

Photo S. Willey

Both sexes Region	2006	2007	Change from 2006 to 2007
Western UP	28,378	33,916	19.5
Eastern UP	6,026	7,473	24.0
NE lower	36,068	37,166	3.0
NW lower	35,765	36,231	1.3
Saginaw Bay	41,576	45,637	9.8
SW lower	43,742	42,258	-3.4
SC lower	56,179	55,875	-0.5
SE lower	13,799	14,267	3.4
Statewide	261,532	272,823	4.3*

* = Does not include deer taken with DMA permits.

DEER HUNTING TOTALS - ANTLERLESS AND ANTLERED BUCKS COMBINED (2007)

Region	Regular Firearm	Archery	Muzzle	Youth	Late Antlerless	Total
Western UP	33,916	7,356	4,089	547	0	47,175
Eastern UP	7,473	1,997	1,264	188	0	10,813
Total UP	41,390	9,354	5,373	735	0	57,988
NE lower	37,166	11,306	3,650	1,310	365	54,600
NW lower	36,231	19,361	3,998	2,182	0	60,993
Saginaw Bay	45,637	21,204	9,107	2,243	470	80,717
SW lower	42,258	21,553	10,275	1,338	733	81,791
SC lower	55,875	30,280	11,018	2,212	966	107,360
SE lower	14,267	11,976	3,752	878	373	33,145

The record for the largest deer taken in Michigan belonged to Alber Tippet for most of the last century. In 1919, he bagged a whitetail in Ontonagon County with a dressed weight of 354 pounds. Estimated live weight: 425 pounds. Because that is only an estimate, the record goes to Gavrill Fermanis. Using a bow he took a deer with a live weight of 416 pounds while hunting in Oakland County in 1993.

More on these and other deer hunting stories can be found in *Michigan Deer Tales: Book One* and *Michigan Deer Tales: Book Four* by U.P. author Richard Smith.

BLACK BEAR HUNTING

The DNR estimates that 13,000 to 17,000 black bear live in the U.P., which represents about 90% of the black bear population of Michigan.

The adult male black bear can range from 150-400 pounds and measure up to five feet tall when standing on hind legs. The female ranges between 100-250 pounds. Life span of the black bear is between 20 to 30 years. Male bears live in area up to 100 square miles, while females usually roam an area of 10-20 square miles. Bear are independent, with the exception of female when raising her cubs.

Bear dine on newly grown green plants in the spring, insects and berries in the summer, and nuts and acorns in the fall. They will take advantage of human food when garbage becomes available.

Bears breed in June and July with cubs born in January when females confine themselves to dens. Litters usually consist of two or three cubs. Females usually breed every other year starting around three years old.

Bears take the winter off, spending much of it asleep in dens which can consist of hollowed-out trees, piles of brush, or ground nests. During this time, usually between late October and late April, they do not eat, drink, or pass waste.

BEAR HARVEST BY BEAR MANAGEMENT UNIT (BMU)

BMU	2000	2001	2002	2003	2004
Bergland	256	284	343	307	283
Baraga	472	587	534	556	426
Amasa	131	171	180	190	168
Carney	161	209	214	237	233
Gwinn	201	228	222	232	248
Newberry	444	357	365	410	452
Drummond	8	14	11	11	11
Red Oak	201	228	313	376	341
Baldwin	10	12	29	27	23
Gladwin	6	20	10	20	19

BEAR HUNTING

	2000	2001	2002	2003	2004
Applicants	45,164	46,336	43,563	41,667	54,797
Tags issued	9,490	9,875	10,844	10,900	11,250
Harvest	1,890	2,110	2,221	2,366	2,204
Male/female %	56/44	57/43	55/45	59/41	59/41
Hunter success	27%	29%	26%	28%	26%

RECORD BEAR

The largest bear on record was taken in Iron County in November of 1950 by Herb Mitchell of South Haven. Mitchell tracked a large bruin's tracks through the snow back to its den. Back then it was legal to shoot denned bear, but now it is illegal to hunt bear during November when most of them are in dens. The bear had a dressed weight of 650 pounds and would have weighed between 715-740 pounds alive.

The second highest-scoring bear overall, based on skull size, was taken in Menominee County on September 25, 2004 by Jason Welch of Perronville. Welch used a bow to bag the bear with a skull scoring 21 12/15, 1/16th smaller than the state record for a bow-bagged bear. (The record is 21 13/16 taken in Montmorency County in north central Lower Peninsula.)

The second largest gun-killed bear was also taken in Menominee County. On October 1, 2000 James Henney of Niles, with the help of hounds, bagged a bear with a skull measuring 22 3/16. The highest-scoring bear was taken in Montmorency County in 1997 by Sharon Agren. It measured 23, and was taken during a dog hunt.

Information courtesy of Understanding Michigan Black Bear, *by Richard Smith (see Culture chapter)*

BOBCAT HUNTING

Bobcat hunting and trapping is permitted in all 15 counties of the Upper Peninsula and in 21 counties of northern Lower Michigan.

BOBCATS REGISTERED – BY COUNTY (2007)

County	Hunters/trappers	Bobcats registered
Alger	49	15
Baraga	41	5
Chippewa	89	29
Delta	74	36
Dickinson	65	29
Gogebic	76	38
Houghton	45	10
Iron	94	41
Keweenaw	6	0
Luce	29	5
Mackinac	62	18
Marquette	82	30
Menominee	81	30
Ontonagon	76	21
Schoolcraft	60	15

SNOWMOBILE REGISTRATIONS – BY COUNTY

County	Registered Snowmobiles (as of May 1, 2007)				
Marquette	6,010	Dickinson	1,971	Iron	1,358
Chippewa	5,523	Alger	1,882	Baraga	922
Delta	3,484	Luce	1,813	Keweenaw	299
Houghton	3,197	Menominee	1,592	U.P.	36,240
Mackinac	2,930	Ontonagon	1,478	Michigan	365,498
Gogebic	2,364	Schoolcraft	1,417		

INTERNATIONAL 500 SNOWMOBILE RACE

SAULT STE. MARIE

An idea that started over a warm cup of coffee on a cold day over forty years ago has evolved into a major event and grand tradition.

A group of Sault Ste. Marie businessmen catching up over coffee at a local restaurant one day were admiring the brand new 1968 Camaro in the auto dealership across the street. It was billed as the Official Indy 500 Pace Car, which led one of the men to wonder if his buddy could run 500 miles on his snowmobile. One thing led to another, and by the end of the calendar year there was an I-500 Committee and land was acquired for a track.

The track was built on Fort Brady's former ammo dump. The National Guard removed two concrete bunkers, and by late fall work crews and volunteers were nearly finished with the one-mile track. The first running of the I-500 snowmobile race offered a total purse of $3,200.

The first race was held on February 8, 1969, the same day that fares to cross the Mackinac Bridge dropped from $3.50 to $1.50. The top qualifying speed among the 47 drivers was 57.1 miles-an-hour. The winner of the first race was Dan Planck of Davidson who completed the 500 miles on a Ski Doo in 13 hours and 42 minutes. At the time Planck crossed the finish line only 26 racers were still on the track. The race attracted an estimated 10,000 spectators. The idea to attract more tourists to Sault Ste. Marie in the winter appeared to be a success.

Today the race is governed by an all volunteer I-500 Committee. Getting the track ready takes three weeks and 1,800,000 gallons of water via a fire hydrant and tanker trucks. During the first 29 years of the event, laps were manually counted. Now, an electronic system keeps track of the number of laps racked up by each sled. The speed of the racing machines has doubled from the first race and the 2009 purse totaled nearly $34,000.

With the higher speeds comes more danger. In 2003, a racer from Munising was killed after falling from his sled and getting hit by another racer. The following year the race was called after 174 laps when a sled careened into a pit crew, killing one women and leaving two other seriously injured. Like auto racing, the speed and danger draw a large crowd; up to 20,000 people turn out each year for the I-500.

The award for the team that moves up the farthest in the standings is named after a Sault, Ontario racer who was seriously injured in the 1979 race. Ladi Filipcic spent six months in the hospital and then tried to qualify for the 1980 I-500. He did not get medical clearance, so he was chosen as Parade Marshall. He went in for corrective surgery the following summer, but died during the operation. In his honor the Alfano Brothers Team sponsors the annual Ladi Filipcic Trophy.

In 2007, a developer proposed a large project to the City of Sault Ste. Marie which would include retail, hotel and recreation space in an indoor setting on the 50 acres now used for the I-500 track. During informal discussions, the developer has said if the deal goes through, he will allow for relocation of the I-500 track. If that happens, organizers are hopeful of building a safer, wider track with new lighting and fences and better parking and accommodations for spectators.

WINNERS OF THE I-500

1969	Dan Planck, Otis Cowles, Leonard Cowles	1989	George Sharrard, Tom Sibbald, Jeff Kipfmiller
1970	Don Brown, Bill Gunsell, Troy Donn	1990	Rick Wezenski, Gary Loar, Steve Holcomb
1971	Mike Nickerson, Gerald Teegarden,	1991	Todd Krikke, Randy Krikke Doug Hayes
1972	LuVerne Hagen, Stan Hayes,	1992	John Wicht III (Polaris) Doug Hayes
1973	Melvin Kitchen, Dan Prevo,	1993	John Wicht III (Polaris) Douglas Bisball
1974	LeRoy Lindblad, Wes Pesek,	1994	Ivan Hansen, Robb Sass Burt Bassett
1975	Buddy Weber, Stanley Shunk,	1995	John Wicht III (Polaris) Jim Crawford
1976	Stan Hayes, Doug Hayes,	1996	Troy Pierce, Todd Krikke Jerry Witt
1977	Grant Hawkins, Mike Chisholm	1997	Troy Pierce, Todd Krikke
1978	Ken Littleton, Ted Ritchie	1998	Corey Davidson, Steve Olson
1979	Robert Dohm Jr, Ron Dohm,	1999	Corey Davidson, Steve Olson Jeff Dohm
1980	Grant Hawkins, Ed Goldsmith	2000	Corey Davidson, Steve Olson
1981	Guy Useldinger, Dan Enns	2001	Russ Chartrand, Tim Leeck
1982	Gerard Karpik, Brian Musselman	2002	Mike Gentz Jr., Gabe Bunke
1983	Duane Baur, Ralph Swartzendruber,	2003	Corey Davidson, Travis Hjelle Paul Swartzendruber
1984	Brian Musselman, Karl Schwartz	2004	John Hoos, Matt Hoos, Corey Furkey, Chris Furkey
1985	Brian Musselman, Chris Daly	2005	Gabe Bunke, Josh Davis, Corey Davidson
1986	Jeff Kipfmiller, Rick Zudell,	2006	Corey Davidson, Travis Hjelle
1987	Mike Staszak, Jeff Kipfmiller	2007	Chad Gueco, Bill Wilkes
1988	John Wicht III	2008	Corey Davidson
		2009	Troy DeWald

UPPER PENINSULA SKI RESORTS

Al-Quaal Ski Area
Ishpeming
Top elevation: N/A
Vertical drop: 70 ft.
Runs: 2
Longest: 600 ft.
Total lifts: 2
Cross-country trails: 17.5 km
Skiable area: 20 acres

Blackjack Ski Resort
Bessemer
Top elevation:
Vertical drop: 465 ft.
Runs: 20, half-pipe, quarter-pipe
Longest: 5,300 ft.
Total lifts: 6
Cross-country trails:
Skiable area: 101 acres

Ski Brule
Iron River
Top elevation: 1,861 ft.
Vertical drop: 500 ft.
Runs: 17 and two terrain parks
Longest: 5,300 ft.
Total lifts: 11
Cross-country trails: 23 km
Skiable area: 150 acres

Big Powderhorn Mountain
Bessemer
Top elevation: 1,840 ft.
Vertical drop: 622 ft.
Runs: 29 and three terrain parks
Longest: 5,260 ft.
Total lifts: 9   Lift capacity per hour: 10,800
Cross-country trails: 17 km
Skiable area: 250 acres

Mount Bohemia
Lac la Belle
Top elevation: N/A
Vertical drop: 900 ft. (highest in Midwest)
Runs: 41
Longest: 9,240 ft. (longest in Midwest)
Total lifts: 2   Lift capacity per hour: 4,800
No Cross-country trails: No
Skiable area: N/A

Gladstone Sports Park
Gladstone
Top elevation: N/A
Vertical drop: 110 ft.
Runs: 3
Longest: 1,000 ft
Total lifts: 5   Lift capacity per hour: 6,500
Cross-country trails: 5 km
Skiable area: 30 acres

Indianhead Mountain Resort
Wakefield
Top elevation: 1,935 ft.
Vertical drop: 638 ft.
Runs: 23 and two terrain parks
Longest: 5,280 ft.
Total lifts: 9
Lift capacity per hour: 8,550
Cross-country trails: No
Skiable area: 195 acres

Norway Mountain
Norway
Top elevation: N/A
Vertical drop: 500 ft.
Runs: 17 and two terrain parks
Longest: 5,300 ft.
Total lifts: 6
Cross-country trails: 5 km
Skiable area: 100 acres

Porcupine Mountains Ski Area
Ontonagon
Top elevation: 1,368 ft.
Vertical drop: 787 ft.
Runs: 42
Longest: 6,000 ft.
Total lifts: 4
Lift capacity per hour: 3,600
Cross-country trails: 42 km
Skiable area: 100 acres

Mt. Zion
Ironwood
Top elevation: N/A
Vertical drop: 300 ft.
Runs: 9
Longest: 3,960 ft.
Total lifts: 2
Cross-country trails: 3 km
Skiable area: 20 acres

Marquette Mountain
Marquette
Top elevation: 1,357 ft.
Vertical drop: 600 ft.
Runs: 25 and three terrain parks
Longest: 8,300 ft.
Total lifts: 4
Lift capacity per hour: 4,600
Cross-country trails: No
Skiable area: 151 acres

Pine Mountain Resort
Iron Mountain
Top elevation: N/A
Vertical drop: 500 ft.
Runs: 23 and two terrain parks
Longest: 5,400 ft.
Total lifts: 4
Cross-country trails: No
Skiable area: 340 acres

Mont Ripley
Houghton
Top elevation: N/A
Vertical drop: 423 ft.
Runs: 16
Longest: N/A
Total lifts: 2
Lift capacity per hour: 1,100
Cross-country trails: No
Skiable area: N/A

THE HURON MOUNTAIN CLUB

Originally called The Huron Mountain Shooting and Fishing Club, this exclusive club was organized in September 1889. The founding members included Marquette pioneer Peter White and prominent citizen and landowner John Munro Longyear. The club initially controlled around 7,000 acres, which included six lakes in the heart of the Huron Mountains of rugged northern Marquette County. Their holdings also included the Superior lakeshore and eventually grew to over 15,000 acres. Today, the Huron Mountain Club (HMC) boasts "30,000 acres of beautiful lakes, woods and mountains."

In the early days, the club roster included 96 members. Eventually the membership dwindled to the "practical maximum" of 50, where it remains today. In the first few years, five private cabins were built along the Pine River. Fifty member cabins exist today along with a clubhouse and other buildings. At first, transportation to the remote location was made exclusively by steamer from Marquette. In 1906, a railway was completed to Big Bay where a team of horse was kept to transport members westward to the club. Automobiles became the main transportation after 1917.

The most famous automaker, Henry Ford, first visited the club while touring the Great Lakes on his yacht in about 1920. Ford tried to gain membership to the club but was at first refused. He kept on good terms with club members and was eventually admitted in the late 1920s. Ford built an ostentatious cabin at a reported $100,000, harvesting the biggest pines off his Upper Peninsula holdings for the logs.

In the late 1930s, famous naturalist Aldo Leopold visited the club and outlined a plan for management of the then 15,000 acres of old-growth forest. In the early 21st Century, the Huron Mountain Club holdings remain virtually unchanged and unspoiled. However, there are changes afoot in the region that has members concerned. A large mining company has plans to open a nickel mining operation on land adjacent to the club. Club members and a number of environmental organizations are seeking to block the mine's development. As of this writing, the Michigan Department of Environmental Quality has issued a mining permit to the Kennecott Eagle Minerals Company. HMC along with environmental groups and the Keweenaw Bay Indian Community have filed appeals, which as of this writing, are being heard before an administrative law judge.

Chapter 14

WILDLIFE

WOLVES

Wolves have been part of the fauna of the Upper Great Lakes from the time the last ice sheets melted. Aboriginal people of the Lake Superior region felt a spiritual kinship with the wolf. Ojibwa legend tells of original man and wolf traveling together to name all the plants and animals on earth. The native people of the region lived compatibly with wolves for countless generations.

With the arrival of Europeans came the views of an agricultural people. That attitude held that wolves were incongruous with human settlement. On the Michigan frontier, killing wolves was acceptable and encouraged. A bounty on wolves was not repealed until 1960. By that time, wolves had virtually disappeared from the Upper Peninsula.

Wolves were given protection when the Endangered Species Act was passed in 1973. A year later, the Michigan Department of Natural Resources (DNR) attempted to relocate four wolves from Minnesota in northern Marquette County. The plan failed when all the wolves were found dead within several months.

In the 1980s, wolf sightings in Upper Michigan were limited to individual animals until 1989. That year, the tracks of two wolves traveling together were verified. The pair produced a litter of pups two years later. It was the first documented natural birth of wolves in Michigan since 1954.

In the early 21st Century, the gray wolf population was estimated at over 400. The wolf recovery has been completely natural. Wolves migrating from Minnesota established packs in Wisconsin and then crossed into the Upper Peninsula. Biologists consider a population of 200 wolves to be self sustaining. A self sustaining population is the first step in removing the wolf from the Endangered Species list.

The reestablishment of the wolf in Michigan has been received with mixed reviews by the general public. Early surveys showed that nearly two-thirds of U.P. residents supported the wolf recovery program. However, just over a third of farmers surveyed supported the initiative. Wolves occasionally take livestock and as the number of wolves increase, this problem has even extended to family pets.

On Isle Royale, the problem is not wolf and human incompatibility. Wolf tracks were first observed on the island in 1948. A cold winter about that time built an ice bridge that allowed wolves to cross from the mainland. A pack was confirmed in the late 1950s and the number of animals reached a peak of 50 in 1980. A couple of years later, the population crashed. Isle Royale is a fully protected National Park with the natural "fence" of the chilly waters of Lake Superior surrounding it. This protection and isolation means the die off was "natural" probably due to a canine virus. In the ensuing years, it is speculated that generations of inbreeding has caused population stagnation.

On the mainland, humans brought the wolf to near extinction. Now, it is humans that will determine whether a healthy wolf population can be preserved in Upper Michigan through the 21st Century.

WOLF—VITAL STATISTICS

Largest member of the Canidae or dog family

Weight: 60 to 115 lbs. (Average 75 lbs. with males slightly larger than females)

Length: Adults about 6 feet long from head to tail

Height: 30-34 inches at the shoulder

Food: Primarily deer, moose, other small mammals

Wolves on Isle Royale: The wolf population was pegged at 21 for the winter of 2006-07, which scientists says is a drop from a peak of about 30 a few years earlier.

MOOSE

The moose was once found over all of Michigan, but human population expansion quickly destroyed the animal's habitat. Given complete protection by the state in 1889, the moose still became extinct in the Lower Peninsula by 1900, with few left in the Upper Peninsula. Those that remained faced diminishing habitat due to clear cutting of the virgin timber. The new growth that sprang up gave way to an additional problem. The young forest became home to a flourishing deer population, which carries a number of parasites including brainworm. This parasite has little effect on deer but is fatal to moose.

In the 1930s, the Michigan Department of Conservation counted 3,000 moose on Isle Royale. In an effort to reduce the herd, animals were live-trapped and transported to the Upper Peninsula in hopes of replenishing the herd on the mainland. That project failed. 50 years later, the Michigan DNR and the Ontario Ministry of Natural Resources with financial help from private citizens and organizations began transporting moose from Canada into the U.P. The first "moose drop" occurred in 1985 over northwestern Marquette County. Another one took place in 1987. A total of 61 radio-collared moose were transplanted in the central Upper Peninsula forests. Since then, the herd has grown but not to the DNR goal of 1,000 by the year 2000.

Moose can be spotted in the rugged terrain of western Marquette and eastern Baraga Counties and over sections of Schoolcraft, Luce and Chippewa Counties. On several occasions moose have found their way into populated areas like Ishpeming and even Marquette. The DNR asks that you report moose sightings to the department. It can be done on-line at:http://www.dnr.state.mi.us/wildlife/pubs/moose_obsreport.asp

MOOSE-VITAL STATISTICS

Size: six feet at the shoulder

Weight: cows up to 1,000 pounds, bulls up to 1,300 pounds

Food: herbivore with a large appetite, estimated to eat 50 to 60 pounds of trees and other plants per day

Antlers: up to a 60-inch spread

Moose on Isle Royale: Michigan Tech biologist, John Vucetich estimates the herd is fewer than 400, a drop from an estimated 1,000 moose in 2002.

THE MICHIGAN COUGAR

The cougar or mountain lion was declared extinct in Michigan in 1906 after decades of trapping and killing to make way for human population expansion. Despite the extinction proclamation, there were a number of "reliable" sightings of large "mystery" cats in the Upper Peninsula over the ensuing years. In 1966, a conservation officer spotted a cougar near Cornell in Menominee County. A plaster cast was made of the animal's track and University of Michigan biologists concluded the track was from a large cat. Other sightings in the ensuing years occurred around Crystal

THE WORKS OF LEWIS HENRY MORGAN THE AMERICAN BEAVER

Cultural anthropologist and legislator Lewis Henry Morgan wrote "The American Beaver and His Works" after being inspired to study the mammal while making periodic business trips to the iron mining district of the Upper Peninsula. Morgan was a director and stockholder of a railroad company which took on the formidable task of opening the rugged wilderness of the north-central Upper Peninsula to a railroad line in the mid-1850s. After the 40-mile rail line was completed, Morgan confessed he could not "withstand the temptation to brook-trout fishing" on the Carp and "Esconauba" Rivers.

The fishing trips "passed through a beaver district, more remarkable, perhaps, than any other of equal extent to be found in any part of North America." Morgan became fascinated with the sheer number of dams as well as the creature's "persevering labors...suggestive of human industry." He eventually put

Falls and the Porcupine Mountains. In 1984, a blood-covered bone fragment of an alleged cougar shot in Menominee County was forwarded to Colorado State University. The sample was identified to be that of a mountain lion.

In the late 1980s, most Michigan Department of Natural Resource (MDNR) biologists denied the existence of cougars in Michigan. Since that time, there have been more documented sightings both in the Upper Peninsula as well as the Lower Peninsula. The National Park Service went so far as to post warning signs at Sleeping Bear Dunes National Lakeshore west of Traverse City advising that the dunes are "cougar habitat." This came after numerous sightings over many years as well as a close encounter with one by a park volunteer. In April 2005, a 1,200 lb. horse was killed by a large predator in downstate Jackson County. Bite and claw marks along with tracks at the scene left little doubt about the cause of death. Later that year, a MDNR official was quoted in an outdoor publication stating that the agency does believe there are cougars in the state, but they have not been able to confirm there is a breeding population in Michigan.

Since then, a peer-reviewed paper co-authored by biologists from the Michigan Wildlife Conservancy and Central Michigan University concludes through DNA evidence the existence of a "remnant" population of cougars in at least Delta, Dickinson, Houghton and Menominee Counties of the Upper Peninsula. This is vindication for residents who have seen the big cats over the years. This also brings up the question of what to do about them. In 1987, despite the agency's denial of a cougar population, the MDNR listed the cougar as an endangered species in Michigan. This declaration by definition seeks to protect the Michigan cougar from extinction. From all the evidence, it appears that the elusive animal has done that on its own for the last 100 years.

COUGAR—VITAL STATISTICS

Common Names: Cougar, Panther, Mountain Lion, Catamount

Range: The cougar has the greatest natural distribution of any mammal in the Western Hemisphere except man

Size: 59-108 inches with a tail 21-36 inches and height of 23 to 28 inches at the shoulder

Weight: can vary greatly from 75 to 250 pounds

DEER

November 15, the opening of Firearm Deer Season, is considered a major holiday in Upper Michigan. Deer hunting has become a tradition in the U.P. over the last century or so. Before the 20th Century, there were few deer in the Upper Peninsula. The thick virgin forest habitat supported a moose and elk population but not deer. After the forest was clear cut, the habitat improved and the white-tail herd grew.

The deer population in Upper Michigan fluctuates, mainly due to the weather. The severe, snowy winters of 1995-97 reduced the U.P. deer herd in some areas by an estimated 80 percent. Deer numbers also parallels timber harvest practices. Increased timber cutting brings an increase in the number of deer. Conversely, as forests mature, deer numbers lower. The Michigan DNR has set up Deer Management Units across the Peninsula to improve the quality of the deer herd. These units were established to address the unique needs of the varied deer habitats of the U.P. The DNR initiates projects like lowland conifer regeneration to improve habitat where deer are scarce. It also regulates licensing, especially antlerless (doe) permits to improve the buck-to-doe ratio. A private, volunteer organization, U.P. Whitetails Association, Inc., works with the DNR in educating the public on sound deer management.

aside fishing and took up study of the beaver. Captivated by the subject, Morgan admitted "no other animal will be allowed to entrap the unambitious author so completely as he confesses himself to have been by the beaver."

Lewis Henry Morgan's definitive book was published in 1868.

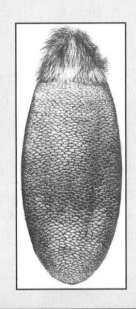

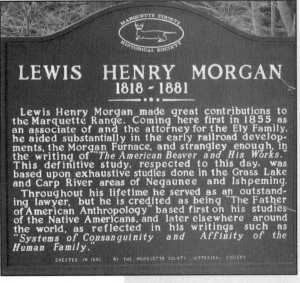

LEWIS HENRY MORGAN
1818 - 1881
• • •

Lewis Henry Morgan made great contributions to the Marquette Range. Coming here first in 1855 as an associate of and the attorney for the Ely Family, he aided substantially in the early railroad developments, the Morgan Furnace, and strangley enough, in the writing of "The American Beaver and His Works." This definitive study, respected to this day, was based upon exhaustive studies done in the Grass Lake and Carp River areas of Negaunee and Ishpeming.
Throughout his lifetime he served as an outstanding lawyer, but he is credited as being "The Father of American Anthropology" based first on his studies of the Native Americans, and later elsewhere around the world, as reflected in his writings such as "Systems of Consanguinity and Affinity of the Human Family."

ERECTED IN 1962   BY THE MARQUETTE COUNTY HISTORICAL SOCIETY

WHITE-TAILED DEER-VITAL STATISTICS

Smallest member of the deer family which contains elk and moose

Size: Healthy adults from 125 to 225 pounds, though largest bucks may be bigger

Range: every county in the State of Michigan

Ideal habitat: areas with open fields and new-growth trees specifically Menominee and parts of Delta Counties

Maximum running speed: 35 mile-per-hour

Deer-vehicle crashes (2005): Highest—Delta (1,068) Menominee (799); Lowest: Keweenaw (21), Gogebic (119), Luce (131), Alger (145)

BLACK BEAR

The Upper Peninsula holds the greatest population of black bear in Michigan. About 90 percent of the state's 15,000-19,000 bear roam the forests north of the Straits. The first people of the Great Lakes region considered the bear part of their relation. However, the animal was also prized for its skin, meat and particularly its fat. As permanent settlement took hold and the land was exploited for minerals and timber, residents of cities and villages eventually looked on this large opportunistic feeder as a pest. Over the last few decades however, the Michigan black bear has also been elevated to prized game species.

Bear claim a lot of territory, particularly males. A male adult bear is a solitary animal with a range of about 100 square miles. Females live in family groups with her cubs in around 10-20 square miles. Adult bear are generally three feet high on all fours and up to five feet when standing upright. Full-grown males weigh between 150-400 pounds, while the smaller females range from 100-250 pounds.

Females breed for the first time at approximately 31/2 years of age in Upper Michigan. Breeding takes place in June or July and the cubs are born in early January when females

are in dens. Den sites may be hollowed out trees, brush piles or even open ground nests. At birth, the cubs weigh less than a pound. By spring, with the aid of mother's rich milk, cubs weigh up to 10 pounds. The sow tends to the cubs through the summer into the fall when she finds a suitable den. Mother and cubs spend the winter together and by the next June, she aggressively forces the yearling bears away in time for the next breeding season.

Bears are not true hibernators, but remain in a state of lethargy during the cold season. They reduce their metabolic rate to the point where they neither eat, drink, pass waste or exercise. The reason for their long winter's sleep is to escape the lack of food. Bears usually bed down in October and emerge from their dens in April or May.

Signs of bear in the vicinity include tracks, droppings, claw marked trees, turned over rocks, torn up stumps or broken limbs of trees, especially fruit trees. Their diets include almost everything. In the wild, bears eat succulent new greens when they leave their dens in the spring. Later, they will feast on colonial insects such as ants and bees, which make up half their diet during early summer. Later in the summer, black bear experience rapid weight gain when wild berries are plentiful. Nuts and acorns are the ideal fall food, since they are high in fats and protein, which prepare the bear for its winter sleep.

The bear is shy by nature. Bear-human encounters are rare since the animal will most likely pick up the scent of a person and run off. Bears take on the role of pest when they associate food with humans. If food is accessible to bear, they may overcome their fear of people and become dangerous.

Bear hunting season begins across the Upper Peninsula on September 10 and runs through mid-to-late October.

LOONS

The loon is a goose-sized, long-bodied bird about 3 feet long with a 5-foot wingspan. A breeding loon, whether male of female, has a black head and neck with a "necklace" of black and white stripes and a white breast.
Its red eyes are said to help with underwater vision, while its eerie, wailing cry is a symbol of the wild northern lakes and marshes of the northeastern United States.

The loon is very much a water bird. Its large, webbed feet make it difficult to move on land where it becomes easy prey for raccoons, coyotes and wolves. A dense bone structure lowers the loon's buoyancy compared to other aquatic birds with hollow bones. This fact allows the bird to swim with only its heads above water when it compresses its feathers and forces air from its lungs. The loon is a very powerful swimmer demonstrating great skill in catching its diet of fish, frogs, crayfish, leeches and aquatic insects. A loon can dive up to 200 feet and stay underwater for as long as two minutes. On the other hand, a loon can move quickly through the air, beating its wings up to 250 times per minute, while achieving a speed of greater than 80 miles-per-hour.

Loons winter along the Gulf of Mexico or southeastern Atlantic Coast and return to Upper Michigan when the ice melts off inland lakes, usually in April to early May. Nesting begins soon after, often in a nest used the year before. The nest must be within a yard of water deep enough to dive into. Nesting pairs prefer lakes larger than 40 acres that contain small islands. They build nests on these islands or bog mat to keep their young safe from predators. One or two (rarely three) eggs are laid in the nest consisting of heaped up vegetation cemented in mud with a shallow depression to hold the eggs. After about a month of incubation, the chicks are hatched. Only one in four make it to six weeks old—an age at which they reach adult size and can fly. Most chicks are lost to predatory fish, hawks, large turtles and eagles.

Loons are easily disturbed and stressed. Adults may abandon a nest if disturbed by a per-

GEORGE SHIRAS III

Pioneer wildlife photographer George Shiras III has roots in Upper Michigan. His grandfather, George I, came to fish the Lake Superior region around the tiny hamlet of Marquette in 1849. He became close friends with Marquette pioneer Peter White. The next two generations of Shirases made regular trips to the U.P., including George, Jr., an associate Justice of the Supreme Court. George III first visited Marquette with his father and grandfather in 1870 at the age of 11. A Pittsburgh native, Shiras attended Cornell and received a law degree from Yale. He served in Congress from 1903-05. Shiras was an avid hunter until 1899 when he put aside his gun and picked up the camera. He developed many of his revolutionary photographic techniques in Upper Michigan.

Shiras's photos caught the attention of Gil Grosvenor, director and editor of the National Geographic Society and its magazine. The July

son. Therefore, shoreline development and recreational use on U.P. inland lakes is an ongoing problem. Loons are sometimes caught in commercial fishing nets. Chemical contamination, particularly through mercury, weakens the bird during migration and makes it susceptible to avian botulism.

Late in the 20th Century, the loon population in Michigan was listed at from 270 to 300 breeding pair. The most concentrated densities of breeding loons are found on Isle Royale, the western Upper Peninsula and the Seney National Wildlife Refuge with a slight decrease in population noted elsewhere. The Michigan DNR listed the bird as threatened in 1987 and a recovery plan was created. It includes protection of current and potential breeding lakes as well as public education programs. One way all Upper Michigan residents and visitors can help is by giving this majestic bird the seclusion it needs and by letting others know if there is a nest nearby so it can be avoided.

CORMORANTS

Photo S. Willey

Once near extinction, double-crested cormorants (cormorants for simplicity) have exploded in population and are being blamed for destroying the fishery around Les Cheneaux Islands off Upper Michigan in Lake Huron. Eleven-thousand of these big black diving birds have been counted on two of the Les Cheneaux island chain alone. A cormorant can eat its own weight in fish in a week. Anglers complain that the birds have decimated the yellow perch population here. In addition, the birds dominate an area stripping trees of all their leaves and driving out other nesting birds. Once the birds deplete an area, they move on. The St. Marys River system had no cormorants back in the 1990s. By 2003, there was a flock of 6,000 hungry birds eating their way through the area.

Cormorants are protected under migratory bird treaties

and cannot be killed without permission from the U.S. Fish and Wildlife Service (USFWS). While the Michigan DNR has had some success at Les Cheneaux with oiling the eggs of cormorants (The bird population was reduced by 25%, while the perch fishery improved 42% over three years.), the USFWS will not allow the practice on Lake Michigan's Beaver Island, another high-concentration cormorant area, citing the possible damage to other nesting birds on the island.

A major question that anti-cormorant forces pose is whether the cormorant is indigenous to the Great Lakes or if it is a sort of invasive species. Excavation of Indian garbage dumps show a variety of bird bones from turkeys to eagles but no cormorant bones. Environment Canada found the first pair of nesting cormorants on the Great Lakes in 1913. Apparently, these birds migrated to Lake Superior from Manitoba's Lake of the Woods. Cormorants were not spotted on Lake Ontario until 1946.

1906 edition of the magazine contained 74 of Shiras's wildlife images—the first photographs to ever appear in National Geographic Magazine. The edition was a hit and became one of only two issues to be reprinted.

However, not all were pleased by the move. Alfred Brooks, a board member and geologist whom the Brooks Range in Alaska is named after, resigned in protest. He deplored the idea that the publication had become nothing but a "picture gallery." Another board member resigned later that year. Grosvenor brushed aside the protests and many years later called the edition "one of the pioneering achievements of National Geographic." Wildlife photography eventually became a hallmark of the publication. He kept an association with Shiras and named him to the Board of Directors in 1911.

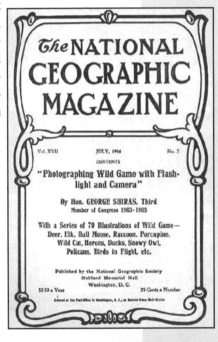

George Shiras II

The remains of the Shiras Zoo, Presque Isle Park

Peregrine Falcon

Kirtland's Warbler

Lynx

ENDANGERED SPECIES – BY COUNTY

ALGER
Round-leaved Orchis	Amerorchis rotundifolia
Acute-leaved Moonwort	Botrychium acuminatum
Hudson Bay Sedge	Carex heleonastes
Piping Plover	Charadrius melodus
Peregrine Falcon	Falco peregrinus
American Burying Beetle	Nicrophorus americanus
Dwarf Raspberry	Dwarf Raspberry

BARAGA
Kirtland's Warbler	Dendroica kirtlandii

CHIPPEWA
Round-leaved Orchis	Amerorchis rotundifolia
Short-eared Owl	Asio flammeus
Wall-rue	Asplenium ruta-muraria
Hart's tongue Fern	Asplenium scolopendrium var. americanum
Piping Plover	Charadrius melodus
Kirtland's Warbler	Dendroica kirtlandii
Peregrine Falcon	Falco peregrinus
Awlwort	Subularia aquatica

DELTA
Piping Plover	Charadrius melodus
Prairie Warbler	Dendroica discolor
Kirtland's Warbler	Dendroica kirtlandii
Peregrine Falcon	Falco peregrinus
Alpine Sainfoin	Hedysarum alpinum

DICKINSON
Round-leaved Orchis	Amerorchis rotundifolia
Slender Beard-tongue	Penstemon gracilis

GOGEBIC
Redside Dace	Clinostomus elongatus
Small Yellow Pond-lily	Nuphar pumila

KEWEENAW
Round-leaved Orchis	Amerorchis rotundifolia
Heart-leaved Arnica	Arnica cordifolia
Keweenaw Rock-rose	Chamaerhodos nuttallii var. keweenawensis
American Rock-brake	Cryptogramma acrostichoides
Smooth Whitlow-grass	Draba glabella
Lynx	Felis lynx
Pygmy water-lily	Nymphaea tetragona ssp. leibergii

Canby's Bluegrass — Poa canbyi
Awlwort — Subularia aquatica
Mountain-cranberry — Vaccinium vitis-idaea

LUCE

Piping Plover — Charadrius melodus
Kirtland's Warbler — Dendroica kirtlandii
Small Yellow Pond-lily — Nuphar pumila

MACKINAC

Hart's-tongue Fern — Asplenium scolopendrium var. americanum
Piping Plover — Charadrius melodus
Lynx — Felis lynx
Lakeside Daisy — Hymenoxys herbacea
Michigan Monkey-flower — Mimulus glabratus var. michiganensis
Hine's Emerald — Somatochlora hineana

Whitefish Point bird observatory

MARQUETTE

Round-leaved Orchis — Amerorchis rotundifolia
Kirtland's Warbler — Dendroica kirtlandii
Peregrine Falcon — Falco peregrinus
Northern Oak Fern — Gymnocarpium jessoense
American Burying Beetle — Nicrophorus americanus
Small Yellow Pond-lily — Nuphar pumila
Fragile Prickly-pear — Opuntia fragilis
Acorn Ramshorn — Planorbella multivolvis
Western Dock — Rumex occidentalis

Prairie Warbler

MENOMINEE

Round-leaved Orchis — Amerorchis rotundifolia
Dwarf Milkweed — Asclepias ovalifolia
Shooting-star — Dodecatheon meadia
American Burying Beetle — Nicrophorus americanus

ONTONAGON

Fairy Bells — Disporum hookeri
Peregrine Falcon — Falco peregrinus
Small Yellow Pond-lily — Nuphar pumila

SCHOOLCRAFT

Black Sedge — Carex nigra
Piping Plover — Charadrius melodus
Prairie Warbler — Dendroica discolor
Kirtland's Warbler — Dendroica kirtlandii
Slender Spikerush — Eleocharis nitida
King Rail — Rallus elegans

American Burying Beetle

BIGFOOT IN THE U.P.?

Over 80 percent of the Upper Peninsula's land is covered in forest. This extensive woodland provides cover for abundant wildlife including, according to some, the legendary "Sasquatch" or Bigfoot.

This legendary man-ape creature has reportedly been spotted in every state and Canadian province. The sightings go back before Europeans arrived on the North American continent. In fact, Native Americans of the Pacific Northwest gave this hairy humanoid creature its name—Sasquatchmen—a primitive tribe of giants.

In Upper Michigan, reports of sightings, foot prints, or strange howling have come from ten counties over the years. One of the most frightening happened to a woman traveling with her baby eastbound down U.S.-2 in Schoolcraft County in September 1978. It was dark and she became sleepy. She pulled her late 1960s SAAB station wagon into a small roadside park near the edge of the Hiawatha Forest to catch a nap. A short time later she was awakened by a horrible smell. She thought her baby had become sick to fill his pants with such a terrible odor. She flipped on the dome light, reached for the diaper bag and then checked his diaper, which was clean. Her infant son was staring out the windshield and she followed his gaze. She glanced out the window and froze, thinking there was a bear standing on its hind legs directly in front of her car. Hoping to scare the creature away, she flipped on the headlights. It was then she realized that what she was staring at was no bear. The creature towered over her small car, was covered in dark brown hair and had a face with a flat snout and eyes in the middle of its face like a human. What's more, the creature seemed unfazed by the headlights. Scared out of her wits, she started the car, slammed it into reverse and sped out of the small park and eastbound down U.S.-2.

Most recently, a Houghton County resident near Nisula spotted what appeared to be Bigfoot in broad daylight. The 72-year-old man was on a riding mower, cutting the lawn for an absent neighbor. He had just made a left turn when straight in front of him, not more than 40 feet away, he spotted a large upright figure walking away from him. He watched the creature, which he described as 7 to 8 feet tall, about 800 pounds and built like a gorilla, for about three seconds. It took a few steps, crouched down, ducked under some bushes and stepped into a ravine. The man turned off the lawn mower and went home. When asked later how he knew the creature weighed so much, he explained that at one time he raised pigs and that "it weighed more than two 300-pound sows."

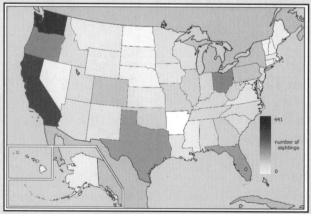

The Bigfoot Field Research Organization led an expedition to the Upper Peninsula during July 2007. Researchers reported recording some strange sounds. However, there apparently were no sightings of the elusive man-ape creature.

Chapter 15

ARCHITECTURE

SANDSTONE ARCHITECTURE

The reddish-brown tint of many older buildings in the Upper Peninsula is from the native sandstone that runs along the southern shore of Lake Superior. The Jacobsville geological formation extends from Sugar Island and Sault Ste. Marie westward to the Keweenaw Peninsula. The formation was named for the town of Jacobsville, which was named after John H. Jacobs, credited with the early development of the sandstone industry around the Keweenaw

Peninsula. Another band of sandstone, the Bayfield group runs from northern Wisconsin into Minnesota.

The sandstone found along Lake Superior consists of sand-sized grains of quartz banded together by iron oxide, calcite, authigenic quartz and silica. It was formed 500 million years ago after Cambrian Streams carried sand and gravel from ancient mountains in the U.P. to the lowlands along the Lake Superior shore.

The sandstone extraction and building industry started in the 1870s after major fires destroyed blocks of wooden buildings in Marquette, Hancock and Red Jacket (Calumet) in 1868. This resulted in building codes calling for fireproof materials such as brick and sandstone. At peak operation there were over seventy companies extracting sandstone from quarries in Alger, Baraga, Houghton, Keweenaw and Marquette counties. The stone was used for local and regional

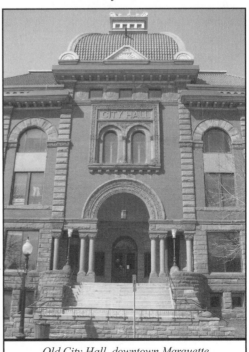

Old City Hall, downtown Marquette

BURT HOUSE

The John Burt House at 220 Craig Street in Marquette is

the oldest surviving structure in Marquette. Built in 1860, this one-story rubble stone cottage has walls two-feet thick. The interior is divided into two rooms, one of which contains a fireplace. Four small windows provide light. The structure served as a warehouse and clerk's office for a quarry business Burt established in 1872.

buildings, and shipped to Midwestern industrial centers including Chicago, Milwaukee, Detroit, and Duluth.

The first major building constructed with Lake Superior sandstone was the Milwaukee County Courthouse, built between 1870 and 1873. Other notable buildings of the era include: The Tribune Building (1872) in Chicago; Germania Bank Building (1890) in St. Paul, Cincinnati City Hall (1893); Chamber of Commerce (1895) in Detroit, and the Waldorf-Astoria Hotel in NYC.

Many of the early sandstone buildings housed government offices, schools, banks, and other businesses. Many of those buildings were designed in the Richardsonian Romanesque style, named after Henry Hobson Richardson who borrowed ideas from the French Romanesque, using a combination of towers, arches, buttresses, and porches.

Architects of the late 19th Century liked the sandstone for its durability, appearance and because it could be carved. The 1870s through 1890s kept architects busy as the mining industry brought more people and more money to the region. By the turn of the century tastes were changing, moving away from the reddish-brown sandstone and the Richardsonian Romanesque style, which brought an end to the sandstone industry in the U.P.

Source: *The Sandstone Architecture of the Lake Superior Region* (copyright 2000, Wayne State University Press)

NOTABLE SANDSTONE BUILDINGS OF THE U.P.

The following are some of the outstanding sandstone buildings catalogued by Kathryn Bishop Eckert in her book, *The Sandstone Architecture of the Lake Superior Region*, (copyright 2000, Wayne State University Press) Eckert's book includes existing buildings and those that have been destroyed in Alger, Baraga, Chippewa, Houghton, Marquette and Ontonagon counties.

MARQUETTE COUNTY

1869-70, Bay Furnace, Onota ** 2

1868, Schoolcraft Furnace, Munising

1860, John Burt House, 220 Craig St., Marquette

1868, Marquette and Ontonagon Railroad Company Shops and Roundhouse

1872, Superior Building (First National Bank Building, Mather Block, Marquette **1

1874-75, St. Paul's Episcopal Church, 201 East Ridge St., Marquette **3

1887-89, Morgan Memorial Church, Marquette

1889, St. Peter's Roman Catholic Cathedral, 311 West Baraga Ave., Marquette **4

1880, Daniel H. and Harriet Afford Merritt House, 410 Ridge St., Marquette

1887, Harlow Block, Washington and Front Streets, Marquette

1885-89, Marquette Prison, Marquette

*1890-92, John Munro and Mary Beecher Longyear House, 425 Cedar Street, Marquette

1890, Marquette County Savings Bank, Front Street, Marquette

1894-94, Marquette City Hall, West Washington Street, Marquette

1902-04, Marquette County Courthouse,

1902-04, Peter White Library, Front and Ridge Streets, Marquette

*The Longyear house was moved in 1903 when the Longyears left Marquette. The entire structure was dismantled and moved by railroad to Massachusetts. In 1937, the home was opened to the public as a museum. The process of moving the stone mansion was included in a Ripley's "Believe It or Not" column.   ** Pictured above

HOUGHTON COUNTY

1899, Shelden-Dee Block, Shelden Ave. & Isle Royale St., Houghton

1898-1900, Finnish Lutheran College and Seminary (Suomi College), Hancock

1898-99, Hancock Town Hall and Fire Hall, Quincy Street, Hancock

1898-99, Red Jacket Fire Station, Sixth Street, Hancock

1899-1900, Red Jacket Town Hall & Opera House (Calumet Village Hall and Calumet
        Theatre, Calumet

1900, St. Anne's Roman Catholic Church (Keweenaw Heritage Center), Calumet Twp.

1895-96, Paul P. and Anna L. Roehm House, 101 Willow Ave., Laurium

1902-03, Sarah Sargent Paine Memorial Library, Painesdale

1909-10, Jeffers High School (Painesdale High School), Painesdale

1898, Calumet and Hecla Library, Red Jacket Road, Calumet

FRANK LLOYD WRIGHT HOMES

The best known American architect has left a fingerprint on the Upper Peninsula. The only Lloyd Wright design is the Abby Beecher Roberts House known as "Deertrack." Located in the woods outside of Marquette, the 1936 design was done for the mother-in-law of one of Wright's students.

The Arthur Heurtley Summer Cottage on Marquette Island in the Les Cheneaux group was built in 1902. Wright did not do the original design, but was contracted for a major remodeling.

ALDEN DOW BOWLING ALLEY

Ornate main entrance to Konteka complex in White Pine

Alden Dow, the Midland, Michigan architect who studied with Frank Lloyd Wright, designed the Konteka Motel, Restaurant, Bar & Grill and Black Bear Lanes bowling alley in Ontonagon County. Dow and his wife Vada spent the summer of 1933 with Wright at Taliesin in Spring Green, Wisconsin. Dow and Wright shared a common interest in nature and its relationship to architecture. Those summer and fall months spent with Wright inspired Dow to return to his hometown of Midland where he designed and built his own studio.

During his career he designed over sixty homes in Midland, and more homes throughout the United States. Dow's style of blending his buildings into existing nature to create a pleasant landscape is displayed in places like the Interlochen Center for the Arts campus outside Traverse City, the Muskegon Community College campus and the University of Michigan botanical gardens. Public buildings designed by Dow include Ann Arbor City Hall and Library; the Phoenix Civic Center and Art Museum in Arizona; the Kalamazoo Nature Center; the original Dow Chemical Company administration building, and the Midland hospital, both in his hometown.

The town of White Pine in Ontonagon County sprang up in the mid-1950s after the White Pine mine was established. Dow designed the restaurant-motel-bowling alley in 1955.

Today the Konteka resort, only six miles south of the Porcupine Mountains Wilderness State Park, is best known as a staging area for snowmobilers. The year round complex includes a 16-room motel, full service restaurant open seven-days-a-week, a bar and grill, and the eight-lane bowling alley all designed by one of the most respected architects of the 20th Century.

JOHN LAUTNER – FRANK LLOYD WRIGHT STUDENT

Noted architect, John Lautner is a native of the Upper Peninsula. Born in Marquette in 1911, he went on to graduate from the local high school and Northern Michigan University.

As a boy he helped his father build a hillside chalet overlooking Lake Superior, which was designed by his mother. He graduated from Northern Michigan University with a degree in English and moved to Spring Green, Wisconsin in 1932. There he was among the first class to study with Frank Lloyd Wright at his Taliesin School.

Five years later he supervised the construction of two of Wright's projects. In 1939, Lautner set up his own architecture practice in Los Angeles. His first project was a house for his own family. The design was called "the best house by an architect under 30 in the United States," by critic Henry-Russell Hitchcock. The respected critic would later remark that Lautner's designs compared favorably with those of his mentor, Frank Lloyd Wright.

Lautner is best known for his unique home designs in and around Los Angeles including the Levy residence, the Elrod residence, Silvertop, and the Chemosphere. Some of his building designs have been featured in James Bond and Diehard movies. Lautner practice architecture for 55 years and was made a Fellow of the American Institute of Architects for Excellence in Design. His work has been exhibited around the world and his buildings featured in numerous publications. In addition, a documentary of his life was produced.

The Marquette native said he maintained fond memories of the woods and water of the U.P. and returned several times throughout his life. He died at 83 on October 24, 1994.

NOTABLE BUILDINGS OF THE UPPER PENINSULA

Beginning in 1987 the State Historic Preservation Office and Bureau of History began the first statewide study of Michigan's architectural history. The study coincided with the state's bicentennial and a project initiated by the Society of Architectural Historians. The project's mission was to document the architectural heritage of the nation through a series of fifty guidebooks, one for each state. The Michigan project was led by Kathryn Bishop Eckert, who at that time was the State Historic Preservation Officer for the Bureau of History. The result was *Buildings of Michigan* (copyright 1993, Oxford University Press), a 600-page highly-detailed, account of Michigan's architectural and cultural heritage from ice shanties in the U.P. to the glass towers of Detroit's Renaissance Center.

The following is a list of Upper Peninsula buildings and structures included in the book.

ALGER COUNTY

MUNISING

Alger County Historical Museum, 203 West Onota Street
St. John's Episcopal Church, 127 West Onota Street
Munising Ranger District Administration Site (Hiawatha National Forest), 601 Cedar St.

OTHER ALGER COUNTY SITES

Wetmore Lookout Tower, 2518 Federal Forest Highway
Teenie Weenie Pickle Barrel Cottage, Lake Ave. and Veteran St., Grand Marais
Au Sable Light Station, Au Sable Point, Burt Township
Pacific Hotel, 101 Rock River Road, Chatham
Bay Furnace, just east of Christmas off M-28, Au Train Township
Charles Paulson House, Au Train Forest Road, Au Train Township

Pickle Barrel cottage, Grand Marais

BARAGA COUNTY
United Methodist Church, Main and Bendry Streets, L'Anse
Arvon Township Hall, Lower Skanee Rd. and Park Rd., Skanee
Michigan Technological University Ford Forestry Center, U.S.-41, Alberta
Holy Name of Jesus Indian Mission, U.S.-41, two miles north of Baraga, Assinins
Hanka Finnish Farmstead, Askel Rd. about ten miles north of Baraga, Pelkie

CHIPPEWA COUNTY
SAULT STE. MARIE
Chippewa County Courthouse, 319 Court St.
Federal Building, 209 East Portage Ave.
St. James Episcopal Church, 533 Bingham Avenue
Eastern Upper Peninsula ISD Building, 315 Armory Place
Sault Locks, St. Marys River
Elmwood (Schoolcraft Home), Water Street eastern edge of Sault Canal
Edison Sault Power Plant, over the Power Canal on St. Marys River
International Railroad Bridge, American Locks Section, over the American Locks
International Railroad Bridge, River Section, over the St. Marys River
International Highway Bridge, over the St. Marys River
Lake Superior State University
Sault Ste. Marie Water Tower, Ryan St. and Easterday Avenue
Robert G. and Christina Bain Ferguson House, 801 Prospect St.
William L. and Cecile Wyman Murdock House, 501 North Ravine Rd.

DRUMMOND ISLAND
The Rock, off Maxson Road
Resort Hotel
Bowling Center
Outdoor Chapel

OTHER CHIPPEWA COUNTY SITES
Hulbert Methodist Chapel, Maple and Third Street, Hulbert
Great Lakes Shipwreck Historical Museum, Whitefish Pt. Road, Whitefish Township
Point Iroquois Light Station, Lake Shore Drive, Bay Mills Township

DELTA COUNTY
ESCANABA
St. Joseph Catholic Church and William Bonifas Fine Arts Center, 700-709 First Avenue
Ludington Street, from Fourth St. to Seventeen St.

East Ludington Gallery/Erickson and Godley Block, 617-619 Ludington St.
American Dream Realty Company, 623 Ludington St.
Delft Theater, 907-913 Ludington Ave.
Delta Building, 1619 Ludington St.

OTHER DELTA COUNTY SITES

Ice Shanty City, Little Bay de Noc
Fayette, company town, Garden Peninsula
Samuel Elliot House, Sac Bay Road off County Rd. 483, Sac Bay

DICKINSON COUNTY
IRON MOUNTAIN

Dickinson County Courthouse and Jail, 500 South Stephenson Ave.
Commercial National Bank and Trust Company Building, 500 South Stephenson Ave.
Iron Mountain Post Office, 101 West Ludington Street
Menominee Range Historical Museum, 300 East Ludington Street
Immaculate Conception Church, 500 Blaine Street

GOGEBIC COUNTY
BESSEMER

Bessemer City Hall and Community Building, 401 South Sophie Street
Frick Funeral Home, 304 South Sophie Street

IRONWOOD

Ironwood Homesteads, Sunset Street
Ironwood Municipal-Memorial Building, McLeod Ave and Marquette St.
Ironwood Theatre, Seaman Block
Ironwood Area Historical Museum, Frederick St. between Suffolk and Lowell Streets
Luther L. Wright High School, 600 Ayer Street

OTHER GOGEBIC COUNTY SITES

Copper Peak Ski-Flying Slide, Black River Road
Black River Harbor Site and Marina, Black River Parkway
Keystone Bridge, over Black River near Bessemer Township Memorial Park
Gogebic Chiefs Hockey Arena, M-28 on Sunday Lake, Wakefield

HOUGHTON COUNTY
HOUGHTON

Houghton County Courthouse
Shelden Avenue district between Franklin Square and Houghton-Hancock Bridge,
Shelden-Dee Block, 512-524 Shelden Ave.

Douglass House Apartments Saloon and Restaurant, 517 Shelden Ave.
Houghton National Bank, 600 Shelden Ave.
Houghton Masonic Temple Building, 616-618 Shelden Rd.
St. Ignatius Loyola Church, 703 E. Houghton Ave.
College Avenue, from Michigan Tech campus to Franklin Square
Allen Forsyth and Caroline Willard Reese House, 918 College Ave.
Michigan Technological University (Michigan School of Mines), East Houghton
ROTC Building, 1416 College Ave.
Daniell Heights Housing, Woodmar Dr. at Division St, eastern edge of MTU
Houghton-Hancock Bridge
Rosa Center, East Houghton Street

HANCOCK

Hancock City Hall, 399 Quincy St.
Detroit and Northern Savings and Loan Association Building, 400 Quincy St.
Suomi College (Finlandia University), Quincy St.
Old Main, Quincy St. at Dakota St.
Nikander Hall
Finlandia Hall, Summit St.
East Hancock, neighborhood of houses bounded by Front, Dunstan, Mason and Vivian
Andrew Kauth House, 318 Cooper Ave.
Temple Jacob, Front St, just east of Houghton-Hancock Bridge

QUINCY AND FRANKLIN TOWNSHIPS

Quincy Mining Company location, Quincy Hill, 1.5 miles from center of Hancock
Mine Agent or Superintendent's House, U.S.-41
Community Action Agency General Office, U.S.-41
Mine Shaft Number Two (Headframe), U.S.-41
Mine Shaft Number Two Hoist House, U.S.-41
Ripley Smelter, Quincy Mining Company, Royce Rd. off M-26, Ripley

CALUMET

Calumet and Hecla Mine Location, Red Jacket Rd. between Sixth and Calumet Ave.
Calumet Clinic (General Office Building of C and H Mining Co.), 100 Red Jacket Rd.
Lake Superior Land Company Office (Library), 101 Red Jacket Rd.
Fifth and Sixth Streets, between Scott and Pine
Bernard Shute's Bar, 322 Sixth St.
Edward Ryan Block, 305-307 Sixth Street
Calumet Village Hall and Calumet Theatre, 340 Sixth St.
Red Jacket Fire Station, Sixth and Elm Streets
St. Anne Roman Catholic Church, Scott and Fifth Streets

LAURIUM

Paul P. Roehm House, 101 Willow St.
Johnson and Anna Lichty Vivian Jr. House, Pewabic and Third Streets
Jukuri's Sauna, 600 Lake Linden Ave.

LAKE LINDEN

Lake Linden Village Hall and Fire Station, 401 Calumet St.
Dad's Home, Front and Fourth Streets
St. Joseph Church, 701 Calumet St.
First Congregational Church of Lake Linden, First and Tunnel Streets

OTHER HOUGHTON COUNTY SITES

Jacobsville Finnish Evangelical Lutheran Church, Jacobsville
Painsedale, M-26, seven miles southwest of Houghton
Redridge Dam, off S-554 in Redridge

IRON COUNTY
IRON RIVER

St. Mary's Assumption Catholic Church, 105 Fifth Ave.,
Houses of Seventh and Eighth Avenues
Wall-Seppanen House, 21 North Seventh Avenue
Iron County Fair Exhibition Hall, West Franklin north of Adams St.

OTHER IRON COUNTY SITES

Iron County Courthouse, 2 Sixth St., Crystal Falls
Joseph Harris House, 165 Washington Ave., Stambaugh
Hiawatha Mine Number One Headframe, Selden Rd. at Fourth Ave.
Pentoga Park Office and Bathhouse, 1630 County Rd. 424
Crooks Run Trout Feeding Station, 180 Crooks Run Road
Van Platen-Fox Lumber Camp, 281 University Road
Italian Society Duke of Abruzzi Hall, McGillis Ave, Caspian
Beechwood Store, 215 Beechwood Road, Beechwood
Camp Gibbs, 129 West Camp Gibbs Rd., Iron River Township

KEWEENAW COUNTY

Keweenaw County Courthouse, Sheriff's residence and Jail, Eagle River
Sand Hills Lighthouse, off Five Mile Point, 3.5 miles southwest of Eagle River
Holy Redeemer Church, South and Fourth Streets
Eagle Harbor Lighthouse
Lake Breeze Hotel, Off Lighthouse Road south of the lighthouse
Central (former mining town), Houghton Township
Brockway Mountain Drive, Grant Township

CLIFF SHAFT HEADFRAMES

While not buildings per se, the Cliff Shaft Mine Headframes in Ishpeming are familiar and unique landmarks and symbols of the mining heritage of the Marquette Iron Range. The Headframes were built in 1919 by Cleveland-Cliffs Iron Company to replace badly deteriorated wooden structures at the site. The prominent structures were featured among the opening shots in the Academy Award-winning movie "Anatomy of a Murder" filmed on location in 1959.

The headframes were constructed of concrete because the material was fireproof. Also, there was an available supply of hard gravel nearby along with plenty of cheap labor. William Mather, the president of Cleveland-Cliffs, insisted that since the mine was in a prominent location, the headframe design should be attractive. An obelisk design was finally chosen, and construction began in late July 1919. The project was completed in December of that year with no interruption in the use of either shaft during the building period.

The Cliff Shaft Headframes are nearly identical and measure 37 feet by 55 feet at the base from which a 37-foot-square tower rises tapering to 21 feet square at the eaves. The tip of the pointed roof is 91 feet above the footings.

Keweenaw Mountain Resort, Copper Harbor
Fort Wilkins, Copper Harbor
Rock Harbor Lighthouse, Middle islands Passage, Houghton Township
Pete Edison Fishery, Isle Royale

LUCE COUNTY

NEWBERRY

Luce County Historical Museum, 411 West Harris
Falls Hotel, 301 South Newberry Avenue
Newberry Correctional Facility (Regional Mental Health Center), McMillan Township

MACKINAC COUNTY

ST. IGNACE

Mackinac County Courthouse, 100 Marley Street
Warren & Florence Highstone House, 100 Trucky St.
St. Ignace Municipal Building, 396 North State Street
Indian Village, 499 North State Street
Marquette Mission Park and Museum of Ojibwa Culture, North State Street at Marquette

LES CHENEAUX ISLANDS

Les Cheneaux Club Subdivision, Marquette Island, Clark Township

MACKINAC ISLAND

Fort Mackinac, Huron Road
Indian Dormitory, Huron Street
William McGulpin House, Fort and Market Street
Mission Church, Huron St at Mission Hill Road
Grand Hotel, West Bluff Road at Cadotte Avenue
O'Neil Cudahy House, Lot 25, West Bluff
Cairngorn Cottage, Lot 22, West Bluff
William D. and Mary Angie Bingham Gilbert Cottage, Lot 21, West Bluff Rd.
Henry Davis Cottage, Hubbard's Annex
Donnybrook Cottage, Lot 17, Huron Rd., East Bluff
Charles C. Bowen Cottage, Lott 22, Huron Rd., East Bluff
Governor's Summer House, West Fort

MARQUETTE COUNTY
MARQUETTE

Marquette County Courthouse, 400 South Third St.
St. Peter's Roman Catholic Cathedral, W. Baraga Ave. and Fourth St.
Washington and Front Streets, commercial district
Marquette County Savings Bank, 107 S. Front St.
Harlow Block, 102 West Washington St.
First National Bank, 101 West Washington
Marquette Post Office, 202 West Washington St.
Old Marquette Hall, 220 Washington St.
Peter White Library, 217 North Front St.
St. Paul's Episcopal Church, 318 High St.
Morgan Memorial Chapel, 318 West High St.
Ridge, Arch, Michigan, and Ohio Streets residential district
Henry R. and Mary Hewitt Mather House, 450 East Ridge St.
Andrew A. and Laura Grenough Ripka House, 430 East Arch St.
Daniel H. Merritt House, 410 East Ridge St.
Julian M. Case House, 425 Ohio St.
Small Fryes Day Care Center, 109 Presque Isle St.
Superior Dome, Northern Michigan University
Lake Superior and Ishpeming Ore Dock and Approach, Lake Shore Blvd.
Marquette Branch Prison, 1960 U.S.-41 South

NEGAUNEE

Negaunee City Hall, 100 Silver St., Negaunee

ISHPEMING

Ishpeming City Hall, 100 East Division St.
The Mather Inn, 107 Canda St.
Edward R. and Jennie Bigelow Hall House, 112 Bluff St.
Cliffs Cottage, 282 Jasper Street
Cliffs Shaft Mine Headframes, Lake Shore Drive at south shore of Lake Bancroft

OTHER MARQUETTE COUNTY SITES

Granot Loma (wilderness camp), off Sauk Head Lake Rd., Powell Township
John and Mary Beecher Longyear Summer House, north shore of Ives Lake, Big Bay
Big Bay Point Lighthouse Bed and Breakfast, Lighthouse Rd., Big Bay

MENOMINEE COUNTY

MENOMINEE

Menominee County Courthouse, 839 Tenth Avenue
First Street Central Business District, from Tenth Avenue to Fourth Avenue
A. D. Paalzow Block, 401 South First Street
Shale Building, 601 First Street
Spies Public Library, 940 First Street
Commercial Bank, 949 First Street

OTHER MENOMINEE COUNTY SITES

John Henes Park, Henes Park Road on Green Bay
Chalk Hill Dam and Hydroelectric Plant, Menominee River, Holmes Township
Hermansville, company town, Meyer Township

ONTONAGON COUNTY

ONTONAGON

Ontonagon Lighthouse, at mouth of Ontonagon River
Ontonagon Elementary School, 301 Greenland Rd.

OTHER ONTONAGON COUNTY SITES

Victoria Mine site, Victoria Rd., 4 miles southwest of Rockland, Rockland Township
Victoria Dam and Hydroelectric Plant, Victoria Dam Rd., Rockland Township
White Pine Townsite, M-64, six miles south of Silver City

SCHOOLCRAFT COUNTY

MANISTIQUE

Manistique Water Tower, in Riverside Park, north side of Deer Street
Manistique paper Company Dam and Flume, Deer Street on Manistique River
Siphon Bridge, Deer St. over Manistique River

OTHER SCHOOLCRAFT COUNTY SITES

Clear Lake Organizational Camp, off Forest Rd, east of M-94, Hiawatha Township
Blaney Park, M-77 a mile north of US-2 and M-77 intersection, Mueller Township

Chapter 16

BIGGEST AND BEST

U.P. SUPERLATIVES

GEOGRAPHY

First permanent city in Michigan: Sault Ste. Marie

Largest county in Michigan (land area): Marquette with a land area of 1,821 sq. mi. and water area of 1,604 sq. mi.

Largest county (water area): Keweenaw County's borderline extends miles away from shore into Lake Superior. Keweenaw's 5,425 water acres combined with 541 acres of land make it the **largest county overall** with 5,966 total acres!

Largest freshwater lake in the world: Lake Superior's surface area covers 31,700 square miles.

Michigan's largest island: Isle Royale

Largest Island in the largest lake on the largest island in the broadest freshwater lake in the world: Ryan Island sits in Siskiwit Lake on Isle Royale in Lake Superior.

County with the most islands in Michigan: There are 105 islands within the boundary of Chippewa County.

Highest Point in Michigan is Mt. Arvon in Baraga County. Hike to the summit and have your photo taken 1,979 feet above sea level.

A view of the Huron Mountains, home of Mt. Arvon,
Photo by R. Poutanen

WORLD'S LARGEST AND OLDEST LIVING ORGANISM?

Indian Ghost Pipe Mushrooms

You can't see it even though it covers 38 acres and weighs about 100 tons. The Armillaria Bulbosa fungus lies underground in a section of forest in Iron County near the Wisconsin Border. It was discovered in 1988 by researchers doing work for the U.S. Navy's proposed ELF (extremely low frequency) underground communication system for submarines.

The humungus fungus attracted national media attention, including a Top Ten List on the David Letterman Show, after it was mentioned in Nature *magazine.*

Estimated to be at least 1,500 years old and possibly dating back 10,000 years, the "Humungus Fungus" may be the oldest living organism on earth, but it is not the largest. Since the publicity of the early 1990s larger fungi have been discovered elsewhere.

Since the discovery of the invisible fungus that produces the honey mushroom, local businesses have produced Fungus Fudge, Fungus Burgers, Fungus T-shirts, and the Humungus Fungus Festival held annually each August in Crystal Falls.

NATURE

Largest stand of old growth hemlock in the Midwest: Porcupine Mountains Wilderness State Park established to preserve the Midwest's largest stand of old growth Hardwood/hemlock forest.

Largest Waterfall in Michigan, Taquamenom Falls: 2nd largest waterfall east of the Mississippi (Niagara is #1)

Largest Springs in Michigan: Kitchitikipi, the Big Springs at Palms Book State Park in Thompson measure 200 feet across and forty feet deep. Water gushes up at the rate of 10,000 gallons a minute.

Ontonagon Boulder: A 3,708 pound copper boulder from Ontonagon is on display at the Smithsonian National Museum of Natural History in Washington D.C. The giant chunk of copper was deposited by retreating glaciers about 35 miles from the mouth of the Ontonagon River. It was surrounded by 100 foot high cliffs, and unreachable by boat.

Native Americans knew of the giant boulder for centuries, but sometime in the early-to-mid 1800s word of the giant copper chunk reached early copper-rush explorers. In 1843, Detroit businessman Julius Eldred organized a party of men to remove the boulder and transport it to Detroit. Eldred had struck a deal with local Indians, paying them forty five dollars in cash and one-hundred five dollars worth of goods. Unbeknownst to Eldred, in his quest to own the giant boulder of copper he was not alone. A Colonel Hammond of the Wisconsin Territory was the first to arrive at the boulder. However, a Colonel White had already been issued a permit for possession of the boulder from the United States government, which had just acquired the land containing the boulder from the Ojibwa nation. Eldred wound up paying more money to Hammond, and more to White for ownership rights to the Ontonagon Boulder. Now all he had to do was haul the boulder up a 50-foot cliff, and over four miles of rough terrain.

Eldred's men worked for a week just to move the 1.5 ton rock up the cliff to flat land. Then he loaded it on to a cart sitting on twenty five feet of track. After moving the cart forward 25 feet his men would pick up the track and lay it down in front of the cart, doing this over and over through four miles of swamp and woods. Once they arrived at a point on the stream where they could raft it to the mouth of the river, Eldred ran into another surprise.

Colonel Hammond was unable to cash the check given to him by Eldred, so Eldred had to accompany him to the bank to clear the matter up. After that he and his men made it to Copper Harbor where they were greeted by a General under orders to give Eldred $700 and seize the rock in the name of the U.S. government. Eldred said he'd give up the boulder, but needed more money for his troubles. While the government decided on a fair payment Eldred had a schooner deliver the copper to Detroit, where he put it on display, charging twenty-five cents a head.

A few months later, Eldred was reimbursed $5,664.98 by the government and the Ontonagon Boulder was delivered to the yard of the War Department. Eventually it was obtained by the Smithsonian. In 1991, the Keweenaw Bay Indian Community filed to have the boulder returned to them, claiming it as a sacred object. In 2000, a ruling denied their request, and the boulder remains at the Museum of Natural History in Washington D.C. (This is one account of the removal of the Ontonagon Boulder, for another version see James Kirk Paul's biography in Chapter 5)

ENGINEERING

Longest locks in the world. The Poe Lock, part of the Soo Locks, is 1200' long, 110' wide and 32 feet deep. It's the only lock on the St. Lawrence Seaway system that can accommodate 1000-foot freighters.

Longest suspension bridge in the western hemisphere: Until 1998 the Mackinac Bridge was the longest suspension bridge in the world; now the third longest in the world.

Largest Wooden Dome in the World: The Superior Dome at Northern Michigan University was built using 781 Douglas Fir beams and includes over 100 miles of fir decking. It stands 14 stories high,

BIG LOUIE MOILANEN: GIANT OF THE COPPER COUNTRY

Louis Moilanen, considered the tallest man in the world of his generation, was born in Finland in 1885. His parents brought him to America four years later and settled on a farm in northern Houghton County.

Louie grew quickly, despite the fact his parents were short in stature—his father was just over 5-feet tall, while his mother was around 4 feet. On the other hand, by the time Louie was nine, he was already as tall as an average man. By the time he was 18 in 1903, Louis Moilanen, Jr. became known as "Big Louie," the world's tallest man at 8-feet, one-inch.

Along with his enormous height, Louie's body was awkwardly shaped. His legs were only three-feet, three-inches long and he wore a size 19 shoe. Louie had trouble balancing himself and often fell. His clothes were individually tailored, mostly by Ed Haas of Houghton who made coats for Louie measuring two feet across at the shoulder and 49 inches around the chest. Louie topped off his apparel with a size 9, wide-brimmed Stetson hat which gave him an even more dramatic, huge appearance.

Louie's careers included work on the family farm and later, as a timber man at a nearby copper mine. The low heights and cramped quarters proved too much for the big man and eventually forced him to quit mining. His fame spread and eventually

brought him employment in circus side shows. He left the Copper Country and was nationally promoted by E.M. Sackrider of Hancock. Later, he toured with the Ringling Brothers, Barnum and Bailey circus. Finally, in 1906 at the age of 21, Moilanen spent a season with the Forepaugh and Sells Circus. Big Louie's shyness hurt him at the box office and put off his promoters. While on the road his father died and Moilanen left the circus and returned home to work the family farm.

Louie later moved to Hancock where he operated a saloon at the corner of Franklin and Tezcuco. A large number of customers came in just to see Big Louie. One of his favorite tricks was to slip off his ring and pass a half dollar through it without touching any edge of the ring. People were amazed at his voice—some said it sounded like it was echoing through a hollow tree! Moilanen eventually tired of the saloon business and returned home again to work the family farm.

Finally in 1911, Big Louie Moilanen sought and won election as Justice of the Peace in Hancock Township. Little is known of his performance in the office because he did not serve long. Two years later in late summer 1913, the Copper Country Giant's health was failing to the point where people began to fear for his life.

On Saturday, September 13, he became so violently ill that he was placed in the county jail for his own safety. People felt he was going insane because of his

the diameter measures 536 feet, and its domed roof covers 5.1 acres. Seating capacity is 8,000, although it can accommodate up to 16,000 people at a time. The dome was built in 1991 and is home to the NMU Wildcat football, soccer, and track teams. The Dome also features the **largest retractable artificial turf carpet in the world**, measuring 120 by 72 feet.

Largest Steam Engine in the World: The Chapin Mine Pumping Engine in Iron Mountain was featured on The History Channel's *Modern Marvels* program in a segment titled World's Largest Machines. The Cornish Pump weighs 725 tons and the engine stands 54 feet tall. The flywheel is 40 feet in diameter and turns slowly, 10 revolutions per minute on average. The high-pressure cylinder has a 50-inch bore, and the low-pressure cylinder is 100 inches in diameter.

The first outboard motor: The first gas-driven outboard motor for boats was built in 1897 at the old Lake Shore Engine Works building in Marquette by Nels Flodin and Carl Blomstrom.

Heaviest Aerial Lift Bridge in the World: The Portage Lake Lift Bridge that connects Houghton and Hancock was built in 1959 as a replacement to the previous bridge built in 1898. (The original bridge was built in 1875, rebuilt in 1898, and repaired and renovated in 1905.) The double deck bridge accommodates vehicular traffic, while the lower deck serves pedestrians and snowmobiles.

Michigan's Oldest Concrete Pavement can be found in Calumet at the southwest corner of Portland and 7th Street. The granitoid blocked concrete was installed in 1906, when the mining industry was booming and the town was known as Red Jacket.

SPORTS

Oldest (unchanged) nine-hole golf course in Michigan: Wawashkamo Golf Course was built on Mackinac Island in 1898. Wawashkamo is a Chippewa word meaning "walk a crooked trail." The clubhouse is built on the site of the 1814 Battle of Mackinac Island.

Longest hole on a golf course: For many years the 6th hole at the former **Chocolay Downs** Golf Course in Marquette, at 1,007 yards, was the longest golf hole in the world. After the owners donated the course to Northern Michigan University, the nearly half-mile long hole was shortened to 440 yards.

Largest putting green in the world: The 9th hole on the NMU Golf Course, formerly Chocolay Downs, has 29,000 sq. feet of groomed putting green.

Highest ski hill in Michigan/Midwest: Mt. Bohemia on the Keweenaw Peninsula offers skiers a 900 foot vertical drop.

Largest artificial ski slide in the world: Copper Peak near Bessemer is the only ski flying hill in the Western Hemisphere. It has the world's largest artificial ski slide at 241 feet above the crest of Chippewa Hill. An 18-story elevator provides access to the observation deck. Climbing the additional 60 feet to the top starting gate will allow the visitor to experience the feelings of the ski flyer about to launch down a 469 foot run.

World's Largest tiger muskie! John Knobla caught a 52 ¼ inch long tiger muskie weighing in at 51 lbs. 3 oz. in Lac Vieux Desert, 4,300 acre lake on the Wisconsin/Michigan border, on July 17, 1919. The fish is mounted on the wall at the Minnow Bucket.

Most Scenic Baseball Diamond: Posted signs declare Steiger Field, near Bessemer, as "the most scenic Little League baseball park in America."

bizarre behavior. A doctor was summoned to the jail to examine him and recommended hospital treatment. Three days later, Big Louie Moilanen was dead. An autopsy revealed he suffered from tubercular meningitis of the brain.

At the time of his death, many in the area thought Big Louie was a wealthy man. However, he had little in reserve to pay his hospital bills, let alone his funeral expenses. The county had to assume some of the burial costs. One of the expenses involved a special-order casket. It was nearly nine feet long and three feet wide. The burial box weighed nearly 300 pounds— about double the weight of an ordinary casket. It took eight men to lift Big Louie's body from the cooling board to the casket. He was laid to rest at Lakeside cemetery.

Big Louie's garments are still prized possessions. A number of items, including Louie's Stetson hat are on display at the Houghton County Historical Museum in Lake Linden.

Big Louie sitting next to an average-size man

ATTRACTIONS

Michigan's Largest State Park: Porcupine Mountains Wilderness State Park covers 60,000 acres.

First roadside park in the nation: Herb Larson, head of the Iron County Highway Department, led an effort to preserve virgin hardwood trees along the county's main roads.

He was successful in convincing major landowners to sell some of their roadside property for this purpose. In 1919 he convinced the county to provide a picnic table and grill along U.S.-2 at a place where drivers could pull off the road, relax, and enjoy the magnificent virgin-hardwood forest.

Longest Front Porch in the world: At 660 feet, the Grand Hotel has the longest porch in the world!

Largest Bear Ranch in the Country: Oswald's Bear Ranch near Newberry is home to about 30 adult bear who roam free behind a chain link fence. Visitors are welcome to walk around and view the bears in their natural habitat. There are also several bear cubs, many of them rescued from the wild and kept in kennels. The Dean Oswald family recently added a trolley to accommodate larger groups of visitors who opt not to walk. Oswald's Bear Ranch was the home of the **Largest Black Bear in the United States** until he died in 2000 after getting info a fight with one of the other bears. At that time Tyson weighed in at 900 pounds.

Largest Running Chain Saw in the World: Big Gus chain saw at Da Yoopers Tourist Trap in Ishpeming is listed in the Guinness Book of World Records. It's powered by a Chevy 350 cubic inch V-8 engine!

Largest Working Rifle in the World: Big Ernie is a 35-foot black-powder muzzle-loader that weighs 4,022 lbs. Located near Big Gus at Da Yoopers Tourist Trap in Ishpeming.

Largest Bear Trap, located in Chassell was created by Ed Sauvola. He calls the 32-foot wide, 9.5-foot tall sculpture the Tourist Trap!

Largest Indian Statue: Hiawatha stands 52 feet high overlooking the town of Ironwood. The 8-ton fiberglass statue was built in Minneapolis and installed at the site of the Old Norrie Iron Mine in June of 1962. Although billed as Largest Indian Statue, a similar statue in Maine stands 10 feet higher.

World's Tallest Santa stands nearly three stories tall outside the entrance to Santa's Workshop in Christmas (Alger County).

World's Largest Concrete Frosty the Snowman also stands outside Santa's Workshop, along with a very large Old Woman in the Shoe statue.

Best Northwoods cap The Stormy Kromer, a wool cap with pull-down flaps, is made exclusively in Ironwood. The distinctive cap is a favorite among lumberjacks, railroad engineers, hunters, skiers, anglers and just about anyone who works or plays in the North Country.

The hat is named after George "Stormy" Kromer. Kromer, born and raised in Kaukauna, Wisconsin, was a railroad engineer who lost a few too many caps due to the icy, arctic winds whipping through his locomotive. He had his beloved wife, Ida, modify one of his caps from his semi-pro baseball-playing days. She sewed flaps on it and also reshaped the visor, which made the hat a great departure from the traditional engineer hats of the day. The best part about it was that it stayed on Stormy's head, high winds and all.

Soon the word spread and Ida was sewing caps for all the engineers, then for hunters and other outdoorsmen. Kromer eventually hired others to help with the sewing and in 1918 he moved his wife and employees to a large manufacturing factory in Milwaukee. Over the years, the company expanded twice. George ran the Kromer Hat Company into the mid-60s when his health began failing. Finally, he sold the business to Richard Grossman in 1965. Five years later, Stormy Kromer passed away.

The Stormy Kromer was manufactured in Milwaukee for the next three decades. Then in 2001, Grossman announced plans to discontinue the original Kromer or "Blizzard" cap because of slow sales. The company would focus on its best-selling line of welding caps.

Over three hundred miles to the northwest, Ironwood businessman Bob Jaquart heard from a local retailer that the Stormy Kromer was being discontinued. Jaquart, who owns a small sewn-products company called Jaquart Fabric Products, Inc., did not want to see a tradition of the North Country die. So he contacted Grossman and purchased the rights to the Stormy Kromer Cap brand as well as the rights to be the sole manufacturer of the product.

Since the Stormy Kromer was acquired by Jaquart, sales have grown steadily and the product line has been expanded. At the time of the purchase, only 3,800 caps were being produced annually, now more than 50,000 caps are made in six styles and 12 colors including blaze orange for hunters. For Packer fans, there even a specially made Kromer in green and gold complete with the Lambeau Field logo.

To learn more about Stormy Kromer caps and clothing go to www.stormykromer.com.

The biggest (and only) outhouse race in the United States

The Alger county community of Trenary hosted the 16th annual Outhouse Classic on February 28, 2009. The event was started in 1994 as an antidote to cabin fever after a particularly severe winter.

Participants construct replicas of outhouses with wood, cardboard and any other material except metal for safety reasons. Inside, there must be a toilet seat and a roll of toilet paper. The entries are then pushed one-at-a-time approximately 500 feet down the main street of Trenary.

Adult racers are awarded cash prizes for the 1st, 2nd and 3rd fastest times. Other prizes are awarded in different categories including a children's division.

Organizers proclaim the event is for "anyone who has a sense of humor or needs one"!

"World's Greatest" Winter Carnival

Held each year at Michigan Tech, the event originated as a one-night Ice Carnival in 1922. The carnival was so well received that students decided to make it an annual affair. In 1936, the biggest and most profound change came with the addition of a snow statue competition. Fraternities, sororities and other campus organizations build statues that have become famous for their size, detail and design. These organizations pass along the "secrets" of statue building from generation to generation of students.

Michigan Tech's Winter Carnival is now a 3-day event with special competitions that take place up to two weeks before the actual carnival. Alumni, parents and tourists from around the Midwest book rooms within a 60-mile radius up to a year in advance and bring a tremendously positive economic impact to the Houghton-Hancock area.

BUSINESS

First Indian-run casino in the U.S. Fred Dakota, a member of the Lake Superior Band of Chippewa Indians, opened for business in a two-car garage on New Year's Eve 1983.

Largest pet casket factory: The Hoegh (hoig) Pet Casket Company in Gladstone produces and ships over 35,000 tiny caskets each year. They also sell over 6,000 cremation urns. The caskets come in eight sizes ranging from ten to 52 inches in length. They are shipped to some 700 locations every day of the week.

The Hoegh Pet Casket Company offers tour of its facility Monday through Friday.

FOOD

The largest pasty on record was made by Northern Michigan University students back in October 1978. It contained 250 pounds of beef, 400 pounds of potatoes, 75 pounds of carrots and 25 pounds of onions all wrapped in 250 pounds of dough.

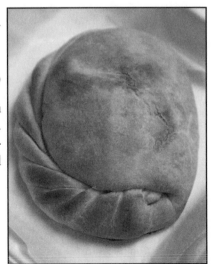

BIBLIOGRAPHY

Chapter 1 HISTORY

Timeline

http://www.borealforest.org/index.php?category=ont_
nw_forest&page=history&content=past
Early history of the Lake Superior region

http://www.dnr.state.mn.us/snas/naturalhistory.html
Early geological information

http://www.law.umkc.edu/faculty/projects/
ftrials/superior/timeline.html
Lake Superior region timeline

For further reading: Michigan Copper, The Untold Story
A History of Discovery
C. Fred Rydholm
Winter Cabin Books and Services
393 Crescent Street, Marquette, Michigan 49855
Copyright 2006

http://www.mnhs.org/places/nationalregister/
shipwrecks/mpdf/mpdf1.html

Early Days in the Upper Peninsula
From Michigan Pioneer and Historical Collections
Volumes 1-40
Vol. 4, 1881 pp. 67-68
Vol. 30, 1905 pp. 83-88
The Upper Peninsula: Historical
Events in Chronological Order
Compiled by John Distuenell
Vol. 7, 1884, pp. 1-2

http://www.geo.msu.edu/geo333/toledo_war.html
The Toledo War

http://huron.lre.usace.army.mil/SOO/lockhist.html
Army Corp of Engineers Detroit District
History of the Sault Locks

http://www.michiganrailroads.com/RRHX/
Timeline/1860s/TimeLine1860sBackUp.htm
Michigan's Internet Railroad History Museum

http://www.geo.msu.edu/geo333/
menominee-iron-range.html
Menominee Iron Range history

http://mattsonworks.com/1888/1888_
Bessemer_history.html
Gogebic Iron Range History
200 Years of the Upper Peninsula
of Michigan and its People
1776-1976
Bill Finlan

http://quickfacts.census.gov/qfd/states/26/26061.html
Houghton County's population

http://hunts-upguide.com/iron_mountain_detail.html
Iron Mountain-Kingsford history

Copper Country Postcards
A View of the Past from the Keweenaw Peninsula
Nancy Ann Sanderson
Keweenaw County Historical Society
Eagle Harbor, MI 2005

http://www.lssu.edu/about/facts.php
Fast facts about Lake Superior State University

City of the Rapids
Sault Ste. Marie's Heritage
Bernie Arbic
Priscilla Press
Allegan Forest, Michigan 2003

Deep Woods Frontier
A History of Logging in Northern Michigan
Theodore J. Karamanski
Wayne State University Press
Detroit 1989

http://www.nmu.edu/facts/history.htm
Northern Michigan University history

http://www.baydenoc.cc.mi.us/bayhistb.html
Bay College history

http://www.chassell.info/histbydecades.htm
Copper Country history

http://www.usmra.com/saxsewell/historical.htm
United States Mine Rescue Association webpage:
facts on the Barnes-Hecker disaster

No Tears in Heaven
The 1926 Barnes-Hecker Mine Disaster
Thomas G. Friggens
Michigan Historical Center, Michigan
Department of State
Lansing, Michigan 1998

http://www.usoc.org/12181_19095.htm
U.S. Olympic Education Center
website: Superior Dome facts

http://www.admin.mtu.edu/urel/
breaking/2000/rozsa.html
Rozsa Center information

http://www.michiganhighways.org/index.html
1-75 extension

The Northern Michigan Almanac
Ron Jolly
University of Michigan Press/Petoskey
Publishing, copyright 2005

Traveling Through Time: A Guide to
Michigan's Historical Markers,
Laura Rose Ashlee,
University of Michigan Press
Ann Arbor, Michigan 2007

Hunt's Guide to Michigan's Upper Peninsula,
Mary and Don Hunt
Midwestern Guides of Albion Michigan 1997

http://www.nps.gov/history/nhl/
designations/Lists/MI01.pdf
National Historic Landmarks

Geology of Upper Michigan

Michigan Today
Its Human and Physical Resources
as They Affect Education
Bulletin No. 307
State of Michigan—Department of
Public Instruction, Lansing 1941
Living with the Lakes
Understanding and Adapting to Great
Lakes Water Level Changes
U.S. Army Corp of Engineers and
Great Lakes Commission
Ann Arbor 1999

http://www.msstate.edu/dept/geosciences/
CT/TIG/WEBSITES/LOCAL/Spring2002/
Michael_Marsicek/geology.htm
Upper Michigan Geology—Michigan State Geosciences

http://hosting.soonet.ca/eliris/
geoforum/superiorshore.htm
Jacobsville Sandstone

http://coppercountry.com/article_42.php
Isle Royale-Keweenaw geology

Chapter 2 Weather

http://mcc.sws.uiuc.edu/climate_midwest/
maps/mi_mapselector.htm
Historical climate summaries for U.P. cities

http://www.tornadoproject.com/alltorns/mitorn.htm
Michigan tornadoes by County

http://www4.ncdc.noaa.gov/cgi-win/wwcgi.
dll?wwevent~storms#NOTICE
NCDC tornado information

http://www.spc.noaa.gov/faq/tornado/f-scale.html
F-scale

U.P. Weather Extremes
Courtesy of the National Weather Service, Marquette

Chapter 3 Land

Cloverland

http://www.nps.gov/archive/piro/adhi/adhi2.htm
History of Pictured Rocks contains
background on Cloverland

A Most Superior Land: Life in the Upper Peninsula
David M. Frimodig
Two Peninsula Press, Lansing 1983

National Forests

http://www.fs.fed.us/r9/ottawa/
U.S. Department of Agriculture—Ottawa
National Forest information

http://www.fs.fed.us/r9/forests/hiawatha/
U.S. Department of Agriculture—Hiawatha
National Forest Information

Timber Industry in Upper Michigan

Deep Woods Frontier
A History of Logging in Northern Michigan
Theodore J. Karamanski
Wayne State University Press, Detroit 1989

http://www.ncrs.fs.fed.us/pubs/gtr/other/
gtr-nc217/gtr_nc217page%20023.pdf
Percent of forested land in Upper Michigan

Seney: One Rough Lumber Town

Deep Wood Frontier
A History of Logging in Northern Michigan
Theodore J. Karamanski
Wayne State University Press, Detroit 1989

Incredible Seney
The First Complete Story of Michigan's
Fabulous Lumber Town
Lewis C. Reimann
Avery Color Studios, Au Train, Michigan 1982

Seney Stretch
A Historical Guide to the Seney Stretch
Jim Carter
The Pilot Press, Marquette, Michigan 2005

Islands

http://www.autrainislandsanctuary.com/
Autrain Island information

http://paddlingmichigan.com/lake_superior_
kayak_trips.htm#presqueisleandpartridgeisland
Partridge Island information

http://www.lhdigest.com/Digest/
StoryPage.cfm?StoryKey=332
Granite Island information

http://www.graniteisland.com/
Granite Island information

http://www.terrypepper.com/lights/superior/
huron_island/huronisland.htm
Huron Island information

http://www.terrypepper.com/lights/
superior/manitou/index.htm
Manitou Island information

http://www.keweenawnow.com/news/klt_projects_

ship_06_05/klt_projects_06_05.htm
Keweenaw Land Trust owners of
Lighthouse Point, Manitou Island

http://www.gullrocklightkeepers.org/gullrock.htm
Information on Gull Rock Island

http://www.terrypepper.com/Lights/superior/
huron_island/huronisland.htm
Seeing the Light
Lighthouses of the Western Great Lakes
Researched and written by Terry Pepper

Superior Heartland
A Backwoods History
C. Fred Rydholm
C. Fred Rydholm, Marquette 1989

Other Sources

Sugar Island Sampler
Bernard Arbic
The Priscilla Press, Allegan Forest, Michigan, 1992
4th printing, 2006 by the Chippewa
County Historical Society

Islands: Great Lakes' Stories
Gerry Volgenau
Ann Arbor Media Group
J.W. Edwards, Inc. 2005

http://www.michiweb.com/drummond/
Drummond Island

http://www.nass.usda.gov/
U.S. Department of Agriculture

http://www.ams.usda.gov
Agriculture statistics

A Most Superior Land: Life in the
Upper Peninsula of Michigan
David M. Frimodig, edited by Susan Newhof Pyle
Michigan Natural Resources Magazine
Department of Natural Resources, 1983

http://www.americanforests.org/
resources/bigtrees/register.php
Largest trees

Chapter 4 Water

Lake Superior

Lake Superior: Story and Spirit
John and Ann Mahan
Sweetwater Visions
Gaylord, Michigan 1998

Thirty Years with the Indian Tribes on
the American Frontier With Notices of
Passing Events, Facts and Opinions
A.D. 1812 to A.D. 1842
Henry Rowe Schoolcraft
Philadelphia: Lippincott, Grambo & Co. 1850

Superior Heartland
A Backwoods History
C. Fred Rydholm
C. Fred Rydholm, Marquette 1989

So Cold a Sky, Upper Michigan Weather Stories
Karl Bohnak
Cold Sky Publishing
Negaunee, MI 2006

http://www.glerl.noaa.gov/data/
Great Lakes

Great Lakes Water Levels

http://www.lre.usace.army.mil/greatlakes/
hh/greatlakeswaterlevels/historicdata/
longtermaveragemin-maxwaterlevels/
Historic Water Levels

http://www.glerl.noaa.gov/data/
now/wlevels/levels.html
Great Lakes Environmental Research Laboratory

Geology of the Great Lakes
Jack L. Hough
University of Illinois Press
Urbana 1958

Rivers, Waterfalls and Inland Lakes

http://www.chrs.ca/Rivers/StMarys/StMarys_e.htm
History and geography of St. Marys River

http://www.ontarioplaques.com/Plaques_
ABC/Plaque_Algoma05.html
Information on Chicora incident

http://www.riverrampage.com/
River Rampage at Sault Ste. Marie

http://www.michigandnr.com/publications/pdfs/
wildlife/viewingguide/up/22Menominee/index.htm
Menominee River information—Piers Gorge

A Guide to 199 Michigan Waterfalls,
Laurie and Bill T. Penrose,
Copyright by Laurie Penrose, Bill T.
Penrose and Ruth Penrose,
Friede Publications, 1988

Canoeing Michigan Rivers: A
Comprehensive Guide to 45 Rivers,
Jerry Dennis and Craig Date,
Copyright by Jerry Dennis and Craig Date
Friede Publications, 1986

http://www.lake-link.com/lakes/
http://www.michigan.gov/dnr/0,1607,7-
153-30301_31431_32340---,00.html
http://www.fishweb.com/recreation/
fishing/lakes/index.html
Inland lakes

http://www.trailstotrout.com/blueribbon.html
Blue Ribbon Trout Streams

Chapter 5 People

Biographies

Peter White
A Great Men of Michigan Book
Herbert Brinks
William R. Erdmans Publishing Company 1970

Superior Heartland
A Backwoods History
C. Fred Rydholm
Published privately by C. Fred Rydholm
Marquette, MI 1989
Louis G. Graveraet

http://www.marquettefiction.com/page7.html
Louis G. Kaufman information

http://www.granotloma.com/
Louis G. Kaufman information

Marquette Monthly Magazine
Feature: "Some of the Finer Things." The
Graveraet High School Lyceum Series
By Frank Richardson
September 2001

Deep Woods Frontier
A History of Logging in Northern Michigan
Theodore J. Karamanski
Wayne State University Press, Detroit 1989
William Bonifas

http://www.escanaba.org/History/bonifasstory.htm
The William and Catherine Bonifas story

History of the Upper Peninsula of Michigan
The Western Historical Company
A.T. Andreas, Proprietor
Chicago, 1883
Biographical information on James Krk Paul,
Capt. Richard Edwards, Daniel D. Brockway,
Capt James Bendry, Jacob A.T. Wendell,
Mary Terry, and Ruel O. Philbrook

Strangers and Sojourners: A History of
Michigan's Keweenaw Peninsula
Arthur W. Thurner
Wayne State University Press, Detroit 1994
Information on Peter Crebassa

http://www.answers.com/topic/henry-schoolcraft
Information on Henry Rowe Schoolcraft

http://www.schoolcraft.edu/archives/
henry_rowe_schoolcraft.asp
Schoolcraft College—the name and its significance
Mary J. Toomey
Information on Henry Rowe Schoolcraft

http://www.infoplease.com/ce6/people/A0844003.html
Henry Rowe Schoolcraft ousted by the Whigs

http://www.michiganhistorymagazine.com/
extra/2008/sandpoint_lighthouse.html
Information regarding Mary L. Terry's
death and subsequent investigation

http://www.gogebic.org/history.htm
Solomon S. Curry biographical information

Native Americans in the Upper
Peninsula/Tribal Treaties

A Guide to the Indians of Michigan's Upper Peninsula
1621-1900
Russell M. Magnaghi
Belle Fontaine Press, Marquette, Michigan 1984

http://www.hannahville.net/
History of the Hannahville Indian Community

http://www.accessgenealogy.com/native/
tribes/chippewa/chippewahist.htm
Chippewa Indian history

http://www.mlive.com/news/grpress/index.ssf?/
base/news-2/1191134413198910.xml&coll=6
2007 agreement upholding the Treaty of 1836

http://www.lvdtribal.com/
Lac Vieux Desert band of Lake
Superior Chippewa history

http://www.1836cora.org/pdf/1820saultstemarie.pdf
Sault Ste. Marie treaty of 1820

http://www.saulttribe.com/index.php?option=com_co
ntent&task=view&id=29&Itemid=205
Sault tribe of Chippewa Indians history

http://www.tolatsga.org/ojib.html
Ojibwe history

http://college.hmco.com/english/lauter/heath/4e/
students/author_pages/early_nineteenth/
johnstonschoolcraftojibwa_ja.html
Susan Johnston's native name

http://www.petoskeynews.com/
articles/2007/10/27/news/news05.txt
Petoskey News-Review
Information on 2007 treaty between the State
of Michigan and Sault Ste. Marie Chippewa

The Find of a Thousand Lifetimes
The Story of the Gorto Site Discovery
James Robert Paquette
AuthorHouse
Bloomington, Indiana 2005

Atlas of Great Lakes Indian History
Edited by Helen Hornbeck Tanner
Published for the Newberry Library by
University of Oklahoma Press
Norman, Oklahoma 1987

Rites of Conquest
The History and Culture of Michigan's Native Americans
Charles E. Cleland
University of Michigan Press
Ann Arbor, Michigan 1992

Bishop Frederic Baraga

The Diary of Bishop Frederic Baraga
First Bishop of Marquette, Michigan
Edited and Annotated by Regis M.
Walling and Rev. N. Daniel Rupp
Translated by Joseph Gregorich and
Rev. Paul Prud'homme, S.J.
Great Lakes Books
Wayne State University Press, Detroit 1990

Kitchi-Gami
Life Among the Lake Superior Ojibway
Johann Georg Kohl
Translated by Lascelles Wraxall
Minnesota Historical Society Press, St. Paul, 1985

So Cold a Sky, Upper Michigan Weather Stories
Karl Bohnak

http://www.bishopbaraga.org/
baragasites.htm#INDIANLAKE
Baraga's Indian Lake Mission

Chapter 6 Counties and Towns

Michigan Place Names: The History of the Founding
and the Naming of More Than Five Thousand
Past and Present Michigan Communities
Walter Romig, L.H.D.
Wayne State University Press
Detroit, Michigan 1986

Michigan: A Guide to the Wolverine State
Writers' Program of the WPA
Copyright by Michigan State Administrative Board
Oxford University Press, New York 1941

What's in a Name?

http://clarke.cmich.edu/
Origin of Houghton, Ontonagon
http://www.pasty.com/discuss/messages/994/1063.html
Origin of Ontonagon

http://www.epodunk.com/cgi-bin/
genInfo.php?locIndex=21814
Germfask origin

http://ipoetry.us/MIAnthology.htm#_Toc115684728
Origin of Menominee and L'Anse

Incredible Seney
The First Complete Story of Michigan's
Fabulous Lumber Town
Lewis C. Reimann
Avery Color Studios, Au Train, Michigan 1982

The Origin of Certain Place Names in the United States
Henry Gannett
Genealogical Publishing Company
Baltimore, Maryland 1973

http://www.rootsweb.com/~michippe/twphist.htm
Origin of Sault Ste. Marie

Chapter 7 Economy

http://www.fedstats.gov/qf/states/26000.html
Employment and income statistics

Louis G. Kaufman

Superior Heartland
A Backwoods History
C. Fred Rydholm
Published privately by C. Fred Rydholm
Marquette, MI 1989
Louis G. Graveraet

http://www.marquettefiction.com/page7.html
Louis G. Kaufman information

http://www.granotloma.com/
Louis G. Kaufman information

Marquette Monthly Magazine
Feature: "Some of the Finer Things." The
Graveraet High School Lyceum Series
By Frank Richardson
September 2001

Mining history

http://www.michiganhistorymagazine.com/
extra/soo/chippewa_county_history.html
Michigan History on line: source
of the Henry Clay quote

http://www.exploringthenorth.com/
cophistory/cophist.html
Vivian Wood: Exploring the North...
Copper mining history

http://www.state.gov/r/pa/ho/time/ar/14313.htm
State Department site: information
on the Treaty of Paris

http://www.minsocam.org/msa/
collectors_corner/vft/mi3d.htm
General copper mining source

http://www.uppermichigan.com/coppertown/history.html
Red Jacket (Calumet) history

http://www.sos.state.mi.us/history/museum/explore/
museums/hismus/prehist/mining/iron.html
General iron mining history

http://www.mg.mtu.edu/shaft3.htm
Information on the Gogebic Iron Range

http://blog.lib.msu.edu/redtape/?p=2127
Sulfide mining permit in Marquette County

http://minnesota.publicradio.org/display/
web/2006/05/15/rangesulfidemining/
Information on sulfide mining

http://hunts-upguide.com/white_pine.html
History of White Pine Mine

http://www.encyclopedia.com/doc/1G1-58915106.html
HighBeam Encyclopedia
The History, Geology and Mineralogy of the
White Pine Mine Ontonagon County, Michigan

Gold and Silver

Michigan Gold Mining in the Upper Peninsula
Daniel Fountain
Lake Superior Port Cities, Inc., Duluth, 1992

http://hunts-upguide.com/white_pine.html
White Pine Michigan's Upper Peninsula

Alexander Henry's Travels and
Adventures in the Years 1760-1776
Edited with historical introduction and
notes by Milo Milton Quaife
The Lakeside Press, Chicago 1922

Wall of Silver
A Treasure Hunter's Dream
Richard Kellogg
Avery Color Studies, Gwinn, Michigan 2004

Henry Ford

The Legend of Henry Ford
Keith Sinard
Rhinehart and Company
New York 1948

Superior Heartland
A Backwoods History
C. Fred Rydholm
C. Fred Rydholm, Marquette 1989

Call it North Country
A Story of Upper Michigan
John Bartlow Martin
Wayne State University Press
Detroit 1944 Copyright renewed by
John Bartlow Martin 1971

Deep Woods Frontier
A History of Logging in Northern Michigan
Theordore J. Karamanski
Wayne State University Press
Detroit 1989

Ford
Expansion and Challenge: 1915-1932
Allan Nevins and Frank Ernest Hill
Charles Scribner and Sons
New York 1957

Howard Shultz

http://www.evancarmichael.com/Famous-
Entrepreneurs/643/The-Coffee-King-
Howard-Schultz-is-Born.html
Howard Shultz biography

Chapter 8 Tourism

Michigan State Parks: A Complete Recreation Guide
for Campers, Boaters, Anglers, Hikers & Skiers,
Jim DuFresne in cooperation with
The Michigan Department of Natural Resources,
Copyright 1989, Jim DuFresne,
The Mountaineers

Michigan State and National Parks: A
Complete Guide, Fourth Edition,
Tom Powers,
Thunder Bay Press, 2007

Hunt's Guide to Michigan's Upper Peninsula,
Mary and Don Hunt,
Midwestern Guides of Albion Michigan 1997

Pictured Rocks

Pictured Rocks Memories
T. Kilgore Splake
Angst Productions
Battle Creek 1985

The Pictured Rocks: An Administrative History
of Pictured Rocks National Lakeshore
Theodore J. Karamanski
National Park Service
U.S. Department of Interior

Dangerous Coast
Pictured Rocks Shipwrecks
Frederick Stonehouse and Daniel R. Fountain
Avery Color Studios, Gwinn 1997

Historic Museums

http://www.bessemerhistoricalsociety.com/
Bessemer Area Heritage Center

http://www.ironwoodmi.org/historical.htm
Old Depot Museum Ironwood

http://hunts-upguide.com/ironwood_
central_ironwood.html
Old Depot Museum Ironwood

http://www.ontonagonmuseum.org/Lighthouse1.htm
Ontonagon Historical Society Museum and Lighthouse

http://www.ontonagonmi.com/historicalsites.html
Rockland Museum

http://www.ontonagonmi.com/oldvictoria.html
Old Victoria Restoration

http://www.exploringthenorth.
com/mine/venture.html
Adventure Mining Company Tours

http://www.museum.mtu.edu/index.html
A.E. Seaman Mineral Museum

http://www.quincymine.com/
Quincy Mine

http://www.keweenaw.info/attractions.aspx
Keweenaw Peninsula historic attractions

http://www.baragacountytourism.
org/attractions.html
Baraga County attractions

http://www.ironheritage.org/
Iron County attractions

http://www.marquettecountry.org/
recreation_artsandculture.php
Marquette County attractions

http://www.ironmountain.org/attractions.shtml
Dickinson County attractions

http://menomineehistoricalsociety.org/
Menominee County historical museums

http://www.exploringthenorth.
com/sandpoint/light.html
Sand Point Lighthouse

http://www.michigan.org/travel/
locations/?city=G3023&m=0
Link to historical museums in
the Upper Peninsula

http://www.exploringthenorth.
com/sandpoint/light.html
Sand Point Lighthouse Escanaba
http://www.exploringthenorth.
com/cornish/pump.html
Cornish Pumping Engine-Iron Mining Museum

Historical Michigan Travel Guide
Historical Society of Michigan
Larry J. Wagenaar, Editor
East Lansing, Michigan 2008

Chapter 9 Transportation
A Drive Down Memory Lane: The Named
State and Federal Highways of Michigan,
LeRoy Barnett, Phd,
The Priscilla Press
Allegan Forest, Michigan 2004

The Great Lakes Car Ferries
George W. Hilton
Howell-North Books
Copyright 1962

Great Lakes Lighthouses American and Canadian
Wes Oleszewski
Avery Color Studios
Gwinn, Michigan 1998

The Northern Lights: Lighthouses
of the Upper Great Lakes
Charles K. Hyde
Michigan Natural Resources Magazine, 1986

http://www.nps.gov/history/maritime/light/mi.htm
Lighthouse information

http://www.michiganhighways.org/
Highway information

http://www.boatnerd.com/
Shipping information

http://michiganrailroads.com/
Railroad information

Shipping

History of the Great Lakes Vol. I
J.B. Mansfield editor
Halton Hills, ON, Canada: Maritime
History of the Great Lakes
2003
Based on the original document:
J.B. Mansfield, ed., History of the Great
Lakes. Volume I, Chicago:
J.H. Beers & Co., 1899

http://www.infomi.com/city/lanse/
Website of L'Anse, Michigan

Deep Woods Frontier
A History of Logging in Northern Michigan
Theodore J. Karamanski
Great Lakes Books edition copyright
Wayne State University Press, Detroit 1989

Dangerous Coast
Pictured Rocks Shipwrecks
Frederick Stonehouse and Daniel R. Fountain
Avery Color Studios, Gwinn, MI 1997

Sault Canal and Locks

To Build a Canal
Sault Ste. Marie, 1853-54 and After
John N. Dickinson
Published for Miami University by the
Ohio State University Press 1981

http://www.saultstemarie.com/soo-
locks-46/#mainPhotoGroup
History of the Sault Ste. Marie locks

Shipwrecks

http://greatlakeshistory.homestead.
com/files/lakegraph.jpg
Graph of Great Lakes shipping
losses as a percent per lake

http://www.michiganhistorymagazine.com/
features/discmich/edmondfitz.pdf
Size of the schooner *Invincible*

Lake Superior Shipwrecks
Dr. Julius F. Wolff, Jr.
Lake Superior Port Cities, Inc.
Duluth 1990

Early shipping/shipwreck information
courtesy of the files of:
The Great Lakes Shipwreck Historical Society Archives
Paradise, Michigan

The Honorable Peter White
A Biographical Sketch of the Lake Superior Iron Country
Ralph D. Williams
The Penton Publishing Co.
Cleveland 1907
Republished by Freshwater Press, Inc.
Euclid, Ohio 1986

So Cold a Sky, Upper Michigan Weather Stories
Karl Bohnak
Cold Sky Publishing
Negaunee, MI 2006

http://www.ship-wreck.com/shipwreck/keweenaw/
Keweenaw Underwater Preserve

http://www.portup.com/~dfount/mqtupc.htm#undisc
Marquette Underwater Preserve

http://www.michiganpreserves.org/alger.htm
Alger Underwater Preserve

Education   Chapter 10

http://www.michigan.gov/hal/0,1607,7-160-
18835_18894_19664---,00.html
Michigan Public Library Statistical Report

http://www.schoolmatters.com/schools.aspx/q/page=hm
Public School statistics

Chapter 11 Government

http://www.wisconsinhistory.org/wlhba/articleView.as
p?pg=1&id=4308&hdl=&np=Chicago+Tribune&adv=
yes&ln=&fn=&q=&y1=&y2=&ci=&co=&mhd=&shd=
Proposed State of Superior—Wisconsin
Historical Society archive

Courage Burning: Incredible Stories
About Incredible People
Sonny Longtine
Sunnyside Publications
Marquette, MI 2006

Stewards of the State: The Governors of Michigan
George Weeks, edited by Robert D. Kirk
Copyright the Historical Society of Michigan
The Detroit News and the Historical
Society of Michigan 1987

Atlas of Michigan
Edited by Lawrence Sommers
Michigan State University Press
Lansing, MI 1977

https://www.msu.edu/~dowj/osborn/osborn.htm
Chase Osborn information

http://politicalgraveyard.com/
The Internet's Most Comprehensive
Source of Political Biography

Chapter 12 Culture

The Hiawatha Legends
Henry R. Schoolcraft
Avery Color Studios
Au Train, MI 1984

Michigan Folklife Reader,
C. Kurt Dewhurst and Yvonne Lockwood
Michigan State University Press
Lansing, MI 1988

Courage Burning: Incredible Stories
About Incredible People
Sonny Longtine
Sunnyside Publications
Marquette, MI 2006

Michigan in Literature
Clarence A. Andrews
Wayne State University Press
Detroit, Michigan, 2002

The Hemingway Review
Fall 1996, p. 33,
Ernest Hemingway Foundation, copyright 1996

Off to the Side,
Jim Harrison,
Atlantic Monthly Press, 2002

Newspapers

Michigan Newspapers on Microfilm
Library of Michigan, Lansing 1986
http://www.genealogia.fi/emi/art/article213e.htm
History of Finnish newspapers in America

http://www.websters-dictionary-online.org/
translation/Swedish/medborgaren
Definition of Medborgaren

http://www.wisconsinhistory.org/wlhba/articleView.
asp?pg=10&id=3126&hdl=&np=&adv=yes&ln=&fn
=&q=&y1=&y2=&ci=Milwaukee&co=&mhd=&shd=
Wisconsin Historical Society—Milwaukee
Free Press story on A.P. Swineford

http://www.ur.umich.edu/9495/Jul10_95/obit.htm
Biographical information on Wesley H. Maurer

http://hof.jrn.msu.edu/bios/maurer.html
More biographical information on Wesley Mauer

Oral taped interview with Marian Strahl Boyer, November 2007

Radio

Oral taped interview with Jay Barry, June 2008

http://www.baymills.org/newspaper/2006/06-01/060106-news-thorne.shtml
Bay Mills News, June 2006 article on Bill Thorne

http://www.michmab.com/pdf/Newsletter/nlSeptOct04.pdf
Ed Kearney biographical information
MAB newsletter Sept./Oct. 2004

http://hof.jrn.msu.edu/bios/kearney.html
Ed Kearney biographical information:
MSU School of Journalism

http://www.alumni.mtu.edu/techalum/2004_05/05_01_03.htm
Dick Storm retirement announcement:
MTU Alumnus newsletter

http://www.keweenawnow.com/news/dick_storm_mtu_04_05/dick_storm_award.htm
Dick Storm biographical information:
Keweenaw Now website

http://www.michiguide.com/history/am.html
History of AM radio broadcasting in Michigan

http://www.angelfire.com/wi/jrosin5765/radio/wupmirad.html
Western Upper Peninsula radio stations

http://www.michiguide.com/dials/up.html
Upper Peninsula radio and TV guide

http://www.tvb.org/rcentral/markettrack/us_hh_by_dma.asp
DMA ranking of television stations

http://en.wikipedia.org/wiki/WBKP
WBKP/WBUP station history

http://www.michiguide.com/dials/tv/wmqf.html
WMQF station history

Musical Groups

http://www.flatbrokebluesband.com/index2.php
Flat Broke Blues Band

http://www.congasemenne.com/index.shtml
Conga Se Menne Group

http://csumc.wisc.edu/exhibit/HeikkiLunta/timeline/1994.html
Conga Se Menne

http://www.white-water-associates.com/music.htm
White Water

Music Festivals

http://www.aurajamboree.com/index.htm
Aura Jamboree

http://www.white-water-associates.com/fortunefest.htm
Fortune Lake Festival

http://www.grandmaraismichigan.com/MusicFestival/index.htm
Grand Marais Music and Arts Festival

http://www.hiawathamusic.org/index.php
Hiawatha Traditional Music Festival

http://www.marquetteareabluessociety.org/festival/index.php
Marquette Area Blues Festival

http://www.pmmf.org/about/index.htm
Pine Mountain Music Festival

http://www.porkiesfestival.org/info.html
Porcupine Mountain Music Festival

http://www.woodtickfestival.com/
Woodtick Music Festival

Writers

http://www.jerryharju.com/author.html
Biographical information on U.P. author Jerry Harju

Email correspondence with Lynn Emerick, August 2007
Biographical information on U.P. author Lon Emerick

The Pasty

http://www.geocities.com/lukefisk.geo/pasty.html
The Upper Michigan informer

Hilltop Sweet Rolls
http://www.sweetroll.com/index.html

Chapter 13 Sports and Recreation

Black Bear Hunting
Richard P. Smith
Stackpole Books
Mechanicsburg, PA 2007

http://www.skiinghistory.org/halloffame.html

http://www.mhsaa.com/
High school records

The Huron Mountain Club

The Book of Huron Mountain
A Collection of Papers Concerning the History of the Huron Mountain Club and the Antiquities and the Natural History of the Region
Edited by Bayard H. Christy
Published by the Club 1929

Chapter 14 Wildlife

http://www.bigcatrescue.org/cougar.htm
Cougar vital statistics

http://www.miwildlife.org/cougarmilestones.doc
Cougar timeline

http://www.co.pima.az.us/cmo/sdcp/kids/gloss.html
Cougar information

http://www.jsonline.com/story/index.aspx?id=189037
Cougar sightings and DNR reaction to sightings

http://www.michigan.gov/dnr/0,1607,7-153-
10370_12143_12185-30966--,00.html
Michigan DNR moose facts

http://www.michigan.gov/dnr/0,1607,7-153-
10370_12145_12205-56904--,00.html
Michigan DNR white-tailed deer facts

http://semcog.org/TranPlan/Safety/
MDCC/assets/MTCF05_Deer2.pdf
Michigan Deer-Vehicle crash information

http://www.upwhitetails.com/index.html
U.P. Whitetails Association, Inc.

http://www.dailypress.net/stories/
articles.asp?articleID=11321
Timber harvest-deer number parallels

http://www.fws.gov/midwest/wolf/recovery/r3wolfct.htm
1995-97 deer die-off in U.P.

The Wolves of Isle Royale
A Broken Balance
Rolf O. Peterson
University of Michigan Press
Ann Arbor, MI 2007

The American Beaver and His Works
Lewis Henry Morgan
University of Chicago Press, Chicago, 1868

http://encyclopedia.jrank.org/Cambridge/
entries/095/Lewis-Henry-Morgan.html
Information on Lewis Henry Morgan

http://photography.nationalgeographic.com/
photography/photographers/first-wildlife-photos.html
George Shiras III information

Superior Heartland
A Backwoods History
C. Fred Rydholm
Biographical information on George Shiras III

http://archshrk.com/2007/07/george-shiras-3d
George Shiras III biographical information

http://www.bfro.net/
Bigfoot Field Research Organization: U.P.
eyewitness accounts of Bigfoot

http://www.hu.mtu.edu/~dkeranen/
revisions/2007fall/fall07pdfs/Zine_Sasquatch.pdf
History of Bigfoot or Sasquatch

http://thatslifeinthecity.blogspot.com/2007/07/
moneymaker-wants-to-find-bigfoot-in.html
BFRO U.P. expedition July 2007

http://deltafarmpress.com/mag/
farming_tale_common_misery/
Cormorant—Delta Farm Press

http://www.freep.com/apps/
pbcs.dll/article?AID=/20080615/
SPORTS10/806150597/1058
Cormorants—*Detroit Free Press*

http://www.michigan.gov/dnr/0,1607,7-153-
10370_12145_12205-59759--,00.html
Black Bear—Michigan Department
of Natural Resources

http://www.michigan.gov/dnr/0,1607,7-153-
10363_10856_10890-105034--,00.html
Michigan Black Bear facts—Michigan DNR

Chapter 15 Architecture

Buildings of Michigan
Kathryn Bishop Eckert
Society of Architectural Historians
Oxford University Press 1993

The Sandstone Architecture of
the Lake Superior Region
Kathryn Bishop Eckert
Wayne State University Press, Detroit 2000
John Burt House

Hunt's Guide to Michigan's Upper Peninsula
Mary and Don Hunt
Midwestern Guides of Albion Michigan, 1997

Chapter 16 Biggest and Best

Cornish in Michigan
Russell M. Magnaghi
Michigan State University Press, East Lansing 2007
Largest pasty

Big Louie Moilanen
Giant of the Copper Country
John H. Forster Press
Houghton County Historical Society, 1989
Louis Moilanen Biography

INDEX